National Geographic Ultimate Adventure Sourcebook

Ultimate

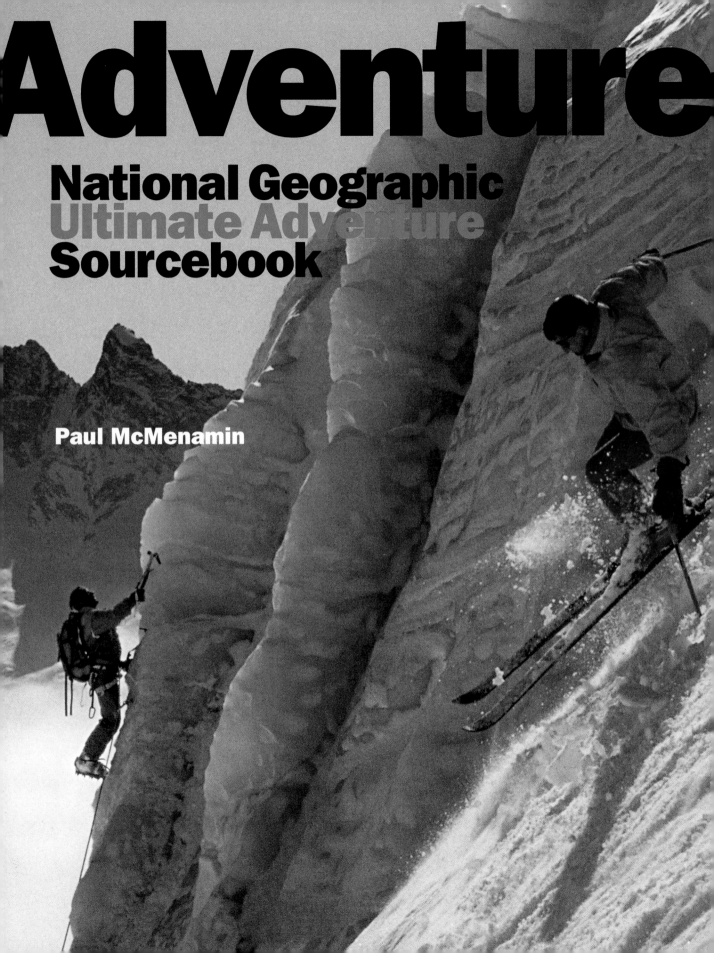

Adventure

National Geographic
Ultimate Adventure
Sourcebook

Paul McMenamin

Contents

267

220

50

17

310

270

The Ultimate Source for Ultimate Adventure

Adventure is a human need. We recognize it as the daring thing which makes us bigger than our usual selves. Adventure is the curiousity of man to see the other side of the mountain, the impulse in him that makes him break his bonds with lesser things and frees him for greater possibility.

WALT BURNETT, *THE SPIRIT OF ADVENTURE*

If you've ever tried to organize an adventure trip to a remote destination—or simply attempted to find a good ski resort overseas—you know that reliable travel information can be elusive. Even with the advent of the Internet, you can spend days tracking down key phone numbers and addresses. And when you finally do come across a list of outfitters or resorts, how do you determine which one is best for you?

The answer lies in the *National Geographic Ultimate Adventure Sourcebook,* an exhaustively researched travel encyclopedia that reveals the best destinations, describes the most rewarding adventure vacations, and recommends the top guide services for dozens of popular outdoor activities. When independent travel is most rewarding, we help you organize your own adventure. When it makes sense to go with an escorted trip, we give you a list of the top-ranked outfitters, along with an idea of how much you'll have to pay—and what kind of services to expect.

ABOUT THIS BOOK

This book is organized alphabetically by activity, not by location. This allows you to learn about your favorite adventures quickly, without having to wade through unrelated topics. If you are intent on visiting a certain part of the world, of course, you can always use the book's index to find the most popular venues for adventure.

Each of the book's 25 chapters begins with a general discussion of the adventure in question, explaining its appeal and pointing out any recent developments in the sport. This introduction is followed by in-depth profiles of seven or eight dream vacations—rafting the Grand Canyon, for example—that include trip sources, itineraries, and prices. Next, most chapters include detailed reviews of the leading outfitters or travel vendors for that activity, as well as details on how to contact them by snail mail, telephone, or Internet. Capping off each chapter is a fact-packed Resources section; this presents a more thorough listing of adventure-travel companies that can introduce you to the activity, supplemented by suggestions for websites, books, magazines, professional associations, and training schools devoted to the adventure. Finally, throughout the book you'll find special features spotlighting the most extreme new adventure sports, from waterfall running, free climbing, and spelunking to bungee jumping, kite surfing, shark diving, and polar exploring.

CRITERIA FOR INCLUSION

With so many adventure trips available today, it can be difficult for the consumer to choose the ideal holiday offered by the best operator. To cut through the clutter, the *Ultimate Adventure Sourcebook* profiles the leading companies in every major category of adventure travel.

We do not live to eat and make money. We eat and make money in order to be able to enjoy life. This is what life means and what life is for.

GEORGE LEIGH MALLORY

The selection process of those companies began in 1989, when I quit my job as a corporate lawyer and began a 10-month journey around the globe. Since that time, assisted by a research team, I have compiled data on more than 3,000 companies and resorts worldwide. I have visited 30 countries on six continents, sampling many of the world's best adventures—bungee jumping in New Zealand, scuba diving the Great Barrier Reef, sailing in the Virgin Islands—along the way. To select the best trips, I interviewed hundreds of active travelers, consulted leading outdoor guides and instructors, and monitored thousands of trip reviews posted by adventure travelers on Outdoor Adventure Online, a travel forum I directed for America Online from 1994 to 2000.

The result is the compendium of outfitters that fills this guide. The *Ultimate Adventure Sourcebook* charges no listing fees, so no company bought its way into the book. Only operators with solid reputations and top-notch activities were considered for inclusion. The following criteria dictated whether or not a firm earned a perch in the guide:

■ A company must have a proven track record. Experience counts.

■ The destinations served must be top-quality, with inherent natural beauty, adventure challenge, or cultural interest.

■ The adventure experience must be superior in terms of excitement, fun, relaxation, and opportunities for learning and discovery.

■ The company must have an excellent safety record and strong customer service.

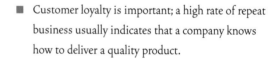

If you reject the food, ignore the customs, fear the religions and avoid the people, you might better stay home.
JAMES MICHENER

■ Trip leaders must be technically proficient, safety conscious, personable, and knowledgeable about the region they serve.

■ Quality food, accommodations, and support services (such as sag wagons on bike trips) are desirable, but luxury is not automatically favored over more basic trips (as long as the pricing is appropriate).

■ Customer loyalty is important; a high rate of repeat business usually indicates that a company knows how to deliver a quality product.

■ Geographic diversity is a plus. The outfitters in this book serve not only popular destinations worldwide, but also many unexplored, little-known, and still unspoiled corners of the globe.

■ Price is not paramount; value is. If two firms offer equally good service, equipment, or itineraries, the one delivering the better value receives the more favorable review.

CHOOSING THE RIGHT OUTFITTER— AND THE RIGHT TRIP

Every trip described in the following pages is a little bit different; choose the one among them that best suits your own interests and needs. Once you have settled on what you want to do and where you want to go, contact some of the outfitters we have identified. Most have websites and toll-free numbers that make it easy to get additional information. Bookmark the sites or collect the catalogs of your top choices, then scrutinize each one. Learn when the various trips depart, and precisely how much each one costs. (Though we have verified the accuracy of all listings, prices or itineraries often change after a guidebook goes to press.) Ask about any hidden expenses: Ground transport, food, park fees, and special equipment (such as rental bikes on cycling trips) often cost extra, and trip prices often vary with group size or departure date. Finally, ask if the company is willing to put you in touch with past customers—then contact those people for their recommendations.

HARD VERSUS SOFT ADVENTURE

As active travel grows in popularity, the definition of adventure is being extended at both ends of the spectrum. At the hard-core end of the spectrum, daredevils are pushing the adventure envelope with intense new high-risk sports such as skysurfing, shark diving, and extreme skiing. At the cushy end of the spectrum, travelers are indulging in luxurious, comfortable forms of active travel. Sometimes called soft adventure, this new style combines outdoor recreation with creature comforts: Just as skiers have traditionally used the hot tub (or hot drinks) of a ski lodge to recuperate from a hard day on the slopes, today's trekkers, rafters, and cyclists often seek the comforts of gourmet restaurants and deluxe inns to restore themselves after a challenging adventure on river or trail.

> *We act as though comfort and luxury were the chief requirements of life, when all that we need to make us happy is something to be enthusiastic about.*
> —CHARLES KINGSLEY

This desire to combine high adrenaline with haute cuisine and posh digs is reshaping the travel industry. Although this sourcebook focuses mainly on wilderness travel and adventure sports, it also covers a wide array of soft-adventure opportunities, from lavish ranch vacations to luxury barge cruises on the canals of Europe.

CUTTING THE COST OF ADVENTURE

Purchasers of the *Ultimate Adventure Sourcebook* qualify for a discount of either $30 or 5 percent of the price of a trip from any participating outfitter or resort listed on pages 370-379. This discount can save you a bundle on the adventure vacation of your choice. Discounts are available through the end of 2002 to any customer who presents a valid sales receipt for this edition of the sourcebook.

LIVE YOUR DREAM

The *Ultimate Adventure Sourcebook* is designed to help people make their dreams a reality. My sincere hope is

> *Whatever you can do, or dream you can do, begin it. Boldness has genius, power and magic in it. Begin it now.*
> JOHANN WOLFGANG VON GOETHE

that it will inspire you to take that trip to a faraway land you've always fantasized about. Because adventure encompasses the unexpected, don't try to anticipate every contingency, and don't worry if everything doesn't turn out as planned: If you forget your camera, buy another; if you can't find a travel partner, go alone—or find an outfitter that sponsors trips for singles. The key is to keep pursuing what you really want.

Having spent 11 years traveling the globe to find, experience, and report on the adventures described in the following pages, I hope you will turn to the *Ultimate Adventure Sourcebook* whenever you are contemplating an adventure of your own. For armchair travelers, too, the book should provide the perfect vehicle for kicking off your shoes and enjoying some virtual voyages both at home and in exotic lands.

—Paul McMenamin

Alpine Mountaineering

MOUNTAINEERING DEFINES HIGH ADVENTURE. TO REACH THE TOP OF A MAJOR SUMMIT, you must transcend fear, conquer gravity, and push yourself to the limit. There is nothing equivocal about a successful climb (when you've made it, you've made it!), which is perhaps why climbing has always appealed to those keen to put themselves to the ultimate test. • Mountaineering encompasses three basic activities: alpine expeditions, rock climbing, and ice climbing. This chapter will review the best climbing schools around the country and dozens of guided summit climbs worldwide. For rock hounds, there's a list of great places to practice their moves, as well as reviews of the top rock-climbing guides. And for climbers with ice water in their veins, there's a description of the winter programs for mastering the gravity-defying art of climbing ice. Whatever your needs, prepare now to leave base camp and set off on your vertical adventure.

LEFT: PEAK EXPERIENCE ATOP THE EIGER IN SWITZERLAND
BELOW: TIROLIAN TRAVERSE, CANYONLANDS NATIONAL PARK, UTAH

Hard Rock

Climbing on Ice

Spelunking

The mountains reserve their choice gifts for those who journey into them and stand upon their summits.

SIR FRANCIS YOUNGBLOOD

Eight Great Alpine Adventures

Certain summits are considered classics—either because they are the highest peaks on a continent or because they hold a special place in the heritage of mountaineering. A number of these ultimate climbs are featured below, including the Matterhorn, Mount McKinley, and Aconcagua. You'll also learn about the world's best training expeditions, such as a climb of Mexico's three volcanoes, which will provide you with the skills needed to tackle a major summit on your next vacation.

NEPAL
Himalayan Trekking Peaks

Every true mountaineer dreams of conquering the great summits of the Himalaya—mountaineering's ultimate challenge. But for the vast majority of climbers, it is a challenge that will go unmet. Expeditions to the highest Himalayan peaks are simply too costly and too dangerous. In 1996, for example, a fierce storm lashed Everest just as several groups of experienced climbers were completing their final assault on the summit, claiming the lives of many.

Thankfully, Everest is not the only worthy hill in the Himalaya: The lesser peaks of Nepal—those in the 20,000-foot range—provide ample challenge and adventure for most climbers. Moreover, these "trekking peaks," as they are called, won't require months of planning, huge teams of porters, and costs of around $60,000. And they won't place you in mortal danger.

Trekking peaks are ideal for relatively small-scale expeditions by climbers with moderate technical skills and some high-altitude experience. Reasonably fit climbers with a budget of around $2,600 to $4,000 can choose among a variety of trekking peaks—from relatively easy walk-ups to tougher peaks requiring technical mountaineering expertise. Nepal offers them all.

Nowhere else in the world will you find more 20,000-foot peaks that can be climbed in ten days or less. Two of the most popular are **Mera Peak** and **Island Peak,** which provide commanding views of the world's tallest mountains: Everest, Makalu, Lhotse, Cho Oyu, and Kanchenjunga. Island Peak is a bit more technical than Mera, finishing as it does with a conical ridge leading directly to the summit.

To the west of Everest—in the Rolwaling region near the border with **Xizang (Tibet)**—lies another popular realm for climbers. But because Rolwaling is only open to those with a peak permit, it does not suffer from the heavy trekking traffic that overwhelms other parts of Nepal. Rolwaling has remained relatively unspoiled.

Ramdung and **Parchemo**—both around 20,000 feet—are the two prime trekking peaks in this region. Ramdung is a long, steady snow climb that steepens dramatically in the final section. Parchemo involves a shorter but more challenging climb that finishes with a steep ice slope up to a pointed summit. (Although the route to the summit of Parchemo passes through many different ecosystems—including jungle, and mountain terrain—some expedition guides consider it too dangerous because of its stone falls.)

A number of Western guide services conduct treks to the peaks of Nepal, among them Britain's **Jagged Globe** (*Sheffield, U.K. 01144-1142-763322. www.jagged-globe.co.uk*). This company—which has guided successful climbs on Everest and other more challenging summits—runs a well-organized and professional operation. Among its expeditions are those to Mera Peak (24 days, $2,500); Mera and Island Peaks combined (30 days, $2,990); and Rolwaling summits (Ramdung and Parchemo, 29 days, $2,990). The success rate for reasonably fit participants under 45 is quite high, particularly for those who have some prior alpine experience. Trips depart in April and October, and prices are for the land cost from the Nepalese capital, Kathmandu.

Another solid British climbing and trekking company is **KE Adventure Travel** (*Keswick, U.K. 0114417-687-73966. Glenwood Springs, CO. 800-497-9675 or 970-384-0001. www.KEadventure.com*). A company with decades of experience in Nepal, KE leads 27-day expeditions to Mera Peak and the Amphu Labtsa Pass; to Ramdung and the Tesi Lapcha Pass; to Island Peak, Lobuche East, and several lesser trekking peaks in **Everest National Park.** All these itineraries are priced at around $3,150. Separate 20-day itineraries for Mera Peak or Island Peak by themselves are available at lower rates.

KE's expeditions—which depart April, October, and November—are rated strenuous, and some alpine experience is recommended, especially for the higher climbs. Before you go, take a short, basic glacier travel seminar to

familiarize yourself with proper ice ax, crampon, belaying and self-rescue techniques.

For the best chance of success on multiple 20,000-foot summits, try the **American Alpine Institute** (*Bellingham, WA. 360-671-1505 or 360-734-8890. www.aai.cc*). AAI offers two exceptional programs in Nepal. The first trip, with ascents of **Lobuche** (20,075 feet) and Island Peak (20,305 feet), rewards participants with one of the Himalaya's supreme vistas—a vast sea of white summits extending far off into Tibet. Its second expedition combines a classic **Annapurna Circuit** trek with two beautiful—and rarely done—climbs: Chulu West (20,341 feet) and Thorong Peak (20,104 feet).

The company runs small groups of four to eight climbers, each of which is led by professional North American and Sherpa guides. Both trips cost $4,200 for 25 days. To ensure success, climbers should have a solid foundation in snow and ice climbing, as well as glacier travel skills.

ANTARCTICA
Climbing the Ice Continent

The most remote of the so-called Seven Summits—the tallest peaks on each of the seven continents—is **Vinson Massif (Mount Vinson)**, Antarctica's highest peak. Perhaps as few as 500 climbers have reached the top of Vinson, which remains one of the world's ultimate climbing destinations.

Climbing Mount Vinson is an arduous quest. The mountain itself is not terribly steep, and a moderately inclined glacier ramp will take you most of the way to the top. But because of the harsh—and unpredictable—Antarctic weather conditions, many climbers consider Vinson a tougher summit than Mount McKinley. When the weather turns nasty, winds can howl at up to 100 miles per hour and temperatures plunge to 40° below zero F—even in the Antarctic's "good" season.

The vast expense of transporting a climbing team to the heart of Antarctica also makes Mount Vinson one of the costliest propositions in mountaineering. Expect to pay at least $25,000 per person plus the cost of air flights to South America. Once the financial hurdle is surmounted, however, qualified climbers have a good chance of overcoming the mountain itself.

Adventure Network International (*Beaconsfield, U.K. 01144-1494-671808. www.adventurenetwork.com*) leads expeditions to the summit of Mount Vinson. To qualify for an expedition, applicants must have several years of mountaineering experience—with peaks over 14,000 feet—and should know the techniques of self-arrest, belays, anchors, crampons, and ice ax. Costs vary with group size, but are around $25,000 per person.

Adventure Network International is the world leader in Antarctic climbing, and its clients enjoy a high success rate. If the company's program is filled, **International**

HIGH AND DRY: MONTANE CAMPSITE IN ANTARCTICA

Mountain Guides (*Ashford, WA. 425-822-5662 or 360-569-2604. www.mountainguides.net*) also offers a Mount Vinson expedition in November and December for $26,000, using Adventure Network logistical support. The 20-day expedition is limited to eight experienced climbers.

If bagging Mount Vinson is not glory enough, there remain numerous virgin (and near virgin) peaks in Antarctica. Many of the summits surrounding Mount Vinson in the **Ellesworth Range,** for instance, have never been scaled. Indeed, the second highest peak in Antarctica, 15,895-foot **Mount Tyree,** has only been conquered a couple of times. Only 165 feet lower than Mount Vinson, Tyree is much steeper and much more challenging. The ascent requires an 8,000-foot technical attack of the West Face, followed by a traverse across razor-edge ridges exposed to high winds. Needless to say, Mount Tyree is for experts only.

Adventure Network International also offers expeditions to the rugged **Queen Maud Range.** Located south of the Ross Ice Shelf, these are the closest mountains to the South Pole. Here, at the bottom of the world, clients can summit one of three peaks. Weather permitting, they may even have an opportunity to ascend one of the unclimbed—and perhaps unnamed—peaks in the area.

Routes on these spectacular mountains vary from a highly technical climb to a moderately difficult trek. The choice is yours. If your climbing resume isn't strong enough to qualify for a major peak, Adventure Network International also offers a unique **Millennium Program,** which enables you to ski or to fly to the geographic South Pole.

THE ALPS
Mont Blanc, the Eiger, and the Matterhorn

Looking for something really worth bragging about at the next class reunion? How about a European Grand Slam—an ascent of the three most famous peaks in the Alps: **Mont Blanc, the Eiger,** and the **Matterhorn?** Every summer, the **American Alpine Institute** (*Bellingham, WA. 360-671-1505 or 360-734-8890. www.aai.cc*) offers a **Grand Slam** expedition that gives intermediate climbers the opportunity to bag all three of these classic European mountains in a single vacation.

During the program, participants stay either in tent camps or in alpine climbers' huts while preparing for each of the major climbs. The first few days will be spent around

the glaciers of Mont Blanc, where climbers practice alpine mountaineering skills, including the use of ropes and anchors, crevasse rescue, and both French and German ice ax and crampon technique.

Next, the group will undertake a two-day ascent of the mountain. Although it is the tallest of the three Grand Slam summits—the tallest in western Europe, in fact—Mont Blanc is not difficult technically. And this summit is also a good way to break in those without much experience of roped ascent.

Then it's on to the Swiss town of Grindewald to climb the Eiger. Before the summit attempt, the group will spend a few days polishing their technical skills. Though the Eiger has a formidable reputation, the West Flank route—a moderate snow ramp leading to the summit—can be mastered by most climbers without too much difficulty.

Finally, it's time for the Matterhorn. This famous peak can be very challenging. However, the group should be able to reach the top in a single day. And with that, the Grand Slam is complete.

American Alpine's program is suitable for most anyone with some alpine camping experience who can carry a 40-pound pack five to six hours a day. Participants should have experience in both glacier climbing and technical rock climbing. The cost for the ten-day adventure is roughly $4,100 plus airfare to Geneva. Climbers must bring all their own personal gear, including crampons and ice ax. American Alpine provides tents, ropes, all collective equipment, some food, and all transport within the climbing areas. Participants must pay for hotels if they overnight before and after the climbing sessions.

Adventures to the Edge (*Crested Butte, CO. 800-349-5219 or 970-349-5219. www.AdventureConsulting.com*) offers a 12-day Grand Slam expedition, as well as shorter trips to the Matterhorn and the Eiger. A professional, English-speaking UIAGM-certified guide costs $300 a day. Other fees for the trip vary according to personal choices of food and lodging, but expect to pay about $5,500 for all three peaks.

The highly respected **International Mountain Guides** (*Ashford, WA. 425-222-4958 or 360-569-2604. www.mountainguides.net*) runs a somewhat less difficult **Alps Classics** trip, combining Mont Blanc with three other summits: 15,204-foot **Monte Rosa,** the highest peak in Switzerland; the 13,650-foot **Jungfrau,** one of the tallest peaks in the Bernese Alps; and the 13,450-foot **Monch,** a shorter but slightly steeper challenge. The cost, including all lodging, is about $3,500 for 14 days.

Intermediate-level climbers looking for a less expensive triple-summit adventure can hire their own European guide, who must be UIAGM certified. With a suitable group of two or three qualified climbers to share costs, you can spend under $170 per day, not including airfare and hotels.

In Europe, you won't have any trouble finding a qualified climbing guide: There are more than 4,000 UIAGM-certified guides in Austria, France, Italy, and Switzerland. A list of guides can be obtained from the **Union International des Associations de Guides de Montagne** (*Via Suot Chesas 6, Champfer, CH-7512, Switzerland. 01141-81833-5680. www.bergtourismus.ch*). Many North American climbing guides also hold UIAGM certification. For referrals, contact the **Alpine Club of Canada** (*Canmore, AB. 403-678-3200. www.alpineclubofcanada.ca*).

NEW ZEALAND
Alps Way Down South

If you *have* to climb a mountain, and it's the middle of winter, how about heading south—way south? Try the Southern Hemisphere. Try New Zealand—the *South* Island, of course. There you'll find a vast range of snowcapped peaks known as the **Southern Alps** that run almost the entire length of the island, encompassing an area greater in size than their better known cousins, the Alps of Europe.

The best mountaineering program in New Zealand is run by **Alpine Guides** (*Mount Cook, 8700, New Zealand. 01164-3435-1834. www.alpineguides.co.nz*). Founded in 1966, the company boasts an international roster of guides and instructors, and offers a full range of activities—including major summit climbs, climbing instruction, glacier travel, and ski mountaineering.

If you're a novice mountaineer, try Alpine Guides' basic **Mountain Experience** course. This week-long program will teach you all the skills necessary for moderate to serious alpine climbing. Your adventure will begin with a helicopter or ski-plane ride to a mountain hut high up on **Mount Cook.** Here, at your base camp, you'll learn the basic knots and rope skills, as well as the wonderful—and initially terrifying—skill of rappeling.

After acquiring these skills, you'll move on to the essential techniques for snow and ice travel. For this, you and the other members of your group will daily trek up the slopes of the Tasman Glacier. There you'll learn how to set snow belays; how to arrest a fall on a shear slope using just your ax and crampons; and how to construct emergency shelters and igloos.

Next, the group will head back down to the base camp—and the rocks—for the technical climbing class. This is where you'll learn how to place "protection"—nuts and jammers—into rock cracks to secure your climbing rope. Instructors will demonstrate all the major belaying techniques, and students will get a chance to climb some pretty vertical rock faces.

The course concludes with instruction in glacier travel and crevasse rescue, carried out on massive ice fields a few

SKIER SCALES AN ICE SERAC ON MONT BLANC.

miles from the base camp. This is the most physically demanding—and *vital*—part of the course. Crevasses claim the lives of more climbers on high-altitude expeditions than any other hazard.

The cost for Alpine Guides' seven-day basic alpine course is about $1,070 (US), including bunkhouse accommodation and most gear. The company also runs a ten-day technical mountaineering course conducted entirely on glaciers and at high elevations. Cost is around $1,400 (US). Successful graduates are eligible to join one of Alpine Guides' major summit climbs. Check out the company's superb website, which contains descriptions of all Alpine Guides' programs and a selection of stunning alpine photography.

MEXICO
Volcanic Trilogy

Rising from the highland valleys east of Mexico City, Pico de **Orizaba** (18,851 feet), **Popocatépetl** (17,887 feet), and **Iztaccihuatl** (17,343 feet) are the third, fifth, and seventh highest peaks in North America. None of these volcanic summits are technically demanding, but the routes can be extremely strenuous, traversing as they do slopes of scree and talus, snowfields and glaciers.

Because of recent volcanic activity in the area, no climbing is currently permitted on Popocatépetl. However, you can still climb Orizaba and Iztaccihuatl, as well as nearby **Malinche,** in a three-summit expedition led by North American guides.

At 14,436 feet, Malinche is smaller than its big sisters—though still higher than all but one peak in the contiguous United States. And it is a perfect tune-up peak for Orizaba and Iztaccihuatl. Climbing all three will prepare you for a major climb like Mount McKinley.

To complete your Mexican trilogy, try the **Colorado Mountain School** (*Estes Park, CO. 970-586-5758. www. cmschool.com*). The company's mountain skills training is thorough, and its program—which features stays with a host family near Mexico City and a trip to local pyramids—allows plenty of time to enjoy the local culture. The cost for the 11-day, triple-summit expedition is in the region of $1,600, with multiple departures between mid-November and early February. Colorado Mountain School also offers a nine-day expedition to Iztaccihuatl and Orizaba for about $100 less.

The **American Alpine Institute** (*Bellingham, WA. 360-671-1505 or 360-734-8890. www.aai.cc*) is another excellent choice for triple-summit expeditions. AAI trips run for 13 days at a cost of $1,700, with six departures from December to March. During the initial few days, the group makes acclimatization treks, then climbs Malinche in a day. With one peak conquered—invariably setting new altitude

records for many team members—the group breaks camp to move on to the bigger objectives: Iztaccihuatl, which it climbs in the first week, and Orizaba, in week two.

The timing of the two larger ascents is significant. Many climbers come to grief by trying to conquer both summits in a hurried eight- or nine-day program. The four or five extra days in the AAI itinerary afford more time for acclimatization, and as a result most participants manage to climb both Iztaccihuatl and Orizaba. Unless you're a two-out-of-three-ain't-bad kind of climber, consider this when you are comparison shopping . You can pay less for a shorter itinerary with an outfitter other than AAI or Colorado Mountain School—but what good is the money saved, if you don't reach the top?

ALASKA
Expedition to Denali

At 20,320 feet, Mount McKinley—the highest peak in North America—is known to mountaineers by its Native American name: Denali, the Great One.

Mountaineers also know that to conquer the Great One, you'll need stamina, a solid grounding in alpine skills—and a wee bit of luck in terms of the weather. The latter can be challenging in the extreme. With little or no warning, whiteouts can blanket the mountain for days at a time, and temperatures can plunge from comfortable to dangerously cold in the space of a few hours.

Tragically, each season some climbers don't make it back from Denali—for the most part, mountaineers who chose to make the climb in a self-guided group. On the other hand, the safety records of the best McKinley guide services are exemplary. A good choice is **Alaska-Denali Guiding, Inc.** (*Talkeetna, AK. 907-733-2649. www.denaliexpeditions.com*).

There are several different approaches to Denali, each with a different degree of difficulty. If this is your first big peak, try the West Buttress approach. Most fit climbers who have completed a basic mountaineering course—and have some high-altitude camping experience—should be able to manage this approach.

Although the West Buttress is the least difficult route to the summit, it is still not an easy climb. You'll have to walk 18 miles and ascend 13,000 feet to reach the top, all the while coping with unpredictable weather, changing snow conditions, threatening crevasses, and steep, icy slopes.

Alaska-Denali Guiding enjoys a high success rate on McKinley: More than 60 percent of its climbers reach the summit. Groups are limited to nine climbers, with three guides. Participants must be in excellent physical condition, have extensive backpacking experience, and be familiar with the use of ice ax and crampons. The company's Denali expeditions last 24 to 26 days and cost around

$3,600. The best time to go is in May and June, before the glaciers get too soft. Make a point of visiting Alaska-Denali Guiding's website, which contains full trip details and many inspiring expedition photos.

Mountain Trip (*Anchorage, AK. 907-345-6499. www. mountaintrip.com*)—which marked its 25th season on Denali in the year 2000—is another recommended guide service. So, too, is the **American Alpine Institute** (*Bellingham, WA. 360-671-1505 or 360-734-8890. www.aai.cc*), which enjoys the highest success rate.

Both companies use progressive techniques, meaning that they travel light yet maintain high safety standards. Their expeditions run about three weeks, and you can choose either the West Buttress route (which costs about $3,500) or the West Rib route ($4,000 to $4,500). Mountain Trip also guides two other approaches—Cassin Ridge and South Buttress—by special arrangement.

ECUADOR
High Andes Adventure

Just as in Mexico, three's a charm in Ecuador, too. But the three major summits here are far more scenic—and considerably more challenging—than the Mexican volcanoes. For novice mountaineers who want to climb some big mountains in a two-week vacation, Ecuador is the place.

The most experienced and successful American guide service in Ecuador is the **American Alpine Institute** (*Bellingham, WA. 360-671-1505 or 360-734-8890. www.aai.cc*). AAI offers 15-day climbing programs November through February every year.

The basic AAI program, designed for those who have been introduced to the fundamentals of climbing, features three superb—volcanic—peaks: 18,997-foot **Cayambe,** 19,348-foot **Cotopaxi,** and 20,703-foot **Chimborazo.** Though no previous high altitude experience is required, participants must be very fit to have a good chance for summit success.

Each AAI expedition includes several days of glacier travel and alpine travel skills conducted on the lower glaciers of Cayambe, at around 15,000 feet. Then it's time for the summit. Climbers must leave well before dawn to make it to the top and back again in a day. Following an easy glacier climb to a saddle, the group must rope up to ascend the 35-degree slopes to the volcano's crater, where a moderate but scenic walk above the clouds leads to the mountain's highest point.

Cotopaxi, the world's highest active volcano, comes next on AAI's agenda. Once again, the push to the summit begins in darkness: By the light of dawn, the group has to climb 30- to 35-degree snow and ice ramps to reach a 17,000-foot glacial platform. Only 2,000 feet remain to the top, but this last stretch puts the climbers' technical skills to the test. The group must belay across snow bridges, skirt crevasses, and then ascend the 40-degree slopes of Cotopaxi's upper glacier. At the summit, the group is rewarded with spectacular views of nine major peaks and Cotopaxi's 1,000-foot-deep summit crater.

Now, only Chimborazo awaits. A massive dormant volcano rising nearly 11,000 feet above Ecuador's central valley, this is the highest peak in the country. Far more challenging than most volcanic summits, Chimborazo has complex faces and glaciers that require careful application of alpine skills. AAI attacks the West Face, a moderately steep and varied approach with 25- to 40-degree slopes and some glacier ice.

AAI's 15-day Ecuador triple-summit programs on Cayambe, Chimborazo, and Cotopaxi will cost about $2,400, including mountain meals, equipment, lodging, and ground transportation in Ecuador. There are at least six departures each year from November through March, and AAI also offers several ten-day expeditions for single summits in Ecuador.

The **Colorado Mountain School** (*Estes Park, CO. 970-586-5758. www.cmschool.com*) also offers excellent one- and two-week trips to the Andes of Ecuador. The major objective of the shorter expedition is Cayambe. However, participants will have the opportunity to acclimatize by climbing **Pinchincha**—the 15,708-foot peak above Quito—and visit the market center of Otavalo before the assault on Cayambe. The cost is $1,200.

CMS's two-week expedition offers more comprehensive alpine training and the chance to climb Cayambe, Chimborazo, Cotopaxi, and Pinchincha. The cost is $2,200, based on a team of five. After completing the first week of skills training and acclimatization on Pinchincha and Cayambe, participants take on Cotopaxi and then Chimborazo.

In between these two ascents, the team enjoys comfortable accommodations in a luxurious, 500-year-old hacienda. Other nights in the mountains are spent in European-style mountain huts, situated 3,000 to 4,000 feet below the objectives. Using these huts as a high camp, climbers can reach the top on summit day carrying just ten pounds of gear.

ARGENTINA
Ascent of Aconcagua

About 1,000 miles south of Ecuador's summits rises mighty **Aconcagua,** the highest mountain in the Western Hemisphere. At 22,841 feet, it is so tall that on a clear day it is visible from the Pacific coast of Chile, 80 miles to the west.

Numerous guide services from around the world run climbing expeditions to Aconcagua every year. Most take the Normal Route, a ridge trail that can—after acclimatization—be negotiated by reasonably fit persons. Unfortunately, the lower sections of the route are often littered with debris from the many expeditions that have passed along the way. As an alternative path, start up the Polish Route along Aconcagua's lower flanks.

Unless you have strong technical and glacier climbing skills, don't plan on completing the climb via the Polish Route, however; it's just too tough. The best plan for most climbers is to traverse back to the Normal Route to finish the last 4,000 feet to the summit of Aconcagua. Although this route does not present much of a technical challenge, the extreme altitude, the lack of oxygen, and the danger of sudden, violent storms (the mountain creates its own climate) make experienced mountaineering judgment and leadership essential.

The **American Alpine Institute** (*Bellingham, WA. 360-671-1505 or 360-734-8890. www.aai.cc*) is the best choice for an Aconcagua expedition. No American guide service has more experience on the mountain or more skilled guides. For the reasons mentioned above, all AAI trips take the Polish Route through the lower elevations. After three days of acclimatizing on the approach march, the team goes to the 13,500-foot base camp. Those with previous alpine climbing experience—and the ability to follow a moderately steep snow and ice route with packs—will attempt a Polish Route ascent to the top. Those with less experience will do a traverse route around the North Face and finish on the less technical upper West Face.

Whatever the route chosen, all participants must be extremely fit to reach the summit. The price, for a team of seven to eight climbers, is roughly $3,600 per person. AAI generally offers three 23-day Aconcagua expeditions annually, with departures in December through February.

Some climbers may prefer the 21-day Aconcagua expedition offered by **Summits Adventure Travel** (*Ashford, WA. 360-569-2992. www.summitsadventure.com*). This program—which employs pack animals to carry the expedition's supplies much of the way—follows a variation of the Polish Route, along the less traveled Las Vacas River Valley to reach base camp. The summit is attempted along the Normal Route.

The company's January expedition costs approximately $4,100. Participants should have previous high-altitude experience and a good foundation in alpine skills.

Free Climbing & Free Soloing

For many rock climbers, the ultimate thrill is "free climbing"—a mode of climbing in which protection (ropes and anchors) is placed but not used.

In short, the goal of free climbing is to ascend the route—typically, a challenging rock face—without ever resting on the rope. Secure in the knowledge that the rope is there in case of a slip, the free climber can concentrate on the ascent itself, testing the limits of endurance and climbing skill.

By contrast, the most extreme (and dangerous) form of climbing is "free soloing"—climbing without a rope or protection of any kind. If free climbing is the equivalent of performing a high wire act above a safety net you hope never to need, free soloing is walking the high wire without the safety net.

Free soloing certainly makes for high drama. But as a sport, it is a questionable practice—no matter how skilled the climber. Though some may view it as a test of climbing courage, most expert alpinists consider free soloing foolhardy. Any error can prove fatal—and when a climber dies free soloing, the repercussions for the sport are always immediate and negative.

World-class climber Paul Piana has no illusions about the dangers of free soloing. His advice should be considered by anyone attracted to this pursuit. "Free climbing and free soloing are different in very important ways," says Piana. "A free climber has the option of safely falling innumerable times, of falling until it is possible to ascend the route as if there was no rope—no safety net. For this reason, because safety equipment and techniques have been developed that are strong and reliable, free climbing is quite safe. On the other hand, a sport like free soloing, where the slightest mistake results in a horrifying death, is more of a stunt than a sport and games as deadly as this attract few participants."

ROCK HOUNDS PERFECT THE ANGLE OF THE DANGLE

Great Mountaineering Schools

Before you attempt any serious mountaineering, you should acquire a strong foundation in technical climbing skills and mountain safety. Watching a video or reading a book is no substitute for hands-on training in the field under the careful supervision of experts. The following programs all offer outstanding novice to advanced training in the major mountaineering disciplines. If you want to stand on the summit someday, these organizations can show you the ropes.

There are only three sports: bullfighting, motor racing, and mountaineering; all the rest are merely games.
—Ernest Hemingway

Alpine Skills International

P.O. Box 8, Norden, CA 95724
800-916-7325 or 530-426-9108
www.alpineskills.com
PROGRAMS: mountaineering, rock, ice, treks, guided climbs, ski mountaineering, winter skills. AMGA accredited with UIAGM-certified guides.

Based in the Sierra Nevada near Lake Tahoe, ASI runs a popular year-round alpine program. While many of its programs are designed for those with strong rock- and snow-climbing skills, ASI also offers a variety of expeditions (Aconcagua, Bolivia, European Haute Route, Mexican volcanoes, Mount Shasta, and Whistler-Blackcomb) that are suitable for those with a limited amount of alpine experience. ASI conducts weekend ice-climbing seminars in the Lee Vining/June Lake area.

American Alpine Institute

1515 12th St., N-3, Bellingham, WA 98225
360-671-1505 or 360-734-8890. www.aai.cc
PROGRAMS: mountaineering, rock, ice, guided climbs, winter skills, ski mountaineering, mountain rescue. AMGA (American Mountain Guides Association) accredited, AMGA-certified guides, some UIAGM guides.

AAI conducts superior alpine mountaineering and technical leadership courses that cover ice- and rock-climbing skills, route-finding, leadership skills, and glacier ascents. AAI leads summit expeditions for novice mountaineers to 20,000-foot-plus peaks in Argentina, Bolivia, Ecuador, Peru, and Nepal, as well as more challenging ascents, including Denali. AAI is a well-established operation that offers the complete spectrum of mountaineering services at moderate prices.

Colorado Mountain School, Inc.

P.O. Box 1846, Estes Park, CO 80517
970-586-5758. www.cmschool.com
PROGRAMS: mountaineering, rock, ice, guided climbs, treks, ski mountaineering. AMGA accredited.

CMS does a great job with novices, yet it also offers challenging, multipitch climbs for intermediates looking to become advanced climbers with the ability to lead. Even expert climbers can learn plenty from CMS's world-class rock guides. In addition to its rock courses, the company offers guiding services in Rocky Mountain National Park and conducts expeditions to major peaks around the world, including Africa (Mount Kilimanjaro), Alaska (Mooses Tooth and Mount McKinley), Mexico (Malinche, Iztaccihuatl, and Orizaba), and South America (Huascaran and Aconcagua). At $1,600, CMS's Mexican volcanoes trip is a bargain-priced introduction to high-altitude climbing.

Exum Mountain Guides

P.O. Box 56, South Jenny Lake
Grand Teton National Park
Moose, WY 83012
307-733-2297. www.exumguides.com
PROGRAMS: mountaineering, rock, ice, winter skills. AMGA accredited.

Exum provides the most experienced and versatile alpine guide service in the northern Rockies. The company can arrange customized training programs for all levels. Basic and intermediate programs are $95 and $115 per day, respectively. Exum also offers guided ascents of 13,770-foot Grand Teton and dozens of local peaks. A Grand Teton climb is $350 with four clients per guide.

International School of Mountaineering

Hafod Tan-y-Graig, Nant Gwynant, Caernarfon LL55 4NW, U.K. 01144-1766-890441. http://dspace.dial.pipex.com/ism/
PROGRAMS: mountaineering, trekking, and ski mountaineering. UIAGM-certified guides.

ISM runs high alpine treks and mountaineering courses for all levels, from beginner to advanced. ISM's major operation is in the Swiss Alps. But the company also offers expeditions to lesser and major peaks in the Andes, the Karakoram, the Pamir, and the Tien Shan Ranges. ISM prefers to explore new areas that offer genuine discovery and adventure.

Jackson Hole Mountain Guides & Climbing School

P.O. Box 7477, Jackson, WY 83002
800-239-7642 or 307-733-4979
www.jhmg.com
PROGRAMS: mountaineering, rock, ice, guided climbs, winter skills, ski mountaineering. AMGA accredited.

This school offers a variety of programs, with small classes and skilled guides. Beginners should try the four-day Grand Teton Climber Course ($850), which features an ascent of Grand Teton. Experts will enjoy one-on-one private guided climbing for $250 per day. For those interested in a wilderness climbing experience, there is the eight-day, $1,500 ascent of Gannet, Wyoming's highest peak.

National Outdoor Leadership School

288 Main St., Lander, WY 82520
307-332-5300. www.nols.edu
PROGRAMS: mountaineering, rock, ice, expeditions, mountain rescue, outdoor survival, ski mountaineering. AEE (Association for Experiential Education) accredited.

The mountaineering programs at NOLS tend to be longer in duration (30-90 days) and more intensive than those of other schools. The climbing instruction is professional and safety oriented, and NOLS gives its clients a thorough grounding in general mountain skills, team-building, and low-impact camping. NOLS operates worldwide, with training centers in Alaska, the Cascades, and Wyoming, plus mountaineering programs in the Andes and the Himalaya.

Rainier Mountaineering, Inc.

535 Dock St., Suite 209, Tacoma, WA 98402 253-627-6242; Mount Rainier National Park, Paradise, WA 98398. 360-569-2227 (May-Sept.). www.rmiguides.com

PROGRAMS: mountaineering, guided climbs, winter skills, mountain rescue, glacier travel.

This is the only climbing school on 14,410-foot Mount Rainier, a good location to develop skills for a major summit climb involving glacier travel. Rainier Mountaineering is best known for its ice and snow training and for its summit work. Among the one-day programs offered are the crevasse rescue program and the basic alpine-climbing school (each $105). Longer programs include a three-day Mount Rainier summit climb ($590), a six-day winter seminar, and a six-day expedition seminar ($1,150) featuring trip planning, logistics, glacier camping, and a summit climb.

Yamnuska, Inc.

50-103 Bow Valley Trail, Canmore, AB T1W 1N8, Canada. 403-678-4164 www.yamnuska.com

PROGRAMS: mountaineering, rock, ice, guided climbs, mountain rescue, glacier travel. UIAGM-certified guides.

Canada's leading mountaineering school, Yamnuska places strong emphasis on training, especially for glacier travel and alpine climbing. The company offers a variety of weekend rock- and ice-climbing courses starting at $190 (CN). Try the three-day Snow and Ice Long Weekend, which culminates with an ascent of 11,452-foot Mount Athabasca for $270 (US). Also popular is the weeklong introduction to mountaineering, a hut-based program on the Wapta Ice Fields that covers glacial ascents, navigation, and crevasse rescue. Cost is $775 (US). Each year, Yamnuska guides a number of major summit expeditions, including Mount Logan, Mount Robson, and a major international peak. The company's Mountain Skills Semester—an intensive three-month field program—is offered in spring and fall and costs $5,750 (US).

EXPEDITION RISK MANAGEMENT

Things can happen while climbing. Common injuries include fractures, frostbite, and concussions. Even altitude sickness can be debilitating for some. You should not undertake any climbing program without good personal medical insurance. (Most accredited climbing schools are bonded and insured, but the type and amount of coverage varies considerably, so you should still have your own insurance.)

Read your policy carefully. Make sure there is no exclusion for high-risk activities, such as climbing. If you need to acquire new medical insurance, carriers specializing in coverage for foreign trips are listed in the last chapter of this book.

You will also want trip cancellation and evacuation insurance. Trip cancellation insurance will cover nonrefundable air and land costs—which are forfeited when you cancel a climbing course because of family or personal illness or disability. Evacuation insurance will cover the cost of emergency medical evacuation from wilderness areas. This coverage is essential: An emergency helicopter evacuation from a remote summit can easily cost $1,000 or more. Ask your guide service if it can place trip cancellation and evacuation insurance for you. Alpine Skills International, for example, provides such insurance to its climbers for approximately $6 per $100 of trip cost.

Rock-climbing Programs

TOP GUIDE SERVICES

Among the general mountaineering schools listed, two stand out for the quality of their rock-climbing programs and for the expertise of their rock instructors: Exum Mountain Guides and Jackson Hole Mountain Guides.

In addition to these well-established programs, here are some other outstanding rock-climbing schools/guide services. Most focus on technical rock and ice climbing, though many also offer programs in alpine expedition skills. For a complete list of accredited climbing programs, contact the **American Mountain Guides Association** (303-271-0984. www.amga.com). An online database of climbing guides worldwide is maintained by **Rocklist** (www.rocklist.com).

Eastern Mountain Sports Climbing School

P.O. Box 514, North Conway, NH 03860 800-310-4504 or 603-356-5433

FREE CLIMBING ABOVE LAKE LOUISE, ALBERTA

www.emsclimb.com
AMGA accredited; AMGA-certified guides.

In business since 1968, the school offers courses on ice climbing, winter skills instruction, mountaineering, and the fundamentals of rock climbing. EMS operates a national program with climbing schools in New Hampshire, New York (New Paltz), Connecticut (West Hartford), and Colorado (Boulder). In North Conway, the EMS Climbing School shares the superb Cathedral and White Horse Ledges with International Mountain Climbing School. Both schools have skilled instructors. For intermediates, the best way to learn is with one-on-one instruction for $150-225 per day. Novices can take the one-day beginner or intermediate IMCS course for $115-125.

High Angle Adventures, Inc.
178 Hardenburgh Rd., Ulster Park, NY 12487.
800-777-2546 or 914-658-9811
www.highangle.com
AMGA accredited; AMGA-certified guides.

High Angle Adventures has top-notch guides and a superb climbing site—a major rock wall 2.5 miles long. High-friction quartzite rock and abundant horizontal striations offer good holds that allow even novices to climb with confidence. A one-day course (three students per guide) costs about $135, including all equipment, even climbing shoes. One-on-one training starts at $175 per day. High Angle's base at New Paltz is less than two hours from New York City.

International Mountain Climbing School
P.O. Box 1666, North Conway, NH 03860
603-356-7064. www.ime-usa.com
AMGA accredited; AMGA-certified guides.

Most courses have a three-to-one maximum student/guide ratio, and IMCS uses progressive techniques and state-of-the-art equipment. Train on weekdays if you can, when the most popular training routes at North Conway's Cathedral Ledge are much less crowded. A day-long rock class runs $135, while a three-day basic course costs $390. The $400, three-day winter mountaineering course is superb, covering ice climbing, snow travel, navigation, and rope skills, culminating in a climb of 6,288-foot Mount Washington.

Mountain Guides Alliance
P.O. Box 266, North Conway, NH 03860
603-356-5310
www.mountainguidesalliance.com
AMGA-certified guides.

This is a small consortium of excellent independent guides who possess strong technical skills and use the latest techniques. Programs are run on a custom basis, with two students assigned to a single guide. In addition to summer rock programs, the Mountain Guides Alliance runs excellent winter ice-climbing programs. Classes range from $120-190 per day.

Sawtooth Mountain Guides
P.O. Box 18, Stanley, ID 83278
208-774-3324. www.sawtoothguides.com
AMGA-certified guides.

The company's two-day basic mountain-craft and rock-craft combination seminar costs $175 per person with a four-person minimum. Custom rock guiding costs about $275 per day. In addition to its May-through-Sept. rock clinics, Sawtooth runs a strong winter program that includes avalanche seminars, telemark clinics, plus backcountry skiing and snowboarding.

Seneca Rocks Climbing School

P.O. Box 53, Seneca Rocks, WV 26884
800-548-0108 or 304-567-2600
www.seneca-rocks.com
AMGA accredited.

Seneca Rocks Mountain Guides

P.O. Box 223, Seneca Rocks, WV 26884
800-451-5108 or 304-567-2115
www.senecarocks.com
AMGA accredited.

The Seneca Rocks in West Virginia's Allegheny Mountains are renowned for their dramatic sandstone pinnacles. With grippy rock surfaces blessed with an abundance of handholds, this is a great place to learn to climb. It is served by the above guide services, both of which merit mention. At the climbing school, instruction is tailored to each student's abilities, with an emphasis on safety. A three-day basic program costs $275. For intermediates and those learning to lead, Seneca Rocks Mountain Guides is your best bet. SRMG operates a remarkable 6,000-square-foot indoor climbing facility, complete with 36-foot-high real rock-climbing walls quarried from the region.

Sky's the Limit

HCR 33 Box 1, Red Rock Canyon, Las Vegas, NV 89124. 800-733-7597 or 702-363-4533
www.skysthelimit.com
AMGA accredited; AMGA-certified guides.

Located 20 minutes west of Las Vegas, Red Rock, Nevada, features a wide variety of rock formations, although most routes are best for intermediates or better. The Sky's the Limit's half-day Discover Climbing course costs $170; the basic rock-craft course (one evening classroom session and two full days of climbing) costs $225; and intermediate and advanced classes featuring two full days of climbing cost $220, including all equipment. Private guiding is also available at $150 for a half day, and $250 for a full day.

Sylvan Rocks Climbing School

P.O. Box 600, Hill City, SD 57745
605-574-2425. www.sylvanrocks.com
AMGA accredited.

Sylvan Rock's primary objective is to give climbers a solid grounding in fundamental skills, rather than just hauling them to the top of the rock. The school offers a variety of programs, starting with a two-day basic rock package priced at $275 for two persons per guide. We recommend the three-day basic novice package, which includes a full day of multipitch training with gear and anchors, plus an optional climb of the

625-foot Devils Tower on the third day. Cost for three days is $395 for two climbers, plus $75 for the Tower.

Vertical Adventures
Rock Climbing School

P.O. Box 7548, Newport Beach, CA 92658
800-514-8785 or 949-854-6250
www.vertical-adventures.com
AMGA accredited; AMGA-certified guides.

In the summer, Vertical Adventures operates out of Idyllwild, climbing granite in the San Jacinto Mountains. In the winter, it moves to Joshua Tree, which offers an incredible diversity of rock formations suited for all levels of climbers. One-day courses for all skill levels cost $85; two-day seminars begin at $165; the Big Wall Seminar—featuring Yosemite-style techniques—costs about $195; and the four-day Rockcraft Seminar costs $315.

Yosemite Mountaineering School

Yosemite National Park, CA 95389
209-372-8435 or 209-372-8344
www.yosemitemountaineering.com
AMGA accredited.

Yosemite is the place to learn big-wall climbing. Yosemite Mountaineering conducts a full range of classes on some of the world's finest granite. The one-day Rock I or Rock II seminars cost $90 based on two persons per guide. The intermediate Rock III program highlights jamcrack skills, direct aid, and self-rescue, and is a prerequisite for the company's guided climbs. For strong climbers (Rock II or equivalent training), Yosemite Mountaineering offers Advanced Rock and Big Wall seminars. The school's signature two-day Big Wall class costs $240 for two climbers per guide; however, one-on-one training is also available.

Great North American Climbing Sites

ROCK CLIMBING

CALIFORNIA
Joshua Tree

Just three hours by car from Los Angeles, Joshua Tree is considered America's leading winter climbing site. The crystal quartz monzonite offers a superb climbing surface—with sharp edges, abundant cracks, and a very high friction factor. With over 3,000 recorded climbs, there is an endless

variety of routes from the beginner's Echo Rock to the classic Walk on the Wild Side. **Vertical Adventures** (800-514-8785. www.vertical-adventures.com) is Joshua Tree's leading guide service.

Tuolumne Meadows

Yosemite remains the heartland of American rock climbing. You'll find a host of well-scouted routes that most novices can master after an introductory weekend of training. The sky's the limit as far as advanced routes are concerned. With some of the longest multipitch climbs in the world, Yosemite is where they wrote the book on big-wall climbing. For guiding, contact **Yosemite Mountaineering School** (209-372-8435 or 209-372-8344. www.yosemitemountaineering.com). Lodging and campsites are conveniently close to the climbing areas.

COLORADO
Boulder Area

With a name like Boulder, you would expect the climbing to be good in this college town—and you'd be right. Although experts will head farther north into Estes Park, there are a number of good training sites close to downtown Boulder, among them Flatirons and Eldorado Canyon. The Wind Tower in Eldorado Canyon is one of the best beginners' pinnacles you can find. For an experienced guide, contact **Front Range Mountain Guides** (303-666-5523. www.mtnguides.com) or **Boulder Rock Club** (800-836-4008 or 303-447-2804. www.boulderrock.com).

IDAHO
City of the Rocks, Burley

While the City of the Rocks offers everything from gentle scrambling to experts-only climbs, the vast majority of routes are suitable for climbers-in-training. The wind-scoured desert granite provides solid holds, and many of the routes have bolted protection. Novices can quickly negotiate Elephant Rock—and within a few days take on the challenging Rye Crisp or Wheat Thins routes. Other popular moderate climbs are the Lost Arrow Spire and Morning Glory Spire. Contact **Sawtooth Mountain Guides** (208-774-3324. www.sawtoothguides.com), which also services Elephants' Ranch in the Sawtooth National Recreation Area, a spectacular 1,000-foot vertical face composed of rare orange granite.

RAPPELING DOWN ROCK FACE IN THE KARAKORAM MOUNTAINS OF PAKISTAN

Alpine Mountaineering

Spelunking

If the opposite of ascent is descent—and the opposite of climbing up is climbing down—can the opposite of mountaineering be…"spelunking"? Apparently, it is.

Spelunking, also known as caving, offers an alternative to all those adventurers disapointed that the world's tallest summits have been conquered. Spelunkers have the chance to discover underground haunts never before viewed by humans.

Caving demands both strength and daring. It combines the techniques of various sports—mountaineering, orienteering, diving—to explore the most remote places on earth. Although popular throughout the world, the sport is just coming into its own as commercial recreation conducted by professional guide services.

The most visited site for caving in the Southern Hemisphere is the vast Waitomo Cave system in New Zealand's North Island. Each year the site draws thousands of adventure-seeking tourists to the underground grottos.

The best way to experience Waitomo is the Lost World tour, which has won the coveted New Zealand Tourism Award. Lonely Planet calls the tour "one of the most amazing things you can do."

The initial rope descent to the cave entrance—the longest commercially led caving rappel in the world—is worth the price of admission alone: You step into space, dangling 330 feet off the ground from a single rope the width of your thumb.

From there the Lost World journey only becomes more enthralling as you climb, crawl, swim, and squeeze your way through the mist-filled cave. While in this surrealistic dreamworld, you'll experience a host of emotions—from paralyzing fear to fascination and ultimately to complete amazement.

THE LOST WORLD OF WAITOMO

For complete information on Lost World spelunking, contact **Waitomo Adventures Ltd.** (P.O. Box 29, Waitomo Caves, New Zealand. 011647-878-7788. www.waitomo.co.nz). A 4–hour Lost World trip costs about $110 (US) and the full 7-hour expedition about $165 (US), which includes lunch and dinner. Do the longer trip if you can—every minute is memorable. Another great program in Waitomo is the Black Water rafting. Chose between a 3–hour family float through the glowworm caves and a 5–hour cave adventure that includes spelunking, rappeling, and a thrilling underground cable traverse. Contact **Black Water Rafting** (P.O. Box 13, Waitomo Caves, New Zealand. 011647-878-6219. www.black-water-rafting.co.nz). General information on all the Waitomo area adventure programs can be obtained from the **Museum of Caves** (P.O. Box 12, Waitomo Caves, New Zealand. 011647-878-7640).

To learn more about caving in the United States and abroad, consult the **National Speleological Society** (Huntsville, AL. 205-852-1300. www.caves.org). This 11,000-member nationwide organization promotes cave preservation, research, and low-impact exploration. For commercial cave-diving adventures in North America, contact **Mad Dog Expeditions** (New York, NY 10028. 212-744-6763 or 212-744-6568. www.mad-dog.net).

NEW HAMPSHIRE

North Conway

Many elite climbers started on North Conway's famed Cathedral and White Horse Ledges. With granite faces of 500 feet and 900 feet, respectively, Cathedral and White Horse offer endless climbing options, many with fixed protection. There are over 200 recorded routes on each ledge. North Conway has some of the best climbing guides in the country, including Rick Wilcox of the **International Mountain Climbing School** (603-356-7064. www.ime-usa.com). North Conway is also an outstanding winter ice-climbing location.

NEW YORK

The Shawangunks, New Paltz

The Shawangunks can be a busy place on weekends, but there's still no better training site close to New York City. The "Gunks" offer sound, high-friction rock and the largest concentration of high-quality moderate climbs in the country. After a few days, novices can set their sights on popular intermediate climbs such as Wild Horses and Arrow. **High Angle Adventures** (800-777-2546. www.highangle.com) is the top guide service in the Gunks, but the **EMS Climbing School** (800-310-4504. www.emsclimb.com) also does a great job.

NORTH CAROLINA

Table Rock, Linville Gorge Wilderness Area

South of the Mason-Dixon Line, you won't find many better places to learn the ropes than North Carolina's Table Rock. The quartzite rock offers a variety of routes, mostly multipitch, and many up to 400 feet. Popular novice climbs include the Cave Route and Jim Dandy on the East Face. If you want to climb in solitude, hike about 45 minutes to the Amphitheater, where you'll find good edges, few crowds, and fine exposure—almost 1,000 feet above the Linville Gorge. For an even greater challenge, head to nearby Looking Glass Rock, which features a wide variety of multilevel, multipitch climbs on faces up to 800 feet, with good crack action. Popular routes are Pins & Needles and The Nose. For both Table Rock and Looking Glass, contact **Asheville's**

Peak Experiences in the United States

Map labels:

Mt. McKinley 20,320 ft
Mt. St. Elias 18,008 ft
Valdez
Mt. Fairweather 15,300 ft
ALASKA

Mt. Baker 10,778 ft
Mt. Shuksan 9,127 ft
Leavenworth
Castle Rock
Mt. Rainier N.P.
WASH.
Mt. Adams 12,307 ft
Terrebonne Smith Rock S.P.
OREGON
Borah Peak 12,662 ft
Grand Teton 13,770 ft
Cody
Devils Tower N.M.
IDAHO
Grand Teton N.P.
Mt. Shasta 14,162 ft
Burley
Jackson
WYO.
Custer S.P.
City of Rocks
Gannett Peak 13,804 ft
NEVADA
Mt. Moriah 12,050 ft
Rocky Mountain N.P.
Tuolumne
Lee Vining
Boulder
Yosemite N.P.
Longs Peak 14,255 ft
June Lake
COLORADO
CALIF.
Canyonlands N.P.
Ouray
Crestone Needle 14,294 ft
Red Rock Canyon N.C.A.
Joshua Tree
Joshua Tree N.P.

Mt. Washington 6,228 ft
North Conway
N.H.
NEW YORK
New Paltz
Shawangunks
Seneca Rocks
W. VA.
Linville
NORTH CAROLINA
Mt. Craig 6,648 ft
Table Rock

Legend:
- ■ Rock Climbing Area
- ▲ Ice Climbing Program
- • City or Town
- + Classic Alpine Climbs

Kauai
Oahu
Molokai
Maui
HAWAII
Mauna Kea 13,796 ft
Hawaii

Black Dome Guides (800-437-2367 or 828-251-9082. www.blackdome.com).

OREGON

Smith Rock State Park, Terrebonne

If you're located in the Pacific Northwest, and would like to learn rock climbing in a dry, sunny environment, Smith Rock State Park is hard to beat. While it's peppered with a variety of easy training routes that can be scouted from the ground, it also has some extremely difficult world-class pitches, which attract many of climbing's noted "rock stars." AMGA-accredited **First Ascent Climbing Services** (Redmond, OR. 800-325-5462 or 541-548-5137. www. goclimbing.com) guides at the park from March through November—and at other local crags on request. Two-day training programs cost $130-290 (depending on group size); private guiding is available.

SOUTH DAKOTA

Custer State Park

Just a few miles southwest of Mount Rushmore National Memorial in Custer State Park, you'll find four of the best rock-climbing sites in the world. Rushmore Needles has the strongest reputation among serious climbers, but Sylvan Lake and Cathedral Spires provide equal challenge and more solitude. Nearby Devils Tower National Monument is a world-class crack-climbing site, yet its 625-foot face can be conquered by well-trained intermediates. With over 600 quality climbs—including multipitch routes, sport climbs, and even free traditional crack climbs—Custer State Park is loaded with options for intermediate to advanced climbers. The top guide service is **Sylvan Rocks Climbing School** (605-574-2425). AMGA-accredited, the school teaches solid technical rock skills and

offers a three-day package with optional multipitch climb of Devils Tower. For general information on Devils Tower, go to www.nps.gov/deto/climbing.htm.

WASHINGTON

Castle Rock, Leavenworth Area

Leavenworth is the premier rock-climbing area in the Cascades, with eight major crags within a 10-mile radius of town. Castle Rock itself boasts over 60 routes. Other great sites are Snow Creek Wall and the Peschastin Pinnacles. Situated on the east slope of the Cascades, Leavenworth is dry and warm, spring through fall. The good weather, combined with short approaches and a wide variety of routes, make Leavenworth a great choice for all classes of climbers. Contact the **American Alpine Institute** (360-671-1505. www. aai.cc) for classes and guided climbs.

WYOMING

Grand Teton Area

Any list of classic American climbs would have to include the Tetons, home to **Exum Mountain Guides** (307-733-2297. *www.exumguides.com*), the nation's oldest climbing school. There are countless climbing options, but the Tetons' most celebrated attractions are its major multi-pitch climbs, ascending 1,000 feet or more above your starting point. Master these complex routes and you can tackle any size mountain. Most novices take Exum's basic mountaineering course, which will—after a couple of days' training—put them atop Grand Teton summit. The views from the top are spectacular. Popular day-climbs include Cube Point, Baxter's Pinnacle, and Guides Wall.

ICE CLIMBING

In the past 15 years, new techniques and more advanced equipment have revolutionized ice climbing, allowing vertical ascents of frozen waterfalls—the ultimate stairways of ice. If you have dreamed of conquering gravity in a winter wonderland, here are the best places to go throughout North America. To learn more about the sport, get *Snow and Ice Climbing* by John Barry, a great primer for newcomers to this most technical of all climbing disciplines. Log on to the Intermountain Ice Project at www.iceclimb.com for reports from 30 major climbing spots and a calendar of ice-climbing festivals nationwide.

Valdez, Alaska

Alaska's ice mecca, Valdez is one of the best ice-climbing venues on the planet. In Keystone Canyon, you'll find dozens of spectacular ice routes, including Bridal Veil Falls and Green Steps (both experts only). Each year in early March, Valdez hosts a major ice-climbing festival attracting many legendary climbers. For festival details, call **Chugach Mountain Adventures** (907-835-5182) or contact the **Valdez Visitor's Bureau** (*800-770-5954 or 907-835-4636. www.alaskagold.com/ice*). A top guide service for Valdez is **St. Elias Alpine Guides** (*Anchorage, AK. 888-933-5427 or 907-345-9048. www.steliasguides.com*). The company also offers summer ice climbing on the Kennicott Glacier in Wrangell-St. Elias National Park, along with major summit climbs, ski mountaineering trips, and glacier travel seminars.

June Lake & Lee Vining, California

Vertical ice is the hallmark of Lee Vining Canyon and June Lake, located on the eastern flank of the Sierra Nevada mountains, near the resort town of Mammoth Lakes. Each winter, water flowing from alpine reservoirs and natural creeks crystallize into columns of glistening blue ice. These frozen cascades—hundreds of feet in height—compose the best ice-climbing area west of the Rockies. **American Alpine Institute** (*360-671-1505. www.aai.cc*) conducts ice-climbing seminars and private climbs throughout the climbing season, generally late December through mid-March. A typical class lasts two days and costs about $220 per person, including all climbing gear. **Alpine Skills International** (*800-916-7325 or 530-426-9108. www.alpineskills.com*) also runs two-day Frozen Waterfalls courses in January and February at a cost of $240. The company provides all the equipment, including the latest high-tech hardware.

Ouray, Colorado

Known as the Ice Capital of the Rockies, Ouray operates the only true Ice Park in America, with regulated water flows and easy access from town. Ouray's ideal conditions attract vertical-ice legends from around the world, yet the reliability and accessibility of Ouray's icefalls makes this a great training ground as well. Telluride-based Michael Covington (*970-728-3546*) is a superb instructor who offers custom guiding for $250 per day or $40 per hour throughout the winter. If you prefer a more structured program, **American Alpine Institute** (*360-671-1505. www.aai.cc*) offers winter ice programs December through April, at a cost of $200 per day for two clients per guide. Because AAI holds permits to operate in the nearby San Juan and Uncompahgre National Forests, its seminars augment Ice Park training with climbs on larger, backcountry ice flows such as Dexter Creek Falls, Camp Bird Mine Falls, and Skylight Falls.

Mt. Washington Valley, New Hampshire

The third week of February each year, you can watch world-class ice climbers tackle impressive frozen waterfalls, as North Conway plays host to the annual Mt. Washington Valley Ice Festival. One of the biggest events of its kind, the festival provides a perfect opportunity to see what this sport is all about. In 2000, festival organizers even built an ice-climbing tower on site at the Sheraton Four Points Hotel so festival visitors could try the sport for free, under the supervision of the **International Mountain Climbing School** (*603-356-7064. www.ime-usa.com*). Along with organizing the festival, the school offers regular ice-climbing and winter mountaineering clinics all winter long.

Cody and Tetons, Wyoming

Generally regarded as Wyoming's best ice venue, Shoshone Canyon near the town of Cody offers an unrivaled diversity of ice-climbing options. In February each year, Cody hosts a Waterfall Ice Campout on the South Fork of the Shoshone River above the town. Elsewhere, the mountains of northwest Wyoming provide excellent opportunities for winter ice climbs. Death Canyon in the Tetons boasts short and medium length practice routes, and Torrey Canyon in the Wind River Range features formidable ice gullies and curtains. **Exum Mountain Guides** (*307-733-2297. www.exumguides.com*) offers a wide range of private climbs to suit every client's interest and skills.

Thunder Bay, Ontario

North of Lake Superior, near Thunder Bay, you'll find great vertical ice and dependable climbing conditions November through April. The winter climbing program is run by **North of Superior Climbing Company** (*Thunder Bay, ON P7B 5E8, Canada. 807-344-9636. www.climbingcentral.com*). The company offers a one-day introduction to ice climbing for $85 (CN); two-day intermediate and advanced courses starting at $275 (CN); and a seven-day Ice Week for $1,000 (CN), including gear but not lodging. You can even arrange a privately guided first ascent of a new local ice fall—and you get to name the climb. Each March, the company hosts the Orient Bay Ice Fest, featuring ice-climbing clinics and competitions.

ORGANIZATIONS

In the United States, certification of mountain guides is regulated by the **American Mountain Guides Association** (*Golden, CO. 303-271-0984. www.amga.com*) and in Canada, by the **Association of Canadian Mountain Guides** (*Canmore, AB. 403-678-2885. www.acmg.ca*).

Certification involves rigorous training and individual field evaluation at a standard recognized by the **International Federation of Mountain Guides Associations** (IFMGA, also known as the UIAGM). In the United States, the AMGA also supervises accreditation of climbing programs. Accreditation, unlike guide certification, evaluates guide services instead of individuals. It is an on-site consultation that determines if safety systems are appropriate for a company's climbing activities.

In IFMGA countries outside North America, a mountain guide is certified by that country's guide association. Each organization can provide you with a list of certified guides in its region. Qualifying guides receive UIAGM certification, which denotes skill in three disciplines: rock, alpine, and ski mountaineering. There are more than 4,800 UIAGM-certified guides worldwide, most of whom guide in the European Alps. For information on UIAGM guides, visit the UIAGM website: www.adventure.ch/ivbv/eivbv.htm.

Other important climbing affiliations include the **American Alpine Club** (*Golden, CO. 303-384-0110. www.americanalpineclub.org*) and the **Alpine Club of Canada** (*Canmore, AB. 403-678-3200. www.alpineclubofcanada.ca*).

ONLINE

The Climbing Archive
www.dtek.chalmers.se/Climbing

This pioneering website features the best directory of climbing partners, plus training tips and articles from *Ravage Climbing* magazine.

Mountain Zone
www.mountainzone.com

This diverse site covers climbing, mountain biking, and snowboarding. Features include live cybercasts, coverage of major climbs, site profiles, plus online books and video sales.

QuokkaSports
www.quokka.com

Quokka offers high-tech, cutting-edge cybercasts of major climbs and expeditions.

RockList
www.rocklist.com

Click on the "links" tab to find a comprehensive directory of climbing guides and outfitters worldwide (more than 130 at last count).

MAGAZINES

Climbing Magazine (800-829-5895 or 970-963-9449. www.climbing.com) is a great bimonthly journal. The emphasis is on rock climbing, with many features on alpine ascents.

Rock & Ice magazine *(303-499-8410. www.rockandice.com)* covers rock climbing, ice climbing, and mountaineering, with regular features on competition and big-wall climbing.

BOOKS

How to Rock-Climb! by John Long (Adventurous Traveler Bookstore, $13.95. 800-282-3963. www.adventuroustraveler.com). A best-selling introductory guidebook that should be in every climber's library.

Climbing Ice by Yvon Chouinard (Chessler Books, 1978, $24. 800-654-8502. www.chesslerbooks.com). Climbing legend Chouinard covers the techniques, equipment, and history of ice climbing and the science of snow and ice formation.

Exotic Rock: The Traveler Guide for Rock Climbers by Sam Lightner, Jr. (Mountain Books, 1995, $24.95. 800-644-5232. www.gearzone.com). This unique travel guide covers prime climbing spots in Greece, Hong Kong, Indonesia, Japan, Malaysia, Morocco, Norway, South Africa, and Thailand.

Mountaineering: The Freedom of the Hills by Don Graydon (Chessler Books, 1997, $24.95. 800-654-8502. www.chesslerbooks.com). This is the most complete guide to alpine mountaineering in print. From rope technique to avalanche rescue, it is the bible of climbing—and a necessary resource for any serious mountaineer.

Rappelling by Tom Martin (Alpenbooks, $16.95. 800-290-9898. www.alpenbooks.com). Written for rescue squads, the military, and sport climbers, this manual covers the use of descender devices, harnesses, ropes, knots, anchors, and belays.

VIDEOS & CD-ROM

Basic Rock-Climbing (Vertical Adventures, $29. 800-514-8785. www.vertical-adventures.com.). Filmed on location in Yosemite, this video shows you the fundamentals needed to challenge a big wall; narrated by John Long, author of *How to Rock-Climb!*

Rock Climbing 101—Basic Skills (Mountain Books, $29.95. 800-644-5232. www.gearzone.com). This CD-ROM covers ropework, technique, types of climbing, and gear.

Everest: Mountain of Dreams, Mountain of Doom (Mountain Books, $39.95. 800-644-5232. www.gearzone.com). A three-part video collection that covers the history of Everest's early climbers and the expeditions of the modern era, including the tragic events of the 1996 climbing season, the deadliest year in the mountain's history. This set includes the Academy Award-nominated documentary of Sir Edmund Hillary's 1953 British expedition.

GET A GRIP!

W HETHER DRIFTING OVER THE QUIET FIELDS OF

BURGUNDY OR CRESTING THE ROCKIES AT DAWN'S

light, balloons possess a singular magic. Ballooning has been around

since the Montgolfier brothers of France soared above Annonay

in 1783, but only in recent decades has the growth of commercial

ballooning allowed the average person to take to the skies in North

America and elsewhere around the world. Balloon operators can be

found near most big U.S. cities, and a number of agents offer tours

on nearly every continent. Many novices get hooked on ballooning

and take up the sport seriously; while some buy their own balloons,

others join a ballooning club. The pages that follow tell you how

to exercise both options. They also give you an idea of what it

will cost to operate your own balloon. • Descriptions of the best

ballooning-vacation packages begin on page 28, followed by listings

of commercial balloon operations worldwide. You'll also find a

comprehensive calendar of ballooning events in the United States.

• For many, going up in a hot-air balloon represents a lifetime

dream. Read on to find out how to make that dream come true.

LEFT: THE THRILL OF BEING A BASKET CASE HIGH ABOVE SNOWMASS, COLORADO.
BELOW: TETHERING THE *YELLOW SUBMARINE* AT THE ALBUQUERQUE BALLOON FIESTA.

French Vineyards

New Mexico Fiesta

An Airborne Safari

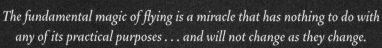

The fundamental magic of flying is a miracle that has nothing to do with any of its practical purposes . . . and will not change as they change.
ANNE MORROW LINDBERGH

Great Ballooning Adventures

Ballooning offers both spectacle and serenity—a celebration of color and an escape from everyday life. The late Malcolm Forbes cherished the tranquil magic of ballooning, popularizing the sport among princes and potentates. But ballooning is not just for the rich and famous. A deluxe champagne flight almost anywhere in America runs from about $130 to $180. For those seeking the ultimate lighter-than-air experience, read on to discover some of the world's greatest ballooning adventures, from Scandinavia to the Outback.

FRANCE
Castles and Vineyards

Nothing epitomizes luxury ballooning better than a flying tour of the famed vineyards and châteaus of **Burgundy.** Such a trip is offered by the Bombard Society, an American company specializing in high-end European ballooning holidays. From Paris, the TGV (*Train à Grande Vitesse*) whisks you first-class to Burgundy. After visiting world-class vineyards, guests make their first balloon ascent, flying over medieval castles and a patchwork of vineyards. In the evening, pilots and passengers dine like royalty in the 14th-century vaulted chambers of Château Savigny-les-Beaune. In short, this trip defines first-class adventure travel.

On your second day, you visit the Patriarche family cellar, home to 10 million bottles representing five centuries' vintage. A wine-tasting precedes lunch with the Countess de Loisy at her country estate. You then fly over the vineyard before sitting down to a candlelight buffet in the ancient cellars of Château Philippe le Hardi. On day three, you visit Château de la Rochepot, a stunning clifftop fortress. After touring the château, fire up your balloon to soar over the intricately patterned tile roofs of nearby Côte d'Or vineyards. The next day, you'll explore the 12th-century fortified city of **Châteauneuf,** then visit more vineyards, including Château Commarin (complete with 13th-century castle and moat). There is one last flight before arriving at Château de Laborde, Buddy Bombard's home in France. Your fifth day is free for exploring **Beaune,** a 14th-century walled city and the ancient capital of Burgundy.

The ultimate ballooning experience comes with a lofty price tag: $6,000 per person. Contact the **Bombard Society** (*333 Pershing Way, West Palm Beach, FL 33401. 800-862-8537 or 561-837-6610. www.bombardsociety.com*).

SWEDEN
Night Flights and City Lights

Stockholm becomes a fantasy destination for balloonists each summer, when they get to enjoy romantic sunset cruises over the city. Stockholm's far northern latitude makes for long hours of summer sun, extending the twilight and allowing safe and spectacular night flying. With predictable air conditions and more than 20 good landing sites in the city's environs, sunset ballooning is not only possible here—it is the custom. Ninety percent of commercial balloon flights lift off at dusk. The evening light combines with the unique sensation of gliding over the glimmering lights of the capital to make this a ballooning vacation to remember.

Visitors to Stockholm are often amazed at the parade of hot-air balloons in the evening sky. On a summer weekend, it's not unusual to spot 25 colorful envelopes cruising over the Stockholm archipelago and the city's skyline at day's end. Of Stockholm's many quality balloon operations, the best are **Scandinavian Balloons** (*01146-8556-40465. http://balloons-sweden.se/*) and **Upp & Ner Balloons** (*01146-8695-0100. www.uppner.se*). Both companies have able, English-speaking pilots. Upp & Nerr boasts one of Europe's most modern balloon fleets. These organizations have carried passengers over the Swedish capital for two decades. A sunset flight of one hour costs roughly $160.

AUSTRIA
Airborne over the Alps

Few European cities can rival the fairy-tale setting of **Salzburg.** On the banks of the Salzach River, Salzburg is tucked between two mountains just a few kilometers from the Austrian Alps. The Bombard Society conducts a superlative five-day balloon tour of the region. On the first day, guests arrive at the elegant Schloss Fuschl Hotel, a tower built in 1450 by the Prince-Archbishops of Salzburg as their private hunting castle and summer residence. In the afternoon, you float over nearby farmlands and foothills.

The next day, the group tours Old Salzburg. This lovely city—an Old World gem — seems far removed from the hustle and bustle of the 21st century. The afternoon features a scenic flight above the foothills of Salzburg, home to some of Austria's most impressive palaces.

On day three, the balloonists visit **St. Gilgen,** at the end of Lake St. Wolfgang, and eat lunch aboard the *Helena* — a privately chartered lake steamer that cruises Lake Mondsee. Dessert is served in a café in the village of Mondsee, wedged between lake and mountain. In the late afternoon, the group goes ballooning over nearby lakes and alpine villages.

The fourth day kicks off with a private yacht cruise to picturesque **Hallstatt,** where Austrian Princess Manni Wittgenstein hosts a lunch in her alpine home. The group then lifts off for a late-afternoon float above the foothills of Salzburg, followed by a four-course dinner at the Jagdhof — a traditional Austrian hunting lodge run by Schloss Fuschl.

The trip costs about $5,500 per person double occupancy; single supplement $600. For details, contact the **Bombard Society** (*West Palm Beach, FL. 800-862-8537 or 561-837-6610. www.bombardsociety.com*). That price is beyond the reach of most travelers, but other balloon operators offer single-day rides in Austria. A favorite of many, **Ballooning Tyrol** (*01143-5352-65666. www.alpennet.com/ballooning-tyrol*), flies from St. Johann and Kitzbuhel, home of a famed ski resort. Winter offers the best flying conditions, and in mid-January you can enjoy *Winterzauber*—Austria's premier balloon festival. More than 45 balloons fill the air; ski competitions add to the fun. Contact the **Austrian National Tourist Office** (*212-944-6880. www.anto.com*).

SWITZERLAND
Château-d'Oex Balloon Festival

Imagine 50 balloons rising simultaneously from the glistening snow of the Swiss Alps, soaring above valleys and 10,000-foot-high peaks. This spectacle takes place every January at the **Château-d'Oex Winter Alpine Balloon Festival** in Gstaad, Switzerland, an event that draws balloonists from more than 15 countries.

The festival lasts 10 days. Special events include a dirigible demonstration, mountain hang-glider flying, and long-distance flights over the Alps (weather permitting). You can visit the event as a spectator or—if you want to fly—join the Bombard Society's nine-day ballooning holiday linked to the festivities. Flights are made every day, with mass ascensions held five times during the festival. Bombard clients stay in deluxe hotels and dine at fine restaurants throughout the region.

The Bombard Society has participated in the festival for six years, making its giant tulip balloons a familiar sight over the Alps. If money is no object, stay the full nine days at $11,471 per person, double occupancy; single supplement $900. When you're not flying, you can ski at nearby resorts. If the cost of a small car seems too much to pay for a vacation, the Bombard Society also offers a six-day, five-night program in the Gstaad region for $7,828

ROAM WITH A VIEW: FLOATING OVER BURGUNDY VINEYARDS

per person, double occupancy; single supplement $590. Guests fly over the same area, but not in conjunction with the festival. Contact the **Bombard Society** (*West Palm Beach, FL. 800-862-8537 or 561-837-6610. www.bombardso-ciety.com*) or the **Swiss National Tourist Office** (*212-757-5944*).

AFRICA
Kenya Balloon Safari

To ascend over Kenya's **Masai Mara Game Reserve** at dawn is without a doubt one of the greatest thrills in bal-looning. Suspended in stillness, you watch the night mist clearing on the plains below as herds of antelope and zebra rise to greet the new day. As you pass above watering holes crowded with all manner of creatures, flocks of birds lift in flight, spooked by the balloon's slow-moving shadow. On the open veldt below, lions stalk their prey while baboons and wild dogs stare in curiosity at your silent craft. It's a remarkable sensation.

Because the Masai Mara is Africa's most popular bal-looning site, flights are available from many locations within the game reserve. These include **Mara Sorova Camp, Mara Serena Camp, Governor's Camp, Keekorok Lodge,** and **Taita Hills Lodge.** At present, no commercial operator runs point-to-point balloon safaris in Africa. Instead, you'll have to settle for 60- to 90-minute dawn flights, which typically cost $350 to $400 per person.

When booking an African balloon excursion, choose an established, bonded operator. Reliable picks in Kenya include **Balloon Safaris Ltd.** (*Nairobi. 01125-4250-2851. http://balloonsafaris.hypermart.net. Departs from Keekorok and Taita Hills Lodges*) and **Musiara Ltd.** (*Nairobi. 01125-4305-2273. Departs from Governor's Camp*). For ballooning over Tan-zania's famed Serengeti Plain, contact **Serengeti Balloon Safaris Ltd.** (*Arusha. 01144-1379-853129 [in the UK] or 57-8578 [in Tanzania]. www.balloonsafaris.com*). All of these com-panies employ American or European pilots, use modern equipment, and carry liability insurance.

Most African safari companies will add a Kenya balloon trip to any East African safari itinerary. You can book through your travel agency, or through a safari-specialty agency, such as **Wildlife Safari** (*800-221-8118 or 925-376-5595. www.wildlife-safari.com*). Wildlife Safari offers ballooning over the Maasai Mara as part of its **Wings over Kenya** tour; alter-natively, this balloon trip can be added to any Kenya safari, time permitting.

Although it is prudent to book balloon flights in advance, you can occasionally save money by waiting until you arrive in Africa to reserve a flight. The staff at your lodge will ordi-narily be able to help you make reservations with local bal-loon operations.

STRIPES HIGH AND LOW: THE VIEW FROM A GONDOLA ABOVE THE MAASAI MARA NATIONAL RESERVE, KENYA

AUSTRALIA
Dawn Flights Down Under

If you're heading into Australia's heartland to visit **Ayers Rock,** make the trip south to Alice Springs for a balloon flight above the dramatic Red Centre. In the still dawn, your hot-air craft carries you above a desert populated with kangaroos, wild horses, and wallabies. You can also watch first light strike the ancient red rocks of the McDonald Range. Champagne-breakfast flights cost about $140 (AU) for a half-hour flight or $220 (AU) for an hour. Balloons lift off each day at dawn, weather permitting. The launch site for **Outback Ballooning** (*01161-8-8952-8723. www.balloons.in. australia.as*) is 12.5 miles (20 km) south of Alice Springs. Australian itineraries that include a visit to Ayers Rock can be booked through the **Adventure Center** (*800-227-8747 or 510-654-187. www.adventurecenter.com*).

In the **Sydney** area, **Balloon Adventures of Australia** (*01161-2-9622-5267. Fax 01161-2-9622-6414*) stages a one-hour flight followed by a deluxe restaurant meal ($180 AU). The company also customizes multiflight itineraries.

To float over the wine country of **Melbourne and Victoria,** try a dawn flight with ace Chris Dewhirst of **Balloon Sunrise** (*41 Dover St., Richmond. 01161-3-9427-7596. www. balloonsunrise.com.au/~hotair/*). In 1991, Dewhirst set a world record by flying his balloon over Mt. Everest. No such peaks beckon in Australia, but the feat attests to the pilot's expertise. Melbourne is one of the few cities that allow dawn balloon flights in its airspace. In the nearby Yarra Valley—one of Australia's premier wine-growing regions—you can waft over a patchwork of Victorian vineyards at dawn, then visit their wineries in the afternoon.

COLORADO
Rocky Mountain High

Superb scenery and an extensive choice of sites make the Rockies one of North America's top spots for ballooning. You can sample a variety of ballooning adventures, from day flights at six different resorts to high-altitude balloon expeditions across the **Continental Divide.**

A number of ballooning events draw participants to the Rockies each year. **Colorado Springs,** for example, hosts a huge Labor Day gathering, which usually features more than 100 balloons. You can arrange to join in the fun by contacting a local balloon service.

It's easy to organize your own Rockies balloon odyssey to the major resort towns: Fort Collins, Boulder, Arvada, Aspen, Vail, Colorado Springs, Englewood, and Denver. To take a break from flying, hit the ski slopes; many Colorado balloon companies offer winter flights, so you can go down the mountain one day and up in the air the next. Outfits to contact include **Unicorn Balloon Company** (*15001 N. 74th St., Scottsdale, AZ 85260. 800-468-2478 or 970-925-5752. www.unicornballoon.com*) or **Life Cycle Balloon Adventures** (*410 19th St., Golden, CO 80401. 800-980-9272 or 303-216-1990. www.lifecycleballoons.com*).

For information about ballooning the Rockies in winter, contact **Camelot Balloons** (*34500 Hwy. 6, Edwards, CO 81632. 800-785-4743 or 970-926-2435. www.camelotballoons.com*). Although it can get chilly aloft, the scenery around Vail looks best under a coat of snow. Camelot's 80-minute flights cost about $225.

NEW MEXICO
Albuquerque Balloon Fiesta

The ultimate balloon festival takes place every October, when **Albuquerque** hosts 800,000 people viewing 625 balloons. With legions of balloons filling the New Mexico sky with color, the nine-day Albuquerque Balloon Fiesta is a photographer's fantasy come true. Spectators can spot everything from small solo balloons to huge cartoon characters, UFOs, and other whimsical creations. Balloons lift off by the hundreds in mass ascensions at dawn. On each Sunday at sunset, more than 300 balloons take to the sky; as night falls, they glow like giant candles in the sky.

Ballooning is just part of the Albuquerque extravaganza. Past events have featured the U.S. Navy Skydiving Team, as well as the Misty Blues, an all-female team of skydivers. The U.S. Army Golden Knights parachute team traditionally performs during the fiesta's final weekend, demonstrating wild free falls and intricate aerial maneuvers.

Fiesta-goers rub elbows with an international ballooning crowd. The Albuquerque event draws pilots and support crews from dozens of countries, including Germany, Luxembourg, France, Great Britain, Switzerland, and Japan.

For information, contact the **Albuquerque International Balloon Fiesta** (*505-821-1000. www.balloonfiesta. com*). For lodging, get in touch with the **Albuquerque Convention & Visitors Bureau** (*800-243-3696 or 505-842-9918*). To arrange a flight, consult the **World Balloon Corporation** (*800-351-9588. www.worldballoon. com*).

After the fiesta, venture up to **Taos** for a low-level flight through the gorge of the Rio Grande with **Pueblo Balloons** (*505-751-9877 or 915-537-2794. www.puebloballoon.com*). Pilot Johnny Lewis, who boasts more than 33 years of flight experience, guides you on a spectacular flight through this canyon measuring 1,000 feet wide and 700 feet deep. You fly over the lip of the gorge at dawn; then, following the river, you gently descend toward the canyon floor. Eagles often glide beside the balloon as it floats next to dramatic rock formations. Finally, you gradually ascend high above the gorge for a climactic view of the entire Rio Grande Valley. All this will set you back about $215.

How to Get Up and Away

Hot-air balloon services operate in most areas of the United States and Canada. The majority of these outfits offer hour-long balloon rides, followed by brunch or a picnic. Almost all flights depart in early morning or at dusk, when winds are calm. The average champagne flight costs $145 per person for a three-hour experience, which includes 60 to 90 minutes in the air. Some companies offer longer, custom-designed balloon tours (such as flights over the Alps from Switzerland to Italy), but these can cost $1,000 or more per day.

When choosing a company, ask if air time is guaranteed, and find out how many passengers ride in the basket. Loaded to maximum capacity, the biggest balloons can make riders feel cramped. Don't hesitate to do some comparison shopping before you commit. Important variables are pilot training, group size, and added charges for shuttles or insurance. Be sure to review the company's accident history—the better companies enjoy perfect safety records. If you cannot find a local company in the listings below, consult your yellow pages.

UNITED STATES

ALASKA

Advanced Balloon Adventures (*Anchorage. 907-455-7433 or 907-346-3495. www.alaska.net/~advanced/Webpage.html*) Since 1979, flights from Fairbanks, May to mid-September. Alaska Range vistas. $180 per person.

ARIZONA

Unicorn Balloon Co. (*Scottsdale. 800-468-2478 or 480-991-3666. www.unicornballoon.com*). Excellent company. Dawn flights year-round, sunset flights in winter only. $135 per person.

Red Rock Balloon Adventures (*Sedona. 800-258-3754 or 520-284-0040. www.redrockballoons.com*). Great Coconino National Forest red-rock scenery. $145 per person.

CALIFORNIA

Above the West Ballooning (*Yountville. 800-627-2759 or 707-944-8638. www.nvaloft.com*). Since 1985. Small-group flights with San Francisco shuttle. $195 per person.

Adventures Aloft of Napa Valley (*Yountville. 800-944-4408 or 707-944-4408. www.nvaloft.com*). Napa Valley wine-country trip for $185 per person.

Skysurfer Balloon Co. (*Del Mar . 800-660-6809 or 858-481-6800. www.skysurferballoon.com*). Since 1978. Inland sunrise and coastal sunset champagne flights. $140 to $160 per person.

COLORADO

Camelot Balloons (*Vail. 800-785-4743 or 970-926-2435. www.camelotballoons.com*). Year-round program, great scenery. 40-min. flight: $150 per person. 80-min. flight with brunch: $225 per person.

Life Cycle Balloon Adventures (*Golden. 800-980-9272 or 303-216-1990. www.lifecycleballoon.com*). Since 1972. Seven balloons. Flight training, rides (great vistas). $175 per person.

Unicorn Balloon Co. (*Aspen. 800-468-2478 or 970-925-5752. www.unicornballoon.com*). Aspen's most experienced balloon company. Summer and winter champagne flights, shuttle service. $175 to $195 per person.

CONNECTICUT

Brighter Skies Hot Air Balloon Company (*Woodstock. 800-677-5114 or 860-963-0600. www.brighterskies.com*). Web- site has good FAQ. $225 per person.

FLORIDA

Big Red Balloon by Fantasy Flights (*Tampa. 813-969-1518. www.bigredballoon.com*). Since 1991. Professional, truly year-round program. $160 per person.

The Bombard Society (*West Palm Beach. 800-862-8537 or 561-837-6610. www.bombardsociety.com*). World's leading balloon-tour operator. Balloon tours in Austria, the Czech Republic (Prague), France, Italy, Switzerland, and Turkey are ultimate vacations for those with the financial means.

GEORGIA

Atlanta Aerosports (*Woodstock. 770-592-7787. www.mindspring.com/~superstu/*). $160 per person.

ILLINOIS

Windy City Balloon Port (*Fox River Grove. 877-933-6359 or 847-639-0550. www.windycityballoonport.com*). Since 1974. $145 to $175 per person.

INDIANA

Upper Wind Balloon Port (*Elkhart. 219-293-5631*). Multiple balloon bases near Chicago on Lake Michigan. Seven days a week. $125 to $175 per person.

KENTUCKY

Balloon Odyssey (*Louisville. 502-245-1588. www.balloonodyssey.com*). Since 1974. Sales and flight training. Five balloons, seven days a week. $175 per person.

MAINE

Balloon Rides (*Portland. 800-952-2076 or 207-761-8373. www.hotairballoon.com*). Flights by appt. May to Oct. $175 per person.

MASSACHUSETTS

Balloon School of Massachusetts (*Brimfield. 413-245-7013*). Country flights; pilot-instructor Clayton Thomas is superb. $200 per person, including breakfast.

MICHIGAN

Sky High Hot Air Balloons (*Middleville. 616-891-8520*). Since 1971, top pilots, flight training. $175 per person.

NEVADA

DreamWeavers (*Gardnerville. 800-386-256. www.nanosecond .com/dreamweaver*). Year-round flights near Reno and Lake Tahoe. $145 per person.

D & R Balloons (*Las Vegas. 702-248-7609. www.drballoons.com*). Flights near the Las Vegas Strip. $125 per person.

NEW HAMPSHIRE

Ballooning Center of New Hampshire (*Derry. 603-434-1910*). Since 1984. Morning and evening champagne flights and training year-round. $175 per person.

AIR-TRAFFIC JAM, ALBUQUERQUE BALLOON FIESTA, NEW MEXICO

NEW JERSEY

Air America Promotions (*Mahwah. 800-424-7871 or 201-818-0266. http://members.xoom.com/AirAmerica*). Since 1988. $175 per person.

NEW MEXICO

Pueblo Balloon Company (*Taos. 505-751-987. www.puebloballoon.com*). Superb, 90-minute flight through Rio Grande gorge and Taos Box area. $215 per person.

World Balloon Corporation (*Albuquerque. 800-351-9588 or 505-293-6800. www.worldballoon.com*). New Mexico's most experienced balloon operation. Rides and training. $135 per person.

NEW YORK

Adirondack Balloon Flights (*Glens Falls. 518-793-6342. www.adkballoonflights.com*). Since 1977. Flights over scenic Lake George and Saratoga Springs area. April through November. $175 per person.

NORTH CAROLINA

Balloons over Charlotte (*Charlotte. 704-541-7058. www.balloonsovercharlotte.com*). Since 1979. Champagne flights. $125 per person.

OHIO

Clear Sky Balloon Port (*Chester. 800-733-2053. www.hotairballoonrides.com*). Since 1981. $129 to $149 per person.

OREGON

Vista Balloon Adventures (*Sherwood. 800-622-2309 or 503-625-7385. www.vistaballoon.com*). Since 1989. Wine-country flights near Portland with picnic. Can handle large groups. $180 per person.

PENNSYLVANIA

Dillon Hot Air Balloon Service (*Camp Hill. 717-761-8820*). Since 1983. Experienced pilots. Sales and instruction. Flights five days a week. $150 per person.

RHODE ISLAND

Stumpf Balloons (*Bristol. 800-942-9411 or 401-253-0111. www.stumpfballoons.com*) Popular coastal champagne flights, May to Oct. Book well in advance. $275 per person.

TENNESSEE

AeroStation Ltd. (*Franklin. 615-799-2323*). Quality program since 1975. Instruction. $300 for two people.

Wind Works Hot Air Balloon Co. (*Morristown. 423-318-8991. www.smokymtnballoons.com*). Since 1984. $120 to $175 per person.

TEXAS

Austin Aeronauts Inc. (*Austin. 800-444-3257 or 512-440-1492. www.austinaeronauts.com*). Champagne flights $175 per person. Lake flights $325, night flights $350.

AirVenture Balloonport (*Plano/Dallas. 800-878-4212 or 972-422-0212. www.airventure.com*). Rides, sales, flight training year-round. $150 per person.

UTAH

Park City Balloon Adventures (*Park City. 800-396-8787 or 435-645-8787. www.pcballoonadventures.com*). Utah's premier balloon operator. Mountain setting. $85 per half hr., $150 per hr. per person.

Skywalker Balloon Company (*www.skywalker.at*). This program for southern Utah includes flights over state parks. Full-day, two-flight programs.

VERMONT

Boland Balloon (*Post Mills. 802-333-9254*). Balloon rides by appointment. Expert pilots. $200 per person.

VIRGINIA/D.C. AREA

Balloons Unlimited (*Oakton. 703-281-2300. www.balloonsunlimited. com*). Shenandoah Valley flights, $150 per person.

Hot Air Balloon A Tics (*Manassas. 703-361-4725*). Since 1980. Private champagne flights, $350 for two people.

WASHINGTON STATE

Airial Balloon Company (*Snohomish. 360-568-3025*). Scenic valley rides. Air time 60 to 90 minutes, weekend champagne brunch, $150 to $175 per person.

Balloon Depot (*Carnation. 425-881-9699. www.balloondepot.com*) Seattle-area flights top-rated by *Ballooning*. Catered meal on weekends. $145-175 per person.

WISCONSIN

Token Creek Hot Air Balloons (*Token Creek. 877-933-6359 or 608-241-4000. www.tokencreekballoon.com*). Since 1981. $145-$180 per person. Also runs Sunbird Balloons, Lake Geneva (*414-249-0660*).

WYOMING

Wyoming Balloon Company (*Jackson Hole. 307-739-0900. balloon@blissnet. com*). Scenic dawn flights. $190 per person.

INTERNATIONAL

AFRICA

Day flights in safari country can be booked through your travel agent as part of a safari itinerary. Use one of the following operators:

Balloon Safaris Ltd. (*Nairobi, Kenya. 011-254-2-502851. Fax 01125-4250-1424. http://balloonsafaris.hypermart.net*). $350 per person at Keekorok, $250 at Taita Hills.

Musiara Ltd. (*Nairobi, Kenya. 01125-4305-2273*). Flies from Governor's Camp, Maasai Mara.

Serengeti Balloon Safaris Ltd. (*Adventure Centre, Arusha, Tanzania. 01144-1379-853129 [UK] or 57-8578 [Tanzania]. www.balloonsafaris.com*). $375 per person.

AUSTRALIA

Balloon Adventures of Australia (*Prospect, NSW 2149. 01161-2-9622-5267*). Camden (Sydney) dawn flights. $180 (AU) per person.

Balloon Sunrise (*Richmond, Victoria 3121. 01161-3-9427-7596. www.balloonsunrise. com.au/~hotair/*). Ride with world-record holder Chris Dewhirst near Melbourne and Victoria wine country.

Outback Ballooning (*Alice Springs, Northern Territory 0871. 01161-8-8952-8723. www.balloons.in.australia.as*). Since 1991. Strong program; also operates in Cairns, Queensland.

AUSTRIA

Ballooning Tyrol (*St. Johann in Tirol. 01143-5352-65666. Fax 01143-5352-65644. www.alpennet.com/ballooning-tyrol*). Since 1990. Alpine flights near Kitzbuhel. Partner pilots in Tirol, Salzburg. Flights year-round; winter is best. 2,500 to 4,200 (OS) per person.

BELGIUM

Ballooning BVBA (*Waasmunster. 01132-5246-2144. http://fly.to/ballooning*). Since 1982; experienced pilots. Flights from Sint-Niklaas. $180 per person.

CANADA

Pegasus Ballooning (*Langley, British Columbia. 604-533-2701*). March to Oct., six days a week. Vancouver-area champagne flight $185 (CN) per person.

Windship Aviation Ltd. (*Edmonton, Alberta. 888-463-5283 or 780-438-0111. www.windship.com*). Edmonton's leading balloon company. Champagne flights $175 (CN) per person.

FRANCE

Air Escargot (*Remigny. 01133-3-8587-1230. Fax 01133-3-8587-0884*). Deluxe trips in Burgundy; daily flights, château lodging, gourmet cuisine. Since 1979.

GREAT BRITAIN

Adventure Balloons (*Hampshire, England. 01144-181-840-0108. www.adventureballoons.co.uk*). Since 1985. Flights in rural counties. Also offers ballooning holidays in Ireland and Normandy from $800.

Virgin Balloon Flights (*Shropshire, England. 01144-990-228-483 [toll-free] or 011-44-1952-200-141. www.virginballoonflights.com*). Balloon flights throughout U.K. include London, Oxford, Scotland.

ITALY

Robert Etherington (*53040 Rapolano Terme [SI]. www.ballooningintuscany.com*). $160 to $220 per person. Can be combined with all-inclusive tours in Tuscany.

LUXEMBOURG

Skylines (*Pierre Tibot, Junglinster. 01135-278-9075. Fax 011-35-278-9909. skylines@pt.lu*). Flights year-round in Luxembourg, Belgium, and France.

NEPAL

Balloon Sunrise Nepal (*Lazimpat Kathmandu. 01197-71-424-131*). Since 1975; still the only balloon company in Nepal. Spectacular vistas. $200 per person.

NEW ZEALAND

Balloon Expedition Company Nz. Ltd. (*Royal Heights, Auckland. 01164-9416-8590*). Auckland vineyard flights; city flights, weather permitting. Top pilots. $200 to $300 (NZ) per person.

Aoraki Balloon Safaris (*Methven 8353. 01164-3302-8172 or 01164-8025-6837 [toll-free]. www.nzballooning.com*). Since 1992. Dawn flights over the Canterbury Plains $255 (NZ).

SWEDEN

Scandinavian Balloons AB (*Stockholm. 01146-8556-40465. http://balloons-sweden.se/*). Since 1979. City sunset flights $180 per person.

Upp & Ner Balloons (*Stockholm. 01146-8695-0100. www.uppner.se*). Scandinavia's most modern fleet. City or country flights from Stockholm, Uppsala, Köpenhamn, Göteborg, and Sao Paulo (Brazil).

SWITZERLAND

Funk's Ballooning (*Wolfwil. 01141-62-92-62277. www.swissballoons.ch/funk*). Central plateau flight $175 (EU), Gstaad mountain flight $410 (EU), full-day crossing of Alps to Italy $1,115 (EU).

ORGANIZATIONS

Balloon Federation of America (BFA) P.O. Box 400, Indianola, Iowa 50125 515-961-8809. www.bfa.net

British Balloon and Airship Club 7 Llewellyn Road, Penllergaer, Swansea SA4 1BB, United Kingdom. 01144-1792-899777. www.bbac.org

Fédération Français d'Aerostation 6 Rue Galilee, 75016 Paris, France. 01133-1472-35620. www.multimania.com/aerostat

Fédération Aéronautique Internationale (FAI) Avenue Mon Repos 24, CH-1005 Lausanne, Switzerland. 01141-2134-5-1070. www.fai.org

ONLINE

Balloon Federation of America (*www.bfa.net*) BFA-sanctioned competitions and seminars; regional ballooning resources; BFA membership information.

Ballooning International (*www.ballooning.net*) Hot air, gas, and experimental ballooning. Site includes links to ballooning events, manufacturers, and associations.

FAI Ballooning Pages (*www.fai.org/ballooning*) Part of the Fédération Aéronautique Internationale's website, this is a good source for international balloon festivals, competitions, and record attempts.

Internet Balloon Database (*www.geocities.com/~dstartz/IBD/IBD.htm*) E-mail addresses and links for pilots, clubs, and chase crews worldwide. Best way to track down sport flyers around the globe.

www.euronet.nl/users/jdewilde
This comprehensive list of ballooning sites includes a searchable database, plus links to balloon festivals, balloon operators, and notable expeditions.

BOOKS

The Balloon Digest (1995). This definitive guide to ballooning covers all aspects of the sport: licensing, instruction, weather, operations, and maintenance. Each chapter is written by a different expert. $30 from the BFA Bookstore (*515-961-8809. P.O. Box 400, Indianola, Iowa 50125. www.bfa.net*).

The Art of Hot-Air Ballooning by Roger Bansemer (*http://bansemer.cftnet.com*). A big, colorful book with great illustrations. $34.95 from 2352 Alligator Creek Rd., Clearwater, FL. 33765.

MAGAZINES

Ballooning, the journal of the Balloon Federation of America (*P.O. Box 150, Ashville, NY 14710. 716-763-0165*).

Skylines, same address as above. This Balloon Federation of America newsletter lists balloon events nationwide.

VIDEOS

Buddy Bombard's half-hour video follows balloons as they float over castles and vineyards in Burgundy, the Loire Valley, and Austria. $20 from the Bombard Society (*800-862-8537. www.bombardsociety. com*).

Phantom Productions (*512-288-1044. www.phantomprod.com*) offers a wide selection of videos on crew training and balloon events, including races and nightglows.

LEARNING TO SOAR

Balloon Basics

Almost all recreational balloons use hot air supplied by a propane burner. The bag, or envelope, is 50 to 80 feet tall. It is made of polyester or nylon fabric, coated with polyurethane to reduce porosity. The basket, or gondola, is made of wicker, aluminum, or heavy-duty synthetic material. A crew of up to eight people uses a blower to inflate the balloon on the ground; a propane burner then heats the trapped air until the envelope stands upright.

During flight, the burner controls the balloon's altitude by warming the air in the envelope. To ascend, you must increase the envelope temperature. You must also burn periodically to maintain altitude (the envelope is constantly cooling). Rapid descents require spilling hot air from a vent at the top. A flight of one to two hours typically uses 15 to 20 gallons of propane.

A balloon's sole means of propulsion is the wind, but it must be gentle. A breeze of 10 miles per hour is the maximum allowed for regular sport flying. During a two-hour flight, a balloon may fly 10 miles overland and ascend to 2,000 feet or so. Higher flights are possible, but there is no real reason for them unless you must clear a mountain.

There is no direct way to steer a balloon — it drifts with the wind. Because the wind blows in different directions at different altitudes, however, expert balloonists can control their path by changing altitude until they find the desired wind.

Getting your license

Balloons are regulated by the Federal Aviation Administration (FAA). To pilot one, you must complete a certification program. FAA licensing requirements demand a minimum of 10 hours of flight training, including at least one hour of solo flight.

The average student needs 15 hours' air time before he or she is ready for certification. Student pilots must also pass a written exam and complete a check flight.

The cost of a good flight-training program, with all equipment provided by the balloon school, ranges from $1,800 to $3,500. The cost drops to $800 to $1,500 if the student supplies the balloon and chase vehicle. Compare prices before you enroll, and choose a school with full-time instructors and an FAA examiner on staff.

Price of Admission

Minimum equipment is a balloon, basket, burner, fuel tank(s), instruments, inflator fan, and trailer. You can pick up the entire rig — used — for less than $10,000. A new outfit will cost at least $15,000 (without trailer); the latest instrumentation and a custom envelope can cost $50,000.

Active balloonists spend $4,500 to $5,000 per year on the sport. The main costs are fuel, insurance, depreciation of the envelope, and annual inspections. Fuel (propane) costs $.60 to $1.30 per gallon; the average balloon burns 12 to 15 gallons per hour. Insurance varies by locale and experience; plan to spend at least $700 per year. A well-maintained envelope will provide 300 to 400 flight hours. If you fly 50 hours per year, the envelope should last about seven years. Chase-vehicle expenses and transportation costs are extra.

BEAR WITH ME: AN ENTRY IN THE SPECIAL-SHAPE RODEO AT ALBUQUERQUE

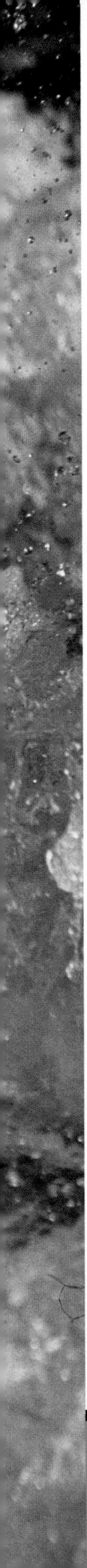

RIVERS ARE FLUID PATHWAYS TO ADVENTURE. WHETHER STEERING A KAYAK THROUGH raging rapids or exploring a remote waterway by canoe, river runners experience both challenge and escape. Shallow in draft and light in weight, canoes and kayaks can negotiate the narrowest tributaries. They can also be portaged, or carried, around difficult rapids or from one wilderness lake to the next, allowing a canoeist or kayaker to venture into unspoiled territories and find refuge from the modern world. • This chapter covers the spectrum of inland paddling, from smooth-water canoe-tripping to Class VI+ white-water kayaking. Eight ultimate river trips are profiled worldwide. (If you are looking for fun closer to home, we review North America's best rivers for self-guided excursions.) Thrill seekers will find descriptions of some very serious white-water trips, as well as write-ups of the top paddling schools in North America—the best places to learn Eskimo rolls and other advanced white-water techniques from the experts.

LEFT: KAYAKING THE CLASS IV SOUTH FORK OF THE PAYETTE RIVER, IDAHO
BELOW: BOW WOWS ON LAKE KEZAR, WESTERN MAINE

**Shooting
the Rapids**

**Wilderness
Canoeing**

**Waterfall
Running**

**Kayak
Clinics**

*Pedal 500 miles on a bicycle and you remain basically a bourgeois;
paddle 100 miles in a canoe and you are already a child of nature.*

PIERRE ELLIOT TRUDEAU

Down Some Not-So-Lazy Rivers

From a peaceful canoe trek through the Canadian wilderness to a thrilling kayak descent of jungle white water, just about any exploit lies within reach of the paddler who seeks adventure. Although expeditions to remote foreign rivers can be costly, most domestic guided paddling trips are relatively inexpensive: Even a fully outfitted trip typically costs less than $100 per day—a fee that includes food, watercraft rental, and guide.

GRAND CANYON
Small Boats, Big Water

Traditionally, the 1,450-mile-long **Colorado River** has been accessible to rafting expeditions only. Thanks to changes in National Park Service regulations, however, it is now possible for advanced paddlers to run the greatest American river of them all on a raft-supported kayaking trip.

Though most of the Colorado is fairly smooth and quiet, certain stretches of it feature the most outrageous hydraulics and standing waves to be found in North America. A large raft can negotiate these with relative ease, but the pilot of something as small as a kayak has to be awfully good to make it through in one piece. For this reason, any kayak expedition should be accompanied by a support raft that can carry the kayaks and their crews through the most hazardous sections.

Despite the easing of restrictions, the waiting period for a properly qualified private kayak group seeking to run the Colorado River can be as long as two years. For all practical purposes, then, the only way to run the river anytime soon is by signing on with a regularly scheduled commercial trip. Indeed, most kayakers and white-water canoeists who run the Colorado now do so in conjunction with a commercial rafting trip.

At present, three outfitters conduct raft-supported kayak trips down the Colorado that are designed for advanced paddlers.

Dvorak's Expeditions (*17921 Hwy. 285, Nathrop, CO 81236. 800-824-3795 or 719-539-6851. www.dvorakexpeditions.com*) runs 225 miles of the Grand Canyon on 12-day adventures that cost $2,225. Even though the company's guides will direct kayakers to the safest sections of the river, cautions owner Bill Dvorak, the Colorado remains a powerful watercourse: Kayakers must be skilled boat handlers—and capable of executing a strong roll. Trips run from May through October and include food and raft support, but not kayak rental. Most of Dvorak's trips are booked six months in advance.

Nantahala Outdoor Center (*13077 US. 19 West, Bryson City, NC 28713. 888-662-1662 ext. 333 or 828-488-2175. www.noc.com*) will escort you down the length of the Colorado River over a 14-day period, providing raft support for advanced kayakers and expert open canoeists. (Paddle rafters can join the group as well.) Nantahala offers two 14-day trips in fall, each costing $3,100, including food and equipment.

Otter Bar Lodge Kayak School (*P.O. Box 210, Forks of Salmon, CA 96031. 530-462-4772. www.otterbar.com*) runs a 13-day river trip for experienced kayakers with a strong roll. This raft-supported trip costs $2,900, including food (but not kayak rental).

MINNESOTA
Wilderness Wayfaring

Sitting athwart the Minnesota-Ontario border, the **Boundary Waters Canoe Area Wilderness** (*877-550-6777. www.bwcaw.org*) is the mecca of North American canoeing. The BWCA and Ontario's adjoining **Quetico Provincial Park** (*807-597-2735. www.queticopark.com*) make up a 2.2-million-acre wilderness that is ideal for canoe exploration. More than 5,000 lakes and 3,000 islands dot the BWCA, affording limitless possibilities for paddling adventures. The BWCA alone features 1,500 miles of canoe routes studded with nearly 2,200 campsites. A canoeist could spend a lifetime of summers here and still not see it all.

For maximum solitude and scenery, head for the Canadian side. Popular Quetico destinations include Lake Kahshahpiwi, Sarah Lake, and Agnes Lake. Great fishing can be found at Basswood Lake, which straddles the border. On the American side, if you've got two or three days to kill, try the 25-mile loop trip that starts at Lake One and returns by way of Snowbank Lake or Moose Lake.

Undertaking a Boundary Waters canoe trip involves much more than driving up to a waterway and setting off. As a strictly controlled wilderness region, the BWCA does not allow motorized transport within its borders. To reach the better destinations, you will therefore have to complete a day's portage (or more) before you can plunk your canoe in the water. That's why those with limited time should consider a fly-in trip: It saves hours of slogging and lets you visit remote hideaways where you are almost guaranteed to have an entire lake to yourself. A week-long fly-in trip costs about

$700 per person. The Quetico side has the most pristine fly-in destinations, including Three-Mile Lake, Wolseley Lake, and Lake La Croix.

Because of the BWCA's popularity, you must reserve early to secure a wilderness permit. In 1998, for example, all summer permits for Quetico had been spoken for by the end of February. (The leading outfitters, by contrast, usually manage to get permits well into the spring—at least for the American side.) To reserve a permit for a self-guided trip in the BWCA, contact the **National Recreation Reservation Service** (*877-550-677. www.bwcaw.org*). The NRRS website provides a complete list of permit-issuing stations, many of which rent canoes or offer outfitted trips, at *www.bwcaw.org/coop.html.*

More than a dozen good canoe outfitters operate in the BWCA. **Canadian Waters, Inc.** (*111 East Sheridan, Ely, MN 55731. 800-255-2922 or 218-365-3202*) is a favorite. Owners Dan and Cathy Waters are friendly and knowledgeable, and they can provision any kind of trip—from a do-it-yourself paddle to a deluxe fly-in—on either side of the border. Other recommended outfitters include **Gunflint Northwoods**

Outfitters (*143 S. Gunflint Lake, Grand Marais, MN 55604. 800-328-3325 or 218-388-2294. www.gunflint.com*); **Piragis Northwoods Co.** (*105 N. Central Ave., Ely, MN 55731. 800-223-6565 or 218-365-6745. www.piragis.com*); **Seagull Canoe Outfitters** (*12208 Gunflint Trail, Grand Marais, MN 55604. 800-346-2205 or 218-388-2216. www.seagulloutfitters.com*); and **Sawbill Canoe Outfitters** (*4620 Sawbill Trail, Tofte, MN 55615. 218-663-7150. www.sawbill.com*).

Rates are more or less standard for all these companies: Canoe rentals average $15 to $35 per day, while an outfitted trip (without guide) is roughly $65 to $100 per day. Air charters run $100 to $150 per person. From Memorial Day to Labor Day, Northwest Airlines operates a daily flight between Minneapolis and Ely for about $250 round-trip.

OREGON
Rogue River Kayak Clinic

There may be no better place west of the Rockies to learn white-water kayaking skills than Oregon's **Rogue River.** Variety is the hallmark of this waterway, which boasts conditions ranging from still-water pools to Class IV rapids that

LAKE-BORNE BIRD-WATCHING IN YELLOWSTONE NATIONAL PARK, WYOMING

challenge experts. Moreover, the Rogue is home to the **Sundance River Center** (*14894 Galice Rd., Merlin, OR 97532. 888-777-7557 or 541-479-8508. www.sundanceriver.com*), a well-regarded facility that houses paddlers-in-training at a back-country lodge, where they enjoy home-cooked meals. In truth, the river-front location and relaxing ambience of the lodge have been as important to Sundance's success as the quality of the kayaking.

Though Sundance offers something for everyone, its most popular program is the nine-day basic seminar. The first five days are devoted to acquiring the skills required to pilot a kayak safely through Class III rapids. You'll practice basic strokes, perfect the Eskimo roll, and learn how to maneuver through eddies and currents. The staff at Sundance is patient, and each kayaker receives individual attention.

After completing this basic-skills training, the group makes a four-day, 40-mile run down the Wild and Scenic Rogue River Gorge. Here students perfect their white-water technique in Class II and III+ rapids under the watchful eyes of instructors. All food and personal gear are carried in support rafts. Water levels have varied considerably over the years, but there is usually a good volume all summer. (Although the high water of spring offers more excitement, the lower water at summer's end is better suited for novices.) This basic seminar costs about $1,800, including meals, lodging, and all gear. A similar training program for women only is offered each summer.

Sundance offers a wide variety of river activities above and beyond its lodge-based kayak training. Single-day and multi-day family rafting trips on the Rogue are popular options. If you're in the market for a major white-water challenge, Sundance is one of only two commercial outfitters permitted to raft the Illinois River—one of the longest continuous runs on the West Coast. The three-day, $575 expedition offers Class IV rapids and true wilderness solitude. Advanced kayak training on the Illinois is also available for qualified paddlers.

TEXAS
Running the Rio Grande

Forming the border between the United States and Mexico, the **Rio Grande** passes through classic canyon country as it flows southeast through **Big Bend National Park**

(*915-477-2251. www.nps.gov/bibe/home.htm*). Although the Class IV upper stretch of the Rio Grande near the New Mexico border (the Taos Box area) demands advanced skills, most of the river is a relatively gentle float that is ideal for first-time canoe-trippers. Overall, a journey down the Rio Grande through Big Bend and the lower canyons is one of the best novice canoe adventures in America.

Expect solitude, spectacular scenery, and fine weather on a week-long Rio Grande trip. Most of your time will be spent within the confines of Big Bend Park, where the landscape is rugged and colorful. There's a fair amount of tourist activity in Big Bend Park—particularly in Mariscall and Boquillas Canyons—but the lower canyons are little traveled. Except during the busiest holiday periods, you should encounter few other boaters on the river.

May and June are the best times of year to canoe the Rio Grande (avoid the low-water period, which usually falls in February). The water is a comfortable 65° to 70°F, while the daytime air temperature ranges between 70° and 90°F. Almost the entire river is suitable for novice paddlers. After a couple of days practicing on the quieter sections, even first-timers should be able to handle all the rapids from Big Bend southward. Most commercial trips offer raft support, allowing you to skirt sections that look too tough.

A number of companies offer raft-supported canoe trips on the Rio Grande. The leading outfitter is **Big Bend River Tours** (*P.O. Box 317, Terlingua, TX 79852. 800-545-4240 or 915-424-3219. www.bigbendrivertours.com*). Trips range from half a day to a week or more, and prices are reasonable; they start at $255 per person for a fully outfitted two-day trip through Santa Elena, Mariscal, or Colorado Canyons. BBRT trips can be customized for families and groups, or you may choose a trip with a special theme such as gourmet food, photography, natural history, or rafting/horsepacking. To reserve a boat or learn the latest river conditions, call BBRT. **Dvorak's Expeditions** (*800-824-3795 or 719-539-6851. www.dvorakexpeditions.com*) runs 45 to 90 miles of the Rio Grande's lower canyons on four- to seven-day adventures in March, April, October, and November. The pace is slow, giving paddlers time to improve their boating skills and to enjoy the many hot springs along the way. Paddlers may also rotate boats, switching from raft to canoe to kayak en route. The four-day trips cost roughly $580 without equipment ($640 with equipment), while the seven-day trips cost $960 without equipment ($1,150 with equipment). **Nantahala Outdoor Center** (*800-232-7238 or 828-488-2175. www.noc.com*) also offers nine-day, $900 raft-supported trips for open canoeists in May, October, and November.

For those on a budget, the Rio Grande is a fine self-guided trip, provided you have some previous canoe-camping experience. You can rent canoes for about $50 per day from Big Bend River Tours. Contact Big Bend National Park for other Big Bend concessionaires who rent canoes and can help you plan an itinerary.

WEST VIRGINIA
Class V Fury

The Allegheny Mountains in West Virginia contain the greatest single concentration of Class IV and V runs in North America. World-class rivers such as the **Cheat,** the **Gauley,** the **Tygart,** and the **Upper Youghiogheny** offer continuous white water with more thrills per mile than you'll find just about anywhere. The upper section of the Gauley, for example, is a solid Class V, with huge waves and high water volume. The Tygart boasts Glens Falls, the most powerful runnable rapid in the Appalachians. The highly technical Upper Yough—once thought to be unrunnable— is the steepest waterway east of the Rockies. (Though located in nearby Maryland, the Upper Yough is served by West Virginia river guides.) The Cheat features tight passages over steep drops; many of its rapids were upgraded to Class V after changes wrought by floods in 1985. The **New River** is popular with beginners and intermediates alike: It offers ideal Class I and II learning conditions in the upper section and reliable Class III and IV water in the lower stretch. In summer the Lower New is a great intermediate play river, with surfable waves and many classic squirt-boating holes.

Along with these well-known rivers, West Virginia boasts many smaller creeks that offer fast flows, dizzying drops, and Class V rapids in the early season or after strong rains. Scenic **Glade Creek,** located not far from the Grist Mill at Babcock State Park near Clifftop, West Virginia, is a demanding Class V run with an outrageous gradient (or rate of regular descent) that ranges from 250 to 400 feet per mile. Very steep and narrow, Glade Creek's toughest rapids become Class VI during high water following hard rainstorms in spring or fall. **Mill Creek**—near Anstead, West Virginia—is another popular small creek that flows well after a rainfall. It boasts a nice 20-foot waterfall that is runnable by advanced paddlers. The first section of Mill Creek up to the falls is a manageable Class II to high III; above there it becomes high IV to low V—definitely for experts only.

The **Meadow River** offers a variety of conditions in its three sections. The technical upper section, which winds through a beautiful hardwood forest, features extremely clear water and many great rapids. Although this stretch is mostly Class III, it can be dangerous at high water. The Middle Meadow is quite popular with locals, given the easy access from the road and its manageable Class III to low Class IV white water. The solid Class IV to Class V Lower

Meadow is assuredly for advanced experts only. It is both very steep and very technical—an extremely tough run that can be a killer at high water. Just consider the names of the Lower Meadow's infamous rapids: "Brink of Disaster" and "Sweet Jesus."

West Virginia's short, steep creeks—Glade Creek and the Lower Meadow among them—require advanced kayaking skills. No matter how good you are, hiring a local guide to help you choose a destination—and make the run safely—is strongly recommended. For guides and safety boats, contact **Ace Whitewater** (*Concho Rd., Minden, WV 25879. 800-223-2641 or 304- 469-2955 . www.aceraft.com*) or **Riversport School of Paddling** (*P.O. Box 95, Confluence, PA 15424. 800-216-6991 or 814-395-5744. www.shol.com/kayak/*). Both companies also offer high-quality personalized instruction for kayakers from novice to advanced.

As a whole, the West Virginia river system is noted for its fast water flow, steep drops, and narrow, technical passages. Unlike many western rivers—where pockets of rapids punctuate long, smooth passages—the rivers of West Virginia are marked by back-to-back rapids with continuous white water. The runs are relatively short, but they yield high-adrenaline excitement that is hard to duplicate anywhere else. To do these runs in a kayak or decked canoe, however, you had better have solid Class IV paddling skills.

If you're new to the sport, both the **Rivermen** (*Lansing, WV 25862. 800-545-7238 or 304-574-0515. www.rivermen. com*) and **Class VI River Runners** (*Lansing, WV 25862. 800-252-7784 or 304-574-0704. www.raftwv. com*) conduct single-day and multiday clinics for novice to intermediate kayakers on the New and Gauley Rivers. The classes cover all essentials: paddle strokes, Eskimo rolls, wet exits, and eddy turns. Clinics run May through October and cost $100 to $160 per day, including food and transport.

Even if you've never paddled a single stroke in a kayak, you can still sample West Virginia's wildest rivers on a raft excursion with any number of competent outfitters such as Class VI, the Rivermen, or **North American River Runners** (*P.O. Box 81, Hico, WV 25854. 800-950-2585 or 304-658-5276. www.narr.com*). For other recommended regional outfitters, see pages 162-179.

CANADA
Nahanni River Nirvana

The **Nahanni** is a dream river—one of the planet's most scenic waterways. From a remote corner of the Northwest Territories, it flows through a wild landscape of legendary scale and beauty. The Nahanni has been called Canada's Grand Canyon, but its forested hills and massive granite

KAYAKING TRIO NEGOTIATES THE MAIN CANYON OF THE CAL SALMON RIVER IN FORKS OF SALMON, CALIFORNIA.

rock faces more closely resemble Yosemite Valley. There is far less recreational activity on the Nahanni than on the Colorado—and never any competition for campsites.

It takes three weeks to navigate the length of the Nahanni, which flows southeast from the Continental Divide, cutting its way through the 150-mile-long **Nahanni National Park** (*P.O. Box 348, Fort Simpson, NWT X0E 0N0 Canada. 867-695-3151*). Even outside the park's boundaries, the Nahanni is truly wild, and you are always quite a distance from civilization—at least 100 miles from the nearest real town.

The white water in the upper half of the river, outside the park, is best suited for experienced paddlers. Starting at Moose Ponds—the Nahanni's source—the river runs approximately 100 miles to the park boundary. In this stretch, paddlers pass through the Rock Gardens, a long section of continuous Class II and Class III white water where the river drops more than 2,000 vertical feet.

As the Nahanni nears the northern end of the national park, the river flattens out and the voyage becomes a peaceful float through impressive granite canyons that harbor elk, moose, and many large species of birds. The section of the Nahanni within the park offers riverside hot springs and good fishing, although the scenery—particularly Virginia Falls—is the main attraction. At twice the height of Niagara, Virginia Falls is perhaps the most spectacular cascade in North America.

A favorite outfitter on the Nahanni is **Nahanni River Adventures, Ltd.** (*P.O. Box 4869, Whitehorse, YT Y1A 4N6, Canada. 800-297-6927 or 867-668-3180. www.nahanni.com*). NRA owner and chief guide Neil Hartling wrote the definitive book about this watercourse (*Nahanni: River of Gold*), and his knowledge of the region is remarkable. His company uses unique expedition-class canoes for excursions that cost about $2,400 (CN) for one week or $3,000 (CN) for two.

Another outstanding guide service for the Nahanni is the **Wilderness Adventure Company** (*R.R. 3, Parry Sound, ON P2A 2W9, Canada. 888-849-7668 or 705-746-1372. www.wildernessadventure.com*). Wilderness Adventure charges $2,800 (CN) for a two-week smooth-water voyage through the whole of Nahanni National Park—including Virginia Falls, the Tufa Mounds, Pulpit Rock, canyons, and hot springs. The company also runs an eight-day **Nahanni Getaway** trip for $2,200 (CN), as well as a three-week Class III Nahanni white-water program for $3,750 (CN). The white-water trip starts at the river's source and traces the entire watershed, including the Rock Gardens. Combining thrills and stunning scenery, this may be the ultimate Nahanni experience for seasoned paddlers.

HONDURAS
Jungle Journeys

Honduras is one of the world's most rapidly developing off-season destinations—a new frontier for adventurous boaters. Almost every year, it seems, pioneering paddlers bent on escaping winter in the north discover new river runs in this Central American nation.

Honduras offers numerous waterways with nearly continuous rapids. Most of the runs are fairly short, so you can sample half a dozen rivers on a white-water safari here. Most trips to Honduras are scheduled for the end of the rainy season—November and December. Although the rainfall can be quite heavy in those months, the storms tend to be brief. With few rivers controlled by dams, however, water levels rise and fall dramatically, constantly presenting new challenges and opportunities for canoeists and kayakers.

Rios Honduras (*P.O. Box 66, La Ceiba, Honduras, C.A. 01150-4443-0780*), founded by guides from Colorado's **Rocky Mountain Outdoor Center** (*10281 Hwy. 50, Howard, CO 81233. 800-255-5784 or 719-942-3214. www.rmoc.com*), has offered canoe and kayak tours in Honduras since 1991. RH's premier offering is its nine-day **Rivers of Honduras** trip, a fully outfitted river sampler that covers a variety of popular jungle waterways. RH offers beginner-intermediate, intermediate, and advanced (Class III to IV+) versions of its Rivers of Honduras tour, so the company is able to accommodate all skill levels. In addition, RH customizes itineraries for boat preference, seasonal water levels, and weather conditions. For those who have only a few days in Honduras or wish to organize their own trip, RH can provide a boat, a guide, and a shuttle vehicle with driver. RH also rents canoes for $25 per day.

Because most Honduran rivers drain into the Caribbean Sea, many trips begin in La Ceiba, on the country's northern coast. A descent of the **Rio Cangrejal**, located just a few minutes from the RH base in La Ceiba, combines classic jungle scenery with intense action. Boaters pass through a dramatic gorge in the heart of original-growth rain forest, encountering 20 miles of steep, technical white water along the way. The upper sections are mostly Class IV; the lower sections are mainly Class III. During high water, Rio Cangrejal kayakers can paddle all the way to the sea, returning to their beachside hotel through ocean surf.

After the Cangrejal, you'll want to sample the **Rio Cuero** and the **Rio San Juan,** two short runs that feature some moderately technical Class II and III rapids and a few small vertical drops. Another popular option is the **Rio Humuya,** a rare dam-controlled river. In the wake of paddling the steep, technical rivers described above, you'll find the Humuya's high volume and large waves an intriguing contrast. Most rapids on the Humuya are rated Class II, but there are great Class III and IV play spots for surfing and enders.

For a unique introduction to the Mayan heritage of Honduras, consider running the **Rio Copan.** This low-volume river passes through a national park containing the ruins of the Mayan city of Copan. The river is both narrow and technical—primarily Class III rapids, with some Class IV.

To venture into the heart of the jungle, check out the **Rio Sico Expedition** put on by RH. You'll experience both wilderness solitude and wild excitement during this four-day descent, which threads more than 60 major rapids. Riverside camping, jungle treks, and wildlife viewing round out your time on the river.

A visit to Honduras offers the best of both worlds—high adventure combined with the laid-back appeal of the tropics. For the independent traveler, Honduras remains an inexpensive destination. Package holidays, too, are reasonable: All Rios Honduras tours—including the company's Rivers of Honduras and Rio Sico Expeditions—cost about $1,400, including boats, guides, food, and accommodations for nine days. Tour participants must provide their own paddling gear, including helmet, paddle jacket, and paddle.

An eight-day Rio Sico Expedition is also offered each January by the **Nantahala Outdoor Center** (*888-662-1662, ext. 333. www.noc.com*). One month after that, NOC runs an eight-day multi-river sampler for advanced paddlers. From a base in La Ceiba, paddlers challenge the steep and technical Cangrejal, **Mame,** and **Yaguala Rivers.** Both NOC programs cost about $1,500, including equipment.

CORSICA
The French Connection

Corsica, the fourth largest island in the Mediterranean, is dominated by a stone massif laced with deep, rocky gorges. For a brief three to six weeks in March and April, snowmelt explodes down these steep channels, forming narrow, twisting chutes of water that are marked by intense vertical drops.

Short the season may be, but tame it is not: Corsica offers some of the world's most extreme white water—demanding technical runs in the Class V to VI range—and some of the wildest waterfalls anywhere. Corsica's larger rivers—notably the Gravona, the Tavignano, and the Golo—boast many less hazardous Class III to VI+ runs that nonetheless pack plenty of white-water punch.

The Gravona, in eastern Corsica, is a long run riddled

with complex Class III to IV boulder fields, runnable water-falls, and a few Class VI drops that only a handful of pad-dlers in the world would dare to take on. Beginning as an easy Class I and Class II float through alpine pastures, the Gravona soon steepens and accelerates as the water moves through a maze of rounded boulders. Scraping against rocks is a constant hazard here.

The Gravona continues with several miles of Class III to Class IV white water. Plan to spend some time on the bank in this section, scouting out the rapids ahead—or pinpoint-ing take-out spots if forced to portage. For an alternative run that is similar to the Gravona, the nearby Golo has count-less Class IIIs and a swift current, even during low water.

Another classic Corsican river is the Tavignano, or "Ta-vo." It features nearly continuous Class III white water run-ning through impressive slot canyons that cut down to the island's bedrock. The upper reaches are particularly tight—sometimes no more than a boat length wide. As you descend to the Tavo's lower sections, you will enter an intricate net-work of narrow channels through boulder fields and more Class III to Class IV rapids.

For the ultimate in extreme boating, the Fium Orbo delivers solid Class V to Class VI action. It begins as a modest, narrow creek flowing through chutes just three feet wide. As the river steepens, it makes several tight bends, generating turbulent rapids and powerful eddies. Here you'll find waterfalls that have attracted top paddlers from around the world. On some of these cascades, water pours out of the top like a pitcher and the paddler becomes airborne, riding a liquid plume before plunging into the roiling waters below. Although most advanced kayakers can safely negotiate vertical drops of 10 to 15 feet, the Fium Orbo also has several pitcher-style drops of 25 to 35 feet that only the most skilled and fearless paddlers should at-tempt to tackle. Such vertical drops give the rivers of Cor-sica some of the steepest gradients of any runnable white-water courses in the world.

Despite the island's reputation as a white-water wonder-land, there are plenty of opportunities for experienced pad-dlers to enjoy other, less demanding runs on Corsica. **Cors' Aventure** (*Suaralta Vecchia 20129, Bastelicaccia, Corsica. 01133-49525-9119. Fax 01133-495-23-8096.*) offers kayak rentals starting at $37 (US) per day and guided tours for roughly $70 (US) per day. A one-week tour with Cors' Aventure, includ-ing equipment rental and lodging, costs about $750 (US). Both **Corsicaventure** (*01133-495-48-8359. Fax 01133-495-57-0734.*) and **Corsikayak** (*01133-495-38-2525. Fax 01133-495-38 2555.*) also offer kayak rentals. Every two years or so, Ameri-can outfitter **Nantahala Outdoor Center** (*888-662-1662 ext.333. www.noc.com*) offers package kayaking tours to Corsica. Contact NOC for current availability and pricing.

LEFT: CLOSE ENCOUNTER WITH A BALD
EAGLE AT CHILKOOT STATE PARK, ALASKA

Notable North American Waterways

Here are North America's finest rivers for self-guided canoe or kayak trips. Many have been officially designated as Wild and Scenic Rivers—the nation's most treasured waterways. Featuring mainly flat water or gentle rapids, the majority of these watercourses can be run confidently without a guide—if, that is, you do your homework ahead of time: Before you set off, talk to local river guides, obtain the best maps available from official agencies, and scout out the more difficult stretches. Above all, don't be too proud to portage!

NORTHEAST

Allagash River, Maine
A north-flowing river with few rapids, the Allagash is one of the best long-distance canoe rivers in the East. A wonderful 90-mile paddle from Telos Lake to Allagash Falls is possible to do in a week.

St. Croix River, Maine
The St. Croix is a New England classic—a waterway with a long heritage of recreational canoeing. A good starter river for building your skills, the St. Croix offers continuous Class I and II white water—fun but never overwhelming.

St. John River, Maine
The St. John offers long stretches of Class I and Class II waters, with many fine camping areas along the way. The St. John is usually less crowded than most other New England rivers in the summertime.

Androscoggin River, New Hampshire
The Androscoggin is New England's only white-water river that runs consistently all summer. Between Errol and Berlin, you'll find about 30 miles of flat water and Class II and III white water through the forested mountains of northern New Hampshire.

Connecticut River, New Hampshire
The upper (New Hampshire border) section of this classic New England canoe river, where gentle rapids alternate with fast water, is best. A good starting point is just below Canaan, Vermont.

Hudson River, New York
More scenic than you might expect, the Hudson is often overlooked as a recreational river, even though it is one of the best rivers in the Northeast for average paddlers. Mostly Class I and II, the Hudson gets rougher north of Glens Falls. Spring offers the best water conditions.

SOUTHEAST

Little River, Alabama
The Little River carves a beautiful gorge in the side of Lookout Mountain in northeast Alabama. The first 6 miles after DeSoto Falls constitute a solid Class IV and V section known as the Avalanche. The next 6 miles are mostly flat water whose occasional rapids can easily be portaged by novices.

Loxahatchee River, Florida
One of the last untamed rivers in South Florida, the Loxahatchee is a pathway into the past. Lined with huge cypress trees hundreds of years old and abundant wildlife, this wilderness river is one of Florida's hidden treasures.

Green River, Kentucky
You can select a variety of easy trips along the Green River, which flows for 370 miles through the heartland of Kentucky. Here's one good choice: the flat-water sections within Mammoth Cave National Park.

Rockcastle River, Kentucky
The Rockcastle is a designated Wild and Scenic River that flows through the Daniel Boone National Forest. Family paddlers will enjoy the Class II upper sections—particularly the 15 miles upstream from the KY 80 bridge. The bridge also makes a good take-out point before you reach the Class III and Class IV waters farther downstream.

Chattooga River, North & South Carolina
The Chattooga (the river in the movie *Deliverance*) is easily one of America's finest waterways—wild and beautiful. The lower stretches are for experts only. Section Two near the Georgia border, however, is an easy Class II run at most water levels. Section Three can be run by intermediates—except at high water.

New River, North Carolina, Virginia, & West Virginia
As it runs through North Carolina and Virginia, the New River is mild enough for beginners. Things get interesting in West Virginia, below Bluestone Lake, with increasing white water. Below Thurmond, West Virginia, lie the biggest rapids in the East; they are suitable for experts only.

Obed-Emory Rivers, Tennessee
The Obed-Emory river system, Tennessee's only Wild and Scenic River, is one of America's prettiest waterways. Although the upper stretches are for experts only, novices can handle the Clear Creek tributary—27 miles of Class II water through unspoiled wilderness.

Shenandoah River, Virginia
The South Fork of the Shenandoah cuts through a scenic valley between the Blue Ridge Mountains and Massanutten Mountain. The 100 miles of smooth but fast water between Port Republic and Front Royal make for a great five-day trip.

CENTRAL

Buffalo River, Arkansas
The Buffalo offers fine Class I and II river running along the 150 miles between Boxley and Buffalo, with many caves and pools to explore. Early in the season, the upper 30 miles can be hazardous during peak flood. By contrast, water levels fall very low over the same stretch in late summer.

Current River, Missouri
The 100 miles of the Current River within Ozark National Scenic Riverways Park make for a marvelous five- to six-day trip year-round. Campsites are numerous, the water is relatively flat but fast flowing, and the river winds through pretty stretches with hardwood groves atop limestone bluffs.

Eleven Point River, Missouri

One of the eight original Wild and Scenic Rivers, the Eleven Point River is fed by more than 20 springs and can be floated year-round. Starting from Thomasville, you can make an easy three-day trip over 45 miles of smooth water, with excellent camping along the way. *Caveat paddlor:* Summer traffic can be quite heavy.

Jack's Fork River, Missouri

A tributary of the Current River, the Jack's Fork can be boated all year—though you may encounter a few shoals. Most of the action is above Alley Spring. The best put-in is at Buck Hollow for either one- or two-day float trips to Alley Spring.

Meramec River, Missouri

One of the best floating and fishing rivers in Missouri, the Meramec is a classic Ozark stream with deep, clear pools, sandy shoals, and fast Class II sections during high water. The Meramec also offers excellent fishing for trophy-class brown trout.

GREAT LAKES

Au Sable River, Michigan

Gentle waters, scenic countryside, and great fishing make the Au Sable one of Michigan's favorite waterways. Paddlers can camp or overnight at notable riverside lodges.

Pere Marquette River, Michigan

Flowing from the western hill country into Lake Michigan, the Pere Marquette boasts good fishing and high-quality campsites. For a one- or two-day trip best suited to intermediate boaters, put in south of Baldwin and paddle to Walhalla.

Boundary Waters, Minnesota

Covering thousands of square miles of unspoiled wilderness, the Boundary Waters Canoe Area Wilderness is a paddler's paradise. Even with 150,000 canoeists visiting each year, there are so many places to go that it never seems crowded. Reserve a permit months in advance.

St. Louis River, Minnesota

One of Minnesota's most scenic rivers, the St. Louis is a fine destination for daytrippers, who will enjoy its varied river dynamics and abundant play spots. Most of the river is Class I; beginners may have to portage the occasional Class III rapid.

St. Croix River, Minnesota & Wisconsin

A designated Wild and Scenic River, the St. Croix flows smoothly from Lake Superior to the river's confluence with the Mississippi near the Twin Cities. Pockmarking the St. Croix are many pools—some as deep as 80 feet—which are connected by narrow sections with faster currents.

Wolf River, Wisconsin

Superb trout fishing combined with more than 30 miles of Class I to III white water make the Wolf River in northeastern Wisconsin a fun and challenging two- to three-day self-guided trip. The US 52 crossing near Lily is a popular put-in.

SOUTHWEST

Verde River, Arizona

From Childs, Arizona, to its confluence with the Salt River, the Verde River offers more than 60 miles of Class I and II paddling between a series of reservoirs. A few Class III rapids lies in wait above Horseshoe Reservoir, but they are nothing that intermediates can't handle. The Verde is best run in March and April, making it an excellent off-season destination.

Rio Grande, New Mexico & Texas

Intermediates can navigate the Pilar section of the Rio Grande, which ranges from flat to Class III, followed by many miles of gentle

DOG PADDLING ON LAKE KEZAR, MAINE

water. Great desert scenery and a long season make this a good family holiday.

Green River, Utah

The Green River flows smoothly for 100 miles south of Green River, Utah, as it winds through red sandstone canyons before joining the Colorado River in Canyonlands National Park. Consider capping off your float trip down the Green with a guided rafting trip through the Colorado's Cataract Canyon.

Middle Colorado River, Utah

No, the Colorado is *not* for experts only. Stick to Ruby and Horsethief Canyons and you can enjoy 27 miles of Class I and II water suitable for open canoes and rookie kayakers (this makes a great two- to four-day trip). Skilled paddlers with permits may continue on to Class IV Westwater Canyon.

San Juan River, Utah

The San Juan River, running through Utah's colorful Canyonlands, offers one of the most dramatic Class I to Class II trips in the world. The steep rock canyons are second in scale only to the Grand Canyon of the Colorado. April is the time to run this river; avoid dangerous high-water conditions.

ROCKIES

Rio Chama, Colorado

The Rio Chama is one of Colorado's best destinations for novices and intermediates. It offers pleasant Class II stretches that are suitable for two- to four-day trips.

Yellowstone River, Montana

The moderate section of the Yellowstone between Livingston and Billings, Montana, makes a fun six-day trip for novices and intermediates. Avoid the dangerous sections in Yellowstone National Park, however.

Upper Missouri River, Montana

Featuring passages through breathtaking canyons, the upper Missouri can be run by canoeists who have a modicum of experience. The stretch from Fort Benton to US 191 is designated a Wild and Scenic River.

Main Payette River, Idaho

The Main Payette near Boise, with Class I and II conditions on warm, dam-controlled waters, is a good one- or two-day novice trip. The rapids of this accessible river can be scouted from nearby roads.

WEST

American River, California

The lower section of the American River is a good training ground for beginning paddlers. Be aware, however, that water levels tend to drop dramatically late in the season.

Russian River, California

Located in northern California's scenic wine country, the Russian River offers 15 miles of gentle Class I water from Asti to Healdsburg. South of Healdsburg, the river widens and the current slows. Water levels in the Russian drop drastically by late summer.

Stanislaus River, California

Beginners will enjoy paddling the Class I section of the Stanislaus from Knights Ferry to Oakdale in the scenic Sierra Nevada foothills. There is one Class II rapid, but novices can easily skirt this by portaging their craft along a nearby trail.

Colorado River (Black Canyon), Nevada

Between Hoover Dam and Lake Mohave, the Colorado courses smoothly through the steep walls of Black Canyon. Everything is strictly Class I or flat water—but there is nothing one-dimensional about the scenery. The put-in near Boulder City, Nevada, is half an hour from Las Vegas.

Deschutes River, Oregon

Although it is also a prime white-water river, the Deschutes is not too demanding in the 100 miles north of Bend, Oregon, where it runs through very pretty country.

Grande Ronde, Oregon

From its junction with the Wallowa River for about 40 miles to the Washington State border, the Grande Ronde is a designated Wild and Scenic River. In this section, it courses through spectacular canyons whose steep walls rise as much as 3,000 feet above river level. The Grande Ronde has mostly Class II and III waters.

Klamath River, Oregon

One of the West's best learning rivers, the Klamath offers many Class I and II sections that are ideal for practicing whitewater skills in relative safety. Because the Klamath also harbors many Class IV and Class V rapids, however, consult a local guide before choosing your route.

CANADA EAST

Grand River, Ontario

The Grand River, about an hour west of Toronto, is a popular choice for single-day or weekend float trips. For a scenic float through Mennonite farm country, try the section between Bellwood Lake and West Montrose. The most popular section is the 25-mile stretch from Glen Morris to Brant, which offers a taste of fast water.

Moisie River, Quebec

On a 260-mile journey from the mountains to the St. Lawrence, the Moisie flows through some of Canada's most beautiful river valleys, complete with spectacular gorges and waterfalls. The Moisie makes a great two-week trip. The Class III to Class IV rapids in the upper section should be portaged.

Ottawa River, Quebec

Flowing west for more than 300 miles among a group of large lakes, the Ottawa is a prime choice for a wilderness tour. Except for some tough rapids in the first 40 miles, the paddling is fairly easy.

CANADA WEST

Okanagan Region, British Columbia

The Okanagan Valley has long been the focus of B.C. canoeing. Paddle Lake Okanagan, or canoe-camp along any of ten nearby rivers. This area offers a great variety of recreational opportunities and classically beautiful, easy-running waterways. Canoes can be rented in Kelowna, B.C. from **Lee's Outfitters** (250-762-8156) or from **Okanagan Canoe Holidays** (250-762-8156).

MacKenzie River, Northwest Territories

Long, wide, and (for the most part) gentle, the MacKenzie is the major river of the Canadian Northwest. It winds through a vast, remote wilderness—you can paddle for days without spying a trace of civilization. Pick a route on the 300-mile stretch between Fort Simpson and Fort Norman.

Big Salmon River, Yukon Territory

Situated deep in the heart of the Yukon Territory, the Big Salmon is hard to reach—but worth the effort. The river begins as a chain of three lakes, then runs for 115 miles. Wildlife galore and nothing above Class II rapids make this an ideal wilderness trip for novices.

North America's Top Paddling Schools

Although canoeing or kayaking on flat water is not difficult, it's a good idea to get some basic paddling training before you head out on your first long-distance float trek. To learn how to negotiate serious rapids—those designated as Class III and above—in either a canoe or a kayak, top-notch professional instruction is essential.

Our list of the best paddling centers in North America starts at right and runs to page 52. Most feature a wide variety of training programs, from half-day clinics to multi-day instructional expeditions. Many schools in the East offer both canoe and kayak training, while those in the West focus primarily on white-water kayaking. The larger schools also tend to offer American Canoe Association (ACA) instructor certification and swift-water rescue training.

EAST

Riversport School of Paddling

355 River Road
Confluence, PA 15424
800-216-6991 or 814-395-5744
www.shol.com/kayak

Riversport offers lessons of one to five days in open canoes and kayaks for paddlers of all experience levels. The costs are reasonable: They range from $100 to $425, which includes lodging at Riversport's camp on the Youghiogheny River. Each class is customized to suit the needs of students. With a maximum of five paddlers per class, you'll get plenty of personal attention from Riversport's instructors. Most training takes place on the nearby Youghiogheny River, but Riversport can also transport paddlers to three West Virginia rivers: the Cheat, the Big Sandy, and the Little Sandy. Intermediate paddlers looking for new challenges should find Riversport—with many steep creeks nearby—a good choice.

Saco Bound

P.O. Box 119
Center Conway, NH 03813
800-677-7238 or 603-447-2177
www.sacobound.com

Established in 1975, Saco Bound is New England's oldest paddling center. Saco Bound's white-water school in Errol, New Hampshire, conducts canoe- and kayak-training seminars for both novices and intermediates on the Class II and III Androscroggin River—New England's only continually running summer white-water river. More intensive training is offered on Class III sections of the Kennebec River near Saco Bound's base camp in West Forks, Maine. Two- to five-day programs operate from June 15 to Labor Day at an average cost of $80 per day. Saco Bound's riverside complex includes a campground, a restaurant, and a motel. This is a high-quality program with a strong history.

LEARNING THE BASICS AT OTTER BAR KAYAK SCHOOL, CALIFORNIA

Waterfall Running

What's a paddler to do when he or she has run the hottest rivers around yet still seeks the extreme river thrill of a lifetime? For those searching out the steepest drops and highest flows, the ultimate riverine challenge is paddling down ferocious waterfalls such as the one shown below. Once the kayak clears the crest of the cascade and becomes airborne, its pilot must maneuver the craft with hair-trigger precision: If the boat hits the water wrong, the paddler can break his paddle, his back, or his neck. This is not for novices! For those who enjoy the extreme thrills of waterfall running, however, here are *Paddler* magazine's picks of North America's wildest kayaking cascades:

ON THE LIP OF THE SPOUT, THE BIGGEST WATERFALL AT GREAT FALLS, VIRGINIA

Spirit Falls
Little White Salmon
River
Washington

Big Falls
White Salmon River
Washington

Steelhead Falls
Deschutes River
Oregon

Curtina Falls
Bald Rock Canyon
Middle Fork of Feather
River
California

McCloud Falls
McCloud River
California

Dream Falls
North Fork of American River
California

Tunnel Falls
Gore Canyon
Colorado River
Colorado

Adrenaline Falls
Lime Creek
Colorado

The Cauldron
Lake Creek
Colorado

Punch Bowl Falls
Crystal River
Colorado

Big Sandy Falls
Big Sandy Creek
West Virginia

Baby Falls
Tellico River
Tennessee

Gorilla Falls
Green River
North Carolina

Singley's Falls
Overflow Gorge
Georgia

Little River Falls
Little River
Alabama

Great Falls
Potomac River
Maryland and Virginia

Agers Falls
Moose River
New York

Wild Waters

1123 Route 28 at The Glen
Warrensburg, NY 12885
800-867-2335, 888-945-3420,
or 518-494-4984
www.wild-waters.com

Located on the banks of the Hudson River, Wild Waters (WW) offers quality training in both kayaks and canoes (both open and decked). Many companies claim to offer personal instruction, but WW delivers. There are four levels of classes, each tailored to a specific degree of skill and experience. WW's American Canoe Association-certified instructors are much better than those found in most schools. Highly recommended are WW's specialty clinics (squirt boat and women-only classes, for example), which are taught by world-class paddlers. Clinics start at $240 for two days, including instruction, meals, lodging, and all equipment. Students stay at WW's Glen House Lodge, which is open to other paddlers and guests for $20 per night (breakfast included).

ZOAR Outdoor Paddling School

P.O. Box 245
Charlemont, MA 01339
800-532-7483 or 413-339-4010
www.zoaroutdoor.com

Led by World Whitewater Champion Bruce Lessels, ZOAR's staff of ACA-certified instructors operate one- to three-day clinics in white-water kayaking and canoeing. ZOAR offers personal instruction with a maximum of four students per instructor. Most training takes place on the Deerfield River, whose conditions—among them numerous Class II and III rapids—are suited for all skill levels. Two-day courses begin at $200. For $500, ZOAR also offers an intensive Introduction to Paddling Week that combines the beginner and intermediate courses. ZOAR's curriculum includes special classes in ACA instructor certification, racing, and river rescue. ZOAR also offers adventures in sea kayaking and rock climbing, as well as a retail store.

SOUTHEAST

Nantahala Outdoor Center
13077 US 19 West
Bryson City, NC 28713
888-662-1662 ext. 600 or 828-488-2176
www.noc.com

Nantahala is the paddling school by which all the rest are judged. Established in 1972, it offers the most comprehensive training program in North America. A partial list of river-skills classes includes: Basic Canoe, C-1 (decked canoe), two- to five-day Beginner to Advanced Canoe/Kayak, seven-day Fast Track Kayak, Racers Workshop, and Raft Guide Training. Nantahala also offers four- and five-day intensive river weeks, which take you down a variety of rivers within a region. Instruction is available on many of the major destination trips (Rio Grande, Costa Rica, and Alaska, for example). Nantahala's instructors are patient and skilled, and many other paddling centers send personnel to Nantahala for workshops and certification. Nantahala has its own on-site retail store and restaurant, and its "bunkhouse" is said to rival many ski-resort condos.

GREAT LAKES

Kayak and Canoe Institute
University of Minnesota at Duluth
121 SPHC, 10 University Dr.
Duluth, MN 55812
218-726-6533
www.d.umn.edu/umdoutdoors/courses/kci

The Kayak and Canoe Institute (KCI) trains more than 7,000 students annually. Year-round instruction in every type of paddling is offered at bargain prices. A three-day weekend kayaking course for beginners, for example, is $265, while a two-day intermediate course costs $170 to $225 (both courses include camping and meals). These prices apply to both white-water and flat-water decked- and open-canoe courses. KCI also offers vacation options such as a three-day intermediate sea-kayak tour to Lake Superior's Apostle Islands for $380, and a variety of Boundary Waters expeditions. For the adventurous, KCI offers a few extended wilderness trips each year: San Juan River canoeing, Lake Powell sea kayaking, British Columbia sea kayaking, and a raft-and-kayak tour of Idaho's Salmon River. These expeditions last 7 to 12 days and are high in both value and camaraderie. KCI also offers instructor training and certification.

ROCKIES

Boulder Outdoor Center
2510 N. 47th St.
Boulder, CO 80301
800-364-9376 or 303-444-8420
www.boc123.com

The Boulder Outdoor Center (BOC) is a mecca for paddle sports. BOC instructors include some of the most talented kayakers in the sport—all-stars with numerous first descents in Central America and Mexico. If you are looking for a school that can push you quickly up to the Class III level and beyond, BOC is a good choice. Seminars are conducted on a number of rivers, including the Colorado, and BOC offers guided trips to the Wild and Scenic Cache La Poudre River near Fort Collins, one of the longest continuous runs in the Front range. BOC offers canoeing and rafting as well, so you can bring the whole family. Classes range from one to five days, accommodations from camping to condos can be arranged, and a fleet of demo kayaks allow paddlers to try out different designs. The three-day Novice River Trip costs $220 with equipment. A week-long tour/clinic is $800 with meals and equipment, or $475 without.

Dvorak's Kayak and Rafting Expeditions, Inc.
17921 US 285
Nathrop, CO 81236
800-824-3795 or 719-539-6851
www.dvorakexpeditions.com

Bill Dvorak's school offers 1- to 12-day instructional seminars on Class II to Class V rivers such as the Green, the Dolores, and the Arkansas. For the serious paddler, Dvorak recommends a five- to seven-day seminar; a three-day program will give a good introduction to white-water technique. On-river seminars begin at about $310 for three days, including food and equipment. Recommended for novices is the six-day program on the Green River ($1,150). All told, the Dvorak operation runs 29 canyons on ten different rivers. You can combine kayak or canoe training with rafting on the same trip.

Four Corners River Sports Paddling School
360 S. Camino del Rio
Durango, CO 81302
800-426-7637 or 970-259-3893
www.riversports.com

Since 1983, Four Corners has offered quality river training in southwest Colorado. Four Corners conducts two- to three-day beginner and intermediate courses, all taught by ACA-certified instructors. Durango's Animas River provides forgiving smooth water for novices and more challenging Class II and III intermediate conditions in the Whitewater Park just south of town. Durango's unique Olympic-class park, a training site for the U.S. Canoeing and Kayaking Team, features a permanent slalom, as well as challenging rapids for intermediate paddlers who'd like to improve their skills. Advanced trainees may also paddle the Class IV Piedre. Courses cost $125 to $325, including equipment, lunch, and transportation to the river. Classes run from April through September, but water levels drop appreciably after July. Four Corners is a quality school that teaches solid fundamentals while maintaining high safety standards. Hiking, mountain-biking, and horseback-riding trails lie just a few minutes from downtown Durango, making this perhaps the best situated paddling center in the Rockies.

WEST

Northwest Outdoor Center
2100 Westlake Ave. N.
Seattle, WA 98109
800-683-0637 or 206- 281-9694
www.nwoc.com

Though Seattle is not known as a haven for white-water sports, the Northwest Outdoor Center (NWOC) runs a strong introductory kayak-training program from spring through fall. Basic training is conducted in heated pools in Seattle; classes then head for the Class II and III Skykomish and Wenatchee Rivers in the Cascades for on-the-water training. The basic Eskimo Roll clinic ($50) boasts a student success rate of 80 percent. Weekend programs cost $175 (plus $50 for kayak rental), while the five-day Total Immersion school costs $550 (meals, lodging, transport, boats, and gear are included). Each summer, NWOC offers a three-day, $675 guided kayak trip down Oregon's Rogue River—a perfect place to hone your intermediate moves in Class II and III rapids. NWOC also operates a busy sea-kayaking program that comprises both clinics and guided trips.

Otter Bar Lodge Kayak School
P.O. Box 210
Forks of Salmon, CA 96031
530- 462-4772
www.otterbar.com

The Otter Bar Kayak School is a high-end white-water destination resort. Challenging rapids right at your doorstep make this a great spot to learn white-water technique. With a student-to-teacher ratio of just three to one, classes are small, serious, and effective, and equipment is new each year. The riverside lodge (limited to 14 guests) offers gourmet meals and deluxe accommodations. Otter Bar offers seven-day clinics for beginners from June through September and seven-day intermediate programs from April through June. Classes run on the emerald green Cal Salmon through midsummer, then shift to the dam-controlled Klamath, which offers more reliable late-season flows. Week-long courses run $1,700, including lodging, meals, and equipment. The advanced courses teach surfing, pirouettes, eddy hopping, and other expert maneuvers. Book early; the center fills up fast during the busy summer months.

Sierra South Mountain Sports

11300 Kernville Rd.
Kernville, CA 93238
800-457-2082, 800-376-7303,
or 760-376-3745
www.sierrasouth.com

Sierra South is southern California's leading white-water kayaking school, training more than 1,000 new paddlers annually on the banks of the Kern—an exciting river three hours from Los Angeles. A two-day basic kayaking course costs $245; novice, intermediate, or advanced weekend classes (such as roll clinics) also cost $245, including all equipment. Flat-water kayak-touring classes are conducted on Lake Isabella; open-top kayak seminars are available, too. Sierra South also runs white-water rafting trips on the Kern. There is no riverside lodge, but inexpensive accommodations are available in Kernville.

Sundance River Center

14894 Galice Rd.
Merlin, OR 97532
888-777-7557 or 541-479-8508
www.sundanceriver.com

Having trained boaters for more than 25 years, Sundance is among the elite of the West Coast kayak schools. Not content simply to run customers through a training regimen, this river center aims to produce skilled, enthusiastic kayakers who will continue with the sport. The training is comparable to that offered at Otter Bar,

and most courses include a long-distance river trip. The majority of classes run on the Rogue River, but Sundance offers clinics on other rivers as well—including the Class IV Illinois, one of the longest continuous runs on the West Coast.

Rapport between students and instructors is excellent. Former Sundance instructor Eric Ludwig and his wife, Laurie, took over operations in 1999. While continuing to offer all of Sundance's key programs, the Ludwigs have added several theme trips and river clinics. The basic nine-day program costs about $1,800 (including permits, lodging, and meals) and culminates with a four-day raft-supported trip down an Oregon river, such as the Rogue. Sundance also runs raft-supported trips on the Middle Fork of the Salmon River in Idaho and on the Colorado for intermediate kayakers and above.

CANADA

Madawaska Kanu Centre

39 First Ave.
Ottawa, ON, Canada, K1S 2G1
613-594-5268
www.owl-mkc.ca

Madawaska Kanu Centre (MKC), Canada's most experienced paddle-sports school, is a great place to learn white-water skills (in canoes as well as kayaks) in a pristine environment. MKC is based on the dam-controlled Madawaska River, just outside scenic Algonquin Provincial Park. The controlled release assures good water flow all summer long. MKC also runs intermediate programs on the fast-moving Petawawa and Ottawa Rivers. Classes are small and the instructors are seasoned. Beginner to advanced courses run two to five days and start at $215 (CN) for a weekend. Five-day residential programs start at less than $450 (CN), with lodging in forest cabins and Continental food. When you factor in the exchange rate, these represent bargain prices for Yanks.

TRAVEL TIPS

Outfitting a Trip

In selecting a canoe outfitter, look for experience and top-notch equipment. If you are headed for an area that requires portaging, take the latest lightweight gear, such as Kevlar canoes and ultralight tents. Established outfitters know the best destinations within a particular region. Many of the paddling schools reviewed above lead

river trips to destinations throughout North America. However, they represent only a small sample of the qualified river guides and outfitters in North America. For example, there are at least 100 canoe outfitters worthy of mention in Canada alone. To locate other qualified river guides and outfitters, consult *Canoe & Kayak Magazine* (800-692-2663 or 425-827-6363. www.canoekayak.com), or contact one of the following organizations:

America Outdoors

P.O. Box 10847, Knoxville, TN 37939
800-524-4814 or 423-558-3595
www.americaoutdoors.org

Represents more than 500 adventure companies in 43 states and 50 countries.

American Canoe Association

7432 Alban Station Blvd., Suite B-232
Springfield, VA 22150. 703- 451-0141
www.aca-paddler.org
Publishes *American Canoeist* newsletter; good source for canoe route guides and local club listings.

Canadian Recreational Canoeing Association

446 Main St. W., Merrickville, ON
K0G 1N0, Canada. 888-252-6292 or
613-269-2910. www.crca.ca
Publishes *Kanawa* newsletter and provides information on waterways and local canoeing clubs.

Canadian River Council (CRC)

c/o New World Expeditions
100 Rivière Rouge
Calumet, PQ J0V 1B0, Canada
800-361-5033 or 819-242-7238
www.newworld.ca

Professional Paddlesports Association

(formerly NACLO)
P.O. Box 248, Butler, KY 41006
(606) 472-2205. www.propaddle.com
Represents more than 500 river outfitters.

Kayak Expeditions

Because of its limited carrying capacity, a river kayak is not a particularly good cruising vehicle. However, multiday kayak trips are feasible if you arrange for a support raft to carry your gear. Nantahala Outdoor Center, Sundance River Center, and the Kayak and Canoe Institute are among the leaders in raft-supported kayak river trips (see addresses above). You'll find a number of additional companies that offer raft-supported trips on pages 162-179.

ONLINE

American Canoe Association
www.aca-paddler.org

This site features an event calendar with white-water rodeos and river festivals, river conservation news, and information on ACA instructor certification.

American Whitewater Affiliation
www.awa.org

This first-rate website hosts the AWA's River Pages Project, a comprehensive review of American rivers including put-ins, take-outs, and white-water classifications. You'll also find an event calendar, as well as directories of manufacturers, tour operators, and U.S. water gauges.

Riversport.com
www.riversport.com

This useful website offers river profiles, message boards, equipment sales, and event news about paddle sports.

U.S. Geological Survey
Water Resources Information
http://h2o.usgs.gov/public/realtime.html

The USGS site features real-time stream-flow conditions for rivers in most U.S. states, plus links to other river-related resources on the Web.

PRINT

The Complete Whitewater Sourcebook ($19.95 from the Boat People, 408-295-2628. www.theboatpeople.com) contains all the information you need for river-running nationwide: phone numbers, water levels, regional guidebooks, access points, and permit requirements. Some listings are dated, but the book is still invaluable.

Classic Northeastern Whitewater Guide by Bruce Lessels ($19.95 from the Appalachian Mountain Club, 800-262-4455. www.outdoors.org) is the leading where-to-go guide for New England paddlers.

Idaho: The Whitewater State by Grant Amaral ($19.95 from the Boat People, 408-295-2628) covers most of the rivers reviewed in Moore and McLaren's older *Idaho Whitewater,* but it offers better maps and more coverage of small creeks.

Performance Kayaking by Stephen U'ren ($15.95 from Stackpole Books, 800-732-3669. www.stackpolebooks.com) is a thorough guide to white-water sport boating written by an expert slalom racer.

Song of the Paddle by Bill Mason ($24.95 from *Canoe & Kayak Magazine,* 800-692-2663. www.canoekayak.com) is a beautiful guide to canoe camping in the wilderness, illustrated with photos. This is classic of the genre.

Western Whitewater: From the Rockies to the Pacific by Cassady, Calhoun, and Cross ($34.95 from the Boat People, 408-295-2628) is the most authoritative guidebook in print for river runners. Fifty top rivers are reviewed and mapped in detail, with basic information on an additional 100 runs. This volume has the best maps and river logs of any current publication.

World Whitewater by Jim Cassady (1999; $22.95 from the Boat People, 408-295-2628). Extensive coverage of Western Europe, Central and South America, plus a few rivers in Australia and New Zealand. A must for overseas trip planning.

Canoeing and Kayaking by Laurie Guillion ($15.95 from Menasha Ridge Press, 205-322-0439. www.menasharidge.com) is a comprehensive guide outlining paddling skills and teaching methods endorsed by the American Canoe Association.

Paddler magazine offers a lively mix of equipment reviews, paddling tips, environmental features, and up-to-the-minute trekking information. The magazine is included with membership in the American Canoe Association (*703-451-0141. www.aca-paddler.org*).

Canoe & Kayak Magazine (800-692-2663 or 425-827-6363. www.canoekayak.com)

VIDEO

PaddleQuest: A Kayaking Adventure ($29.95 from Adventurous Traveler Bookstore, 800-282-3963. www.adventuroustraveler.com). This video features action from Chile, Mexico, Idaho, Montana, and Alaska. The footage from Chile's Futaleufu River alone is worth the price.

The paddling series from Placid Videos ($19.95 each from 2139 Tapo St. #109 Simi Valley, CA 93063. 800-549-0046) covers many of the best flat-water destinations: California, the Florida Everglades, Hawaii, and the Boundary Waters.

USING ONE'S HEAD NEAR LAKE TAKIJUQ IN CANADA'S NORTHWEST TERRITORIES

BICYCLE TOURING IS BOOMING. DOZENS OF TOUR COMPANIES OFFER HUNDREDS OF GUIDED TRIPS, with off-the-saddle extras that range from sailing cruises to rafting excursions. Despite the road-bike origins of cycle touring, many outfitters now run mountain-bike tours both in the United States and abroad. • The quality of commercial tours is generally quite high; most customers seem satisfied with the package-tour experience. As guided tours—especially those in Europe—have become more deluxe, however, the cost of taking them has crept ever upward. • If you've already scouted out some cycling tours, the hard part is probably over: Picking the right trip can be more difficult than pedaling it. To ease the process, this chapter steers you to the best outfitters and tours for your budget and interests. You'll also find advice on how to organize a tour of your own, as well as a list of North America's prime mountain-biking spots.

LEFT: MOUNTAIN BIKER DAN DIEZ HEADS DOWNHILL NEAR SEDONA, ARIZONA.
BELOW: FIRST LEG OF A 65-DAY, 3,135-MILE ODYSSEY ACROSS AMERICA

Touring for Roadies

Mountain Biking

Plan It— and Pedal It— Yourself

The bicycle is a vehicle for revolution. It can destroy the tyranny of the automobile as effectively as the printing press brought down despots of flesh and blood.

DANIEL BEHRMAN

Life Cycles

The most efficient conveyance ever invented, the bicycle is also the perfect way to reach new destinations. You ramble rather than rush, interacting with the environment instead of passing it in a blur. From the mild to the wild, the world's best bicycle tours and destinations appear below. Any one of them could become the trip of a lifetime.

SAN JUAN ISLANDS
A Northwest Passage

The scenic **San Juans,** about an hour's drive north of Seattle, may well be the premier coastal-cycling destination in North America. The islands offer just about everything: moderate terrain, plentiful parks and campgrounds, charming country inns, boat rides, and easy access to major cities.

A good starting point is Port Townsend, where you can roll aboard a ferry and cross Admiralty Inlet to reach **Whidbey Island.** Many resorts dot Whidbey, which is also home to excellent campgrounds at Fort Casey, Fort Ebey, Oak Harbor, and Deception Pass State Parks. Whidbey gets crowded in summer, so you'll probably want to move on after a day or two. Cross the bridge at the north end to Fidalgo Island, then head north along Burrows Bay to the campground at Washington Park. An island loop that takes in the town of Anacortes makes a nice day trip.

You can also include the **Gulf Islands** of British Columbia in your trip. In that case, take the ferry to Sidney and make the easy ride south to Victoria, or catch a different boat and head for Saltspring Island, Galiano Island, or another Gulf Island to the north.

If you stay on the American side, hop off the ferry at **Shaw Island,** in the middle of Puget Sound. There's a nice campground here, and Shaw is also a good base from which to explore San Juan Island, Lopez Island, and Orcas Island. (Orcas has the nicest scenery, Lopez the easiest peddling, and San Juan the best restaurants and facilities.) On Orcas Island, the long climb to the top of 2,400-foot-high Mount Constitution is rewarded with a 360-degree view of the entire area. San Juan's west-side road is notable for its unobstructed views; elsewhere in the San Juans, you'll ride between thick stands of trees most of the time.

Given the understandably extreme popularity of the San Juans, the thinking cyclist will reserve lodging well in advance. You can also avoid crowds by traveling in May, September, or October, when the weather cooperates and the price of an inn or resort stay tends to be lower. The indispensable *Touring the Islands* by Peter Powers and Renee Travis (*Adventurous Traveler Bookstore,* 800-282-3963) has 3-D maps of the San Juan and Gulf Islands; it also lists lodgings and campgrounds.

If you prefer a guided tour with a sag wagon, consider the eight-day trip to the San Juans, **Vancouver Island,** and the **Olympic Peninsula** offered by **Bicycle Adventures** (*Olympia, WA 98508. 800-443-6060 or 360-786-0989. www.bicycleadventures.com*). You can customize the itinerary with sailing or sea-kayaking excursions. The eight-day trip costs $2,000 (add $128 for bike rental); six-day and four-day versions of the tour are available for $1,600 and $1,000, respectively. **Backroads** (*Berkeley, CA 94710. 800-462-2848 or 510-527-1555. www.backroads.com*) also offers a good six-day Puget Sound trip for $1,900 if you stay at inns or $1,000 if you camp.

OREGON AND CALIFORNIA
Pedaling the Pacific Coast Highway

Riding down the **Pacific Coast Highway** is the ultimate cycling adventure. Although the car traffic gets worse every year, there is still plenty of stunning scenery once you leave the big cities behind. Best of all, by riding the route from north to south you can keep the prevailing wind at your back.

Ambitious riders often start as far north as Vancouver, but a more reasonable pedaling-off point is Portland, Oregon. Follow Highway 6 through the Coast Range to reach Tillamook, then turn left on Highway 101 to begin your journey south. Though seaside development blights the first leg of this ride, you'll be breaking out the camera by the time you hit the **Otter Rock** area north of Newport. Try to arrange your arrival here—the most dramatically beautiful stretch of the Oregon coast—for the afternoon, when the fog has lifted.

Farther south, the **Gold Beach** area below Port Orford is a great spot for camping and beach walks. (If you plan to camp in the state parks in summer, reserve a spot well in advance.) After crossing the Oregon-California border, you are in for a treat: a 40-mile stretch of road that threads the heart of **Redwood National Park** (*707-464-6101. www.redwood.national-park.com*). South of the park, the road climbs through the Coast Range before joining Highway 1 at Leggett. The next few days' riding take you down the Mendocino coast—a scenic highlight of the trip. Twenty miles south of Mendocino, for example, the quiet outpost of **Elk** on the far side of the Russian River boasts the best ocean views on the West Coast.

From here on, the road snakes along rugged headlands toward San Francisco. Stop in the eateries of **Bodega Bay** to sample some of their great local oysters. Then, if you have an extra day to spare, make the 85-mile round-trip to **Point Reyes.** As you approach San Francisco, resist the temptation to bomb across the bridge; instead, stop just short of the span to explore **Golden Gate National Recreation Area** (*415-556-0560*)— a perfect place for a midday picnic, with views that will leave you amazed.

If you press on south of San Francisco, take time to explore **Monterey, Carmel,** and **Point Lobos Nature Preserve.** Once you see **Big Sur** and **San Simeon,** you will have hit all the highlights, so you may want to wrap up the tour.

If a week on the coast is all the cycling you need, consider the seven-day Eureka-to-San Francisco tour offered by **Backroads Bicycle Touring** (*800-462-2848. www.backroads.com. $1,250 inn to inn, $750 camping*). Another good California trip, put on by **VBT Bicycling Vacations** (*800-245-3868. www.vbt.com*) for roughly $1,275, spends six days visiting wineries along the coast between Napa Valley and San Francisco.

UTAH CANYON COUNTRY
Mountain Biking in Moab

Few landscapes can match the drama of Utah's Canyonlands, where rivers course through serpentine canyons, haunting rock formations perch atop windswept mesas, and snowy peaks crenulate the horizon. The beauty and variety of this terrain—which makes for challenging climbs, chilling descents, and eminently crankable flats—have transformed Moab, Utah, into a mountain-biking mecca.

When it comes to routes, Canyonlands cyclists enjoy an embarrassment of riches. One of the most popular routes is the 140-mile-long **Kokopelli Trail,** which is primarily single track. From its start in the sandstone canyons of the Colorado River near Grand Junction, the trail ascends through the green forests of the La Sal Mountains (12,700 feet) before dropping into the red desert of Moab. The Kokopelli Trail ends at Sand Flats Road, which features red-rock panoramas and sandstone spires.

Sand Flats Road also happens to be the starting point for the 10-mile **Slickrock Trail,** one of the most challenging bike routes in North America. You can test your bike-handling skills on a 2-mile practice loop before committing yourself to the trail itself.

A number of outstanding outfitters offer guided mountain-bike expeditions in Canyonlands. **Kaibab Mountain Bike Tours** (*391 So. Main St., Moab 84532. 800-451-1133 or 435-259-7423. www.kaibabtours.com*) offers a four-day, $775 camping tour of the Kokopelli Trail segment that runs along the Colorado River corridor from Grand Junction to Dewey Bridge.

CYCLING THROUGH THE NORTH ALGODONES DUNES WILDERNESS AREA, SOUTHERN CALIFORNIA.

To experience the entire Kokopelli, try the four-day camping trip from Loma to Moab offered by **Nichols Expeditions** (*497 N. Main, Moab 84532. 800-648-8488 or 435-259-3999. www.nicholsexpeditions.com*). You can also bike the Kokopelli at a slower (but still challenging) pace on a five-day, $695 camping trip from Grand Junction to the Slickrock Trail run by **Rim Tours** (*1233 So. Highway 191, Moab 84532. 800-626-7335 or 435-259-5223. www.rimtours. com*).

Just southwest of Moab, in the heart of the Colorado plateau, lies **Canyonlands National Park.** The park's 100-mile-long **White Rim Trail** is a premier vantage point for panoramic views of Utah's red-rock wilderness. The trail begins atop the high mesas of the park's **Island in the Sky District,** then descends through deep canyons carved by the Green and Colorado Rivers. Portions of the trail parallel the canyon rim a dizzying 1,000 feet above the river below. Rim Tours, the mountain-bike company that blazed the White Rim Trail, offers three- and four-day trips that make a 90-mile loop along the trail for $495 and $595, respectively. (Nichols and Kaibab offer similar White Rim excursions.)

To explore Moab at your own pace, stay at **Pack Creek Ranch** (*Box 1270, Moab 84532. 435-259-5505. www.pack-creekranch.com. $135 to $300 per cabin in season, $100 to $200 per cabin off-season*), a reasonably priced, comfortable retreat that lets you cycle from your doorstep directly into the foothills. From the ranch, you can easily jump into a half- or full-day guided bike ride with Rim Tours or Kaibab Mountain Bike

Tours. Renting a mountain bike can be arranged through Rim Tours, Kaibab Tours, or **Poison Spider Bikes** (*800-635-1792*) for $25 to $45 per day, depending on season and equipment.

VERMONT
Green Mountain Getaway

Cyclists don't visit Vermont—they make pilgrimages here. The state's landscape is legend: Dairy farms and forests unroll from either side of the road, white-sided buildings cluster on village greens, and steep climbs spur riders to put their mettle to the pedal. From the gentle hills of the Connecticut River Valley to the daunting slopes of the Green Mountains, most Vermont roads are ideally suited for two-wheeled touring. Each year, a spectacular display of fall foliage graces the state's backcountry byways. To top it all off, Vermont abounds with cozy inns, country stores, bike shops, and cycle-tour companies.

Many Vermont cycling holidays focus on **Lake Champlain** and its environs. Forming a watery border between New York and Vermont, the 110-mile-long lake anchors a fertile valley that is rich in both history and scenery. Rides in this region follow narrow country roads over gentle hills, through farmlands and apple orchards, and along meandering creeks. Don't miss visiting scenic North Hero Island and South Hero Island at the lake's northern end.

The **Green Mountains**—the spine of Vermont—furnish many fine biking routes through farmland and dense

forests of pine, maple, and oak. For a moderately difficult ride with a large dose of mountain scenery, take Route 125 east from Middlebury to the 2,100-foot-high Middlebury Gap, then pick up Route 100—the state's most scenic road—and follow it in either direction. You'll pass countless towns and country inns that invite you to use the word "quaint" without a trace of embarrassment.

Weather in the Green Mountains is predictable: It varies wildly without exception. To cope with cold snaps in the upper elevations, cyclists should pack silk long underwear. For more information about bike routes in the Green Mountains, contact the **Green Mountain National Forest Headquarters** (*231 N. Main St., Rutland 05701. 802-747-6700*) or the **Middlebury Ranger Station** (*R.D. 4, Box 1260, Middlebury 05753. 802-388-4362*).

For a laid-back look at the state, **Bike Vermont** (*P.O. Box 207, Woodstock 05091. 800-257-2226 or 802-457-3553. www.bikevt.com*) offers three- to five-day tours around the southern part of Lake Champlain and into the Green Mountains. All trips feature inn lodging, gourmet cuisine, scenic routes, and visits to historic sites such as Fort Ticonderoga.

If you've heard horror stories from your friends about their two-wheeled run-ins with the rugged terrain of northern and western Vermont, you might want to explore the gently rolling hills of southern Vermont's Connecticut River Valley. **VBT Worldwide Bicycling Vacations** (*614 Monkton Rd., Bristol 05443. 800-245-3868 or 802-453-4811. www.vbt. com*) has a six-day, $795 tour of the region that explores historic Woodstock, Windsor, and the countryside around them. For a pleasant weekend getaway in the valley, take VBT's Brookfield trip, which is designed for mountain bikes and hybrids. (Bike Vermont stages some equally enjoyable trips in the Connecticut River Valley.)

IRELAND
Round the Emerald Isle in Low Gear

Like an arcadia glimpsed in a dream, Ireland is a sea of green punctuated by tame villages and wild coasts. Throughout the uncrowded island, family-run bed-and-breakfasts offer cozy accommodations at modest rates—normally less than $35 a night. With no mountain ranges to cross and no heavy traffic to navigate, the land seems designed for cycling.

Ireland's small scale makes it possible to see a large part of the country in just a week or two. Conveniently, much of the prettiest scenery is packed into **County Kerry,** the magical southwestern corner of Ireland. Most tours of the region begin in Shannon, a small city that is served by direct flights from the United States.

From Shannon, ride south to Tralee and Killarney; both towns are known for their colorful pubs. After meeting the locals and tasting the local brew—Ireland boasts hundreds of regional beers—you can explore the **Ring of Kerry,** a coastal route pocked with quaint harbors, peaceful villages, and high, rocky headlands. Don't miss the **Dingle Peninsula,** where the road snakes along sheer hillsides that plunge into Dingle Bay on one side and the Atlantic on the other.

If you have time to kill once you complete the Ring of Kerry, put your bike on a train and head north to **County Donegal,** the land of Keats. From Donegal Town, ride northeast to Letterkenny, then follow the western shore of **Lough Swilly** to land's end at **Fanad Head.** This region has a timeless quality, with few settlements (and even fewer tourists) in sight. From Fanad Head, follow the coastal roads southwest. You'll skirt isolated bays and cross the rugged, forbidding terrain of the **Bloody Foreland,** where Gaelic is still the mother tongue. This is the one stretch of Ireland where you may have trouble getting a room without a reservation.

Continue along the coast to Sligo, then pedal due west to reach **County Mayo.** They say the sun never shines in County Mayo, but now and then it does—and on that occasion you'll find yourself in one of the prettiest places on Earth. Take time to explore the county's remote western coast (the offshore islands make good day trips), then work your way south to dramatic **Killary Harbour**—the gateway to **County Galway.**

Once you reach County Galway, it's time to turn east and head back toward Shannon. You can follow the coast or swing inland past Ballynahinch and **Lough Corrib,** which offers some of the best trout fishing in Ireland. It's possible to cross from the west coast to Galway in a day, and from there it's only another day's pedaling to reach Shannon Airport and your flight home.

You can see virtually all of western Ireland in three weeks. Two weeks should suffice to take in most of the highlights in the southwest and far north of the country—provided you make the leap from County Kerry to County Donegal by train or bus. Either scenario should yield a memorable trip for about $60 per day. If you prefer the convenience of a packaged trip, **Euro-Bike Tours** (*800-321-6060 or 815-758-8851. www.eurobike.com*) runs an 11-day loop tour out of Shannon for approximately $2,750 all-inclusive, while **VBT Bicycling Vacations** (*800-245-3868. www.vbt.com*) offers a moderate to challenging seven-day County Galway trip for about $2,000. The latter price includes breakfasts, most dinners, and bike rental.

FRANCE
Down a Lazy *Rivière*

France is the place to combine the high life with the bike life. By day you can pedal from one world-class vineyard to the next, pausing to picnic on the banks of the Rhône, Loire, or Dordogne Rivers. By night you can watch the stars come

A TRANSPLANTED VERMONTER ADMIRES DROMOLAND CASTLE IN COUNTY CLARE, IRELAND.

out—the Michelin stars gracing the evening's restaurant, that is—before bedding down in a fine château.

France's castle-packed **Dordogne River Valley**—home to 1,000 châteaus within 100 square miles—has made it one of the country's most popular bike-touring venues. A typical itinerary leads downstream from Beaulieu or Argentat to Rocamadour, La Tryne, Sarlat-la-Canéda, and Les Eyzies-de-Tayac (site of the Font-de-Gaume cave) before finishing up in Bergerac or Tremolat.

The Dordogne's high-caliber hotels and restaurants lend themselves to deluxe touring. **Bike Riders Tours** (*800-473-7040 or 617-723-2354. www.bikeriderstours.com*) offers an eight-day, $3,300 luxury tour that features a hot-air balloon ride over Rocamadour and the surrounding countryside. The company's "standard" version follows the same itinerary—and at $2,500, it is still fairly steep. **Backroads** (*800-462-2848. www.backroads.com*) offers an excellent eight-day exploration of the Dordogne, with lodging in deluxe inns, for $2,700.

For the value-conscious, **Euro-Bike Tours** (*800-321-6060 or 815-758-8851. www.eurobike.com*) runs a ten-day trip that takes you the length of the Dordogne—from Argentat to Bordeaux—for $2,150.

Fit cyclists from adventurous amateurs to hard-core hammerheads will want to check out the **Great Gorges** trip put on by **Europeds** (*800-321-9552 or 831-646-4920. www.europeds.com*). The fairly aggressive itinerary leads riders from the Dordogne River Valley into the remote hills of France's **Massif Central.** After a climb like that, you deserve to descend the corniche that winds down the 1,000-foot-high walls of the **Tarn River Gorge** to the crystal-clear **Tarn River.** The seven-day journey costs roughly $2,600.

To experience two cultures in one trip, explore the **Alsace** region in the northeast corner of France. If you follow the historic **Route du Vin**, you can sample the output of vineyards on both sides of the Rhine while visiting Strasbourg, the Black Forest, Mont Sainte-Odile, and many other villages. Continuing south, you can stop in Riquewhir and Munster for some food and drink that are decidedly non-French. **Chateaux Bike Tours** (*800-678-2453 or 303-393-6910. www.chateauxbiketours.com*) offers a six-day deluxe tour of Alsace for about $2,250, including breakfasts and most dinners. Chateaux guides are fluent in French and are commendably familiar with the history of every stop along the way.

NEW ZEALAND
Of Glaciers and Gravel

Hardy bicycle travelers—those who take both hail and hills in stride—get their earthly rewards in New Zealand, where the scenery defies description and the hospitality of the residents is world renowned. Budget motels are scarce, but the country's network of conveniently located youth hostels (a misnomer—they're open to all ages) gives cyclists a clean place to crash for less than $20 per night. Camping, a sure way to make Kiwi friends, is plentiful as well.

Whereas the North Island offers better weather and flatter roads, the South Island boasts finer scenery. If you're pressed for time, spend most of it in the south. A favorite South Island itinerary begins at **Picton**—the disembarkation point for ferries arriving from Wellington, New Zealand's capital. From Picton, ride west through the Marlborough Sounds area, stopping in Havelock for a boat ride before continuing on to Nelson, a sunny community on the Tasman Bay.

Many cyclists wend their way down the lush western coast, but be forewarned—the coast is lush because it's usually gray and wet, so if possible travel with a support vehicle that can shelter you from showers. After passing **Franz Josef Glacier** and **Fox Glacier** about halfway down the coast, your legs should be tough enough to climb the spectacular **Haast Pass** through New Zealand's 12,000-foot-high **Southern Alps.** The road conditions here can be rough, making sag-wagon backup essential once again.

The road to the pass leads to lakeside Wanaka and then **Queenstown,** a magnet for the adventurous. With your bike in tow, you can board a gondola and ascend the ridge overlooking the city, then coast back down into town. **Gravity Action** (*01164-3441-1021*) will haul you and your wheels to the top of the 4,200-foot crest near Coronet Ski Resort; from there it's a thrilling single-track descent through Skipper's Canyon. Halfway down, fearless riders can pause to bungee jump 270 feet into the canyon.

After a few days in Queenstown, you can follow the coast or the eastern base of the Alps to **Christchurch,** where flights depart for the outside world. If you're a fat-tire geek, plan on visiting Queenstown during the annual Easter week mountain-biking festival sponsored by **A. J. Hackett Bungy** (*01164-3442-7100. www.ajhackett.com*).

A number of outfitters offer New Zealand bike tours. **Backroads** (*800-462-2848. www.backroads.com*) runs a 15-day, $3,400 tour that hits virtually all the scenic highlights on the South Island. Trips depart from December through March. A leading Kiwi bike-touring company, **New Zealand Pedaltours** (*888-222-9187 in U.S. or 01164-9302-0968 in NZ. www.pedaltours.co.nz*), offers a variety of road-bike tours throughout both islands. Pedaltours' 6- to 19-day trips are just as good as the American-run tours—and, at the exchange rate prevailing in 2000, they tended to cost less (U.S. $750-2,600, roughly).

When it comes to **mountain-bike tours** of New Zealand, family-run **Pacific Cycle Tours** (*13 Trent St., Avonside, Christchurch. 01164-3389-0583. www.bike-nz.com*) is highly rec-

ommended. Pacific Cycle offers 8-day and 17-day fat-tire extravaganzas in the South Island (*$1,430 and $2,450, respectively*) in addition to a 15-day mountain-bike tour of the North Island. (Trips are available for roadies as well.) The mountain-bike routes—particularly those on the South Island—take you deep into the unspoiled heartland of New Zealand to explore regions of the country that are visited by no other cycling operator. Riding alpine trails with spectacular vistas of the Southern Alps is exhilaration incarnate.

Pacific Cycle's owners—a German couple who emigrated to New Zealand in 1994—treat each rider like family and constantly fine-tune tour logistics. As a result, their trips possess a certain refinement: A scenic flight, a boat cruise, or a winery tour often enliven the proceedings, while a four-wheel-drive Land Cruiser serves as the sag wagon.

The ultimate New Zealand cycling adventure is **heli-biking** in the Wanaka area. While descending the slopes of Mt. Alpha, you can enjoy striking views of Wanaka Lake and the Upper Clutha Basin.

CANADA
Rockies Cycling Adventure

One question for those who have never cycled the Canadian Rockies: What are you waiting for? The alpine scenery is spectacular, and the trip cost can be minimized by staying in one of the area's many youth hostels, campgrounds, or lodges.

With four national parks to ride through (**Kootenay, Yoho, Banff,** and **Jasper**), you can design a tour lasting a few days or several weeks. To cover a lot of ground in a short period on fairly flat roads, cycle the **Icefields Parkway** from Jasper to Banff. Along the way, you'll pass Sunwapta Falls, the Columbia Icefields, and Lake Louise. Excellent campgrounds punctuate the route, and numerous trails lead directly from the main road on beckoning day hikes into the mountains.

For a bigger challenge, ride from Banff over Vermillion and Sinclair Passes, then head south through Kootenay National Park. The steep road is hard on the legs, but the montane views are easy on the eyes. Stop at **Radium Hot Springs** for some R and R before heading north through the **Columbia River Valley** to Golden, a hot spot for white-water rafting.

Golden is also a good staging point for excursions into Yoho National Park. Take time to hike into the nearby mountains to see one of Yoho park's aquamarine alpine lakes (many area trails are open to mountain bikes). Leaving Yoho, head on to Lake Louise and then back to Banff. The youth hostel in Banff is good and therefore often full, so call ahead.

Truly adventurous types often start their Rockies trip in the United States, passing through **Glacier National Park** in Montana and then **Waterton Lakes National Park** in Alberta. The scenery on both sides of the border is majestic, and first-rate lodges operate in both parks. The pedal-

ing is no picnic, however; you'll need a third chain ring on Glacier Park's famous **Going-to-the-Sun Road,** and you can expect fierce winds throughout the border region.

With so much to see and do in Canada's Rockies—and with good accommodations so easy to find in all price ranges—devoted amateurs should not hesitate to tackle this trip themselves. You'll want to do enough hill work in advance, of course, to be able to climb serious mountain passes without sag-wagon assistance. The touring books listed on page 69, among others, will help you plan the best itinerary.

Rocky Mountain Worldwide Cycle Tours (*Squamish, BC V1L 4H6, Canada. 800-661-2453 or 604-898-8488. www. rockymountaincycle.com*) runs a variety of six-day bicycle tours in the Rockies for $800 (camping) to $1,600 (quality inns). Either way, the trips are a good value, thanks in part to favorable exchange rates.

If you want to go with an American outfitter, **Backcountry Bicycle Tours** (*Bozeman, MT 59715. 800-575-1540 or 406-586-3556. www.backcountrytours.com*) offers a six-day, $1,800 trip that takes in both Glacier and Waterton Lakes National Parks. This itinerary, combining exceptional scenery and deluxe lodging, has earned rave reviews from customers.

The **Adventure Cycling Association** (*Missoula, MT. 800-755-2453 or 406-721-1776. www.adv-cycling.org*) offers a challenging 22-day, $900 camping tour that guides riders from Glacier National Park all the way to Jasper, at the northern end of the Icefields Parkway. This trip is a good choice for dedicated cyclists who want to rack up some serious miles.

COSTA RICA
Two-Wheeling in the Tropics

Costa Rica may be the most ecologically rich and geographically diverse country of its size on Planet Earth. In this unique bridge between two continents thrives an astonishing variety of plant and animal species from both the Northern Hemisphere and the Southern Hemisphere. Towering volcanoes, high-altitude cloud forests, pristine beaches, raging white-water rivers, and dense tropical rain forests are all packed into an area the size of West Virginia.

Such extreme ecological variation in such a small landmass means challenging terrain for bicyclists. Adding to the fun, much of Costa Rica is both hilly and unpaved. But the rewards are rich: superlative views of the abundant, exotic wildlife and scenery that distinguish Costa Rica as "the Eden of the Americas."

Given the difficulty of biking in Costa Rica—think dust, insects, heavy rains, and hilly dirt roads—it makes sense to go with a tour. A planned route can keep you from stum-

MOUNTAIN BIKERS RAPPEL A CLIFF FACE IN
BLUE MOUNTAINS NATIONAL PARK, AUSTRALIA.

bling into areas that are inaccessible by bike, while the presence of a guide comes in handy when torrential rains wash out the day's road or trail and you need someone familiar with the terrain to redirect you.

For a cycling tour that samples the region's variegated ecosystems, try the eight-day, $2,400 Costa Rica trip offered by **Backroads** (*800-462-2848 or 510-527-1555. www.backroads.com*). Cyclists begin the trip in the capital, **San Jose,** then roll on to **Arenal**—one of the world's most active volcanoes. The tour then climbs to misty **Monteverde Cloud Forest,** filled with tropical birds, butterflies, and white-faced monkeys. The trip concludes on the coast, where you can bike, snorkel, swim, or just loll about admiring your new iron thighs on the beaches of the **Nicoya Peninsula.**

To take advantage of Costa Rica's scenic roads and wild rivers, many cycle-touring companies stage trips that combine biking with rafting. Such a hybrid adventure is an ideal way to experience all that Costa Rica has to offer. For example, a nine-day, $1,500 combo tour offered by **REI Adventures** (*P.O. Box 1938, Sumner, WA 98352. 800-622-2236 or 253-437-1100. www.reiadventures.com*) begins atop the **Irazu Volcano.** Things—and people—go quickly downhill from there, as you descend 11,000 feet to reach the lush **Turrialba** area of coffee plantations and small villages. Enjoy the view from here of the **Reventazon River,** because you'll be rafting its Class III rapids the next day. Other side trips during the tour include a raft descent of the **Rio Pacuare**—a protected wilderness waterway that flows through virgin jungle—and a hike around the **Tiskita rain forest.** For an additional $575, you can tack on a five-day visit to Arenal Volcano and the Monteverde Cloud Forest.

For a shorter combo trip, **Adventures LLC** (*P.O. Box 1336, Bozeman, MT 59771. 800-231-7422 or 406-586-9942. www.adventuresllc.com*) offers four-day, $630 pedal-paddle trips run by **Rios Tropicales,** a premier Costa Rican rafting company. Guests cycle through the area around Arenal Volcano and Arenal Lake, then float down the Rio Sarapiqui.

SUMMER BIKING AT SKI RESORTS
All Tired out on the Slopes

Ski resorts in the Alps have opened their lifts to summer hikers and glacier skiers since the mid-1980s. Many North American ski centers followed suit, inviting mountain bikers and their machines to hop aboard their chairlifts in summer. Here are some spots where you and your wheels can crest the mountain without getting cranky.

Deer Valley Resort

Wednesdays through Sundays from June to September,

Deer Valley Resort (*P.O. Box 889, Park City, UT 84060. 800-424-3337 or 435-649-1000. www.deervalley.com*) throws open 19 trails for mountain bikers of all ability levels. Cost is $15 per day for lift use, $8 for a single ride, and no charge for trail access only.

Mammoth Mountain Ski Area

Mammoth Mountain—70 miles of snowcat trails, single tracks, and fire roads—is open for mountain biking from July through October. An unlimited all-day pass (gondola and bike shuttle) is $27 per day, a two-ride pass is $23, and trail access only is $10 per day. **Mammoth Adventure Connection** (*Box 24, Mammoth Lakes, CA 93546. 800-228-4947 or 760-934-0606. www.mammothmountain.com*)

Mt. Snow Ski Resort

Mountain biking on more than 100 miles of trails is a reality here from June through mid-October. Lift tickets are $25 per day; trail access only is $8 per day. Contact **Mt. Snow Vacation Services** (*Mt. Snow, VT 05356. 800-245-7669 or 802-464-8501. www.mountsnow.com*).

Squaw Valley U.S.A.

Most of the 4,000 acres at **Squaw Valley U.S.A.** (*P.O. Box 2007, Olympic Valley, CA 96146. 888-766-9321 or 530-583-6985. www.squaw.com*) are open to mountain bikers from May to September. Unlimited cable-car access is $26 per day; one cable-car ride costs $19 (all cyclists must purchase a cable-car pass). Trails are intermediate to advanced.

Vail

The extensive network of marked mountain-biking trails on the front side of Vail opens to cyclists from late May to October. You'll pay $25 per day to use the ski lift (no charge for trail access only). Guided tours and equipment rental are available. Contact **Vail Associates** (*P.O. Box 7, Vail, CO 81658. 800-525-2257 or 970-476-9090. www.snow.com*).

Whistler Resort

June through October, Whistler and Blackcomb Mountains offer guided and unguided lift-served biking, as well as heli-biking. Most trails are intermediate to advanced single tracks or double tracks that wind through coastal forests. Great routes include **River Runs Through It** and the **Sea to Sky Trail,** a 60-mile off-road trip through canyons. Programs cost $60 (CN) per day for guide, lift, and bike rental, or $21 (CN) per day for lift only. Contact **Whistler Backroads** (*P.O. Box 43, Whistler, BC V0N 1B0, Canada. 877-932-3111 or 604-932-3111. www.whistlermountainbiking.com*).

Best Ways to Spin Your Wheels

The following North American bike-touring companies were chosen from more than 100 candidates. Some run tours worldwide; others specialize in a limited region. All are well-established outfits that offer a high level of service and have been recommended by past customers. You can feel confident booking a tour with any one of them, keeping in mind that the cost of a tour tends to rise in tandem with the cushiness of the accommodations.

Adventure Cycling Association
150 E. Pine St., Missoula, MT 59807
800-755-2453 or 406-721-1776
www.adv-cycling.org

Formerly known as Bikecentennial, the Adventure Cycling Association offers no-frills trips for hardy cyclists. Adventure Cycling's trips tend to cover more miles, cross more mountain ranges, and offer more challenge than do other tours. Many trips offer no van support—hence the modest cost.

Asian Pacific Adventures
9010 Reseda Blvd., Northridge, CA 91324
800-825-1680 or 818-886-5190
www.asianpacificadventures.com

More than a mere bike-touring company, Asian Pacific offers a wide range of adventure trips to some of the world's most exotic destinations. Having pioneered bike tours in Asia, the company can arrange custom small-group tours to China, Russia, India, Thailand, Mongolia, and Vietnam. The China trips (two road-bike tours in the south, a mountain-bike excursion in Yunnan, and a mountain-bike tour in Inner Mongolia) have been popular with past customers and are available from few—if any—other outfitters. Two-week trips (excluding air fare) cost $2,700 to $3,000.

Backcountry Bicycle Tours
1408 Gold Ave., #6, Bozeman, MT 59715
800-575-1540 or 406-586-3556
www.backcountrytours.com

Backcountry is a small, family-run business, but nearly every trip in its catalog is a clear winner. Top tours include the San Juans, Glacier National Park/Canadian Rockies, Yellowstone, Bryce Canyon/Zion National Parks, and a Montana Rockies trip that packs cycling, horseback riding, and rafting into six days. All trips are supported by a sag wagon, and each night guests bed down in a superb country inn or bed-and-breakfast. Five- to six-day trips, covering 35 to 60 miles daily, run $800 to $1,500.

Backroads
801 Cedar St., Berkeley, CA 94710
800-462-2848 or 510-527-1555
www.backroads.com

Backroads is the Microsoft of bicycle touring: The company has the nicest catalog, the shiniest vans, and one of the largest tour selections worldwide—28 countries in all. If you are looking for a reliable trip that offers high-quality accommodations, easy pedaling, and a top-notch van-shuttle service, Backroads is an obvious choice. There are blemishes on this beauty, however: Backroads tour groups can swell to large numbers (20 or more guests, in some cases), and the company's prices—particularly for some of its shorter domestic inn tours—are steep as well. Nonetheless, we recommend Backroads very highly—with the caveat that some destinations command premium prices.

Bicycle Adventures
P.O. Box 11219, Olympia, WA 98508
800-443-6060 or 360-786-0989
www.bicycleadventures.com

Bicycle Adventures concentrates on the Pacific Northwest (U.S. and Canada), offering more itineraries there than any other company. (Trips are also available in California, Utah, and Hawaii.) Prices range from $150 to $250 per day and include lodging, van support, meals, and all activities. Prices are 10 to 20 percent lower than those of the big outfitters, the trip leaders are terrific, and the itineraries are well planned. You can add special activities such as kayaking and sailing to most tours.

Bike Riders Tours
P.O. Box 130254, Boston, MA 02113
800-473-7040 or 617-723-2354
www.bikeriderstours.com

Bike Riders Tours specializes in scenic European tours for small groups. With a maximum of 16 people per tour, cyclists stay at small, luxurious inns and dine at intimate restaurants. Though Bike Riders hasn't yet broken into the big leagues, the outfit works much harder than others to scout the best routes and find the most memorable local features. Destinations include France, Italy, Portugal, Ireland, and Spain. Most tours follow quiet back roads through lovely landscapes, with little or no traffic. The knowledgeable guides set a reasonable pace; you generally won't ride more than 35 miles per day. Costs for five- to eight-day tours are $900 to $2,500.

Bike Vermont, Inc.
52 Pleasant St., Woodstock, VT 05091
800-257-2226 or 802-457-3553
www.bikevt.com

Bike Vermont is one of the oldest bicycle touring companies in the country, and the only one that still concentrates almost exclusively on its home state. All Bike Vermont inn-to-inn tours cater to cyclists of varying ability by offering a range of routes. Overnight stops are at the state's finest inns, known for delicious dinners and hearty country breakfasts. Tour prices range from $330 for a summer-weekend tour of Vermont to $1,825 for eight days in Ireland. The group size varies from 10 to 20 riders, and bikes can be rented for about $40 per tour.

Butterfield & Robinson
70 Bond St., Toronto, ON, M5B 1X3, Canada
800-678-1147 or 416-864-1354
www.butterfieldandrobinson.com

Butterfield & Robinson, a major player in the bike-touring industry, offers deluxe tours throughout Canada, Asia, Africa, Central America, the Pacific, and Europe. B&R built its reputation on European trips featuring the very best hotels, superb cuisine, and excellent tour guides. As you would expect, most B&R tours are quite expensive: An eight-day tour in France costs over $3,000 per person—more than most competitors. In 1998 and 1999, the readers of *Travel & Leisure* magazine ranked B&R their favorite biking company. So sign up if you want a consistently good trip—but expect to pay for the cachet.

Chateaux Bike Tours

P.O. Box 5706, Denver, CO 80217
800-678-2453 or 303-393-6910
www.chateauxbiketours.com

Founded by French owners in 1980, Chateaux Tours specializes in luxurious, easy-paced tours through France. Many outfitters offer the same type of trip, but Chateaux features Michelin-star restaurants and superb accommodations in beautiful châteaus. Ranging from $2,300 to $3,350 for five to nine days (meals included), the trips aren't cheap—but they constitute a first-class adventure.

Classic Adventures

2844 Roosevelt Hwy., Hamlin, NY 14464
800-777-8090 or 716-964-8488
www.classicadventures.com

Founded in 1979, Classic Adventures is a "boutique" outfitter specializing in trips to less trendy destinations such as Greece, Québec, Prince Edward Island, and New York's Finger Lakes region. Other adventures include Ireland, Italy, Germany, France (the Dordogne and Loire Valleys), and Mississippi. Prices average about 20 percent less than some of the big companies: Six-night trips start at $1,300, while 12 days' cycling in Greece will set you back only $2,400.

Euro-Bike & Walking Tours

212 Sycamore Rd., Dekalb, IL 60115
800-321-6060 or 815-758-8851
www.eurobike.com

Euro-Bike Tours is a bit like a bicycle supermarket: Pick a place in Europe, and Euro-Bike can take you there. All guides are multilingual, and they really know their way around. Founded in 1974, Euro-Bike Tours has one of the strongest track records in Europe, with well-chosen itineraries and reasonable prices. Six-day tours begin at $1,600, while two-week trips range from $2,600 to $3,000. Accommodations are very good, but not super luxurious. The cuisine never disappoints, however—one reason why Euro-Bike enjoys many repeat customers.

Europeds

761 Lighthouse Ave., Monterey, CA 93940
800-321-9552 or 831-646-4920
www.europeds.com

Although many commercial bike tours in Europe feature more noshing than riding, Europeds offers not only luxury tours but faster-paced, more challenging rides as well in France, Switzerland, and Italy. From the company's large selection of family adventures, you can choose a relatively flat, easy pedal through the Dordogne River Valley or Provence (a bargain at $2,000 for seven days) or a more intense ride such as the Great Gorges Route in France. Compared with the competition, Europeds' tours generally cover more ground, and they spend more time in hilly country—a bonus, since the scenery there is best. Europeds is the only American tour operator that offers mountain-biking trips through the Alps. Prices are reasonable, yet lodging and food are of a high standard.

Rocky Mountain Worldwide Cycle Tours

Box 268, Garibaldi Highlands, Squamish, BC V0N 1T0, Canada. 800-661-2453 or 604-898-8488. www.rockymountaincycle.com

Founded in 1977, Rocky Mountain Worldwide Cycle Tours (RMWCT) is one of Canada's premier bike-touring companies. RMWCT specializes in week-long inn-to-inn and camping tours in the Canadian Rockies, but it also leads tours to six European countries and Hawaii. The routes through Canada are superb, support services are top-notch, and the accommodations are luxurious. This is probably the best choice for an organized, sag-supported cycling vacation in the Canadian Rockies. Canadian

MAN, MOUNTAIN BIKE, AND MOSS: MARIN COUNTY, CALIFORNIA

trips cost $800 (US) for camping, $1,400 (US) for hotels. European holidays run $1,700 to $2,500.

Timberline

7975 E. Harvard, Unit J, Denver, CO 80231
800-417-2453 or 303-368-4418
www.timbertours.com

This is a down-to-earth touring company for real riders—those who want to travel the best roads, regardless of elevation, at their own pace. If you're a strong rider and good climber who enjoys the challenge of cycling an average of 55 miles per day over mountain passes, Timberline is worth a look. The company also offers some interesting and reasonably priced mountain-bike tours in the western United States and Canada, as well as hiking tours in 34 national parks. Trips range from five to ten days and cost $1,000 to $1,700. If you love to ride and are looking for a bargain adventure, call Timberline first.

VBT Worldwide Bicycling Vacations

614 Monkton Rd., Bristol, VT 05443
800-245-3868 or 802-453-4811 www.vbt.com

Founded in 1971, Vermont Bicycle Touring (VBT) was a pioneer in the bike-touring industry. That may explain why few companies can match its overall excellence today. VBT offers numerous well-planned trips nationwide, as well as overseas (France, Austria, the Netherlands, Ireland, Italy, England, New Zealand, and Nova Scotia).

VBT hasn't been spoiled by success, so its prices have remained in line. A weekend domestic tour costs $270 to $490, while a domestic trip of five to six days costs $800 to $1,300. Prices for international trips of 7 to 17 days range from $1,700 to $2,100. Since 1990, VBT has acquired several other cycling companies, among them Open Roads Bicycle Touring and Travent International. A solid outfit, VBT is a reliable first choice for many destinations.

Mountain Biking

Mountain biking has emerged from its homegrown origins in Marin County, California, to become one of the most popular forms of outdoor recreation. Most bikes sold in the U.S. each year now feature the trademark fat tires, upright handlebars, and (often) single or double suspension of

a mountain bike. These rugged, go-anywhere machines allow backcountry explorers to travel farther and faster than they could on foot. North America's best spots for off-road riding are profiled below, as are a host of companies that specialize in mountain-biking holidays.

NORTH AMERICAN MOUNTAIN BIKING AREAS

Especially scenic mountain-biking destinations are described below. Most are suitable for cyclists of all levels, but some will challenge even super-hardcore riders. For a list of 1,000 wilderness trails open to mountain bikes, pick up *Mountain Bike* magazine's *Trail-Finder Directory* (free with a $20 IMBA membership). Compiled by the magazine's editors and the International Mountain Bike Association (*303-545-9011. www.imba.com*), this is a must resource for backcountry adventuring.

ALASKA

Chugach National Forest

TERRAIN: More than 200 miles of trails through glaciated terrain, forests, rivers, and wetlands.

BEST ROUTE: Resurrection Trail System.

GETTING THERE: Head south and southeast from Anchorage to the Kenai Peninsula and the Chugach Mountains.

CONTACT: Chugach National Forest, 3301 C St., Suite 300, Anchorage, AK 99503 907-271-2500.

ARIZONA

Coronado National Forest

TERRAIN: Two advanced, rugged trails plus hundreds of miles of forest roads through desert, canyons, and mountains.

BEST ROUTES: Arcadia Trail, Chiva Falls Loop.

GETTING THERE: Head south on I-19 from Tucson.

CONTACT: Coronado National Forest, Box 709, Safford, AZ 85548. 520-428-4150.

CALIFORNIA

Angeles National Forest

TERRAIN: Hilly to steep single tracks and roads through coastal forests of pine and fir.

BEST ROUTES: Mt. Wilson Toll Road, Wrightwood and Big Bear areas.

GETTING THERE: Head east from Los Angeles to the San Gabriel Mountains.

CONTACT: Angeles National Forest, 701 Anita Ave., Arcadia, CA 91006. 626-574-1613.

Lake Tahoe Basin

TERRAIN: Everything from reasonably flat to straight up and down. Mostly rugged single tracks, but also some manicured trails.

BEST ROUTES: Mr. Toad's Wild Ride, The Flume Trail.

GETTING THERE: Located on the California-Nevada border, east of Sacramento and south of Reno. Take U.S. 50.

CONTACT: Forest Service Visitor Center, 870 Emerald Bay Rd., South Lake Tahoe, CA 96150. 530-573-2600. Trail guide expert: 530-573-2615. Recreation guide expert: 530-573-2621.

COLORADO

Crested Butte

TERRAIN: Steep climbs and downhills; rocky, forested, high-altitude passes; great vistas.

BEST ROUTES: Farris Creek, Trail #409, Upper Loop.

GETTING THERE: Trails start from Aspen, Colorado.

CONTACT: Crested Butte Chamber of Commerce, Box 1288, Crested Butte, CO 81224. 800-545-4505 or 970-349-6438.

GEORGIA

Chattahoochee National Forest

TERRAIN: Forest Service roads and challenging, sometimes steep single track.

BEST ROUTES: Rich Mountain Trail, Mountain Town Creek and Bear Creek, Bull Mountain Trail.

GETTING THERE: Head NE from Atlanta to the border of Georgia and Tennessee.

CONTACT: Southern Off-Road Bicycle Association, P.O. Box 671774, Marietta, GA 30067. 770-565-1795. www.sorba.org. Georgia Forestry Commission, 770-528-3195.

HAWAII

The Big Island

TERRAIN: Steep hills, ridge trails, solidified lava flows; soft dirt trails in valleys.

BEST ROUTES: Kilauea Crater Rim Drive, Chain of Craters Road, Waipio Valley Trail, Kumukahi Lighthouse Trail.

GETTING THERE: Start from Kilauea Crater Park.

CONTACT: Hawaii Visitors Bureau, 808-923-1811; Hawaii Bicycling League, 808-735-5756; Mauna Kea Mt. Bike, 808-883-0130.

IDAHO

Ketchum District, Sawtooth National Forest

TERRAIN: Easy to challenging single track and old jeep roads and mining roads. Some stretches are quite technical—everything from smooth to rocky through mountain ranges full of lakes, rivers, and streams.

BEST ROUTES: Corral Creek, Adams Gulch, Greenhorn Gulch.

GETTING THERE: Head N from Twin Falls, Idaho, on Idaho 75/US 93 to Ketchum.

CONTACT: Sun Valley/Ketchum Chamber of Commerce, P.O. Box 2420, Sun Valley, ID 83353. 800-634-3347 or 208-726-3423.

CROSSING THE ROUGH MELT ICE OF BLACK RAPIDS GLACIER, SOUTHERN ALASKA

NEBRASKA

Nebraska National Forest

TERRAIN: 70 miles of mountain-biking routes through ponderosa pines, canyons, buttes, and streams. Graduated degrees of difficulty; 200 miles of Rail Trails.

BEST ROUTES: Pine Ridge Trail, Bordeaux Creek, Black Hills Overlook Trail.

GETTING THERE: Located 100 miles south of Rapid City. Take Rte. 79 south to US 385 south to Chadron.

CONTACT: Nebraska National Forest, 125 N. Main St., Chadron, NE 69337. 308-432-0300. Chadron Chamber of Commerce, 706 W. 3rd St., Chadron NE 69337. 308-432-4401.

NEW MEXICO

Santa Fe National Forest

TERRAIN: Mostly primitive and gravel roads through mountain forests. Steep grades in many areas.

BEST ROUTES: Lower Colonias and Barillas area: Forest Road 83. Rowe Mesa area: State Road 34. Cow Creek area: Forest Road 92, Willow Creek. Elk Mountain: Forest Road 645 to Forest Road 156.

GETTING THERE: Take Highway 285 or I-25 north to Santa Fe.

CONTACT: Santa Fe National Forest Supervisors Office, 1220 St. Francis Dr., Santa Fe, NM 87504. 505-438-7840. New Mexico Public Lands Information Center, 1474 Rodeo Dr., Santa Fe, NM 87105. 505-438-7542. Maps available.

NORTH CAROLINA

Pisgah and Nantahala National Forests

TERRAIN: Unlimited single track through dense forest. Trails range from rolling to steep and challenging.

BEST ROUTES: Tsali Trail along Fontana Lake has switchbacks, rolling climbs, and banked turns. Also try Swing Bridge Trail Loop along the Little Tennessee River Trail.

GETTING THERE: From Asheville, North Carolina, head S on Blue Ridge Pkwy.

CONTACT: Pisgah National Forest, North Mills River Area, 1001 Pisgah Highway, Pisgah Forest, NC 28768. 828-877-3265. Nantahala Outdoor Center, 13077 Highway 19 W., Bryson City, NC 28713. 888-662-1662 or 828-488-2175.

OREGON

Deschutes National Forest, Bend-Fort Rock Ranger District

TERRAIN: Beginning to advanced. Scenic and challenging single-track and double-track roads wind their way through the high Cascade country of Central Oregon.

BEST ROUTES: Sparks Lake, Lava Lake, Edison Butte Trail System, Cache Mountain Trail.

GETTING THERE: Many trailheads are located just outside Bend. You'll also find several good trails off the road as you travel south from Bend on Cascade Lakes Hwy. 46.

CONTACT: Supervisor, Deschutes National Forest, 1645 Hwy. 20 E., Bend, OR 97701. 541-388-2715. www.fs.fed.us/r6/deschutes.

TENNESSEE

Big South Fork National River and Recreation Area

TERRAIN: Gravel and dirt roads; disused horseback-riding trails. Low plateaus with flat, easy trails and steep, rugged trails that drop into side canyons and gorges.

BEST ROUTE: Duncan Hollow Loop.

GETTING THERE: Northwest of Knoxville. Take Tenn. 92 off US 27.

CONTACT: Bandy Creek Visitor Center, 4564 Leatherwood Rd., Oneida, TN 37841. 931-879-3625. Stearns Visitor Center, Stearns, KY. 606-376-5073.

TEXAS

Sam Houston National Forest

TERRAIN: All ability levels through pine forests.

BEST ROUTE: Double Lake Trail (usage fee required).

GETTING THERE: Head north from Houston to eastern Texas.

CONTACT: Sam Houston National Forest, Raven District, 394 W. FM Road 1375, P.O. Drawer 1000, New Waverly, TX 77358. 409-344-6205.

UTAH

Moab

TERRAIN: Mostly flat, but the uphills are steep; trail surfaces are sand, gravel, and rock. Jeep trails and some single track.

BEST ROUTES: Gemini Bridges Trail,

Porcupine Rim, Amasa Back Trail, Arches National Park loop, White Rim Trail, Slickrock Trail. If you head upcountry to the La Sal Mountains, Warner Lake is a good starting point and Bachelor Basin has scenic trails.

GETTING THERE: Drive from Moab to the trailheads.

CONTACT: Moab/Green River Visitor Information Line, P.O. Box 550, Moab, UT 84532. 800-635-6622. www.canyonlands-utah.com. Rim Tours, 800-626-7335. www.rimtours.com.

VERMONT

Randolf

TERRAIN: 240 miles of intermediate to expert, very hilly (1,000 feet to 2,900 feet) single track, double track, and fourth-class roads through thick forest.

BEST ROUTE: Cushman Trail going over Braintree Mountain into Rochester.

GETTING THERE: From I-89, take exit 4 to Randolf.

CONTACT: White River Valley Trails Association, Box 284, Randolph, VT 05060. 802-728-9667. The Chamber of Commerce (802-728-9027) has maps detailing bike trails.

WASHINGTON

Methow Valley, Okanogan National Forest

TERRAIN: Multiuse logging roads and spur roads through mountainous forests. Trails access open meadows and old homesteads. Higher altitudes are extremely scenic. Beginning to expert terrain, single track and double track.

BEST ROUTES: Sun Mountain Trail system, Buck Mountain Trail, Blue Buck Mountain area.

GETTING THERE: In summer, take I-5 N, then E on Wash. 20 (No. Cascades Hwy.). In winter (Dec.-March), cross Snoqualamie Pass, then U.S. 97 N; turn left on Wash. 153.

CONTACT: Okanogan National Forest, P.O. Box 579, Winthrop, WA 98862. 509-826-3275. Winthrop Mountain Sports, 257 Riverside Ave., Winthrop, WA 98862. 509-996-2886. Methow Valley Sports Trails Association, P.O. Box 147, Winthrop, WA 98862. 509-996-3287. Methow Valley Visitor Center for the Forest Service, 509-996-4000.

WEST VIRGINIA

Slatyfork, Monongahela National Forest

TERRAIN: Lushly forested Appalachian area, well known for its tight, technical single track. There are also dirt roads and old railroad grades that accommodate all ability levels.

BEST ROUTES: Gauley Mountain Trail, regional Rail Trails.

GETTING THERE: Located on W. Va. 219, one hour south of Elkins and 75 minutes north of Lewisburg.

CONTACT: Elk River Touring Center, HC 69 Box 7, Slatyfork, WV 26291. 304-572-3771 www.ertc.com

WISCONSIN

Chequamegon National Forest

TERRAIN: Rolling to hilly single-track and double-track backwoods riding over more than 300 miles of mapped and marked trails. Trails range from gravel roads to hard-packed single track. There's also a fair amount of overgrown double-track forest roads.

BEST ROUTES: Rock Lake Trail, West Fork Trail, Firetower Trail.

GETTING THERE: 75 miles southeast of Duluth and 150 miles northeast of Minneapolis. From US 63, exit at Cable or Hayward.

CONTACT: Chequamegon Area Mountain Bike Association, P.O. Box 141, Cable, WI 54821. Chamber of Commerce, 800-533-7454 or 715-798-3599. www.cable4fun.com/camba.

OFF-ROAD TOURS

A number of tour operators specialize in mountain-biking (MB) holidays. Some feature deluxe inn-to-inn trips in several locales, while others offer more rugged backcountry trips with wilderness camping. Sag-wagon support is provided in most cases, but ask in advance about a particular itinerary just to make sure.

Alaska Bicycle Tours/Sockeye Cycle

P.O. Box 829, Haines, AK 99827
907-766-2869. www.cyclealaska.com

DESTINATIONS: Southeast Alaska, Canada (Yukon and British Columbia). Gateway to vast wilderness area near Glacier Bay National Park

PROGRAMS: Day trips and camping tours of up to nine days. Featured trip to Tatshenshini- Alsek Park. Also rentals and sales.

Alaskan Bicycle Adventures

907 East Dowling Rd., Anchorage, AK 99518
800-770-7242 or 907-243-2329
www.alaskabike.com

DESTINATIONS: Southeast Alaska

PROGRAMS: Eleven-day camping tour from Fairbanks to Prudhoe Bay. Excellent itineraries, well-planned logistics on seven- to twelve-day MB trips. Also: custom trips.

Elk River Touring Center

HC 69, Box 7, Slatyfork, WV 26291
304-572-3771. www.ertc.com

DESTINATIONS: Forest Service roads and Rail Trails in backcountry West Virginia

PROGRAMS: Weekend to six-day inn-to-inn MB tours ($269-699) and self-guided rides. Touring Center offers B&B lodging or cabins ($50 per person per night) and a restaurant.

Kaibab Mountain Bike Tours

391 S. Main St., Moab, Utah 84532
800-451-1133 or 435-259-7423
www.kaibabtours.com

DESTINATIONS: Southwestern U.S., Belize

PROGRAMS: Four- to eleven-day fully

supported inn-to-inn and camping tours for all ability levels.

The Mountain Bike School

Route 100, Mount Snow, VT 05356
800-245-7669 or 802-464-3333, ext. 328
www.mountsnow.com

DESTINATION: Vermont

PROGRAMS : Weekend tours and race training (summer only).

Nichols Expeditions

497 N. Main St., Moab, UT 84532
800-648-8488 or 435-259-3999
www.nicholsexpeditions.com

DESTINATIONS: Utah, northern Arizona, Idaho, Ecuador, Peru, Chile, Galápagos islands, Alaska, Italy, Spain, and Colorado

PROGRAMS: Four- to fifteen-day vehicle-supported trips with daily clinics on MB riding and maintenance. Nichols also offers rafting, sea kayaking, and backpacking trips.

Pacific Cycle Tours Ltd.

13 Trent St., Avonside, Christchurch, NZ
01164-3389-0583. www.bike-nz.com

DESTINATIONS: North Island and South Island of New Zealand

PROGRAMS: Inn-to-inn MB tours through farmland and scenic wildlands with many single-track segments. Lift-served and heli-biking options available in Wanaka area.

Paragon Guides

P.O. Box 130, Vail, CO 81658
877-926-5299 or 970-926-5299
www.paragonguides.com

DESTINATION: Colorado Rockies

PROGRAMS: Hut-to-hut MB tours through alpine backcountry between Vail and Aspen. Standard five-day trip covers 100 miles and costs $1,330. Paragon also runs llama treks and backcountry skiing trips.

Rim Tours

1233 S. Highway 191, Moab, UT 84532
800-626-7335 or 435-259-5223
www.rimtours.com

DESTINATIONS: Canyon Country (Utah), Colorado Rockies, Grand Canyon (Arizona), Hawaii.

PROGRAMS: Bike rentals and two- to six-day tours on great routes through the most scenic regions of the Southwest and Rockies.

Western Spirit Cycling

478 Mill Creek Dr., Moab, UT 84532
800-845-2453 or 435-259-8732
www.westernspirit.com

DESTINATIONS: Arizona (Grand Canyon), Colorado (Durango, Telluride), Idaho (Sun Valley), South Dakota (Black Hills), Utah (Canyonlands, Bryce, Zion, and Capitol Reef National Parks)

PROGRAMS: WSC claims to offer more destinations and departure dates than any other MB touring company. Pedal-paddle option in Utah. Small groups; mostly overnight wilderness camping.

TRAVEL TIPS

Planning your own bike tour

Don't freak at the price tags for some of the deluxe guided tours above. Staging your own van-supported tour is easier than you might think: Choose your riding partners wisely, and the experience need not be an ordeal. By heeding the half-dozen rules of thumb that follow, you can map out a trouble-free bicycle tour that should save you $50 to $150 per day.

1. Select the overall area you wish to tour, then consult a regional cycling guidebook and plot an itinerary. Most commercial bike-touring companies won't divulge route specifics, but their catalogs come in handy for mapping a course of your own creation.

2. Once you've settled on a route, order a specialized bike-touring map from the **Adventure Cycling Association** (*800-755-2453. www.adv-cycling.org*). Customized for each route, these handy references include elevation charts and suggested daily itineraries. For a $30 annual membership, the ACA will send you the *Cyclists' Yellow Pages,* which contains state- and country-specific listings of bike shops and touring groups, as well as sources for maps and regional guidebooks.

3. Assemble the equipment you'll need: roof rack, tire-changing kit, heavy-duty bicycle pump, first-aid kit, cooking kit, stove, and (if camping) sleeping bags, pads, and tent. Get a youth hostel card. (Contrary to urban myth, "youth" hostels are open to all ages.)

4. If you plan to camp in popular spots such as national parks, reserve in advance with the park offices to secure a site.

5. If your final destination is a plane ride away, comparison shop to find the cheapest air tickets (booking well in advance can help you get the best value). Call the air carrier to determine bicycle-packing requirements and any extra shipping charges (some airlines send the bikes gratis). A good place to start your search for discount fares is **Cheap Tickets** (*www.cheaptickets.com*).

6. A week before you depart, call the inns and hostels you plan to visit to confirm your reservations. Buy the extras you'll need on the trip—spare tubes, a spoke wrench and extra spokes, handlebar tape, a chain tool, and power snacks.

Do a 50-mile shakedown ride with your group to get those first few flats over and done with.

Dollars and sense: How much should two couples expect to pay for their own 14-day, vehicle-supported tour? Assuming an even mix of camp-outs, hostel stays, and hotel overnights, the price tag will probably total about $3,600. That's $65 per person per day—a far cry from commercial tours charging as much as $300. Read on to double-check our math:

- Sag-wagon rental and gas ($55 per day, including mileage): $770
- Camping and hostels (9 nights at $10 per person per night): $360
- Deluxe inn with hot showers—yippee! (4 nights at $50 per person per night): $800
- Food ($20 per person/day): $1,120
- Airline baggage fees ($50 per bike each way): $400
- Roof rack or spare wheel: $150

Total cost per person for 14 days: $900

ONLINE

Adventure Cycling Association
www.adv-cycling.org

Offers touring maps, proposed routes with detailed day-by-day itineraries, and touring stories, technical features, and essays from the pages of *Adventure Cyclist* magazine.

Away.com
www.away.com

This active-travel website has a searchable database of trips, including hundreds of cycling holidays worldwide. Moon Handbooks are available online from this site.

MountainZone.com
www.mountainzone.com/mtbiking

Dedicated mainly to fat-tire racing, this site offers good destination reports for the U.S., Canada, and abroad. Also: gear reviews, technical advice, expedition reports.

BOOKS

Bicycling the Pacific Coast by Tom Kirkendall and Vicky Spring (The Mountaineers, 1998, $14.95). The bible of West Coast touring covers British Columbia to Mexico. Good maps and hill profiles.

Backcountry Biking in the Canadian Rockies by Doug Eastcott (Rocky Mountain Books, 1999, $16.95, 403-249-9490). A thorough guide with good maps and excellent route descriptions.

New Zealand by Bike by Bruce Ringer ($16.95). Detailed maps and tour write-ups make this the best resource for the North and South Islands.

Europe by Bike by Ken and Terry Whitehall (The Mountaineers, 1993, $14.95). Profiles 18 great European bike tours from 100 to 800 miles in length.

Full Tilt: Ireland to India with a Bicycle by Dervla Murphy.

IN KATHMANDU, NEPAL, THE PIE AT THE END OF THE ROAD SMOOTHES EVEN THE ROUGHEST JOURNEY.

Family Adventures

A THEME PARK RIDE MAY BE FUN, BUT A FAMILY ADVENTURE VACATION OFFERS A WHOLE LOT MORE. Exploring new countries and encountering new cultures broadens a child's horizons and challenges her or his preconceptions. Kids discover that North America is just one corner of the planet—and that we have much to learn from other places and peoples. As future caretakers of the Earth, children can explore some of the world's wild places while delving into environmental issues. • An adventure vacation can also be a living classroom. Kids can retrace the paths of the pioneers, spend a week in a Native American village, explore a coral reef from a submarine, or visit Darwin's stomping grounds in the Galápagos islands. • Adventure travel stretches the body as well as the mind. It inspires children to achieve challenging physical goals—and invites parents to take part in those accomplishments. Family adventuring offers time to talk, to explore, to reconnect. Chances are that everyone will return home a little more relaxed—and more than a little transformed by the experience.

LEFT: YOUNG SNORKELERS BASK IN THE THRILL OF A NEWFOUND SKILL AT CASA DE CAMPO RESORT IN THE DOMINICAN REPUBLIC. BELOW: A MODERN-DAY WAGON TRAIN HITS THE OREGON TRAIL.

Wagon Trains

Llama Trekking

River Runs

Barging About

Beach and Island

Eco-friendly Tours

Farm Stays

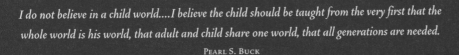

I do not believe in a child world....I believe the child should be taught from the very first that the whole world is his world, that adult and child share one world, that all generations are needed.

PEARL S. BUCK

Great Family Adventures

The world is a vast place, with an almost infinite number of adventures awaiting discovery. An adventure trip can take a family to the edge of civilization, or it may lead to the discovery of natural wonders close to home. Some favorite family adventures are described below. Each of these options maximizes fun and learning for children while offering parents a relaxing respite from the hustle and bustle of daily life.

COVERED WAGON ADVENTURES
Pioneer Pathways

A wagon train holiday combines outdoor fun with the lure of the Wild West while letting you relive the experience of the early pioneers and Native Americans—complete with authentic, horse-drawn covered wagons.

Although most wagon-train guests travel on horseback each day, the littlest dudes (and any saddle-sore adults) can opt for cushioned perches on the wagons. This makes the wagon train a good choice for families with small children or nonriding grown-ups. Along the trail, you'll see antelope, deer, rabbits, eagles, and maybe even a buffalo herd. During your backcountry journey, the kids will make new friends while you enjoy the freedom of ranging the open plains. And at the end of the day, children and adults alike sleep soundly under the stars.

A number of wagon-train outfitters offer quality family programs. **Kelly's Place** (*Cortez, CO. 800-745-4885 or 970-565-3125. www.kellyplace.com*) is an adobe-style lodge and outdoor education center 45 miles from Durango. One-week holidays include a four-day wagon train through Ute Mountain Park, where guests explore Anasazi ruins with Native American guides.

Kelly's Place also offers classes, such as Navajo pottery, Hopi culture, and ethnobotany. Just 20 miles from four parks — **Mesa Verde, Hovenweep National Monument, Anasazi Heritage Center,** and **Ute Tribal Park** — Kelly's Place makes an ideal base for exploring the **Four Corners Canyon Country.** The wagon train costs $300 per person per day, with a six-person group minimum. Additional nights at the lodge cost $75 for a room for two, plus $10 for each additional person, and $7 for children under 12.

Oregon Trail Wagon Train (*Bayard, NE. 308-586-1850. www.prairieweb.com/oregonwagon*) is a good choice for families looking for a classic living history experience at a moderate price. On one- to four-day journeys, covered wagons follow the historic **Oregon Trail** across the Nebraska plain, passing near towering **Chimney Rock.** Special activities for youngsters (*age 4 and older*) include hunting for arrowheads, watching black-powder rifle drills, learning Native American arts and crafts, and cooking over a campfire. (Remember to warn children about the mock Indian attack!) Another treat for kids is mail delivery via Pony Express. Guests can either sleep in tents or bed down in the wagons. Rates for a four-day trip are $525 for adults and $425 for kids under 12.

Since 1991, **Powder River Wagon Train & Cattle Drives** (*Broadus, MT. 800-492-8835, 800-982-0710, or 406-436-2404. www.powderrivercattledrive.com*) has operated one of the best family wagon trains in the West. Each August, 60 guests join the **Premier Wagon Train** for a six-day, six-night journey through the wide open country of eastern Montana. From May through September, Powder River usually runs one five-day wagon train each month for 10 to 20 guests. These excellent programs feature authentic wooden-wheeled wagons, abundant wildlife, lots of fun activities for the kids, and nightly Western-style entertainment. The Premier Wagon Train costs $1,450 per person; monthly trips are $1,250 per person. Powder River costs more than the competition, but perks such as hot showers, deluxe food, and personal attention compensate for the expense.

A leading Wyoming outfitter since 1971, **Wagons West-Yellowstone Outfitters** (*Afton, WY. 800-447-4711 or 307-886-9693*) offers two-, four-, and six-day wagon-train journeys through the spectacular **Bridger-Teton National Forest** near Jackson, Wyoming. Guests ride horseback about half the time, but small children and nonriders can also enjoy the experience from a stable wagon with rubber tires for added comfort. Suitable even for younger kids, this program offers many supervised children's activities: Guides recount the history of the early settlers and of the Sioux and Crow tribes. Two-day trips cost $325 for adults, $285 for children under 14; four-day trips cost $635 for adults and $540 for children; six-day trips run $835 for adults and $735 for kids.

For additional information on wagon trains, cattle drives, and other western holidays, contact the **Dude Ranchers' Association** (*La Porte, CO. 970-223-8440*).

LLET ME LLEAD THE WAY: LLAMA TREKKING NEAR RAINY PASS IN THE NORTH CASCADES.

LLAMA PACK TRIPS
Furry Friends on the Trail

Combine hiking with a traveling petting zoo and you'll understand the appeal of llama trekking. Pack trips let families enjoy scenic backcountry without having to carry heavy loads up steep trails. Moreover, the added carrying capacity of pack animals lets you bring along all those special items, such as medications, coloring books, even teddy bears.

Llama treks are particularly appealing to families with young children. These user-friendly animals have gentle dispositions and, unlike packhorses and mules, they are easy for children to lead and care for throughout the trek. In fact, many youngsters will report that making friends with their llama was the highlight of their holiday.

Since 1985, **Hurricane Creek Llama Treks** (*Enterprise, OR. 800-528-9609 or 541-432-4455. www.hcltrek.com*) has led llama treks into northeast Oregon's **Eagle Cap Wilderness Area,** an alpine region with glaciated peaks and flower-filled meadows. Trips last six or seven days, with the first and last nights spent in a comfortable bed-and-breakfast. Family trips feature day treks from a backcountry base camp, so you don't have to set up camp every day. This makes it easier to spend more time with your kids. Customized trips can also be arranged for families as long as children can hike 4 to 8 miles of easy to moderate terrain. The six-day trip costs $710 for adults, $570 for kids ages 6 to 18.

An excellent program, **Jackson Hole Llamas** (*Jackson, WY. 800-830-7316 or 307-739-9582. www.jhllamas.com*) is run by a friendly and knowledgeable couple who lead small groups of eight to ten guests into the high country near **Yellowstone National Park.** Jackson specializes in family trips, and itineraries can be customized for all levels— even grandparents can join in the fun.

The scenery, particularly in the Bechler region, is exceptional. You'll travel near 21 waterfalls and cross meadows exploding with wildflowers in season. There are ample opportunities for day-hiking and relaxing near lakes and hot springs, and the food is excellent. Kids will enjoy the "mountain man" trip offered each summer. Given the brevity (*mid-July–Sept.*) of the llama-trekking season, book early. For both adults and children, the cost is reasonable: $895 for five days, $720 for four days.

In July and August, **Telemark Inn and Llama Treks** (*Bethel, ME. 207-836-2703. www.telemarkinn.com*) offers a six-day **Mountain and Lakes Trip** designed for families. The guides are trained ecologists. You spend the first three days exploring **Caribou Speckled Wilderness Area** within the **White Mountain National Forest.** Each guest leads her

own pack llama. From a base camp near a waterfall, the group day-hikes and tent-camps for two days, returning on the third day to the 100-year-old deluxe inn. The remaining three days are spent canoeing on the **Richardson Lakes.** The six-day combo vacation is $975 for adults, $750 for kids under 14. The three-day llama trip can be done separately at $475 for adults, $350 for kids 14 and under. One-day llama treks are also available at $85 per adult, $65 per child.

Yellowstone Llamas (*Bozeman, MT. 406-586-6872. www.yellowstone-llamas.com*), the outfitter that pioneered llama trekking in Yellowstone National Park, is a perfect way for your family to experience the natural history and beauty of the Yellowstone region. Since 1983, geologist Will Gavin and his wife, llama breeder Renée, have offered three- to five-day llama treks into the backcountry of **Yellowstone National Park** and the **Crazy Mountains** of Montana's Absaroka range. Parents will appreciate the Gavins' gourmet camp cooking, while kids can fish, hike, explore alpine lakes, and of course, bond with the llamas. Daily rates are about $195 per adult and $135 per day for children 12 and under. These trips are suitable for kids age 5 or older who can hike at least 3 miles at a stretch. The Gavins' trips—a superb combination of scenery, companionship, challenge, and fine dining—are highly recommended.

RIVER TRIPS
Water Worlds

Wilderness river trips are an endless source of wonder. Floating downstream on a raft or in a canoe or inflatable kayak, children experience a constantly changing natural backdrop with new items of interest around every river bend. Moreover, little ones are spared the typically rigorous pace and heavy burdens of backpacking. Rolling down a river is a comfortable, relaxing way to introduce kids to the joys of water sports and the beauty of wild lands.

Perhaps the ultimate river adventure for kids is a float trip down the Amazon through the Brazilian rain forest. We tried it with a ten-year-old and a five-year-old and heartily recommend it.

If you go on a trip sponsored by **Brazil Nuts** (*Naples, FL. 800-553-9959 or 941-593-0267. www.brazilnuts.com*), as we did, a four-hour direct flight from Miami lands you in the Brazilian city of **Manaus.** After an overnight stay in the luxurious **Tropical Hotel,** you travel by steamer up the **Rio Negro** tributary to the **Ariau Jungle Tower Lodge.** With its aerial catwalks through the jungle canopy, the lodge is the world's biggest tree house. An ideal base for jungle exploring, it boasts fine international cuisine, multilingual guides, and a helicopter launching pad for emergencies. Morning and

afternoon river excursions range from bird-watching to alligator hunting. Air from Miami and all land charges for six days and five nights costs $1,300 for adults and $1,100 for kids.

It's hard to top the Amazon, but plenty of other fabulous waterways beckon to be explored with your brood. If you decide to visit northern Minnesota's **Boundary Waters Canoe Area Wilderness**, go with **Gunflint Northwoods Outfitters** (*Grand Marais, MN. 800-362-5251 or 218-388-2296. www.gunflintoutfitters.com*). Since the 1920s, the Kerfoot family has been guiding trips through America's premier canoeing venue. On a typical week-long adventure, families paddle from lodge to lodge while guides handle the heavy gear. Kids' activities include fishing, hiking, riding, and naturalist programs.

If you're looking for a more rugged holiday, wilderness camping and fly-ins are optional. The guide sets up camp and does all the cooking, so you can spend time with the kids. A seven-day, six-night lodge-based canoe package costs $775 per adult and $580 per child ages 5 to 12 (there is no charge for kids under 5).

Flamingo Lodge Marina and Outpost (*Flamingo, FL. 800-600-3813 or 941-695-3101. www.flamingolodge.com*) lets you explore the wildlife-rich waterways of **Everglades National Park** in comfortable houseboats operated by **Flamingo Lodge Marina.** (With only eight houseboats chartered in the park, you won't be bothered by noisy neighbors.) A 40-foot houseboat sleeps eight and is equipped with a skiff or canoe for exploring mangrove canals. The cost for four nights is $570 to $800. The best time to visit the Everglades is December through April.

Outdoor Adventure River Specialists (**OARS**) (*Angels Camp, CA. 800-446-7238 or 209-736-4677. www.oars. com*) organizes special family-only floats in **California, Idaho, Oregon, Wyoming,** and **Utah.** All trips feature a "fun director" who entertains the kids (*age 5 and older*) with activities from magic to geology lessons. One of the best trips for kids age 7 and older is the **Lower Salmon River** in Idaho, which combines great scenery, abundant wildlife, fishing, and riverside camping. Itineraries range from one to five days; the daily cost is $100 to $200. Discounts are available for children and groups.

For kids 4 and up, **Turtle River Rafting Company** (*Mt. Shasta, CA. 800-726-3223 or 530-926-3223. www. turtleriver.com*) offers **Kids' Klamath** and **Kids Trinity** river programs. These easy overnight trips, which are for families only, are a good introduction to river travel. They also allow plenty of time for hiking, paddling, and swimming, so the kids never get bored. The two-day trips cost $196 for adults and $142 for kids. A three-day family trip for kids 6 and older costs $322 for adults and $286 for children.

BARGE HOLIDAYS
European Canal Adventure

As Toad said in *Wind in the Willows,* "There is nothing—absolutely nothing—half so much worth doing as simply messing about in boats." For children, barging is a carefree adventure with days of drifting down canals, negotiating locks, and mooring at new places. For parents, it's an ideal way to experience the beauty of the European countryside.

The long, narrow barges with their homey cabins, compact galley, and cozy living room remind children of a floating playhouse; parents enjoy the privacy and quiet provided by the aft cabin and foredeck. For a change of pace, you can jump ashore and bike or jog along the riverbank, keeping up with the barge—not difficult at the boat's stately speed of about 4 miles per hour.

Barges vary in size and price. A fully crewed, height-of-luxury barge cruise for two four-member families typically costs $1,500 to $2,500 per person for one week during summer, meals included. In **France,** a full-boat charter (with only the guests in your own party on board) starts at around $10,000 per week.

A less expensive, albeit less romantic, option is a self-drive canalboat, which looks like a stretched cabin cruiser. Rentals start at about $2,000 per week. After an orientation, you'll know how to enter a lock, secure the boat for the changing water level, and leap aboard before the water surges from the lock doors. Two adults can handle the job competently and you'll find plenty of helping hands at each lockkeeper's house.

When thinking about a barging destination, consider **Ireland** and **Holland.** On the Emerald Isle, a popular itinerary navigates the **River Shannon** and **Shannon-Erne Canal,** from the town of **Carrick on Shannon.** In Holland, the vast network of canals offers myriad opportunities to explore small towns and quiet agricultural regions.

Many brokers offer European barge vacations. Shop around and ask about meal plans. (On a piloted cruise, consider a cost-saving half-board plan, which covers breakfast and lunch on board; dinner is ashore, at your own expense.) Also ask about extras, such as side trips to historic sites, and time your trip for art fairs and local festivals. For self-drive boats, inquire about accessory equipment—you'll want to have a bicycle or moped on board for quick jaunts away from your floating home. (*For information on booking a barge vacation in Europe, including the United Kingdom and Ireland, see page 95.*)

BEACH AND ISLAND VACATIONS
Family Fun in the Sun

A beach vacation is one of the easiest family getaways. Kids entertain themselves building sand castles, collecting shells, chasing waves, and burrowing in the sand—and parents actually get to relax. There are many family beach resorts

THREE GENERATIONS RAFT IDAHO'S SALMON RIVER.

around the United States and the Caribbean. A growing number of them offer custom eco-adventures for children and adults.

When choosing a beach destination, ask about dangerous currents, undertow, and jellyfish at the time you plan to travel—and avoid hurricane season. Be sure that the resort provides lifeguards, recreational options, and a good child-care program.

Two excellent sources for North American beach resorts are Jane Wilford's *What to Do with the Kids this Year* and *Super Family Vacations* by Martha Shirk and Nancy Klepper. Also worth looking into are the following unique, moderately priced resorts in the Caribbean and Central America.

A first-class resort in the **Dominican Republic,** 7,000-acre **Casa de Campo** (*Premier Resorts & Hotels, Miami, FL. 800-877-3643 or 809-523-3333. www.casadecampo.cc*) is known for its excellent children's programs. There are 50 nannies on staff for toddlers. A two-division kids club (for youngsters ages 5 to 12) features swimming, riding, sailing, and arts and crafts classes. Teens enjoy tennis, riding, shooting, polo, and windsurfing. Rates start at $190 per room per night in summer, including all activities and meals.

Beachfront options at **Club Med Family Villages** (*Coral Gables, FL. 800-258-2633 or 305-925-9000. www.clubmed.com*) include **Eleuthera, the Bahamas; Punta Cana, Dominican Republic; St. Lucia;** and **Huatulco** and **Ixtapa, Mexico.** While parents swim, golf, water-ski, windsurf, kayak, snorkel, or sail, children have their fun in the Petit Club (ages 2 to 3), the Mini-Club (ages 4 to 7), or the Kids Club (ages 8 to 11). Children's offerings include water sports, arts and crafts, drama, and circus activities. At Ixtapa and Eleuthera, the Baby Club offers babysitting for toddlers at least one year old.

For a more exotic adventure, check out **Journeys International** (*Ann Arbor, MI. 800-255-8735 or 734-665-440. www.journeys-intl.com*). The **Belize Family Explorer** trip offers a naturalist-led introduction to Mayan culture and the idyllic islands of Belize as well as snorkeling and a jungle river trip. Land fee for one week is $1,900 for adults and $1,000 for children under 12. The week-long **Costa Rica Natural Wonders** trip combines rain forest hikes, jungle river-running, and beach exploring on the Caribbean and Pacific coasts. The land cost is $1,600 for adults, $1,500 for ages 12 to 15, and $900 for kids under 12.

Scuba divers with preteenagers should consider the **Dolphin Discovery Camp** run by **Anthony's Key Resort** and the **Institute of Marine Sciences** on **Roatan** island in **Honduras.** Booked through **American Wilderness Experience** (**AWE**) (*Boulder, CO. 800-444-0099 or 303-444-2622. www.awetrips.com*), the program lets kids feed, train, and swim with dolphins.

The camp also features marine-science presentations,

riding, boat trips, nature hikes, and water sports. Week-long dive packages for adults cost about $850 per person, including meals; children ages 8 to 11 who share a room with an adult on this package can join the Dolphin Discovery Camp for an all-inclusive price of $500.

ENVIRONMENTAL VACATIONS
Adventures in Ecotourism

Environmental vacations teach children to appreciate nature, sparking a lifelong interest in ecology and conservation. Eco-adventures range from rugged jungle treks to cushy lodge-based holidays. You can also join an ecocruise, which lets you visit a variety of locales. If you opt for the rugged route, make sure the trip is family friendly.

For a world-class eco-adventure to the country that pioneered the concept, consider a trip to safe and stable **Costa Rica.** The nation's vast parks and preserves harbor an amazing diversity of ecosystems—and abundant possibilities for adventure. In Costa Rica's rain forest—a giant zoo without bars—kids can see monkeys, sloths, macaws, and iguanas in the wild. You can also raft or kayak from the highlands to the black-sand coast and explore various animal habitats, such as the sea-turtle rookery in **Tortuguero National Park.**

While many fine companies offer ecotours in Costa Rica, one of my favorites is **Wildland Adventures** (*Seattle, WA.*

BARGE PASSENGERS KEEP PACE WITH THEIR CRAFT ON THE CANAL DU RHÔNE AU RHIN IN FRANCE.

800-345-4453 or 206-365-0686. *www.wildland.com*). This firm offers a wide variety of multiactivity adventures led by knowledgeable guides. Groups are small and prices are reasonable, with a 20 percent discount for kids under 12.

The ten-day **Caribbean Highlands and Jungles** trip visits **Arenal Volcano, Monteverde National Park, Poas Volcano, Cano Negro Wildlife Refuge,** and Tortuguero park, with a jungle river trip along the way. ($1,600-1,800 for adults, $1,200 for ages 6-16, $600 for kids under 5.)

Other good environmental and wildlife trips are sponsored by the **National Wildlife Federation** (*Vienna, VA. 800-245-5484 or 703-790-4000. www.nwf.org/*), whose **Conservation Summit and Teen Adventure** programs feature wilderness trips in Alaska, Colorado, and elsewhere for four age groups. Fees range from $150 for preschoolers to $400 for adults, excluding lodging.

Nature Expeditions International (NEI) (*Plantation, FL. 800-869-0639 or 954-693-8852. www.naturexp.com*) specializes in small-group ecotourism for all age groups. Tours are led by expert naturalists, biologists, or geologists. NEI's **Costa Rica** and **Galápagos** programs are great family trips, but at $2,800 to $3,000 per person they are fairly pricey.

Less expensive **Sierra Club Outings** (*San Francisco, CA. 415-977-5522 or 5630 (after hours). www.sierraclub.org/outings*) also offer expert-guided family adventures suitable for toddlers to grandparents. Prices for one-week trips average $620 to $790 for adults and $400 to $600 for children. A favorite is the annual **Alaskan camping/van trip,** which costs about $1,500 for both adults and children.

The popular **YMCA of the Rockies** (*Snow Mountain Ranch, Winter Park, CO. 970-887-2152. www.ymcarockies.org*) offers economical family wilderness experiences for children ages 3 to 17. Located in **Estes Park** near Denver, the ranch offers guided nature hikes in beautiful Colorado backcountry with easy access to rock climbing, horseback riding, and other outdoor activities. The ranch is very popular in summer, so book early.

FARM STAYS
Greener Acres for Your Family

No matter how stressed your existence or how active your toddler, a farm vacation sends you home rejuvenated. Children experience the simple pleasures of rural life, from gathering eggs to riding a tractor, while parents can go exploring or antiquing or just hang out on the porch swing. Think of it as an adventure in serenity: You'll share home-cooked meals with your host family, tranquil and quiet evenings, and early bedtimes.

The farm you select should offer a full range of activities for both you and your children. Spend time interviewing

potential host families by phone; you'll be spending a lot of time together, so a good personality fit is important. Also, try to choose a family whose kids match yours in age.

North America has a number of first-rate farm stays. Since 1820, eight generations have operated **Bluffdale Vacation Farm** (*Eldred, IL. 217-983-2854*). Set on 320 rolling acres near the Illinois River, it offers hayrides, canoeing, horseback riding, and paddleboating. Farm holidays, including meals and activities, start at $72 per day for adults and $48 per day for children.

Family Circle magazine has named **Harvey's Mountain View Inn and Farm** (*Rochester, VT. 802-767-4273*) one of the top ten farm vacations in the United States. Founded in 1809, Harvey's has been serving guests since 1900. Families enjoy swimming, fishing, and pony rides in summer, and cross-country skiing in winter. The cost per day, including two meals, is $65 per person for adults and $35 for children; toddlers under 2 are free.

At **Ingeberg Acres** (*Weston, WV. 304-269-2834. www.spikeworld.com*), a 450-acre working farm, children can feed and care for livestock or pick fresh berries and vegetables. The price is a bargain: A double room for adults is $59, a single $39. Kids under 6 share the room for free. Hunting and fishing are popular on the farm; parents will enjoy the many craft fairs nearby.

Established in 1834, the **Inn at East Hill Farm** (*Troy, NH. 800-242-6495 or 603-242-6495. www.east-hill-farm.com*) has operated as a resort since 1945. In 1997, the New Hampshire Hospitality Association named the proprietor "Innkeeper of the Year." This year-round country retreat offers excellent hiking trails, swimming, hay rides, horseback riding, waterskiing, and boating. In winter, there's cross-country skiing, ice skating, and sleigh rides. One week's lodging and meals start at $510 per adult and $365 for children.

The owners of remote **Mountain Dale Farm** (*McClure, PA. 570-658-3536*) treat you like family. The farm dates to the late 1800s and is home to goats, chickens, roosters, ducks, and kittens. There's boating and fishing on the Susquehanna River, a 45-minute drive away. A forest cabin for four costs $80, and the farm is open year-round.

SKI VACATIONS
Alpine Adventures

A ski trip is sure to be one of your most memorable family vacations. Everyone can do their own thing during the day, then meet for an après-ski warm-up in the hot tub or a hot chocolate around the fire.

Children as young as 3 can learn to downhill ski. Cross-country skiing requires more strength, endurance, and balance, so it's generally advisable to wait until they are a bit older. Make sure your children are dressed comfortably;

AN AERIAL-TRAM VIEW OF THE COSTA RICA RAIN FOREST

parents tend to overdress kids, hampering their movement — and consequently their fun. Whether you rent or purchase skis (look for a buy-back program that allows you to trade in equipment each year), let your kids get used to the equipment at home before they hit the slopes.

One of the keys to successful family skiing is to start kids off with professional lessons. Many resorts offer Montessori-style skiing schools, which teach basic ski techniques by playing games such as soccer, red rover, and relay races.

Cost is a major factor when it comes to family ski trips, so we've listed popular ski resorts (*see pp. 80-81*) that offer special family discounts and excellent children's services. (*Note: Specials are subject to change. For additional information on skiing and ski resorts, see pp. 242-263.*)

HISTORICAL ADVENTURES
Back to the Future

The concept of time travel captivates most children, and visiting a site of historical or archaeological significance is a fun way to teach them about history and geography. You can choose from a variety of exciting vacations that will challenge kids to actively engage with the past rather than remain passive observers of it.

If you have a young dinosaur fan in the family, consider an expedition back to prehistoric America. Planning a dinosaur adventure can be be as simple as car-camping near **Dinosaur National Monument** (*Dinosaur, CO. 970-374-3000*). You can see 350 tons of bones in ongoing digs at the Visitor Center.

Utah's **Dinosaurland** (*Vernal, UT. 800-477-5558 or 435-789-6932*) contains many famous fossil sites, including the **Dinosaur National Monument Quarry,** which boasts more than 2,000 dinosaur bones. Visitors can also camp, hike, and ride horses nearby.

At **U-Dig Fossils** (*Delta, UT. 435-864-3638*), visitors age 8 and older can hunt for trilobites on half- or full-day digs. Fees start at $20 for four hours.

Another time-travel trip suitable for youngsters is a guided journey through ancient **Native American cultural sites** in the Northeast, the Rockies, the Great Plains, or the Southwest. Options range from guided day hikes to week-long tribal homestays.

Blackfeet Historical Site Tours (*Browning, MT. 406-338-2058*) offers one- to three-day excursions with Native American guides to tribal areas near scenic **Glacier National Park.** You can visit **Lewis & Clark historical sites,** climb sacred **Chief Mountain,** observe a sun-dance ceremony, and see buffalo herds. Tours start at $50 per person per day, plus $40 for overnight lodging.

At **Ute Mountain Tribal Park** (*Towoc, CO. 800-847-5485 or 970-565-3751*), programs present the culture of the Ancestral Puebloans. This is a scenic area of Colorado, with many recreational opportunities nearby.

Represented by the National Park Service, **Canyon de Chelly Guide Association** (*Chinle, AZ. 520-674-5500*) features local Native American guides who lead tours to Ancestral Puebloan sites. You can opt to walk, ride horses, or take a motorized tour. Canyon de Chelly is near many other important Ancestral Puebloan sites.

Anthropologist and "adopted" native son Robert Vetter runs **Journeys into American Indian Territory** (*Westhampton Beach, NY. 800-458-2632 or 516-878-8655. www.indianjourneys.com*). He arranges 3- to 12-day full-immersion visits to Native American settlements in Massachusetts, New York, Montana, Wyoming, South Dakota, New Mexico, Oklahoma, and Texas. Trips feature traditional crafts and tipi-camping or homestays. The most popular kids program is the three-day family affair in New York's Catskill Mountains. (*For more information on Native American site visits, contact the state Native American Tourism Office.*)

You can delve into another chapter of American history at **Colonial Williamsburg** (*Williamsburg, VA. 800-447-8679 or 757-229-1000. www.history.org*). Here, at America's most famous museum of living history, children immerse themselves in 18th-century culture — whether it's riding in a horse-drawn carriage, participating in a courthouse trial, enjoying special workshops, playing colonial games such as hoop-rolling, or visiting with the resident farm animals.

Williamsburg's **Kids' Clubs** offer miniature golf, swimming, arts and crafts, and a special **Family Fun** tour of the 173-acre historic site. Quality hotels, tennis facilities, and nearby golf courses keep parents happy, too. Colonial Williamsburg is a national treasure that every family should visit at least once. Check the calendar for special events that can enhance your holiday.

Another favorite with families, **Old Sturbridge Village** (*Sturbridge, MA. 800-733-1830 or 508-347-3362. www.osv.org*) is an authentic re-creation of an early colonial village. The villagers dress, talk, and conduct themselves as the original New England settlers would have. The 200-acre site is home to more than 40 vintage structures, including a blacksmith shop, a gristmill, and a schoolhouse. The **Museum Education Department** runs five-day summer workshops for children ages 8 to 14 (*the cost is about $200*) and several week-long family programs.

As long as you're in the neighborhood, plan to visit nearby **Plimoth Plantation** (*Plymouth, MA. 508-746-1622*). Here kids will find a full-scale reproduction of the *Mayflower,* as well as a re-created Pilgrim settlement and a Native American encampment.

Adventuring with Kids

Children are citizens of the world, and travel at a young age helps to bring that message home. Not every parent would characterize traveling with children as a relaxing vacation, but if the trip is well planned, bringing the kids along can make for a rewarding and memorable adventure.

The key to success is to be realistic in your expectations. Don't push young children — or yourself — too hard. Also, try not to do too much in the allotted time. Choose one or two locations, then stay in each for at least a week. This spares you the rigmarole of packing and unpacking every day.

Select a destination that offers plenty of activities for everyone in the family. Then prepare for your trip together using books, storybooks, videos, and other resources.

Nurture your kids' powers of observation. Bring some disposable cameras; the waterproof versions are ideal for water trips. Encourage children to keep a journal; younger ones can draw pictures or dictate their impressions to you.

A fun and useful exercise is to make "best" and "worst" lists summarizing the trip. This teaches kids that tough times make the best stories, that mistakes can be opportunities for learning, and that life itself is an ongoing adventure.

FAMILY TOUR COORDINATORS

The following organizations offer a range of adventure activities and travel assistance for families and teens.

Grandtravel
800-247-7651 or 301-986-0790

International and domestic tours for grandchildren ages 7 to 17 and their grandparents. Most are fairly pricey "soft adventure" trips, such as lodge-based safaris.

Off the Beaten Path
800-445-2995 or 406-586-1311.
www.offbeatenpath.com

Bill and Pam Bryan plan made-to-order family holidays. Specializing in the Rockies and Southwest, Off the Beaten Path will hook you up with the best ranches, fishing lodges, and other resorts, or arrange unique programs such as tribal homestays.

Rascals in Paradise
800-872-7225 or 415-978-9800.

www.rascalsinparadise.com

This agency designs customized family vacations. It can handle special needs, such as providing nannies and tutors for children.

SAFEGUARDING YOUR FAMILY

Comprehensive travel insurance, including medical coverage, should be the first thing on your packing list when traveling with children. Many plans do not cover injuries sustained overseas or while engaging in adventure sports, such as scuba diving or parasailing. For a complete travel insurance package, contact:

Travelex
11717 Burt St., No. 202, Omaha, NE
800-228-9792 or 402-491-3200
www.travelexinsurance.com

The Cruise & Tours program and the Travel Assure Policy for independent travelers offer comprehensive accident insurance for tourists. Coverage includes most medical and evacuation costs, lost baggage, and trip cancellation.

Worldwide Assistance
1133 15th St. NW, Suite 400, Washington, DC
20005. 800-368-7878 or 202-331-1609

This outfit covers foreign medical expenses and emergency medical evacuation. Among its offerings are a 24-hour travelers' aid service to help with legal problems, lost passports, and visas. You can also purchase coverage for trip cancellation, lost baggage, and accidents.

BARGE

European Waterways
New York, NY. 800-217-4447 or
212-688-9489.
www.europeanwaterways.com

Mostly piloted cruises. Watch for the "value special" for big savings.

French Country Waterways, Ltd.
Duxbury, MA. 800-222-1236 or 781-934-2454

Mostly large, deluxe barges.
Competitive prices.

Le Boat
Ramsey, NJ. 800-992-0291 or 201-236-2333.
www.leboat.com

Large, modern self-drive and luxury barges.

Remote Odysseys Worldwide (ROW)
Coeur d'Alene, ID. 800-451-6034 or 208-765-0841.
www.rowinc.com

Continental barge tours, as well as adventure cruises in the Turkish Mediterranean.

The Barge Cruise Company
Bristol, UK. 800-688-0245 or
01144-1275-474034 in England
www.bargecompany.com

Operates 50 barges in the United Kingdom, Ireland, and France.

CAMPING

These resources can help you plan a great camping trip or other outdoor adventure.

Outside *Magazine's Guide to Family Vacations* (IDG Books, 1997, $15.95). Good for planning vacations in and around the national parks, as well as for Alaska and the Rockies.

Wilderness with Children by Michael Hodgson (Stackpole Books, 1992, $12.95). Rated the "best book of its kind in recent years" by the *San Francisco Chronicle/Examiner.*

Woodall's Campground Directory. (Woodall's Publications, $17.95. 708-362-6700.) Updated annually, this resource reviews campgrounds and RV parks throughout North America. Includes maps.

SKIING

Copper Mountain
Copper Mountain, CO. 800-458-8386 or
970-968-2882. www.ski-copper.com

Crested Butte
Mount Crested Butte, CO. 888-223-3530 or
970-349-2333. www.crestedbutteresort.com

Diamond Peak
Incline Village, NV. 800-468-2463 or
775-832-1177. www.diamondpeak.com

Children 18 and under ski and stay free with a three-day, three-night minimum.

Grand Targhee
Alta, WY. 800-827-4433 or 307-353-2300. www.grandtarghee.com

Children 14 and under ski and stay free with a three-day, three-night minimum.

Purgatory/Durango
Durango, CO. 800-982-6103 or 970-247-9000. www.ski-purg.com

Schweitzer
Sandpoint, ID. 800-831-8810 or 208-263-9555. www.schweitzer.com

Children 6 and under ski and stay free.

Snowbird
Snowbird, UT. 800-453-3000 or 801-742-2222. www.snowbird.com

Steamboat
Steamboat Springs, CO. 800-922-2722 or 970-879-6111. www.steamboat-ski.com

Kids 12 and under ski free when parents purchase a minimum five-day lift ticket.

Stowe Mountain
Stowe, VT. 800-253-4754 or 802-253-3000. www.stowe.com

Children 6 and under ski free.

Sun Valley
Sun Valley, ID. 800-786-8259 or 208-622-4111. www.sunvalley.com

Waterville Valley Resort
Waterville Valley, NH. 800-468-2553 or 603-236-8311. www.waterville.com

Children 5 and under ski free all winter; in January, children age 12 and under ski free.

White Mountains
North Woodstock, NH. 800-367-3364

A five-day mid-week **Family Pass**, good except for December holidays, is available at five resorts.

For more information on ski holidays, visit www.skinet.com

ONLINE

Family.com
www.family.com

Travel bargains, destination reports, and articles from *FamilyFun* magazine.

Family Travel Files
www.thefamilytravelfiles.com

Unique and affordable destinations, plus recommended travel gear.

Family Travel Forum
www.familytravelforum.com

The leading family-travel website. Subscription-based service features resort reviews, a message board, and member discounts on travel services and lodging.

BOOKS

Adventuring with Children by Nan Jeffrey with Kevin Jeffrey (Foghorn Press, 1995, $14.95). A valuable how-to for hiking, biking, sailing, or international travel.

Family Travel Resorts: The Complete Guide by Pamela Lanier (Ten Speed Press, 1998, $19.99).

Farm, Ranch and Country Vacations by Pat Dickerman (Adventure Guides, Inc., $19.95 plus $3.00 shipping. 800-252-7899 or 480-596-0226). Handy reference to farms that offer children's programs.

National Geographic Guide to Family Adventure Vacations by Candyce H. Stapen (National Geographic Books, April 2000, $25). Spotlights all sorts of interactive family adventures — wildlife encounters, cultural explorations, and learning escapes — in 327 destinations across the United States and Canada. Includes 100 photos and five detailed regional maps .

100 Best Family Resorts in North America by Janet Tice (Globe Pequot Press, 1999, $17.95). Complete profiles of 100 ski lodges, lake cottages, inns, ranches, and B&Bs.

Super Family Vacations/Resort and Adventure Guide by Martha Shirk and Nancy Klepper (Harper Perennial, 1995, $17.95). Perhaps the best guide for conventional resort vacations; includes ratings.

Take 'em Along: Sharing the Wilderness with Your Children by Barbara J. Euser (Johnson Books, 1987, $7.95). Shows how to enrich children's lives by introducing them to new environments.

Travel with Children by Maureen Wheeler (Lonely Planet, 1995, $11.95). Packed with practical tips, this is required reading for families planning third-world itineraries.

TAKING A BREAK FROM DINOSAUR HUNTING IN DINOSAURLAND, RED CANYON, ASHLEY NATIONAL FOREST, UTAH.

Fishing

AMERICA'S ESTIMATED 45 MILLION ANGLERS SPEND BILLIONS OF DOLLARS EACH YEAR ON THEIR SPORT. Yet just 10 percent of those anglers catch as much as 80 percent of all the fish. Skill and the right equipment are vital to success, of course. But the key to a rewarding fishing trip is finding the right fishing hole: Unless you go where the fish are biting, you can spend a small fortune on tackle and still walk away empty-handed, no matter how advanced your angling skills. This chapter is designed to point you in the right direction. • Giving a whole new meaning to the term *fly-fishing*, the following pages will transport you to more than 50 of the finest river, lake, and ocean fishing sites around the world. From the streams of Montana to the shores of Mauritius, there's enough here for a lifetime of angling. • This chapter will also take care of you once you reach your destination: You'll find information on recommended guides and outfitters, as well as lodges where, after a long day's fishing, you can chat with fellow anglers—about the one that *didn't* get away.

LEFT: REEL-TIME ADVENTURE IN ALASKA
BELOW: FLY-FISHING IN THE ADIRONDACKS, NEW YORK

Fishing on the Fly

Freshwater Fishing

Saltwater Fishing

I fish because I love to...because trout do not lie or cheat but respond only to endless patience; because there are no telephones on trout waters.
JOHN VOELKER

Fishing Around for the Best

You don't have to travel to the four corners of the Earth to catch fish. But if you're thinking of devoting precious vacation days to a fishing trip, you want a destination that delivers game fish reliably, year in and year out. Here are eight truly superior picks—places where you're virtually guaranteed to hook quality fish in large numbers, whether you're a longtime angler or a relative newcomer to the sport.

ALASKA
Where Salmon Is King

When most city folks head to Alaska on a fishing vacation, they've usually got one thing in mind: salmon—preferably very big salmon, the type known as Alaskan kings.

There are scores of king-salmon fisheries in the state. Perhaps the most accessible—and still one of the most productive—is the **Kenai River.** Easily reached by car or bus from Anchorage, the Kenai flows into Cook Inlet at the town of Soldotna. Happily, the fish seem to find the river accessible too. Each year the world's largest kings—weighing in at around 90 pounds—return to the Kenai in May, June, and July.

To book charter trips and local guides, contact **Kenai Peninsula Fishing** (*Soldotna, AK. 888-285-2665 or 907-283-2665. www.alaska.net/~trophy/*). This company also operates the comfortable Homestead Trophy Lodge. Here, guests can stay either in the central lodge or, at a cost of $50 per night, in one of the smaller wood cabins. The lodge offers several different options for the visiting angler: drift-boat trips, river fishing, and fly-outs to sites upriver. An eight-day package promises all the fish you can catch.

Another great destination for salmon fishing is **Iliamna Lake,** on the other side of Cook Inlet. Kings up to 50 pounds run in great numbers in the lake from June through August. Although cheaper options are available, most visitors to Iliamna Lake go the deluxe lodge route, which can set you back a whopping $3,650 to $5,150 per week. These prices usually include fly-out fishing and guides, as well as all meals and accommodations. The leading Iliamna-area lodge is the Valhalla (*907-243-6096*), but many other fine, less costly alternatives exist. Contact the full-service travel agency **Alaskan Experience** (*Anchorage. 800-777-7055 or 907-276-5425. www.alaskanexp.com*).

If trophy silver salmon is your calling, the Karluk River on windswept Kodiak Island is the place to go. With the biggest silver run in Alaska, the Karluk has yielded virtually every world-record silver salmon. The silvers run all summer long, but the biggest specimens often come late, in the month of September, just as the seasons begin to change.

Alaska offers more than just great salmon, however. Anglers keen to fish for trout as well should head for **Lake Creek.** Famed for its rainbow trout, June kings, and August silver salmon, Lake Creek is a beautiful, remote waterway running from the slopes of Mount McKinley 65 miles to the Yentna River.

Near Lake Creek, Ed and Judy Sharpe maintain a simple but lovely lodge called the **Wilderness Place** (*Lake Creek. 907-248-4337. www.windriverak.com*). Here you can pull on your waders and fish from the creek side or, as many anglers prefer, cast your line from a drift-boat floating on the creek. Cost for a six-night stay at the Wilderness is $2,675—solid value by Alaska standards.

In this great state, salmon might be king. But for fans of big fish—really big fish—halibut is a weighty pretender to the throne. Here, a halibut doesn't get a second glance unless it tips the scales in the hundreds of pounds. Just how big are they? Well, a 200-pounder can easily be 6 feet long. When you first hook one, you'll feel like you're trying to land a small submarine.

A number of Alaska ports cater to anglers in search of halibut, but Homer is the prime fishery. Day trips aboard Homer's larger vessels cost around $150 per person, which is about the same price as some of the port's private charter boats that operate with a minimum of four people. To reserve a spot or arrange a charter, contact **Central Charter** (*Homer. 800-478-7847 or 907-235-7847. www. ptialaska.net/~central/*).

MONTANA
Classic American Trout Streams

The heartland of American trout fishing is Montana, where you'll find more excellent streams and first-rate outfitters than in the rest of the Rocky Mountain states combined.

Among Montana's many blue-ribbon trout rivers, the **Bighorn** may be the best of them all. With a population of more than 5,000 fish per mile, it has earned a reputation as one of the most productive fly-fishing destinations in the country. Although the river is accessible to the general public, you may want to hire a guide, both to help you choose

the best flies and to lead you to its most productive stretches. Contact the **Bighorn Trout Shop** (*Fort Smith. 800-235-5450 or 406-666-2375. www.bighorntroutshop.com*).

The **Bighorn River Lodge** (*Fort Smith. 800-235-5450 or 406-666-2368. www.bighornriverlodge.com*) is the oldest resort on the Bighorn—and the only one that is streamside. The lodge has a fly shop and fishing license. A four-night, three-day package—which includes meals, lodging, and guides—costs $1,275 per person.

The **Big Hole River** area is another legendary Montana trout destination. Here you can fish the Big Hole itself, as well as half a dozen other top streams, including the Beaverhead, the Upper Clark Fork, and the Wise. July, August, and September are generally the best months.

A 45-minute drive south of Butte on I-15 takes you to the highly recommended **Big Hole Outfitters** in Wise River. "Excellent fishing in magnificent country," one Outfitters customer declared, "with topnotch guides and first-rate accommodations, including meals and airport pickup." Big Hole Outfitters offers anglers six days and seven nights—based on double occupancy and a shared guide—for $1,600 per head. Book through **Frontiers** (*Wexford, PA. 800-245-1950 or 724-935-1577. www.frontierstrvl.com*).

A third top spot in the state is the Madison River, where you'll find the trout biting a little earlier in the year, in June.

The first few miles of the river below Earthquake Lake are particularly rich. An outstanding outfitter on the Madison is **Henry's Fork Anglers** (*Island Park, ID. 800-788-4479 or 208-558-7525. www.henrys-fork.com*).

Before you head off to Big Sky country, pick up a copy of the *Montana Angling Guide* by Chuck Fothergill and Bob Sterling. The guide provides detailed maps of all the classic fishing holes and many lesser known ones as well. (A companion book for Wyoming is available.) Also worth a look is *The Fabulous Bighorn with Gary Borger.* In this informative 55-minute video, Borger visits some of his favorite spots along the Bighorn River and illustrates proper fly selection and casting.

COSTA RICA
Billfishing Paradise

For many anglers, big game fishing means one thing—billfish. And on Costa Rica's Pacific coast—thanks to a fish-friendly ocean current that hits the country's Osa Peninsula and then turns west into the ocean—you'll find one of the world's richest billfishing areas. Behind it, in the happily placed **Dulce Gulf,** the current deposits its bounty: large numbers of blue marlin, black marlin, and Pacific sailfish.

Roosterfish, snapper, tuna, tripletail, dorado, and all types of jack also prowl these warm waters. Seven rivers

ALASKA IS JUST A CAST AWAY.

and 25 smaller streams feed the Dulce Gulf, which make it a natural hatchery for the bait fish that draw the bigger—carnivorous—game fish.

Situated on a private beach on the Dulce Gulf is the **Golfito Sailfish Rancho** (*Tampa, FL. 800-450-9908 or 813-249-9908. www.sailfishrancho.com*). The Rancho can accommodate up to two dozen anglers at a time with its superb fleet of 27-foot, 300-horsepower Ocean Masters, all custom rigged to the best American standards. A week's stay at the Rancho—with five full days' fishing—starts at about $2,100 per person, based on double occupancy.

The billfishing is excellent in the **Gulf of Papagayo,** too, about 200 miles or so farther north along the Pacific coast. "We raised about 40 sailfish and two marlin, landing one blue that was about 250 pounds," one visitor reported. "There is also great light-tackle fishing for dorado, wahoo, and yellowfin."

The leading resort in the Gulf of Papagayo is the Ocotal Resort at Flamingo Beach. The resort offers serious anglers a high-tech fishing program with comfortable onshore facilities. The price for six nights and five full days of fishing—aboard 32-footers complete with all gear and tackle—is $1,675, based on double occupancy and a party of four anglers.

Also recommended are the nearby Flamingo Beach Hotel and the luxurious resort of Maria Playa Conchal. The resort offers six nights and five days of fishing for around $1,600, again based on double occupancy (meals not included). Boat charters on the Gulf cost $500 to $800 per day.

Fishing vacations in Costa Rica can be booked through **Fishing International** (*Santa Rosa, CA. 800-950-4242 or 707-542-4242. www.fishinginternational.com*), **World Wide Sportsman** (*Springfield, MO. 800-327-2880 or 305-664-4615. www.outdoorworld.com*), or **Costa Rica Experts** (*Chicago, IL. 800-827-9046 or 773-935-1009. www. crexpert.com*).

VENEZUELA
The Atlantic Angle

If you're really serious about hooking billfish—and you'd like to try your hand in the Caribbean—look no farther than Venezuela. An hour's cruise north from one of the ports serving the capital, Caracas, brings you to La Guaira Bank. This offshore underwater plateau is home to hordes of bait fish, which attract to the area all of the major species of Atlantic billfish.

During the fall white-marlin season, catches of ten or more billfish are common, and the coveted Grand Slam—

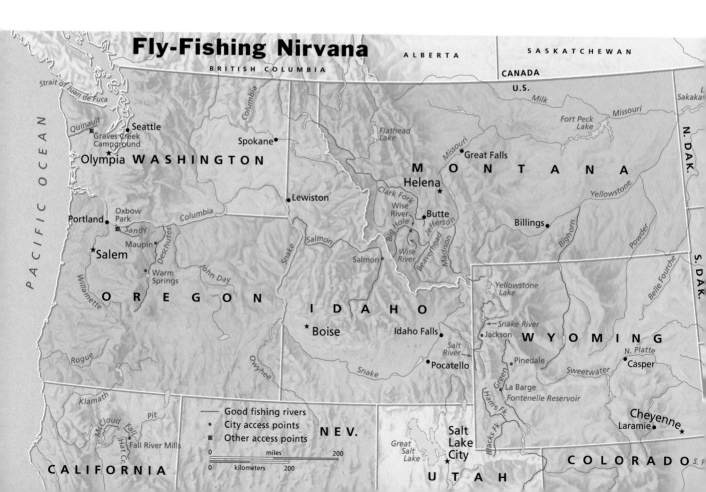

white marlin, blue marlin, and sailfish—is an everyday possibility. In February and March, blue marlin predominate, typically weighing in at 300 to 800 pounds. Sailfish and swordfish run year-round.

The premier charter base for fishing La Guaira Bank is the harbor at Caraballeda, several miles outside Caracas. From here a number of local sportfishing boats can take you out for $500 to $800 per day. Or you can book a package trip with **Club Gigi.** The club maintains a number of speedy twin-diesel sportfishers that are tournament-rigged and equipped with full electronics and the best tackle.

Club Gigi's five-day trip with four days' fishing costs anywhere between $800 and $3,350 per person; the price depends on the size of the vessel. The club arranges side trips to other points of interest as well, such as the magnificent Angel Falls—where you'll see plenty of water but precious few opportunities for angling—and the capital. Book Club Gigi through **Quest Global Angling Adventures** (*Marietta, GA. 888-891-3474 or 770-971-8586. www.fishquest.com*). This agency also offers an attractive package from another of the Caracas-area ports, Macuto: three nights and two days of fishing for $795 per person.

For other angling holidays in Venezuela, contact **South Fishing** (*Miami, FL. 800-882-4665 or 305-279-3252. www.southfishing.com*), which offers some of the best deals. South Fishing is also one of the organizers of the annual **La Guaira Billfish Shootout,** a fall event with more than $100,000 in prizes. Advance reservations are a must if you want to visit during the time of this popular event.

Venezuela offers more than just billfishing, however. There's world-class tarpon fishing at Rio Chico and bonefishing at Los Roques. **Fishing International** (*Santa Rosa, CA. 800-950-4242 or 707-542-4242. www.fishinginternational.com*) and Quest Global Angling Adventures offer package fishing vacations at these top shoreside resorts.

For mainland adventure extensions, including rafting and jungle trekking—or even fishing for peacock bass—contact **Lost World Adventures** (*Decatur, GA. 800-999-0558 or 404-373-5820. www.lostworldadventures.com*). Lost World has specialized in Venezuelan travel since 1986, and its staff knows more about the myriad adventure opportunities in this part of the world than any other North American agency.

ARGENTINA
Trout Fishing's Best-Kept Secret

If you had to choose one trout-fishing destination—a place where just about anyone could catch lots of jumbo-size trout—Argentina would have to be the place: "The best trout water I've ever seen," proclaimed one recent visitor, "and I've fished everywhere you could name. I caught 22 rainbows and browns in two pools in three hours. Only six of them were under 15 inches."

The country's prime trout fisheries are located along the eastern flank of the Andes near the Chilean border, between the towns of Esquel and Junin de los Andes. Here, in the cool mountain rivers, you'll find browns, rainbows, and brook trout, as well as a smattering of landlocked salmon. The average size of the fish is about two pounds, with some as big as eight pounds. A number of the rivers are catch-and-release only.

If you do some research and learn a little Spanish before setting out, there is no reason why you can't do the trip independently. For anglers with money to burn, however, there are always other options: The **Frontiers** agency (*Wexford, PA. 800-245-1950 or 724-935-1577. www.frontierstrvl.com*) books a number of superior itineraries through Patagonia Outfitters.

Between November and April, Patagonia arranges five-, six-, and eleven-day excursions in the beautiful **Los Alerces National Park** area—in the heart of the country's unspoiled lake district. In this area, west of Esquel, anglers regularly land brown trout as large as 15 pounds and brooks up to 6 pounds. Catch-and-release tallies of two dozen per day are common.

Frontiers' trips are limited to small groups of anglers, so it's essential to book early. The prices are steep: For two anglers sharing one guide, six nights and five days of fishing cost about $3,900. Another recommended operation is the **Esquel Lodge,** which offers a week of custom-guided fishing for around the same price. For reservations, contact **The Fly Shop** (*Redding, CA. 800-669-3474 or 530-222-3555. www.theflyshop.com*).

If you want to combine fishing with other backcountry adventures, consider **La Rinconada,** an 880-acre ranch located in an alpine valley just 5 miles north of Los Alerces National Park. The fishing on crystal-clear alpine streams is outstanding. But the ranch has more to offer: A unique multisport facility, La Rinconada is a place where guests can also enjoy horse trekking, jeep tours, mountain biking, kayaking, and canoeing—all within sight of the breathtaking backdrop of the Andes.

A week at La Rinconada costs about $1,750 per person, which includes meals and use of all equipment and horses—a great way to experience this region at half the cost of the exclusive fishing lodges. Those on tight budgets can save even more by preparing their own meals. Camping is available, too, and day visitors can rent gear or horses separately. Contact **La Rinconada** (*Santa Fe, NM. 505-989-3359. E-mail: LaRiconada@red42.com.ar*).

CHRISTMAS ISLAND
Bonefishing Bonanza

When anglers agree on anything, it is a noteworthy event. However, many would acknowledge that the single most prolific bonefishing destination in the world is Christmas Island, a tiny atoll 1,300 miles south of Hawaii.

Noted angler Lefty Kreh, writing in the *Baltimore Sun*, remarked: "The flats are huge, composed of hard sand and provide good wading. On these flats roam probably the most bonefish you'll see in a lifetime. A good saltwater angler should be able to average at least 20 bonefish a day."

Because of its proximity to the equator—just 90 miles distant—Christmas Island offers excellent angling year-round. Reflecting the tidal conditions, two weeks of each month are noticeably better than the other two, so time your arrival accordingly.

Should you get tired of the flats, try your hand at the offshore light-tackle fishing. On an island so renowned for its bonefish, this is a real Christmas bonus: The good-eating yellowfins are abundant here, and a catch of ten wahoo a day is common.

Lodge accommodations on the island are fairly rustic, and there isn't much shoreside nightlife. Still, most visitors to this exotic part of the world come to fish—not to party. Trips can be booked with a variety of agencies, including **The Fly Shop** (*Redding, CA. 800-669-3474 or 916-222-3555. www.theflyshop.com*), **Kaufmann's Streamborn Fly Shop** (*Tigard, OR. 800-442-4359 or 503-639-6400. www.kman.com*), or **Fishing International** (*Santa Rosa, CA. 800-950-4242 or 707-542-4242. www.fishinginternational.com*). Package trips to Christmas Island start at approximately $2,500 per week, which includes round-trip airfare from Honolulu.

NEW ZEALAND
Kiwi Trout

Boasting scores of great rivers and spring creeks teeming with wild trout, New Zealand represents the best in fly-fishing. This destination is less than ideal for novices, however. Kiwi trout are notoriously shy, and a fly-fishing novice—even one who has paid thousands of dollars to fish at a top lodge—can come away frustrated.

Still, few places combine trophy angling with unspoiled natural beauty as well as New Zealand. The country's South Island in particular is recognized as the country's angling mecca, even though fewer than 6,000 foreign anglers a year make the journey to the trout-laden streams of the Southern Alps. There are many great lodges in this region, but the Lake Rotorua Lodge is hard to beat. Here, in scenic **Nelson Lakes National Park,** you can catch truly big fish on 42 different streams. The average trout caught here weigh in at 4.5 pounds.

Another superior South Island lodge is the Lake Brunner, which boasts many world-class spring creeks. If only the best will do, though, make your way to Dick Fraser's Cedar Lodge. Located on the banks of the Makarora River near Mount Aspiring National Park, the lodge caters to just eight anglers a week and employs helicopters to access some of New Zealand's most pristine trout waters. The price, including fly-outs, is a hefty $3,600 to $4,000 (US) for six days and seven nights, or about $1,900 (US) for three days and four nights.

For those who have time to cross Cook Strait to visit the North Island, make sure you head to **Lake Taupo.** There you can either hire a local guide or fish on your own. (Ask the local shops for recommended trout streams and flies.) If you prefer a deluxe lodge, try Tony Hayes' Tongariro Lodge, which has fishing rights to the area's best river. The Tongariro costs $380 (US) per day, double occupancy. The Poronui Ranch is also a top North Island lodge. Located near the **Rangitaiki**—the north's major wilderness river—the Poronui offers its guests some of the most prolific brown-trout fishing in the country.

Lodge-based vacations start at about $300 (US) per day. To book any of the lodges listed, call **Frontiers** (*Wexford, Pennsylvania. 800-245-1950 or 724-935-1577. www.frontierstrvl.com*), **The Fly Shop** (*Redding, CA. 800-669-3474 or 530-222-3555. www.theflyshop.com*), or **Kaufmann's Streamborn** (*Tigard, OR. 800-442-4359 or 503-639-6400. www.kman.com*).

When considering a trip to New Zealand, remember that the fishing scene there is not only for the rich. True, prices for the top lodges are high. But don't let that deter you: Many anglers—locals and visitors alike—cannot afford such places either, but they still manage to catch plenty of trout. Lots of great trout streams can be reached by four-wheel-drive vehicle or on foot over New Zealand's extensive network of wilderness trails.

For general travel information and advice, contact the **New Zealand Tourism Board** (*800-388-5494. www.new-zealand2000.com*). A complete list of the country's fishing guides and lodges appears in the *New Zealand Outside Directory*, which you can order for $20 (NZ) from **New Zealand Outside Ltd.** (*01164-3326-7516. www.outside.nz.com*).

MAURITIUS
Exotic Marlin Magnet

Few North American anglers ever make the long trip to Mauritius, which is located in the Indian Ocean about 1,800 miles off the east coast of Africa. The same cannot be said of the record-setting billfish that regularly ply the waters around this tropical island. Here you will find large populations of swordfish, tuna, and black marlin, as well as the blue marlin for which Mauritius is renowned.

Blues caught off the coast of Mauritius have always ranked among the largest of the world's billfish. For anglers keen to pit their wits against these great sport fish, you won't find a better place to hook a marlin of a thousand pounds or more.

Because Mauritius is a mid-ocean volcanic seamount, deep water and big game fish are never more than a short boat ride from shore. Nor are the tuna, dorado, and several species of shark that live in the island's fish-rich waters year-round. With quick runs to the blue water, anglers don't have to wait long for the action to start.

The best times for billfishing in Mauritius are the spring and summer months. Year-round water and air temperatures are very comfortable—both usually in the mid-80s (though the summer months can be humid).

Competitive sportfishing enthusiasts should consider visiting Mauritius at the time of the **Marlin World Cup.** Held each December during peak marlin season, the World Cup attracts a large international field of anglers and is one of the top sportfishing tournaments in the world.

Most participants during the five-day competition hook at least a 500-pound blue, and on occasion some have recorded a Mauritian Grand Slam: a black marlin, a blue marlin, a sailfish, and a short-bill spearfish. Winning teams and individuals receive cash prizes, in addition to airfare and accommodations for return trips to the island.

Mauritius may be remote, but that doesn't mean visitors have to settle for rustic accommodations. There are many large luxury resorts on the island, most of which offer fishing charters or special sportfishing packages. Luxury hotels range from $175 to $225 per person per night. Large charter boats cost between $750 and $1,200 per day.

For those who make the journey, Mauritius is well worth the effort. In addition to world-class fishing, it boasts spectacular beaches and exciting nightlife and casinos. English is the official language on the island—which is part of the British Commonwealth—though French and Creole are also common. The island's eclectic mix of Indians, Africans, and Europeans produces a remarkable blend of cultures that is apparent in its architecture, food, and art.

For package vacations in Mauritius, contact **Rod & Reel Adventures** (*Copperopolis, CA. 800-356-6982 or 209-785-0444. www.rodreeladventures.com*). For information about the Marlin World Cup, airfare, and accommodations, contact **Air Mauritius** (*800-537-1182 or 201-871-8382. www.airmauritiususa.com*).

HOOKING A BLUE MARLIN

Go Fish!

This collection of saltwater fishing destinations has a strong foreign emphasis because the best big game fishing is found in the tropics—where warm waters and abundant bait fish attract the big species—and because fewer anglers tend to compete for the fish in foreign waters. The freshwater destinations that follow are closer to home.

UNITED STATES

ALASKA

DESTINATION: **Cook Inlet/Deep Creek**

GAME FISH & SEASONS: Jumbo king salmon (*mid-May-July*); giant halibut to 200 pounds.

LODGES & CHARTERS: Alaskan Adventure Fishing Charters (*800-438-6257. www.alaskanadventures.com*), Alaskan Experience (*Anchorage. 800-777-7055 or 907-789-5977. www.alaskanexp.com*), Chihuly's Charters (*Ninilchik. 907-567-3374. www.ptialaska.net/~chihuly/*).

COST: $135-150 per person per day for guided trips, including boats and equipment, at Alaska Halibut Fishing (*Homer. 800-438-6257. www.alaskahalibutfishing.com*). Lodgings at Alaskan Experience run to about $500 per night. Alaskan Adventure Fishing Charters books trips in three other area lodges.

FISHING HIGHLIGHTS: King salmon and halibut fishing on the same trip. Kenai kings to 80 pounds are caught every season.

CALIFORNIA

DESTINATION: **San Diego to Baja**

GAME FISH & SEASON: April through September for albacore, yellowtail, yellowfin tuna, bluefin tuna, and dorado. Spring is best for yellowtail; tuna peaks late summer.

LODGES & CHARTERS: Point Loma Sportfishing (*619-223-1627. www.pointlomasportfishing.com*), Fisherman's Landing (*619-221-8500. www.fishermanslanding.com*).

COST: $75-160 per day for overnights; half days start at $25.

FISHING HIGHLIGHTS: Most fishing is in Mexican waters. Productive 10- to 20-day trips to Mexico's southern islands.

FLORIDA

DESTINATION: **Key West**

GAME FISH & SEASON: Sailfish, black and blue marlin (*Sept.-Nov.*); grouper, kingfish, yellowtail (*Dec.-Jan.*); snapper (*spring*).

TOP CHARTERS: Oceanside Marina (*305-294-4676, ext. 709*), Captain Jim Sharpe (*800-238-1746 or 305-745-1530*).

COST: $450-650 per day for deep-sea fishing.

FISHING HIGHLIGHTS: Mid-September to early November good for blue marlin, winter for kingfish.

HAWAII

DESTINATION: **Kona Coast**

GAME FISH & SEASON: Striped and blue marlin, yellowfin tuna, wahoo, dorado, mahimahi, amberjack; summer is best.

CHARTER: Kona Charter Skippers Assoc. (*800-762-7546 or 808-329-3600. www.konabiggamefishing.com*).

COST: $625 per boat per full day, $416 per half day (40-foot Bertram or Hatteras).

FISHING HIGHLIGHTS: Blue marlin average 150 to 300 pounds; yellowfin tuna and mahimahi are strong at South Point. Kona hosts an International Billfish Tournament each August.

NORTH CAROLINA

DESTINATION: **Hatteras**

GAME FISH & SEASON: Mahimahi (*April-Nov.*), white and blue marlin (*June-July*), yellowfin tuna (*April-May*), wahoo, king mackerel (*March-June, late Sept.-Dec.*).

CHARTERS: Tuna Duck (*252-986-2257. www.tunaduck.com*), Hatteras Marina (*252-986-2166. www.hatterasharbor.com*).

COST: $650-950 per day for boat with six anglers. Winter is the best time for giant tuna expeditions, which run about $1,000.

FISHING HIGHLIGHTS: Productive fishing grounds for mahimahi, wahoo, and tuna. On a good day you can raise 20 tuna and more than 60 mahimahi. Only an hour from the Continental Shelf.

VIRGIN ISLANDS

DESTINATION: **St. Thomas**

GAME FISH & SEASON: Blue marlin (*July-Oct.*); white marlin, mahimahi, bonefish.

LODGE & CHARTER: Cruise and Gold. Accommodations at Sapphire Beach Marina. Contact Fishing International (*800-950-4242 or 707-542-4242. www.fishinginternational.com*).

COST: $1,100-1,200 per day for boat (36-foot Hatteras and other American sportfishers) and skipper. $2,500-4,200 per week for fishing and lodging package.

FISHING HIGHLIGHTS: Surprisingly productive billfish grounds. Good boats average four to ten billfish shots per day. The fishing grounds are a mere 45 minutes from port, and the shoreside amenities will keep non-angling travel partners happy.

INTERNATIONAL

AUSTRALIA

DESTINATION: **Cairns, Queensland**

GAME FISH & SEASON: Marlin and sailfish (*Aug.-Jan.*); wahoo, tuna, dorado, mackerel (*year-round*); trevally, barracuda, queenfish.

CHARTERS: Capt. Calvin Tilly—contact Frontiers (*800-245-1950 or 724-935-1577. www.frontierstrvl.com*); Capts. Bobby Jones and Frank Thompson—contact Fishing International (*800-950-4242 or 707-542-4242. www.fishinginternational.com*).

COST: $2,250 per day for deluxe four-person live-aboard; light-tackle fishing for smaller billfish averages $1,100 per day for boat and skipper.

FISHING HIGHLIGHTS: Small black marlin from 40 to 250 pounds are found inshore most of the season. But if you want to catch 1,000-pound trophy blacks, go late September through early December and count on spending some time at sea.

BAHAMAS

DESTINATION: **Andros Island**

GAME FISH & SEASON: Bonefish (*Nov.-July*), tarpon, permit, barracuda, shark. Late spring and summer are best because winter cold fronts can take fish off the flats and obscure water visibility.

LODGES: Andros Island Bonefish Club (best fishing)—contact World Wide Sportsman (*800-327-2880 or 305-664-4615. www.outdoorworld.com*); Kemps Bay Club (best lodging)—contact Fishing International (*800-950-4242 or 707-542-4242. www.fishinginternational.com*).

COST: $2,200 for six days fishing with shared guide; $1,900 for five days fishing (based on double occupancy).

FISHING HIGHLIGHTS: Andros is the best spot in the eastern Caribbean for large bonefish. There are also 50- to 100-pound tarpon. Both major clubs feature excellent rooms, guides, and equipment.

BELIZE

DESTINATION: **Manta Reef, Barrier Reef**

GAME FISH & SEASON: Bonefish and permit in 80-square-mile lagoon (*Nov.-July*); barracuda, snapper on reefs; tuna, marlin, and sailfish offshore; tarpon at Barrier Reef.

LODGES: For bonefish, Manta Reef Resort (*800-342-0053*) and Turneffe Flats

(contact *World Wide Sportsman. 800-327-2880 or 305-664-4615. www.outdoorworld.com*); for bonefish and tarpon, El Pescador on Ambergris Cay (*Fishing International or Frontiers*).

COST: El Pescador, Manta Reef, and Turneffe Flats cost $1,850 per week (six days fishing, shared guide).

FISHING HIGHLIGHTS: Some of the best bonefishing in the Caribbean—both at Manta Reef and Turneffe Flats. Manta's vast shallow lagoon is a casting delight, and 20 strikes in an afternoon are common. The shallow-water tarpon fishing at Ambergris Cay is also excellent.

BRAZIL

DESTINATION: **Victoria (north of Rio de Janeiro)**

GAME FISH & SEASON: White and blue marlin (*Dec.-April*); Atlantic sailfish, dorado, yellowfin tuna (*Sept.-Feb.*).

LODGES: Three- to five-star hotels. Book through Rod & Reel Adventures (*800-356-6982 or 209-785-0444. www.rodreeladventures.com*).

COST: Deluxe hotels start at $200 a night. World-class boats in the 40-foot to 48-foot range are between $1,100 and $1,500 per day.

FISHING HIGHLIGHTS: Uncrowded and prolific marlin fishing, if trip is planned at the correct season. The marlin are extremely large, with yearly catches in excess of 1,000 pounds.

COSTA RICA

DESTINATION: **Gulf of Papagayo**

GAME FISH & SEASON: Blue and black marlin (*April-Nov.*); dorado, yellowfin, roosterfish, snapper (*year-round*).

LODGES: Bahía Pez Vela—contact World Wide Sportsman (*800-327-2880 or 305-664-4615. www.outdoorworld.com*); Tamarindo—contact Fishing International (*800-950-4242 or 707-542-4242. www.fishinginternational.com*).

COST: Pez Vela runs from $1,900-3,000 per week; a charter typically costs $450-850 depending on boat size.

FISHING HIGHLIGHTS: The Gulf of Papagayo may offer the best billfishing in the world. Ten to thirty billfish shots per day and multiple hookups happen regularly. Crack crews operate large, high-performance sportfishers. The resorts rank among Costa Rica's most deluxe.

DESTINATION: **Quepos**

GAME FISH & SEASON: Sailfish, dorado, wahoo, mackerel, tuna, and roosterfish (*Jan.-May*).

LODGES & CHARTERS: La Mariposa is the best hotel. There are many world-class, twin-engine sportfishers with experienced crews. World Wide Sportsman acts as agent for a number of boats in Quepos.

COST: $1,060-1,320 per person for three days fishing with four anglers, depending on size of boat. $550-1,200 per day for top boat and skipper.

FISHING HIGHLIGHTS: Quepos offers prime sailfishing. Raising 10 to 15 sails per day per boat is common. Dorado are plentiful as well, but Americans come for the billfish, which never disappoint. Though prices in Quepos are rising, they remain on the low end of Costa Rica's top fishing areas.

KENYA

DESTINATION: **Malindi (north of Mombasa)**

GAME FISH & SEASON: Striped, black, and blue marlin, sailfish (*fall*), bonefish, tarpon.

LODGE: Hemingway's Resort. Book through Rod & Reel Adventures (*800-356-6982 or 209-785-0444. www.rodreeladventures.com*).

COST: $2,600-3,000 for four nights, three days, including accommodations, food, boats, and guides.

FISHING HIGHLIGHTS: In terms of billfish size and numbers, Kenya is similar to Hawaii and Cairns. All the deep-sea fishing is done out of Hemingway's—a first-class, modern beachfront resort with excellent service and amenities.

MAURITIUS

DESTINATION: **Mauritius**

GAME FISH & SEASON: Blue and black marlin (*Oct.-April*); wahoo (*Sept.-Jan.*); mako, hammerhead, and blue sharks (*Aug.-Sept.*); skipjack tuna (*March-May*); yellowfin tuna and dorado (*year-round*).

IN COLORADO, THREE GENERATIONS, THREE POLES, ONE DOG

TOP LODGES & CHARTERS: La Pirogue Hotel, Club Santre de Peche, and the Meridien Paradise hotels all book fishing charters. Contact Rod & Reel Adventures (800-356-6982).

COST: $150-200 a night for hotels and $750-1,200 a day for boats ranging from 30 to 43 feet.

FISHING HIGHLIGHTS: December billfish tournament attracts top crews. Mauritius has large populations of marlin, swordfish, and tuna. A 50-minute run gets you to deep water and big game fish.

MEXICO

DESTINATION: **Ascension Bay, Yucatán**

GAME FISH & SEASON: Bonefish and barracuda year-round; permit (if you're lucky); tarpon at Casa Blanca.

LODGES: Pesca Maya Lodge and Casa Blanca Lodge; contact Fishing International (*800-950-4242 or 707-542-4242. www. fishinginternational.com*) or The Fly Shop (*Redding. 800-669-3474 or 916-222-3555. www.theflyshop.com*).

COST: Pesca Maya is $2,000-2,350 per week (high season), Casa Blanca $2,200-3,100 per week, including transportation from Cancun.

FISHING HIGHLIGHTS: The opulent Pesca Maya Lodge, near Cancun, is a superb bonefish and permit destination rivaling any

fishery in the world. Head to the Casa Blanca for equal luxury and deluxe cuisine. Both are quality American-run lodges for serious anglers. Try nearby Boca Paila or Pez Maya for outstanding saltwater fly-fishing for bonefish and tarpon.

DESTINATION: **Cancun, Yucatán**

GAME FISH & SEASON: Offshore—mackerel, Atlantic sailfish, dorado, blue and white marlin, yellowfin tuna, swordfish, wahoo, and sharks (*April-July*). Inner waters—tarpon, snook, bonefish, and permit (*March-June*).

LODGES: Melia Cancun Hotel—contact Fishing International.

COST: $200-250 per night. Fishing is $355 per day (three-day minimum) for flats fishing with guide.

FISHING HIGHLIGHTS: White marlin are prolific in this part of Mexico, and the wide variety of shallow-water fish guarantee light-tackle fun. A family-oriented area, Cancun also offers safe beaches and good shopping.

DESTINATION: **Loreto, Baja**

GAME FISH & SEASON: Dorado, Spanish mackerel, roosterfish (*year-round*).

LODGES & CHARTERS: Baja Fishing Adventures (*800-458-3688*); Corporate Adventures (*800-875-4114. www. corporateadventures.com*). Corporate Adventures specializes in VIP groups, and

can organize a tournament for just six to eight people .

COST: Hotel and air packages from Los Angeles start at $500. Customized trips are also available. Contact South Fishing (*800-882-4665 or 305-279-3252. www. southfishing.com*).

FISHING HIGHLIGHTS: The best fishing value around. Wild dorado runs in July. Nearby islands are rich fisheries.

NEW ZEALAND

DESTINATION: **Bay of Islands/Whitianga, North Island**

GAME FISH & SEASON: Striped, black, and blue marlin (*Jan.-April*); shark, kingfish, yellowtail (*Oct.-May*); yellowfin tuna (*Dec.-May*); mahimahi, wahoo (*Jan.-March*).

CHARTERS: Harlequin, Tagit, Triple-B—all based out of Bay of Islands. Book through Pacific Promotions (*01164-9402-8336. www.fishingpro.co.nz*).

COST: $440-1,000 (US) per day for full-boat charter of 32-foot to 45-foot sportfisher, dawn to dusk, all gear and tackle provided. A 44-foot Tagi costs around $900 (US) per day for live-aboard cruising and fishing, including all meals for up to four guests.

FISHING HIGHLIGHTS: All world records for striped marlin were set here. New Zealand's large game-fish grounds include 300 miles of the North Island's northeast coast, an unspoiled area of great beauty.

VENEZUELA

DESTINATION: **Los Roques Archipelago**

GAME FISH & SEASON: Bonefish, tarpon, barracuda, pompano, mackerel. Avoid November to March (high winds and unpredictable water levels).

LODGES: Pez Raton Lodge, Macabi Lodge on El Gran Roque—contact Frontiers (800-245-1950) or The Fly Shop (800-669-3474).

COST: $2,400 for seven nights, six days fishing; $1,600-1,700 for four nights, three days fishing.

FISHING HIGHLIGHTS: Los Roques may well offer the Caribbean's best flats fishing. Forty-eight islands create a huge area of flats harboring three- to seven-pound bonefish that school by the hundreds.

DESTINATION: **Rio Chico**

GAME FISH & SEASON: Tarpon (*Aug.-Dec.*), snook, white marlin (*fall*).

LODGE: Rio Chico Tarpon Club—contact South Fishing (*800-882-4665 or 305-279-3252. www.southfishing.com*) or Fishing International (*800-950-4242 or 707-542-4242. www.fishinginternational. com*).

COST: $1,500-1,650 for five days of fishing.

FISHING HIGHLIGHTS: Spectacular tarpon fishing—expect between 20 and 50 strikes per day, 10 percent of them 10 to 30 pounds in size. Fish tarpon in the mangroves one day, then try your hand at the blue and white marlin fishing offshore.

Freshwater Fishing

UNITED STATES

ALASKA

LOCATION: **Iliamna Lake**

ACCESS: Fly-in from Anchorage.

GAME FISH & SEASONS: Sockeye, king, and humpback salmon (*June-Aug.*), rainbow of over 5 pounds common (*June and Sept. best*).

LODGES & GUIDES: Valhalla Lodge (*907-243-6096*) is between Iliamna Lake and Lake Clark; for Wildman Lake Lodge, book through Alaskan Experience (*800-777-7055 or 907-276-5425. www. alaskanexp.com*).

COST: $5,000 per week, including all meals, fly-outs, and river jetboats; guided one-day float trips are around $200 per day for two anglers. Wildman Lake Lodge costs $3,750 per week with daily fly-outs, or $2,450 per week with guided jetboat river trips.

FISHING HIGHLIGHTS: This is prime salmon country. The summer sockeye run brings 50-pound jumbos. Fly-outs and float trips are included in many of the lodge deals.

LOCATION: **Katmai Wilderness**

ACCESS: Fly-in from Anchorage to King Salmon.

GAME FISH & SEASONS: Sockeye, king salmon (*July-Sept.*), grayling, Dolly Varden, and rainbow trout (*May-June, Sept.-Oct.*).

LODGES & GUIDES: For Brooks Lodge, Grosvenor Lodge, and Kulik Lodge, contact Katmailand, Inc. (*Anchorage, AK. 800-544-0551 or 907-243-5448. www.katmailand. com*).

COST: $1,800-3,500 per week (low-price basic cabins, no fly-outs).

FISHING HIGHLIGHTS: The Katmai region boasts some of Alaska's most renowned lodges and most of its best guides. Count on a massive sockeye run every year.

CALIFORNIA

LOCATION: **Fall River**

ACCESS: Fall River Mills, CA.

GAME FISH & SEASONS: Rainbow, some browns (*April-Nov.*).

LODGES & GUIDES: Contact The Fly Shop (*Redding, CA. 800-669-3474 or 916-222-3555. www.theflyshop.com*).

COST: $1,200 per week—consult The Fly Shop; guide and boat $285 per day for two anglers.

FISHING HIGHLIGHTS: Wild trophy trout up to five pounds, barbless or artificial lure only; excellent fishing on nearby Hat Creek and McCloud River.

COLORADO

LOCATION: **Roaring Fork River**

ACCESS: Drive from Basalt, CO.

GAME FISH & SEASONS: Rainbow, brown, and brook trout (*July-Aug.*).

LODGES & GUIDES: Contact Frying Pan Anglers (*Basalt, CO. 970-927-3441. www.fryingpananglers.com*).

COST: $325 per day float, $265 per day wade trip with guide, two anglers.

FISHING HIGHLIGHTS: Probably the most productive trout stream in Colorado. Good fishing in nearby Frying Pan River and alpine streams.

IDAHO

LOCATION: **Main Salmon River**

ACCESS: Plane from Boise to town of Salmon, then a 70-mile bus trip to the wilderness area.

GAME FISH & SEASONS: Steelhead (*spring and fall*), cutthroat, bull, and rainbow trout (*summer*).

LODGES & GUIDES: Silver Cloud Expeditions (*Salmon, ID. 877-756-6215 or 208-756-6215. www.silvercloudexp.com*).

COST: $1,500 for five days of steelhead fishing (less in summer). Includes airfare from Boise to Salmon, food, deluxe camping, equipment, and guides.

FISHING HIGHLIGHTS: A unique experience with some of the biggest steelhead in the U.S. (8 to 12 pounds on average). You raft an 80-mile stretch of the Salmon, running through the second deepest canyon in North America. Spectacular scenery and wildlife.

MICHIGAN

LOCATION: **Au Sable River**

ACCESS: Drive from Grayling, MI.

GAME FISH & SEASONS: Rainbow and brown trout (*April-Oct.*).

LODGES & GUIDES: Gates Au Sable Lodge (*Grayling, MI. 517-348-8462. www.gateslodge.com*).

FISHING HIGHLIGHTS: Michigan's best trout fishing.

COST: About $1,500 per week all-inclusive with guide.

NEW MEXICO

LOCATION: **San Juan River**

ACCESS: A 20-mile stretch near Navajo Dam, NM.

GAME FISH & SEASONS: Rainbow and brown trout, 19 inches and 4 to 7 pounds average (*Aug.-Nov. best*).

LODGES & GUIDES: Contact San Juan Troutfitters (*Farmington, NM. 505-326-3454*), Abe's Fly Shop (*Navajo Dam, NM. 505-632-2194. www.sanjuanriver.com*).

COST: $45-75 per night, motel only; $275 per day for guided trips (for two anglers). San Juan Troutfitters: $250 per day for wading trip with two anglers, $285 for float trip with one or two anglers and a guide.

FISHING HIGHLIGHTS: Abundant, big trout. Some consider the San Juan to be the best trout stream in the western U.S.—catching ten five-pounders in a day is not uncommon. Three miles of expert trophy waters require barbless hooks and artificial lures; only one "keeper" (of 20 inches or bigger) allowed per day.

OREGON

LOCATION: **Deschutes River**

ACCESS: Warm Springs to Maupin, OR.

GAME FISH & SEASONS: Steelhead fishing year round, catch-and-release on wild fish. Rainbows on the upper river (*May to June*); steelheads on lower river (*Aug.-Sept., Dec.-Jan.*).

LODGES & GUIDES: Contact High Desert Drifters Guides (*Bend, OR. 800-685-3474 or 541-389-0607. www. deschutesflyfishing.com*).

COST: Guide and drift boat are $300 per day for two anglers. The Fly Fishing Shop (*Welches, CO. 800-266-3971 or 503-622-4607. www.flyfishusa.com*) boats the whole lower 100 miles of the Deschutes River. Two people pay $500 per day, which includes gear, guide, and food.

FISHING HIGHLIGHTS: Summer and winter runs of trophy native rainbows.

LOCATION: **Sandy River**

ACCESS: Dodge Park to Oxbow Park (float); Marmot Dam (walk-in).

GAME FISH & SEASONS: Splendid steelhead fishing year-round with catch-and-release for wild fish.

LODGES & GUIDES: Contact The Fly Fishing Shop (800-266-3971).

COST: Guide and drift boat are $350 per day for two anglers. Walking trips run $25 an hour with a four-hour minimum.

FISHING HIGHLIGHTS: The state's oldest scenic waterway, the Sandy ranks among the top three most productive steelhead rivers in the Northwest.

PENNSYLVANIA

LOCATION: **Fishing Creek**

ACCESS: Start at Benton and work up to Grassmere Park.

GAME FISH & SEASONS: Brown and rainbow trout (*late May-June*).

LODGES & GUIDES: Contact Fishing Creek Angler (*Benton, PA. 570-925-2709. www.fishingcreekangler.com*).

COST: Wade trip with guide runs $150 for one angler, $225 for two.

FISHING HIGHLIGHTS: Fishing Creek wasn't named by accident. This is one of the most productive trout streams in the eastern United States.

WASHINGTON

LOCATION: **Quinalt River**

ACCESS: Go upstream from the Graves Creek Campground along the Quinalt and tributaries.

GAME FISH & SEASONS: Famed for large winter steelheads; summers offer Dolly Varden and cutthroat trout.

LODGES & GUIDES: No riverside lodges. The lower river from the ocean to Quinalt Lake is reserved for the Quinalt Indian Tribe; hire a registered tribal guide from Quinalt Guide Services (*Amanda Park, WA. 360-288-2513*).

COST: Typical guide charges are $125-150 per person, two person minimum.

FISHING HIGHLIGHTS: Catch salmon and trout in the same day.

WYOMING

LOCATION: **Green River and Upper Snake River**

ACCESS: Jackson, WY.

GAME FISH & SEASONS: Rainbow and brown trout on the Green River in August. Cutthroat on the Upper Snake in late summer and early fall.

LODGES & GUIDES: Contact High Country Flies (*Jackson Hole, WY. 877-732-7210 or 307-733-7210. www.highcountryflies.com*).

COST: Guides charge $325 per day for one or two anglers.

FISHING HIGHLIGHTS: The Green is one of Wyoming's finest trout streams. Fish Pinedale to La Barge and below Fontenelle Reservoir. Fishing is also good on the nearby Salt, Black Fork, and Hams Fork Rivers.

CANADA

ALBERTA

LOCATION: **Amethyst Lake, Moat Lake, Tonquin Valley, Jasper National Park**

ACCESS: 250 miles from Calgary; drive to Jasper, then cover 14 miles by horse.

GAME FISH & SEASONS: Rainbow and brown trout (*July-Sept.*).

LODGES & GUIDES: Contact Tonquin Valley Pack and Ski Trips (*Jasper, Alberta. 780-852-3909. www.tonquinvalley.com*).

COST: A five-day trip runs about $650 (US), including food, guide, and horse-pack services.

FISHING HIGHLIGHTS: A little-known spot, Amethyst boasts some of the best alpine fly-fishing in Canada. Rainbows run to ten pounds, brook trout to three to four pounds. Raising 50 catch-and-release in an afternoon is not uncommon.

LOCATION: **Bow River**

ACCESS: Drive from Calgary.

GAME FISH & SEASON: Rainbows and brown trout (*May, July, Sept.*). Late October is good for browns. Catch-and-release.

LODGES & GUIDES: Contact Great Waters (*403-256-3090. E-mail: andreasen@tucanada.org*).

COST: Great Waters—$320 (US) for two people for one day. Overnight trips on custom basis only. Prices on request.

FISHING HIGHLIGHTS: The Bow may offer the finest dry fly-fishing for rising rainbows in North America; 16- to 18-inchers are abundant. The river is placid and easily floated in 14-foot John boats.

QUEBEC

LOCATION: **George River/Helen's Falls**

ACCESS: Fly from Montreal to Kuujjuaq; Helen's Falls is 40 miles upriver. Guests go by van to the log cabin near the falls.

GAME FISH & SEASONS: Brook, char, and lake trout (*July-Aug.*), Atlantic salmon (*Aug.-Sept.*).

LODGES & GUIDES: Contact Ungava Adventures (*Pointe-Claire, Quebec. 514-694-4424*). Pioneer Ungava Bay Outfitters (*Kuujjuaq, Quebec. 819-964-2761*).

COST: Ungava Adventures—$2,300-5,300 (US) per week. Pioneer Ungava Bay Outfitters—$2,600 (US) per week for both trout and salmon, $2,200 for just salmon; either option includes food, lodging, boats, and guides.

FISHING HIGHLIGHTS: Fantastic August Atlantic salmon runs yield 15- to 20-pound fish in great numbers. Remote site means little competition. Bring spinning tackle in July.

OTHER INTERNATIONAL DESTINATIONS

IRELAND

LOCATION: **Counties Sligo and Mayo**

ACCESS: Northwest from Dublin or north from Shannon Airport.

GAME FISH & SEASONS: Brown trout, sea trout, salmon. Fly-, lure-, or bait-fishing is permitted.

LODGES & GUIDES: Gillaroo Lodge in Sligo Town offers quality and value: $130 per day includes all meals, licenses, guide, and even instruction. This area boasts access to Loch Melvin, Loch Assaroe, and Loch Erne, as well as many hill lochs, as the Irish call their lakes. Combine this with salmon fishing on the nearby River Drowes, River Duff, and River Eany. Visit Mount Falcon Castle in Mayo. The nearby River Moy hosts Ireland's most prolific Atlantic salmon run. Book either lodge through Fishing International (*800-950-4242 or 707-542-4242. www.fishinginternational.com*).

COST: Six nights at Mount Falcon is $2,500 per person. This includes guided fishing, breakfast, and dinner.

NOTE: Most Americans underestimate the quality of fishing in Europe. France boasts chalk streams equal to those of Britain; there is good trout fishing in Austria, the Pyrenees, and the Julian Alps; and the salmon fishing in Iceland, Norway, and Russia is world class. All of these European destinations, plus Scotland (salmon, sea trout, and trout), are served by agencies such as Fishing International.

ANGLING TOUR AGENCIES

The following agencies all offer package holidays at North America's major fishing centers, as well as tours to angling venues around the world. Listed for each agency are the major destinations served.

Angler Adventures (*800-628-1447 or 860-434-9624. www.angleradventures.com*). Freshwater: Alaska, Canada, Montana, New Zealand, Russia. Saltwater: Bahamas, Belize, Brazil, Christmas Island, Costa Rica, Guatemala, Mexico, Venezuela.

Fishing International (*800-950-4242 or 707-542-4242. www. fishinginternational.com*). Freshwater: Canada, Central and South America, Europe, New Zealand, United States. Saltwater: Australia, Bahamas, Belize, Canada, Christmas Island, Costa Rica, Mexico, Venezuela.

Frontiers (*800-245-1950 or 724-935-1577. www.frontierstrvl.com*). Freshwater: Australia, Argentina, Chile, England, New Zealand, Russia. Saltwater: Australia,

Brazil, Christmas Island, Iceland, Mexico, Puerto Rico, Venezuela.

Kaufmann's Streamborn Fly Shop *(800-442-4359 or 503-639-6400. www.kman.com).* Freshwater: Argentina, Canada, Chile, New Zealand, Russia, United States (Alaska, Idaho, Montana, Oregon, and Washington). Saltwater: Bahamas, Belize, Bikini Atoll, Christmas Island, Mexico, Seychelles, Venezuela.

Rod & Reel Adventures *(800-356-6982 or 209-785-0444. www.rodreeladventures. com).* Freshwater and Saltwater: Argentina, Australia, Belize, Brazil, Canada, Chile, Costa Rica, England, Honduras, Ireland, Mexico, New Zealand, Panama, Scotland, United States, Venezuela.

South Fishing *(800-882-4665 or 305-279-3252. www.southfishing.com).* Saltwater: Australia, Bahamas, Belize, Bermuda, Brazil, Costa Rica, Guatemala, Hawaii, Honduras, Mexico, Panama, South Pacific, Venezuela, Virgin Islands.

ONLINE

Anglers Online
www.streamside.com

This popular site features active chat forums, product reviews, a list of outfitters, tackle and travel services, and angling links. Upload your own trophy shot to the online gallery.

FisherNet
www.thefishernet.com

FisherNet features original articles on all aspects of sportfishing, a large outfitter directory, and a handy database with game-fish tables, weather information, and fishing license information for the United States and Canada.

Fly & Field
www.flyfield.com

Sponsored by Chicago's Fly & Field store, this site offers fly-tying techniques, tools, and materials, plus useful tips for anglers.

Flyfish.com
www.flyfish.com

Flyfish.com provides tackle reviews, hatch and weather reports, and comprehensive listings of gear suppliers, flyshops, charters, and guide services throughout North America.

Virtual Flyshop
www.flyshop.com

This well-designed and authoritative site

features technical articles, outfitter listings, and an excellent "Riverkeeper" destination guide that profiles fishing waters around the world.

BOOKS

Alpine Angler: Fly Fisher's Guide to the Western Wilderness by John Shewey (Frank Amato Publications. $24.95). Here's all you need to know about alpine lake trout, including their feeding habits and how to access the best lakes in the West. *(800-541-9498. www.amatobooks.com.)*

Fly Fishing in Saltwater by Lefty Kreh (Lyons Press. $27.95). One of the world's leading anglers shares his knowledge of the best angling techniques for particular saltwater species. *(212-697-3133.)*

Montana Angling Guide, $29.95, *Wyoming Angling Guide*, $27.95, and *Colorado Angling Guide*, $27.95, by Chuck Fothergill and Bob Sterling. They provide detailed profiles and maps of all the prime fishing spots in these three states. Order from Stream Stalker Publishing Company *(970-923-4552).*

Orvis Fly Fishing Guide by Tom Rosenbauer (Lyons Press. $17.95). This popular work is the how-to bible on fly-fishing for beginners and intermediate anglers. *(212-697-3133.)*

MAGAZINES

American Angler, Fly Tyer, and *Saltwater Fly Fishing* are quality journals packed with good advice on the best tackle, flies, and fishing holes. All three magazines are produced by Abenaki Publishers *(802-447-1518. www.flyfishmags.com).*

Fly Fisherman (800-829-3340), the leading fly-fishing monthly, offers good destination reports and photos. *Marlin (800-879-0483)* profiles bill-fishing spots around the world, with angling advice from leading sportsmen. *Sport Fishing (800-879-0496)* concentrates on big game salt-water angling. All three journals are produced by Primedia Publications *(www.cowles.com).*

Fly Rod & Reel (207-594-9544). Published six times a year, this handsome publication covers equipment, destinations, and casting techniques.

VIDEOS

Gary Borger *(800-567-4279. www.garyborger.com.)* offers an excellent series of videos on fly-fishing, including *The Fabulous Bighorn with Gary Borger* and *South Island Sampler*, the latter a 56-minute video on spotting, stalking, and landing trophy New Zealand trout.

CUTTING UP THE SPOILS AT THE KENAI AND RUSSIAN RIVERS, ALASKA

POWERED FLIGHT IS LARGELY UTILITARIAN—

GETTING FROM POINT A TO POINT B. "FREEFLIGHT"—

paragliding, hang gliding, and soaring—is a different kind of experience: The means *is* the end. The very challenge associated with gliding (as all three pursuits are also known) captures our imagination and stirs our sense of adventure. • Boosted by new technology and lighter, faster, better-flying craft, the popularity of paragliding, hang gliding, and soaring grows steadily every year. Though still considered somewhat elite sports—they require considerable training and skill—paragliding, hang gliding, and soaring offer participants an exhilaration that few other activities can match. • In this chapter, you'll find out how to get started in all three freeflight disciplines. In addition to telling you how to go about earning your pilot's license, the text explains how to compare the top training centers for paragliding, hang gliding, and soaring in North America. So until you strap on your harness, sit back, enjoy the armchair ride—and let your imagination take flight.

LEFT:HANG GLIDING ABOVE THE FORESTS OF THE SAN JUAN MOUN-
TAINS NEAR TELLURIDE, COLORADO. BELOW: GLIDER SOARING
OVER BALD EAGLE RIDGE IN PENNSYLVANIA.

Paragliding

Hang gliding

Soaring

Paragliding is the nearest thing to flying without wings this side of an out-of-body experience.
RICHARD BACH

Paragliding: Breaking the Bonds of Gravity

Standing on the crown of a 1,000-foot-high dormant volcano, you look at the desert floor far below. With a quiet prayer, you propel yourself down the slope, straining against the 250-square-foot nylon wing billowing up behind you. Suddenly, the wing comes to life, hauling you airborne. Free of the bonds of gravity, you glide outward into the void, rising aloft on the warm desert winds.

Welcome to the world of **paragliding.** Flying from ridge or mountaintop with a foot-launched canopy, or "wing," has emerged as one of the world's hottest adventure sports. It is also the simplest way to fly. Less expensive than hang gliding—and much easier to learn—paragliding offers beginners a simple attraction: the prospect of flying on the very first day of taking up the sport.

If you're new to paragliding, a **tandem flight** is the way to start. Accompanied by a trained instructor flying alongside you on the same wing, you can immediately experience the thrill of this aerial sport. The learning process is fast: After just a few hours of orientation, you will be able to make short flights on your own. After a couple of weekends, you'll be flying moderate hills, gradually working your way up to greater distances and climbing to higher altitudes.

You can get your basic paragliding pilot's rating for approximately $800 to $1,000, typically after just four or five weekends of flying. By contrast, most hang-glider pilots spend many months, and considerably more money, to complete their training.

Paragliding gear is compact and light. There is no large rig to assemble, and you don't need a car to reach your launch site. In the European Alps, where the sport is particularly popular, many fliers simply carry their 15 or so pounds of equipment in a backpack and hop on a cable car to reach their takeoff point.

TAKING FLIGHT

A paragliding flight begins with reassuring terra firma beneath your feet—ideally, a smooth, grassy slope. The first task is to deploy your canopy on the ground behind you, facing into the prevailing wind. Next, check that the **canopy lines** are straight. Hoisting the lines above your head, you are ready to go.

Now you must summon all your energy to inflate the canopy—and propel yourself into the air. One deep breath, and you begin running down the slope to inflate the **scoops** that open in the canopy's leading edge and taper to a close toward the rear. As air fills the canopy, you keep running, as hard as you can, until you feel your weight lift off your toes.

To the casual observer, it can all look a little awkward—and often it is. Much depends on the action of the wind, the paraglider's invisible hazard. With no wind, it is difficult to inflate the canopy into its recognizable wing shape. If the wind is too strong, the canopy assumes a mind of its own: It can rotate backward, turning a launch into a running tug-of-war; or it can veer violently off to one side, sometimes dragging the pilot embarrassingly—and painfully—along the slope.

But wind is also the paraglider's best friend. Given the right breeze—a steady, 5 to 10 mile per hour headwind—an experienced pilot can inflate the canopy in seconds with a few well-timed tugs of the canopy lines. As long as the wing remains centered overhead, the pilot can be airborne within a few yards of the starting point.

Once in the air, the pilot controls the flight by steering the wing. For this purpose, the wing is equipped with two **brake lines,** which are attached to the canopy lines and run either side of the pilot's harness. The pilot pulls down on the left brake line to turn left and on the right brake line to turn right. To descend, and ultimately to land, the pilot pulls on both brake lines together, stalling the canopy just before touching down on the ground.

TRAINING PROGRAMS

First flights for beginners will be exciting—but brief. In most cases, you will remain aloft for only a minute or so. Taking off from gentle training slopes, you'll rarely be more than 50 feet above the ground or beyond the watchful eye of an instructor. But don't be disappointed. As you progress to launch sites at higher altitudes, flights of 20 minutes or longer will become possible.

For beginners impatient with bunny slopes, tandem training provides an attractive alternative: The chance to start with high-altitude flights right away. And for more experienced fliers with a taste for altitude, there are some schools that use towplanes to pull pilot and canopy up to heights of 1,000 feet or more.

The extended air time made possible by such **aero-towing,** as it is known, allows pilots to practice increasingly complex maneuvers. For the same reason, seasoned fliers also make use of **thermals.** By locating and riding these rising columns of air, pilots can paraglide over long distances—often for hours on end.

EVOLUTION OF THE SPORT

Paragliding started in Europe in the 1970s, when Alpine mountaineers hit upon an easier—and faster—way down from the summits they had labored so hard to scale. They chose the direct route: soaring back down under brilliantly colored canopies. Having come up the slopes like mountain goats, these hardy souls glided back to earth in the company of hawks.

Europe's paragliding pioneers at first made do with old-fashioned round canopies. But soon they were flying the distinctive wing shape of today, which provides vastly superior lift and maneuverability. These canopies are a common sight in Europe, where paragliding enthusiasts outnumber hang-glider pilots by as many as ten to one. Every summer weekend in the Alps, hundreds of these paragliders can be seen high above the range's snow-covered glaciers and lush green valleys.

So-called **ski paragliding** is also popular in Europe, particularly on the lift-served glaciers of Switzerland, Austria, and France. Most paragliders in other parts of the world begin their rides when they launch themselves by foot off a grassy slope and end them when they touch back down to earth. Ski paragliders add to their fun by donning a pair of skis for the ride, part flying and part skiing down the snow-covered slopes.

In North America, lift-served ski paragliding is offered at the **Aspen, Sun Valley,** and **Whistler** resorts, where spectacular 5,000-foot vertical descents are commonplace.

THE RIGHT STUFF

Beginners to the sport of paragliding generally start on training wings, which are smaller and more boxlike than other canopies. This makes them easier to inflate and significantly more stable and forgiving in the air.

Measuring 25 to 30 feet from wingtip to wingtip, intermediate and competition canopies fly faster and soar better than training models, but they require considerable piloting skills. In expert hands, these canopies can be flown in strong winds, when lift is best, for stretches of more than 50 miles.

Paragliding canopies and harnesses are colorful, well made, and surprisingly durable. Exposure to the sun will degrade the fabric over time, but with proper care a quality wing can last many years. Most canopies are made in Europe, where design and manufacturing standards are strictly regulated. A quality, intermediate-level wing will typically

A TANDEM PARAGLIDER FLIGHT OVER THE SWISS ALPS

cost you between $2,500 and $3,500 new—or around $2,000 used. Top wing manufacturers include **Airwave** (England), **Edel** (Korea), **Firebird** (Germany), **ITV** (France), **Paratec** (Switzerland), **Pro Design** (Austria), and **Wills Wing** (U.S.).

For an introductory paragliding lesson, however, all you need are jeans, a windbreaker, and a sturdy pair of shoes with good ankle support. When you get serious about the sport, the price tag climbs quickly. In addition to your wing, essential accessories include a helmet ($100-200), a harness ($350-800), a reserve parachute ($600), instruments such as an altimeter and anemometer ($400-500), and a flight suit ($200).

Don't scrimp when it comes to safety, though: Invest in a full-coverage helmet and one of the latest impact-absorbing harnesses, which help protect the spine and pelvis from serious injury. Some harnesses even have airbags. Many pilots also carry VHF radios ($150-300) for air-to-ground communication.

Hang Gliding for Beginner Pilots by Peter Cheney, the flight-training manual approved by the U. S. Hang Gliding Association, covers the proper operation and maintenance of paragliding equipment .

Hang Gliding

Since its origins in the late 19th century, the sport of **hang gliding** has progressed enormously. The equipment is stronger, safer, and offers dramatically improved performance. Using new, high-performance cantilevered or rigid-wing gliders, advanced pilots can easily climb to 10,000 feet or higher, where they can soar for hours at a time. Hand- and ballistic-launched parachutes have added to the safety of the sport, and the development of tandem training has cut the time needed to achieve an intermediate pilot rating by up to a third.

As with paragliding, a tandem flight is the best way to go hang gliding for the first time. A certified instructor will take you up in the air for 15 to 30 minutes, flying at altitudes of 2,000 feet or more. Under the instructor's guidance, you will help steer the craft through 360-degree turns and other basic maneuvers. Depending on location, an initial tandem ride ranges from $100 to $200.

If that first flight stirs your soul, the next step is to sign up for a formal training program. This is not a do-it-yourself sport: Like any form of aviation, hang gliding is serious business, and you must learn from certified professionals. You should choose a training center with instructors certified by the **U. S. Hang Gliding Association** (*Colorado Springs, CO. 800-616-6888 or 719-632-8300. www.ushga.org*).

A HANG GLIDER RIDES THE RIDGE LIFT OVER NGORONGORO CRATER IN TANZANIA, EAST AFRICA.

CHOOSING A SCHOOL

Given that 90 percent of hang-gliding students never advance past the novice stage, picking the right flight school can make the difference between becoming a skilled pilot and abandoning the sport early.

When selecting a school, consider the list of training centers that begins on page 104. The school you choose should have experienced, certified instructors and good physical facilities, including gentle training hills that are flyable in a variety of wind conditions. Beginners in particular will appreciate training programs conducted on sand dunes, which make for gentle landings even when technique is poor.

Unless you're a complete newcomer to the sport, look for a school that offers **aero-towing,** which will maximize your air time and let you practice more maneuvers on each flight. Class size is key, too. With more than seven people flying the same hill, you may find yourself spending more time waiting than learning.

For most people, price is also a valid consideration. But you should remember this: Choosing a flight school with what appears to be a reasonable hourly rate for lessons may be less desirable than one that offers a fixed price guaranteeing all the lessons necessary to reach a particular level of training.

Good equipment is vital, of course. Training gliders should be of recent vintage—ideally with wheels to ease the task of hauling them back up the hill. Some schools have flight simulators that give you the feel of maneuvering the glider before you leave the ground. The best schools also offer tandem training, which (as you will see later in the chapter) is an important consideration for those students keen on making rapid progress.

Finally, a good training center will provide a thorough ground-school curriculum—covering flight theory, site discipline (deciding when and where to fly), weather conditions, and equipment assembly and care. Printed flight manuals should be supplied as part of ground school, and course fees should include membership in the USHGA for those new to the sport.

GETTING THE HANG OF THE TERMINOLOGY

The U.S. Hang Gliding Association classifies pilots according to the following rating system: **Hang I** (Beginner); **Hang II** (Novice); **Hang III** (Intermediate); **Hang IV** (Advanced); and **Hang V** (Master). A similar rating system (Para I, Para II, etc.) exists for paragliding.

Completion of the Hang I level, which will cost between $350 and $500, allows the student to make low-level flights over gentle slopes. The learning process begins with a couple of hours of ground school. Next, you make your first runs across a stretch of level ground to become familiar with the feel of the glider. Then it's time to attempt your first flight.

On day one, expect to make five to 15 trial takeoffs, each lasting 10 to 20 seconds, depending on wind and terrain. You'll experience very little glory in these first few hours of hang gliding; managing a 30-foot wing isn't easy, even for experts. The glider will seem heavy and awkward, and your harness restrictive. You'll also find it hard to make smooth and positive movements of the control bar. Don't be discouraged; all have gone through this stage.

After a few more days of training, each time building to longer, higher flights, you will take an obligatory written exam; once this is passed, you'll have earned your Hang I rating. Now you are certified for flights of up to 150 feet, on gradual, open slopes. (In case this doesn't sound like much, remind your earthbound friends that 150 feet is the height of a 15-story building.)

You should make no delay in progressing to the Hang II rating, which qualifies you for high-altitude flights. (Flying skills can get rusty if you wait too long before getting back in the harness.) Hang II flight programs vary in length according to the flight conditions and the ability of the student pilot. Most students should expect to pay between $900 and $1,500 for a program of 10 to 15 lessons. And, as mentioned above, some flight centers offer unlimited lessons until you attain your rating.

To achieve Hang II status, you must be able to make smooth 90-degree S-turns over selected points, land within 40 feet of a designated target, and demonstrate controlled flight 40 feet above ground level. Once you've done this—and passed another written exam—you can consider yourself a real flier, permitted to operate at heights up to 300 feet and in winds of 18 miles per hour.

TANDEM INSTRUCTION

Traditionally, new pilots have struggled to progress to the next hang-glider rating, Hang III. That's because the more difficult skills required at this intermediate level had to be self taught—and performed while in the air.

For many Hang II novices, achieving a Hang III rating became a frustrating process of trial and error. Without the hands-on guidance of a skilled instructor, novices typically experienced a long learning curve that discouraged them from continuing with the sport. All this has changed thanks to **accelerated training**—or tandem training, as it is more commonly known.

Tandem training allows students to progress much more quickly than they could if they had to learn on their own. In the company of an instructor, they can climb to higher altitudes and perform more advanced turns and landings, all the while benefiting from the expertise of their more seasoned flight partner.

Once student and instructor are harnessed to an oversize glider, a towplane pulls them up to an altitude of around 2,000 feet—seven times as high as the Hang II pilot is allowed to fly alone. The pair fly side by side for 15 minutes or so, while the instructor demonstrates a series of maneuvers—360s, riding thermals, making landing approaches—that the student then practices.

After four or five tandem sessions, most novice pilots will have mastered Hang III flying skills. Even so, another 20 hours or so of air time is required to actually attain the Hang III certification.

BUYING A HANG GLIDER

If you plan to continue with the sport, you should consider buying your own hang glider as early as the completion of your Hang II rating . A basic **single-surface design,** good for novices, costs about $3,000.

If you are a strong Hang II flier, however, you may want to consider a **double-surface hang glider.** High-quality models have a glide ratio of at least 14:1—meaning that they will glide for 14 feet through the air for every foot that they descend toward the earth—and cost around $4,000 new, less than $3,000 used.

For $5,000 to $6,000, you can own one of the latest generation of cantilevered gliders with no top-rigging, such as the Seedwing Sensor 610CF or the Moyes Lightspeed. These elegant "topless" designs boast a glide ratio of 15:1 or better. Those with at least $10,000 to spend will find that the new **rigid-wing hang gliders** deliver the ultimate in performance: With glide ratios approaching 20:1, these high-tech craft fly nearly as well as the conventional sailplanes used for soaring.

Whatever your choice, arrange for a test flight from a local dealer before you make any purchase. And if possible, try to use the glider at a launch site with which you are familiar. Every year, on Memorial Day weekend, Utah's **Cloud 9 Soaring Center** offers a demo day at the renowned **Point of the Mountain** site. This popular event allows certified pilots to test out a variety of hang gliders and paraglider wings for a modest registration fee.

MEET THE MAKERS

For details on the latest hang gliders on the market, visit a flight center nearby or contact one of these manufacturers:
Altair Hang Gliders, Draper, UT. 801-523-9544.
Moyes Delta Gliders, Botany, NSW, Australia.
01161-2-9316-4644. www.moyes.com.au.
Seedwings, Goleta, CA. 805-681-0604.
www.seedwings.com.
Wills Wing, Orange, CA. 714-998-6359.
www.willswing.com.

Soaring: Fixed-wing Flight

Thrilling and serene, **soaring** is freeflight in its most advanced form. With soaring centers located in many of America's most scenic destinations, you can fly the spectacular Hana coast of Maui, soar over the Colorado Rockies, or circle above the vineyards of California's wine country.

The modern gliders, or sailplanes that will take you over these picturesque locations have themselves been called "the most beautiful machines ever crafted by humans." And their performance matches their looks. In the hands of an expert, a modern sailplane can fly hundreds of miles and stay aloft for hours.

The essence of soaring is the quest for lift. To stay in the air, all gliders—whether a basic trainer or the most sophisticated of models—must have lift. Without it, no matter how exceptional the pilot may be, gravity will prevail and the ship must land.

There are three basic kinds of lift: thermal, ridge, and wave. **Thermal lift** is produced when the sun warms the ground, causing the surface air to rise. Thermals take many forms, from large masses of rising air to narrow, turbulent shafts no more than 100 feet across.

Ridge lift is produced by winds blowing against the vertical face of a mountain or cliff. As the wind hits the land mass, it deflects upward, while on the opposite side of the crest, it veers down. Accordingly, ridges can be soared on the windward side only.

Wave lift arises when a large mass of air spills, like a waterfall, over a mountain range. When the wave of air hits the valley floor, it bounces upward, sometimes ascending for miles. Wave lift, the strongest form of lift, permits spectacular ascents of 2,000 feet per minute to altitudes of around 35,000 feet. Little surprise that flying a wave is considered the ultimate soaring experience: Once past the **rotor**—an area of turbulence lurking at the bottom of the wave—the air is incredibly smooth and stable, and the glider cruises as if on rails.

WHAT'S IN STORE WHEN YOU SOAR

The first time you climb into a glider, it may seem cramped and ungainly—little more than an oversize toy. That perception will quickly change. As soon as you and your glider are released from the towplane—typically about a mile and a half above the ground—you will realize that you are in a sophisticated machine designed to ride the air.

On your first flight, the craft will likely be a two- or three-seat Schweizer glider, an American craft that has been the mainstay of commercial soaring for decades. At some of the larger facilities, you can also fly in a high-performance

two-seater such as the maneuverable Grob 103, which is capable of speeds up to 120 miles per hour.

Choosing the right school begins with selecting the right type of glider—and that means a choice between high performance and low performance. Most flight schools and clubs train new pilots in Schweizer 232s or 233s—forgiving ships with a glide ratio of about 24:1. Though they do not soar as well as fiberglass sailplanes, which have glide ratios approaching 40:1, Schweizers are much easier for beginners to fly.

The majority of students, however, take up soaring with the objective of eventually flying high-performance gliders. If this is the case for you, then the best idea might be to start in one. Among the schools that feature training in fiberglass gliders are **Arizona Soaring, Caracole Soaring** in California, **Soar Minden** in Nevada, and **Southwest Soaring Enterprises** in Texas.

WHAT FREEFLIGHT COSTS

In order to fly on your own, you must enter a formal flight-training program with an instructor certified by the Federal Aviation Authority (FAA). During this training, student and instructor practice together in a **dual-control glider.** The process normally takes 8 to 12 days of flying and around 20 to 35 flights. Learning to fly on your own at a commercial flight school costs somewhere in the neighborhood of $1,400 to $2,000, while learning to solo with a club costs about half that amount.

Securing a Private Pilot Glider license is the next stage in soaring training. The FAA requires seven hours of **solo flight** to get your pilot's license, followed by the student's successful completion of both a written exam and an in-flight test.

Achieving pilot status usually takes 20 to 25 flights—which amounts to at least two weeks of flying for the majority of students. At a commercial school, this level of training can cost a solo-qualified student from $1,000 to $1,600, depending on the aircraft flown and the ability of the would-be pilot.

For those with less free-flying ambitions, there are always **scenic rides.** A half-hour ride in a training-class glider will cost approximately $70 to $90, while a similar ride in a high-performance fiberglass glider will run from $90 to $120.

Not all soaring schools are located in Hawaii, the Rockies, or Napa Valley; there are hundreds of schools throughout North America. Most are listed in the Yellow Pages under Gliding or Aviation. To help you choose among them, page 106 profiles the top schools nationwide.

For a complete list of soaring sites in the United States, request the "Soaring Site Directory" (a booklet available for $3.00) from the **Soaring Society of America** (*P.O. Box 2100, Hobbs, NM 88241-1308. 888-335-7627 or 505-392-1177. www.ssa.org*). The Soaring Society also has information on foreign soaring centers, which is available to SSA members upon request.

A PILOT TAKES WING IN A SOLO GLIDER OVER THE FORESTS OF CENTRAL PENNSYLVANIA.

Paragliding and Hang Gliding Flight Centers

It is recommended that you learn the sport at a well-established freeflight center. The following schools offer certified instruction under the USHGA rating system for hang gliding, paragliding, or both. To ensure national coverage, some worthy programs in hot spots such as California have been omitted.

Contact the USHGA for a list of certified instruction programs. Before committing to a program, comparison shop and talk to several instructors. Try to find a patient teacher with whom you can develop a rapport. If you are keen to get your Hang II rating, look for a school that can tow you to high altitudes for extended airtime.
Note: **HG** *indicates that hang gliding is offered;* **PG** *denotes paragliding.*

ARIZONA
Dixon's Airplay Paragliding
520-526-4579.
www.paraglide.com
One of the country's top paragliding schools, Airplay operates in Arizona in winter and in Cashmere, Washington (509-782-5543), in summer. The immersion-style program gives you all the skills needed to fly safely on your own. An introductory tandem flight is $125; a Para II package costs $800. PG, TANDEM

CALIFORNIA
High Adventure
San Bernardino. 909-883-8488.
www.flytandem.com
Try the sampler program: tandem lessons in both paragliding and hang gliding for $120 to $190. The training is extremely thorough. HG, PG, TANDEM

Mission Soaring Center
Milpitas. 408-262-1055.
www.hang-gliding.com
Classes are conducted on excellent inland training hills with consistent weather. Mission Soaring has specialized training gliders, a winch towing system for novice training, and flight simulators. An introductory class costs $140, a five-lesson new-pilot package $600, and a tandem lesson $175-200. HG, PG, TANDEM

Torrey Pines Gliderport
La Jolla. 858-452-9858.
www.flytorrey.com
Paragliding dominates the flight training at Torrey Pines. An introductory tandem flight is $125. The facility also offers advanced training in thermal, ridge, and mountain flying. HG, PG, TANDEM

Western Hang Gliders
Marina. 831-384-2622.
www.westernhanggliders.com
Western Hang Gliders conducts year-round classes on the forgiving sands of Marina Beach near Monterey Bay. All levels of instruction are offered. Basic classes start at $100, while a six-lesson package costs $525. HG, PG, TANDEM

Windsports Soaring Center
Van Nuys. 800-426-4454 or 818-988-0111. www.windsports.com
Tandem instruction allows a student to gain intermediate flying skills in two-thirds the normal time. Simulators and videos also speed progress for Hang IIs. An introductory class is $99, a two-day training course $299. HG, PG, TANDEM

COLORADO
Aspen Paragliding and Expeditions
Aspen. 970-925-7625.
www.aspen.com/paragliding
One of only two lift-served, year-round paragliding sites in the United States. The site is less desirable for novices in training: There is no suitable training hill, and flying from the mountaintop requires strong flight skills. PG, TANDEM

Parasoft Paragliding School
Boulder. 303-494-2820.
http://parasoft.boulder.net
Parasoft boasts two nice training hills, with both a 250-foot and 750-foot launch, and tow-launch capacity for flights up to 3,000 feet. Parasoft also offers winter flying safaris to Mexico. PG, TANDEM

FLORIDA
Miami Hang Gliding
Miami. 305-285-8978.
www.serioussports.com/miamihg
Launched from a platform on a powerboat, a tandem glider is towed 1,200 feet above Biscayne Bay, allowing plenty of airtime for practice. At the end of the lesson, you land gently on the water, supported by floats on the glider frame. An introductory flight is $95, while the six-flight Level I program or eight-flight Level II program each cost $395. For advanced training, land flying sites are available. HG, TANDEM

Wallaby Ranch, Inc.
Davenport. 863-424-0070.
www.wallaby.com
This popular school uses powered aero-towing to 2,500 feet. From this height, one tandem lesson offers airtime equivalent to 75 training hill flights. Six microlight aero-tugs mean short waits for flights, and the weather permits year-round training. Glider rentals are available. HG, TANDEM

GEORGIA
Lookout Mountain Flight Park
Rising Fawn. 800-688-5637 or 706-398-3541. www.hangglide.com
Offers excellent ramp-launch novice hills. Both conventional and tandem instruction are available at around $150 for an introductory class. The $599, 50-flight Mountain Package takes novices from their first class through high-altitude flight and a Hang II rating. The $899 Eagle Package allows an unlimited number of flights needed to reach the Hang II rating. HG, TANDEM

NEW HAMPSHIRE
Morningside Flight Park
Charlestown. 603-542-4416.
www.cyberportal.net/morningside
Morningside offers four-hour introductory hang-gliding lessons for $100. The training area is a grass slope that allows launches as high as 250 feet, with a higher plateau launch at 430 feet. A six-day Hang I program costs $530, a five-day Paragliding course $650. HG, PG, TANDEM

NEW YORK
Mountain Wings Hang Gliding and Eastcoast Paragliding Center
Ellenville. 914-647-3377.
www.flightschool.net
The largest paragliding school on the East Coast offers a full flight park, repair serv-

ice, and certified instruction for all levels. Classes use simulators and videotape reviews. Winch towing allows higher altitudes. Costs are $125 for an introductory hang-gliding or paragliding class, $925 for the eight- to ten-day hang-gliding Mountain Package, $985 for Para II-rating program (unlimited lessons). HG, PG, TANDEM

NORTH CAROLINA
Kitty Hawk Kites
Nags Head. 800-334-4777 or 252-441-4124. www.kittyhawk.com
This hang-gliding school, the world's largest, has trained more than 250,000 students since 1974. All levels of certified instruction are offered, with a focus on beginner/novice training. A half-day, $75 beginner lesson includes ground school, video review, and five short flights. Three lessons cost $175, and an eight-lesson package—usually enough for a Hang I rating—is $399. A $449 winter package offers unlimited training flights November through March. HG, PG

UTAH
Cloud 9 Soaring Center
*Draper. 801-576-6460.
www.paragliders.com*
One of the few schools that offer excellent training in both hang gliding and paragliding from a site ideal for both disciplines. An introductory tandem flight is $90, full Para II $650, and Hang II $850. HG, PG, TANDEM

WASHINGTON
Dixon's Airplay Paragliding: (See Arizona opposite)

WISCONSIN
Raven Sky Sports
Whitewater. 262-473-8800 or 312-360-0700. www.hanggliding.com
Aero-tow is the primary method of instruction. An introductory tandem flight costs $125 and a first-time paragliding class $105. Raven offers an attractive "100-flight Hang II+" package combining 90 hill-launch flights plus 10 tandem aero-tow lessons for $1,150. For the same price, a 72-flight paragliding program is available. HG, PG, TANDEM

CANADA
Parawest Paragliding
*Whistler, BC. 604-932-7052.
www.parawest.bc.ca*
Fliers can ride the ski-lift to the tops of

HANG GLIDER PREPARES TO LAND
NEAR WINDMILL, EASTERN WYOMING.

Whistler Mountain and Blackcomb Mountain year-round. This allows high-altitude launches with impressive air time. An introductory tandem flight costs $130 (CN), a novice rating program $800 (CN).

Muller Hang Gliding and Paragliding
Cochrane, AB. 403-932-6760.
www.muller-hang-paraglide.com
Based east of the Rockies, this is another quality Canadian program, a good choice for intermediates wishing to improve.

Soaring Schools

There are many schools where you can learn to soar and obtain your private pilot's license. However, it is recommended that you enroll with one of the leading flight schools listed below. All offer professional instruction, good equipment, and superior soaring conditions.

ARIZONA

Arizona Soaring
Maricopa. 520-568-2318 or 480-821-2903. www.azsoaring.com
Train in a Schweizer or a fiberglass ship, depending on your interests. Lift is 80 percent thermal, with ridges 2 miles away. The flight school runs year-round. Glider rides start at $70. Training costs: $35/hr. (pilot), $36/hr. (S 233), $50/hr. (Grob 103).

Turf Soaring School
Peoria. 602-439-3621.
www.turfsoaring.com
One of the largest soaring academies in the country. Instruction is offered year-round, seven days a week. All basic training is done in Schweizer 233s. An introductory ride costs $75 in a Schweizer, or $110 in a fiberglass ship. Training costs: $36/hr. (S 233), $50/hr. (Grob 103).

CALIFORNIA

Caracole Soaring
California City. 619-373-1019.
http://members.aol.com/soarca/
caracole.htm
Enjoying world-class thermal and wave lift, Caracole specializes in personalized, in-depth training. The school operates year-round, with wave flying in the winter. An introductory lesson is $60, while the cost to solo averages $2,000. Training costs: $25/hr. (pilot), $42/hr. (ASK 21).

Sky Sailing
Warner Springs. 442-782-0404.
www.skysailing.com

One of the top soaring centers in North America. Lift at Warner Springs is mostly thermal, with some ridge and wave. A 20-minute introductory ride in a Schweizer costs $59, or $40 per person for two passengers. Training costs: $33/hr. (pilot), $26/hr. (S 233), $45/hr. (Grob 103).

COLORADO

Mile High Gliding
Boulder. 303-530-2208.
www.milehighgliding.com
Located near the Continental Divide, Mile High offers great scenery as well as good lift year-round. From May through August, look for good thermal conditions; in winter, wave lift is abundant. Scenic introductory rides over the Rockies cost $60 to $195. Training costs: $35/hr. (pilot), $35/hr. (S 233), $50/hr. (Pegasus).

FLORIDA

Seminole Flying and Soaring
Claremont. 352-394-5450.
www.soarfl.com
Training conditions are excellent year-round. Spring and fall are best for altitude and duration. Training costs: $25/hr. (pilot), $24-$50/hr. (aircraft); about $1,300 to solo, $2,300 to license.

HAWAII

Soar Hawaii, Ltd.
Honolulu. 808-637-3147.
www.soarhawaii.com
Instruction is in Schweizer 233s and Grob 103s, the latter for aerobatic training. Trade winds provide excellent ridge lift most of the year. Training costs: $45/hr. (pilot), $35/hr. (S 233), $60/hr. (Grob 103); approximately $1,900-2,500 from first flight to license.

NEVADA

High Country Soaring
Minden. 775-782-4944
One of the best soaring sites in the world, High Country Soaring draws 60 to 70 percent of its clientele from overseas. Thermal soaring is reliable, but when the wave kicks in, even novices can fly for hours. High Country offers a superb 40-minute Tahoe scenic ride. Training costs: $30+/hr. (pilot), $60/hr. (Grob 103).

Soar Minden
Minden. 800-345-7627 or 775-782-7627.
www.soarminden.com
A full training program is offered, from first flight to advanced aerobatics. Most training is done in Grob 103s, but a

Schweizer 232 is also available. Lift is predominantly thermal, with wave flying November through May. Training costs: $1,800-3,000 to solo.

NEW YORK

Harris Hill Soaring Center
Elmira. 607-734-0641.
www.harrishillsoaring.org
Harris Hill hosts many major soaring events each year and offers scenic rides in Schweizer 233s ($55) and in ASK 21s ($65). Training is conducted at the nearby Schweizer Soaring School.

PENNSYLVANIA

Ridge Soaring Gliderport
Julian. 814-355-2483.
www.eglider.org
Pilots come from all over the world to enjoy Julian's exceptional ridge-soaring conditions. An introductory ride in a Grob 103 costs $60. The flight center is active March through November. Training costs: $36/hr. (pilot), $42/hr. (Grob 103).

SOUTH CAROLINA

Bermuda High Soaring School
Lancaster. 803-475-SOAR.
www.bermudahighsoaring.com
A top choice for those seeking a reasonably priced training program from first flight to pilot rating. The site offers soarable conditions nine days out of ten during the principal flying season, March through November. All basic training is conducted in Schweizers. Training costs: basic course to solo, 32 flights—about $1,500.

TEXAS

Southwest Soaring Enterprises
Caddo Mills. 903-527-3124 or 972-251-5079. www.southwestsoaring.com
All flight training is done in high-performance Grob 103s. Introductory rides start at $40 for a 2,000-foot tow, plus $20 for each additional 1,000 feet. Training costs: $23/hr. (pilot), $42/hr. (Grob 103).

VERMONT

Sugarbush Soaring
Warren. 802-496-2290.
www.sugarbush.org
New England's leading soaring center is renowned for its spring and fall wave conditions. Scenic rides are offered in various aircraft, starting at $70 for 20 minutes. Sugarbush provides complete novice training, as well as wave and mountain flying instruction for licensed pilots.

ORGANIZATIONS

Soaring Society of America (*P.O. Box 2100, Hobbs, NM. 888-335-7627 or 505-392-1177. www.ssa.org*) oversees international competitions and maintains a global directory of pilots and flight centers.

United States Hang Gliding Association (*P.O. Box 1330, Colorado Springs, CO. 719-632-8300. www.ushga.org*) issues standards for hang gliding and paragliding and maintains a directory of schools, pilots, and manufacturers.

Paragliding Assoc. of Canada/Assoc. Canadienne de Vol Libre (*Surrey, BC V3W 0T6. 604-507-2565. www.hpac.ca*) is a federation of seven provincial associations. It offers a quarterly publication, *AIR,* that is free with membership, $35 (CN) for nonmembers.

British Hang Gliding and Paragliding Assoc. (*P.O. Box W3, The Old School Room, Loughborough Rd., Leicester LE4 5PJ, England. 011-44-116-261-1322. www.bhpa.co.uk*) maintains on its website a list of registered freeflight centers in the United Kingdom.

Fédération Française de Vol Libre (*4 rue de Suisse, 0600 Nice, France.01133-4-9703-8282. www.ffvl.fr*) keeps a directory of hang gliding and paragliding schools and clubs.

Federazione Italiana Volo Libero (*Via Salbertrand 50, 10146 Torino, Italy. 01139-011-744991. www.fivl.it*).

ONLINE

U.S. Hang Gliding Association
www.ushaga.org
Features news, technical articles, events, and photos, plus directories of USHGA chapters, flight clubs, and flight schools.

Hang Gliding Server
www.sky-adventures.com
An excellent resource with a comprehensive guide to schools, a photo gallery, FAQs, chat room, and air-sport links.

Big Air International Paragliding
www.bigairparagliding.com
Includes a freeflight FAQ, paraglider specifications, links to other sites, manufacturers' addresses, an event calendar, and product tests.

Soaring Society of America
www.ssa.org
Articles from *SOARING* magazine, news, training standards, competition results, and links to SSA affiliates and the FAA.

Sportflyer.com
www.sportflyer.com/soar.htm
Provides a comprehensive set of links to worldwide soaring flight centers and clubs, plus low-cost soaring books and supplies.

Torrey Pines International Glider Port
www.flytorrey.com
Offers how-to primers for paragliding and hang gliding, along with a comprehensive FAQ, gear reviews, and great photos.

MAGAZINES

Hang Gliding and *Paragliding* are journals of the **U.S. Hang Gliding Association** (see above).

SOARING, the journal of the Soaring Society of America, features technical articles, sporting news, and photos.

BOOKS

Hang Gliding for Beginner Pilots by Peter Cheney (USHGA, $29.95) is the USHGA-approved flight-training manual, essential for all new fliers. Available from Lookout Mountain Flight Park (*706-398-3541.*

www.hangglide.com) or the USHGA.

Hang Gliding Training Manual: Learning Hang Gliding Skills by Dennis Pagen (Sport Aviation Publications, $29.95). A must for hang-glider pilots.

Paragliding Flight by Dennis Pagen (USHGA, $19.95). Another excellent manual for new pilots.

The Joy of Soaring by the Soaring Society of America (SSA, $19.95). An authoritative primer for first-time fliers.

Cloud Dancing: Your Introduction to Gliding and Motorless Flight by Robert Whelan ($14.95). A good introduction to gliding. Available through www.sportflyer.com.

VIDEOS

Starting Hang Gliding: Fly Like an Eagle! (Adventure Productions, $29.95) is a good video guide for novice training, tandem instruction, and basic in-flight skills. Contact Adventure Productions (*775-747-0175. www.adventurep.com*).

The **Soaring Society of America** offers instructional videos on navigation, instruments, and the transition from powered flight to gliding.

PARAGLIDERS AT POINT OF THE MOUNTAIN, UTAH

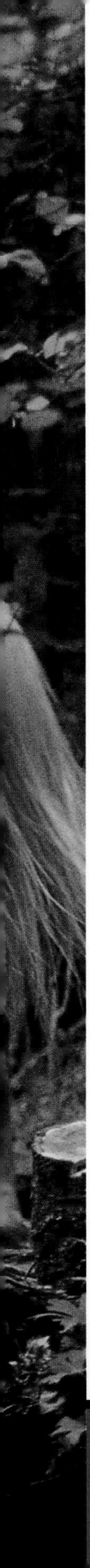

Horseback Riding

FOR CENTURIES, HUMANS HAVE RELIED ON HORSES AS BEASTS OF BURDEN AND MEANS OF transport. But in today's developed countries, horses rarely serve these functions. The exceptions can be found on an ever dwindling number of working ranches or in places where people ride for sport or to experience the adventure of traveling as their ancestors did. • For both novice and expert riders, plenty of riding opportunities are available on nearly every continent. Imagine trekking through New Zealand, chasing foxes in Ireland, or climbing the Andes along the border between Chile and Argentina. How about riding to the palaces of Rajasthan's warrior kings or exploring glaciers and volcanoes in Iceland? All these adventures and more are described in the pages that follow. • You will also find a complete guide to the premier western guest ranches, to cattle drives, and to covered-wagon trips, along with ratings for the top wilderness pack outfitters in North America.

LEFT: CREEK CROSSING IN LIMBERLOST AREA OF SHENANDOAH NATIONAL PARK, VIRGINIA. BELOW: SADDLE-HORSE ROUNDUP, MONTANA

Riding Adventures

Western Adventures

Cattle Drives

Wagon Trains

Trail Rides

Wilderness Horsepacking

You can get in a car to see what man has created, but you have to get on a horse to see what God has made.
CHARLES RUSSELL

Six Great Riding Adventures

In an era of jet travel and superhighways, riding a horse is admittedly old-fashioned. Even so, it is still one of the best ways to travel in the wild backcountry, where roads are few and far between. And riding is one of the few forms of adventure that allow you to work with animals, not just watch them. Many riding tours are relatively gentle, slow-paced outings suitable for every family member. If you're an experienced rider looking for something beyond the ordinary, however, you'll find a host of challenging adventures in these pages as well.

IRELAND'S WEST COAST
Riding Country Supreme

On the west coast of Ireland—a region of craggy hillsides, emerald valleys, quick-change weather, and traditional Celtic culture—is the Connemara Peninsula, the setting for director John Ford's *The Quiet Man*. It is also a near-legendary center for horse breeding.

To sample Connemara's best riding opportunities, head to County Galway, home of the **Aille Cross Equestrian Center** (*Aille Cross, Loughrea, County Galway, Ireland. 01135-3918-41216. Fax 01135-3918-42363*). Here, noted horseman Willie Leahy maintains a stable of a hundred horses, and he matches these horses to the individual likes and abilities of his guests. Leahy's showcase offering, the six-day **Connemara Trail Ride,** follows bridle paths, beaches, and mountain tracks at a moderate pace, with overnight stops at comfortable country inns. The highlight is a visit to **Mweenish Island,** a national wilderness preserve. Seaside fields with stone walls invite jumping, and the broad beach at low tide inspires informal racing. Leahy now offers a "relaxed" version of the ride; guests can go at their own leisurely pace and ride English or Western. The Connemara Trail Ride is offered April through August for roughly $1,050 to $1,400.

The best time to visit is in August, when the largest town, Clifton, hosts the annual pony show, an event that draws equine enthusiasts from around the world. In the winter, Leahy runs an even more adventurous tour for skilled riders: the **Aille Cross Country Trail.** The O'Deas Hotel serves as your base for a week of cross-country jumping, with an optional three days of foxhunting. The Aille trail week costs about $1,400, with a $125 surcharge for foxhunting. **Hidden Trails** (*5936 Inverness St., Vancouver, BC, V5W 3P7, Canada. 888-987-2457 or 604-323-1141. www.hiddentrails.com*), a fine Canadian agency specializing in riding tours, also offers the Aille Cross Country Trail week.

If you want something really special, consider a riding holiday at the **St. Clerans Manor House.** Once owned by John Huston, this restored 18th-century mansion is part of a 45-acre estate. A four-day stay, including riding, costs about $1,350.

For roads a bit less traveled, head north to Sligo for the **Beaches, Dunes, and Trail Ride.** Guests are briefed at the stables, given maps and lists of farmhouses offering prebooked B&B accommodations, and allowed to ride independently along well-marked paths and country roads. The cost is $910 to $980 for eight days. Contact **Equitour** (*P.O. Box 807, Dubois, WY 82513. 800-545-0019 or 307-455-3363. www.ridingtours.com*). North of Sligo is Donfanoghy, where the coastline is even more dramatic. Equitour offers a **Donegal Saddle Tour** including a ride from the Donegal highlands to the sea. Cost for the eight-day trip is $1,100 to $1,200.

For a luxurious, castle-based tour, try Cross Country's **Kinnitty Castle Trail Ride** in central Ireland's County Offaly. Tours range from three to six days and from $1,115 to $1,835. Each day riders venture into the 60,000-acre Kinnitty Forest, a vast preserve filled with deer, pheasants, badgers, and foxes. Contact **Cross Country International** (*P.O. Box 1170, Millbrook, NY 12545. 800-828-8768 or 914-677-6000. www.equestrianvacations.com*).

ICELAND
Land of Fire and Ice

Ninth-century Vikings brought the first horses to Iceland, and the surefooted descendants of those animals afford a practical means of travel in this land of geysers and glaciers, mountains and waterfalls, and black lava and green valleys.

If you decide to see Iceland from the back of a horse, you should expect to rough it. Backcountry riders stay at rustic farms or in shepherd huts, and in the most remote areas, they bathe in natural hot springs because showers are not available. Fortunately, a branch of the Gulf Stream touches the southwest coast and affects the climate in a positive way, producing summer temperatures that are remarkably hospitable despite Iceland's location near the Arctic Circle. The midnight sun also affords long days for exploring.

If you want to ride for a day or two, simply visit any number of farms outside Reykjavik, the capital city. You can get a listing of farm-stay locations from the **Iceland Tourist Board** (*www.goiceland.org*). To take longer trips, contact **Ishestar Icelandic Riding Tours** (*Sorlaskeid 26, 220, Hafnarfjordur, Iceland. 01135-4555-7000. www.ishestar.is*). For novices, the four-day volcano tour from Leirubakki Farm offers diverse terrain and views of Mount Hekla. Riders with more experience may prefer the six-day **Hekla-Landmannalaugar Tour** of black lava fields, natural hot springs near Mount Hekla, and a Viking settlement. You ride from four to seven hours a day and stay at farms or mountain huts. The price, roughly $1,060, includes the horse, tack, English-speaking guide, lodging, and all meals. A wide variety of other itineraries up to 16 days are offered. Both **Equitour** (*800-545-0019. www.ridingtours.com*) and **Hidden Trails** (*888-987-2457. www.hiddentrails.com*) book trips with Ishestar and other stables in Iceland. To combine riding with glacier tours and other such adventures, contact the **Iceland Tourist Bureau** (*Lagmuli 4, P.O. Box 8650, Reykjavik, Iceland. 01135-4585-4300. www.icelandtravel.is*).

SOUTH AMERICA
Andes Riding Adventure

The horsemen of South America—Argentina's gauchos and Chile's *huasos*—carry on a tradition of horsemanship dating from the age of the Spanish conquistadores. In both countries you can book tours that let you join these able riders for a great equestrian adventure: trekking in Patagonia.

Although you can make your own arrangements with private *estancias*, you should consider booking a package tour if you are a first-time visitor to South America. **Hidden Trails** (*888-987-2457. www.hiddentrails.com*) markets a host of excellent rides in southern Chile and Argentina. For the most spectacular scenery, take the Torres del Paine trek through **Chilean Patagonia.** On this seven-day, $1,760 journey, you'll ride between remote inns, crossing high passes and enjoying breathtaking views of Grey Glacier, the Towers of Paine, Laguna Azul, and other natural wonders.

Farther north, in the **Lake District,** Hidden Trails offers a ride across the Andes following the path of outlaws Butch Cassidy and the Sundance Kid. The adventure begins on the famous **Gaucho Trail,** which leads through the Valdivian rain forest into the Andean wilderness, and after a few days

TRAIL RIDING ON THE GROUNDS OF MOUNT JULIET, COUNTY KILKENNY, IRELAND of climbing, you reach **Valle Leon** ("lion's valley"), the pass from Chile to Argentina. The trip ends with a ride on the Patagonia Express steam train and a visit to the historic homestead of Butch and Sundance near Lago Cholila. The cost of this challenging 11-day tour is $2,975 per person.

Equitour (*800-545-0019. www.ridingtours.com*) has also put together a flexible riding program in **Argentine Patagonia.** You stay a minimum of four days at 15,000-acre Estancia Huechahue in the foothills of the Andes. Adventurous types can add a four-day pack trip to **Lanin National Park** to see Huanquihue Volcano, the thermal springs at Epulaufquen, and the towering Lanin Volcano. The cost is $240 per day, all-inclusive, and trips are offered November through April.

COLORADO ROCKIES
Wilderness Horsepacking

Colorado is among the premier places in North America for a horsepacking adventure. Here you will find abundant wildlife, beautiful alpine scenery, and trails that are less heavily traveled than those in the Sierra, the Tetons, or in some other well-known areas of the continent.

One of the best outfitters in southwestern Colorado is

Rapp Guide Service (*3635 County Rd. 301, Durango, CO 81301. 877-600-2656 or 970-375-1250 or 247-8923. www.rappguides. com*). Owner and chief guide Pete Turner takes small groups (typically six riders) to a number of less traveled destinations in the **San Juan National Forest.** The loop through Silver Mesa and the Needle Mountain Range is a six-day journey in which you travel over rugged and dramatic mountains, cross two 11,000-foot passes, and spend 80 percent of the time above timberline. The cost is about $1,300.

Rapp's premier pack trip is a five- to six-day Continental Divide tour. From the trailhead east of Silverton, you ride along the Divide to a remote alpine valley, home to large herds of elk. After five days at two different high camps, your group returns by rail to Durango. The $1,200 cost is substantial, but people rave about the scenery, the wildlife, and the well-trained horses. For gourmet pack trips, make reservations early because those trips fill up quickly.

Another recommended operation is the **Bear Basin Ranch** in south-central Colorado. Guides Amy Finger and Gary Ziegler, trained naturalists and former Outward Bound instructors, lead three- and five-day trips into the rugged Sangre de Cristo range. Behind these razor-edge peaks lie alpine meadows, shimmering lakes, and miles of trails. Fin-

ger and Ziegler specialize in seldom-used routes, and their **Ultimate Pack Trip** follows game trails into incredibly remote areas. On all trips, they teach wilderness skills, saddling techniques, and orienteering. To make reservations, contact the agent for Bear Basin, **American Wilderness Experience** (*P.O. Box 1486, Boulder, CO 80306. 800-444-0099 or 303-444-2622. www.awetrips.com*).

SPAIN
Rides of the Conquistadores

With its numerous fine stables and broad, open countryside networked by bridle paths, Spain is a natural choice for a riding vacation. A wide variety of options await those who wish to ride here: Stables, ranches, and haciendas throughout the country offer everything from trail rides to lengthy overland treks.

Many people here consider Andalusia, in southern Spain, to be the region that best preserves classic Spanish heritage. Famed for its horse breeds, Andalusia certainly remains the heartland of Spanish riding culture, for it is a land of great horses and great riding destinations. From the olive groves, farmlands, and vineyards of Sevilla to the high mountain pastures in the Sierra Nevada, this region offers wide-open country with countless routes that beckon explorers.

To help you sample the best of southern Spain, **Equitour** (*800-545-0019. www.ridingtours.com*) offers **Trails of Andalusia,** an eight-day ride through the heart of Andalusia. The ride begins in Seville and moves through farm country along a historic pilgrimage route. Accommodations on this luxurious tour include some of the great showplaces of the Spanish aristocracy, more than justifying the $1,900 cost of the trip. The route proceeds to **Doñana National Park,** a biosphere reserve, and then to Palacio del Rey, a royal residence. Another great tour through the provinces of Granada and Almeria is Equitour's **Alpujarra Ride.** Departing from Granada, this eight-day trek (six riding days) follows ancient Moorish bridle paths to small villages little changed since the time of Columbus. The ride offers great scenic diversity as you climb from sea level to the crest of Spain's Sierra Nevada, where you overnight at Trevelez, the highest village in the country. Emerging high above the Poqueira Valley, on a clear day you can see across the Mediterranean Sea to Morocco. Price for the Alpujarra Ride is $1,350 for eight days, seven nights.

Equitour and **Hidden Trails** (*888-987-2457. www.hiddentrails.com*) offer numerous riding tours in Andalusia and other parts of Spain. Most rides feature a moderate to fast pace. Riders should have intermediate or better skills, and they should be comfortable with English saddles. With some advance planning, you can arrange your riding holiday to coincide with one of Spain's many equestrian events. For a listing of horse events, schools, and tours call the **Tourist Office of Spain** (*8383 Wilshire Blvd., Suite 960, Beverly Hills, CA 90211. 323-658-7188. www.okspain.org*).

INDIA
Land of Kings

Traveling in the style of a bygone era, riding tours reveal the magic of India far more vividly than motorized travel does. A riding tour also bypasses the country's heavily populated cities, which tend to overwhelm first-time visitors here. But an Indian riding adventure is not only for the rich and famous: You can experience a "luxury" trip on horseback for a few hundred dollars more than the price of a week's stay at a deluxe guest ranch in the United States.

Once composed of separate kingdoms, India's northwestern state of **Rajasthan** is an ideal destination for a tour on horseback. Carriage paths cross open terrain to connect historic forts and temples just a day's ride apart, and riders can spend evenings in the former palaces of Rajasthan's warrior kings (Rajputs). But Rajasthan is not the ideal place for a self-guided riding tour; you won't find it easy to locate or reserve many of the best places to stay, many of which have only recently opened to tourism from the West. You will also need a reliable local contact to secure mounts and transport to the hinterlands. To experience the best of Rajasthan, you should therefore consider a package tour from a reliable company such as **Equitour** (*800-545-0019. www.ridingtours. com*) or **Hidden Trails** (*888-987-2457. www.hiddentrails.com*).

The 19-day Rajasthani riding tour, offered by both Equitour and Hidden Trails, begins in the semidesert **Marwar** region. Traveling far from the urban world, riders visit remote villages, the lakeside resort of the Maharaja of Jodhpur, the **Kumbalgarh Wildlife Sanctuary,** and several ancient temples, palaces, and fortresses. Virtually every detail of the trip is conducted in grand style: Guests stay in luxurious castles and fortresses and are entertained by local musicians, dancers, and magicians. Lovers of fine horses delight in strong, intelligent mounts, many of which are impeccably groomed polo ponies from the maharajas' stables. Superb cuisine is prepared by a caterer who travels with the group.

A 22-day itinerary explores more of the Rajasthan region. From Delhi, riders cross the **Thar Desert** (near Pakistan) to visit the **Nagaur Camel Fair.** Rarely attended by tourists, this event features 25,000 lavishly decorated camels in Central Asia's largest gathering of camel traders. The ride continues to Jaisalmer, a picturesque walled town, and Jodhpur, a famed riding center that lent its name to the breeches. The price for Rajasthani riding tours ranges from $2,400 to $4,500, depending on the season and duration.

HORSEPACKING IN CHILE'S TORRES DEL PAINE NATIONAL PARK

Horseback Riding

Western Adventures: Working Ranch Vacations

If you want more action than a conventional dude ranch vacation provides, consider spending a week at a working ranch. You will round up strays, check fences, punch dogies, and help with other day-to-day operations of the ranch. If you visit during a seasonal roundup, you can join a real cattle drive. During the day you'll move the herd, and at night you'll camp out under the stars.

To learn more about working ranches, pick up the fifth edition of *Gene Kilgore's Ranch Vacations* (John Muir Press, 1999, $23) from Kilgore's Ranchweb (707-939-3801. www.ranchweb.com). The author visited all of the ranches included in the book, identifying those spreads that specialize in working holidays, roundups, and cattle drives.

ARIZONA

Grapevine Canyon Ranch
P.O. Box 302, Pearce, AZ 85625
800-245-9202 or 520-826-3185
www.grapevinecanyonranch.com

Grapevine Canyon Ranch is an authentic working cattle ranch located high in the Dragoon Mountains, about 85 miles southeast of Tucson. Skilled riders can work the range alongside real cowboys, riding herd and rounding up strays. Much of the terrain is steep and rugged, offering a challenge for even experienced trail riders. Although the Grapevine is open year-round, spring and fall are the best times to visit. Accommodations are first-class. You may ride like a hardworking cowboy here, but you can still enjoy a little luxury at day's end. For the best deals, book directly with the ranch. The owners offer two-week packages beginning at $2,016; shorter stays cost $130-170 per person per day, including meals.

CALIFORNIA/NEVADA

Hunewill Circle H Ranch
Winter: 200 Hunewill Lane, Wellington, NV 89444. 775-465-2201. Summer: P.O. Box 368, Bridgeport, CA 93517. 760-932-7710
www.guestranches.com/hunewill

One of the most well-known dude-and-cattle ranches in California, Hunewill Circle H Ranch is a family-run operation nestled on the eastern slope of the Sierra Nevada. Guests are welcome to help with the cattle work; however, horseback riding is the main activity, with organized rides twice daily. You won't have to rough it too much, because guests stay in comfortable cottages and can take advantage of plenty of opportunities to relax after ranch duties. Participate in the two-day cattle roundup in September, or join the five-day cattle drive in November. The all-inclusive price is about $150 per day or $992 per week; children under age 10 pay half price.

COLORADO

Lost Valley Ranch
29555 Goose Creek Rd., Box KRW
Sedalia, CO 80135-9000. 303-647-2311
www.lostvalleyranch.com

For a working ranch vacation that seems to have it all—amenities, ranch and cattle duties, fishing, quality accommodations, great staff, riding instruction, strong programs for young children and teens, beautiful natural surroundings, and lots of charm—Lost Valley ranks among America's very best ranches. Guests stay in individual cabins, each having a fireplace and a bath. With over 150 horses and special horsemanship weeks with expert trainers, Lost Valley is a top choice for serious equestrians. The ranch, set high in the Pike National Forest, offers outstanding fishing on the nearby South Platte River, a heated swimming pool, and tennis. This premier American cattle ranch has been perfecting the dude ranch experience for five decades. Cost is $100-200 per day, all-inclusive, and requires a one-week minimum stay in summer.

IDAHO

Bar H Bar Ranch
1501 Eight Mile Creek Rd., Soda Springs, ID 83276. 800-743-9505 or 208-547-3082
www.barhbar.com

"They come as guests and leave as friends," says fifth generation rancher-owner Janet Harris. And it is true. This family-run working cattle ranch only takes four to six visitors at a time, assuring guests a great deal of personal attention. Located in the Bear River Range Wilderness of the Wasatch Mountains in Idaho, Bar H Bar Ranch provides an authentic ranching experience for its guests. Be prepared to log some hours in the saddle while you ride fence lines, move cattle to pasture, and help during calving and branding. But also be sure to leave plenty of time to explore the beautiful high country on nature walks and fishing trips. Guests stay in comfortable, renovated bunkhouses. Cost is $800 per week.

MONTANA

Bridger Mountain Ranch
15100 W. Rocky Mountain Rd., Suite 310, Belgrade, MT 59714. 406-388-4463
www.bridgeroutfitters.com

The Bridger Mountain Ranch is a good choice if you're looking for a rustic working ranch situated in the high country near Bozeman, about 100 miles from Yellowstone park. Learn wrangling skills at the ranch, take guided day rides and fishing trips, or join guide Dave Warwood on a four- to eight-day wilderness pack trip. These pack trips, which typically run from $700-1,100 per week, are especially popular with fly-fishing enthusiasts. (Warwood's knowledge of local fishing holes is without peer; his great-grandfather guided in these mountains almost a century ago.) In the fall the ranch offers elk and deer hunting in the Lee Metcalf Wilderness bordering Yellowstone. The price is $2650 for six days.

Hargrave Cattle & Guest Ranch
Thompson River Valley, 300 Thompson River Rd., Marion, MT 59925. 406-858-2284.
www.hargraveranch.com

Located in a scenic valley just 70 miles from Glacier National Park, the Hargrave Ranch offers one of the most authentic Western vacations in the northern Rockies. Guests help drive the herds to summer pastures. They can also participate in the fall roundups that bring cattle down from

A PALAMINO JUMPS IN THE AIR AS A SPOOKED CALF RUNS UNDER ITS LEGS ON A RANCH NEAR GRAND STAIRCASE-ESCALANTE NATIONAL MONUMENT, UTAH.

the high country. (Each night, however, everyone returns to the ranch.) The cost is $1,120 per person for six days, Sunday to Saturday. The ranch takes no more than 19 guests each week, so personalized service is assured. The Hargraves are great hosts: Enjoy the down comforters and "Gramma's best Sunday cooking."

OREGON

Ponderosa Cattle Company & Guest Ranch

P.O. Box 190, Hwy 395, Seneca, OR 97873
541-542-2403
www.ponderosaguestranch.com

Cowboys and cowgirls of all ages can keep themselves busy working the Ponderosa Cattle Company's 4,000 head of cattle. Branding, sorting, and moving cattle from forests to pastures are just some of the many tasks guests perform on this working ranch. You will also discover plenty of opportunities for fun: Go horseback riding, fishing, and cross-country skiing on 120,000 acres of meadows and forests in the Seneca backcountry. The ranch is open year-round, but most of the cattle work happens during spring and summer. Cost is $1,200 per week.

WYOMING

High Island Ranch & Cattle Co.

346 Amoretti, No. 10, Thermopolis, WY 82443.
307-867-2374 www.gorp.com/highisland

If you want to experience cowboy life, head up to Wyoming's High Island Ranch, a no-compromise working ranch where they'll put you in the saddle the day you arrive and test your mettle until you leave. You may help with the branding, a prairie-to-mountain roundup, or moving the herd on a long-distance cattle drive from mountain pastures to Cottonwood Creek. This is the real thing, not a roundup staged solely for the guests. The spring drives run in June and July, with the last three trips from late August through mid-September. The ranch also offers fly-fishing, horseback riding, and hunting. The price for one week is $995-1,550 per person.

Schively Ranch

1062 Road 15, Lovell, WY 82431
307-548-6688. www.schivelyranch.com

The Schively Ranch is another destination where you can help authentic cowboys perform actual ranch work. Using well-trained quarter horses, guests ride the range every day, assisting with activities that

include roping, branding, and cattle drives. In spring and fall, guests help move the herd 60 miles to the ranch site, which is located on the east slope of the Pryor Range on the Wyoming border. A small, family-run operation, the Schively Ranch handles no more than 14 guests at a time. The reputation of this ranch has been spreading, so you should book your stay well in advance. The cost per week is about $750-950.

GUEST RANCHES

If you want more rest and relaxation than a working ranch might offer, then consider making a visit to an old-fashioned guest ranch. With dozens of fine ranches from which to choose, you may wish to consult an agency for help in picking a destination.

American Wilderness Experience (800-444-0099. www.awetrips.com) represents more than 65 guest ranches in Arizona, Colorado, Idaho, Montana, Oregon, New Mexico, Wyoming, and British Columbia. **Off the Beaten Path** (27 E. Main St., Bozeman, MT 59715. 800-445-2995 or 406-586-1311. www.offthebeatenpath. com) will also help you select the best ranch for your interests. A directory describing

over a hundred ranches is published by the **Dude Ranchers' Association** (*P.O. Box F-471, La Porte, CO 80535. 970-223-8440. www.duderanch.org*). Another great resource, with hundreds of Web listings, is **Guest Ranches of North America** (*www.guestranches.com*).

ARIZONA

Rancho de los Caballeros

1551 S. Vulture Mine Rd., Wickenburg, AZ 85390. 800-684-5030 or 520-684-5484
www.sunc.com

Well-known for its 18-hole championship golf course and rated as one of America's top 75 resort courses by *Golf Digest,* Rancho de los Caballeros is also one of the best alternative-season guest ranches in the United States. The ranch is situated on 20,000 acres of scenic southwestern desert land, and you'll find the terrain ideal for horseback riding, whether you're a city slicker or a seasoned rider.

In addition to golf and horseback riding, the many other recreational activities offered here include tennis, swimming, guided nature walks, and skeet and trapshooting. Open from October through May, the Rancho de los Caballeros costs $199-499 per day with a three-night minimum.

COLORADO

Skyline Guest Ranch

7214 Hwy. 145, P.O. Box 67, KRW, Telluride, CO 81435. 888-754-1126 or 970-728-3757
www.ranchweb.com/skyline

One of the most beautiful ranches in North America, the Skyline is hard to top as a destination for a Western vacation. Guests at the ranch have the option of riding through green meadows in the lower elevations of the Rocky Mountains or venturing as high as 14,000 feet on a wilderness peak climb. Mountain biking and hiking are also very popular activities among visitors. If you wish to devote a few hours of your vacation to fishing, be sure to try your luck in the excellent streams and lakes located nearby.

During the winter months, Skyline offers nordic skiing on the grounds of the ranch. It will also make arrangements with nearby resorts for guests who prefer downhill skiing. Accommodations and meals here are decidedly first-class. In summer, adults pay about $1,400 per week; for children 3 to 7 years old, the cost is $700 per week. Reservations for summer are recommended nine months to one year in advance.

SEASIDE CANTER ON PUERTO RICO'S PALOMINO ISLAND

Wind River Ranch

P.O. Box 3410, Estes Park, CO 80517
800-523-4212 or 970-586-4212
www.windriverranch.com

The Wind River Ranch offers its guests deluxe facilities in a breathtaking setting just 7 miles from Estes Park. You can ride through the spectacular high country of Rocky Mountain National Park and then return to the ranch to enjoy delicious food and relax in cozy rooms. Although you can find better places for challenging riding opportunities (no overnight pack trips are offered), you'll soon discover that the Wind River Ranch offers virtually all the extras you expect. Special features include a stocked fishpond, nightly campfires, and a hayride.

This place is a Christian family dude ranch offering a kids' club and an optional early morning Bible study with a different speaker each week. Other activities include access to golf and white-water rafting (for additional fees). Make your reservations well in advance. Prices start at about $1,125 per person per week for adults.

IDAHO

Wapiti Meadow Ranch

Diana and Barry Bryant, H.C. 72,
Cascade, ID 83611. 208-633-321.
www.guestranches.com/wapiti

Located near Idaho's remote River of No Return Wilderness Area, the Wapiti Meadow Ranch provides an outstanding setting for high alpine horseback riding, as well as fishing and rafting on the nearby Middle Fork of the Salmon River. The ridgetop pack trips are super, with great scenery and fine angling in a number of alpine streams and lakes. Near the ranch lodge are miles of trails for day rides, a stocked trout pond, a salmon stream, and plentiful wildlife to watch or photograph. The "hearty gourmet" cooking will delight the palate. Wapiti Meadow is a good choice for people seeking high-country solitude. A three-day stay costs $1,000 per person; six days add up to $1,500. The six-day fly-fishing package costs $2,250.

MONTANA

Lone Mountain Ranch

P.O. Box 160069, Big Sky, MT 59716
800-514-4644 or 406-995-4644
www.lmranch.com

Lone Mountain operates in summer and winter. From June through October you can enjoy ranch activities and ride trails on the outskirts of Yellowstone National Park,

about 20 miles away. An Orvis-endorsed fly-fishing resort, this ranch offers angling on the Madison and Gallatin Rivers, two of the best trout streams in the United States. In winter, you can cross-country ski from Lone Mountain into the Spanish Peaks Wilderness. Prices start at $2,600 for two guests ($1,665 for the first adult and $935 for the second).

Mountain Sky Guest Ranch

P.O. Box 1128, Bozeman, MT 59715
800-548-3392 or 406-587-1244
www.mtnsky.com

The Mountain Sky Guest Ranch is a deluxe, AAA four-diamond facility in the aptly named Paradise Valley. Guests enjoy numerous amenities, including a pool, tennis courts, gourmet dining, and great fishing. Wranglers are very skilled and the horses are first-rate. The cost ranges from $2,240-2,660 per week, with special rates for children.

OREGON

Baker's Bar M Ranch

58840 Bar M Lane, Adams, OR 97810
888-824-3381 or 541-566-3381
www.barmranch.com

Situated in the Blue Mountains and the North Fork of the Umatilla River Wilderness, Baker's Bar M Ranch is a family-oriented, family-run operation in eastern Oregon. Each guest is assigned a horse for a week and encouraged to groom and saddle the animal. There are plenty of daily riding opportunities, plus fishing, hiking, and swimming. A special attraction is the natural hot springs pool, a wonderful soak for muscles tired from riding.

An average of 32 guests per week enjoy the Bar M's accommodations, which include a historic ranch house that served as a stop for stagecoaches in the 1800s, a 19th-century homestead, and two modern family cabins. Rooms run $835-975 per week for adults and $720-795 per week for children 9 to 15 years old.

WYOMING

Absaroka Ranch

P.O. Box 929, Dubois, WY 82513
307-455-2275

Nestled between the Absaroka Mountains and the headwaters of the Wind River, the Absaroka Ranch offers a scenic, isolated alpine experience. Guests stay in private cabins, with hiking, fishing, and riding opportunities close at hand. The ranch's pack trips to the Washakie Wilderness east of the Tetons are among the best in the

country. Owners Budd and Emi Betts take small groups through pristine river valleys and over 11,000-foot plateaus. Cost is about $150 per day for pack trips or $1,200 (based on three people in the cabin) per week at the ranch.

CANADA

Top of the World Guest Ranch

P.O. Box 29, Fort Steele, BC, V0B 1N0, Canada. 888-996-6306 or 250-426-6306
www.topoftheworldranch.com

The 70,000-acre Top of the World Guest Ranch offers unrivaled scenery, fine horses, and memorable hospitality in southeastern British Columbia. Tucked in a green valley overlooking the Purcell Mountains, this vast and lovely ranch is perfect for horseback riding. A full trail-riding program runs from May through September, and seasonal cattle work is available. Guests can swim, canoe, and fish in the ranch's three private lakes. Arrangements can be made nearby for visitors who wish to play golf or go skiing, mountain biking, and white-water rafting. Guests stay in six comfortable log cabins equipped with private baths. Holidays range from $1,195 to $1,280 per week, with discounts for children.

Ts'yl-os Park Lodge

c/o Hidden Trails, 5936 Inverness St.
Vancouver, BC, V5W 3P7, Canada
888-987-2457 or 604-323-1141
www.hiddentrails.com

Guests at Ts'yl-os Park Lodge enjoy one of the most beautiful locations in North America. Situated at the north end of the vast, glacier-fed Chilko Lake, the lodge commands the gateway to newly created Ts'yl-os Provincial Park. A private airstrip serves the lodge, a true wilderness outpost where guests have the surrounding region to themselves. The area offers excellent fishing, riding, hiking, and hunting.

Four individual guest rooms and three cabins, all furnished with private baths, accommodate 16 guests. The lodge is very nice but not ultraluxurious, and most of the people who stay here are experienced riders. Riding groups are usually small. Even novices enjoy the ride to Mount Tullin, which provides spectacular views from its summit. Other trails offer equally impressive scenery, and the nearby Chilko River offers great trophy trout fishing. The cost is $1,195-1,595 per week, depending on the season (this includes round-trip air travel from Vancouver).

Cattle Drives, Wagon Trains, & Trail Rides

If you really want to get away from it all, an organized cattle drive, wagon trip, or trail ride may hold more appeal than a stay at a dude ranch. You see more country and get a hands-on Western experience that will both challenge and reward you.

CATTLE DRIVES

Imagine rising at dawn, mounting your trusty quarter horse, and guiding a herd across the open prairie to new pastures. Many people want to do just that, thanks to *City Slickers*, a comedy that made cattle drives a favorite choice for those seeking an active, fun-filled Western adventure.

Epic Trails

7875 170th Place N.E., Redmond, WA 98052
425-861-9969
www.serioussports.com/epictrails

Connie Cox, Montana's legendary cowboy, founded Epic Trails—authentic cattle drives that can't be beat. Each drive moves about 250 head, covering 55 miles as it travels from the open plains of southern Saskatchewan, in Canada, to the big sky country of Montana. Epic takes up to 20 guests and accepts all levels of ability for a cattle drive lasting five days and costing about $1,100; group discounts are available. Epic Trails also represents three different ranches in Montana that offer authentic activities such as branding, roping, and gathering cattle.

High Island Ranch & Cattle Co.

346 Amoretti, No. 10, Thermopolis, WY 82443. 307-867-2374
www.gorp.com/highisland

The High Island Ranch, 60 miles southeast of Cody, Wyoming, runs our favorite cattle drives. Starting from an upper mountain lodge at 9,000 feet or from the main ranch at 6,000 feet, the cattle drives move through the Wyoming high country. Participants spend the first couple of days bunching up the herd and then hit the trail for the remaining three days. Each summer, High Island offers a unique 1800s cattle drive during which "you will eat, sleep, dress, ride, and live" in Wild West style. Six cattle drives are scheduled for June and July, August and September, although the ranch hosts guests all summer. Prices for the drives range from $1,250 to $1,550 per person.

Hondoo Rivers & Trails

c/o A.W.E., P.O. Box 1486, Boulder, CO 80306. 800-444-0099 or 303-444-2622
www.awetrips.com

Hondoo Rivers & Trails, based at Torrey, Utah, runs a cattle drive through Capitol Reef National Park and the Dixie National Forest. Participants enjoy diverse and spectacular canyonlands scenery ranging from red-rock buttes to cool aspen forests above 9,000 feet. A maximum of ten guests accompany several full-time cowboys on the six- or seven-day journeys, which Hondoo offers in May and again in October. The price is a bargain, roughly $1,100, and it includes all gear and meals.

Powder River Wagon Trains & Cattle Drives

P.O. Box 676, Broadus, MT 59317. 800-492-8835, 800-982-0710, or 406-436-2404
www.powderrivercattledrive.com

Offering what it calls the "Cadillac of cattle drives," Powder River is ideal for people who not only want the adventure of a real cattle drive but also need a bit of luxury at the end of the day. While you help guide the 80-head herd across Montana's broad plains, members of the Powder River staff set up a tented camp complete with generators, showers, toilets, a dining commons, a saloon, and a dance hall. (They also provide the entertainment.) When you arrive from the trail, you will find everything ready and waiting for you. Approximately 40 to 60 guests accompany Powder River each year as it moves the herd of cattle on its major drive in August. Adults pay $1,450 for six days.

Powder River also runs popular wagon train trips. Each August, 60 guests join the Premier Wagon Train for a six-day journey through the scenic high country of Montana. From May through September, Powder River usually runs one five-day wagon train each month for 10 to 20 guests. The Premier Wagon Train costs $1,450 per person, while other wagon train trips cost $1,250 per person.

WAGON TRAINS

Wagon trains offer a chance to relive an experience of Western pioneers. On most trips, you can ride in a wagon or saddle up your own mount as an outrider. These trips are great for families because small children can safely ride in the wagon under the watchful eyes of the wagon masters, while teens can handle their own mounts.

Teton Wagon Train & Horse Adventure

Double H Bar Inc., P.O. Box 10307, Jackson Hole, WY 83002. 888-734-6101 or 307-734-6101. www.tetonwagontrain.com

Employing three wagons, and 10 to 25 horses for outriders, the Teton Wagon Train makes a four-day loop tour around Grand Teton National Park. Trips cover about 20 miles on the Grassy Lake Trail and Reclamation Road, reaching elevations of 8,000 feet. Camp is made early each afternoon, allowing plenty of time to hike, swim in mountain lakes, or take short pleasure rides. Though most of the 20 to 30 guests prefer to ride horseback, the wagons offer a secure, comfortable ride for kids and anyone who happens to need a break from the saddle. Evenings feature Dutch oven cookouts, campfire singing, and surprise visits by "Indians" and "mountain men." The four-day adventure costs $745 for adults and $645 for kids under 8 years of age.

Wagons West—Yellowstone Outfitters

P.O. Box 1156, Afton, WY 83110. 800-447-4711 or 307-886-9693; or contact American Wilderness Experience (800-444-0099. www.awetrips.com)

Wagons West offers two-, four- and six-day journeys through the Bridger-Teton National Forest near Jackson, Wyoming. Guests ride horseback about half the time, but small kids and nonriders can enjoy the experience from a stable wagon with rubber tires for added comfort. The Wagons West program is quite suitable for families. Guides recount the histories of the early settlers, the Sioux, and the Crow, and kids enjoy supervised activities just for them. Four-day trips cost $635 for adults and $540 for children under 14.

TRAIL RIDES

On a trail ride, you can join a trail boss and his wranglers for a four- to ten-day adventure by horseback, often following a historic trail used by early homesteaders. Experienced equestrians who like to canter and gallop will prefer trail rides over horsepacking trips or cattle drives, which tend to travel at a much slower pace.

Anchor D Guiding & Outfitting

Dewy and Jan Matthews, Box 656
Black Diamond, AB, T0L 0H0, Canada
403-933-2867. www.anchord.com

Anchor D offers great riding vacations in the Kananaskis area of the Alberta Rockies, a realm of breathtaking natural beauty. The showcase adventure is the seven-day Great

Divide Trail Ride, which ventures across high mountain passes to elevations of 8,000 feet. Unlike most pack trip outfitters, Anchor D hauls supplies by wagon, so riders can range freely from moving high-country camps, enjoying a brisk gallop now and then. Wagons carry comfortable cots with foam mattresses, ensuring a good night's sleep after each day's ride. This superior operation relies on two decades of experience. The horses are great, groups are limited to 12 clients, the food is first-rate, and owner-guide Dewey Matthews is a local legend known for his great passion for riding. Anchor D also offers a six-day Lost Trail trip featuring day rides from an alpine base camp beside a lovely waterfall. Experienced "horse people" who love to ride and ride fast will enjoy both of these trips. The Great Divide trip costs about $1,200 and the Lost Trail trip costs about $1,050. Shorter two- to four-day base-camp trips provide ideal weekend getaways.

Box K Ranch

Winter: Walt Korn, c/o Box K Ranch, 6716 Calle de la Mango, Hereford, AZ 85615. 800-729-1410 or 520-803-9694. Summer: P.O. Box 110, Moran, WY 83013. 800-729-1410 or 307-543-2407. www.jaycreek.com/boxranch

The Box K's Jackson Hole Trail Ride is celebrating its 30th year of operation, which means that this journey is one of the most enduring adventure trips in the high country of Wyoming. Much of the five-day ride is spent above timberline on alpine routes in the Tetons. Although the trip is certainly suitable for so-called greenhorns, the Trail Ride remains very popular with men and women who are skilled riders. Most of the people who choose to take this journey are horse owners themselves or have plenty of trail-riding experience. The trip runs for seven days in August and costs approximately $600; horses and packs are not included in the price, but you can rent a horse for $300. Box K also offers pack trips throughout the summer in the Teton Wilderness area.

Don Donnelly Horseback Vacations & Stables

6010 S. Kings Ranch Rd., Gold Canyon, AZ 85219. 800-346-4403 or 480-982-7822 www.dondonnelly.com

Don Donnelly Stables offers three-, five-, and seven-day horseback vacations in scenic Monument Valley, the Superstition Wilderness, the White Mountains, and the Mogollon Rim (Zane Grey country). The best way to experience Monument Valley, by far, is on horseback. Get up early to witness the play of light on the valley's massive red-rock formations. Valley tours run for seven days in spring and fall for about $1,600. The other programs run about $1,000-1,200 for five days, while three-day trips cost $575. On all trips you make daily rides from a comfortable base camp that features good Western cooking and hot showers. Don Donnelly, say those who have ridden with him, "is basically John Wayne reincarnated, only he's bigger—and a better horseman!"

Wilderness Horsepacking

Although purist backpackers may scoff at the use of burdened beasts, horsepacking is a sensible and rewarding way to experience the wilderness. You can travel farther and faster into the mountains than you can on foot, and your horse can easily carry four times the load you could manage with a backpack. Comfort levels vary: On some trips you sleep on the ground, and in other cases, you may bed down on cots set up in comfortable wall tents.

CALIFORNIA
**Pine Creek Pack Station/
Sequoia Kings Pack Train**
P.O. Box 968, Bishop, CA 93515
800-962-0775 or 760-387-2797
www.395.com/packers.htm

Brian and Dee Berner run low-impact pack trips into the eastern and southern Sierra Nevada range, near Yosemite and Kings Canyon National Parks. You can join a trans-Sierra crossing over high passes or follow the John Muir Trail along the Sierra Crest and through Kings Canyon National Park. In addition to their guided horseback and hiking trips, the Berners offer daily trail rides and guided pack trips. Prices range from $70 to $395 per day, depending on destination and type of trip.

COLORADO
Rapp Guide Service
3635 County Rd. 301, Durango, CO 81301.
877-600-2656, 970-375-1250,
or 970-247-8923. www.rappguides.com

Many people consider Rapp Guide's horsepack trips among the best in Colorado. Trips run through the San Juan and Rio Grande National Forests and the Weminuche Wilderness, and they cost about $200 per day for gourmet food, expert guiding, and all the necessary gear. Horsepackers discover great diversity in the terrain and in spring see abundant wildflowers. Groups are small—no more than six in wilderness areas or ten in national forests—and this outfitter customizes all trips so that they match the guests' interests and riding experience. Heading a staff of qualified wranglers is expert horseman and guide Pete Turner. Together they maintain a fine stable of strong, amiable horses. You will also find that excellent cuisine is served on the deluxe trips. Four-day trips range from $895 to $995. In winter, the Rapps also offer horse-drawn sleigh rides.

IDAHO
Mystic Saddle Ranch
Stanley, ID 83278. 888-722-5432 or 208-774-3591. Winter: P.O. Box 736, Challis, ID

83226. 208-879-5071
www.mysticsaddleranch.com

You can venture into Idaho's rugged Sawtooth Mountains with Jeff and Deb Bitton, extremely able and personable outfitters who have been running quality pack trips since 1969. The terrain here features alpine meadows, cobalt blue lakes, and towering peaks. Itineraries of one to seven days can be arranged for riders of all skill levels and ages (kids 6 and older). Mystic Saddle Ranch also lets you combine pack trips with rafting on the Payette River or fishing at some of the 180 lakes in the Sawtooth wilderness. The spot-pack program drops hikers off at an isolated campsite and later picks them up on a prearranged date. Pack trips cost roughly $170 per person per day. Base-camp trips and day rides are also offered.

Pioneer Mountain Outfitters

3267 East, 3225 North, Twin Falls, ID 83301. Summer: 208-774-3737. Winter: 208-734-3679. www.pioneermountain.com.

Pioneer operates daily trail rides plus multiday pack trips out of the historic Idaho Rocky Mountain Ranch, one of the state's first guest ranches. On the pack trips, guides Tom and Debbie Proctor lead guests on three- to fifteen-day adventures into the White Cloud Mountains of the Sawtooth Range. This region is dotted with alpine lakes offering some of the best high-country trout fishing in the state.

Most itineraries are customized, small-group adventures involving 8 to 12 miles of riding each day and allowing plenty of time to enjoy the scenery, the wildlife, and the fishing. You can choose from easy family outings or rugged back-country treks. Pack trips run $185 per day. The Proctors make an enormous effort to guarantee that each trip matches their clients' particular interests.

MONTANA

7 Lazy P Outfitters

P.O. Box 178, Choteau, MT 59422. 406-466-2044. www.7lazyp.com.

From a comfortable ranch near scenic Glacier National Park, Chuck and Sharon Blixrud have operated pack trips through the Bob Marshall Wilderness Area since 1958. The mountains of the "Bob," which are prime habitats for moose, elk, and bighorn sheep, are among North America's most dramatic natural features. The Blixruds' pack trips run from seven to ten days and cost an average of $210 per day.

Fishing trips are also offered to some of Montana's prime alpine fishing spots. Given the popularity of these trips, it's not a bad idea to book them well in advance. The Blixruds also welcome guests who wish to stay at their 7 Lazy P guest ranch.

Wilderness Outfitters

3800 Rattlesnake Dr., Missoula, MT 59802. 406-549-2820
www.recworld.com/wildout

Author of the definitive *Packing In on Mules and Horses*, Smoke Elser is perhaps the most renowned wilderness guide in Montana. Since 1964, he and his wife, Thelma, have outfitted and run outstanding pack trips through the Bob Marshall Wilderness Area, a vast sanctuary where grizzlies, wolves, and wolverines still roam. The pack trips are exceptionally popular: About 90 percent of riders are repeat customers. The Elsers run a roving program each summer, covering the entire length of the wilderness area from north to south. Trips run six to ten days at a cost of $230 per day. Specialty photography and fishing itineraries are also available.

OREGON

Outback Ranch Outfitters

P.O. Box 384, Joseph, OR 97846. 541-886-2029. www.catsback.com/outbackranch.

Ken Wick of the Outback Ranch is one of eastern Oregon's most knowledgeable outdoorsmen. He guides first-rate horse trips into the state's Wallowa Mountains, the Wenaha-Tucannon Wilderness on the Oregon-Washington border, and the Hell's Canyon region along the border between Oregon and Idaho.

The Wallowas encompass a little-known but beautiful region of high-Alpine lakes that some people like to call the Switzerland of America. If you are looking for places where you can do some trout fishing, consider the wild and still unspoiled Imnaha and Wenaha Rivers, which are superb fisheries for Dolly Varden and brook trout. In Hell's Canyon you can combine horsepacking with white-water rafting and fishing on the Snake River. Basic three- to ten-day horsepack trips cost about $200 per day, all-inclusive. High-lakes fishing trips, limited to four anglers, run $250 per day.

UTAH

Ken Sleight Pack Trips, Pack Creek Ranch

P.O. Box 1270, Moab, UT 84532. 435-259-5505. www.packcreekranch.com

Ken Sleight offers wilderness trips from his ranch situated near Arches and Canyonlands National Parks. His two- to three-day overnight trips venture out from the Pack Creek Ranch to Ken's South Mountain cabin from June through August, while horse-supported hiking tours, lasting from two to six days, are offered in the Grand Gulch Primitive Area and canyon country. (You get to walk and the horses have to carry all of your gear.)

This region of Utah—in the state's southeastern corner—offers some of the most dramatic scenery on the planet. As a result, first-time visitors here find themselves almost continually marveling at the often incredible vistas and red-rock formations. Ken Sleight's trips cost about $175 per day; the best times to travel in this part of Utah are late spring and early fall.

WASHINGTON

North Cascade Safaris

P.O. Box 250, Winthrop, WA 98862. 509-996-2350. E-mail: clod@methow.com

For three decades, Claude Miller has run horsepacking excursions out of Winthrop, Washington, and into the verdant high country of the Okanagan National Forest (Paysaten and Lake Chelan Sawtooth Wildernesses) midway between Seattle and Spokane. Miller knows the Cascade Range like the back of his hand, and he can put together just about any kind of trip you would want—from three days to two weeks.

Two of the most popular routes offered by North Cascade are the Sawtooth Ridge Trail to Lake Chelan and the Pacific Crest National Scenic Trail to the Canadian border—a spectacular trek through 8,000-foot-high passes. On most of the trips you cover less than 15 miles a day, so you won't have to spend all of your time sitting in the saddle. Miller tries to follow a day of hard riding with some rest and relaxation, allowing you time to fish and unwind. Pack trips cost about $150 per day.

WYOMING

Lazy Boot Outfitters

P.O. Box 7595, Fort Smith, MT 59035
800-665-3799 or 406-666-9199
www.forrester-travel.com

Using a running pack string, Lazy Boot Outfitters goes much farther into the wild than many other horsepackers do. From a wilderness base camp at 9,600

BRINKMANSHIP IN HELL'S CANYON NATIONAL RECREATION AREA, IDAHO feet, Lazy Boot trips explore the distant corners of the Cloud Peak Wilderness Area and Big Horn National Forest. Led by a family-run outfitting team, these outings offer excellent opportunities for wildlife photography, so bring a camera and watch for elk, deer, and moose. Guided bow hunting (for elk) is an option, and fly-fishing is also available. Go casting for the plentiful brook, cutthroat, rainbow, and golden trout.

The pack trips are all customized, with no more than six persons per group. Most trips run four to seven days at a cost of about $250 to $300 per day per person, all-inclusive. Guests can also combine a pack trip with a stay at the Big Horn River Resort.

CANADA

Wild Rose Outfitting

P.O. Box 113, Peers, AB, T0J 1W0, Canada 780-693-2296. www.wildroseoutfitting.com

Wild Rose is a small, family-run enterprise that can claim two decades of experience in the Jasper National Park/Willmore Wilderness Area of northern Alberta. Dave Manzer, owner of Wild Rose Outfitting, personally leads each one of the trips into the Willmore Wilderness Park.

The Willmore region, on the northern edge of Jasper National Park, is a true mountain wilderness in which you will find no roads, buildings, or bridges. The scenery, according to many people who visit here, rivals anything else in North America. The horse treks take you to the shores of pristine high-Alpine lakes, prime trout-fishing country where one-and-a-half-pound cutthroats and rainbows are abundant. A guide plus two to four wranglers and two cooks accompany each group of eight to fourteen riders, affording truly personalized attention.

The trips run from June through mid-September and cost $175 (CN) per day, or about $770 (US) for six days. If you have never traveled to the Canadian Rockies, prepare to belly up to a visual feast: These trips offer some of the finest scenery in the world.

Warner Guiding & Outfitting

P.O. Box 2280, Banff, AB, T0L 0C0, Canada 403-762-4551 www.horseback.com/localride.html

Among the leading horse outfitters in Alberta, Warner Guiding & Outfitting offers a broad range of wilderness pack trips and riding vacations in Banff National Park. You can combine pack trips with lodge vacations. You can also take advantage of one of the special wildlife-viewing programs that are available. The season runs from May through October, and the prices average about $225 (US) per day, all-inclusive. Half-day rides that include breakfast run about $40 (US). The stock is excellent, and the guides are very experienced.

NEW ZEALAND

Hurunui Horsetreks

Taihoa Downs, Hawarden RD, North Canterbury, New Zealand. 01164-3314-4204. www.horseback.co.nz.

Run by Rob Stanley and Mandy Platt since 1987, Hurunui Horsetreks is the leading backcountry riding operation on New Zealand's scenic South Island. From a comfortable high-country farm, Hurunui offers two- to eight-day pack trips into the foothills above the Canterbury Plain. Potential trekkers can choose from a wide variety of trips, one of which is a five-day wagon trip that is ideal for families with small children.

Hurunui runs a group of 70 horses, supported by a first-class team of trained, professional guides. The food is hearty, but it is not gourmet. You will find that this is a solid operation, with very friendly staff and excellent stock. Both experienced and novice riders are welcome. Hurunui Horsetreks offers a ride that is one of the most interesting and enjoyable activities you can do on horseback in New Zealand. The prices are modest—approximately US$100 to $150 per day.

PLANNING YOUR RANCH VACATION

Before you head for the West, ask your ranch boss or outfitter to recommend personal gear for your trip. You should plan on bringing any personal items you require, including hats, sunglasses, sunscreen, and medicines. Many ranches stock a few sundries, but you will pay a premium price if you run out of the toothpaste or hand lotion you brought with you. On working ranches or cattle drives be prepared for cold and dirty conditions. Dress in layers and remember that cotton, unlike wool or fleece, won't keep you warm if the fabric gets wet. If your outfitter or the ranch where you are staying does not provide work gloves, you'll want to bring long, gauntlet-style leather gloves that cover your sleeve cuff.

Handkerchiefs are a necessity. You will use them for wiping away sweat and trail dust, and if you wet one of them and wear it around your neck, it will cool you and keep the sun's rays off your skin. When rain begins to fall, rubberized fabric coats provide the best protection; so-called "water-resistant" fabrics or nylon ponchos are too flimsy. Tall boots are also essential. Make sure you have a comfortable pair that you break in before your trip.

If you plan to hunt or fish on your trip, ask your outfitter if he or she will provide all of the necessary equipment. Also remember to find out whether you need to obtain any licenses. Another good idea is to ask whether the insurance the ranch or outfitter provides will cover you if you injure yourself in an accident. If you are required to sign a waiver, check your own insurance because some personal policies have exclusions for hazardous activities. Families with small children should find out if there are minimum age requirements for riding and whether their hosts offer children's programs or lessons.

ORGANIZATIONS

British Columbia Guest Ranchers Association, P.O. Box 4501, Williams Lake, BC, V2G 2V5, Canada. 604-398-7755. www.bcguestranches.com.

Colorado Dude and Guest Ranch Association, P.O. Box 2120, Granby, CO 80446. 970-887-3128. www.coloradoranch.com.

Dude Ranchers' Association, P.O. Box F-471, La Porte, CO 80535. 970-223-8440. www.duderanch.org.

ONLINE

Equinet

http://horses.product.com

A strong website, Equinet features original articles and news items, provides extensive classified listings of horses and riding centers that are for sale, and includes information on boarding, training, breeding, and veterinary services.

Gene Kilgore's Ranchweb

www.ranchweb.com

Created by the author of the definitive guidebook on ranch vacations, this website includes descriptions of hundreds of

ranches and Western vacations.

Guest Ranches of North America
www.guestranches.com

This site contains profiles of hundreds of guest and working ranches in the United States and Canada. Many of the best ranches in North America are found here, and multiple large photos illustrate most of them.

The HayNet
www.haynet.net

Hay.net delivers the most comprehensive collection of the horse-related URLs found anywhere. You'll find links for virtually all equine topics.

Horse Net
www.horsenet.com

This is a full-featured site that includes a growing list of riding tour vacations and equestrian events worldwide. You'll also find horse-related news, classifieds, and veterinary advice.

PRINT

Gene Kilgore's Ranch Vacations (John Muir Press, 5th ed., 1999, $23). "[T]he guidebook of guidebooks for anyone interested in a ranch vacation," say the editors of *The Western Horseman*. A saddlebag-stretching 528 pages, the tome features detailed profiles of more than 250 ranches visited by Gene Kilgore. Using the book's rock-solid reviews, photographs, and thorough index, you can choose the ideal Western venue, including working ranches and those that cater to anglers or skiers. *Ranch Vacations* can be ordered from **Ranchweb** (*707-939-3801. www.ranchweb.com*).

Farm, Ranch and Country Vacations by Pat Dickerman (1995, $19.95). This publication is a photo-illustrated directory of country lodgings in North America, ranging from rugged working ranches to deluxe B&Bs near popular resort areas. Dickerman's work is a good complement to *Gene*

Kilgore's Ranch Vacations, particularly for farm stays. The book can be ordered from **Adventure Guides** (*7550 E. McDonald Dr., Scottsdale, AZ 83250. 800-252-7899*).

Packing In on Mules and Horses by Smoke Elser and Bill Brown (Mountain Press, $18. P.O. Box 2399, Missoula, MT 59806. 800-234-5308 or 406-728-1900. www.mtn-press.com). Professional outfitter Smoke Elser teaches his readers how to make their pack trips more enjoyable, safe, and comfortable. The book is easy to read and includes instructional photos and sketches.

VIDEOS

EquiVid (*800-872-9462 or 713-812-1242. www.equivid.com*) offers more than 1,000 videos on riding and the West, for rent or for sale. Topics include dressage, equine health, racing, competition, rodeos, and breed histories.

DUDE AND DOG CHILL ON A UTAH RANCH.

RUGGED AND RELIABLE, OFF-ROAD VEHICLES TAKE YOU WHERE YOU WANT TO GO IN HIGH style—and surprising comfort. To maximize your enjoyment of four-wheeling, we've drawn up a detailed guide to the top off-road destinations in North America. These touring areas and parks let you get back to nature in a 4WD vehicle without incurring the wrath of farmers, ranchers, or bureaucrats. Along with this North America guide, you'll find a number of jeep safaris and fully outfitted overland odysseys to exotic venues worldwide, from Tasmania to Tennessee. • Granted, many adventurers find two wheels better than four. Millionaire motorcyclist Malcolm Forbes, for one, dismissed car travel as "driving around in your living room." If you're a like-minded soul, motorcycle touring is the ultimate escape. Beginners as well as experienced riders will be able to find a suitable tour in our comprehensive guide to motorcycle travel worldwide, which begins on page 136. We also offer tips on planning your own two-wheeled adventures.

LEFT: COLBERT PEPPER ROARS DOWN A GRAVEL ROAD IN ARGEN-
TINA'S PATAGONIA ON HIS HONDA XR650.
BELOW: KICKING UP A LITTLE FOUR-WHEEL DUST IN MAUI, HAWAII.

Motorized Adventures

Four-Wheel Drives

Jeep Jamborees

Getting Off-*Piste*

Motorcycle Madness

[T]he two greatest illusions among American males are, first, that they are good in bed, and second, that they can drive anything.

CRAIG VETTER

America's Best 4WD Destinations

Deluxe four-wheel-drive machines get justifiably dissed as "urban assault vehicles" when their new owners waste all that traction on runs to the dry cleaner and day-care center. If you want to put your own 4WD machine through the paces for which it was really designed, read on to discover the best off-road destinations in the U.S. and Mexico.

ARIZONA & UTAH
Grand Canyon Region

The northwest corner of Arizona, along the **North Rim** of the Grand Canyon, is an off-roader's dream, with 7,600 square miles of high desert wilderness, scores of accessible jeep trails, and the splendor of the Grand Canyon. From St. George, Utah, a rough road takes you south toward the canyon overlook at Tuweep Point. There you can see the Colorado River snaking along 3,000 feet below. Heading back north, you will connect with paved Ariz. 67 at Jacob's Lake. This can take you to the North Rim in summer, but the road is usually closed in winter. If you've got the time, continue east to the **Marble Canyon** area, where a number of fun routes take you over reservation roads and through sand washes near the banks of the Colorado. You can also book a river float trip from Marble Canyon or continue up to **Lake Powell,** worth a visit in itself.

Camping information and maps for the North Rim and Marble Canyon are available from the **Arizona Strip Interpretive Association** (*St. George, UT. 435-688-3246*). Short, guided South Rim jeep excursions are offered by **Grand Canyon Outback Jeep Tours** (*520-638-2052*). Good guidebooks include Roger Mitchell's *Grand Canyon Jeep Trails I: North Rim* (*La Siesta Press*) and Rick Harris's *Discover Arizona* (*Golden West Publishers, 800-658-5830. www.goldenwest.cc*).

Monument Valley

Everyone should visit **Monument Valley** at least once. You'll be awestruck the first time you drive beneath its giant sandstone pinnacles, formed by millions of years of wind erosion. Located in northeast Arizona right on the Utah border, the valley's scenery is straight out of the age of the dinosaurs. A network of jeep trails takes you to scenic vistas and a variety of old Native American sites. For a nominal fee, you can take your own 4WD; for a bit more, you can book a guided 4WD tour at the park's parking lot, which overlooks the entrance to the valley. We recommend the guided tour unless you are experienced running in sand.

Try to visit at sunrise or sunset to experience the rich colors and rugged beauty that have drawn countless Hollywood film crews to this area. Accommodations and camping sites are limited, so book in advance if you're planning to stay more than a day. Monument Valley is only a few hours' drive from the Grand Canyon and other major southwestern parklands. **Monument Valley Tribal Park** (*435-727-3287*)

Canyon Country

For colorful rock formations and sheer rugged beauty, we can't think of a better destination than the canyonlands region. One of North America's premier 4WD routes is the 100-mile **White Rim Trail,** located in the Island in the Sky District of **Canyonlands National Park.** The two-day route winds through red-rock canyons, buttes, mesas, and plateaus with 1,000-foot overlooks above the Colorado and Green Rivers. Camping is authorized, but you should apply months in advance for a camping permit.

In the Needles District of Canyonlands National Park lie **Salt Creek Canyon** and **Horse Canyon,** two routes offering vistas of magnificent arches, sandstone canyons, ancient Anasazi ruins, and petroglyph sites. Don't miss nearby **Arches National Park** (*435-259-8161. www.nps.gov/arch*), located just outside Moab, Utah. With hundreds of richly colored sandstone spires and arches carved by eons of wind erosion, the park is a high desert wonderland that no nature-loving visitor should miss. The main route through the park is paved and therefore suitable for civilian vehicles. However, off-roaders can enjoy the **Salt Valley** and **Klondike Bluffs** routes—sandy, wilderness-area tracks specially designated for 4x4s. On any venture into canyon country, bring plenty of water and essential spare parts; you'll be quite isolated on many of your excursions. Good maps and regional guidebooks are available through the **Grand County Travel Council** (*Moab, UT. 800-635-6622. www.canyonlands-utah.com*).

Capitol Reef

In **Capitol Reef National Park** (*Torrey, UT. 435-425-3791. www.nps.gov/care*) you'll find stunning red-rock canyons, huge sandstone rock formations, one of the world's largest natural arches, and many other geological oddities. There are many good off-highway routes. One of the best is **Notom-Bullfrog Road,** an easy-driving dirt road through red-rock country. The road runs north-

JEEPS CRAWL ALONG THE SLICK ROCKS OF MOAB, UTAH, DURING THE ANNUAL JEEP SAFARI IN APRIL.

south along a geological formation called the Waterpocket Fold, which looks like giant plates that erupted from the earth. The Waterpocket Fold is best appreciated from a high elevation such as the Strike Valley Overlook, which can be reached by turning off Notom-Bullfrog Road. Take Burr Trail for 2 miles, then follow a signed road for 3 miles to the overlook trailhead. The overlook is about 20 minutes away by foot. For four-wheeling, the **Bull Creek Pass National Backcountry Byway** is spectacular. Some 60 miles long, the byway climbs to 10,485 feet as it crests the Henry Mountains overlooking Capitol Reef. For information, contact the **Henry Mountains Field Station** of the Bureau of Land Management in Hanksville (435-542-3461).

The park boasts a network of hiking trails, as well as dirt and gravel roads laid out expressly for 4WD touring. You can easily spend a week exploring these roads. There's also plenty of open country to run, but check with the Park Service before venturing off any designated route. One of Utah's best campgrounds is in the middle of Capitol Reef National Park. If you plan to camp, reserve early. The nearest motels are 13 miles away and are often fully booked. Tony Huegel's *Utah Byways* (*Wilderness Press*, 800-443-7227) and Wade Roylance's *Seeing Capitol Reef National Park* are good resources.

CALIFORNIA
Rubicon Trail

The Rubicon Trail runs for 65 miles over the crest of the Sierra Nevada from Georgetown in the west to Lake Tahoe in the east. This challenging and historic route, an old wagon road, will test your patience—and your machine's low-speed agility—through lengthy sections of steep boulders. The rocks can be so tough in places that dirt-bikers have been spotted turning around in defeat. Once you've passed the rocky sections, however, the rest of the run is relatively easy, and it offers great views and excellent campsites in the **Eldorado National Forest.**

For company on the Rubicon Trail, join the annual **Jeepers Jamboree** (530-333-4771. *www.jeepers-jamboree.com*) in late July. This has been one of the premier 4WD events in California for more than 40 years. If you miss the July Jamboree there is another major Rubicon 4WD outing in August.

Death Valley National Park

Death Valley National Park (760-786-2331. *www.nps.gov/deva*), as its ominous name suggests, can be an unforgiving, punishing place where survival is never certain. But Death Valley is also a land of stark and primeval beauty—particularly in the winter and spring, when temperatures moderate and the desert blooms. With few places like it on

Earth, a visit to America's newest national park should be near the top of any serious off-roader's wish list.

First-time visitors may want to start at Ubehebe Crater and proceed south on **Racetrack Road,** which climbs 4,000 feet to the open playa called the Racetrack. There, large rocks—loosened by rain, of all things—fall from the surrounding cliffs and tumble into the playa's bed. Intense late afternoon winds push the rocks, which roll in mysterious trajectories like dice tossed by invisible giants. Racetrack Road is a fairly easy 55-mile round-trip, but there are long rocky stretches that will test your rig's suspension. The road also passes by a Joshua tree forest at Tin Pass in the Panamint Range, and offers access to another Joshua tree forest in beautiful Hidden Valley (turn off at Teakettle Junction).

Another popular route through Death Valley is the 100-mile **Saline Valley Road,** a national backcountry byway that runs from Calif. 168 east of Big Pine in Owens Valley through Death Valley National Park. The road rises and falls along the way, affording rare views of spectacular desert valleys and nearby mountain ranges.

WASHINGTON
Wenatchee Forest

Some hair-raising trails are found in the backwoods of the **Wenatchee National Forest** (*509-662-4335. www.fs.fed. us/r6/wenatchee*), which bristles with tricky sidehills, tough slopes, sheer ridge lines, and lots of rocks and streams. The Shoestring Trail near Cliffdell—route of the annual Northwest 4WD Jamboree—is said to be rougher and more challenging than California's Rubicon Trail (*see p. 127*). The Devil's Gulch area is also a hot spot for off-roading. The trails here are not as forbidding, but the scenery is exceptional.

Throughout the Wenatchee Forest, prepare for rain at any time of the year—especially in the spring, when the snowmelt runoff can present some real problems. You'll therefore need all the ground clearance you can get. For tips on routes, contact the ORV Manager for the **Naches Ranger District** (*509-653-2205*).

IDAHO
Owyhee County

With ghost towns galore, impressive canyons, rocky peaks, and even some sand dunes, Owyhee County is 4WD paradise. Besides more good trails than you can count, you're right next to the Snake River, one of the world's best rafting runs. A great drive is the **Owyhee Uplands** (also known as Mudflat Rd.), a national backcountry byway that travels 105 miles between Jordan Valley near the Oregon border, along US 95 past Juniper Mountain to the town of Grand View on Idaho 78. The route affords beautiful views of the north fork of the Owyhee River Canyon and the Owyhee

Mountains. Wildlife, fishing, and camping abound. The nearby Leslie Gulch-Succor Creek Rd. winds through a spectacular canyon carved by centuries of erosion. Another favorite drive begins at Murphy on US 78: A rough but exciting gold-mining road threads the mountains west to the Oregon border, where you end up at US 95. You'll have about 50 miles of off-roading over tough, wet, and rocky tracks—a real challenge for human and machine. Request maps from the **BLM Boise field office of the Lower Snake River District** (*Boise, ID. 208-384-3300*).

WYOMING
Tetons & Yellowstone

Nestled beside the Snake River in the shadow of the Grand Tetons and just south of Yellowstone National Park, Jackson is a great starting point for off-road exploration. Old logging roads and backcountry routes crisscross the area. One of the best routes is **Reclamation Road**—an unpaved scenic byway that begins in Ashton, Idaho, crosses the border into Wyoming, then passes through a corridor just north of Grand Teton National Park. From there it emerges just south of Yellowstone and links up with US 89/191/287 near Jackson. Travel the road in autumn, when the grasslands, marshes, and pine forests are ablaze with color. **Targhee National Forest** (*Ashton, ID. 208-652-7442*).

Off-road driving is not allowed inside the national parks themselves, but you'll find 2,000 miles of unpaved logging roads in the **Bridger-Teton National Forest** (*Jackson, WY. 307-739-5500. www.fs.fed.us/btnf*), which encircles Yellowstone and Grand Teton parks. Rugged 35-mile **Union Pass Road,** off US 26/287 out of Dubois, Wyoming, takes you to high, remote forests dotted with alpine meadows and lakes. The route offers vistas of the rugged Wind River Range to the east and the distant Grand Tetons.

The side roads off Union Pass Road are also worth exploring. Try the 187-mile, day-trip loop to Union Pass Road from Jackson, or take a multiday trip and camp at the excellent Green River Lakes campground. **Flagstaff** and **Spread Creek Roads**—45 miles north of Jackson off US 287 in the Togwotee Pass area—lead to great spots for fishing, hunting, and mountain biking. Camping, with reservations, is allowed along both roads. Information is also available through the **Buffalo Ranger District** (*Moran, WY. 307-543-2386*).

COLORADO
San Juan Mountains

In the San Juan Mountains of southwestern Colorado—often called the Switzerland of America—you'll find plenty of old mining trails and abandoned railroad beds perfect for backcountry forays. Ouray, Colorado, makes a good starting point for 4WD trips into the San Juans. Head west from town up Imogene Pass for a splendid day trip with great overlooks and a number of large waterfalls. Along the way, you can sample the mining roads that crisscross the area or continue all the way up the pass and switchback down the west slope to Telluride. Through the end of June, expect snow at high elevations and tricky stream crossings. Ouray is one of the few places in the country where you can rent a roll-bar-equipped 4WD jeep for exploring narrow-track backcountry routes. **Switzerland of America Tours** (*226 7th Ave., Ouray, CO. 800-432-5337 or 970-325-4484. www. soajeep.com*). **Ouray Chamber of Commerce** (*970-325-4746. www.ouraycolorado.com*)

There are so many superlative routes in this area you'll find plenty of options from any starting point. **Black Bear Pass** between Red Mountain Pass and Telluride is one of the most famous drives in this area. Another challenging trail is the route from Telluride to Silverton via the 12,350-foot-high **Ophir Pass.** From Silverton, a great run crosses the 12,500-foot-high **Stony Pass**—a route that carried thousands of miners and covered wagons in its heyday. To get to Stony Pass, head north from Silverton to Howardsville, then turn south through Cunningham Gulch. Follow the signs to Cunningham Pass (another name for the Stony Pass route). You'll start climbing right away, as you begin a 28-mile journey through forests and alpine meadows that boasts some of the best overlooks in the Rockies.

From the summit, you'll want to continue on Forest Road 520, notable for the network of 4WD trails that radiate from it. You can then pick up Colo. 149, which eventually gets you to Creede. From there, you can head to Lost Lakes, Regan Lake, or other wilderness destinations. The Rio Grande National Forest Map clearly indicates the Stony Pass Route as well as fire roads and jeep trails to lakes and camping areas. Contact the **San Juan National Forest** (*15 Burnett Ct., Durango. 970-247-4874*). A good local trail guide, *Jeep Roads and Ghost Towns of the San Juans*, and information on local 4WD outfitters and off-road events are available from the **Silverton Chamber of Commerce** (*970-387-5654. www.silverton.org*).

NEW MEXICO
Chokecherry Canyon

The best kept secret in New Mexico is Chokecherry Canyon, just outside of Farmington. Chokecherry is small—not more than 15 square miles—but it is packed with boulders, stepped rocks, sandstone ledges, and slickrock that provide hours of fun for intrepid four-wheel drivers. The main feature of the canyon is the **Waterfall Trail,** the ultimate in 4WD craziness: One or two miles of ledges, camber scram-

bles, steep descents, and rocks all provide a supreme test for drivers and their rigs. Other challenging trails—ranging from 100 yards to a mile long—include Ball Hanger Trail, Stairsteps, Groundspring, Playground, Harley's Wash, and Beaver Falls. You can bypass obstacles on most trails or piece together your own set. Chokecherry Canyon is a fun outing for a summer afternoon, best finished beside a campfire while you watch the sun go down over this high desert land of mesas, mountains, and valleys. **Southwest 4WD Association.**

TENNESSEE
Great Smoky Mountains

Great Smoky Mountains National Park straddles the border between North Carolina and Tennessee. The park itself is closed to most off-road travel, but it is bordered by Forest Service lands with many good 4WD routes. Some of the most popular trails are found in Tennessee's **Cherokee National Forest** (*Cleveland, TN. 423-476-9700*), which attracts 4WD fans from around the country. In the **Nolichucky-Unaka Ranger Districts** (*Greenville, TN. 423-638-4109*), take the Horse Creek ORV Road to Cold Springs Mountain. At the summit you'll enjoy great views and access to the Appalachian Trail (foot traffic only).

In North Carolina, routes along the headwaters of Tellico Creek are very popular, with good trout streams nearby. The Great Smoky Mountains are still relatively unspoiled, but you're never too far from civilization, making it easy to locate a good campground or country inn. Contact the **Tusquitee Ranger District, Nantahala National Forest** (*Murphy, NC. 828-837-5152*).

FLORIDA
The Panhandle

In Florida's Panhandle wilderness between the Gulf Coast and the southern edges of Alabama and Georgia, you'll find lots of good 4WD destinations in the Apalachicola and Osceola National Forests. Located near Tallahassee and Lake City, both forests contain a network of off-road trails, along with many camping and fishing spots.

Florida wildlife-management areas on the panhandle also allow four-wheel-drive use over unpaved backcountry roads—fairly rugged, often muddy tracks. You'll need a permit to hunt in the game preserves, which are operated by the Florida Fish and Wildlife Conservation Commission (*Tallahassee, FL. 850-488-4676*). Permits are available from local hunting and fishing shops. For Apalachicola: **Apalachicola Ranger District** (*Bristol, Fl.. 850-643-2282*). For Osceola: **Osceola Ranger District** (*Olustee, FL. 904-752-2577*)

130

Motorized Adventures

SAND DUNE DWARFS OVERLAND EXPEDITION VEHICLE IN NIGER, WEST AFRICA.

HAWAII
Maui & the Big Island

If you're planning a vacation to Hawaii, take time out for a little tropical four-wheeling. The two best islands for off-roading are Maui and the Big Island of Hawaii. Both have high peaks, lush valleys, and rugged coastal sections accessible only by 4WD vehicle. Get a good map of either island—one that shows fire roads and ranch roads—and you're ready to go. Most major car-rental agencies rent Suzuki Samurais or equivalent small 4WD vehicles.

On Maui, you'll want to take the spectacular road to **Hana.** It is paved, but mud slides are common, so you'll be glad you're in a jeep. From Hana, proceed southwest along the coast toward the edge of Haleakala National Park. You'll soon find yourself in real 4WD country with thick jungle and rugged stretches of lava. Continue along the shore, passing the County Rd. 31 junction, while keeping to the coastal dirt road. You'll have fun exploring the windswept, wild southern end of the island, which is not passable by normal cars. Try **Maui Adventures Rent-a-Jeep** (*Puunene, HI. 800-701-5337 or 808-877-6626. Jeeps $60 per day or $260 per week*).

Three of the best backcountry routes on the Big Island are **Saddle Road** between Hilo and Kona, the steep **Waipio Valley Trail** (guided tours only), and **Green Sand Beach** at the island's southernmost point. Check out the track leading off Saddle Road to the summit of Mauna Kea, as well as the route from Hawaii 11 to Kilauea crater—great for lava-watching in **Hawaii Volcanoes National Park** (*808-985-6000. www.nps.gov/havo*). Most car-rental agencies forbid you to drive their vehicles on these trails; to rent a 4WD vehicle that is permitted off-road, call **Harper Car and Truck Rental** (*Hilo, HI. 800-852-9993 or 808-969-1478. www.harpershawaii.com*).

Overseas Overlands

To explore the most remote reaches of Africa, Mexico, South America, and Australia, a 4WD vehicle is often the only alternative to saddling up a camel or striking out on foot. An overland 4WD tour is one of the last great adventures, taking you deep into the heart of a continent, far from the watering holes frequented by Westerners. (All costs are in U.S. dollars.)

AFRICA
The Ultimate Expedition

It could be the most ambitious 4WD journey on Earth: a 19-week overland trek through the heart of eastern and southern Africa. Using large, heavy-duty 4WD expedition vehicles, the group drives through Egypt, Sudan, Kenya, Tanzania, Malawi, Zambia, Zimbabwe, Botswana, Namibia, and South Africa, visiting wildlife parks and local villages all along the way. The **Cairo-to-Capetown** trip is run by **Dragoman,** a leader in African trips. Much of the route is through open country with no charted roads—only *pistes,* or tracks left on the ground by previous vehicles.

This is not a trip for luxury-seekers. You camp in tents most of the time, and everyone joins in the work to be done, whether it's changing a tire or cooking a meal. Expeditions depart in January; the cost is about $6,900, plus $1,600 for the food kitty. You can also opt to do the lower half only (in reverse, from **Capetown to Nairobi**). This 11-week return leg includes East Africa's classic safari destinations and costs $4,800, plus $1,300 for the food kitty. Both Dragoman tours can be booked through the **Adventure Center** (*800-227-8747 or 510-654-1879. www.adventurecenter.com*).

AUSTRALIA
Voyages into the Wild Interior

Trans-Continental Safaris (*01161-8-8842-3469. Fax 01161-8-8842-2586*) offers 1- to 37-day off-road expeditions into Australia's central outback. Destinations include Ayers Rock, the opal mining fields, the Simpson Desert, and—closer to the coast—Litchfield National Park and the Flinders Ranges. The rugged expedition vehicles are piloted by expert local guides, who double as chefs during the tours. Crocodile Dundee may be an invention of Hollywood, but these hardy Outback drivers come close.

Other 4WD outback tours are offered by **AAT Kings Australian Tours** (*Anaheim, CA. 800-353-4525. Fax 714-456-0501. www.aatkings.com*). Destinations include the Red Centre (Alice Springs and Ayers Rock), Kakadu, Western Australia, Victoria, Queensland, the Northern Territory, and Tasmania. Local outfitters used by AAT King's include **Sahara Tours** (*Alice Springs. 01161-8-8953-0881*) and **Odyssey Safaris** (*Darwin. 01161-8-8948-0091*).

On Australia's east coast, many local guides offer jeep treks out of Cairns into Queensland's tropical rain forests. The **Adventure Center** (*Emeryville, CA. 800-227-8747 or 510-654-1879. www.adventurecenter.com*) runs a 14-day **Cape York** adventure from Cairns to Cape York—Australia's northernmost frontier. The journey begins with a seven-day **Barrier Reef** cruise aboard an 82-foot catamaran, the *Kangaroo Explorer.* Participants return overland from Cape York in 4WD expedition vehicles, tent-camping along the way. Trips run May to October and cost $2,460 to $3,000.

MEXICO
Baja California

With terrain ranging from high-altitude ridges in the Sierra Madre to high dunes on the west coast, Baja is a four-

wheeler's dream. You can explore the coast along the **Golfo de California (Sea of Cortés),** camping on the beach, or venture inland on rugged, rock-strewn routes. Along the coast road to San Felipe, you can cruise for miles on lake beds that are dustier versions of the Bonneville Salt Flats. There's endless variety for any 4WD taste, from mild to wild. You can even sample desert racing during the **San Felipe 250,** one of off-roading's premier competitions. Run in March, this race draws hundreds of competitors and spectators every year.

If you like to cap off your adventuring with nightlife, head all the way south to **Cabo San Lucas,** where you can explore remote surfing and fishing beaches with your four-wheel drive by day, then motor back to your hotel in time for that night's party. Another nice spot is halfway up the coast at Bahia de los Angeles. Major overland routes can be explored from here, and there is superior fishing and diving offshore. Cut across to Santa Rosalillita on the west coast to investigate miles of deserted beaches, or camp out at nearby Scammon Lagoon for winter whale-watching.

The **American Automobile Association** (*800-222-4357*) produces a good general guide for motor tourists in Baja, available free to AAA members. *The Baja Book III*, by Tom Miller and Carol Hoffman, describes campsites and contains dozens of maps illustrating jeep trails, as well as the best spots for fishing, diving, and surfing. Look for it in travel bookstores or order it directly from **Baja Source** (*619-442-7061*).

SOUTH AMERICA
Continental Circuit

Imagine traversing South America in military-class Mercedes 4WD vehicles. You'd have to ford jungle streams, penetrate dense rain forests, and scale mountain passes 17,000 feet high. That's just what happens on **Exodus Expeditions'** remarkable 23-week odyssey, the **South American Circuit,** which takes you to Argentina, Paraguay, Brazil, Bolivia, Chile, Peru, Ecuador, Colombia, and Venezuela. Trip highlights include Torres del Paine National Park in Patagonia; Carnival in Rio; the Atacama Desert in Chile; the Gran Sabana in Venezuela; and Brazil's Pantanal and Amazon River basins. The Inca ruins at Machu Picchu are optional.

The South America Circuit runs from the headwaters of the Amazon to the tip of Patagonia and back, covering 20,000 miles of Earth's wildest terrain. If you don't have time for the full expedition, you can join the tour for shorter segments of three weeks and up by meeting the group somewhere along the route. Total price is approximately $6,200, plus $2,400 for the food kitty—roughly $55 per day. Exodus is represented by **SafariCentre** (*Manhattan Beach, CA. 800-223-6046 or 310-546-4411. www.safaricentre.com*).

The Dragoman company offers a similar but less demanding seven-week overland journey down the length of the **Andes.** The trip begins in Quito, Ecuador, and finishes in Santiago, Chile. Along the way, you visit Machu Picchu, Cuzco, and the Atacama Desert. The cost is about $3,400, plus $800 for the food kitty. Book through the **Adventure Center** (*800-227-8747. www.adventurecenter.com*).

Ultimate Motorcycle Tours

I don't believe in a risk-free society, where the thrills of living are traded for the safety of existence. A long life is good only if it's chock-full of memories. . . . Motorcycle riders are in touch with the need to live life, this need to experience something potentially dangerous and master it. . . .

Nick Ienatsch, in *Motorcycling* magazine

Both as a sport and as a form of exploration, motorcycling is an adventure—one in which the process of getting there is its own reward. For most motorcyclists, the joys of riding far outweigh any risks.

ARIZONA & UTAH
The Great Southwest

The **Great Circle Tour** through Arizona and southern Utah may be America's ultimate open-road odyssey. You can hit five national parks in less than a week, viewing the most spectacular scenery in the West. A good starting point for the tour is Flagstaff, Arizona. Head north from there to the Ariz. 64 junction, then go west into Grand Canyon National Park. Excellent hotels and campsites are available, but book in advance between May and September. Double back from the Grand Canyon, then take US 160 and US 163 northeast toward Monument Valley (*see p. 126*), near the Utah-Arizona

border. (Don't attempt to ride a street bike into the valley unless you want to be towed out.) For relatively cheap lodging, try the San Juan Inn (*435-683-2220*) in the town of Mexican Hat, about 18 miles east on the banks of the San Juan River.

Just out of town, follow Utah 261 through the Valley of the Gods. (A section of this road is unpaved as it switchbacks up the face of a mesa.) After reaching the spectacular vistas at the crest, go north along 261 to connect with Utah 95. If you've got an extra day or two, head east on 95 and then north on US 191 to Moab and Arches National Park; if not, head west toward Glen Canyon and Lake Powell. The next 30 miles are motorcycling heaven—wide-open sweepers with excellent road surface. After Lake Powell, pick up Utah 24 toward Capitol Reef National Park. The park has an excellent campground, or you can stay in a motel down the road in Torrey. For the final leg of the tour, pick up Utah 12 south, which takes you way up to ridge line—close to 9,000 feet— for some superb views. Utah 12 takes you through Bryce Canyon National Park to US 89 south, which in turn leads toward Zion National Park; both parks are spectacular.

No commercial tour follows this route precisely, but **Edelweiss Bike Travel** (*Tri-Community Travel, Wrightwood, CA. 800-582-2263 or 760-249-5825. www.edelweissbike. com*) runs a nine-day, $2,300 tour that takes in the Grand Canyon, Monument Valley, Bryce Canyon Park, and

Mt. Zion Park. Tours leave from Las Vegas. For a self-guided vacation, **Western States Motorcycle Tours and Rentals** (*Phoenix, AZ. 602-943-9030. http://members.aol.com/azmcrent*) rents BMW, Harley, and Suzuki touring bikes for $65 to $175 per day, or $400 to $750 per week. Bikes must be rented from, and returned to, Phoenix. Registered members of the **Harley Owners Group** (*800-258-2464 or 414-343-4896. www. hog.com*) can rent Harley touring bikes at many Southwest locations, including Los Angeles, Las Vegas, and Phoenix. Rentals start at about $95 per day, or $570 per week with a two-day minimum. Arizona and Utah are year-round destinations, but some of the most scenic motorcycling routes reach altitudes where the weather ranges from harsh to unpredictable. Late March through late October is good, but May and September are ideal. July and August are very hot at lower elevations.

CALIFORNIA & OREGON
A Pacific Coast Odyssey

The famed **Coastal Highway**—Calif. 1 and US 101 along the California and Oregon coasts—offers more than 1,000 miles of verdant scenery and challenging curves. From Los Angeles, head north on US 101, then cut over to Calif. 154 at Santa Barbara. You'll be rewarded with breathtaking ocean vistas as you climb a 2,224-foot-high pass. Just beyond the top of the pass is the Cold Springs Tavern, a legendary watering hole for bikers. After 25 more miles of two-lane asphalt, 154 reconnects with US 101 northbound. When you reach San Luis Obispo, follow the signs for Calif. 1 and Big Sur.

North of Morro Bay (a good place for a seaside lunch), you'll head through open country toward San Simeon. Some of the nicest bends on the trip are just north of town. Once you pass the Hearst Castle Park Center, the traffic thins out and you feel like you're riding through the California of a bygone era. After Big Sur, however, you reenter civilization in the form of Carmel, Pacific Grove, and Monterey. Take your time in Pacific Grove, where the shoreline route is perfect for picnicking or exploring tide pools.

From San Francisco, be sure to explore the Marin Headlands at the north end of the Golden Gate Bridge. When you cross the bridge, turn to the right almost immediately and cross back under the roadway. The headlands road then climbs to the ridge, offering million-dollar views of the bridge, the bay, and beyond.

You're in for some serious riding north of San Francisco. Stay on Calif. 1 where it splits off for Stinson Beach. From Stinson, proceed north to Point Reyes Station. If you've got the time, head west to the lighthouse—a two-hour side trip. When you return to Calif. 1, you've hit the big time: The next 100 miles north to Mendocino is probably America's best coastal motorcycle road. Stunning rock formations dot the coast at Elk, and in Albion you can sample the region's best cuisine at the Albion River Inn. Just north of there, Mendocino is home to many romantic bed-and-breakfasts. North of Ft. Bragg, Calif. 1 switchbacks through the redwoods until you rejoin US 101.

Just inside Oregon, you'll find great beaches between Brookings and Port Orford. North of Reedsport, the road crosses the Umpqua River and winds along sheer cliffs high above the water. Stop for a photo and you can hear the surf pounding the rocks hundreds of feet below. Otter Rock, near Newport, boasts excellent campgrounds. You may want to continue north as far as Tillamook before heading inland on Oreg. 6 to conclude your tour in Portland.

No commercial trip duplicates this itinerary, but you can rent BMW and Harley touring bikes at **Dubbelju Motorcycle Rentals** (*San Francisco, CA. 415-495-2774. www. dubbelju.com*). If you're starting farther south, BMWs are available from **California Motorcycle Rental** (*La Jolla, CA. 858-456-9577. www.calif-motorcyclerental.com*). An R1100R costs $700 per week with unlimited mileage. **EagleRider** (*Torrance, CA. 800-501 8687 or 310-320-3456. www.hogrent. com*) offers Harley rentals in Los Angeles and San Francisco, as well as at other locations nationwide. For those with limited time but big budgets, **Edelweiss Bike Travel** (*800-582-2263. www.edelweissbike.com*) offers a seven-day, $2,900 loop tour from San Francisco that includes the Napa Valley and the best of Highway 1 from the Golden Gate to the Oregon border. Riders stay in five-star hotels.

MONTANA & CANADA
Edelweiss in Alberta

For spectacular alpine scenery, Canada's Rockies rival anything in the European Alps. A good place to kick off a motorcycle odyssey of the Canadian range is just south of the border in Kalispell, Montana. From there, head east through Glacier National Park. The route through the park follows the justifiably famed Going-to-the-Sun Road. Hugging sheer granite walls, you climb to Logan Pass at 6,646 feet, with waterfalls and scenic lookouts every few hundred yards.

Once out of Glacier Park, head north on US 89 to Canada. On the far side of the border, visit Waterton Lakes National Park and the Prince of Wales Hotel. Heading west on Hwy. 3 takes you across the Continental Divide and into British Columbia. At Cranbrook, pick up Hwy. 93 north, which leads to Kootenay National Park and the heart of the Rockies.

Continue on Hwy. 93 through the high passes to Lake Louise. This is the jumping-off point for the **Icefields Parkway**—a modern scenic highway that runs all the way to Jasper, 145 miles north. Snowcapped peaks 12,000 feet high line the route, and in places the ice fields march right down

HOG WILD IN THE HEARTLAND: 1,340CC HARLEY-DAVIDSONS MOTOR INTO MILWAUKEE.

134

Motorized Adventures

A PERUVIAN MAN WEAVES A PONCHO ON THE ROAD TO
OLLANTAYTAMBO. THE PHOTOGRAPHER'S BMW F/650 SITS NEARBY.

to the road. Although the Icefields Parkway is an easy one-day ride, pause to explore some of the high-country foot trails you'll find along the way. The trailheads, clearly marked, crop up every 5 miles or so; just park your bike by the side of the road, and head for the hills. Within an hour or two you can be sitting in an alpine meadow carpeted with wildflowers, gazing down on a glacier-fed lake of bright turquoise. Although Canada's parks have been protected from overdevelopment, there's no lack of places to rest your head. Canada has an extensive system of campgrounds, and many quality lodges are located near the roads. The "youth" hostels—nothing of the sort—accept travelers of all ages.

Rocky Mountain Motorcycle Holidays (604-938-0126. www.rockymtnmoto.com) offers the best escorted motorcycle tours in western Canada. The routes are ideal, the Triumph bikes are new, and the customer service is second to none; the guides wash your bike each day and carry your bags to your room in very nice hotels.

For a self-guided tour, rent a bike in Vancouver or Calgary from Great Canadian Motor Corp. (800-667-8865 or 250-837-6500. www.gcmc.com). For $55 to $130 per day, GCMC rents a wide selection of bikes, including BMWs, Honda Goldwings, and full-dress Harleys. GCMC also offers a ten-day U-ride vacation for $1,600, a fee that includes bike rental, lodging, and detailed maps. For another $700, you can run the route as part of an escorted tour.

EUROPE
Touring the Alps

Because the boundaries of France, Switzerland, Austria and Italy converge in the Alps, you can experience four different national cultures—and cuisines—in a few days. If you plan to travel for three weeks or less, an organized tour is the way to go. The best operations have spent years developing itineraries that take you over spectacular passes to the nicest hotels and most charming towns. The best time to go is in June, July, or September; August is the busiest vacation period for Europeans. Start in Austria or Germany, work your way west to Switzerland, then head south to the French coast. After soaking up some sunshine, you can return northeast through Italy and Austria. Don't miss Austria's Tyrol, a land of high peaks, lush valleys, and reasonably priced alpine chalets.

A number of companies offer excellent escorted Alps tours. Among American tour companies, Beach's Motorcycle Adventures (Grand Island, NY. 716-773-4960. www.beachs-mca.com) has the best track record on the Continent. Tours cost about $5,100 for three weeks or $4,200 for two weeks, including deluxe hotels and the use of a new BMW. For a no-frills tour on your own, you can rent just a bike for about $850 per week. Edelweiss Bike Travel

(800-582-2263. www.edelweissbike.com) offers many Alps tours. The best is the 12-day Alpine Mediterranean trip, which starts in Munich, crosses the Austrian Tyrol into Switzerland, then visits French ski areas before blasting south to the Riviera. This itinerary leads riders to the Matterhorn and Chamonix via Europe's most challenging passes. The price is about $3,200 for a solo rider on a 650.

Both Beach's and Edelweiss tours offer a moderate pace. To ride at a faster clip—and save up to $50 per day—choose one of the major German tour companies such as: Bosenberg Motorcycle Excursions (01149-6716-7312. www.bosenberg.com) or HIT-Motorradreisen (01149-911-28-78-505. www.hit-motorradreisen.de). Bosenberg also offers BMW, Ducati, Harley, Honda, and Triumph rentals at Frankfurt and Munich, Germany; Bern and Zurich, Switzerland; and Milan, Italy.

NEW ZEALAND
Unspoiled Paradise

New Zealand is the perfect destination for motorcycle touring in the Kiwi summer (November through March). The North Island evokes the California of an earlier day, while the South Island combines the best of Colorado and the Pacific Northwest. With only 3.5 million people inhabiting a landmass the size of California, many spots are still virtually undeveloped. If you start in the north from Auckland, New Zealand's largest city, head north to visit the Bay of Islands. Keep to the smaller roads through farmlands along the coast. At the northernmost tip of the country is a 100-mile beach that should not be missed. Looping back south, most tourists head straight for the geysers and sulphur pools near Rotorua. Instead, try exploring the rugged and sparsely populated west coast: It offers isolated beaches, verdant tropical vegetation, and even a snowcapped volcano or two.

At the southern tip of the North Island is Wellington, New Zealand's capital. A city of hills, much like San Francisco, Wellington is the departure point for the ferry trip across the Cook Strait to Picton in the South Island. This is notoriously rough water; make sure your touring rig is well secured, for 25-foot seas and 50-knot winds are not uncommon. From Picton, enjoy the winding road (south, then west, then north) to Havelock, where you can board a small boat for a day tour of nearby island farms. If you continue down the west coast, be prepared for serious downpours—some spots receive more than 200 inches of rain every year. About halfway down the coast, cross inland along the scenic Haast Pass and make for the lovely village of Wanaka, in the heart of the Southern Alps. Continue south to Queenstown—New Zealand's mecca for outdoor recreation, including paragliding, rafting, and jet-boating. Try to

set aside a day to visit nearby Milford Sound. (You may want to park the bike and hop a tour bus; the Milford Highway is awash with water and gravel even in summer.) Your last stop should be Christchurch and its international airport.

The circuit described above covers 1,800 miles and requires a couple of weeks to complete. You can rent a bike in Auckland or Christchurch, or join a group tour. **Adventure New Zealand Motorcycle Tours and Rentals** (*01164-2196-9071. www.thunderbike.co.nz/anzmtr*) runs the best trips, which start at $2,600 per person for ten days. Operated by enthusiastic Kiwis who seem to have uncovered every "secret spot" in the South Island, this program has earned lavish praise from recent customers. For an independent twin-island trip, contact **Motorcycling Downunder** (*800-788-6685 or 01164-3366-0129. www.adventour.com*). Based in Christchurch, this firm also has facilities in Auckland, so you can cruise both islands without backtracking. Motorcycling Downunder rents a full range of bikes from 250cc (*about $65 per day*) to the 1500cc Honda Gold Wing (*about $125 per day*).

If you want a fully escorted two-island tour, both **Beach's Motorcycle Adventures** (*716-773-4960. www.beachs-mca.com*) and **Edelweiss Bike Travel** (*800-582-2263. www.edelweissbike.com*) offer fine programs that hit the highlights of each island. Such trips last two to three weeks and start at about $3,800, including lodging, motorcycle rental (road or dual-purpose), and sag-wagon support.

CHILE AND ARGENTINA
Patagonia and the Southern Andes

What country on Earth can top the geographic diversity of Chile? Almost 3,000 miles long and about 120 miles wide, Chile is bordered on the west by the Pacific and on the east by the Andes—the second highest mountain range in the world. The result: climates and habitats ranging from vast glaciers to the world's driest desert.

Given these conditions, you would expect motorcycling in Chile to be challenging, and the country does not disappoint. The roads have a habit of changing suddenly from asphalt to gravel, dirt, or sand. The weather is notoriously unstable, and elevation changes brutalize the unacclimated.

So what are you waiting for? Two South American tours represent the next frontier of motorcycling. **Pancho Villa Moto-Tours** (*800-233-0564*) leads a month-long expedition from Santiago, Chile, to the tip of South America and back. Billed as an "expedition class" tour, this trip demands fitness and a familiarity with riding on rugged, unimproved roads. Riders cover 4,500 to 6,000 miles, about a third of them on unpaved surfaces. The cost—$5,900 per solo rider—includes lodging, most meals, and round-trip ocean transport of your motorcycle. If the PVMT tour is booked, contact **Edelweiss Bike Travel** (*800-582-2263. www.edelweissbike.com*). In January and February, Edelweiss offers a two-week, 2,000-mile loop tour of the Andes through Chile and Argentina for seasoned off-road riders.

Two-Wheelin' to the Four Corners of the Earth

A number of veteran motorcycle-tour companies offer guided two-wheel holidays worldwide. Itineraries can be customized in many cases, or you can simply rent a bike and travel on your own. Dozens of other motorcycle tours and rentals can be found on the web at www.mcguide.com/tourlist.asp. When comparing tour prices, be sure to ask whether gas, insurance, and motorcycle use are included. And don't forget to find out about rental qualifications before you leave home: Some companies require two years' riding experience on a large-displacement bike. (Costs are in U.S. dollars.)

Adventure New Zealand Motorcycle Tours and Rentals
P.O. Box 674, 82 Achilles Ave., Nelson 7001, New Zealand. 01164-2196-9071 or (in NZ) 021-969-071
www.thunderbike.co.nz/anzmtr
DESTINATIONS: North Island and South Island, New Zealand
EQUIPMENT: 250-1450cc BMW, Harley, Suzuki, and Triumph road or road/trail bikes

Owned and operated by Kiwis John and Ian Fitzwater, Adventure New Zealand Motorcycle Tours (ANZMT) offers the kind of personalized service and local knowledge that transforms a good vacation into a great one. Choose 7-, 10-, 14-, or 18-day fully escorted tours starting at $2,400, or self-guided holidays with bike rentals starting at $100 per day. Recent customers (including America's Cup crews) have raved about the tours, which feature New Zealand's best roads and most magical secret spots (many of which you won't find on the map, much less on any other tour). Route planning is exceptional. With group size limited to ten, you stay in scenic inns and B&Bs far from the usual tourist traps. ANZMT also provides a motor coach for nonriding family members. Itineraries can be customized to a group's special interests. ANZMT features a wide variety of mounts from the Fitzwaters' full-service motorcycle emporium, Thunderbike Powersports. Highly recommended.

Australian Motorcycle Adventures (AMA)
424 Samford Road, Enoggera, Brisbane, Queensland 4051, Australia. 01161-7385-3542. www.austmcycleadventures.com
DESTINATIONS: Cape York Peninsula, Brisbane region, Ayers Rock
EQUIPMENT: Yamaha road and road/trail bikes

Founded in 1988, AMA offers both on-road and off-road tours, and maintains one of the largest motorcycle rental fleets in Australia. This is a great choice for those looking to explore the outback and rain forest areas of Queensland. Guides are knowledgeable and enthusiastic. The off-road tours, such as the 11-day Cape York trip, are challenging outback adventures: 90 percent of the route is on dirt tracks, and you camp out under the stars. For road riders, we recommend the five-day Taste of Australia tour, with its wide open roads, great scenery, and four-star accommodations. Bike rentals start around $80 per day.

Baja Off Road Tours
25108 Marguerite Pkwy., Suite B-126, Mission Viejo, CA 92692. 949-830-6569
www.bajaoffroadtours.com
DESTINATIONS: Baja California
EQUIPMENT: KTM 250, 300 (2-stroke); 400, 620 (4-stroke)

Former Team Honda dirt-bike racer Chris Haines operates four- and seven-day tours to Baja Mexico for $1,800 and $3,600, respectively. The four-day trip begins just across the Mexican border in Ensenada and runs to San Felipe, with an overnight in Mike's Sky Rancho, a well-known off-roaders' hacienda. The seven-day tour continues on to Cabo San Lucas, where the group spends the evening. These trips are fairly pricey, but everything—meals, hotels, even gas for the off-road bikes—is included. Group size is typically 12 riders; a support vehicle accompanies all tours. Riding conditions are moderately difficult, so off-road experience is recommended. Custom Baja road-bike tours arranged on request.

Beach's Motorcycle Adventures, Ltd.
2763 West River Pkwy., Grand Island, NY 14072. 716-773-4960. www.beachs-mca.com
DESTINATIONS: Alps, New Zealand, Norway
EQUIPMENT: BMW 650-1100cc road; Honda sport-touring bikes (VFR, CBR) in Norway; Suzuki and Yamaha in New Zealand

Known best for its outstanding alpine tours, the Beach family also runs trips to New Zealand and Norway. The tours are popular—more than half of Beach's clients return for another ride. Routes are well-scouted, a member of the Beach family accompanies almost every tour, and daily distances are moderate. On a three-week tour, you visit Germany, Austria, Switzerland, France, and Italy. Most Beach tours feature high-quality BMW bikes. Alps tours cost $5,100 for three weeks ($4,000 extra for a passenger) or $4,200 for two weeks ($3,250 extra for a passenger), including motorcycle, lodging, most meals, and van support. On-your-own motorcycle rental is available from $850 per week, with pick-up and return in Munich.

Bosenberg Motorcycle Excursions
Mainzer Strasse 54, 55545 Bad Kreuznach, Germany. 01149-6716-7312
www.bosenberg.com
DESTINATIONS: Germany (Bavaria); Swiss, Austrian, French, and Italian Alps; Alsace region of France
EQUIPMENT: BMW, Harley-Davidson, Honda, Suzuki, and Yamaha, 500-1500cc; tour, sport, cruiser, and dual-sport models

Bosenberg conducts tours in six European countries. It also offers individual motorcycle rentals in Germany (Frankfurt and Munich), Switzerland (Bern and Zurich), and Italy (Milan). Rental centers are located near airports, letting you fly in and ride out. Escorted tours run May through September, with itineraries that take in Germany's Black Forest, the Austrian Tyrol, and three regions of France: Alsace, Savoie, and Haute-Alpes. You can rent almost any late-model BMW, Harley-Davidson, or Japanese machine—even dual-sports and cruisers—through participating dealers. Rental bikes cost $110-230 per day, depending on model and length of rental.

AYERS ROCK, AUSTRALIA, AS IT APPEARS FROM THE SEAT OF A BMW R80 G/S.

EagleRider Motorcycle Rentals

20917 Western Ave., Torrance, CA 90501
800-501-8687 or 310-320-3456
www.hogrent.com
DESTINATIONS: United States
EQUIPMENT: Harley-Davidson

With showrooms in Los Angeles, San Francisco, Chicago, Orlando, and Las Vegas, EagleRider is the world's largest motorcycle-rental company specializing in Harley-Davidson rentals. EagleRider also offers many notable guided tours: Outlaw Trails of the Wild West (AZ, CA, NV, UT), Baja 1000, Sturgis (SD), Route 66, Coast-to-Coast Jazz Festival (New Orleans to Los Angeles), and Florida/Key West. Most rentals are $125 per day; tours average about $2,000 per week, including bike, lodging, support vehicle, and guides. This is a big, solid company with good customer service.

Edelweiss Bike Travel

P.O. Box 2, A-6414 Mieming, Austria. 01143-5264-5690. www.edelweissbike.com
U.S.: Tri-Community Travel, P.O. Box 1974, Wrightwood, CA 92397-1974
800-582-2263 or 760-249-5825
DESTINATIONS: Africa, Austria, France, Germany, Ireland, Italy, Mexico, New Zealand, Spain, Switzerland, United States (AK, CA, WY, AZ, CO, NV)
EQUIPMENT: BMW road and dual-purpose bikes; some other makes outside Europe

Edelweiss Bike Travel offers well-organized escorted tours worldwide. Having featured the Alps since 1980, Edelweiss added many new itineraries in the 1990s, including some great trips in Mexico. Edelweiss prices are competitive; the 12-day Best of Europe tour starts at $2,700 for a solo rider, including food, hotels, and BMW motorcycle rental. Other great European trips are the Royal Spanish Castle Tour and the Alpine Mediterranean trip. Challenging off-road tours in Australia, Chile, and Argentina are available for experienced dirt riders; Edelweiss also throws open its scouting tours to new destinations, such as Morocco. A support van is on hand for all tours. Despite Edelweiss's professional, well-managed approach, its more popular group tours tend to be fairly large.

Freedom Tours

P.O. Box 848, Longmont, CO 80502
800-643-2109 or 303-682-9482
www.indra.com/freedom
DESTINATIONS: Colorado, Utah, Arizona, New Mexico
EQUIPMENT: BMW, Harley, and Honda

Since 1990, Freedom Tours (FT) has run 3- to 14-day tours through Colorado and the Southwest. Most tours begin and end in Longmont, Colorado, north of Boulder. FT's premier trip—the two-week Heart of the Southwest Tour—visits southwest Colorado, the red-rock canyons of Utah, Arizona's Monument Valley, and the high desert of New Mexico's Sangre de Cristo and San Juan Mountains. This June-only itinerary, limited to 20 people, costs $5,920 per couple ($3,800 for a solo rider) and includes hotels, most meals, and vehicle support. Prices do not include the motorcycle, but FT offers daily rentals starting at $85 and weekly rentals (through Cruise America in Denver and Phoenix) starting at $550.

Lotus Tours

1644 N. Sedgwick St., Chicago, IL 60614.
312-951-0031. www.lotustours.com
DESTINATIONS (partial list): Australia, Austria, Bhutan, Canada, Chile, Egypt, France (including Corsica), Italy (including Sicily), India, Israel, Jordan, Mexico, Morocco, Peru, Switzerland, Thailand, Tibet, U.K., U.S., Vietnam
EQUIPMENT: BMW, Ducati, and many dual purpose makes

Since 1984, Lotus Tours has offered unique, upscale trips to every corner of the planet. Trips feature spectacular routes and unique accommodations. Founded by former architect Burt Richmond, Lotus Tours delivers a truly ultimate adventure—the kind of trip that can change your life. These trips are not for dilettantes; Lotus clients tend to be successful businesspeople who are passionate about travel and motorcycles. Prices are high—typically $5,000 for two weeks—but you may find yourself resting your head in a palace in Rajasthan (or a castle in the Côte d'Azur) or handpicking your bike at the Ducati factory. Every tour is customized, and new trips are offered every season. Highly recommended.

Northeastern Motorcycle Tours

P.O. Box 574, Saxtons River, VT 05154. 802-869-3999. www.motorcycletours.com

DESTINATIONS: New England, Adirondacks, Nova Scotia, New Brunswick, Gaspé Peninsula

EQUIPMENT: BMW, Harley, or Honda large touring bikes.

Northeastern Motorcycle Tours (NMT) offers deluxe trips along the most scenic routes in New England and Canada's Maritime Provinces—a clear choice for a fall foliage ride or an exploration of the rugged Atlantic Coast. The tours feature the best inns (and most celebrated chefs) in the region. It's hard to pick a favorite from the many good tours the company offers, but the Gaspé Peninsula trip combines great scenery with splendid inns and fantastic cuisine. (At $1,465 for seven nights, including all meals, it's also an excellent value.) NMT's basic price does not include bike rental (available at extra cost) because many customers prefer to ride, ship, or haul their machine to the tour base. In 1999, *Motorcyclist Magazine* rated NMT one of its four favorite tour operators worldwide.

Pancho Villa Moto-Tours

4510 Hwy. 281 North, No. 3, Spring Branch, TX 78070. 800-233-0564 or 830-438-7744 www.panchovilla.com

DESTINATIONS: Mexico (Baja, Copper Canyon, Yucatán), Chile, Argentina

EQUIPMENT: BYO motorcycle; rental of BMW, Harley, Honda, or off-road bikes is optional.

In operation since 1981, Pancho Villa Moto-Tours (PVMT) is the leader in Mexico motorcycle touring. PVMT's Latin American tours range from 4 to 29 days. Strongly recommended are PVMT's

Colonial tour and Sierra Madre Expedition, both of which last a week and cost $1,280; the latter visits Mexico's majestic Copper Canyon, which is four times larger than the Grand Canyon. The 32-day Andes Patagonia expedition begins and ends in Santiago, Chile. Riders venture to Tierra del Fuego, then return through Argentine Patagonia and lake district. The price is $5,880 per person (bike rental extra). On most trips, PVMT can arrange motorcycle rental for an additional $55-100 per day. Mexico tours depart from a variety of gateways along the U.S.-Mexico border.

Rocky Mountain Motorcycle Holidays

103-4338 Main St., Suite 124, Whistler, BC, V0N 1B4, Canada. 604-938-0126 www.rockymtnmoto.com

DESTINATIONS: Canada (Alberta, British Columbia)

EQUIPMENT: 750-1100cc Triumph road bikes

If you're about to undertake a group tour of western Canada, Rocky Mountain Motorcycle Holidays is the clear choice. The routes, personally scouted by owner Mike Ciebien, are spectacular. The bikes, new Triumphs, are superb. Food and accommodations are consistently excellent, and the guides even wash your bike at day's end. From its base in Whistler, British Columbia, Rocky Mountain offers tours of four, seven, and ten days. If you have the time, do the ten-day, $3,350 Best of the West tour. On this trip the group typically rides four to five hours each day, leaving it plenty of time to enjoy golf, mountain biking, water-skiing, horseback riding, and even white-water rafting. More than a road trip, this is a complete vacation in one of the most beautiful regions on Earth. Highly recommended.

OVERSEAS SHIPPING PROGRAMS

For an overseas tour of three weeks or more, it may pay to purchase a motorcycle abroad and bring it home, or ship your own bike to your destination and freight it home at tour's end. You can usually airfreight a motorcycle from a major U.S. gateway to Europe for about $2,000 round-trip. Contact these agents:

Michael I. Mandell, Inc.

6800 Jericho Tpk., Suite 201 W, Syosset, NY 11791-4488. 800-245-8726 or 516-682-9220 www.mandellinc.com

Airfreight between North America and Europe, Australia, New Zealand, and South

America; also provides insurance.

Warren Motorcycle Transport

10395 Utopia Circle East, Boynton Beach, FL 33437. 800-443-7519 or 561-737-4954 www.gate.net/~bikeship

Since 1972, airfreight from the United States to most European gateways, including Scandinavia and the United Kingdom.

4WD GROUPS IN NORTH AMERICA

To find a four-wheel-drive club in your area, contact the **United Four Wheel Drive Association** (*4505 W. 700 South, Shelbyville, IN 46176. 800-448-3932. www.UFWDA.org*). A $25 membership fee buys you a year's subscription to a 4WD magazine and qualifies you to receive UFWDA discounts on 4WD supplies.

RIDER ORGANIZATIONS

American Motorcyclist Association

13515 Yarmouth Dr., Pickerington, OH 43147 800-262-5646 or 614-856-1900. www.ama-cycle.org

BMW Motorcycle Owners of America

P.O. Box 489, Chesterfield, MO 63006 636-537-5511. www.bmwmoa.org

Gold Wing Road Riders Association

P.O. Box 42450, Phoenix, AZ 85080 800-843-9460 or 623-581-2500 www.gwrra.org

Harley Owners Group

P.O. Box 453, Milwaukee, WI 53201 800-258-2464 or 414-343-4896 www.hog.com

TRAINING PROGRAMS

The Motorcycle Safety Foundation

800-446-9227. www.msf-usa.org

The MSF offers training for new motorcyclists. The beginner course costs $120-145 for a 16-hour program conducted over 2 to 3 days. The price includes use of a 175cc to 250cc machine. For those with previous street-riding experience, MSF stages a one-day Experienced RiderCourse for $60.

ONLINE

4x4now.com or www.4x4now.com

This site features trail reports, an off-road event calendar, Jeep Jamboree/ 4WD rally coverage, and an online store with 4WD books and videos. You'll find lots of photos and video clips of popular off-road events such as the Moab Jeep Safari.

Four Wheeler On-Line
www.fourwheeler.com

Surf your way here for 4WD events, truck reviews and best buys, off-road driving schools, a race calendar, technical Q&A, and online bulletin boards.

Off-Road.com
www.off-road.com

Although it focuses primarily on hardware and off-road racing, this site posts hundreds of trip and trail reports by amateur correspondents around the country.

Best Roads in the USA/the World
hea-www.harvard.edu/motorcyclist/roads.html

Great list of fine two-wheeled destinations, written by bikers. There are no pictures or maps, but the text describes most U.S. states plus Spain, Italy, and Canada.

MCguide.com
www.mcguide.com/tourlist.asp

This is the best Internet directory of motorcycle tours. It lists nearly 100 tour operators worldwide, including hard-to-find services in Africa, Asia, and South America. The best North American and European operators are here, and nearly all the links work. Worth bookmarking.

Motorcycle Online
www.motorcycle.com

Heavy on products and engineering, this site is aimed mostly at "gearheads." However, it also offers a travel section with tour reports from around the world.

Motorworld Online
www.motorworld.com

This full-featured website devoted to motorcycles offers news and feature articles on the latest models, product reviews, rides and events, competitions, parts and accessories, and motorcycle clubs.

PRINT

America's Best Roads by Harley-Davidson is a short (98 pages) but useful guide to 50 of America's best touring routes. This book contains color photos and detailed maps of all 50 routes. Available from Harley dealers.

4 Wheel Drive and Sport Utility Magazine (*P.O. Box 68033, Anaheim, CA 92817-0833. 714-693-1866*). Aimed at the hard-core off-roading set, this magazine is filled with trail reports and technical articles.

Motorcycle Touring: International Directory 1993/4 lists commercial motorcycle tours worldwide. The listings are a tad dated, but the book remains a valuable resource. Motorcycling books and videos are available from **Whitehorse Press** (*P.O. Box 60, North Conway, NH 03860. 800-531-1133. www.whitehorsepress.com*).

Tony Huegel's excellent guidebooks feature color-coded maps and detailed route descriptions for dozens of backcountry drives in the western U.S. Huegel has driven every route, most of which are graded roads suitable for popular sport-utility vehicles. Titles include: *Idaho Off-road, Sierra Nevada Byways, California Desert Byways,* and *Utah Byways.* Order from **Wilderness Press** (*800-443-7227*) or from 4x4books.com (*308-381-4410*). For more information, contact **Tony Huegel** (*208-524-4245. byways@srv.net*).

VIDEO

The Off Highway Adventure Series (produced by Rick Russell) and *Sidekick*

OffRoad Videos are destination-specific videos. $24.95 from **Sidekick Offroad** (*909-628-7227. www.sidekickoffroad.com*)

MAPS

Trails Illustrated (*800-962-1643. www.trailsillustrated.com*) produces high-quality topographic maps for major parks and recreation areas in North America.

4x4books.com (*308-381-4410*) offers USGS topographic maps on CD-ROM. A CD-ROM pack ($100) covering the entire U.S. contains more than 1,500 maps.

MapLink USA (*805-692-6777. www.maplink.com*) stocks more than 200,000 maps that cover the globe. Check here for maps of exotic destinations.

Sidekick OffRoad Maps (*909-628-7227. www.sidekickoffroad.com*) offers excellent, specialized maps for off-road adventuring. Venues include the Rubicon Trail, Santiago Canyon, and Dumont Dunes. All maps include trail-difficulty ratings and information on campgrounds.

JEEP AND CARGO BRAVE MINING-CAMP TRAILS ABOVE TELLURIDE, COLORADO.

MORE AND MORE PEOPLE ARE DISCOVERING THE SIMPLE JOYS OF NORDIC, OR CROSS-COUNTRY, skiing—a catchall term for skiing without a lift. A less expensive and less cumbersome alternative to downhill, nordic skiing is easy to master and offers excellent fitness benefits. Many physicians call it nearly ideal as an aerobic activity. • Whether you ski the backcountry or on groomed trails, you travel closer to nature, experiencing greater solitude and serenity than is possible with many other winter sports. Skilled ski mountaineers don nordic gear and trade long lift lines for empty, untracked slopes of virgin powder. Cross-country skiers, from novices to experts, enjoy the thousands of miles of groomed trails at nordic centers around North America and in Europe. • Ten tantalizing nordic ski destinations around the world are featured in this chapter. We also review the top-rated cross-country ski areas in North America. Finally, we profile quality ski-mountaineering programs that will teach you the skills to ascend—and descend—the toughest slopes.

LEFT: A FREE-HEELING NORDIC ENTHUSIAST IN CALIFORNIA
INSET: CROSS-COUNTRY SKIING IN NEW YORK'S ADIRONDACKS

Nordic Skiing

Good Norwegian Woods

Off the Beaten Track in Turkey

Ski Mountaineering

Telemarking

The white magnificence yields to the clean motion of our skis, and we glide over the glistening dome of the world and launch our long descent....
ANSEL ADAMS

Ten Great Nordic Ski Tours

With all the glitz and gear associated with skiing these days, it's hard to conjure up the sport's austere and practical beginnings. Way back when, skiing was invented as a mode of travel, not play. Cross-country is all about getting back to the basics of ski travel: It opens pristine backcountry to the winter explorer and invites the venturesome to wander empty wildlands. If this sort of adventure speaks to you, consider the following options:

NORWAY
Birthplace of Skiing

Norway is cross-country skiing heaven. The country's extensive network of huts and well-maintained trail systems afford a nearly endless variety of itineraries.

In western Norway the **Hallingdal** region rewards intermediate-level skiers with glaciers, forests, and moderate foothills flanked by rugged mountains.

Expert nordic skiers will enjoy **Finnmark,** the northernmost county in Norway—and home to the reindeer-herding Sami nomads. Here you can join a high-Arctic wilderness expedition complete with dogsled teams to carry your gear.

Spitsbergen, an archipelago off Norway's northern coast, offers true adventure for hardy skiers. A rugged and untamed land of ice and polar bears, Spitsbergen is about as wild as Europe gets.

Given Norway's generally high prices, package ski tours tend to offer visitors the best vacation value. One good agent is **DNT,** represented in the United States by **Borton Overseas** (*5412 Lyndale Ave. S., Minneapolis, MN 55419. 800-843-0602 or 612-822-4640. www.bortonoverseas.com*).

A government-subsidized equivalent of the Sierra Club, DNT maintains trails and warming huts all over Norway and offers excellent—and affordable—ski tours through four scenic national parks.

DNT tours are led by able volunteers, most of whom speak fluent English. Eight-day trips cost $600 to $700 per person, with lodging. (Note: When selecting a ski tour, keep in mind that the Norwegian system tends to underrate difficulty levels; a rating of "moderate" in Norway, for example, would probably translate into an "advanced" rating in the United States.) DNT also offers tours in the **Geilo** area and in Spitsbergen.

Inn-to-inn touring is also popular in Norway. Experienced mountain guide **Torger Moller Foss** (*U.S. agent: Borton Overseas, 5412 Lyndale Ave. S., Minneapolis, MN 55419. 800-843-0602 or 612-822-4640. www.bortonoverseas.com*) leads comfortable but strenuous seven-day inn-to-inn tours in the Hallingdal Mountains.

This is a good choice for skiers who want a solid daily workout followed by a bit of luxury each evening; the cost is $1,633 per person.

Also recommended is **Fitness by Fisher** (*P.O. Box 596, New York, NY 10028. 212-744-5900*). An expert skier, owner Sandra Fisher has toured extensively throughout Norway. (She personally considers this the best place in the world to ski-tour because of the vast, undeveloped tracts.)

Fisher runs a week-long tour with Torger Foss; the cost is $1,550 per person. She can also arrange customized ski vacations.

AUSTRIA
Tirolean Inn to Inn

Austria's spectacular **Tirol** region offers one of the world's largest networks of cross-country ski trails. Miles of groomed tracks connect picturesque alpine villages. Many of the country's major downhill resorts feature nordic programs—at valley level as well as at higher elevations served by lifts and cable cars.

You're never far from a country inn, a chalet, or a heated climbers' hut. And with the many reasonably priced rooms available in small hotels and in private homes, you can enjoy an Austrian ski holiday for less than $75 per day (if you bring your own equipment).

A variety of itineraries is available for "skinny-ski" fans. One recommended route takes you over well-maintained trails through the foothills of the **Karwendel Alps.** After a day's warm-up just outside **Innsbruck,** follow the **Leutasch River Valley** to the village of **Scharnitz,** then cross by car into Germany and ski back across the border to the village of **Hinterriss.** From there, drive to **Lake Achensee,** your starting point for a 30-mile circuit through beautiful valleys.

Take your time on this trip and consider an overnight in **Steinberg am Rofan** or **Thiersee.** Both of these towns are noted for their baroque architecture.

Although you can easily arrange your own ski holiday in Austria, you'll probably save considerably on airfare if you go with a package tour. Package ski vacations in Austria may

be arranged through **Adventure Sport Holidays** (*815 North Rd., Westfield, MA 01085. 800-628-9655 or 413-568-2855. www.advonskis.com*). This experienced, Austrian-owned operation offers ski-holiday packages to destinations all over the country.

A one-week nordic holiday costs about $900 per person, including round-trip airfare from New York and lodging at Innsbruck's four-star Alpotel. With more than 310 miles of groomed trails, the resort is a popular retreat for cross-country skiers.

Another recommendation is to contact **Ski Europe** (*1535 West Loop S., Suite 319, Houston, TX 77027-9509. 800-333-5533. www.ski-europe.com*). This company offers a variety of high-quality package ski tours that range in price from budget to deluxe.

For a comprehensive list of nordic ski areas and chalets in Austria, contact the **Austrian National Tourist Office** (*P.O. Box 1142, New York, NY 10108. 212-944-6880 or 310-477-2038 in Los Angeles. www.anto.com*).

In Austria, the **Tirol Tourism Office** has an extensive network of excellent travel-information centers. These are located in Innsbruck and elsewhere around the country. English-speaking clerks provide local trail maps as well as information about lodging, winter sports opportunities, and other travel-related questions.

FRANCE & SWITZERLAND
The Haute Route

Europe's classic **Haute Route** through the Alps links the Swiss resorts of **Saas-Fee** and **Zermatt** with the **Chamonix** ski area in France.

This is the ultimate Alpine adventure—and a real test of a skier's skill, stamina, and determination. Haute Route skiers must carry heavy packs and climb as much as 3,300 feet each day up steep slopes more than 30 degrees in grade. Strong powder skills are essential.

Haute Route tours normally run from May to June, when high-altitude snow conditions are optimal. Climbers' huts fill up during holidays, so avoid these busy times. You'll find qualified guides at major resorts along the route, or you can check the web before you go for a list of internationally accredited guides (*www.adventure.ch/ivbv/addromg.htm*).

The French organization **Atalante** (*36/37, Quai Arloing, 69256 Lyon Cedex 09, France. 01133-472-5324-80. www.atalante.fr*) runs Haute Route tours. It also offers private guiding.

If you prefer an American outfitter, **Alpine Skills International** (*888-274-7325. www.alpineskills.com*) offers a nine-day trek along the route from Chamonix to Zermatt.

The trip begins with a two-day, off-trail skiing seminar at Chamonix. You then set off for a full week of steep

PEAK EXPERIENCE: A TELEMARK SKIER PLIES VIRGIN POWDER AT LA PLAGNE IN THE FRENCH ALPS.

climbing and descend from the **Aiguille du Midi** and the **Grandes Jorasses.** Eventually you arrive at Zermatt via the **Matterhorn.**

The cost is about $1,925 per person, and the program runs from late April to early May.

If you're not up to the Haute Route but still want a Swiss ski-touring experience, contact **Bill Russell's Mountain Tours** (*404 Hulls Hwy., Southport, CT 06490. 800-669-4453. www.russelltours.com*).

This company has led nordic tours in Switzerland's **Upper Engadine** region for more than 20 years. Experienced guides take you through four spectacular valleys on trails that link numerous small villages; skiers venture as far afield as they like before taking public transport back to the village of **Pontresina,** where they can glide right to the door of a four-star hotel. All skiers receive a Swiss Pass, which entitles them to unlimited use of public transport.

TURKEY
Traverse of the Taurus

Looking for a real adventure on skis? How about a multi-summit ski-mountaineering expedition in eastern Turkey's **Taurus Mountains?** This little-traveled region sees few tourists, even in summer. In winter you and your group (just six or seven skiers plus a guide) are guaranteed to have the mountains to yourselves.

Designed for skilled adventurers with a taste for unusual destinations, this is a novel ski program. It's also the perfect escape for those who have had their fill of crowded ski resorts.

Each day your destination is the next village. Skiers travel by horse or by truck as far up the mountain as possible; from there you continue the climb to the summit on skis. The daily regimen includes an 11,500-foot (3,500 m) ascent to a summit using randonée equipment—alpine gear modified for touring—followed by a full-tilt, alpine-style descent.

This program, intended for only the strongest and most capable wilderness skiers, is offered by the French outfitter **Atalante** (*C.P. 701, 36037, Quai Arloing, 69256 Lyon Cedex 09, France. 01133-472-5324-80. www.atalante.fr*). Participants tend to be primarily French or Italian, but the guides speak at least some English.

This challenging program runs for eight days in March and costs about $2,000 per person.

Atalante also runs an established ski-mountaineering program in **Morocco's High Atlas Mountains** every year, but the snow is generally more reliable in Turkey—and the scenery more varied.

NEW ZEALAND
Skiing the Southern Alps

For a world-class, hut-to-hut vacation, ski New Zealand's **Southern Alps.** You traverse high mountain passes, learn the basics of ski mountaineering, and even get a taste of glacier skiing. And you stay in provisioned, heated huts, so you need to carry only minimal gear.

Alpine Guides (*Mt. Cook Ltd., P.O. Box 20, Mt. Cook 8770, New Zealand. 01164-3435-1834. www.alpineguides.co.nz*) runs ski tours from June through October—New Zealand's winter season. Six-day trips cost about $1,000 per person.

Alpine designs custom itineraries for everyone one from novices to expert skiers. It also provides private guides for those who wish to explore virgin wilderness areas. If you are planning to travel this far, consider signing up for one of Alpine Guides' excellent courses in winter camping or ice-climbing.

If you can afford the expense (and only if you have the skill), consider hiring a helicopter for a day of wilderness heli-skiing. In New Zealand the higher you go, the better the snow. Thanks to the country's notoriously fickle weather, the snow regularly melts and refreezes at lower altitudes, causing frustratingly crusty conditions. No worries, though. The spectacular scenery more than compensates for a little crust.

YOSEMITE
Touring Ansel Adams Country

If **Yosemite National Park's** summer crowds get you down, try the place in the winter. Yosemite boasts 90 miles of groomed and marked trails and offers daily cross-country classes for skiers of all ages and all skill levels.

For those who want to learn telemark technique—basically, a turning position in which you drop one knee and slide one ski ahead—drive over to nearby **Badger Pass ski area** (209-372-1000) for a lesson.

To get into the high country, try an overnight hut trip to **Glacier Point** or scenic **Ostrander Lake.** The Glacier Point hut can be booked at a cost of $110 for one night or $150 for two nights, including food. The popular hut at Ostrander Lake costs $20 per person per night. For reservations, contact the **Yosemite Association** (*P.O. Box 545, Yosemite, CA 95389. 209-372-0740. www.nps.gov/yose*). For even more solitude, bring your tent and snow-camp under the stars.

The ultimate Yosemite skiing adventure is a six-day trans-Sierra crossing that is organized by the **Yosemite Cross-Country Ski School** (*Yosemite Concession Services, Yosemite National Park, CA 95389. 209-372-8444 winter only. www.yosemitepark.com*). Starting from the eastern slope, you ski across **Tioga Pass** (9,041 feet) and down to **Yosemite Valley.** (The Tioga Pass road is closed in winter, so you and your fellow skiers will have the route to yourselves.)

Skiers overnight in alpine huts, with a night or two of tented snow-camping if conditions permit. The program costs about $600 per person. Participants should have strong alpine-skiing skills and good stamina to keep up with all the climbing. Previous snow-camping experience is also helpful. Although seasoned backcountry skiers can make the journey on their own, it's better to go with a guide who can offer assistance with directions, avalanche avoidance, and making camp if you can't reach a hut.

Sierra Mountain Center (*P.O. Box 95, Bishop, CA 93515. 760-873-8526. www.sierramountaincenter.com*) does a slightly different six-day trip. Starting at **Mammoth Lakes,** this tour crosses the crest of the Sierras at **Tioga Pass,** takes you into Yosemite National Park, and exits at **Lee Vining.** The cost is $695 per person.

CALIFORNIA
Hut-to-Hut in the Sierras

Perched at a lofty 9,373 feet near Bishop, California, **Rock Creek Lodge** (*Rte. 1, Box 12, Mammoth Lakes, CA 93546. 760-935-4170. www.rockcreeklodge.com*) offers one of the best backcountry ski programs in the **Sierras.** Rock Creek maintains two huts that sit 3 miles apart and more than 10,000 feet above sea level.

You can ski the relatively flat trails between huts, or you

MAKING TRACKS ON PACKED POWDER, GALENA, IDAHO

can venture off into empty powder bowls. Self-guided hut trips cost a reasonable $27 per person per night (minimum two people per hut); the huts comfortably accommodate up to six people. Snowmobile support is available to transport you to the lodge and haul your supplies.

A nice route for strong skiers is the high passage from Rock Creek to **Mammoth Lakes. Sierra Mountain Center** (*P.O. Box 95, Bishop, CA 93515. 760-873-8526. www.sierramountaincenter.com*) offers this five-day trip as well as other high-Sierra crossings on a custom basis throughout the winter season.

If you prefer groomed routes, nearby **Tamarack Lodge Resort** (*P.O. Box 69, Mammoth Lakes, CA 93546. 800-237-6879 or 760-934-2442. www.tamaracklodge.com*) has 25 miles of tracked trails that start at an elevation of 8,600 feet. Rates start at $90 per night for comfortable, fully equipped, and heated cabins, plus a $16 trail fee. Private ski instruction is available at $35 per hour. A shuttle bus provides regular service to the cozy lodge.

In the **Lake Tahoe** area, **Alpine Skills International** (*P.O. Box 8, Norden, CA 95724. 888-274-7325 or 530-426-9108. www.alpineskills.com*) stages a variety of nordic programs from its own deluxe lodge. ASI's backcountry itineraries range from mild to wild; custom trips can be arranged for $85 to $150 per person per day.

If you don't find these programs sufficiently challenging, try the high route through the Sierras in April or May. Higher, tougher, and more remote than the Haute Route in France (*see pp. 259-250*), the **Sierra High Route** demands considerable strength, stamina, and preparation. Take the three- to seven-day, 40-mile route from the **Symmes Creek Trailhead** near **Independence** and ski west to **Wolverton.**

Unlike the popular Haute Route, the Sierra High Route is far less traveled by other skiers—despite the fact that spring skiing in the Sierras is about as good as it gets. The weather tends to be sunny, the corn snow is easy to navigate, storms are short lived—and you have a seemingly endless number of spectacular routes from which to choose.

OREGON
Crater Lake Ski Odyssey

Crater Lake in winter is one of the most beautiful spots in North America. The lake's icy waters—tinted blue by the big sky—mirror the jagged, white peaks of the crater's 6-mile-wide rim, a sight right out of a Sierra Club calendar. Teeming with tourists in summer, **Crater Lake National Park** is a far different place in the wintertime—particularly on weekdays, when it is nearly deserted. If you're looking for a getaway from civilization, this is it.

Although there are many ways to reach the crater's rim,

CROSS-COUNTRY SKIER CRUISES WHITE GRASS SKI TOURING CENTER IN CANAAN VALLEY, WEST VIRGINIA.

smart skiers approach from the east, park their vehicles a few miles from the crest, and then ascend the steady but fairly gentle grade to the top. The best ski-touring follows 33-mile **Rim Drive.** Snowmobile trails along much of this route allow for easy skiing, even if you are carrying a pack.

The area features four well-marked trails that range in difficulty from beginner to expert. Although they see a fair number of travelers, these trails promise beautiful views of the lake and the surrounding backcountry.

About two and a half hours southwest from Crater Lake, you'll find **Outdoor Odyssey** (*373rd St., Ashland, OR 97520. 541-488-1202. www.outdoorstore.com*). Operating out of **Ashland Outdoor Store,** this outfitter offers guided cross-country skiing tours and ski lessons in the **Rogue River Forest.**

Each year in early spring, Outdoor Odyssey leads a four-day circumnavigation of Crater Lake. This is a fine opportunity to do some extended ski-touring and pick up skills in winter camping. The cost is $250 per person, which includes food but not equipment.

Outdoor Odyssey also offers telemark-skiing classes and tours; the minimum group size is four people.

If you plan to ski the Crater Lake area on your own, check the ski conditions in advance with the **Rim Village Visitor Center** (*541-594-2211. www.nps.gov*). The Park Service occasionally offers guided snowshoe walks; participants must bring their own gear.

COLORADO
Tenth Mountain Telemarking

The Colorado Rockies offer boundless options for wilderness ski enthusiasts. Expert telemarkers will enjoy the **Tenth Mountain Division Hut System,** a 300-mile network of high ski trails and huts. All routes offer superb views, great powder, and a chance to ski the best of the Rockies away from the downhill crowds. Ski lifts access the trailheads to some of the more popular huts, including **Janet Cabin** and **Barnard Memorial Hut** near **Copper Mountain** resort.

Backcountry skiers on the trail at Tenth Mountain can overnight at any of the area's 22 well-equipped huts, which are maintained by the **Tenth Mountain Division Hut Association** (*1280 Ute Ave., Unit 21, Aspen, CO 81611. 970-925-5775. www.huts.org*). This is the most extensive hut network in the country.

If you prefer, you can stay in one of 18 privately owned cabins. Four of these are operated by the **Summit Huts Association** and may be reserved through the TMDHA.

Alternatively, you can stay at one of the seven huts south of Aspen. Maintained by the **Alfred A. Braun Hut System,** they must also be reserved through the TMDHA. Most huts range from $17 to $35 per person per night.

One of the most popular stretches at Tenth Mountain is the 50-mile run from **Vail** to **Aspen.** Experienced ski mountaineers can make the trek unguided; anyone else should hire an experienced guide.

If you decide to go with **Paragon Guides** (*P.O. Box 130, Vail, CO 81658. 877-926-5299 or 970-926-5299. www. paragonguides.com*), a ski tour will cost $630 per person for three days, $1,300 for six days. **Aspen Alpine Guides** (*P.O. Box 659, Aspen, CO 81612. 800-643-8621 or 970-925-6618. www.aspenalpine.com*) charges $575 per person for four days, all inclusive. Both outfitters also offer other winter adventures in the Rockies.

Those without expedition-caliber telemarking and climbing skills may prefer to sample the **Rockies Grand Tour.** This 90-mile trail network links the region's main ski resorts. Ski lifts deliver you to the major passes; from there, you traverse from one resort to the next with relative ease.

The idea of letting the lifts do most of the work is appealing; however, you spend evenings at downhill resorts, which diminishes some of the wilderness appeal.

NEW YORK
Adirondack Cross-Country

Planning a nordic holiday in the Adirondacks is easy: The region boasts hundreds of fine bed and breakfasts and lodges that cater to winter-sports enthusiasts.

One of the best lodges is operated by the **Adirondack Rock and River Guide Service** (*P.O. Box 219, Keene, NY 12942. 518-576-2041. www.rockandriver.com*). Located in the heart of the **Sentinel Wilderness Area,** the ARRGS Lodge offers easy access to one of the best-known cross-country-ski trails in the East. In fact, the 25-mile-long **Jackrabbit Trail** starts right outside the door.

The first section of the Jackrabbit Trail climbs 5 miles to a mountain saddle, passing beaver ponds and ice cliffs en route. From the top of the pass you can turn around and glide back down to the lodge. Alternatively, you can continue on to beautiful **Lake Placid,** which is 15 miles farther down the trail. Hardy skiers can run the entire length of the trail with an overnight at one of the many country inns along the route.

Another popular day trip from the ARRGS Lodge is the 10-mile, intermediate-level loop to **Avalanche Pass,** where you get a stunning overview of **Avalanche Lake.**

Expert skiers will enjoy the trail up **Mt. Marcy,** which offers great telemarking on the return descent.

The cost for all of this backcountry fun is very reasonable. Rooms at the lodge cost $45 to $55 per night for a single or $65 to $75 per night for a double, including breakfast. ARRGS also provides nordic ski guides and ice-climbing guides for $140 to $150 per person per day. You need not be a guest at the lodge to book a guide.

The Skinny on Nordic Skiing

Nordic skiers may not need ski lifts, but who could turn down a little pampering at the end of a day's exertions on the trail? If you're a novice, groomed tracks help you get into the cross-country groove. A few well-earned amenities and a cozy lodge are just the ticket to elevate your spirits and enhance your skinny-ski holiday—without spoiling your solitude. Here are the top nordic ski centers in North America.

EAST

MAINE

Sugarloaf/USA Outdoor Center
In uncrowded and unspoiled Carrabassett Valley, **Sugarloaf/USA Outdoor Center** (*Kingsfield. 800-843-5623 or 207-237-2000. www.sugarloaf.com*) features warming huts and 56 miles of excellent machine-tracked trails, plus a 4.6-mile racing loop and a skating rink. Also rentals, lessons, and clinics, as well as night skiing (with headlamps).

NEW HAMPSHIRE

Jackson Ski Touring Foundation
A major cross-country center, **Jackson Ski Touring Foundation** (*Jackson. 800-927-6697 or 603-383-9355 for ski report. www.jacksonxc.com*) offers more than 93 miles of premium trails for all levels. Trails cover a variety of terrain and connect with inns, such as the **Inn at Thorn Hill, Nestlenook Farm,** and **Whitney's Inn,** and resorts, including **Nordic Village.**

NEW YORK

Mt. Van Hoevenberg Cross-Country Center
This center boasts 31 miles of Olympic-quality groomed trails, snow-making facilities, expert instruction, and 13 racing loops, plus bobsled runs and other sporting options. Linked with two regional trail systems, it is near the Jackrabbit Trail (*see p. 253*). Daily and weekend trail fee is $12, $10 for seniors and children. Rentals are $16 per day. Contact the **Olympic Sports Complex** (*Lake Placid. 518-523-2811*) or the **Lake Placid Visitors Bureau** (*800-447-5224 or 518-523-2445. www.lakeplacid.com*).

VERMONT

Mountain Top Inn
Romantic and picturesque **Mountain Top Inn** (*Chittenden. 800-445-2100 or 802-483-2311. www.mountaintopinn.com*) offers 52 miles of mostly tracked and groomed trails, plus snow-making facilities, in the Green Mountains. Other features include sleigh rides, ice-skating, and training seminars. Rooms range from $176-226. Ski rentals are $15 per day; trail fees for nonguests are $14 per day.

Stowe
This major downhill resort boasts one of America's best cross-country networks. Four touring centers are linked by 87 miles of groomed trails and 62 miles of back-country trails.

The centers include: **Edson Hill Touring Center** (*800-621-0284 or 802-253-7371. www.stowevt.com*); **Stowe Mountain Resort Cross-Country Center** (*800-253-4754 or 802-253-3000. www.stowe.com*); **Topnotch at Stowe Resort & Spa** (*800-451-8686 or 802-253-8585. www.topnotch-resort.com*); and **Trapp Family Lodge** (*800-826-7000 or 802-253-5719. www.trappfamily.com*).

WEST VIRGINIA

White Grass Ski Touring Center
Situated on a 4,000-foot-high plateau in Dolly Sods Wilderness Area, **White Grass Ski Touring Center** (*Davis. 304-866-4114. www.whitegrass.com*) occupies a former downhill resort. Along with the hills, there are 80 miles of groomed flats. The café is excellent; reserve for dinner. Day fee is $10; rentals are $10-20 per day. Both telemark and cross-country lessons are offered.

CENTRAL STATES

MICHIGAN

Garland Resort
The only AAA-rated four-diamond resort in the Midwest, this upscale complex features more than 24 miles of groomed tracks through 3,500 acres of pristine backcountry—and a private airstrip. The rate for room, two meals, and skiing is about $140 per person per night. Extras include the romantic **Zhivago Tour**—a horse-drawn sleigh ride to **Buckhorn Lodge** for a feast of wild game and fine wine. Contact **Garland Resort** (*Lewiston. 877-442-7526 or 517-786-3584. www.garlandusa.com*).

Traverse City
Michigan's nordic capital, Traverse City boasts hundreds of miles of groomed public and private trails and six nordic resorts, which range from basic to deluxe and offer ski instruction. Trails cover varied terrain, including frozen waterways at Sleeping Bear Dunes National Lakeshore.

Recommended are **Shanty Creek-Shuss Mountain Resort** (*Bellaire. 800-678-4111 or 231-533-8621. www.shantycreek. com*); **Sugar Loaf Resort** (*Cedar. 800-952-6390 or 231-228-1808. www.theloaf. com*); and **Grand Traverse Resort** (*Acme. 800-748-0303 or 231-938-2100. www. grandtraverseresort. com*).

For information, contact the **Traverse City Convention & Visitors Bureau** (*Traverse City. 800-872-8377 or 231-947-3134. www.tcvisitor.com*).

MINNESOTA

Bearskin Lodge
A true wilderness area at the northern end of the Boundary Waters Canoe Area Wilderness, spacious **Bearskin Lodge** (*Grand Marais. 800-338-2292 or 218-388-4170. www.bearskin.com*) has 31 miles of groomed tracks. Off the trail, you'll find hundreds of frozen lakes to ski. Other amenities here include a lighted trail and ice-skating.

THE ROCKIES

COLORADO

Breckenridge Nordic Ski Center
Enjoy every kind of nordic and backcountry skiing at **Breckenridge Nordic Ski**

Center (*Breckenridge. 970-453-6855*). Ski the 17 miles of trails, groomed for classical and skate-skiing, then head over to nearby **Frisco Nordic Center** (*970-668-0866. www.colorado.net/~nord/*), which has 26 miles (42 km) of groomed track. (No trail connects the two, but a free shuttle bus does.)

The $10 daily trail pass is good at both locales. Off trail, you can traverse mountain ranges between old mining towns. Breckenridge offers certified ski instruction for all levels.

Crested Butte Nordic Ski Center

Expect gentle flats to steep alpine trails at **Crested Butte Nordic Ski Center** (*Crested Butte. 970-349-1707. www.visitcrestedbutte.com/nordic*).

There are 25 miles of groomed trails for skating and classical cross-country; nearby Gunnison National Forest and the adjoining high-country wilderness promise vast reaches of virgin powder. Cost for trail use is $9 per day. Equipment rentals and guided backcountry tours are available. Inquire about reservations at **Forest Queen Hut;** the cabin stands four miles north of **Mt. Crested Butte.**

Telluride

Ski for free on 25 miles of groomed trails at **Telluride Nordic Center** (*Telluride. 970-728-1144*). Along with guided day trips and ski instruction, the center offers access to a five-hut, 45-mile trail network through the **San Juan Mountains** (*San Juan Hut Systems, Inc. 970-728-6935. www.sanjuanhuts.com*). Guide rates are $50 to $150 per day; hut fees are $22 per person per night. **Faraway Ranch Foundation** (*970-728-9640. www.farawayranch.org*) runs backcountry ski tours for $75-150 per day.

MONTANA
Lone Mountain Guest Ranch

A premier ski ranch, **Lone Mountain Guest Ranch** (*Big Sky. 800-514-4644 or 406-995-4644. www.lmranch.com*) features more than 40 miles of wide, groomed trails. Wilderness routes access vast tracts of pristine powder. Other options are ski tours through **Yellowstone National Park,** ski instruction, and fly-fishing trips. A week on the ranch at **North Fork Cabin,** with meals and sleigh-ride dinner, starts at approximately $2,600 for two people.

SKIER DOGGEDLY CROSSES FROZEN LAKE COLDEN, UPSTATE NEW YORK.

W E S T

CALIFORNIA

Kirkwood Cross-Country Ski Area

Part of a ski complex, **Kirkwood Cross-Country Ski Area** (*800-967-7500 or 209-258-6000. www.skikirkwood.com. Nov.-April*) is the perfect place for a combination nordic and alpine ski vacation. The area offers about 50 miles of groomed track at an average altitude of 7,800 feet. Terrain varies from flat valley trails to alpine and mountaineering routes. The nordic center provides three warming huts and quality instruction for all levels.

Montecito-Sequoia Cross-Country Ski Resort

A good choice for skiers of all levels, **Montecito-Sequoia Cross-Country Ski Center** (*Kings Canyon National Park. 800-227-9900. www.mslodge.com*) features 37 miles of groomed trails and 125 miles of backcountry routes that link **Sequoia** and **Kings Canyon National Parks.** Other activities include night skating and tube-riding. Cost is about $120 per person per day, double occupancy, including all meals.

Royal Gorge Cross-Country Ski Resort

America's largest cross-country venue (only about three hours from San Francisco), **Royal Gorge Cross-Country Ski Resort** (*Soda Springs. 800-500-3871 or 530-426-3871. www.royalgorge.com*) boasts 90 groomed trails totaling about 205 miles. Set at 7,000 feet, it also enjoys a long season. Top-rate facilities include private cabins, two lodges, a ski school, and ten warming huts. We recommend **Royal Gorge's Wilderness Lodge.** Skiers pay $129-169 per person per day; two-, three-, and five-day packages include lodging, meals, instruction, and a sleigh ride.

OREGON

Mount Bachelor Cross-Country Center

Known for its good, dry snow and sunshine, **Mount Bachelor Cross-Country Center** (*Bend. 800-829-2442 or 541-382-2442. www.mtbachelor.com*) is the U.S. Ski Team's spring-training site. Along with 34 miles of machine-laid tracks, groomed trails through Deschutes National Forest in the Cascades offer great backcountry skiing. Instruction and competition programs are excellent here, as is the downhill skiing at Mount Bachelor ski resort.

WASHINGTON

Cascades Methow Valley

Only four hours from Seattle, Methow Valley is a superb destination for nordic skiers, who enjoy great scenery, dry snow, and 110 miles of groomed trails on the trail system maintained by the nonprofit Methow Valley Sport Trails Association. Recreational options are many: You can ski hut to hut, along old logging roads, through high meadows, on valley flats, or via helicopter. This is a perfect spot for telemarking.

Area lodging ranges from luxurious **Sun Mountain Lodge** (*Winthrop. 800-572-0493 or 509-996-2211. www. sunmountainlodge.com*), a four-star resort, to backcountry **Rendezvous Huts** (*Winthrop. 800-257-2452 or 509-996-8100. www.methow.com/huts*). Rates for the five cozy huts start at $25 per person per night (*maximum of eight per hut; gear-freighting is optional*). For more lodging information, contact **Methow Reservations** (*800-422-3048 or 509-996-2148. www.mvcentralres.com*).

C A N A D A

BRITISH COLUMBIA

Wells Gray Provincial Park

For those seeking a high-alpine, backcountry adventure, **Wells Gray Chalets** (*Clearwater. 888-754-8735 or 250-587-6444. www.skihike.com*) promises superb snow and scenery at bargain rates.

Operating from three comfortable chalets in the Cariboo Mountains, Wells Gray offers guided and unguided routes through untracked wilderness, as well as drop-offs by Snowcats or helicopters for spectacular alpine traverses. Cost for five days is about $500 per person, including lodging, meals, guide, and gear.

QUÉBEC

Parc du Mont-Sainte-Anne

With about 140 miles of marked trails through the Laurentian forest, **Parc du Mont-Sainte-Anne** (*Beaupré. 800-463-1568 or 418-827-5281. www.mont-sainte-anne.com*) boasts the largest single nordic system in Canada. Well-maintained trails—including about 84 miles groomed for skating—suit skiers of all levels.

At the trail hub, **L'Auberge du Fondeur** offers skiers charming accommodations and excellent food. The park also maintains a skating rink and seven heated trailside cabins.

Ski Mountaineering

Ski mountaineering—ascending a peak with the goal of skiing down—demands special skills, including randonée and telemark ski techniques, climbing, route-finding methods, glacier travel, and winter survival. Here are some of North America's best ski-mountaineering programs.

ALASKA

Ruth Glacier

Each April **Mountain Madness** (*Seattle. 800-328-5925 or 206-937-8389. www.mountainmadness.com*) leads nine-day fly-in trips to **Ruth Glacier** in Denali National Park. Even though this trip is open to skiers of all levels, those with backcountry skiing experience and good telemark technique will benefit most. Focus is on vertical ascents and descents; glacier travel skills and telemarking technique are also taught. Cost is about $1,500. Outfitter Gary Bocarde's **Mountain Trip** (*Anchorage. 907-345-6499. www.mountaintrip.com*) also leads ski tours in this region.

CALIFORNIA

Summit Skiing Adventures

Based in the California Sierra, **Alpine Skills International** (*Norden. 888-274-7325 or 530-426-9108. www.alpineskills. com*) offers a full range of programs. ASI's two-day climb/ski trips in the eastern Sierras are ideal for novice ski mountaineers with some downhill experience. The cost is about $250. The more adventuresome three-day Mount Shasta descent costs about $300.

IDAHO

Skiing the Sawtooths

Renowned instructor Kirk Bachman directs the **Sawtooth Mountain Guides** (*Stanley. 208-774-3324. www. sawtoothguides.com*) winter program in the **Sawtooth Wilderness.** Ski to a 8,000-foot-high yurt and enjoy unlimited telemarking opportunities. Or continue on to high-altitude routes accessible from two yurts (with saunas). Fully guided tours cost $150 per person per day (*three-person minimum*); yurt rental is $30 per person per night (*eight-person minimum*); the rate for a private guide is $400 per day. Sawtooth also offers international expeditions, avalanche seminars, telemark clinics, and backcountry skiing.

ALBERTA

Rockies Ski Mountaineering

Yamnuska, Inc. (*Canmore. 403-678-4164. www.yamnuska.com*) offers ski-mountaineering instruction in the heart of the Canadian Rockies. The seven-day introductory program is run from base huts and tents in the **Wapta Icefield** and focuses on equipment, avalanche awareness, search and rescue, glacier travel, and navigation. Cost is about $725 per person. Experienced skiers can try the six-day, hut-to-hut **Wapta Traverse** program, which traces the ice field into remote backcountry. Cost is about $570. Custom programs are available. Guides are internationally certified.

TRAVEL TIPS

Trip Planning

Nordic ski-touring takes a lot of preparation, whether you go with a guide or not. If you're heading for the backcountry, review this checklist before you depart.

Day Trip

Bring a lightweight (2,000 cubic inches) day pack that won't impede your movements, plus a water bottle and insulated carrier; food, including nonfreezing energy snacks; sunscreen and lip protector; maps, compass, camera, and first-aid kit. For a high-country outing, pack an avalanche beacon, extra clothes for layering, and a space blanket. Cell phones can be useful, but tell someone where you are going— and when you expect to return.

Overnight

A moderately large internal- or external-frame backpack (5,000 cubic inches) is appropriate. Pack for a day trip and bring a winter sleeping bag that *exceeds* the region's temperature requirements. Also take a sleeping pad, four-season tent, food, stove, cooking equipment, fuel, toiletries, candles, and headlamp. Kicker shins are helpful for climbing hills. A lightweight trenching tool is handy for snow-camping.

Expedition

You'll need a bigger pack (6,000 to 7,000 cubic inches) plus extra clothing, fuel (a quart per day per skier in winter, a pint in spring), food, and repair kits. Bring a water filter, altimeter, and insulated pants and jacket. You must be able to bear a third of your weight for up to eight hours a day, and you should be knowledgeable about navigation, snow safety, first aid, weather, equipment repair, and water purification.

ONLINE

Cross Country Ski Areas Association

www.xcski.org

Information on ski shops, equipment, travel, instruction, resources, and regional snow reports.

Ski Central

skicentral.com

Quick-reference site indexes nearly 2,000 web pages. A good source for ski clubs.

SkiNet

www.skinet.com

Features destinations plus reprints from *Skiing* and *Ski* magazines, but the emphasis is on downhill.

U.S. Ski Reports

America Online, Sports Area, Keyword: Ski Report

Daily snow reports at resorts nationwide. For destination profiles and ski vacation specials, go to to keyword: ski zone.

BOOKS

Backcountry Skiing California's High Sierra by John Moynier (Falcon Books, 1999, $14.95. 800-725-8303. www.falconbooks.com). Ski guide presents day trips to expeditions, plus elevation graphs and photos.

Cross-Country Skiing by Ned Gillette and John Dostal (The Mountaineers, 1988, $14.95. 800-553-4453 or 206-223-6303. www.mountaineers.org). A fun, informative manual by two pros.

Free-Heel Skiing: Telemark and Parallel Techniques for All Conditions by Paul Parker (The Mountaineers, 1995, $19.95. 800-553-4453 or 206-223-6303. www.mountaineers.org). This solid resource recounts trips to Denali, the Haute Route, and more.

MAGAZINES

Cross Country Skier Magazine (Stillwater, MN. 800-827-0607 or 612-361-6760. www.crosscountryskier.com). The premier journal for the nordically inclined.

Skitrax Magazine (Toronto. 416-530-1350. E-mail: pedal@passport.ca). Calendar, buyers' guide, race news, ski destinations.

Backcountry (Arvada, CO. 303-424-5858. www.backcountrymagazine.com). Backcountry and telemark skiing, with gear reviews and articles

VIDEO

Dryland Training with Olympic Champion Vegard Ulvang ($24.95. 800-321-1671. www.nordicequipment.com). Roller-skating, running, speed and interval training.

SKIERS ON TOUR CAMP OUT IN ALASKA'S DENALI NATIONAL PARK AND PRESERVE.

outdoorSkills

O UTDOOR-SKILLS INSTRUCTION TAKES MANY FORMS: SURVIVAL TRAINING, LEADERSHIP TRAINING, BACK- country sports training, and emergency medical training. In a classic survival school, students learn to live off the land with virtually no aid or gear. The goal is to find food and water, make a fire, and build a shelter. Knowledge of these skills is found in everything from military manuals to Native American lore. • A general outdoor- skills program teaches you to fend for yourself in the wilderness, but the focus is on adventure: The curriculum may include an extended backpacking trip, telemarking in the Tetons, paddling a canoe, sailing, or scaling a mountain peak. • Leadership training— designed for people who aspire to be professional guides or group leaders—involves more formalized instruction: Leaders-in-training learn specific guiding skills, as well as general techniques on how to work with large groups outdoors. • Wilderness medical training teaches advanced first aid and rescue techniques to outdoor professionals and serious backcountry enthusiasts. • The best facilities for all these types of outdoor learning are reviewed in this chapter. Whether you want to live like a Native American or cope with a medical emergency on the trail, you'll find a way to do it here.

LEFT: PRACTICING SNOW-SURVIVAL SKILLS IN NEW YORK'S ADIRONDACKS
BELOW: CAMPSITE BY THE *MERLIN*, A ROCK FACE IN WYOMING'S BIGHORN MOUNTAINS

Learning to Lead

Outward Bound

Survival Schools

There is nothing training cannot do, nothing is above its reach. It can turn bad morals into good. It can destroy bad principles and re-create good ones. It can lift men to angelship.
MARK TWAIN

Getting Schooled in the Great Outdoors

Key skills are needed to summit a major peak or undertake a wilderness expedition, and you can learn them from the pros. Whatever your passion—climbing, backcountry skiing, sea kayaking—training centers such as the National Outdoor Leadership School and Outward Bound can give you the necessary techniques and conditioning.

Does this mean you shouldn't venture outdoors without a survival-school diploma? Of course not. Modern outdoor equipment has made it possible for the average person to complete a weeklong backpacking expedition without suffering anything more serious than sore feet. One need not be a latter-day Daniel Boone to enjoy the wilderness.

Why, then, subject yourself to the rigors of a wilderness training school? Because you're likely to emerge from it not only a stronger person but a better one—a person who sets high goals in life and has the confidence to achieve them. One student called Outward Bound her "most meaningful personal experience ... more cerebral and spiritual than anything else. In every way, I learned I was much greater and more capable than I thought."

Does a wilderness experience have everyday applications? Most who have completed a wilderness course insist that it does. "The work you are doing goes far beyond the extent of the trip," noted one student. "It shapes attitudes, affects lives, and inspires careers." Outward Bound and similar programs tap human potential by forcing us to summon our courage, thereby finding new limits.

The best wilderness and survival schools are profiled below. For general information on guide training for a particular activity, contact **America Outdoors** (*P.O. Box 10847, Knoxville, TN 37939. 423-558-3595. www.americaoutdoors.org*), which represents more than 550 outfitters nationwide; some of them operate guiding schools devoted to specific pursuits, such as horse packing, river running, or rock climbing.

NATIONAL OUTDOOR LEADERSHIP SCHOOL (NOLS)

Do you yearn to lead a mountain ascent or a sea-kayak expedition? If so, the **National Outdoor Leadership School** (*288 Main St., Lander, WY 82520. 307-332-5300. www.nols.edu*) is probably the place for you. Because NOLS is the only wilderness institute designed with the express purpose of training professional outdoor guides, it is the best choice for those heading into an outdoor career.

Programs are conducted year-round in mountaineering, backpacking, sea kayaking and white-water kayaking, telemark skiing, winter camping, and sailing. Certain courses even offer college credit. School directors lead two-week to three-month expeditions in Alaska, Arizona, Washington, and Wyoming, as well as Australia, Canada, Chile, Kenya, and Mexico. If Outward Bound is boot camp, NOLS is officer-candidates school. You learn by doing—and you are then shown how to teach what you have learned.

NOLS is not a survival school where you must live off the land or undergo rugged conditioning treks and solos. Instead, it strives to "teach the skills and judgment that should prevent you from ever getting yourself into a survival situation." This kind of training is delivered via hands-on experiences in the wilderness. Mountaineering is taught through month-long courses conducted in the North Cascades, the Wind River Range (Wyoming), Alaska, British Columbia, and Chile. Shorter courses are available for those over 25. NOLS also offers climbing expeditions to Denali (Mount McKinley) in Alaska. The **Denali Expedition** is a serious high-altitude climb for those who have already completed a NOLS course. The cost is $4,550; four hours of college credit are available.

Kayak training programs range from 14-day tours of Baja, the Rio Grande, or Alaska to a full semester (83 days) in Baja, during which you also learn sailing and climbing skills. Other multiactivity semester programs (16 to 20 hours of credit) are run in Alaska, Wyoming, the Cascades, Australia, Africa, and Chilean Patagonia. Semester programs cost $7,800 to $8,900 and feature kayaking or rafting, rock or ice climbing, and alpine hiking and camping. Shorter, month-long wilderness courses combine hiking with kayaking or rock climbing and cost $2,700 to $3,000. Once you have completed a basic wilderness class, you can apply for the NOLS instructor's course (*34 days, $3,300*).

Those without unlimited time should investigate the three-week specialty courses offered by NOLS. These include a $2,775 rock-climbing session in the Wind River Range, a wilderness horse-packing course (*$2,950*), and the exceptional Wyoming winter ski course, which is available in two versions: standard (*two weeks, $1,255*) and age 25 and up (*10 days, $1,450*). Ski-course participants learn how to telemark in powder, build snow caves and igloos, and navigate open wilderness areas.

NOLS is a unique program. Its highly qualified instructors teach a range of activities—56 courses in six countries on four continents. If you're serious about learning outdoor skills in enough depth to teach others, contact NOLS. Getting college credit was never so exciting—or rewarding.

OUTWARD BOUND

Founded in 1941, Outward Bound (*100 Mystery Pt. Rd., Garrison, NY 10524. 800-243-8520 or 914-424-4000. www. outwardbound.org*) now encompasses more than 50 schools and training centers worldwide. It is by far the largest outdoor-skills program, and it boasts the most offerings.

Although the core of the Outward Bound curriculum remains a one- to four-week wilderness adventure in which students learn self-sufficiency in the outdoors, that theme now has many variations: Programs focus on ocean skills, rock climbing, river rafting, winter camping, canoeing, mountaineering, sea kayaking, sailing, desert backpacking, cross-country skiing, and dogsledding. There are also three-month semester courses, as well as specialty programs for families, young adults, and even corporate groups.

Most programs involve four distinct training stages:

First, students are led through an instruction-and-conditioning phase in which they learn the skills needed for their principal activity, be it paddling, rock climbing, or hiking.

Next, the students (in groups of 8 to 12) set off with their instructors on an extended wilderness journey—down a river, up a mountain, or into a forest. Along the way, the students practice and refine their wilderness skills.

Phase three is the solo—the aspect of Outward Bound that has received so much media attention. This individual retreat may seem risky, but instructors monitor the students daily to guarantee their safety. The solo is designed to be a challenge, not an ordeal. It is a chance to get away from everything, with a minimum of equipment, and reflect on one's resources and capabilities. Many Outward Bound alumni credit the solo as the best part of the course.

At the conclusion of the solo, the last phase begins. The students are divided into small groups to complete short expeditions, either on their own or with minimal supervision. When all groups have completed their treks, there is a final group activity called a personal-challenge event—a paddle, a climb, or a hike. Participants then depart for home, family, and civilization.

Outward Bound has an excellent reputation for safety and professionalism. All instructors are Red Cross and CPR trained. Many have Wilderness First Responder certificates. The typical staff-to-student ratio is 1 to 5.

With five major schools nationwide, Outward Bound offers an enormous variety of courses. Here are some perennial favorites: backcountry skiing in the Rockies (*Colorado School, eight days, Feb.-March, $1,100*); combined mountaineering, canyon trekking, and white-water rafting in Utah

(*Colorado School, 23 days, June-July, $2,700*); canoe expedition and trekking (*Voyageur School, 7-29 days, summer, $1,000-2,500*); combined mountaineering and white-water rafting in the Cascades and Deschutes River, Oregon (*Pacific Crest School, summer, 14-25 days, $2,100-2,700*); backpacking, rock climbing, and white-water canoeing (*North Carolina School, summer, 21 days, $2,400*). Mountaineering-only programs are also offered in California's Sierra Nevada, Washington's North Cascades, and British Columbia's Coastal Range. Prices vary by destination.

Outward Bound also conducts outdoor leadership courses, many of which offer high-school or college credit. Ranging from four days to a full semester, these programs are designed for professional educators and would-be outdoor guides. Contact the **North Carolina Outward Bound School** (*800-841-0186*). The affiliated **Kurt Hahn Center for Educational Services** (*800-438-9661, ext. 120*) specializes in leadership training and curriculum development for teachers and staff of community agencies.

REGIONAL OUTWARD BOUND PROGRAMS

Colorado Outward Bound School
945 Pennsylvania St., Denver, CO 80203
800-477-2627 or 303-837-0880. www.cobs.org
Primarily mountaineering courses.

Hurricane Island Outward Bound School
75 Mechanic St., Rockland, ME 04841
800-341-1744 or 207-594-5548.
www.hurricaneisland.com

Also runs winter programs in the Florida Keys.
North Carolina Outward Bound School
2582 Riceville Rd., Asheville, NC 28805
800-841-0186 or 704-299-3366. www.ncobs.org.
Staff training is a specialty here.

Pacific Crest Outward Bound School
0110 S.W. Bancroft St., Portland, OR 97201
800-547-3312 or 503-243-1993. www.pcobs.org

Voyageur Outward Bound School
111 Third Ave. S., Minneapolis, MN 55401
800-328-2943 or 612-338-0131. www.vobs.org

SIR EDMUND HILLARY OUTDOOR PURSUITS CENTRE OF NEW ZEALAND

Although primarily an outdoor-activity center for the general public, the **Hillary Center** (*Private Bag, Turangi, New Zealand. 01164-7386-5511. Fax 01164-7386-0204. www.opc.org.nz*) also offers leadership training for future guides. Novices can learn a variety of skills, including mountaineering, kayaking, wilderness first aid, and sport climbing. Guides-in-training will find a full curriculum of leadership-training courses, among them kayak instruction, white-water guiding, and mountain guiding. Prices range from $200 for two-day programs to $1,050 for the full, week-long **Skills for Outdoor Leaders** course. Outdoor professionals should seriously consider the five-day, $560 **Risk Management Seminar.** New Zealand's unique geography allows students to train in a variety of environments, from sea to summit. The center will also customize guide-training programs upon request.

CANYONLANDS FIELD INSTITUTE (CFI)

The nonprofit **Canyonlands Field Institute** (*P.O. Box 68, Moab, UT 84532. 800-860-5262 or 435-259-7750. www. canyonlandsfieldinst.org*) teaches outdoor skills as part of its general mission to promote the proper use and conservation of wilderness areas. Programs run the gamut from weekend sessions to a graduate residency program offering credit through the University of Utah.

CFI's land-based seminars feature history, Native American culture, geology, and the life zone of the Colorado plateau. The river-based programs include paddling, rowing, and river ecology. All seminars teach how to set up camps and plan expeditions. Instructors may include naturalists, anthropologists, wildlife biologists, geologists, archaeologists, or experts in desert ecology and river ecology. For working adults, we recommend CFI's annual **Special Expeditions.** These multiday journeys through spectacular scenery are offered four times each year for $100 to $200 per day; participants must sign up as a group of eight or more.

Popular with youngsters are the institute's five-day whitewater academy for teens and five-day outdoor-science program for grades 4 through 12. Student fees are low because CFI receives funding from the National Park Service. CFI also sponsors Elderhostel programs such as rafting, canoe trips, land-based programs, a guest ranch, and cultural tours.

JERRY MALSON'S MONTANA GUIDE TRAINING CENTER

Seasoned wilderness guide Jerry Malson offers hands-on training for hunting, fishing, and horse-packing guides. His Montana state-licensed training center (*22 Swamp Creek Rd., Trout Creek, MT 59874. 406-847-5582. Fax 406-827-3789*) gives students the skills to start their own outfitting businesses or secure employment as professional guides or wranglers. (Malson even offers job-placement services to his students.) You'll learn how to outfit wilderness expeditions and how to run a horse or mule string in the backcountry. The month-long program covers wrangling and packing, first aid, animal tracking, camping, and serving as camp jack—that is, choosing and setting up a camp, then cooking the meals. Most students also obtain American Red Cross and CPR certifications during their stay at the center. The fee for a four-week program is $2,750, including room and board. Although some students enroll purely for the Western experience, the Montana Guide Training Center is a serious school that graduates skilled, self-sufficient outdoor leaders.

WILDERNESS EDUCATION ASSOCIATION (WEA)

The nonprofit **Wilderness Education Association** (*P.O. Box 158897, Nashville, TN 37215. 615-531-5174. www.wildernesseducation.org.*), founded in 1977, sponsors environmental-education and outdoor-leadership programs. The leadership courses focus on low-impact recreation methods, conservation strategies, and environmental awareness. The WEA offers a variety of courses year-round, including one- to seven-day wilderness education workshops; seven- to 10-day wilderness-steward programs; and 10- to 14-day instructors' courses. Prices range from $120 to $200 per day. Most programs require no previous experience, but the instructors' courses require some wilderness travel skills, and prior experience in handling groups is preferred. For more information, contact the WEA National Office for dates, locations, and application procedures.

Survival Schools

The more you know the less you need. Americans are into gimmicks. But in the end, there is very little you can buy that replaces knowledge.... A thousand years ago, if you didn't learn this stuff, you died.
—Cody Lundin, *USA Today*

True self-sufficiency in the wild demands mastering such aboriginal skills as building a fire, gathering food, and making shelter. These abilities were second nature to Native Americans and pioneers, but they are lost arts for modern urbanites. Fortunately, a number of specialty survival schools have kept the lore alive, and they can teach you what it takes to survive in the wild.

All of the schools profiled below offer courses in outdoor survival using basic tools and subsistence provisions. Some emphasize Native American culture and spirituality; others employ a more mainstream approach, teaching general wilderness skills both ancient and modern.

Getting Ready

Survival schools involve tough, strenuous activity—mountaineering and backpacking over long distances with a limited supply of food and water. To a large degree, the object is to live off the land as early peoples did. This can be quite a shock, even to experienced backpackers: The average weight loss on a three-week survival course sponsored by the Boulder Outdoor Survival School (*see p. 158*) is 10 to 15 pounds.

You need not be an Olympic athlete to endure these courses, but you should do your best to arrive fit and mentally prepared for the challenges that lie ahead. Courage and will—more than physical abilities—will pull you through the program. And though it's true that a survival school challenges the body, it also tests the spirit. Unless you are ready to extend your limits, you may resent what you're being asked to do.

ABORIGINAL LIVING SKILLS SCHOOL (ALSS)

Chief guide and survival guru Cody Lundin offers a serious outdoor-survival program in Arizona's backcountry—from desert to high mountain terrain. Relying on a combination of basic skills, modern devices, and lots of common sense, Lundin's preparedness seminars equip average people with the tools they need to survive in the wilderness.

Still, the **Aboriginal Living Skills School** (*P.O. Box 3064, Prescott, AZ 86302. 520-636-8384. www.alssadventures.com*) is no Rambo-style school: Most courses combine classroom lectures with field experience. The program emphasizes practical training, borrowing methods and materials from both ancient and modern eras. Participants learn key skills such as starting a fire, constructing a shelter, and navigating in the wilderness. No previous experience is required, and according to Cody "you don't have to be a fitness nut."

Prepare to be impressed by the cleverness and simplicity of Lundin's solutions to survival challenges. His "fanny-pack survival kit," for example, includes everything from a condom for water storage to 100 feet of nylon dental floss (think of it as "ultralight cordage with a thousand uses," says Lundin). Costs range from $320 for the two-day **Staying Alive** course to $1,200 for the more demanding nine-day field seminar. ALSS courses reflect Lundin's passion for life; all programs teach responsibility to self, others, and the natural world.

BOULDER OUTDOOR
SURVIVAL SCHOOL (BOSS)

For more than 30 years, the **Boulder Outdoor Survival School** (*P.O. Box 1590, Boulder, CO 80306. 800-335-7404 or 303-444-9779. www.boss-inc.com*) has been the place to gain traditional survival skills—living off the land as Native Americans did. BOSS conducts one-week traditional arts and skills courses in southern Utah, Mexico, and Canada; one-week marine- and desert-skills courses in Mexico; and one- to four-week intensive field courses in Canyon Country, Utah.

BOSS's core curriculum features Native American cultures' clothing-making methods, tool and hunting-weapon construction, food gathering, shelter building, and ecological awareness. The one-week basic earth-skills courses cost $775; the two-week field-skills courses are $1,500. The popular week-long Mexican desert and Sonoran living-skills course covers surf and spear fishing, boat operation, snorkeling and surf diving, Seri Indian food preparation, water gathering, and coastal living techniques. The $950 course is conducted in small groups, using 14-foot-long inflatable rafts to navigate the Kino Bay of Sonora, Mexico. A land-based living-skills course is also offered in Mexico's spectacular Copper Canyon.

Far to the north, BOSS now offers a winter living-skills and nature-awareness course in Canada. For $950, students construct winter shelters, make snowshoes, navigate overland, and learn winter first aid. BOSS also offers a women's course, as well as traditional technology workshops that focus on specific skills such as animal tracking. These specialty courses typically last five days; call for rates.

The most challenging BOSS operation is its 28-day field course in the Utah high desert (*$2,625*). The goal of the program is to travel light, making little use of modern technology—and minimal impact on the environment.

The course consists of six phases:

The initial orientation-and-impact phase is spent on a rigorous immersion hike, carrying no food, water, or modern equipment.

The next 10 to 12 days are spent traveling overland, with the class learning and practicing basic survival skills along the way.

Phase three consists of an independent hike.

During phase four, each student spends three to four days on a solo survival quest, carrying only minimal tools and supplies.

In phase five of the course, student teams make a five-day wilderness trek without instructors.

The last phase is a challenge that requires students to implement all the skills they have acquired in the weeks leading up to it.

Sports Afield labeled the BOSS field course the "most challenging and toughest school in the nation." *America* magazine has dubbed it "the supreme challenge." Despite the rigor, most participants find the program enormously rewarding. As one student mused, "It was hard...the most intense experience I have ever had.... I don't believe I have ever felt more alive."

BREAKAWAY SURVIVAL SCHOOL

The **Breakaway Survival School** (*17 Hugh Thomas Ave., Holmer, Hereford, England HR4 9RB. 01144-1432-267-097. www.specialforces.co.uk/breakaway2.htm*) offers a military-style survival-training experience in the Welsh countryside. This is the real thing: using your wits to stay alive in the bush. Instructor Mick Tyler, a former SAS commando, has served with the British Special Forces from the Arctic to Borneo.

Breakaway's weekend and five-day courses encompass basic survival techniques: building a weatherproof shelter, making a fire, hunting by bow and arrow, mountain navigation and rescue, finding edible plants, purifying water, and preparing food in the wild. The price is about $140 for a weekend, or $295 for a full five-day course.

All instruction is carried out in the wilds of Brecon Beacons National Park, Wales' scenic waterfall country, just four hours from London. Participants must supply their own backpacks and sleeping bags. If you want modern, practical survival training without shaman ceremonies—and you aren't squeamish about chowing down on the local fauna and flora—the Breakaway School is a good choice.

EARTHWALK NORTHWEST

Frank and Karen Sherwood, former head instructors of Tom Brown's Tracker School (*see below, right*), operate **EarthWalk Northwest** (*P.O. Box 461, Issaquah, WA 98027. 425-746-7267. www.earthwalknorthwest.com*). Here you can get the authentic Tracker experience in the scenic wilds of the Pacific Northwest. Mentor Tom Brown endorses Earthwalk: "Frank and Karen's classes are a tremendous complement to the Tracker classes. In my experience, they are the best out there. I cannot recommend these classes enough to my students. Frank and Karen teach from experience, not from theory. When they were not teaching at the Tracker School, they were working on their skills, living their skills, and thus brought those skills to a level of excellence I rarely see."

Earthwalk offers a wide variety of field seminars, spring through fall, primarily along the Oregon and Washington coast. Most programs run three days and cost $200 to $550. Recommended programs include **Wilderness Skills, Wild Edible Plants, Primitive Fishing,** and **Bow-Making** (*$550 each*). Sea kayakers and coastal campers can learn to harvest and cook local sea plants and shellfish in the **San Juan Islands Seminar.** Earthwalk's "graduate course" is a six-day, $650 "semi-survival trek," offered in Washington in June or Idaho in November.

HARDT SCHOOL OF WILDERNESS LIVING AND SURVIVAL

The **Hardt School** (*766 Smead Rd., Salisbury, VT 05769. 802-352-1033*), in the Green Mountains of Vermont, specializes in six-day outdoor-skills courses for people of all ages, with or without prior wilderness experience. Students learn the essential survival skills: building a fire, finding water, constructing a shelter, finding natural food sources, tracking and hunting animals, and cooking in the wilderness. The goal is to use your hands, your imagination, and the tools you can find in nature to achieve complete self-reliance. However, you will not be expected to endure long periods in the outdoors—there are no extended solos requiring you to forage for food or water. When classes are in camp, students enjoy cabin accommodations and hot meals.

Regular six-day programs, costing $475, are offered twice monthly in July, August, and October. For those with less free time, Hardt conducts two-day, $150 weekend introductory programs during the same months. The Hardt School also offers summer programs for young adults. Themed classes such as canoe trips (for graduates of the basic course) are scheduled from time to time throughout the year and by special request. One graduate of the school observed that "one week with Ron [Hardt] is like reading one hundred books on how to survive in a wilderness area."

NORTHWEST SCHOOL OF SURVIVAL (NWSOS)

The **Northwest School of Survival** (*39065 Pioneer Blvd., Suite 300, Sandy, OR 97055. 503-668-8264. www.nwsos.com*) emphasizes full preparedness for those venturing into the wilderness. Though NWSOS teaches people how to live off the land, it downplays minimalist survival using aboriginal skills and emphasizes expedition planning and organization. Strategies learned here will prove useful in all sorts of situations, not just if you're stranded and forced to forage and find shelter. NWSOS courses cover a wide variety of activities: mountaineering, rock climbing, cold-weather and wilderness survival, avalanche training, map-and-compass and GPS training, desert survival, backpacking, and executive team-building. Most classes last two to seven days and cost about $200 per day. It is common for students to take a series of seminars, beginning with basic skills and moving on to more specialized or advanced training. NWSOS also offers instructor-certification and guide-training courses, plus specialized programs for the military.

TOM BROWN'S TRACKER SCHOOL

Tom Brown, Jr., operates a traditional, Native American skills and philosophy school (*P.O. Box 173, Asbury, NJ 08802. 908-479-4681. www.trackerschool.com*) designed for those seeking self-reliance in the outdoors. Field training is conducted in the Pine Barrens region of New Jersey. This is true minimalist survival training—learning to live in the wild without equipment or supplies. Along with survival skills, Brown and his instructors teach tracking and navigation techniques that benefit hunters, orienteering enthusiasts, and those engaged in search and rescue.

Most of the programs heavily emphasize Native American spirituality. For many, this is one of the primary attractions of Brown's school. If this philosophy is not your cup of tea, however, you may want to consider another program.

The Tracker School offers 18 courses. The **Standard Course** lasts seven days, costs $650, and offers the basics of wilderness survival (camouflage, tracking, stalking, survival skills, nature observation, and Native American philosophy). The Standard Course is a prerequisite for higher-level courses such as **Advanced Tracking, Search and Rescue,** and the **Philosophy Workshop** (*$700 each*). Instructor Brown has written two leading survival texts, *The Science and Art of Tracking* and *Tom Brown's Field Guide to City and Suburban Survival*, both available at the Tracker School website.

Wilderness Medical Training

Sooner or later, those who spend much time in the wilderness will confront a medical emergency. Especially if you're leading a group, it's essential to know how to cope with everything from poison ivy to a broken bone—or even a heart attack. Thankfully, North America boasts some unsurpassed wilderness-medicine programs. The top three, profiled below, collectively educate 90 per cent of the wilderness-medicine students in the United States.

Stonehearth Open Learning Opportunity (SOLO)
Box 3150, Conway, NH 03818
888-765-6633 or 603-447-6711
www.stonehearth.com

Where do Outward Bound staffers and National Park Service rangers get their rescue training? They go to Stonehearth Open Learning Opportunity, an advanced wilderness and emergency-medicine training institute that offers two-day, $150 seminars at sites in Colorado, New Hampshire, Tennessee, North Carolina, Wyoming, Canada, the Caribbean, and Europe. SOLO also offers a three-week, $1,700 wilderness Emergency Medical Technician (EMT) certification course.

SOLO teaches outdoor guides how to prevent wilderness emergencies—or, when that's not possible, how to cope with them. Stonehearth students learn how to get themselves and their charges out of tough situations that require specialized skills and medical knowledge. The SOLO curriculum focuses on backcountry rescue, backcountry medicine (treating altitude sickness and exposure), and emergency medicine (advanced first aid, including setting fractures, treating major wounds, and extended care). SOLO also offers two-day and longer specialized rescue courses, including Search and Rescue (SAR), High-Angle Rescue, and Swift-Water Rescue. Though SOLO is not geared to the general public, anyone involved in high-risk outdoor sports will benefit from its programs.

Wilderness Medical Associates (WMA)
189 Dudley Rd., Bryant Pond, ME 04219
888-945-3633 or 207-665-2707
www.wildmed.com

Wilderness Medical Associates provides high-quality medical instruction to emergency-care providers and outdoor professionals working in remote areas of the wilderness. WMA boasts an impressive pedigree of past clients, among them the FBI, the National Park Service, and Outward Bound. "The program developed by WMA," says the emergency medical coordinator for Grand Canyon National Park, is "one of the best training programs available to prehospital care providers." WMA programs include Wilderness First Aid ($150-250), Advanced First Aid ($275-550), Wilderness First Responder ($450-750), and Wilderness EMT ($450-750; participants must be certified EMTs). The courses last two days to one week.

Seminars are conducted in various locations nationwide. Typically, a sponsoring organization hires WMA to develop a seminar that is tailored to the sponsor's special needs. WMA then furnishes the textbooks and instructors, and supervises the training and certification process.

Wilderness Medicine Institute, Inc. (WMI)
P.O. Box 9, 413 Main St., Pitkin, CO 81241.
970-641-3572. http://wmi.nols.edu

The Wilderness Medicine Institute (WMI), an affiliate of the National Outdoor Leadership School (NOLS), takes a hands-on approach in training students to recognize, treat, and prevent all types of wilderness emergencies. The institute emphasizes the practical application of information, not the rote memorization of medical procedures. All instructors have experience in prehospital medicine, outdoor guiding, and education.

Seminars are held in all states west of the Rockies, including Alaska and Hawaii, as well as abroad (Australia, Costa Rica, Kenya, and South Africa). WMI's key programs are Wilderness First Responder (ten days, $450), Wilderness First Aid (two to three days, $125), and Wilderness EMT (four weeks, $1,820). The Wilderness First Aid class—a bargain, since it teaches skills that could save a life—is recommended for the outdoors enthusiast. Outdoor professionals should take the First Responder course; WMI's textbook for this class, *The Wilderness First Responder,* was the first comprehensive reference for outdoor medical professionals. WMI trains guides for outfitters nationwide and has conducted medical training for Outward Bound and the U.S. Forest Service's Wilderness Ranger Training Center. Though WMI staffs and operates its own seminars, it coordinates its programs with those of NOLS, its parent organization.

INTERNATIONAL

Wilderness First Aid Consultants (WFAC)
P.O. Box 320, Katoomba, NSW, Australia 2780
01161-2478-24419
www.wfac.aust.com/~wfac

Wilderness First Aid Consultants is the leading organization of its kind in Australia, having trained more than 3,000 clients since 1984. WFAC's hallmark program is the highly regarded seven-day, $550 Leaders' First Aid Course, designed primarily for professional guides and outdoor education leaders. WFA also offers a three-and-a-half day, $250 Remote Area First Aid Course that is suited for the general public.

Employing a curriculum similar to Wilderness First Responder seminars in the United States (see WMI, above), WFAC courses focus on accident management and patient treatment. Programs are conducted throughout Australia, with seminars customized to the needs of the group in training. River-accident simulations are used to train white-water guides, for example, while ski guides train in an alpine environment. All courses cover the gamut of emergency-response and patient-care skills.

Because WFAC courses deal primarily with how to assist an injured or ill person in the wilderness, they do not ordinarily cover specialty rescue disciplines such as victim tracking, vertical rescue, or long-distance evacuation.

ONLINE

Dining on the Wilds
www.edibleplants.com

This is a helpful online guide to foraging, including how to prepare plants gathered in the wild for human consumption. The site also features survival tips and expert advice.

Mountain Rescue Association (MRA)
www.mra.org

MRA is a group of 60 volunteer organizations that conduct mountain search and rescue in a dozen U.S. states. The MRA website provides information about the association's educational programs, as well as how to become a member.

Outward Bound Home Page
www.outwardbound.org

Maintained by the Outward Bound National Office, this site features information on Outward Bound's regional schools and the courses available at each one.

**Princeton University
Outdoor Action Program**
www.princeton.edu/~oa

This thorough outdoor-information directory contains concise, fact-filled guides for low-impact camping, orienteering, animal tracking, and wilderness first aid.

Wilderness Way Magazine
www.pioneerpc.com/wildernessway/

The magazine's website offers articles from past editions as well as sections for classified ads, survival tips, and links to dozens of other outdoor-survival sites.

PRINT

Are We Having Fun Yet? by Brian Baird (Mountaineers Books, 1995, $12.95. www.mountaineersbooks.org). Baird's insightful and humorous book explores group dynamics in the outdoors.

Medicine for Mountaineering, by James Wilkerson (Mountaineers Books, 4th ed., 1993, $18.95). This comprehensive manual for wilderness medicine is useful for all backcountry travelers.

NOLS Cookery by Claudia Pearson ($12.95). This classic pocket cookbook from the National Outdoor Leadership School offers recipes and tips for food planning on wilderness expeditions. Order from NOLS (*307-332-6973*) or Stackpole Books (*800-732-3669. www.stackpolebooks.com*)

NOLS Wilderness Mountaineering by Phil Powers (Stackpole Books, 1993, $14.95). Although this text will benefit all alpinists, those training to be mountain guides will find it particularly valuable.

Outdoor Survival Skills by Larry Dean Olsen (6th ed., 1997, $14.95). This is the official text of the Boulder Outdoor Survival School (*303-444-9779*).

Packin' In on Mules and Horses by Smoke Elser and Bill Brown (Mountain Press, $18.00. 800-234-5308). Professional outfitter Smoke Elser shows how to increase the safety, comfort, and enjoyment of a pack trip. Easy to read, with instructional sketches and photos.

Primitive Outdoor Skills: More Wilderness Techniques from Woodsmoke Journal by Richard L. Jamison (Horizon Publishing, 1985, $17.95.). This text explains and demonstrates aboriginal living skills.

Primitive Wilderness Living and Survival Skills by John and Geri McPherson. This excellent field guide is used by the Northwest School of Survival (503-668-8264. www.nwsos.com).

Tom Brown's Field Guide to Wilderness Survival by Tom Brown with Brandt Morgan. The main text for the Tracker School (908-479-4681. www.trackerschool.com).

Wilderness Way magazine Four issues per year feature a range of topics for the primitive backpacker (713-667-0128).

Most of the books listed above can be ordered from the **Adventurous Traveler Bookstore** (800-282-3963. www.adventuroustraveler.com).

VIDEO

Land of One Season: The Basics of Mountain Safety. This award-winning video is hard to find but worth the search. It covers hypothermia, avalanche survival, overland navigation, weather, shelter building, and proper food, fuel, and clothing. Mountain guides and backcountry medicine experts demonstrate survival and rescue skills.

Wilderness 911 (Chessler Books, $20. 800-654-8502. www.chesslerbooks.com). This 40-minute instructional tape covers the basics of wilderness emergency: dealing with hypothermia, building a fire, ice self-rescue, and locating an avalanche victim.

Winning the Avalanche Game (Chessler Books, $20) is a complete course in avalanche survival, with dramatic footage of real avalanches. This 60-minute video covers interpreting snow conditions, route selection, and rescue techniques.

BIG ROCK, BIG SKY, LITTLE SHELTER IN THE BIGHORN MOUNTAINS OF WYOMING

WHITEWATER RAFTING IS SYNONYMOUS WITH HIGH ADVENTURE. IT COMBINES PHYSICAL challenge, raw excitement, and the chance to explore pristine wilderness areas. Rafting also offers a special measure of camaraderie; when you have to rely on your fellow paddlers to make it through serious white water, bonding occurs almost instantaneously. • Hundreds of rafting companies now operate around the world. By and large, they have skilled crews and good safety records. Choosing where to go and whom to go with can still be a difficult task, however. By assessing the operations of the main outfitters, this chapter aims to make the selection process a bit easier, helping you plan precisely the kind of river trip you want. • As you'll see, much depends on your definition of rafting—whether it's plunging through rapids in your own cataraft, rowing as part of a team, or enjoying the views while leisurely motoring down a scenic waterway.

LEFT: PULLING TOGETHER ON IDAHO'S SALMON RIVER
BELOW: RAFTING THE WHITE WATER OF THE ARKANSAS RIVER, COLORADO

White Water, White Knuckles

Class V Fun

Putting Your Oar In

Motor Rafting

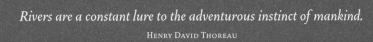

Rivers are a constant lure to the adventurous instinct of mankind.
HENRY DAVID THOREAU

Eight Ultimate Rafting Adventures

From gentle Class I rapids to plunging Class Vs and from half-day trips near home to 200-mile wilderness expeditions into the jungles of South America, rafting offers a heady freshet of vacation experiences. Here are eight river trips that promise big rapids, incredible scenery, and the ultimate in riverine adventure.

NEW ZEALAND
Black Water Rafting

In the upside-down world of down under, rafters navigate pitch-black rivers 300 feet underground. In New Zealand, they call it black water rafting. It's not really rafting at all, however: "Rafters" actually paddle inner tubes, not rafts. And there are no scary hydraulics or boat-flipping rapids. But there *is* plenty to write home about: The mystery, the darkness, and the serenity of riding the water under the surface of the Earth.

The village of Waitomo in the center of New Zealand's North Island boasts an extensive cave system, with more than 60 miles of underground passages, waterways, and caverns. **Black Water Rafting** (*Waitomo Caves, New Zealand. 01164-7878-6219. www.blackwaterrafting.co.nz*) offers two decidedly adventurous ways to view the caves: Blackwater I and Blackwater II.

Blackwater I, which costs about $35 (US), is a three-hour floating voyage through a dark and strange netherworld. Blackwater II (about $70) is the more challenging trip, combining the thrill of mountaineering and rafting with the mystery of spelunking.

The Blackwater II trip begins with a drop down the entrance of 5-mile-long Ruakari Cave. Inside the cave you rappel down eight stories of total blackness to a steel platform. Next comes a wild, 100-foot Tirolean traverse across a very black, very deep chasm. Then, holding your inner tube like a hula hoop, you hurtle 16 feet into the water below, creating a thunderous splash that echoes through the cavern. Soon you arrive at the scenic highlight of the trip, the main glowworm chamber, where a thousand pin-dots of light appear like stars in a distant night sky.

After 45 minutes or so of quiet drifting—interspersed with a few gentle rapids—it's time to leave the cave. That's the toughest part of the trip. On Blackwater II, you don't float out of the cave—you leave your tube behind and climb out through some amazingly tight passages. If you like rock-climbing, you'll love this part of the experience. But it's hard on the knuckles—and it is most certainly not for the claustrophobic.

New Zealand's South Island has caves, too. Part of a vast network beneath **Paparoa National Park,** the Metro Cave offers an underworld rafting experience every bit the equal of Waitomo. The stalactite- and stalagmite-filled Metro boasts a concentration of glowworms that is the best in the country. (During peak season, the light from the glowworms is bright enough to cast shadows inside the cave.)

Guided tours through the Metro are run by **Norwest Adventures** (*Westport, New Zealand. 01164-3789-6686. www.voyager.co.nz/~schurr/nwa.html*). Norwest's basic Underworld Rafting tour ($45) is similar to the Blackwater I trip in Waitomo with one important exception: You float right out of the Metro and into daylight, merging with a stream running through the virgin bush of Paparoa Park. **The Wild West Adventure Company** (*Kiata, New Zealand. 01164-3768-6649. www.newzealandholiday.co.nz*) also offers underground tubing for about $50 year-round.

If cave cruising in the South Island whets your appetite for adventure, there's plenty more to experience in this part of the country. New Zealand's adventure mecca is Queenstown, a day's drive south along the coast from Westport. Here, in the course of 48 hours, you can sample a dozen different adventures, ranging from bungee jumping to paragliding to Class V white-water rafting.

For conventional rafting trips in Queenstown and elsewhere on the western coast of the South Island, contact **Buller Adventure Tours** (*Westport, New Zealand. 01164-3789-7286. www.adventuretours.co.nz*); **Challenge Rafting** (*Queenstown, New Zealand. 01164-3442-7318. www.raft.co.nz*); or **Queenstown Rafting** (*Queenstown, New Zealand. 011643-442-9792. www.rafting.co.nz*).

ZAMBIA/ZIMBABWE
Zooming Down the Zambezi

Warm, jade-green waters. Powerful rapids. Stunning scenery and wildlife. These are just some of the attractions of a trip down the **Zambezi River.**

For an 80-mile stretch from **Victoria Falls** in the west to **Lake Kariba** in the east, the great river cuts through a deep gorge that separates Zambia and Zimbabwe. Here you'll find ten of the world's biggest rapids, including the notorious **Number 5.** These rapids are similar to the Grand Canyon section of the Colorado River, and they promise nonstop, boat-flipping action.

The Zambezi also offers variety. The river alternates between rollicking Class IV-V white water and quiet stretches teeming with wildlife, including crocodiles, hippos, fish eagles, and antelope. It also boasts two spectacular waterfalls that cascade over 20-foot-high basalt cliffs; short portages are made around these sections.

You can raft this part of the Zambezi in a day—billed as the world's most exciting day trip—or as part of a six-day river safari. Both begin at the base of Victoria Falls. Known to the locals as **Mosi-O-Tunya** ("the smoke that thunders"), the falls are 350 feet high and more than a mile wide. Put in from the Zambian side of the river and you'll be directly below the falls. The view is a highlight of the trip.

From here you raft through the biggest commercially run white water in the world, with huge rapids separated only by short pools. At this point, those who opt for the six-day trip continue on to run all the rapids of the middle Zambezi downstream from the falls—leaving the crowds of the one-day trip far behind. Along the way, rafters will camp on the sandy riverbanks, and there will be opportunities to hike, relax, and visit Zambian fishing villages. The trip finishes with an easy float out of the river gorge.

The wildest rafting near the falls comes in low-water season, around mid-October, when the rapids are at their trickiest—and the drops at their most aggressive. The rainy season starts in December, and water levels build throughout the spring. At peak high water, the river is more of a gentle roller coaster. High-water trips put-in about 6 miles below Victoria Falls and are fun, bouncy, Class III-IV rapids, rather than the Class V challenge of the low-water run. In particularly wet years, however, water levels can rise so much that some sections of the river become unrunnable from late May through early July.

Mountain Travel-Sobek (*El Cerrito, CA. 800-227-2384, 800-282-8747, or 510-527-8100. www.mtsobek.com*) offers the Zambezi through Zimbabwe's leading river outfitter, **Shearwater** (*Victoria Falls, Zimbabwe. 01126-313-4471 or 4472. http://africanadrenalin.co.za/shearwater*). Shearwater, the most popular rafting company on the river, enjoys a good safety record. Its boaters have an average of five years' experience, and most are trained in CPR and swift-water rescue. Mountain Travel-Sobek offers a 14-day Zambezi expedition with Shearwater for $2,700, which includes six days of rafting plus three days of kayaking on the lower Zambezi. Trips depart from August through November. **Bio-Bio Expeditions** (*Truckee, CA. 800-246-7238 or 530-582-6865. www. bbxrafting.com*) also offers a few trips each year with logistical support from Shearwater.

Half-day, full-day, and 2.5-day journeys are staged by Shearwater year-round as well. You can combine rafting with river boarding, canoe trips, or even bungee-jumping

from the **Victoria Falls Bridge.** Other African rafting companies running the Zambezi include **Supreme Raft** (01126-313-3300) and **Safari Par Excellence** (01126-313-4510) on the Zambian side, and **Frontiers** (011263-134772) on the Zimbabwe side. All these companies, as well as Shearwater, charge $150 for a full-day trip, with not much price variance for the longer river trips. Mountain Travel-Sobek puts on land safaris that can extend your African river holiday.

ARIZONA
Grand Canyon of the Colorado

A rafting trip down the Grand Canyon is America's greatest river odyssey. The journey takes you through 161 named rapids and past spectacular scenery—sheer walls that rise a full mile above the river. Along with the rapids, the Grand Canyon offers serene smooth-water sections, as well as amazing side canyons with waterfalls and grottoes.

Running the Grand Canyon has become big business. More than 20 concessionaires take thousands of visitors down the Colorado River every year. In planning a trip, your primary concerns should be the length of the trip, the type of craft (motor, oar, paddle, or dory), and the price.

Seeing the entire canyon will take seven to nine days in a motor-raft, and up to two weeks in an oar boat or paddle boat. The full river trip takes you at least 226 miles downriver from **Lee's Ferry** to **Diamond Creek.** Those with limited time can raft half the canyon, from Lee's Ferry to **Phantom Ranch;** or you can start at Phantom Ranch and voyage to the lower take-out.

The upper-half Grand Canyon trip takes about five to seven days in an oar or paddle boat. This stretch boasts quality rapids and is considered more scenic than the lower half. However, running the upper also involves an arduous 12-mile hike out of the canyon. And the lower half does have the lion's share of the big rapids. Can't choose between them? Do the full trip—you'll not regret it.

Most Grand Canyon rafting brochures emphasize the thundering waters of **Lava Falls** (*shown below*) or the **Crystal** and **Horn Creek** rapids. Bear in mind, however, that most of your time on the river will be spent floating long stretches of relatively still water. For this reason, your decision as to what type of craft to take can be all-important.

Big motor-rafts travel fast, enabling you to see more canyon in less time. Carrying 20 or so passengers, these 30- to 40-footers can seem like cattle boats, however. They're also noisy, though most people say they get used to the sound of the motor within a few hours and it ceases to bother them. Oar rafts provide a more personal experi-

ence—and they're more exciting in the rapids. Paddle rafts are the most adventurous option, but they're not for everyone: Unless you're incredibly fit, you'll quickly get tired of paddling through the canyon's long flat-water sections.

Last but not least, dories offer the most traditional Grand Canyon experience. Dories are pretty to look at and can be exciting in big rapids. They aren't the most comfortable of craft, though, and they're slow to boot: Running the Grand Canyon in a dory takes from 14 to 21 days. (In August, the water is generally higher and the flat water moves considerably faster, so the trip may take less time.)

For a motorized trip, contact **Arizona River Runners** (*800-477-7238. www.raftarizona.com*); **Western River Expeditions** (*800-453-7450. www.westernriver.com*); or **Grand Canyon Expeditions Co.** (*800-544-2691. www.gcex.com*). For an oar-raft trip, the top outfitters are Grand Canyon Expeditions; **Outdoor Adventure River Specialists** (*800-346-6277 or 209-736-4677. www.oars.com*); and **Colorado River & Trail Expeditions** (*800-253-7328 or 801-261-1789. www.crateinc.com*).

If you're really hard-core, you can paddle your own raft with the last two outfitters, as well as with **Arizona Raft Adventures** (*800-786-7238. www.azraft.com*). **Grand Canyon Dories** (*800-877-3679 or 209-736-0805. www.grandcanyondories. com*) is the top choice for dory trips.

Because it is dam controlled, the Colorado is runnable year-round. But the best time is probably April and May or September and October. The river is less crowded in these months, and temperatures will be in the high 80s as opposed to more than 100° F in midsummer.

Prices for Colorado River trips vary considerably. A three- or four-day motorized trip averages between $650 and $800. A six- to eight-day, full-canyon motor journey costs between $1,500 and $1,800. A half-river oar-boat trip of seven to eight days runs about $1,800, while a full-river oar-boat or paddle-boat trip costs $1,600 to $2,500.

WEST VIRGINIA
Class V Fury

Those seeking continuous action with back-to-back Class IV to V rapids (Class VI is considered unrunnable) will find it along West Virginia's **New, Gauley,** and **Upper Youghiogheny (Upper Yough) Rivers.** The upper section of the Gauley is a solid Class V, with huge waves and very high water volumes during the fall dam release in the months of September and October. The Upper Yough—a challenging, technical run from top to bottom—is the steepest waterway east of the Rockies.

Making West Virginia rivers unique are the steep drops, the nonstop rapids, and the narrow passages, which all require the utmost in boat-handling skill by the guide—and

careful coordination by the paddling team. During the spring runoff and late-season dam releases, rafters will encounter powerful water flows. All this puts a premium on river skills and safety: It's essential to have first-class equipment (preferably a self-bailing raft) and expert boat crews to run these rivers at high water levels.

Most West Virginia rivers have fairly short runs—no more than 15 miles or so—and are rafted on a day-trip basis only. Some outfitters offer overnight river tours, but these generally consist of a double run of the same river or a two-river combination with overnight accommodation in a lodge. Because the West Virginia rafting industry is so competitive, prices have remained reasonable, considering the quality of the white water. A typical day's run on the New or the Gauley will cost $85 per person, including lunch. Head for the Gauley in late September for big-water fun and boat-flipping excitement. The Upper Yough may cost a bit more because it is more remote and more difficult.

Numerous good outfitters operate in West Virginia. For the Upper Yough, contact **Appalachian Wildwaters** (*Rowlesburg, WV. 800-872-7238 or 304-454-2475. www.usaraft.com*). For the New River and the Gauley River, try **Class VI River Runners** (*Lansing, WV. 800-252-7784 or 304-574-0704. www.raftwv.com*); **North American River Runners** (*Hico, WV. 800-950-2585 or 304-658-5276. www.narr.com*); or **the Rivermen** (*Lansing, WV. 800-545-7238 or 304-574-0515. www.rivermen.com*). For a complete list of licensed rafting companies, call the West Virginia rafting hotline (*800-225-5982*).

IDAHO
Best of the Rockies

Idaho is a wonderful river venue for those seeking both exciting white water and wilderness solitude. The **Selway**—a waterway of exceptional beauty and diversity—is Idaho's gem. A designated Wild and Scenic River that flows through the **Bitterroot Wilderness Area,** it is the least crowded and most serene of Idaho's waterways; even in peak season you can travel the entire river and not see another group of rafters.

A typical trip on the Selway lasts four to six days. Over the course of 50 miles, you descend through steep, tree-lined canyons and alongside sandy riverbanks. Along the way, you'll see great wildlife—elk, moose, bears, and birds of prey—but very few humans, thanks to U.S. Forest Service regulations that allow only one launch per day.

The best times to experience the Selway are June and July, when the water is up. But this waterway is so exceptional that you should not hesitate to run it in late summer or early fall, when the water is lower. For river-guide services, contact **American River Touring Association** (*Groveland, CA.*

WHITE-WATER HOT SPOT: LAVA FALLS, GRAND CANYON

800-323-2782 or 209-962-7873. www.arta.org); **Northwest River Company** *(Boise, ID. 800-867-7238 or 208-344-7119. E-mail: mail@maravia.com);* or **Masoner's Whitewater Adventures** *(Boise, ID. 800-432-4611 or 208-939-4324. www.selway.net).* A four- to five-day trip costs between $1,450 and $1,850.

After the Selway, the **Middle Fork of the Salmon** is probably Idaho's finest rafting destination, with exciting Class III to IV rapids and outstanding wildlife. The voyage begins with a descent down a steep Alpine section. For the next five days, you will pass spectacular rocky gorges, sandy beaches, and hot springs. In the calm stretches there is excellent fishing for rainbow, cutthroat, and Dolly Varden trout.

The Middle Fork is an ideal choice for those looking for a luxury rafting holiday. Some of America's top river outfitters operate on the Middle Fork. Three family-owned operations are **Rocky Mountain River Tours** *(Boise, ID. 208-345-2400. www.rafttrips.com),* **Hughes River Expeditions** *(Cambridge, ID. 800-262-1882 or 208-257-3477. www.hughesriver.com),* and **Middle Fork Wilderness Outfitters** *(Ketchum, ID. 800-726-0575 or 208-726-5999. www.idahorapids.com).* A six-day trip on the Middle Fork of the Salmon costs between $975 and $1,600.

CALIFORNIA
White-Water Gold Mine

The **American River** is Califronia's most popular rafting river for good reason. The river boasts three commercially run branches—the **South, Middle,** and **North Forks**— that are conveniently rated: easy, moderate, and difficult.

The **South Fork** of the American is a great river for learning to raft while still providing plenty of challenge to intermediate paddlers. More than 50 Class II-III rapids are strung out along 20 miles of the South Fork, blending with sections of calm water and still pools. The South Fork is usually run from April through June, but it can also be run during low-water levels through October.

Among the many fine companies running the South Fork, **Beyond Limits Adventures** *(Riverbank, CA. 800-234-7238 or 209-869-6060. www.rivertrip.com)* stands out for its splendid two-acre riverside campground with full amenities—even hot showers, electricity, and a beer garden. Other good operators include **American River Touring Association** *(Groveland, CA. 800-323-2782 or 209-962-7873. www.arta.org)* and **Whitewater Voyages** *(El Sobrante, CA. 800-488-7238 or 510-222-5994. www.whitewatervoyages.com).*

A handful of Class IV rapids makes the **Middle Fork** of the American River a tougher challenge than the South Fork. The rest of the river, however, offers more flat water than the South Fork and relatively few intermediate rapids. **All-Outdoors Rafting** *(Walnut Creek, CA. 800-247-2387 or 925-*

932-8993. www.aorafting.com) offers one- or two-day trips from May through September for $130 to $270.

To make the jump to experts-only rafting, try the **North Fork.** Here , in a wilderness canyon with 2,000-foot walls, the river courses through continuous Class V rapids among steep and narrow boulder fields. This one-day, 15-mile trip is highly technical and requires previous Class IV paddle raft experience. The trip is run from April to June and costs $255 with **Sierra Mac Outfitters** *(Sonora, CA. 800-457-2580 or 209-532-1327. www.sierramac.com).*

Another challenging and steep Sierra river is the **Tuolumne.** Pouring out of Yosemite National Park through a canyon of giant white granite boulders, the river drops at an average of 110 feet per mile and boasts one Class V rapid after another. **Sierra Mac** *(Sonora, CA. 800-457-2580 or 209-532-1327. www.sierramac.com)* offers the Cherry Creek run on the Upper Tuolumne with Sotar catarafts for $255 per person. The company also offers one-, two-, and three-day trips on the Main Tuolumne for $180 to $455.

The longest river in the Sierra is the **Kern,** southernmost of California's first-rate white-water rivers. The premier section of the river is the **Forks of the Kern**—a spectacular run that flows through the pristine **Golden Trout Wilderness** area. This section of the waterway is accessible only by boat, and a strenuous two-mile hike down a steep ravine is required to reach the put-in. The Forks of the Kern features many Class IV-V+ rapids, some of which require portaging during high water. The river here is highly regulated by the Forest Service, which allows no more than two parties to launch per day. The 18-mile trip can be run in two or three days and costs $575 to $650 with Whitewater Voyages.

COSTA RICA
Tropical Rafters' Paradise

With more than a tenth of its territory set aside as national parks or wilderness preserves, Costa Rica has been called Central America's outdoor playground. Thanks to its tropical climate and reliable winter water levels, it's also a great off-season getaway, offering world-class rafting on four major rivers: the **Reventazón, Chirripo, Rio General,** and **Pacuare.**

The Reventazón offers the most challenging rafting in Costa Rica, with numerous major rapids. The river's remarkably steep gradient (it drops more than 100 feet per mile in the first three miles) generates back-to-back rapids that test the most expert boaters. Because the river is dam-controlled, water flow on the Reventazón is consistent season to season, allowing good paddling year-round. By contrast, the Chirripo—50 miles of rapids and waterfalls—is best in the second half of the year.

The Rio General is a good choice for a family vacation:

Few of the rapids exceed Class III, and there are many opportunities to explore nearby villages and scenic waterfalls. But there's still plenty of action. With a gradient of more than 50 feet per mile, the Rio General offers close to 100 runnable rapids in a 40-mile stretch.

The more challenging Pacuare is considered a Class IV+ river at high water. Yet the river has smooth stretches, too, where you can relax and enjoy the beauty of the tropical jungle—home to tapirs, jaguars, ocelots, and South American deer. Enjoy it while you can: There are plans to dam the Pacuare in the near future.

You can run Costa Rica's rivers with a number of reputable outfitters. The leading local company, **Ríos Tropicales** (*01150-6233-6455. www.riostropicales.com*), has the lowest prices and runs all the top rivers year-round. Among the American companies operating in Costa Rica are: **Mountain Travel-Sobek** (*800-227-2384. www.mtsobek. com*), which offers a ten-day trip to the country with seven days on the Pacuare for $2,300; **Nantahala Outdoor Center** (*Bryson City, NC. 800-232-7238 or 828-488-2175. www.noc.com*), which runs a multiriver Costa Rica trip every October for both rafters and kayakers; and **Serendipity Adventures** (*Ann Arbor, MI. 800-635-2325 or 734-995-0111. www.serendipityadventures.com*), which offers custom vacations that combine rafting, ballooning, and canyoning with mountain biking, horseback riding, and jungle-canopy treks.

CHILE
Andes River Adventure

Chile's stunning **Futaleufu River** pours through one of the most challenging river canyons in the world. Located in a region untouched by large-scale tourism, this adrenaline-pumping river boasts rapids that are long, powerful, steep, and technical, with nearly three dozen major Class IV and V drops—some as long as a mile. And when you need to catch your breath? The Futaleufu's calm stretches give you a chance to enjoy the river's aquamarine water and the canyon's breathtaking Patagonian scenery.

Most expeditions include hiking and horseback riding, as well as a training day on the lower Futaleufu; flip drill, swim tests, and miles of Class IV+ white water will help you prepare for the more difficult sections upstream. Expeditions depart from mid-January to the end of March, last 10 to 14 days, and cost between $2,100 and $3,500 without airfare. Oar-paddle combination rafts are used. Contact **Earth River Expeditions** (*Accord, NY. 800-643-2784 or 914-626-2665. www.earthriver.com*) or **Bio-Bio Expeditions** (*Truckee, CA. 800-246-7238 or 530-582-6865. www.bbxrafting.com*).

Unfortunately for the Futaleufu, the Chilean power company, Endessa, hopes to tap the river's powerful flow for a major hydroelectric project. If Endessa succeeds, the Futaleufu will be dammed, and the beautiful canyon through which it now courses will swallowed up.

North America: Rivers Run Through It

River	Rapids Class/ Gradient/% WW	Trip Miles/Trip Days Season/Raft Type	Cost Range	Accommodations	Outfitters
ALASKA *Caribou migration in the Arctic National Wildlife Refuge and spectacular scenery on the Alsek from the Elias Mountains to Glacier Bay.*					
TATSHEN-SHINI/ALSEK	I-III/mild/ low	160/10-12/ summer/OR, PR	$2,500 (Tat), $1,650 (Alsek); + $500-$800 air	Wilderness camp	Alaska Discovery; MT-Sobek; Canadian River Expeditions; Nahanni River Adventures
KONGACUT	I-III/ mild/low	100/10/June-July/OR, PR	$3000 including bush plane	Wilderness camp	Alaska Discovery Wilderness Alaska
ARIZONA *More than 160 rapids in the mile-deep Grand Canyon; granite gorges of the Salt River in the Sonoran Desert.*					
COLORADO (Grand Canyon)	I-VI/ 9/10%	Up to 280/6-8 typical/Mar-Nov/MR, OR, PR	$225/day, MR or OR	Quality camping; average to deluxe meals	Colorado River & Trail Exped.; Grand Canyon Exped.; O.A.R.S.; Western River Exped.
SALT	III-IV/ 22/20%	90/1-5/Feb-May/PR	$75-$85/day; $245-$650 (2-5 days)	Wilderness camp	Far Flung Adventures
CALIFORNIA *Four-thousand-foot cliffs along the Forks of Kern, ghost towns along the Tuolumne, and cliffs, gorges, and pine forests along the American.*					
KERN (Upper & Forks)	IV-V/ 55-60/65%	17-20/1-3/ Apr-Aug/PR	(Upper) $100-$250; (Forks) $575-$650	Riverside camp; deluxe meals	Kern River Tours; O.A.R.S.; Whitewater Voyages
STANISLAUS		10/1-2/ Apr-Jun/PR	$109-$275	Riverside camp, quality meals	All-Outdoors; Beyond Limits Adventures
TUOLUMNE (Main Cherry Creek)	IV/40-60/ 60% (Main) V/120-200/ 95% (Creek)	9 Creek, 18 Main/ 1-3/Mar-Oct/CR, OR, PR	$235 (1 day upper); $175-$455 (lower)	Riverside camp; deluxe, meals	ARTA; ECHO; Sierra Mac
AMERICAN (North Fork - Giant Gap)	IV-V/75 /75%	9 or 18 (repeat)/ 1-2/Apr-Jun/ PR, OR	$125-$385 (lower run, 2-day); $255-$410	Riverside camp; quality meals	ARTA; O.A.R.S.; Sierra Mac
COLORADO *Black basalt canyon of the Colorado, 7,000-foot put-in on the Cache la Poudre, more than 50 major rapids on the Yampa.*					
ARKANSAS (Leadville to Canon City)	III-V/100 upper, 55 aver./45%	10-15/1/May-July/PR; 1-3/ May-Sept/KO	$35-$40 (half day); $67-$259 (1-2 days)	Camp, motels and lodges	Dvorak Expeditions; Mad River Rafting; RMOC
COLORADO (Westwater Canyon)	III-IV/NA/ 25%	20-30/2-3/May-Aug/OR, PR option	$255-$450	Riverside camp, deluxe meals	Colo. River & Trail; Sheri Griffith River Expeditions; Western River Exped.
CACHE LA POUDRE	II-V/ varies/85%	18/1/May-Aug/PR	$50-$85	Snack or deluxe lunch	Rocky Mountain Adventures
YAMPA (Cross Mountain Gorge)	IV-V/45/ 80%	72/3-5/May-June/PR, OR	$629-$725	Wilderness camp, deluxe meals	Adrift Adventures; ARTA; Holiday Exped.; O.A.R.S.
IDAHO *After the remote put-in on the Selway, expect narrows with big boulders; choose the Salmon that's right for you.*					
SALMON (Middle Fork)	III-IV/ NA/35%	100/5-6 (or fly-out)/June-Sept/PR, OR, inflatable KO	$1,200-$1,625 (less with early fly-out)	Wilderness camp, deluxe meals	ARTA; Hughes River Expeditions; Rocky Mountain River Tours
SALMON (Main)	III-IV/NA/ 20%	96/6/Jun-Sept/ OR, PR, KO; WW dory	$650-$1,150	Wilderness camp, deluxe meals	ARTA; ECHO; Orange Torpedo; River Odysseys West
SELWAY	IV/30-50/35%	48/4-5/May-Aug/ PR, OR, decked canoe, KO	$1,400-$1,800	Wilderness camp, deluxe meals	ARTA; Masoner's Whitewater Adventures; Northwest River Co.
SNAKE (Hell's Canyon)	IV/10-15/ 10%	32-85/3-6/May-Oct/PR, OR, McKenzie drift boat, WW dory	$750-$1,365	Wilderness camp or lodge, deluxe meals	Holiday Expeditions; Hughes Expeditions; River Odysseys West
MAINE *The Penobscot features a 90-foot gorge and a dozen waterfalls; the Kennebec flows through unspoiled wilderness.*					
PENOBSCOT (West Fork)	IV/60/ 50%	14/1/May-Oct/PR	$80-$120	Day trip, deluxe lunch; riverside lodges	New England Outdoor Ctr.; North Country Rivers; Unicorn Expeditions
KENNEBEC	IV/30/ 40%	13/1/May-Sept/PR	$80-$120	Day trip. Riverside lodge available.	New England Outdoor Ctr.; Maine Whitewater; North Country Rivers
MARYLAND *Narrow, fast, and beautiful, the Upper Youghiogheny boasts the steepest drop east of the Rockies.*					
UPPER YOUGH	IV-V/115/ 70%	11/1-2/ Apr-Nov/PR	$100 (1 day); $250 (overnight)	Day trip, deluxe meal	Appalachian Wildwaters; Precision Rafting Expeditions
MONTANA *The Flathead runs through the alpine wilderness of Glacier National Park; keep an eye out for moose, elk, and bighorn sheep.*					
FLATHEAD Middle & North	II-IV/ 22/20%	10-50/1-4/ May-Sept/ PR, OR	$50-$895 (up to 4 days)	Riverside tent camp, deluxe food	Glacier Wilderness Guides/ Montana Raft Co.
NEW MEXICO *On the Rio Grande, Taos and La Junta Box Canyons are tight and wild; the Rio Chama takes you through 7,000-foot forested mountains.*					
RIO GRANDE	II-IV/ NA/50%	18-35/1-3/Mar-Sept/OR, PR on request	$100-$360, $40 half-day	Taos Box day trip/overnight forest camp	Far Flung Adven.; Native Sons Adven.; Southwest Wilderness Adven.

CODES: White Water (**WW**), Paddle Raft (**PR**), Oar Raft (**OR**), Motorized Raft (**MR**), Twin-hulled Cataraft (**CR**), Kayak Option (**KO**).

River	Rapids Class/ Gradient/% WW	Trip Miles/Trip Days/ Season/Raft Type	Cost Range	Accommodations	Outfitters
NEW MEXICO					
RIO CHAMA	II-III/ 8/25%	24-32/2-3/ May-Aug/PR, OR, canoe & KO	$225-$350	Wilderness camp	Far Flung Adven.; Native Sons Adven.; Southwest Wilderness Adven.
NEW YORK *The Moose has exciting rapids in a pleasant, unspectacular setting. The remote, heavily forested Hudson River Gorge has steep canyon walls.*					
MOOSE	IV/85 max/50%	12/1/Apr-May/PR	$90-$100	Day trip, no lunch	Adirondack River Outfitters; Whitewater Challengers
HUDSON	IV/40/ 40%	18/1/May-July/PR	$65-$75	Day trip	Adirondack River Outfitters
OREGON *The Deschutes runs through an arid grassland canyon, the Illinois through a forested canyon near the Oregon coast.*					
DESCHUTES	II-IV/ 12/20%	13-98/1-3/ Apr-Oct/PR, OR	$55-$70 (1 day); $210-$695 (3-5 day)	River camp; day trip or overnight	Deschutes River Adventures; Orion Expeditions; Ouzel Outfitters
GRANDE RONDE	II+/ 18/20%	39/1-6/Apr-July/ PR, OR, KO, dory	$60-$85 (1 day); $240-$950 (3-5 day)	Day trip or overnight river camp	Downstream River Runners
ILLINOIS	III-IV/ 40/40%	40/3-4/ May-June/PR	$400-$500	Wilderness camp	ARTA; Sundance River Center
UPPER OWYHEE	III-IV/ 25/50%	35/3-4/Apr-June/PR, OR	$450-$850	Riverside camp and cabins, hot springs	Downstream River Runners; Hughes River Expeditions; River Odysseys West; Sevy Guide Service
SOUTH CAROLINA *Remote and mysterious, the "the Deliverance river" has major rapids with big drops. Variable flows demand strong local knowledge.*					
CHATTOOGA	III-IV+/ 30/35-50%	10-21 (Sec. 3,4)/ 1-2/PR, OR, KO	$55-$100 (1 day); $240 (2 day)	Day trip or overnight river camp	Nantahala Outdoor Center; Wildwater Ltd.
TENNESSEE *In spring high water, the Nolichucky promises big waves, constant action; the Ocoee has controlled dam release through Cherokee Nat. Forest..*					
NOLICHUCKY	III-IV/ 30-60/60%	8.5/1/Mar-July/PR, KO	$50-$75	Day trip with lunch	Nantahala Outdoor Center; USA Raft
OCOEE	III-IV/ 60/60%	5/1/Apr-Oct/PR	$35-$40 (half-day)	Day trip, no lunch	Appalachian Wildwaters; Nantahala Outdoor Center; Wildwater Ltd.
TEXAS *Mostly smooth water through the massive limestone canyons of the Chihuahua Desert. Good wildlife and fishing.*					
RIO GRANDE (Big Bend)	II-III/ low/low	10-85/1-7/Varies with trip/PR, OR, canoe option	$85-$1,000	Riverside campsites	Big Bend River Tours; Dvorak Expeditions; Far Flung Adventures
UTAH *North section has large waves, many rapids, but Desolation Canyon is mostly smooth. A great family trip.*					
GREEN	II-IV/ 20/20%	42/2-4/May-Sept/PR, OR	$480-$730	Riverside camp, deluxe meals	Adrift Adventures; Holiday Expeditions; O.A.R.S.; Sheri Griffith River Expeditions
VIRGINIA *One of the wildest short rivers in the United States, with back-to-back rapids.*					
RUSSELL FORK	V+/210/ 90%	7/1/Sept-Oct/ PR, KO	$150-$225	Day trip with lunch	Upper Yough Expeditions
WASHINGTON *Rafting in rugged wilderness. The challenging white water of the Klickitat requires previous river experience.*					
KLICKITAT	II-IV/47/ 90%	16/1-2/May-July/PR	$75-$100	Day trip with lunch	All Rivers Adventures; Whitewater Adventures
SAUK	III-IV/ 38/75%	8.3/1/June-Aug/PR	$70-$95	Day trip with lunch	Downstream River Runners; Orion Expeditions
SKYKOMISH	III-V/40/ 60%	7/1/Mar-July/ PR, OR	$75-$85	Day trip	Downstream River Runners; Orion Expeditions
WEST VIRGINIA *With possible boat-flipping hydraulics, the Cheat requires previous experience. Top 10 day-trip during dam release (Sept.- October).*					
CHEAT	III-IV/ 26/65%	11/1/Mar-July/ PR, inflatable KO	$79-$99	Day trip with lunch	USA RAFT
NEW	III-V/18/ 50%	15 or 30/1 or 3/Apr-Nov/PR	$65-$110 (1 day); $285-$350 (3 day)	3-day camp or country inn; deluxe meals	Appalachian Wildwaters; Mountain River Bluewater Tours; Class VI River Runners
UPPER GAULEY	III-V/38/ 90+%	15/1/Sept-Oct/ OR, PR, Oar-paddle hybrid	$90-$155	Day trip, deluxe meal	Appalachian Wildwaters; Class VI River Runners; Mountain River Bluewater Tours; The Rivermen
WYOMING *You'll need 4WD for access to this wilderness river, which flows north from Colorado into Wyoming.*					
NORTH PLATTE	III-IV/ 25-30/65%	40+/1-3/May-July/PR, OR	$85 (1 day); $240-$360 (2-3 days)	Day trip or over-night wilder--ness camp	Dvorak's Expeditions; Rocky Mountain Adventures
CANADA *Superb scenery of British Columbia, with roller-coaster rapids. On Quebec's Rouge, the lower section has the best white water.*					
KICKING HORSE LOWER CANYON (B.C.)	IV/steep/ 70%	7/1/Aug-Sept/PR, OR	$85-$100	Day trip with steak BBQ	Alpine Rafting Co.; Glacier Rafting Co.
ROUGE (Quebec)	III-V/35-47/55%	8-16/1-2/June-Oct/PR, KO	$89-$179	Day trip or overnight camp	New World River Expeditions
CHILCO/CHIL-COTIN (B.C.)	IV/20/35%	120+/6-11/June-Sept/Oar CR with motor	$1,250 (6 days); $2,620 (11 days)	Riverside camps, deluxe meals	Canadian River Expeditions; Hyak Expeditions

A Raft of River Runners

Planning a river-rafting holiday often involves addressing a series of crucial do-yous: Do you want to paddle the raft yourself, or let a guide do the heavy pulling? Do you want mostly gentle sections, or only the roughest rapids? Do you want continuous white water, or will two or three big drops a day suffice? Do you want to cover a lot of distance or a little? Finally, do you seek other activities too, such as swimming, fishing, and general vegging out?

When you contact outfitters, give them your answers to these questions, and they will help select the best river for your interests. In general, rivers in the Idaho Rockies offer the longest continuous runs, and California and Oregon rivers are more suited for weekend tours. The best white-water rivers in the East (Maine, West Virginia) have relatively short but intense runs, with nearly continuous rapids. It's impossible to generalize about foreign rivers, of course. Most are not run as regularly as those in the United States, and they can have unexpected conditions that can present special challenges.

To help with your planning, you may wish to contact the following guides associations:

America Outdoors
P.O. Box 10847, Knoxville, TN 37939
423-558-3595. www.americaoutdoors.org

California Outdoors
P.O. Box 401, Coloma, CA 95613
530-295-0102. www.caloutdoors.org

Colorado River Outfitters Assoc.
P.O. Box 1662, Buena Vista, CO 81211
303-280-2554. www.croa.org

Idaho Outfitters and Guides Assoc.
P.O. Box 95, Boise, ID 83701
303-280-2554. www.ioga.org

Recommended Outfitters Worldwide

Good organization, skilled, personable guides, and quality equipment are the hallmarks of a top outfitter. On the roughest Class IV to V rivers, state-of-the-art boats are essential. Choose a company that uses modern self-bailing rafts, so you won't struggle through the rapids half-submerged. On longer river tours, particularly those with lengthy flat-water

stretches, the interaction between guide and customers is what makes or breaks the trip. Look for a company that employs guides who understand the local history, archaeology, and ecology of the river that you're running.

The listings below use the following codes: **M** (large, motorized raft); **O** (oar-raft); **P** (paddle-raft); **K** (raft-supported kayak trip). Trip durations are listed in days (3, 4, 5, etc.).

EAST

MAINE

New England Outdoor Center
P.O. Box 669, Millinocket, ME 04462
800-766-7238 or 207-723-5438
www.neoc.com
RIVERS: Dead, Kennebec, Penobscot.
The New England Outdoor Center has been a mainstay of New England rafting since 1982. The Penobscot and Kennebec runs are the most popular. The center has excellent guides and operates comfortable riverside lodges on both rivers.

Unicorn Expeditions
Route 201, Jackman, ME 04945
800-864-2676 or 207-668-7629
www.unicornraft.com
RIVERS: Dead, Kennebec, Penobscot.
Unicorn offers popular river trips April through October. The company operates two deluxe base camps where you can unwind after riding the rapids. Group and family trips are a specialty.

NEW YORK

Adirondack River Outfitters
P.O. Box 649, Old Forge, NY 13420
800-525-7238 or 315-369-3536
www.aroadventures.com
RIVERS: Black, Hudson, Moose, Sacandaga.
Since 1980, Adirondack River Outfitters has guided more than 100,000 rafters down New York's Adirondack rivers, establishing a solid program with a strong

safety record. From April through October the company offers half- and full-day trips for about $65-85 per day. The Black and the Hudson are most popular. All rafts are manned by New York State-licensed guides, and all trips are escorted by an expert kayaker.

NORTH CAROLINA

Nantahala Outdoor Center
13077 Hwy. 19W, Bryson City, NC 28713
800-232-7238, 828-488-2175, or 888-662-1662. www.noc.com
RIVERS: French Broad, Nantahala (NC); Nolichucky, Ocoee, Pigeon (TN); Chattooga (GA, SC); Grand Canyon Colorado (AZ); Rio Grande (TX); also worldwide.
Nantahala Outdoor is a world leader in river-running. Choose from weekend or day-trips on southeastern rivers (the Ocoee or Section 4 of the Chattooga offer the best white water) or destination tours throughout North America. This company is the first choice for the rivers of southern Appalachia.

WEST VIRGINIA

Class VI River Runners
P.O. Box 78, Lansing, WV 25862
800-252-7784 or 304-574-0704
www.raftwv.com
RIVERS: New, Gauley (WV); Rio Grande (TX).
Class VI concentrates on two of the finest West Virginia rivers, the New and the Gauley. For its scenery and big water thrills, the New has been called the "Grand Canyon of the East," and the Gauley has been rated one of the 10 best white water runs in the world. For maximum thrills, hit the Gauley during the dam-release in September and October. Class VI maintains its own base camp with a restaurant.

North American River Runners, Inc.
P.O. Box 81, Hico, WV 25854
800-950-2585 or 304-658-5276
www.narr.com
RIVERS: New, Gauley.

This company offers quality trips at competitive prices and a wider selection of departures than other regional outfitters. It uses self-bailing boats and provides camping facilities and cabins in West Virginia.

The Rivermen

P.O. Box 220, Lansing, WV 25862
800-545-7238 or 304-574-0515
www.rivermen.com

RIVERS: New, Gauley.

The Rivermen maintains a quality riverside resort with a campground, hotel, catered meals, volleyball court, laundry, and more. You can take 1- to 2-day trips down the New and Gauley Rivers, then return to the resort for relaxation and land-based fun. This company takes as many as 400 people rafting in one day. You can rely on the quality of its service and equipment.

USA RAFT and Appalachian Wildwaters

P.O. Box 277, Rowlesburg, WV 26425
800-872-7238 or 304-454-2475
www.usaraft.com

RIVERS: **USA Raft:** Cheat, Gauley, New, Potomac (WV); Nolichucky, Ocoee, Pigeon (TN); French Broad, Nantahala (NC). **Appalachian Wildwaters:** Cheat, Gauley, New, Tygart (WV); Nolichucky (TN), Upper Youghiogheny (MD).

USA RAFT and sister company Appalachian Wildwaters jointly run a dozen or so rivers in the Southeast. One call can arrange any kind of river experience, from family float trips to advanced, steep creeks. The most popular rivers are the New, Gauley, Nolichucky, Upper Yough, and Cheat. Appalachian Wildwaters specializes in full-day and overnight trips, and USA Raft specializes in half-day "Express" runs.

NORTHWEST

ALASKA

Alaska Discovery Wilderness Tours, Inc.

5310 Glacier Hwy., Juneau, AK 99801
800-586-1911 or 907-780-6226
www.akdiscovery.com

RIVERS: Alsek, Noatak, Kongacut, Tatshenshini.

Multi-day float trips with this top Alaskan outfitter cost about $200 per day. On longer trips, floatplane charges can bring the cost up to around $300.

Nova, The Adventure Company

P.O. Box 1129, Chickaloon, AK 99674
800-746-5753 or 907-745-5753
www.novalaska.com

RIVERS: Chickaloon, Copper, Lionshead, Matanuska, Six-Mile Creek, Talkeetna, Tana.

Nova offers 1- to 12-day wilderness trips ranging from mild (Matanuska) to Class V white water (Six-Mile Creek). A popular choice is a combo rafting/hiking trip on the Lionshead River and Matanuska Glacier. Also recommend is the 3-day, $950 Talkeetna fly-in trip. The 75-mile voyage combines great white water with excellent fishing and wildlife.

Wilderness Alaska

P.O. Box 113063, Anchorage, AK 99511
907-345-3967. www.wildernessalaska.com

RIVERS: Alatna, Canning, Hulahula, John, Kobuk, Kongakut, Koyukuk, Killik, Nigu, Noatak, Wild.

Wilderness Alaska runs scheduled and semi-custom small-group trips, including backpacking trips in the Brooks Range and kayak tours in Prince William Sound. Don't expect to be pampered with nouvelle cuisine. But do expect to enjoy the best Alaska has to offer with a colorful guide who knows the region and its indigenous wildlife.

IDAHO

Hughes River Expeditions
P.O. Box 217, Cambridge, ID 83610
800-262-1882 or 208-257-3477
www.hughesriver.com
RIVERS: Bruneau, Owyhee, Salmon (Middle and Lower Fork), Snake (Hell's Canyon). This is a small, family-run operation. For guides, food, equipment, and service, it's hard to beat its trips on the Middle Fork of the Salmon and Snake River/Hell's Canyon A 3-day trip costs about $775, and longer trips run roughly $250 per day per person.

River Odysseys West
P.O. Box 579, Coeur d'Alene, ID 83816
800-451-6034 or 208-765-0841
www.rowinc.com
RIVERS: Bruneau, Lochsa, Moyie, Owyhee, Salmon (Middle Fork), Salmon River

Canyon, Snake, St. Joe (ID); Clark Fork, Missouri (MT), Rio Upano (Ecuador). The company's Salmon River Canyon trips are ideal for first-timers, and the Lochsa River expedition offers almost continuous Class IV and V rapids. Both oar- and paddle-rafts are available (plus duckies on some rivers), and you can switch from one to the other during the trip. Programs range from $80 day trips to 6-day tours costing $1,450. Each year, 80% of clients are repeat customers.

Rocky Mountain River Tours, Inc.
P.O. Box 8596, Boise, ID 83707
208-345-2400. www.rafttrips.com
RIVERS: Salmon (Middle Fork).
A family operation with a two-decade track record, Rocky Mountain River Tours is renowned for its fabulous cuisine and great guides. Trips run from June through September each year, and cost $975 for 4 days, $1,565 for 6 days. June's high water means maximum white-water excitement, but families should go later in the season. Book well in advance.

Salmon River Outfitters
P.O. Box 519, Donnelly, ID 83615
800-346-6204 or 208-325-3400
www.salmonriveroutfitters.com
RIVERS: Main Salmon.

From its remote riverside guest lodge on the main Salmon River, the company runs 6-day trips through more than 80 miles of the roadless section of the Frank Church Wilderness area. Trips are available in oar rafts (5 person), paddle rafts (7 person), and inflatable single and double kayaks. Particularly popular are the specialty trips, including natural history, Indian lore, wine tasting, storytelling, and gourmet food.

MONTANA

Glacier Wilderness Guides and Montana Raft Co.
P.O. Box 330, West Glacier, MT 59936
800-521-7238 or 406-387-5555
www.glacierguides.com
RIVERS: Flathead (North and Middle Fork).
Running the Flathead is the specialty of Glacier Wilderness Guides/Montana Raft Co., based near Glacier National Park. The Middle Fork offers more white water, and the North Fork is a scenic float trip. These 1- to 8-day trips offer excellent fishing and wildlife-viewing opportunities. Late spring is best for white water.

OREGON

Ouzel Adventures
P.O. Box 827, Bend, OR 97709
800-788-7238 or 541-385-5947

www.oregonrafting.com

RIVERS: Deschutes, McKenzie, North Umpqua, Owyhee, Rogue (OR); Lower Salmon (ID).

In business since 1979, Ouzel offers deluxe, active rafting vacations on Oregon's most beautiful rivers. With Ouzel you can expect everything to be a step above—gourmet food, experienced guides, and new equipment. Most trips run paddle rafts down moderate Class II to IV rivers, and family trips are a specialty. Trips range from 1 to 5 days.

Orange Torpedo Trips

P.O. Box 1111, Grants Pass, OR 97528
800-635-2925 or 541-479- 5061
www.orangetorpedo.com

RIVERS: Lower Klamath, North Umqua, Rogue (OR); Salmon (Main & Lower) (ID).

This company operates comfortable riverside lodges on the Klamath, Rogue, North Umpqua, and Salmon Rivers for those who enjoy a bit of comfort at the end of the day. Duckies are available on nearly all the runs, and the guides are skilled kayak mentors, not just raft jockeys. Most of Orange Torpedo's river trips make fine intros to solo paddling, and good family vacations.

WASHINGTON

Downstream River Runners

13414 Chain Lake Rd., Monroe, WA 98272
800-234-4644 or 360-805-9899
www.riverpeople.com

RIVERS: Sauk, Skaggit, Skykomish, Suiattle, Tieton, Wenatchee (WA); Grande Ronde, Owyhee (OR).

Washington's rivers may be the best kept secret in the rafting world. Most of the runs are fairly short, however (8-12 miles on average). All Downstream's guides are certified in swift-water rescue, and rafts are self-bailing. Prices average $85 for single day trips, $125 per day for multiday trips.

Orion Expeditions, Inc.

5111 Latona Ave. N.E., Seattle, WA 98105
800-553-7466 or 206-547-6715
www.orionexp.com

RIVERS: Green, Methow, Sauk, Skagit, Skykomish, Tieton, Wenatchee (WA); Deschutes (OR).

Orion offers the full spectrum of river-running, from gentle floats to serious white water. With top-quality equipment, and seasoned guides, Orion is a solid choice in the Northwest.

WYOMING

Barker-Ewing River Trips

P.O. Box 450, Jackson, WY 83001
800-448-4202 or 307-733-1000

www.barker-ewing.com

RIVERS: Main Salmon (ID); Snake River (WY).

Operating since 1962, Barker-Ewing enjoys a strong reputation for safety and customer service. The company specializes in easy day trips on the Upper Snake River priced at $30-40 per person. Overnight trips on the Snake cost $112. One-week trips on the Main Salmon are also available for $1,200 per adult.

SOUTHWEST

ARIZONA

Arizona Raft Adventures, Inc.

4050 E. Huntington, Flagstaff, AZ 86004
800-786-7238 or 520-526-8200
www.azraft.com

RIVERS: Grand Canyon Colorado (M,O,P,K;6-14) (AZ); San Juan (UT).

Arizona Raft Adventures is a major Grand Canyon concessionaire that is used by a number of other outfits marketing Colorado river trips. Although it runs mostly oar-raft trips, the company also offers paddle-raft, kayak, and motor-raft trips.

Arizona River Runners

P.O. Box 47788, Phoenix, AZ 85068
800-477-7238 or 602-867-4866
www.raftarizona.com

RIVERS: Grand Canyon Colorado (M,O;3,6-8) (AZ).

This is one of the premier motorized raft operators on the Colorado, with more than 50 river trips per year. Prices are: $1,405 for 6 days, 190 miles, including heli-flight out; $1,535 for 8 days, 280 miles; and $695 for 3 days. Book well in advance.

COLORADO

Adrift Adventures

P.O. Box 192, Jensen, UT 84035
800-824-0150 or 435-789-3600
www.adrift.com

RIVERS: Gunnison, Yampa (CO); Green (CO, UT).

Adrift Adventures runs small trips that manage to preserve the serenity of the backcountry. The Yampa trip is a true wilderness journey on Colorado's last free-flowing river. The Gunnison, recently designated a National Conservation Area, provides little tourist traffic, good fishing, and even some Class IV white water. Raft-supported kayak trips are also offered on all rivers. Sample prices: 5 days on the Yampa, $699; 4 days on the Green, $639; 2 days on the Gunnison, $275. Family rates are available.

Mountain Waters Rafting

P.O. Box 2681, Durango, CO 81302
800-748-2507 or 970-259-4191
www.durangorafting.com

RIVERS: Upper and Lower Animas, Piedra (CO).

This small, family operation runs two great rivers, the Class V Upper Animas and the Class IV Piedra. Customers must have prior river-running experience, and a swimming test is mandatory for the Upper Animas. The company uses high-tech catarafts and modern 14-foot self-bailers. Cost is $375 for 2 days on the Upper Animas, including transport on the Durango-Silverton Railroad to and from the river. Peak water flow is mid-June for the Animas, mid-May for the Piedra. One-day Piedra trips are $125.

Peregrine Outfitters

64 Ptarmigan Lane, Durango, CO 81301
800-598-7600 or 970-385-7600
www.peregineriver.com

RIVERS: Animas (Upper and Lower), Dolores, Gunnison, Piedra, San Juan, San Miguel, Upper Colorado.

Experienced boaters should try Peregrine's day trips on the Class IV-V Upper Animas. Families should opt for the company's 1- to 6-day trips on the Dolores River for about $150 per day. The San Miguel is an alpine river near Telluride with very scenic camps. Inflatable kayaks are offered on all rivers except the Upper Animas and Piedra. A family business, Peregrine runs small groups, usually around 12-16 participants including guides.

Rocky Mountain Adventures

P.O. Box 1989, Fort Collins, CO 80522
800-858-6808 or 970-493-4005
www.omnibus.com/rma.html

RIVERS: Arkansas (Royal Gorge, Browns Canyon, Texas Creek), Cache la Poudre, Delores, North Platte, Upper Colorado.

Rocky Mountain Adventures offers a full range of rafting trips, including half- and full-day trips on the Arkansas River. For serious white water, the company has full-day and overnight trips on the scenic Cache la Poudre, whose upper section is Class V at high water.

Rocky Mountain Outdoor Center

10281 U.S. Highway 50, Howard, CO 81233
800-255-5784 or 719-942-3214
www.rmoc.com

RIVERS: Arkansas (Browns Canyon, Cottonwood, Parkdale, Royal Gorge) (CO); Dolores (CO, UT).

Guides are personable and very skilled, and the company uses new, high-quality boats.

It operates a nice riverside facility with activities for non-paddlers. For nonstop major rapids, try the Royal Gorge or the Brown's Canyon sections, which are run only at high water in the spring. The Cottonwood section is an excellent choice for younger children and families. Inflatable kayaks are offered on the easier sections of the Arkansas.

NEW MEXICO

Southwest Wilderness Adventures
P.O. Box 9380, Santa Fe, NM 87504
800-869-7238 or 505-983-7262
www.white-water-rafting.net
RIVERS: Rio Grande (Taos Box, La Junta, Rio Grande Gorge, Whiterock Canyon), Rio Chama.
This leading outfitter provides half-day ($42) and full-day ($84) rafting trips through Taos Box, Rio Grande Gorge, and Whiterock Canyon. Taos box is a classic, full-day Class IV run. Overnight rafting is also available on the Rio Chama and Whiterock Canyon, starting at $225.

TEXAS

Big Bend River Tours
P.O. Box 317, Terlingua, TX 79852
800-545-4240 or 915-424-3219
www.bigbendrivertours.com
RIVERS: Rio Grande.
Big Bend's specialty gourmet, naturalist, and photo trips are popular, and a combo raft/horseback trip is available. The company provides raft support and outfitting for canoeists. It rents rafts for $25 per day per person, and canoes for $45 per day per boat. Hiking and jeep tours are available as well.

Far Flung Adventures
P.O. Box 377, Terlingua, TX 79852
800-359-4138 or 915-371-2489
www.farflung.com
RIVERS: Salt (AZ); Arkansas (CO); Rio Chama and Rio Grande Gorge (NM); Big Bend/Lower Canyons (TX); Rio Antigua, Rio Filo Bobo, Octopan, Chiapas waterways (Mexico).
Far Flung Adventures offers a diverse range of river experiences, from Class IV white water on the Rio Grande Gorge to gentle floats in Big Bend National Park. Modern self-bailing rafts are used on the whitewater runs. Try the company's specialty programs—naturalist workshops, gourmet, and music trips. Far Flung runs a strong program south of the border with sister company Eco Expediciones. The Rio Antigua and Octopan are classic one-day white-water runs. The Rio Filo Bobo is a

scenic, multi-day jungle adventure featuring Aztec archaeological sites.

UTAH

Colorado River & Trail Expeditions
P.O. Box 57575, Salt Lake City, UT 84157
800-253-7328 or 801-261-1789
www.crateinc.com
RIVERS: Colorado (Grand Canyon M, O, P, K; 4-13, Cataract and Westwater Canyons) (AZ, UT, CO); Green (Desolation Canyon) (UT); also, Alsek, Noatak, Hula Hula, and Tatshenshini (AK).
This small, family-run business offers better service and prices than most of its high-volume competitors, plus less-crowded motor rafts. It also provides some of the best oar- and paddle-raft journeys on the Colorado. Colorado River & Trail stresses personal service and quality rather than hauling the maximum number of customers.

Grand Canyon Expeditions Company
P.O. Box O, Kanab, UT 84741
800-544-2691 or 435-644-2691
www.gcex.com
RIVERS: Grand Canyon Colorado (M,dory;8,14) (AZ).
Although the largest commercial rafting operation on the Grand Canyon, the company offers a level of personalized service not found with other big operators. Customers can request a guide with special expertise in photography, geology, archaeology, or other outdoor science. Cost for the 8-day motor trip is $1,820; the 14-day dory trip is $2,555.

Holiday Expeditions
544 E. 3900 S., Salt Lake City, UT 84107
800-624-6323 or 801-266-2087
www.bikeraft.com
RIVERS: Yampa (CO); Colorado, Green, San Juan (UT); Salmon (Main and Lower), Lochsa, Snake (ID).
Holiday's highly rated 1- to 6-day trips average about $160 per day. This is above average, but the trips are high quality, with skilled staff, excellent food, and great attention to detail. Something for everyone is offered—from rugged big-water runs to gentle family floats. In Utah, Holiday also offers 4- or 7-day itineraries that combine rafting with mountain biking or rafting with guest ranch stays.

Western River Expeditions
7258 Racquet Club Dr., Salt Lake City, UT 84121. 800-453-7450 or 801-942-6669
www.westernriver.com.
RIVERS: Colorado (Grand [M; 3, 4, 6], Cataract, and Westwater Canyons) (AZ, UT, CO ; Salmon (Main and Middle Fork) (ID);

Green (UT).
Western River Expeditions is the nation's largest rafting company, with over 40 years of experience running the Grand Canyon. It uses big J-Rig motor rafts, the best craft for negotiating the Colorado's major rapids. The company offers range of itineraries, but try the full-river trip if you can afford it. It's staff, trip organization, and cuisine are superior. Grand Canyon trips begin or end with a helicopter flight, and Western River maintains its own lodge atop the Canyon Rim. For a Grand Canyon motor trip, WRE is an excellent choice. However, WRE packs a lot of people into its boats, and the pace on the 6-day trip can be a bit hurried.

WEST

CALIFORNIA

All-Outdoors Rafting
1250 Pine St., Suite 103, Walnut Creek, CA 94596. 800-247-2387 or 925-932-8993
www.aorafting.com.
RIVERS: American (Middle, South Fork), Kaweah, Lower and Upper Klamath, Merced, Stanislaus (Goodwin Canyon, North Fork), Tuolumne (Main, Cheery Creek) (CA).
One of California's leading outfitters, family-owned All-Outdoors offers 1- to 3-day trips on a dozen California rivers. Since it was founded in the early 1960s, All-Outdoors has guided over 12,000 trips for more than 135,000 guests. This is a rock-solid company with a great inventory of waterways for every skill level. Choose from easy family trips like the Lower Klamath, or Class V adrenaline runs like the Cal Salmon.

American River Touring Association (ARTA) River Trips
24000 Casa Loma Rd., Groveland, CA 95321
800-323-2782 or 209-962-7873
www.arta.org
Rivers: American (Middle and South Fork), Merced, Tuolumne (CA); Yampa (CO); Illinois, Rogue, Umqua, Upper Klamath (OR); Green (UT); Salmon, Selway (ID).
One of the country's finest rafting companies, ARTA selects guides not only for their white-water skills, but also their knowledge of wilderness ecology and geology. Custom trips can be arranged for experienced paddlers. The Green and Yampa Rivers both flow through Dinosaur National Monument, which boasts awe-inspiring scenery.

Beyond Limits Adventures
P.O. Box 215, Riverbank, CA 95367
800-234-7238 or 209-869-6060

www.rivertrip.com

RIVERS: American (South Fork), Stanislaus, Kaweah, Trinity (Burnt Ranch Gorge), Yuba (North Fork), West Walker (CA).

Beyond Limits offers the full spectrum of California white water, from mild to wild. On the American River it provides good family rafting supported by a superb riverside resort. The Kaweah is a high-energy run near Sequoia National Park. Burnt Ranch Gorge is a supreme test of paddling skills—technical, with Class V drops. Beyond Limits also runs many moderate 1- and 2-day trips, such as the Stanislaus, that are suitable for families. Water levels are best in late spring, so book early.

Outdoor Adventure River Specialists (O.A.R.S.), Inc.

P.O. Box 67, Angels Camp, CA 95222
800-346-6277, 209-736-2924, or 4677
www.oars.com

RIVERS: Colorado (O, P, K; 5-13) (AZ, CO, UT); American, Upper and Lower Klamath, Merced, Cal. Salmon, Tuolumne (CA); Salmon (Main and Middle Fork), Snake (ID); Rogue (OR); Snake to Grand Teton (WY); Cataract Canyon of the Colorado, Dolores, Green, San Juan, Yampa (UT).

Founded in 1970, O.A.R.S. is a major player in the rafting industry, with sizable operations throughout the American West. The company's guides, service, and cuisine are excellent, although some trips can be crowded. The O.A.R.S. staff does a good job of helping you plan the ideal river vacation, from a family float on Oregon's Rogue to a high-adrenaline outing on the Class V Tuolumne. The excellent oar-raft trips on the Grand Canyon remain one of the cornerstones of O.A.R.S. river inventory. O.A.R.S. also offers dory trips on many western rivers with sister company Grand Canyon Dories.

Sierra Mac River Trips

P.O. Box 366, Sonora, CA 95370
800-457-2580 or 209-532-1327
www.sierramac.com

RIVERS: Tuolumne (Main, Cherry Creek), North Fork American (Giant Gap, Chamberlain Falls).

Since 1972, Sierra Mac has stood out as one of the premier river companies in the United States. Their guides (who average 10-12 years of river experience) are top notch, and so is the cuisine. This outfitter pioneered two of the hardest commercial rivers run in the United States, Cherry Creek and Giant Gap, and its safety record is flawless. Using the latest equipment, including catarafts, Sierra Mac runs exciting rivers that many lesser companies can't handle.

Whitewater Voyages

5225 San Pablo Dam Rd., El Sobrante, CA 94803. 800-488-7238 or 510-222-5994
www.whitewatervoyages.com

Rivers: American (all forks), Cal. Salmon, Giant Gap, Kern (Forks, Upper, Lower), Kaweah, Lower and Upper Klamath, Merced, Tuolumne (Main, Cherry Creek), Yuba (North Fork).

Founded in 1975, Whitewater Voyages runs more trips on more rivers than any other California outfitter. This outfitter offers everything from Class V white-knuckle runs (Cherry Creek or Giant Gap) to specialty family trips on the Lower Klamath (discounts for groups and juniors are available). Equipment is state-of-the-art, with new boats every season. Not all of the guides are seasoned veterans, but most are quite good and a third are EMTs and/or swift-water rescue certified. The food is first rate, and prices are moderate, starting at $85 per day. The most popular river is the Kern, just three hours from Los Angeles. Inflatable kayaks are offered on the Kern when conditions permit. Teens will enjoy the company's unique white water summer camp on the South Fork of the American. Five days of fun and skills training costs $595-695.

FOREIGN RAFTING

CANADA

Alpine Rafting Company

P.O. Box 1272, Golden, BC V0A 1H0
888-599-5299 or 250-344-6778
www.kickinghorseriver.com

DESTINATIONS: Kicking Horse, Blaeberry, Columbia.

The town of Golden, British Columbia, is the center of Canadian white-water rafting, and Alpine is the top operator in this scenic part of the Rockies. The Kicking Horse is a Class III-IV run. All single day trips range from $25-90.

Canadian River Expeditions

P.O. Box 1023, Whistler, BC B0N 1B0
800-898-7238 or 604-938-6651
www.canriver.com

DESTINATIONS: Chilcotin, Fraser, Skeena, Gataga-Kechika (BC); Firth (Yukon); Tatshenshini/Alsek (AK/Yukon); Taku (AK)).

Canadian River Expeditions offers spectacular river runs. Sections of the Chilco/Chilcotin rival the Grand Canyon for big water excitement, and the Tatshenshini/Alsek is the ultimate, far northern float trip. The company has very skilled guides and decades of experience.

Hyak River Adventures

203-3823 Henning Drive, Burnaby, BC V5C 6N5. 800-663-7238, 604-734-8622 (Vancouver), or 206-382-1311 (Seattle)
www.hyak.com

RIVERS: Chilko/Chilcotin/Fraser, Chilliwack, Thompson (BC); Firth, Nahanni (Yukon); Tatshenshini (AK/Yukon); Middle Fork Salmon (ID).

Hyak River Adventures is an outstanding outfitter running exceptional rivers. The Chilko/Chilcotin/Fraser run is a 6-day, 3-river adventure combining big white water with scenic splendor. The Firth, pioneered by Hyak, flows from Alaska's Arctic National Wildlife Refuge through Inuvik National Park at the northern tip of Canada's Yukon Territory. The Tatshenshini is a classic high northern river that winds through remote, unspoiled wilderness. Hyak handles the logistical challenges of these big rivers with aplomb, and the company's guides are well-versed in the history and ecology of the region.

Nahanni River Adventures, Ltd.

Box 4869, Whitehorse, YT Y1A 4N6
800-297-6927 or 867-668-3180
www.nahanni.com

RIVERS: Nahanni (NWT), Firth, Snake (Yukon), Tatshenshini-Alsek (Yukon, BC, AK), Burnside, Coppermine, Horton (NWT), Stikine (BC/AK), Snake (Yukon), and other sub-Arctic waterways.

Nahanni River Adventures is the top guide service on many of the great rivers of Canada's Yukon and Northwest Territories, especially on the mighty Nahanni. The company's expeditions are long (1- to 3-week) wilderness camping trips offering great solitude and scenery. Expect to rough it a bit more than on an Idaho or Grand Canyon trip. Depending on the river, you may use an oar-raft, tandem canoes, or Voyageur canoes (31-foot replicas of the freighter craft paddled by fur traders). Crossing the path of migrating caribou herds, these far northern rivers flow through spectacular wildlife habitats.

New World River Expeditions

100 Rouge River Rd., Calumet, PQ J0V 1B0
800-361-5033 or 819-242-7238
www.newworld.ca

DESTINATIONS: Rouge, Batiscan Rivers (Quebec).

There is plenty of great white water in eastern Canada, though in this part of the country you'll be limited to short day-trips or overnighters. Good water flow allows long seasons, and there is good fishing, hiking, or canoeing near the rafting runs. New World runs two of the best short rivers in Quebec and has a great riverside activity center with many land-based activities for the whole family. The company offers 1-day rafting and kayaking trips, multi-day kayak clinics, and a 5-day Adventure Package that includes rafting, horseback riding, kayaking, mountain biking, and hiking. Cost is $400 (CN) per person, including campsite and all meals.

INTERNATIONAL

Bio-Bio Expeditions
Box 2028, Truckee, CA 96160
800-246-7238 or 530-582-6865
www.bbxrafting.com
Rivers: Cal. Salmon, Scott (CA); Futaleufu (Chile); Apuramac (Peru); Katun (Siberia); Marsyangdi, Sun Kosi, Karnali (Nepal); Zambezi (Zambia).

Bio-Bio Expeditions runs rivers worldwide, from Chile to Siberia, offering rafting and kayaking expeditions for novice paddlers and seasoned veterans alike. The Zambezi operation is one of the few multiday run with North American guides. South America is one of Bio-Bio Expeditions' specialties. In Chile, Bio-Bio runs the Futaleufu 1.5 times per tour from a base camp, with day shuttles to the river. Peru is a combo trip with the Apuramac and the Inca Trail. One of the Zambezi trips includes an ascent of Kilimanjaro. Bio-Bio uses the most experienced local operator in Nepal.

Earth River Expeditions, Inc.
180 Towpath Rd., Accord, NY 12404
800-643-2784 or 914-626-2665
www.earthriver.com
RIVERS: Colca (Peru); Futaleufu (Chile); Great Bend of the Yangtze (China); Headwall Canyon (BC); Magpie and Great Whale (Quebec); Primrose (Yukon); Rufigi (Tanzania); Upano (Ecuador); Upper Yangtze and Po Tsangpo (Tibet).

Earth River Expeditions made the first raft descent of Chile's Futaleufu and, in the last decade, it has pioneered commercial rafting on many world-class foreign rivers, including the Futaleufu, Colca, Upper Yangtze, and the Great Bend of the Yangtze and Po Tsangpo. The company introduced a number of important safety measures that have become standard in the rafting industry. British Columbia's Headwall Canyon is a spectacular new discovery, one of the most impressive, remote rivers in

North America. Patagonia's Futaleafu River is a world-class run featuring azure waters, stunning scenery, and 39 major rapids. Earth River's outstanding Futaleufu operation is profiled earlier in this chapter.

Faszinatour Magerbach
Allee Strasse Be1, D-87509, Immenstadt, Germany. 01149-8323-51271 or 01143-5266-87188 in Austria. www.faszinatour.de
RIVERS: Various runs in Tirol, Austria.

Faszinatour is a top European adventure company offering half-day to week-long river adventures on the glacier-fed rivers of the Tirol. Day-trips run about $80, and overnight excursions cost about $120 per day, including indoor lodging. Rafting can be combined with rock climbing and mountain biking. The office staff and most guides speak English.

Mountain Travel-Sobek
6420 Fairmont Ave., El Cerrito, CA, 94530
800-227-2384, 800-282-8747, or 510-527-8100. www.mtsobek.com
RIVERS: Alps Rivers (Austria, France, Italy); Alsek, Tatshenshini (AK); Apurimac, Tambopata (Peru); Blue Nile, Omo (Ethiopia); Coruh (Turkey); Franklin (Tasmania); Futaleafu (Chile); Karnali (Nepal); Pacuare, Reventazón (Costa Rica); Rio Tuich (Bolivia); Rio Upano (Ecuador); Zambezi (Zambia).

MT-Sobek's Alaska trips are classic journeys through spectacular, remote wilderness areas. Sobek offers a wide selection of great rivers in South America, and it works with the top outfitters in Costa Rica. MT-Sobek's African river trips are unique adventures; the Zambezi is profiled in this chapter. The new Alps Rivers package is a great introduction to European white water, and the Karnali in Nepal is a spectacular Class IV descent through the foothills of the Himalayas. MT-Sobek offers such a wide range of rivers worldwide by employing local outfitters in many destinations.

Norwegian Wildlife and Rafting
Randsverk 2680 Vaga, Norway
01147-6123-8727. www.nwr.no.
RIVERS: Asengjuvet, Sjoa, and many other destinations in Norway.

Norwegian Wildlife and Rafting is the leading rafting service in Norway, having pioneered many Norwegian rivers. Servicing roughly 3,000 clients yearly, the company offers 1- to 2-day trips on Class II-IV rivers that are some of the most exciting in western Europe. Norwegian Wildlife and Rafting has great boats (self-bailers and

catarafts). The scenery can be stunning. Be ready for steep, steady gradients and icy water, though, even in the summertime.

Saga d'Aventures
46 bis rue de la Rébublique, 92170 Vanves, France
011331-4108-1490; Fax: 011331-4529-0326
www.webexpert.fr/raft
RIVERS: Allier, Allier Supérieure, Doron, Isère, Les Dranses (France); Dora Baltée (Italy); Noguerra Palaresa (Spain); Sun Kosi (Nepal).

Saga d'Aventures pioneered commercial white-water sports in France, and is one of the biggest rafting companies on the continent. Employing able guides, Saga runs the major white-water rivers of southern Europe. On the Doron, Dranses, and Isère rivers, Saga also offers hydro-speeding, a wild new way of running white water with a body-board (plus wet suit and helmet, of course). It's fast, inexpensive, and combines the thrill of kayaking with the athleticism of body-surfing.

Ríos Tropicales
Contact Rafael Gallo or Fernando Esquivel, INTERLINK #124, P.O. BOX 526770, Miami, FL 33152. 506-233-6455
www.riostropicales.com
RIVERS: General, Pacuare, Reventazón (Costa Rica).

Ríos Tropicales is Costa Rica's largest river outfitter, and one of its owners, Rafael Gallo, co-wrote *The Rivers of Costa Rica,* the definitive white-water guidebook for this region. Ríos Tropicales is used by many U.S.-based adventure companies, particularly for combo trekking/rafting or rafting/sea kayaking adventures. You may cut costs by booking directly.

PREPARING FOR YOUR RAFTING TRIP

Day trips
Single-day trips are the most popular form of rafting. However, be sure to ask how much time you'll actually be on the water. On some trips billed as full-day adventures, you'll spend hours riding a bus to and from the river. While most outfitters will serve up an ample lunch, don't skip breakfast—you'll need the energy. Pack light, but be sure to bring athletic shoes (not sandals), sunscreen, and sunglasses with a safety strap. An inexpensive waterproof disposable camera will deliver great action shots. Where the water is cold, bring along polypropylene underwear to layer

under a wet suit (many outfitters rent wet suits), and don't forget a hat that covers your ears, polypro socks, and gloves (simple household rubber gloves work fine in really cold water).

Multi-day trips

Over the years, multi-day river trips have become more deluxe, serving up gourmet cuisine in comfortable tent camps. Moreover, many guide services now offer speciality river trips—everything from music cruises to fly-fishing seminars. Having a musician, story-teller, ace photographer, or archaeologist on the trip can help entertain the kids and add something special to your vacation. Before leaving on a multi-day outing, ask your outfitter for a recommended gear list. Don't forget any special medications you may require, and bring reading material, a deck of cards, or other diversions for the hours spent shoreside. A small headlamp such as the Petzl is great at night, and bring lightweight binoculars for wildlife watching and star-gazing.

RIVER SKILLS TRAINING

In the Canoe and Kayaking chapter, you'll find a list of excellent paddling schools, many of which offer paddle raft training. If you are interested in becoming a river guide, the following facilities offer professional white-water river training.

ARTA

24000 Casa Loma Rd., Groveland, CA 95321. 800-323-2782 or 209-962-7873. www.arta.org. Programs: 7-day white-water basics course, $600; 12-day pro guide training, $1,080; 10-day Oregon whitewater school, $820, 16-day Idaho river training, $1,350.

Nantahala Outdoor Center

13077 Hwy 19 W., Bryson City, NC 28713. 800-232-7238 or 828-488-2175. www.noc.com. Extensive guide training program, including swift-water rescue. Riverside lodge with restaurant.

Rocky Mountain Outdoor Center

10281 Highway 50, Howard, CO 81233. 800-255-5784 or 719-942-3214. www.rmoc.com. Conducts a 10-day raft guide training course for about $600.

Whitewater Voyages

5225 San Pablo Dam Rd., El Sobrante, CA 94803. 800-488-7238 or 510-222-5994. www.whitewatervoyages.com. American and Kern River clinics: 7-day intro class,

$800. For guides in training and private boaters looking to learn boat-handling and river safety.

ONLINE

American Whitewater Affiliation

www.awa.org

This first-rate web site hosts a comprehensive review of American rivers, an event calendar, plus directories of manufacturers, tour operators, and U.S. river water gauges.

Great Outdoor Recreation Pages

www.gorp.com

This company offers a complete summary of Wild and Scenic Rivers plus links to outfitters, river gear suppliers, and weather and flow information.

Riversearch

www.riversearch.com

Sponsored by several large, well-established river outfitters, this cooperative site offers a searchable index of rivers worldwide in addition to feature articles on destinations and travel.

U.S. Geological Survey Water Resources Information

http://h2o.usgs.gov/public/realtime.html

This site features real-time streamflow conditions for rivers in most U.S. states, plus links to other river-related internet resources.

BOOKS

Whitewater Rafting in North America by Lloyd Armstead (Globe Pequot Press, $16.95). This is the definitive guide to river vacations in the United States. Painstakingly researched, it recommends guides and describes 200 rivers in detail. (*888-249-7586, www.globe-pequot.com.*)

The Whitewater Rafting Manual by Jimmy Johnson (Stackpole Books, $16.95). This manual covers nearly every rafting topic from basic paddle strokes to advanced river tactics. Also covers repair and maintenance of equipment. (*800-282-3963. www. adventuroustraveler.com.*)

Western Whitewater: From the Rockies to the Pacific by Cassady, Calhoun, and Cross (The Boat People, $34.95) is an authoritative guidebook for river runners. Fifty top rivers are reviewed and mapped in detail, with basic information on 100 other runs. This volume has the best maps and river logs of any current publication. (*408-295-2628. www.theboatpeople.com.*)

VIDEOS

An award-winning series of white-water videos from **Camera One** (*8523 15th Ave. N.E., Seattle, WA 98115. 800-726-3456 or 206-523-3456*) covers many of the greatest U.S. rivers, including the Grand Canyon Colorado. All videos are $19.95.

KICKING BACK ON THE COLORADO

SAFARI. THE VERY WORD CONJURES IMAGES OF AN

AFRICAN **E**DEN WHERE REGAL BEASTS ROAM FREELY

on an endless open plain. • Let's face it: This is adventure travel at

its most romantic. If your inner explorer yearns to answer the call

of the wild, an array of commercial safari companies stand ready

to help you place that call. Their offerings range from whirlwind

wildlife tours to month-long odysseys on which you journey across

numerous frontiers in East and southern Africa. • Most modern

safaris are well planned and expertly guided. The biggest challenge

lies in ferreting out the truly wild places—spots where great herds

still roam, and the flocks you see are birds, not tourists. Though

Kenya and Tanzania remain the most popular safari destinations,

heavy tourism in each country has diminished the intensity of the

experience. • In this chapter you will find tips on less traveled—

but gloriously game-rich—safari regions, including Botswana,

Zambia, and Namibia. You'll also learn the current status of such

classic East African game parks as the Serengeti's Masai Mara

Reserve, and find out how to design a safari itinerary of your own.

LEFT: SAFARI-GOERS CAPTURE A PERFECT MOMENT ON THE SERENGETI PLAIN.
BELOW: ELEPHANTS IN BOTSWANA'S CHOBE NATIONAL PARK

*While photographing elephants...I recognized in them a kindred spirit—
...the unabashed pleasure they seem to take at just messing around in water.*

FRANS LANTING

Great African Adventures

This section features both classic safaris—where you game-watch from a vehicle and stay in traditional lodges— as well as edgier, more exotic adventures that take you to Africa's most remote and untamed territory. The trips described below represent but a small fraction of the safaris available in East and in southern Africa. Moreover, there are safaris for all budgets—from bargain camping expeditions to luxury safaris that cost as much as a small car. However you go, whatever your resources permit, you are guaranteed a thrilling and memorable journey.

KENYA & TANZANIA
The Classic Safari

A tour of the great game parks of Kenya and Tanzania is the quintessential safari experience. Although poaching and diminished grazing lands have taken their toll on East Africa's game herds, during annual migrations you can still see animals by the tens of thousands in the parklands of Kenya and Tanzania.

Modern safaris are carefully orchestrated. After arriving in Nairobi or Mombasa, Kenya, you are transported by air or by van to staging points in **Amboseli** in Kenya or **Arusha** in Tanzania.

Accommodations typically consist of large, permanent lodges situated near watering holes—natural gathering places for a diversity of species. Alternatively, and increasingly popular, tent camps feature semipermanent facilities that often are located closer to the largest groups of animals. You sacrifice some luxury in a tent camp, but the experience is far from rugged.

Each day you travel from base by Land Rover or by minivan to scout for wildlife. Game parks are frequently located miles apart; be prepared to endure long stretches of dusty, bumpy roads.

Also, don't be surprised to encounter other tour vehicles when you arrive at your destination: Game reserves are popular places these days—particularly during the cooler peak season. If you go to East Africa expecting solitude, you may be disappointed.

Kenya

The game parks in Kenya are the best known safari destinations. Lodges and tent camps are comfortable, sophisticated, and, in general, among the finest to be found in Africa.

A must-see stop is **Masai Mara National Reserve.** An extension of the **Serengeti Plain,** the reserve holds Kenya's largest and most diverse big game population. In August, zebra and wildebeest herds pursued by lions migrate north across the dusty flats as far as you can see.

Two other recommended safari destinations are **Amboseli Game Reserve** and **Tsavo West Park.** The former, a historic crossroads, lies at the foot of **Mount Kilimanjaro.** Watering holes in Amboseli are few and far between, so any site with exposed groundwater is a good bet for spotting lions, elephants, rhino, giraffes, and other game. Tsavo is famous for its large elephant herds.

Among Kenya's many fine lodges, two complexes near **Mount Kenya** deserve special mention. They are **Mountain Lodge** (*Kiganjo. 011-254-171-4248*) and **Naro Moru River Lodge** (*Naro Moru. 011-254-176-62622*).

The **Nyeri** area offers several hotels, including **The Ark** (*011-254-2-216940 for reservations*) in **Aberdares National Park.** Located near popular watering holes and salt licks, the hotel offers superb game-viewing. If you're feeling flush, about 40 miles away near Nanyuki, **Mount Kenya Safari Club** (*Nanyuki. 011-254-2-216940 for reservations*) offers classic luxury lodging—with few rivals in East Africa.

Tanzania

While Kenya is the overwhelming choice of most tourists, those in the know seem to prefer Tanzania. Although the tourist facilities aren't quite as refined, the country's primary draw is the Serengeti Plain. Covering 5,610 square miles [14,530 sq km], it is home to more than three million animals, including 35 major species.

A trip to Tanzania should include the **Ngorongoro Crater,** probably the single best site for game viewing in East Africa. Remnants of the world's largest volcano, the crater's 2,000-foot-high walls shelter the largest concentration of nonmigratory wildlife in Africa—more than 20,000 animals.

From the rim, the land below resembles a Garden of Eden, with green forests and open savannah surrounding **Lake Magadi,** a shallow soda lake. You have the option of staying in one of the luxury lodges up on the rim.

If you're willing to rough it a little, you can tent-camp at one of four campsites in the crater. You enjoy the double ben-

efits of saving money and getting closer to the wildlife: lions, elephants, cheetahs, hyenas, hippos, zebras, wildebeests, Cape buffalo, bushbuck, black rhino, gazelles, impalas, ostriches, and flamingos.

A typical, 14-day safari in Kenya or Tanzania will visit four or five game parks, each featuring different types of animals. The daily cost ranges from about $150 to more than $350 per person.

It pays to shop around. Prices for similar itineraries can vary by thousands of dollars. You can often save by using a less known safari agency, such as **SafariCentre International** *(800-223-6046. www.safaricentre.com)*, rather than a big name outfitter like **Abercrombie & Kent.**

Substantial savings can also be gained by traveling during East Africa's spring *(Sept.-Oct.)* rather than the peak winter season *(May-Aug.)*.

ZAMBIA & ZIMBABWE
Heart of East Africa

Zambia and Zimbabwe have become increasingly popular safari sites—as add-ons to a Kenyan or a Tanzanian trip, but also as primary destinations.

Victoria Falls is the hub for most safaris here. An extended trip, however, will also allow you to visit major game preserves and perhaps to take a river trip on the mighty **Zam-bezi,** which forms the boundary between the two countries.

Most visitors fly to Zambia's Livingstone Airport because of its proximity to Victoria Falls, which is twice the height of Niagara Falls and twice as wide. Allow at least two days to explore the sites and recreational opportunities around the falls, then travel north to tour **Kafue, North Luangwa,** and **South Luangwa National Parks.**

Kafue is classic East Africa—a vast, open rangeland, where dozens of species, including the rare roan antelope, roam free. North Luangwa to the east offers excellent game-viewing opportunities, especially along the **Mwaleshi River.** At the southernmost reaches of the **Luangwa Valley,** South Luangwa park preserves a woody region covered with coarse grasses and bush.

Cross the river into Zimbabwe, where the premier safari destination is **Hwange International Park.** The country's largest game reserve boasts a remarkable array of birds and mammals, including Zimbabwe's largest elephant population, plus sizable numbers of lions, leopards, white rhino, and wild dogs. An elevated observation platform provides prime viewing of park animals.

Hwange is directly west of Harare International Airport. You can depart from here or return to Zambia and fly out of Livingstone.

A popular alternative adventure in Zimbabwe is a river

RISING ABOVE THE SAVANNA, MOUNT KILIMANJARO PROVIDES THE BACKDROP FOR A MASAI COUPLE.

safari. Most trips run the Lower Zambezi River between **Kariba** and **Kanyemba** on the Mozambique border.

In Zambia, **Lower Zambezi National Park** is a protected wilderness area that is home to a diversity of birds and large mammals. Among the activities offered here are day and night game drives, fishing, walking safaris, and sundowner cruises.

If you are interested in traveling to this region, many commercial safaris are available. **Abercrombie & Kent** (*1520 Kensington Rd., Suite 212, Oak Brook, IL 60521. 800-323-7308 or 630-954-2944. www.abercrombiekent.com*) offers an excellent, 14-day **Zimbabwe Adventure.**

The program features a Zambezi River cruise, bush walks, canoe treks, rafting, horseback riding, and game viewing on the back of an elephant. It's quite a package for $3,570 per person.

SafariCentre International (*800-223-6046. www. safaricentre.com*) offers moderately priced, 3- to 17-day safaris in Zambia and Zimbabwe that focus on the Zambezi River. The cost for a four-day tour is $895 per person.

Zambezi River safaris as well as game-tracking safaris can be booked through **Mountain Travel-Sobek** (*6420 Fairmont Ave., El Cerrito, CA 94530. 800-227-2384 or 510-527-8100. www.mtsobek.com*).

BOTSWANA
Delta Wildlands and the Kalahari Desert

Botswana offers an unspoiled safari experience that is unique on the continent. About the size of France with a population of just over a million people, this landlocked nation in southern Africa is often hyped as the "real" Africa.

Perhaps its reputation is due to the fact that nearly a fourth of the country has been set aside as parkland and game preserves. And Botswana boasts a wealth of flora and fauna that you're not likely to see elsewhere on safari.

Tourist facilities may be generally less deluxe than those you'll find in Kenya or in Tanzania. But if you can forgo a little comfort, you'll discover one of Africa's best kept secrets.

Most of the country is covered by the **Kalahari Desert,** the world's largest mantle of sand. Herds of zebra, springbok, gemsbok, and desert antelope can be seen in the desert's salt pans.

At the edge of the Kalahari sprawls the vast **Okavango Delta.** This floodplain is actually the inland terminus of a river that begins 600 miles away in the Angolan highlands. The waters here run crystal clear and support floating gardens of reeds, palms, papyrus, bulrushes, giant leadwoods, and acacia. Animal life abounds in this rich ecosystem. Hippos swim through tree-lined lagoons and the birdlife is staggering.

Safaris generally travel through the Okavango by truck, plane, or boat. Some groups ply the delta in *mokoros*—traditional canoes punted by Okavango boatmen.

North of the Okavango Delta lies scenic **Chobe National Park.** An obligatory stop on any Botswana itinerary, here you will see roaming buffalo and enormous elephant herds that surpass even those in Kenya. The park is also home to rare puku and lechwe. Of cultural interest are Bushmen rock paintings, which you'll see on some safaris.

Another highlight of a Botswana safari is the magnificent **Victoria Falls,** just across the Zimbabwe border. The falls are known locally as Mosi-oa-Tunya—"the smoke that thunders."

If you are interested in a tour, **Capricorn Safaris** (*011-267-661-165. http://wildnetafrica.com/travelbots/capricorn*) is a leading Botswana-based company that offers quality tented safaris led by experienced bush guides. Capricorn's most complete safari covers the Kalahari, Okavango, Chobe, the Zambezi, and Victoria Falls in 14 days (on land). The cost is about $2,925 per person.

Capricorn trips may be booked through the **Safari-Centre** (*3201 N. Sepulveda Blvd., Manhattan Beach, CA 90266. 800-223-6046 or 310-546-4411. www.safaricentre.com*).

Another recommended safari in Botswana—and a good choice for the budget-minded traveler—is offered by the **Adventure Center** (*1311 63rd Street, Suite 200, Emeryville, CA 94608. 800-227-8747 or 510-654-1879. www. adventurecenter.com*).

The center's three-week-long **Kruger, Okavango, and the Falls** trip takes you through Chobe National Park and the Okavango Delta by boat, canoe, and bush walk. This is a basic, camping-style trip, but the price is right: just $1,800 for 22 days.

If you prefer a deluxe experience, go with **Ker & Downey** (*2825 Wilcrest Dr., Suite 600, Houston, TX 77042. 800-423-4236 or 713-917-0048. www.kerdowney.com*). For decades K&D has operated first-class safari camps around Botswana.

The company specializes in fine lodges and equipment as well as some of the best guides in the business. But be prepared to pay: A one-week tent safari with K&D runs about $3,200 per person.

SOUTH AFRICA
The Safari Frontier

Since its emergence as a democratic state, South Africa has become a popular destination for safari adventuring. Its expansive wildlands harbor large and vast herds of game and its parks have not suffered the heavy tourism that has plagued parts of Kenya and Tanzania.

South Africa is a land of remarkable diversity. The country boasts a range of distinct ecosystems that span subtropical forest to arid desert to temperate grasslands, where the large herds roam.

The lands preserved within South Africa's 17 national parks are also widely varied. In the northeast sector lies **Kruger National Park.** One of the continent's largest and most diverse wildlife reserves, Kruger boasts more mammal species than any other park in Africa. It is also home to countless birds, reptiles, and amphibians. Established in 1926, Kruger is ranked internationally as a model of wildlife management.

You'll find plenty to do at this park. Kruger has an excellent trail network. You can hike on your own or join a ranger-guided bush walk. If a self-drive excursion appeals, this is a good place to do it. Maps are available at park entrances and the roads are well posted. Among the wildlife you can expect to see here are Cape buffalo, elephants, leopards, giraffes, lions, rhino, impala, and antelope.

Twenty-one camps are located within the park. Accommodations range from camping to luxury-style, air-conditioned guest lodges, complete with restaurants, shops, and swimming pools.

Walking safaris and nighttime game drives are popular in the many private reserves adjacent to Kruger, including **Sabi Sabi, Mala Mala,** and **Londolozi.** The wildlife viewing on these private tracts is as good as you'll find at Kruger, so be sure to include them in your safari itinerary.

Kalahari Gemsbok National Park, an untamed wilderness region in the north, is another popular safari destination. Here you'll find rugged, semidesert dominated by vast, red-sand dunes, grassy plains, and a scattering of acacia trees.

The park shares an unfenced boundary with an equally rugged sanctuary in Botswana, which facilitates seasonal game migrations. Resident wildlife includes the Kalahari lion, blue wildebeest, eland, springbok, red hartebeest, leopard, and cheetah.

Roads in Kalahari park run along dry riverbeds and across relatively open terrain, presenting excellent opportunities for wildlife observation and photography.

The best times to visit this region are between March and May, when temperatures are moderate, or in September and October. During this time, you'll see the largest herds of animals.

Accommodations at three main camps consist of rustic cabins and campgrounds with bathroom facilities and camp stores. Cars are available for rent but should be reserved well in advance.

To the east near the Indian Ocean, **Phinda Resource Reserve** (*Conservation Corporation Reservations Office, Sun-*

ninghill Park. 011-27-11-803-8421) is one of South Africa's biggest success stories. Owned and operated by the Conservation Corporation, Phinda Resource Reserve exemplifies what can be accomplished with enlightened wildlife-management policies. The reserve boasts high-quality lodges and unique scenery.

When it comes to booking a trip to South Africa, one of the finest tour agencies is **David Anderson Safaris** *(30 W. Mission, Santa Barbara, CA 93101. 800-927-4647 or 805-563-7943. www.davidanderson.com)*. An experienced safari leader in East and southern Africa, director David Anderson knows all the game parks and he visits South Africa regularly to review safari camps.

A two-week customized safari that includes Kruger National Park, private game reserves, and Cape Town, ranges from $4,000 to $6,250 per person, excluding airfare.

A smaller, but also excellent agency, is **Fish Eagle Safaris** *(11191 Westheimer, No. 349, Houston, TX 77042. 800-513-5222 or 713-467-5222. www.fisheaglesafaris.com)*. Run by South African Bert du Plessis, Fish Eagle offers a variety of trips. The daily cost starts at about $200 per person.

Highly recommended is the fly-in safari, an 11-day adventure at $2,850 per person. Fish Eagle designs custom safaris with multiple-destination itineraries, so you can explore South Africa's parks as well as those in Botswana, Namibia (see p. 193), or elsewhere.

Multi-destination combo safaris are also a specialty of **African Travel** *(1100 E. Broadway, Glendale, CA 91205. 800-421-8907 or 818-507-7893. www.africantravelinc. com/MainIndex/MainIndex.html)*. This company represents many of South Africa's top private parks, plus **Gametrackers** luxury safari camps in Botswana.

To make reservations at one of South Africa's national parks, contact **South African National Parks** *(01127-12-343-1991. www.parks-sa.co.za)*. General tourist information regarding travel in South Africa is available on the Web *(www.southafrica.net)*.

ADVENTURE SAFARIS
Treks Atop Elephant and Camel

If sitting in a Jeep or a minivan doesn't exactly satisfy your adventure craving, forget about a conventional safari and consider a classic bush safari that puts you in the driver's seat—on an elephant or a camel. Imagine viewing the wilds of Botswana atop a regal pachyderm or traveling through the Kenyan countryside by camel convoy.

There are many advantages to a nonmotorized safari. First, traveling with animals allows you to venture into untracked bush. It also allows you to get closer to animals in the wild, including elusive species.

Second, many seasoned travelers feel that the more

leisurely pace of an animal safari is better suited to the African milieu than is a motorized trip.

Third, the higher perch afforded by your camel or elephant mount frankly offers a better vantage point for viewing animals in the field.

In the southwestern part of Botswana's **Okavango Delta, Elephant Back Safaris** conducts a unique program from its Abu Camp on the banks of the **Nxabega River**.

Thirteen well-trained elephants mounted with comfortable riding platforms each carry two guests on day-long excursions into the wild. Every evening you return to the comfort of a deluxe tent camp. The six-day elephant safari costs $6,500 per person.

The program is directed by noted wildlife conservationist Randall Moore, a leading force in the preservation of African elephant habitats. Animal welfare is also a high priority: All of the elephants used in the EBS program were orphans. They were shipped to the United States for training, then returned to Africa.

In recognition of its conservation efforts, EBS was awarded a 15-year lease on 500,000 acres of some of Africa's most pristine land.

EBS also offers daytime and nighttime wildlife expeditions with transport provided by four-wheel-drive vehicles. The company also runs a trip through the Okavango Delta in dugout canoes.

For more information about this and other EBS programs, contact **Esplanade Tours** *(581 Boylston St., Boston, MA 02116. 800-426-5492 or 617-266-7465)*. In Africa, contact **Elephant Back Safaris** *(Private Bag 333, Maun, Botswana. 01126-766-1260)*.

A less costly—but equally exotic—alternative safari is a camel expedition. **SafariCentre International** *(800-223-6046. www.safaricentre.com)* runs a six-day **Samburu Camel Safari** in Kenya, accompanied by Masai handlers.

This rugged camping adventure takes you into the remote northern frontier district of **Lewa Downs Conservancy** and across Samburu tribal lands. The expedition costs $1,550 per person.

If you prefer a shorter trek, **Baobab Safari Company** *(210 Post St., Suite 911, San Francisco, CA 94108. 800-835-3692 or 415-391-5788. www.baobabsafaris.com)* offers a fun, three-day camel safari in northern Tanzania.

Camel safaris are a relatively new activity in this beautiful region, where you are treated to a spectacular backdrop of snow-capped Mount Kilimanjaro. From a scenic base camp at the foot of **Mount Meru,** participants do a loop tour across the veld.

Note that this is primarily a hiking trip. Although you do get to ride the camels, they are used principally as pack animals. The cost is $950 per person.

Mount Kilimanjaro Diversion

Snow-capped and solitary, Mount Kilimanjaro is a dramatic backdrop for many East African safaris. Rising 19,340 feet above the Tanzanian plain, Africa's highest peak dominates the horizon for miles around and stands as a symbol of the continent. Kilimanjaro is also an adventure destination in itself—and an ideal detour for climbers on safari.

Suprisingly, Kilimanjaro is the easiest of the world's great peaks to climb. The summit can be reached in a few days by any reasonably fit person—and you don't need to have previous mountaineering experience.

The ascent is a study in contrasting ecosystems. From the dry savannah base, you hike through rain forest and moorlands, and eventually arrive at a mile-wide, snow-covered caldera. When you reach the nearly four-mile-high summit, you feel as though you've been transported to another continent—and the panoramic view is breathtaking.

You can organize your own ascent, starting from either the northwestern (Kenyan) or the southern (Tanzanian) flank. You will need to acclimate yourself to the high elevations, so plan to spend a couple of days at an altitude between 9,000 and 12,000 feet.

Although Kilimanjaro has no steep pitches that require special technical skills or equipment, it helps to have some alpine experience. Good boots are a must. An ice ax is useful as you spend at least two days hiking through snow with some icy stretches.

Foreign climbers must hire a local guide. You can find one, as well as porters to carry your gear, through the **Marangu Hotel** (011-255-55-51307). The best times to climb Kilimanjaro are January through March and July through October.

If you prefer to climb with an organized group, **Journeys** (*Ann Arbor, MI. 800-255-8735 or 313-665-4407. www.journeys-intl.com*) offers a seven-day trip that departs from **Arusha** in Tanzania. The cost—including guide, porters, and provisions—is about $1,400 per person.

A good second choice is **Mountain Madness** (*Seattle, WA. 800-328-5925 or 206-937-8389. www. mountainmadness.com*). This agent's 11-day climb costs $3,350 and is offered year-round.

If you want to climb 17,058-foot **Mount Kenya** as well, **Himalayan Travel** (*Stamford, CT. 800-225-2380 or 203-359-3711. www.gorp.com/himtravel.htm*) offers a 17-day, twin-peak expedition for $2,850. This company can also add a wildlife safari to your climbing expedition at reasonable cost.

The best reference for a Kilimanjaro expedition is *Kilimanjaro and Mount Kenya: A Climbing and Trekking Guide* by Cameron M. Burns (Mountaineers, 1998, $18.95).

For an entertaining and informative account of a Kilimanjaro expedition, log on to *Chris Wee's Internet African Journal* (*http://seclab.cs.ucdavis.edu/~wee/east-africa.html*).

YELLOW-BILLED STORK, MOREMI WILDLIFE RESERVE

EAST AFRICA
Masters Photo Safaris

All safaris cater to some extent to photography because almost everyone wants to take pictures. If you're really serious about getting those once-in-a-lifetime shots, though, consider a specialized photo safari led by a recognized wildlife photographer. You spend more time in the field under the best shooting conditions. (Especially in Africa, it's the light that makes the magic.)

Before choosing a photo tour, check the itinerary. Make sure that you'll be viewing the species you want to shoot. Determine the guest-to-guide ratio; it should be less than six to one.

Ask about equipment: Does the tour operator provide tripods and specialty lenses? Find out what you get for the price; photo tours are expensive and should include food, lodging, and all ground transportation.

Bring two, if not three, camera bodies to save time, avoid dust contamination, and eliminate the hassle of frequent lens changing (see sidebar, p. 189).

A leading operator is **Joseph Van Os Photo Safaris** (*Vashon Island, WA. 206-463-5383. www.photosafaris.com*). The Van Os photographer-guides are world-class—and Joe personally leads many of the African trips. The company limits the number of photographers to three per vehicle.

Trips are scheduled to ensure the best conditions for wildlife viewing. Unfortunately, Van Os runs just one or two African photo safaris a year, so book early. The cost varies; a 16-day Kenya safari runs about $6,000 per person.

Another top agent, **Voyagers International** (*Ithaca, NY. 800-633-0299 or 607-273-4321. www.voyagers.com*) offers specialized photo safaris in **Kenya, Tanzania, Botswana, Namibia,** and **Zimbabwe.** Founder Dave Blanton served in the Peace Corps in East Africa for two years and worked as a photographer-writer in Nairobi for five years.

Voyager's safaris are designed by and for photographers. Professional shooters lead the trips. Locations are scouted in advance and schedules coincide with major migrations. You aren't rushed from place to place, either; clients can spend long days in the field to capture the best light at dawn and in late afternoon.

A typical two-week photo safari ranges from about $4,000 to $5,000 per person, plus airfare.

Rafiki Safaris (*Camden, ME. 207-236-4244. www.gorp.com/rafiki*), which operates in Kenya and in Tanzania, is a good choice for travelers who wish to combine wildlife photography with other activities, such as bird-watching, walking tours, or night game drives.

Rafiki specializes in birding, with services provided by its partner company in Africa, **East African Ornithological Safaris.**

Itineraries include visits to many of Africa's most exclusive wildlife areas rarely visited by conventional tours. Highlights include **Rukinga Wildlife Conservancy** in Tsavo, **Delamere Camp** near Lake Nakuru, and **Mara River Camp**. In most of these locations, participants can pursue the perfect shot during day or night bush walks with trained local naturalists.

Although Land Rovers are used as transport, you are not confined to a vehicle as you would be on many conventional driving safaris. The cost for a 13-day trip starts at about $3,000 per person.

How to Shoot on Safari

There's no doubt that a safari is an extraordinary adventure. For the photographer, it can also be a lot of work. You're up early and out late in the field to catch the light, burdened with cameras and long lenses. What preparations should you make to maximize your comfort?

When it comes to clothing, think comfortable—and practical. The roads are dusty beyond belief. And "formal" at most game lodges means a clean shirt at best.

Jeans or khakis, a long-sleeved shirt, a sweatshirt and windbreaker (it can get cool at night in game parks at higher elevations), and a good hat are about all you need. Add toiletries, sun- block, and a pair of small binoculars.

Cameras

Don't take any equipment that you have not tested out at home first. Make sure it's all working—and make sure you know how to use it. The Serengeti is no place to learn what all those buttons really do. Run several rolls through the camera, practice loading and rewinding film, and test that new lens.

Don't even think of going to Africa with only one camera. Bring at least two bodies, preferably with motor drives; a third body for backup wouldn't hurt. You'll probably be happiest with one standard body and one autofocus.

If your one and only camera quits, you're out of luck. For practical purposes, there will be no possibility of camera repair on your safari. Take lots of batteries for the camera and motor drives. Such things will not be available in safari country.

Lenses

You won't need many short focal lengths. A medium wide-angle or a normal lens in the 35- to 50-mm range will do—particularly if you have a popular camera model and can borrow a true wide-angle lens for one or two shots. Other-

wise, slip a small 28-mm lens in your bag.

Absolutely bring a zoom in the 80- to 200-mm or 70- to 210-mm range. Zooms are great for safaris; you'll be doing most of your shooting from vehicles and the ability to crop in the camera is paramount.

Bring any big lenses you have. If you double up on any focal lengths, make it the long ones. The most useful lens is a reasonably fast, 400-mm, f3.5 or f4 lens. A 300-mm lens is worth bringing as well.

A 200- to 400-mm zoom, such as the f4 Nikon, can be ideal, particularly if it has constant aperture throughout the zoom range.

By all means bring a 1.4X teleconverter. This will take your 300-mm to 420-mm, offering great versatility.

Accessories

Pack your camera gear in a good case and carry it on the plane. You'll fit more into a soft, padded bag than a foam-filled, hard-sided case. Also, look for a bag with a zipper-close top as well as a large overflap. This feature enables you to leave the top unzipped for easy access, while the flap will keep the dust out when you're in the field.

Pack a tripod in your suitcase. You'll want it at the lodges, but it's useless in the vehicles. For working out of a van, bring a bean bag about the size of a loaf of bread. Window mounts work fine, but bean bags are more handy and versatile.

One important item is a dust bag in which you can keep your camera ready with long lens attached but avoid a coating of dust. A finely woven pillowcase works fine if you keep it clean.

Clean your camera nightly. Take a squeeze-bulb blower, lens tissue, lens cleaner, some Q-tips, and an old toothbrush for cleaning.

Film

Take whatever you normally like to shoot. You don't really need several kinds of film, although you may want to take some print film and some slides.

Pack double the amount you think you would use. An absolute minimum would be three rolls per day in the field. You can always bring film back with you, but don't count on buying any in Africa. Take all your film home as carry-on luggage and ask for a hand inspection.

A final tip on getting the shots you'll prize for a lifetime is to shoot freely when you have a good subject and the conditions are right. Film expense is but a tiny fraction of the cost of your trip. The attitude you should have is that your next shot will be the definitive photo of your subject.

WATER HOLE AT SUNSET IN BOTSWANA'S CHOBE NATIONAL PARK

Safari So Good

The key to getting the most from your safari adventure is choosing the right outfitter to suit your style and comfort quotient. Do your research—and ask lots of questions. Listed below are recommended outfitters in North America. Most agents contract with African guide services who actually run the tours in country.

If you're prepared to shell out $3,500 to $8,000 for a couple of weeks on a safari holiday, you owe it to yourself to comparison shop.

Don't assume that the most expensive trip is necessarily the best: Competing outfitters often offer virtually the same safaris —for a surprisingly wide range of prices. Moreover, many domestic safari companies employ the same guides and overland services in Kenya and Tanzania.

And be reasonable: If you're going to travel all the way to Africa—and really see something of the place—you need to stay a minimum of two weeks.

You should plan to visit more than one country, if possible. Look for an itinerary that combines multiple destinations: Kenya and Tanzania, for example, or Tanzania and Botswana.

It's also a good idea to find a trip that offers additional activities to riding around in a van for five to ten days. Some companies, for instance, feature balloon rides, canoe trips, or flight-seeing as options.

Chances are you will be spending a fair amount of time on the move. Ask how many people are assigned to a vehicle.

Be realistic about what you are looking for and what you can afford. If you prefer to stay in luxury lodges, go with an elite outfitter, such as Ker & Downey (Botswana) or Abercrombie & Kent (Kenya, Tanzania).

If you want a more physically challenging safari trip that might include a walk in the bush or an ascent of Mount Kilimanjaro or Mount Kenya, Mountain Travel-Sobek or the Adventure Center would be your best bets.

Read the brochures carefully; many "16-day safaris" can in reality mean as few as 11 days in the wild—with the remainder of the time spent in a city hotel or on an airplane.

Finally, and certainly not least, you should determine how close to the animals you'll really get and what species you can actually expect to see. After all, that's the reason you're going on safari.

Experienced adventure travelers may find organized tours too soft, too pricey, and too insulated from Africa's edgier side. If your inclination is to rough it rather than to luxuriate, consider custom designing your own safari for a more personally rewarding experience (see pp. 192-94).

Abercrombie & Kent
1520 Kensington Rd., Suite 212, Oak Brook, IL 60521 800-323-7308 or 630-954-2944
www.abercrombiekent.com

This is an upper-end operation, with years of experience in Africa. Trips are deluxe—and the prices reflect it. Customer service is excellent. Unlike most other agencies, Abercrombie & Kent operates many of its own facilities in Africa.

African Travel, Inc.
1100 E. Broadway, Glendale, CA 91205
800-421-8907 or 818-507-7893
www.africantravel.com/MainIndex/
MainIndex.html

With nearly three decades of experience, African Travel is highly recommended for Botswana, Namibia, and southern Africa. It also represents Gametrackers, a collection of luxury camps in Botswana. A wide range of prices is offered.

Adventure Center
1311 63rd St., Suite 200, Emeryville, CA 94608 800-227-8747 or 510-654-1879
www.adventurecenter.com

Adventure Center runs reasonably priced trips for many excellent foreign outfitters. It is one of the few agencies offering multi-nation, four-wheel-drive overland safaris. As a plus, the company employs specialists with extensive African travel experience.

Baobab Safari Company
210 Post St., Suite 911, San Francisco, CA 94108. 800-835-3692 or 415-391-5788
www.baobabsafaris.com

Baobab, formerly AfricaTours, conducts wildlife safaris to the continent's more remote regions. The company's African itineraries tend to avoid the most heavily touristed game parks. Camel treks are a unique feature.

Big Five Tours and Expeditions, Ltd.
1551 S.E. Palm Ct., Stuart, FL 34994
800-244-3483 or 561-287-7995
www.bigfive.com

Operating since 1973, Big Five is a good, general agency, with its own guides and vehicles. It specializes in photo tours throughout **East** and **southern Africa,** plus many programs in **Egypt** and **Ethiopia.** Big Five maintains offices in **Kenya, Tanzania,** and **South Africa.**

Borton Overseas
5412 Lyndale Ave. S., Minneapolis, MN 55419
800-843-0602 or 612-822-4640
www.bortonoverseas.com

A top outfitter for **Tanzania,** Borton runs its own show in East Africa. The company's unique *Roots* safari visits locations mentioned in Alex Haley's popular book. Inquire about gorilla safaris in **Uganda.**

David Anderson Safaris
30 W. Mission, Santa Barbara, CA 93101
800-927-4647 or 805-563-7943
www.davidanderson.com

This experienced safari agency offers customized safaris in Africa for a discerning clientele. Director David Anderson regularly visits Africa's best game parks and is extremely knowledgeable about the region.

Esplanade Tours
581 Boylston St., Boston, MA 02116
800-426-5492 or 617-266-7465

In business since 1954, Esplanade arranges African travel from Egypt to South Africa, including elephant-back safaris. Esplanade offers a diverse tour catalog.

Fish Eagle Safaris
11191 Westheimer, No. 349, Houston, TX 77042 800-513-5222 or 713-467-5222
www.fisheaglesafaris.com

Fish Eagle Safaris specializes in southern Africa: Botswana, Namibia, and South Africa. Company founder Bert du Plessis, a South African, custom designs wilderness safaris led by the region's top guides. Other destinations include Kenya, Malawi, Mozambique, Tanzania, Uganda, Zambia, and Zimbabwe.

Himalayan Travel

110 Prospect St., Stamford, CT 06901
800-225-2380 or 203-359-3711
www.gorp.com/himtravel.htm

Like the Adventure Center, Himalayan
Travel principally offers value-oriented
trips for established foreign safari operators. Overland expeditions and camping
safaris are also a speciality.

International Expeditions

1 Environs Park, Helena, AL 35080
800-633-4734 or 205-428-1700
www.ietravel.com

International Expeditions offers serious
wildlife tours featuring trained naturalist
guides—and plenty of time in the bush.
This is a good choice for serious wildlife-
watchers. The company also runs unique
cultural and environmental workshops.
These include hands-on construction and
agriculture projects with local villagers.

Ker & Downey

2825 Wilcrest Dr., Suite 600, Houston, TX
77042
800-423-4236 or 713-917-0048
www.kerdowney.com
In Botswana:
P.O. Box 27, Maun, Botswana
01126-766-0375.

Ker & Downey runs its own programs and
offers a variety of safaris at medium to high
prices. Nobody does **Botswana** better,
where K&D operates private camps. The
company also represents many of the best
lodges in **East** and **southern Africa.**

Mountain Travel-Sobek

6420 Fairmont Ave., El Cerrito, CA 94530
888-687-6235 or 510-527-8100
www.mtsobek.com

MTS offers some of the more unique itineraries, from **Zimbabwe** walking safaris
to **Kilimanjaro** expeditions to raft trips
on the **Zambezi River.**

Overseas Adventure Travel

347 Congress St., Boston, MA 02210
800-493-6824 or 617-346-6799
www.oattravel.com

OAT is a major player in the safari market,
with its own offices and guides in **South
Africa.** The company offers a broad range of
African trips, from rugged to luxurious. It
generally caters to an older clientele.

SafariCentre International

3201 N. Sepulveda Blvd.
Manhattan Beach, CA 90266
800-223-6046 or 310-546-4411
www.safaricentre.com

SafariCentre offers a wide selection of

UNEXPECTED CAMP VISITOR AT
NGALA GAME RESERVE, SOUTH AFRICA

safaris, from economy to deluxe. This is a good choice for the budget traveler or for those seeking something different, such as a four-wheel-drive overland safari or a camel trek.

Wilderness Travel

1102 Ninth St., Berkeley, CA 94710
800-368-2794 or 510-558-2488
www.wildernesstravel.com

This popular company has good safari guides and exciting itineraries, including a **Kilimanjaro** climb, a canoeing trip down **Zimbabwe's Zambezi River,** and walking safaris in **Zambia.** Prices are fairly high.

Wildlife Safari

346 Rheem Blvd., Moraga, CA 94556
800-221-8118 or 925-376-5595
www.wildlife-safari.com

This well-established broker offers mainly medium- to high-end trips to all popular safari destinations. Flight-seeing safaris are a specialty.

Safari Destinations

If you are designing your own African safari, use this shorthand list to help plan the ideal itinerary. The sites were selected based on the quantity and the variety of observable wildlife. Since crowds can spoil any safari, the emphasis here is on lesser known regions, where tourism may be low but the game-watching is outstanding.

BOTSWANA

Chobe National Park

Chobe remains an untouched wilderness where game runs free. At least for now, the park is not yet overrun with safari tourism. A particularly scenic area, Chobe's hallmark is large herds of elephant and sable antelope, plus strong populations of giraffe. Some lions and cheetahs follow the antelope herds, and you can also expect to see white rhino, although their numbers are small.

Okavango Delta

The Okavango Delta, a 7,000-square-mile inland floodplain, contains one of the richest concentrations of wildlife in Africa. On the plains graze large herds of buffalo, kudu, oryx, and sable antelope. In the waters of the delta—which can be traversed only by dugout canoes, or *mokoros*—you'll find crocodiles and countless hippos. Elephants, lions, and leopards are common, but in lesser numbers than in the large game parks of Tanzania.

DEMOCRATIC REPUBLIC OF THE CONGO

Virunga National Park

The nation's first national park is also one of the most well-planned preserves in Africa. Known for its beautiful moun-

African Safaris

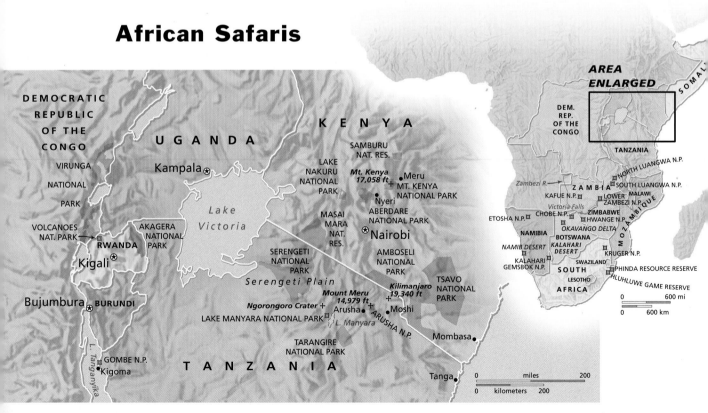

tains, lakes, and rivers, Virunga is also notable for its large and diverse wildlife populations. The number of resident hippos, for example, is at least 30,000—a world-class count. Along the park's many waterways, you'll find thousands of water buffalos and five species of antelope. Monkeys and baboons gather in the forest. Gorilla safaris have been offered in the **Virunga Mountains** area, although Uganda is now probably your best bet for observing mountain gorillas. Hundreds of bird species nest in the park, while elephants, lions, and leopards are present in limited numbers.

KENYA

Amboseli Reserve

Kenya's Amboseli Reserve lies beneath snowcapped Mount Kilimanjaro. Although the reserve is quite dry, there are many water holes, which attract elephants, rhinos, lions, giraffes, and countless bird species. Because of its plethora of permanent lodges and its proximity to Nairobi, however, Amboseli suffers from heavy tourism and lacks some of the wilderness ambience found at other sites. Still, it's worth a visit just to see Kilimanjaro—best done at dawn or at dusk.

Lake Nakuru

Centrally located in the Great Rift Valley, Lake Nakuru is famed for its huge flocks of lesser and greater pink flamingos. (More than half of the world's five million flamingos nest here, concentrated at the lake.) The soda lake is ringed by acacia groves and dense forest. You see herds of waterbuck, gazelle, and impala at water's edge, along with many shorebirds, including pelicans, storks, and fish eagle. Giraffe herds range close by. Lake Nakuru was recently designated as a sanctuary for the endangered black rhino.

Masai Mara Reserve

Situated on the northern edge of the Serengeti Plain at an elevation of 5,200 feet, the Mara justly enjoys its fame as one of the few remaining areas in Africa where you can still see game in vast numbers. The diverse terrain—savanna, forests, rolling hills, and water courses—supports a wide variety of animals, including the big cats—lions, leopards, and cheetahs—which prey on migrating herds. If you visit during the August wildebeest migration, you can see

as many as 150,000 animals in one area. The Masai Mara is also home to virtually all of the other major players—elephants, rhino, giraffes, zebras, and gazelles.

Mount Kenya National Park

At 17,058 feet, Mount Kenya is East Africa's second highest summit. The surrounding lowlands and foothills, with their lakes and rain forest and dense woodlands, encompass one of Kenya's most scenic regions. This is one of the best spots in East Africa for a walking tour. Although the game viewing is not as good as that at Samburu or Masai Mara to the south, you can still expect to see elephant, buffalo, bushback, and a rhino or two if you're lucky. If you can afford it, stay at the Mount Kenya Safari Club, a classic colonial-era lodge—one of the best in Africa.

Samburu Reserve

Samburu, together with nearby Buffalo Springs and Shaba, compose what many consider the best game-viewing area north of Nairobi. Hence, most Kenyan safari itineraries include a stop at Samburu. All the major big game species are here, plus hippos and crocodiles. There are large herds of zebra and antelope, many giraffes, and ostriches are quite common. Try to visit a Samburu village. The women wear elaborate, colorful necklaces, and the tribal dances are inspiring, to say the least.

Tsavo National Park

A huge (8,034 square miles) and very arid park, Tsavo boasts some of Africa's largest elephant herds, but they can be hard to locate. Tsavo West, dominated by the Yatta Plateau, an ancient lava flow, contains the more interesting terrain, but you'll see more wildlife in Tsavo East, which consists of mostly open savanna. Along with elephants, look for rhino, lions, and lesser kudus. Don't miss the Mzima Springs oasis, where hippos and crocodiles can be viewed from a submerged tank and observation platform.

NAMIBIA

Etosha National Park

One of the world's largest game parks, but still not widely known, Etosha is what Kenya and Tanzania were 25 years ago. Centered around the Etosha Pan, a 72-mile-long lake bed, the park contains a number of spring-fed water holes that

attract a variety of animals throughout the year. You'll see large populations of kudus, wildebeest, oryx, and zebras, along with elephants, lions, springbok, giraffes, ostriches, cheetahs, and leopards. With less human intrusion in their environment, the animals here are relaxed, affording excellent photo opportunities.

Namib Desert; Damaraland

The otherworldly landscape of the Namib Desert is quite unlike anything else in Africa. Here you find a landscape of massive dunes, high mesas, and giant rock formations. The world's tallest sand dunes, piled hundreds of feet high, stand at Sossusvlei. At Sandwich Harbor, huge hills of red sand tower above a lagoon, where thousands of flamingos, pelicans, and other species congregate. North of the Kuiseb River, the sand gives way to the windswept isolation of the Skeleton Coast. Farther inland is Damaraland. A region of dramatic contrasts—desert, grasslands, high mountains—it is home to elephants, springbok, rhino, and the rare Hartmann's mountain zebra.

SOUTH AFRICA

Hluhluwe Game Reserve

In the heart of Zululand lies the Hluhluwe Game Reserve, home of the famous white rhino and shy, deer-like nyala. Along with these animals, you will also find buffalo, antelope, elephant, and other species. The large herds of elephant favor the dense forests around the reserve. Located just southeast of Swaziland, Hluhluwe boasts seven distinct ecosystems, which range from mountain bushveld to wetlands. The best time to visit Hluhluwe is after the severe heat in early fall, when the animals gather in herds.

Kruger National Park

One of the largest wildlife reserves in Africa, Kruger National Park is known for the abundance and diversity of its fauna. Bush walks and game drives are excellent ways to view the "big five": elephants, lions, leopards, rhino, and buffalo. The park's distinct ecosystems also harbor a great variety of smaller species. In and adjacent to Kruger are several private, richly populated game reserves, including Londolozi, Singita, and Ngala. These are under the jurisdiction of particular semi-exclusive safari companies. If you visit during South Africa's summer (*Dec.-March*), expect thunderstorms.

TANZANIA

Gombe National Park

If you want to see chimpanzees in the wild, Gombe, one of Tanzania's lesser known parks, is probably your best bet. But be aware that these elusive creatures are a good deal harder to locate than the gorillas of Rwanda or Zaire. Another chimpanzee habitat in Tanzania that you may also wish to explore is Mahale Mountains National Park.

Lake Manyara National Park

Situated in Tanzania's Rift Valley, Lake Manyara is known for its big cats and abundant birds. The park's numerous lions often rest high above ground in the acacia trees, although this habit seems to have been discouraged somewhat by increased numbers of tourists. This relatively small park also boasts the highest concentration of elephants in East Africa—but don't expect to see them roaming anywhere near the permanent lodges. Lake Manyara's alkaline waters attract many types of birds; more than 340 species have been observed in the park. Monkeys and baboons also abound in this region. For some great photos, head for a hippo pool, where you'll see these creatures cavorting in the mud, while zebras, giraffes, and buffalo gather nearby.

Ngorongoro Crater

A one-of-a-kind wildlife preserve, Ngorongoro was once the site of the world's largest volcano—a giant cone more than three times the height of MountEverest. In a catastrophic explosion, the volcano erupted, leaving a huge, 100-square-mile crater with a rim reaching to 7,000 feet. The crater now harbors the largest concentration of nonmigratory wildlife in Africa. Across the plains of the crater roam huge herds of wildebeest, antelope, and zebra, which, in turn, attract predatory lions, leopards, and cheetahs. The crater's lakes and flowing waters abound with hippos and waterfowl. Protected by the high rim, elephants and rhino have managed not only to elude poachers, but to proliferate in great numbers. For optimal proximity to the animals, opt for a tent-camping safari in the heart of the crater. You can also stay at one of the luxury lodges along the rim.

Serengeti National Park

Perhaps the most famous of all the African game parks, the Serengeti adjoins Masai Mara Reserve to the north. Encompassing more than 5,000 square miles of savanna and plain, the Serengeti is unrivaled when it comes to sheer numbers of migratory animals and big game—more than 35 species—as well as 350 types of birds. You'll find antelope of all varieties, and huge herds of gazelle, zebra, and wildebeest. The Serengeti Plain boasts more lions than any other reserve in Africa, and leopards and cheetahs also abound. A must for any Tanzanian itinerary.

Tarangire National Park

Tanzania's newest—and wildest—game reserve, Tarangire is refreshingly free of development. The park offers fine game viewing, especially along the Tarangire River, where elephants, lions, buffalo, and kudus mingle in cooling, muddy pools. Whether you're an ornithologist or just a bird lover, you're in for a treat: The resident bird population exceeds more than 260 species, including the bateleur eagle, the secretary bird, and the Masai ostrich.

ZAMBIA

South Luangwa National Park

The Luangwa Valley—part of the 6,000-mile-long Great Rift Valley—is known as the Valley of the Elephants. Along with its impressive pachyderm herds, this wild—and little-known— 3,500-square-mile reserve also boasts significant populations of hippos and crocodiles. The Luangwa River, which runs through the center of this outstanding park, has numerous lagoons and mud holes. At any time of year, you're sure to see a variety of animals gathered at these watering holes.

ZIMBABWE

Victoria Falls

Twice as high as Niagara Falls and more than a mile wide, Victoria Falls is considered one of the Seven Wonders of the World. Locally known as Mosi-oa-Tunya—"the smoke that thunders"—the falls were discovered in 1855 by explorer David Livingstone and they were named in honor of Queen Victoria. You can approach Victoria Falls either from Zambia or from Zimbabwe. Many Botswana safaris include a trip to the falls as an optional feature.

While you're in the area, a flight-seeing excursion over the falls is highly recommended. If you're looking for something more physically challenging, popular activities include rafting the Class V Zambezi River or bungee jumping from Victoria Falls Bridge.

Travel Tips

What to Bring

Pack lightweight and durable cotton clothes, comfortable walking shoes, two pairs of quality sunglasses, and a hat for the sun. Pack a sweater or a windbreaker for the evenings, which can be quite cool in the highlands. If you happen to travel during the rainy season (April and May in Kenya), a small folding umbrella will come in handy. Guests at luxury lodges should take one "better" outfit (a sport coat and a tie for men, a lightweight dress for women). Bring all the personal items you will need; items such as cosmetics and medicines are difficult to obtain. If possible, limit your luggage to one medium-size bag under 25 pounds, plus a day pack or a shoulder bag.

Ground Transport

Virtually all safari operators transport their guests in small minivans or in Land Rovers. If the vehicle is seriously overcrowded, it can spoil your entire vacation. Ask your outfitter the maximum number of persons assigned per vehicle. Some outfitters guarantee a window seat—a good practice. For taking photographs, open safari trucks are preferable; however, they are less comfortable than minivans in the heat and dust.

When to Go

Kenya/Tanzania

Most tourists visit Kenya and Tanzania in the winter months, June through August, when temperatures moderate to highs in the 70s and lows in the 50s. Highly recommended, though, are the spring months—September through November. This is a great time to see blossoms and newborn animals, and temperatures are still tolerable in the upper 80s. December through March on the plains is hot—90° to 100°F—but it's actually pleasant in the higher altitudes, where many of the game reserves are located. Summer is the time of the great migra-

tions on the Serengeti—a good reason to brave the heat. Although April and May are considered the rainy months, the weather rarely turns severe and you benefit from off-season rates and fewer tourists.

Botswana

Avoid Botswana during the worst of the rainy season—generally late December through February—when the Okavango Delta is heavily flooded. The best time to visit the delta is April through June, when animals congregate around the watering holes. The weather is generally good and temperatures are moderate from April through November.

Namibia

The prime time for a visit to Namibia is in September or October. Game herds have gathered and the wildflowers are in bloom. This is also the season to see newborn animals. The least crowded period is the summer rainy season, from November through March. You'll encounter fewer tourists then, but the wildlife also tends to be more dispersed. Water holes at Etosha are most active during the dry season, from April until the rains come. Weather conditions along the rugged Skeleton Coast can be cold and windy at anytime of the year.

South Africa

While South Africa is a year-round destination, most safari visitors prefer to travel during the spring season, September through November, or in the fall, March through May, to avoid the worst heat. Animal viewing is best in the winter months, June through August, when the watering holes are active. September is the month for wildflower blooms. Safari destinations in the interior, such as Kruger National Park, see thundershowers during the summer months of January and February, while coastal regions, such as Capetown, get rain in the winter.

ONLINE

Africa Travel Desk
www.africadesk.com

This site covers Botswana, Malawi, Namibia, South Africa, Swaziland, Tanzania, Uganda, Zambia, and Madagascar. Search by geographical location or by type of safari.

Classic Safari Camps of Africa
www.classicsafaricamps.com

The website's detailed descriptions and photographs of dozens of quality tent camps and lodges allow you to check out potential accommodations before you book.

OnSafari.com
www.onsafari.com

A comprehensive, one-stop resource for all things safari, this site features numerous photos and maps. This one is definitely worth a bookmark.

Travel Organization: Africa
www.travel.org/africa1.html

A very extensive travel resource where you'll find profiles of more than 50 African nations, plus maps, travel reports, and health information.

BOOKS

The African Safari: The Ultimate Wildlife and Photographic Adventure by P. Jay Fetner (St. Martins Press, 1989, $60) is the most complete resource for safaris throughout Africa.

Lonely Planet East Africa by Hugh Finlay (Lonely Planet, 2000, $24.95) is an essential guide to Kenya, Tanzania, Zaire, and Botswana.

Field Guide to the National Parks of East Africa by J. G. Williams (Collins Press, 1988, $25) is the best standard text available on big-game viewing in Kenya and Tanzania.

Fielding's African Safaris (Fielding Travel Books, 1987, $18.95) provides comprehensive descriptions of dozens of African safaris for all budgets. The guide also contains valuable information on wildlife, health, and safety.

The Safari Companion by Richard Estes (*Chelsea Green, 1999, $25*) is an indispensable tool for safari travelers to Africa, with detailed information on African wildlife.

Guide to Southern Africa Game and Nature Reserves by Chris and Tilde Stuart (*Passport Books, 1997, $24.95*). This definitive resource describes transport, lodging, facilities, wildlife, and game seasons for 400 reserves in southern Africa.

YOUNG RANGER IN LAND ROVER AT NGALA GAME RESERVE

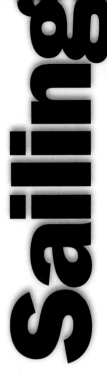

Sailing

ONE OF THE GREATEST PLEASURES IN LIFE, SAILING PRESENTS AN IMMENSE VARIETY OF POSSIBLE adventures when you consider that water covers three-quarters of the planet's surface. Bareboating—that is, skippering your own boat—is generally the least expensive sailing holiday, as well as the most liberating way to enjoy the wind and the water. Free to plan your own itinerary, you can sail when the wind is good and relax on a deserted beach when you want to take a break. • Operating a large yacht is not child's play, but most people with some keelboat experience will be allowed to charter a boat in a destination such as the Virgin Islands. You may have to bring a skipper aboard for the first day or two, however. • On pages 198-203, author Brian Fagan introduces you to seven nautical wonders of the world—the seven best bareboat-cruising grounds on the planet. You will also find a comprehensive chart that provides information on 29 of the world's greatest sailing destinations; a directory of recommended charter companies around the globe; a guide to windjammer cruises available worldwide; and, finally, a list of sailing schools.

LEFT: BAREBOAT-CHARTER SAILBOAT, BRITISH VIRGIN ISLANDS
BELOW: SEA SPRAY ON THE FOREDECK IN THE CARIBBEAN

Charters

Windjammers

Tall Ships

Bareboating

We must be at the helm at least once a day; we must feel the tiller-rope in our hands, and know that if we sail, we steer.
HENRY DAVID THOREAU

Charter Sailing Vacations

If you truly want to get away from it all—even from the confines of a land-based resort—a bareboat charter cruise is the ideal vacation. Hire a skipper for a few days if your cruising skills are rusty, or experiment with flotilla sailing, in which a group of boats follow a leader who handles the navigation chores. Fun can be had in any boat of 25 feet or larger, but we recommend a yacht in the 34- to 44-foot range. At this size, you can get private cabins for two or three couples—a modicum of privacy that will keep you all on speaking terms until the end of an extended cruise.

VIRGIN ISLANDS
Sailors' Cruising Mecca

Many cruising sailors call the **U.S. Virgin Islands (USVI)** and the **British Virgin Islands (BVI)** the best bareboating area in the world. These islands offer superlative sailing in relatively sheltered waters, predictable winds, exceptional diving and snorkeling, and a rich social life ashore.

A Virgin Island charter usually starts at **St. Thomas** in the USVI or at **Road Town** on **Tortola Island** in the BVI. St. Thomas and **St. John** lie at the southwest end of the **Sir Francis Drake Channel,** the waterway that bisects the Virgins. Mountainous Tortola dominates the north side of the channel, while a string of lesser islands, the largest of them **Virgin Gorda,** protects the south edge. Running east to west, the islands shelter you from the Atlantic swells that sweep toward the Lesser Antilles across thousands of miles of open ocean. Novice crews can thus enjoy trade-wind sailing in relatively flat water, with plenty of safe anchorages nearby.

For pure sailing fun, we recommend the beat to windward in the Sir Francis Drake Channel or the crossing from Tortola to nearby **Jost Van Dyke Island.** Wherever you sail, though, the choice of anchorages is endless. For evening entertainment, check out Foxy's Beach Bar on Jost Van Dyke or Stanley's at Cane Garden Bay on Tortola. You can also try such internationally famous resorts as the Bitter End on Virgin Gorda—the climax of many bareboat cruises. Anchor or moor offshore, and treat yourself to lobster at the resort.

Smart sailors work their way to windward against the prevailing trades from St. Thomas and Tortola over the first few days, then take their time sailing home downwind. This allows time to snorkel the wreck of the R.M.S. *Rhone* or to enjoy dinner at **Marina Cay,** where the evening social life is fast and furious. Sailors craving peace and quiet will find it at the Bight on **Norman Island,** alleged to be the prototype for Robert Louis Stevenson's *Treasure Island,* or in **Gorda Sound,** where your only companions will be sea creatures and the gentle sough of the trades.

During the high season (December through early April) you will encounter crowded anchorages and resorts. You'll also be confronted by a bewildering array of charter companies from which to choose. **The Moorings** (*19345 U.S. Hwy. 19 N., 4th floor, Clearwater, FL 33764. 800-535-7289 or 727-530-5424. www.moorings.com*) is famous for its fine service and large, well-maintained fleet, and it has the largest charter base on Tortola Island, complete with hotel. **Sunsail** (*980 Awald Rd., Annapolis, MD 21403. 800-327-2276 or 410-280-2553. www.sunsail.com*) is based at Soper's Hole on Tortola's West End, an easy ferry ride from St. Thomas. Other recommended charter companies include **Tortola**

EDENIC ANCHORAGE IN THE BAY OF ISLANDS, NEW ZEALAND

Marine Management (TMM) Bareboat Vacations (*P.O. Box 3042, Road Town, Tortola, BVI. 800-633-0155 or 284-494-2751. www.sailtmm.com*) and **Quest Marine Group** (*2401 W. Bay Dr., Suite 410, Largo, FL 33770. 800-225-2520 or 727-559-7142. www.cycyachtcharters.com*), based on St. Thomas. If you prefer a multihull vessel, we strongly recommend TMM or the **Catamaran Company** (*4005 N. Federal Hwy., Suite 200, Fort Lauderdale, FL 33308. 800-262-0308 or 954-566-9806. www.catamaranco.com*), both of which feature French-built catamarans offering abundant deck space. On the twin sterns of a catamaran (*see p. 202*), steps lead down to the waterline and make good swimming platforms. TMM and the Moorings also charter spacious, well-equipped catamarans from 35 feet to nearly 60 feet.

It's best to work with a larger company in these waters, especially on a first-time charter. Large companies have the facilities to back up their yachts, and if you have a problem with one of their boats they can bring you a replacement. The most popular charter yachts are in the 38- to 50-foot range. A party of six people can share a yacht this size in comfort, divvying up the cost to make the vacation affordable. Typical bareboat expense for a newer 42-footer is about $3,800 per week, but prices drop as low as $2,300 per week in the low season of midsummer. For current weather information in the Virgin Islands, log on to www.caribwx.com.

NEW ZEALAND
Cruising the Bay of Islands

New Zealand is one of the few charter destinations where you can sail in the morning and ski in the afternoon. It may also be the most distant cruising ground accessible to the bareboater—14 hours' flying time from the West Coast. But the country that awaits you at the other end more than compensates for the long hours aloft.

You will want to spend a minimum of two weeks in New Zealand, at least one of them ashore and the remainder afloat. Most charterers land at Auckland, spend a day there, rent a car, then drive three and a half hours north to the **Bay of Islands** (*below*). Host to the 2000 America's Cup regatta, **Auckland**—the City of Sails—is a world-class yachting center, with a huge new waterfront complex built for the race. You can sail from Auckland or take a week-long coastal charter, but it's probably better to start in the Bay of Islands your first time around. The charter base, located at the village of Opua, offers a good selection of yachts in the 27- to 40-foot range. Most cruises make their first stop at the old whaling town of **Russell,** a short sail away. Take time to visit the museum and the church, the oldest in New Zealand. Across the water lies **Waitangi,** the country's most important historical site. The Treaty House and Maori meetinghouse are national monuments well worth a visit.

The anchorage off Russell can be uncomfortable, so sail into the sheltered waters in the Bay of Islands itself. You beat out into the prevailing winds and anchor in one of six coves in nearby Manawaora Bay. The bay offers everything from uninhabited islands to small coves hemmed in by steep hills. You can sail around Cape Brett to Whangamumu Harbor, which was a whaling station until the 1930s. But the highlight of your charter is a visit to **Kerikeri,** where missionary Samuel Marsden founded a mission station in 1819. The stone mission store still stands beside a quiet pool reached by a long, tidal channel. High overhead broods the great *pa* (fortified village) of the Maori chief Hongi Hika. Spend a day here, touring the mission and the pa. The bay is a compact cruising ground—so much so that Kerikeri Inlet is only 7 miles from Russell. Few charter areas offer such variety in so small a compass.

New Zealanders take pride in the quality of their sailing craft, and you will find a good inventory of bareboats in the 28- to 40-foot range. Two of the country's leading charter companies maintain fleets in the Bay of Islands. Contact **the Moorings** (*800-535-7289. www.moorings.com*) or **Charter Link NZ** (*P.O. Box 32501, Devonport, Auckland, New Zealand. 01164-9445-7114. www.charterlink.co.nz*).

For general information on travel in New Zealand, contact the **New Zealand Tourism Board** (*501 Santa Monica Blvd., Suite 300, Santa Monica, CA 90401. 800-388-5494 or 310-395-7480. www.purenz.com*). The staff is very helpful, and the office maintains a current computer database of travel information. The official website also contains descriptions of award-winning land and sea adventures on both the North Island and the South Island.

GREECE
Classical Sailing Adventures

Greece is a magical place for chartering, especially if you have an interest in colorful ports and archaeology. You can anchor in the shadow of a classical temple, explore remote islands, dance till dawn in local tavernas, or simply relax on sandy beaches to your heart's content.

This all sounds heavenly, and indeed it is. But Greece is not a cruising ground for the novice. The weather, even in summer, can be stormy, frustrating, and at times downright uncomfortable. For a first-time visit, try a week's flotilla charter. Guided by an experienced flotilla leader, you sail from port to port in the company of half a dozen yachts or more. You can charter in the **Ionian Islands,** in the **Saronic Gulf,** in the **Sporades** in the northern Aegean, and along the **Turkish coast.** Flotilla charters being especially popular with British and German sailors, you'll find plenty of attractive package deals in European sailing magazines. If you prefer to bareboat by yourself, you can't go wrong with

Kavos (*800-535-7289. www.moorings.com*), an Athens-based company that merged with the Moorings. Other recommended charterers: **Sunsail** (*800-327-2276. www.sunsail.com*) and **GPSC Charters, Ltd.** (*600 St. Andrews Rd., Philadelphia, PA 19118. 800-732-6786 or 215-247-3903. www.gpsc.com*).

Experts prefer to charter at either end of the high season (May to early June, or September). The sheltered Saronic Gulf affords an ideal introduction to Greek waters. Your first stop is the island of **Aegina,** a short sail from Athens. In late afternoon, take a cab to the ancient Temple of Aphaia high on a hill to the northeast. The fluted columns of the temple shine pink in the sunset as you gaze out over the mountains and bays of the Peloponnesus.

Aegina is half a day's sail from **Epidauros,** a small port close to the amphitheater and shrine of Aeskepios, the god of healing. The theater's acoustics are so good that you can hear a stage whisper when you're sitting in the upper tier. After half a day of archaeology, sail east to **Poros,** a charming town perched above a narrow channel that takes you east toward **Hydra,** one of the highlights of a Saronic charter.

Hydra is invisible until you are just outside the harbor entrance, a semicircular cove that has been a trading center for many centuries. A stone quay shelters the tiny port, where you moor among a crowd of yachts large and small. There are no automobiles on the island—only heavily laden mules wending their way through narrow streets. This picturesque harbor is busy by day but blissfully quiet at night.

Your Saronic cruise takes you as far as **Naplion,** an old Venetian town overlooked by an imposing fortress—the Palamidi. Your passage homeward will bring you to the island of **Spetsae,** where you can wander through small boatyards that still build traditional wooden fishing craft. There are quiet anchorages, too—places where the only sound you hear is likely to be the wind. On the last day, sail along the eastern shore of Aegina to **Agia Marina** and perhaps savor another visit to the Temple of Aegina. Greece is addicting, a place where the magic of history comes to life. The great thing is that you can return again and again, exploring different charter grounds each time.

PACIFIC NORTHWEST
Gunkholer's Paradise

To many people, the Pacific Northwest is a region of gray skies, fir trees, and rain. True, the weather is often rainy, but the summers can bring weeks of predictable winds, calm seas, and brilliant blue skies. For sailing, you can catch the best winds in spring and fall, before and after the high season between Memorial Day and Labor Day. Summer winds are lighter and tend to blow from the southwest through northwest, with calms and light land breezes in evening, night, and early morning hours, and a pleasant sea breeze that comes up about noon. This is a cruising ground for people who like rugged, unspoiled scenery, superb fishing, and sailing among myriad small islands.

Most U.S. charterers take a boat out of **Anacortes, Washington,** while Canadian fleets operate from **Vancouver** and **Vancouver Island.** Distances can be large here, so many people prefer to rent a diesel trawler rather than a sailing yacht in these waters—particularly if they are departing from Washington, bound for British Columbia.

Anacortes is a superb base for exploring the **San Juan Islands,** only 10 miles away across the **Rosario Strait.** The tides run strongly through the strait, which should be crossed only in clear weather. Once among the islands you will find a good anchorage every few miles. **Friday Harbor** is the main town, a small and crowded tourist community where you can buy supplies; you can clear customs here if inbound from Canada's Gulf Islands to the north. The best sail charter operation is **Anacortes Yacht Charters** (*P.O. Box 69, Anacortes, WA 98221. 800-233-3004 or 360-293-4555. www.ayc.com*). Alternatively, **ABC Yacht Charters** (*1905 Skyline Way, Anacortes, WA 98221. 800-426-2313 or 360-293-9533. www.abcyachtcharters.com*) also operates from Anacortes, but it mostly charters powerboats. **Roche Harbor,** on the northwest coast of San Juan Island, is famous for its resort hotel and many sheltered coves. There are no fewer than 11 state parks in the San Juans, all accessible from your yacht. One of the best is **Spencer Spit,** just over 10 miles from Anacortes. The San Juans can also be reached easily from Bellingham, the base for an excellent smaller operation, **San Juan Sailing** (*1 Squalicum Harbor Espl., Bellingham, WA 98225. 800-677-7245 or 360-671-4300. www.sanjuansailing.com*).

You can explore the San Juans in a week, but a longer charter will tempt you to sail north across the border into the **Gulf Islands.** Clear customs on South Pender Island and then head north. The Gulfs are more sparsely populated than the San Juans, and you should be prepared to motor during the calm summer months. The lovely anchorages—places like Glenthorne Passage or Conover Cove on **Saltspring Island**—are worth it, however. Some people spend but a day or two in the Gulf Islands and then head west for Victoria, at the southern end of Vancouver Island.

Many charterers plan more ambitious cruises north from Anacortes and Vancouver along the mainland **Sunshine Coast.** You can also cross the Strait of Georgia, but watch the tides and weather. One favorite cruise takes you up the narrow **Agamemnon Channel** to Egmont, then 40 miles up spectacular **Jervis Inlet,** through the narrow Malibu Rapids at slack water, and into **Princess Louisa Inlet,** with its 120-foot waterfall. For a longer trip, make your way back down Jervis Inlet and head north into **Desolation Sound,** where you can choose from numerous scenic anchorages.

For more information on cruising in the Pacific Northwest, check out *North Puget Sound; South Puget Sound;* and *The San Juan Islands Afoot and Afloat,* all by Marge and Ted Mueller. These 200-page guides cover marina facilities and regional highlights. You can buy them for $14.95 each from The Mountaineers Books (*1001 S.W. Klickitat Way, Suite 201, Seattle, WA 98134. 800-553-4453 or 206-223-6303. www.mountaineersbooks.org*). For cruising farther north, Robert Hale's *The Waggoner Cruising Guide* is a superb annual cruising guide with coverage from Olympia, Washington, to the northern end of Vancouver Island. Price is $14.95 from Weatherly Press (*1803 132nd Ave. N.E., No. 4, Bellevue, WA 98005. 800-733-5330 or 425-881-5212. www.waggonerguide.com*).

WINDWARD ISLANDS
The Other Caribbean

The rugged Windward Islands, from St. Lucia in the north to Grenada in the south, offer some of the finest sailing in the West Indies. Most bareboat charters in the Windwards start in St. Lucia or St. Vincent. **Tortola Marine Management (TMM) Bareboat Vacations** (*800-633-0155. www.sailtmm.com*) is generally considered the best operation in St. Vincent, while **the Moorings** (*800-535-7289. www.moorings.com*) has large fleets in St. Lucia and Grenada. St. Lucia is a favorite. On the first evening of your charter you can anchor in Anse des Pitons, one of the world's most spectacular anchorages, where sugarloaf peaks tower 2,000 feet above the ocean. Anchoring there is quite a challenge, because the water is 600 feet deep only 400 yards from the beach. You should anchor 50 yards offshore and secure a stern line to a nearby tree.

From Anse des Pitons, most people sail south to Blue Lagoon or Young Island at the southern tip of **St. Vincent** before taking off for the **Grenadines.** The prevailing trades allow you to reach comfortably down-island, even if the inter-island passages are a trifle bumpy. Coming home, you will be hard on the wind, so allow time to work your way north.

The best time to sail here is between November and April, when the northeast trades blow steadily at a constant 15 to 25 knots. You sail down the westerly side of the islands, spending your first night at **Bequia,** only about 9 miles from Blue Lagoon. Admiralty Bay, near the main town, is a fine anchorage, and there are simple restaurants ashore. No visit to Bequia is complete without an excursion to **Friendship Bay** and the island of **Petit Nevis** off the south coast.

Most charterers head south from Bequia to **Tobago Cays** and **Union Island.** Tobago Cays consists of four islands inside Horse Shoe Reef. Avid snorkelers spend days here, anchored off **Baradal Island** or in the narrow cut between **Petit Rameau** and **Petit Bateau Islands.** You can walk ashore and admire the aloes, collect shells on the beaches, or snorkel for hours on end. Nearby **Palm Island,** Union Island, and **Petit St. Vincent** offer a pleasant mix of island resorts, with the best anchorage in Clifton Harbor sheltered behind the reefs, just off the resort hotel.

From Union Island south to Grenada is a comfortable day's run. The best anchorages are along the southwestern coast, so plan to visit **St. George's** first. Take a leisurely tour of the town, enjoying its Dutch-style architecture, or go shopping. The public market on Wednesdays and Saturdays is always a treat. A gunkholer's paradise, the southwestern coast offers many sheltered anchorages; the one west of Hog Island is among the best. At **Hog Island,** you eyeball your way between reefs, conning from the bow through brilliantly clear water. Once inside, anchor in about 25 feet of water, and use your dinghy to explore the channel into Clarke's Court Bay. Most sailors work their way as far east as Bacaye Harbor, having explored such secluded anchorages as Port Egmont. The reefs are tricky here, so enter the harbor when the sun is high so you can detect changing water colors.

TONGA
South Pacific Paradise

Tonga's South Pacific islands known as the **Vava'u Group** offer a unique opportunity to experience tropical sailing at its best. The people are friendly, onshore activities are plentiful, the trade-wind sailing is magnificent, and the snorkeling and diving are unforgettable. All you need to sail here is some expertise with eyeball navigation through reefs and in shallow water. Anchoring presents few problems, and you can always check your set with a pair of goggles and a snorkel. You can charter anytime, but it's best to avoid January through March—hurricane season.

The islands are a scenic mixture of the Bahamas and the Virgins, but with a profusion of shallow coral reefs and fine white beaches. You will find yourself sailing in the Pacific's last independent monarchy, still largely untouched by modern civilization. The missionary influence here is very strong, and the islanders observe the Sabbath with Victorian rigor. The highest islands, in the north and west, offer deepwater

anchorages and an ever changing vista of cliffs, beaches, and sheltered coves. Sail to the east to view the great coral reefs that protect **Vava'u Island** itself, and you will cruise among tiny islets capped with a few palm trees surrounded by gleaming white beaches. Many visitors spend their nights in the sheltered anchorages to the north and west, then sail down during the day for snorkeling and beachcombing.

The Moorings (*800-535-7289. www.moorings.com*), the charter company of choice here, will supply a modern Beneteau yacht and, if you prefer, a professional crew. **Sunsail** (*800-327-2276. www.sunsail.com*) also operates a charter fleet in Tonga, and its modern French yachts may be more affordable than the Moorings' vessels of similar size. There is much to be said for hiring Tongan skippers, especially if you want to fish or dive. They know the best spots and have good contacts in local villages. The charter base at Neiafu lies up the 5-mile-long, fjordlike waterway that virtually bisects Vava'u. You will find plenty of places to anchor along the fjord, and be sure to allow time for a visit to **Swallow Cave** on Kapa Island. The late afternoon sun reaches inside, illuminating coral formations deep in the water.

Take a couple of days to get used to local conditions before sailing eastward into shallower water. The **Fanua Tapu Passage** takes you to the heart of the reefs, an easy trip if you have a rising tide under you and high sun to see the shallows. Spend a night at nearby **Makave** village, and visit the **Ofu** village. Its thatched huts sit on a gently curving beach where fishermen mend their nets.

You can spend a fascinating day sailing the 10-mile passage inside the chain of reefs and islands to **Maninita.** To anchor there, you will need a local guide to eyeball you into a small cove surrounded by coral heads and a beach. Alternatively, head over to **Euakafa** 5 miles away, where you can tramp over a 300-foot summit plateau and get some exercise. More ambitious charterers sail to Hunga Lagoon on the western island of **Ava Pulepulekai.** Its narrow entrance should be attempted only at high tide.

For more information on cruising in Polynesia, read *Landfalls of Paradise* by Earl Hinz. The fourth edition is $44.95 from the University of Hawaii Press (*888-847-7377. www. uhpress.hawaii.edu*).

WHITSUNDAY ISLANDS
Aussie Cruising Haven

The Whitsundays lie near Townsville in northern Queensland, a tropical region with warm, clear waters. The charter fleet is based at Shute Harbor, which can be reached by air from Sydney or Brisbane. On the other side of the Whitsunday Channel is the **Great Barrier Reef,** one of the world's natural wonders. Crewed charters are quite popular here, and many fine yachts are available. But more adventurous sailors head out on their own, on bareboats in the 30- to 45-foot range. Try to reserve a yacht well ahead of time, because local demand is strong throughout the year.

The Whitsundays themselves are not part of the barrier reef. They are craggy islands with bays, rugged hills, and snow-white beaches protected by coral reefs. The trade winds blow steadily here, lighter in summer and with greater, more predictable force during the Australian winter (May through August). This is not a cruising ground for beginners: Currents run strongly between islands, and sudden downslope winds can put you on the coral at the entrance to an anchorage in seconds. A newcomer is best advised to engage a local skipper, at least for a couple of days. Having said that, anyone with solid anchoring experience and some familiarity with eyeball navigation and reefing should adjust rapidly. Anchoring here requires care, and you will find yourself using plenty of chain and running your engine more than you might in home waters.

Note, incidentally, that the barrier reef is 15 to 40 miles offshore, and bareboats are forbidden to visit it. But an Air Whitsunday seaplane will meet you at your yacht and take you there for a half-day excursion.

In the Whitsundays you can combine days of solitude with congenial evenings ashore at the various resorts, such as **Hamilton Island.** Many maintain moorings, and dinner and a few drinks is a wonderful way to meet the locals on their own turf. If your tastes run to the unspoiled, have no fear. There are 74 Whitsunday Islands, and you can lose yourself for days among them. This is a "lunch hook" charter area where you can anchor off any number of pristine white beaches and walk ashore, your feet scuffing sand that may have gone untrodden for months. The choice of overnight anchorages is unending, including such famous spots as **Butterfly Bay** and **Macona Inlet,** where you can lie in solitude and snorkel among colorful coral heads.

A number of decent charter companies operate in the Whitsundays, but they seem to change ownership often. Now that **Sunsail** (*800-327-2276. www.sunsail.com*) has a modern fleet there, overall quality can be expected to improve. Many sailors favor **Queensland Yacht Charters** (*P.O. Box 293, Airlie Beach, Queensland 4802, Australia. 01161-7494-67400. www.yachtcharters.com.au*). Recipient of a 1999 Queensland Tourism Award, QYC maintains a strong fleet of bareboats and crewed yachts, its prices are competitive, and its staff is excellent. If you want a complete air, land, and sea package, however, you should also consider **Whitsunday Rent-a-Yacht** (*P.O. Box 357, Airlie Beach, Whitsunday, Queensland 4802, Australia. 01161-7494-69232 or 800-075-111 in Australia. www.rentayacht.com.au*), which offers multiactivity holidays including airfare, resort accommodations, sailing, golf, fishing, and scuba diving.

GULL'S-EYE VIEW OF FLYING SPINNAKER AND CATAMARAN, VIRGIN GORDA, BRITISH VIRGIN ISLANDS

Super Sailing Destinations: A Nautical Chart

Location/Charters	Phone	Recommended Boats	Cost per week	Shoreside	Season
ALASKA *Many destinations offer snowcapped volcanic peaks and rugged shorelines. Cruising is for the hardy soul.*					
58°22′ N. Sailing Ch. ABC Alaska	907-789-7301 800-780-1239	Catalina 36 Bayliner 32 32-footer	$2,200-2,750	Vast distances separate ports, facilities in Glacier Bay and Juneau.	Summer is best; temperatures 40°-50° F; minimal fog.
ANTIGUA *April Race week is big draw; weather may be unpredictable. Open-water sailing skills are helpful.*					
Sunsail Sun Yacht Charters	800-327-2276 800-772-3500	Sun Odyssey 42 Centurion 41 41-footer	$2,175-4,000	Hotels and restaurants are numerous. Visit the museum of Antigua/Barbuda.	Dec.-Mar.; April is also excellent; June temperatures are 80°-88° F.
AUSTRALIA (WHITSUNDAYS) *Currents are strong and winds erratic; sailing expertise is essential. Moorings are in place on many islands.*					
Sunsail	800-327-2276	Oceanis 400 40-footer	$2,800-4,100	Lodging and services are available on some islands. Make advance reservations.	Best sailing is with stronger winds May through October.
BAHAMAS *Keep a good lookout in the shoal waters. Watch out for Chigaterra poisoning. The Exuma Chain is safe and unspoiled.*					
Catamaran C&S The Moorings	800-262-0308 800-535-7289	Privilege 39 Moorings 413 40-footer	$2,800-4,250	50 miles from Florida, it has high visitor rate. Find an out-of-the-way spot.	Year-round mild sailing conditions; avoid hurricane season.
BAJA *Sail in deep waters with sheltered anchorages. Enjoy good fishing and view marine life such as whales and dolphins.*					
The Moorings	800-535-7289	Moorings 413, 405 3800 Cat 40-footer	$2,600-4,000	Cabo San Lucas offers exciting nightlife.	Winter to spring; summers very hot; minimal provisioning elsewhere.
BVI (TORTOLA, VIRGIN GORDA) *Learn cruising skills in this good first-time charter venue. Don't miss Sandy Cay, Green Cay, and Baths.*					
Catamaran Company The Moorings Sunsail	800-262-0308 800-535-7289 800-327-2276	Privilege 43 Moorings 433 Sun Odyssey 42.2	$2,300-4,200	Provision in Tortola or Gorda. Visit Bitter End and island nightspots.	July-October. Year-round; watch for hurricanes
CALIFORNIA (CHANNEL ISLANDS) *Blue-water skills are a must; high winds, big seas mid-channel; bow/stern anchoring in most popular harbors.*					
Marina Sailing Santa Barbara Sail Charter	805-985-5219 800-350-9090	Hunter 41 Catalina 36 36-footer	$1,575	Shoreside facilities are rare. Enjoy good diving and some hiking. See sea caves and much wildlife.	Year-round; summer is best; fog in June and storms Dec.-Feb.
CHESAPEAKE BAY *Largest estuary on East Coast, the bay has over 3,000 miles of shoreline, great shallow-water cruising.*					
AYS Charters Harbor View Boat & Breakfast	800-382-8181 800-877-9330	C&C 30 Hyliss 40 40-footer	$3,500	Annapolis dates from 18th century; excellent museums and historic preservation.	April-June, Sept.-Nov.; avoid midsummer heat and low winds.
FLORIDA KEYS *Shallow and unpredictable, the shoal waters are tricky. Keys are great for diving, snorkeling, and windsurfing.*					
Florida Yacht Centers Spinnaker Bay	800-537-0050 800-584-4432	Chinook Cat, Athena 38 Hunter 430 40-foot cat	$3,000-3,650	watch the sunset from southernmost point in conterminous U.S. Enjoy nightlife, dancing.	Year-round; summer is hot and humid.
FRANCE (RIVIERA) *Some open-water experience is essential, plus ability to moor or raft in tight harbors. Strong winds affect some areas.*					
Sun Yacht Charters	800-772-3500	Moorings 405 37-footer	$1,550-3,500	Tourists flock here in high season; destinations offer facilities, marinas, and historical monuments.	May-July
GREAT LAKES *Lake Erie is known for short, steep chop. The region is relatively unpopulated; visit Superior's Apostle Island, Bass Island.*					
Bay Breeze Sailboats, Inc.	231-941-0535 800-826-7010	Morgan 41 Catalina 36 C&C 41 41-footer	$2,350-2,950	Lakes are a major tourist destination; state parks line shores of the lakes; hiking is good.	Summer; good westerlies.
GREECE *A nice loop begins in Athens, goes through the Cyclades, then the Saronic Islands by way of Hydra and Poros.*					
GPSC Charters The Moorings	800-732-6786 800-535-7289	Gypsy 126 Moorings 464 44-footer	$2,950-4,450	Hike the islands and discover sleepy fishing villages or stop in one of the lively taverns.	Year-round; spring and fall are best.
GRENADA *Strong trade winds and sailing conditions are for more experienced sailors; it's a good step up from the Virgins.*					
Barefoot Yach Chrtr. The Moorings	784-456-9526 800-535-7289	Moorings 463 Moorings 405 45-footer	$2,520-4,500	The Grenada Yacht Club welcomes charterers; provisions are reasonable.	Dec.-April; avoid hurricane season.
GUADELOUPE *Big island provides numerous anchorages. Many charters sail south to Marie Galant and Les Saints Islands.*					
Sunsail Trade Wind Yachts	800-327-2276 800-825-7245	Beneteau 40.5 Sun Odyssey 42 42-footer	$2,100-3,800	Point à Pitre is cosmopolitan port; French influence is great; provisions are plentiful.	Dec.-April; avoid hurricane season.

Location/ Charters	Phone	Recommended Boats	Cost per week	Shoreside	Season
ITALY (TUSCAN IS., CORSICA) *Encounter variable wind/sea conditions, busy harbors in high season, and lots of water-sports activity.*					
GPSC Charters The Moorings	800-732-6786 800-535-7289	Hunter 336 Moorings 464 Oceanis 510 46-footer	$2,775- 5,000	Visit Elba's Palazzina Museum and many waterfront cafes and shops. Kayak Corsica in spring.	April-August
MAINE *The state offers 50 miles of coastline with thousands of coves on more than 3,000 islands. Watch for tricky tides and fog.*					
Bay Islands Hinckley Morris	207-596-7550 800-492-7245 207-244-5509	Hinckley 42 Hinckley 49 49-footer	$4,950- 5,500	Maine has fishing villages, deserted beaches, and many accessible coastal inns and restaurants.	July-early Sept.; moderate SW winds.
MARTINIQUE *Trades blow NE in winter, SE in summer at steady 10-25 knots. Some experience is necessary.*					
Barefoot Yacht Charters Catamaran Co. The Moorings	784-456-9526 800-262-0309 800-535-7289	Privilege 42 Moorings 464 46-footer	$2,450- 4,500	Balata Gardens are near Fort de France. St. Pierre has a wonderful museum.	Year-round trades; avoid hurricane season.
NEW ZEALAND (BAY OF ISLANDS, HAURAKI GULF) *Small islands dot gulf; in bay, seas are mostly calm. Passages are short, winds variable.*					
Charter Link NZ The Moorings	01164-9445-7114 800-535-7289	Privilege 42 Moorings 463 46-footer	$2400- 4,350	Many facilities are on shore; well-maintained trails are on Gulf Islands; fishing is good.	Best chartering at summer's end; high season is congested.
PACIFIC NW (SAN JUAN) *Gunkholing in the San Juans is great. Here are calm waters and short passages but strong currents and extreme tides.*					
ABC Yacht Charters Anacortes Yacht Chrtrs.	800-426-2313 800-233-3004	Beneteau 36 Cascade 44 44-footer	$1,600- 2,300	Friday Harbor is busy haven with complete services. See island parks, fine scenery.	May-Sept.; Aug.-Sept. offers best wind and sun.
SOCIETY ISLANDS (RAIATEA) *Open-water sailing, deep-anchoring (90 ft.), and navigation skills are required. Reef passages need good lookouts.*					
The Moorings	800-535-7289	Moorings 464 Hylas 49 46-footer	$4,025- 6,100	Beaches are superb but local shopping limited. Visit ancient Polynesian shrines.	April-Nov.; trade winds are year-round.
SPAIN *Charter fleets move from Balearics to Canaries in winter. High winds and open anchorages are found in Canaries.*					
The Moorings Sunsail	800-535-7289 800-327-2276	Moorings 405 Moorings 510 40-footer	$1,925- 3,500	Majorca offers wild nightlife with lively discos and bars. Many beaches are topless.	Summer is best; watch for strong NW mistrals.
ST. LUCIA *Trades are solid 10-20 knots. Consider a one-way charter to avoid long return passage to windward.*					
The Moorings	800-535-7289	Moorings 405 Moorings 510 40-footer	$2,150- 3,750	Visit the fruit and vegetable market, mineral baths, and Pitons.	Year-round; high season is midwinter.
ST. MARTIN *Cruise between ports with moorings, or anchor in secluded coves.*					
The Moorings Sun Yacht Charters	800-535-7289 800-772-3500	Centurion 49 Hunter 336 49-footer	$2,650- 4,975	Provisioning and shopping are better at Phillipsburg, in the Dutch section.	Dec.-April
ST. VINCENT *Grenadines stretch south from here in a row of 32 islands, cays, and reefs; one uses Bahamian moor.*					
Sunsail Trade Wind Yachts	800-327-2276 800-825-7245	Jeanneau 12.5 Sun Odyssey 42 Beneteau 432 42-footer	$2,000- 3,800	Visit black-sand beaches, lovely waterfalls, a 4,000-foot volcano, resorts, and excellent markets.	Year-round; high season is midwinter.
TAHITI *Rugged NE coast is exposed to intense, pounding surf. Southern coast is gentle, open, and protected by barrier reef.*					
The Moorings Sun Yacht Charters	800-535-7289 800-772-3500	Moorings 405 Oceanis Moorings 510 40-footer	$2,650- 3,900	Papeete, the main harbor, is a political, economic, and cultural hub.	Nov.-June
THAILAND *Phuket is the most popular cruising area. Avoid long offshore passages; pirates can be a risk.*					
Sunsail Thai Marine	800-327-2276 01166-7623-9111	Hunter 43 43-footer	$3,100- 5,470	Developments and marinas are few. Thai cuisine and wild Phuket nightlife are big draws.	Nov.-April; avoid winter monsoons.
TONGA *Ocean crossings between island groups demand experience with passage-making and navigating coral channels.*					
Sunsail The Moorings	800-327-2276 800-535-7289	Beneteau 30 Moorings 405 40-footer	$2,750- 3,400	Small tribal villages offer very few conveniences; snorkeling and fishing are great.	Year-round; avoid hurricane season.
TURKEY *Some sailing experience and basic knowledge of piloting are necessary. Turkey is great for flotilla charters.*					
GPSC Charters Sunsail	800-732-6786 800-327-2276	Sun Odyssey 40 Moorings 405 40-footer	$1,800- 2,500	Visit colorful restaurants and markets; see classical ruins; enjoy lively nightlife.	April-late Sept.; May and Sept. are less crowded.
U.S. VIRGIN ISLANDS *St. Croix involves 35-mile open passage and requires basic sailing and anchoring skills, with some ability at navigation.*					
VIP Sail & Power Yacht Island Yachts	800-524-2015 800-524-2019	Beneteau 45 Hunter 43 Privilege 12 45-footer	$2,750- 4,750	Shop duty-free; walk white-sand beaches; see a rain forest; visit resorts and hotels.	Late spring, early summer; avoid hurricane season.

All the Bareboat You Can Bear

Presented below are the major players in the world of bareboat chartering. All of them are good, but their prices vary considerably—as do the features of the yachts they offer. The boat you choose will be your home for a week or more, so it must be comfortable and reliable. In general, the newer the boat, the better it will be.

You will also find that the latest French designs (Beneteau, Fountaine-Pajot, Jeanneau) offer enhanced comfort and privacy. With superior stability and deck space, catamarans have become quite popular and are ideal for families. Multihulls are generally more expensive to charter than monohulls of the same length, but a well-designed multihull will have as much interior and deck space as a monohull that is 7 to 10 feet longer overall. Moreover, shoal draft allows cats to anchor conveniently close to the beach and to navigate shallows that may be off-limits to large monohulls.

We use these codes to describe features: **BB** (bareboat), **CC** (crewed charter), **SK** (skippered charter), **FLO** (flotilla), **CB** (chaseboat), **DIO** (dinghy with outboard included), **MH** (multihulls), **PROV** (provisioning), **REFR** (refrigeration), and **TRAV** (air/land package can be arranged). High- and low-season prices, listed for comparison purposes, give an idea of what you should expect to pay for a one-week charter in the Caribbean. Prices, regrettably, are subject to change.

Anacortes Yacht Charters

P.O. Box 69, Anacortes Marina, 2415 T Ave., Anacortes, WA 98221
800-233-3004 or 360-293-4555
www.ayc.com

Founded 1978; 90 yachts (half sail), BB, CC, SK, FLO, CB, PROV, REFR (half). Base: Anacortes, adding Bellingham in 2001. Best boats: Lagoon 35 Cat, Freedom 38, Taswell 50. Pricing: below average.

With the largest sailing fleet in the Pacific Northwest, Anacortes is highly rated by the readers of *Cruising World*. Its well-maintained yachts and excellent customer support give it a high rate of repeat customers. Because the region's fickle winds and strong currents present challenges to sailors, Anacortes offers an excellent three-day Introduction to Cruising course. Most boats over 35 feet have GPS; larger yachts have radar as well.

Catamaran Company

4005 N. Federal Hwy., Suite 200, Ft. Lauderdale, FL 33308
800-262-0308 or 954-566-9806
www.catamaranco.com

Founded 1988; 50 yachts, 35 to 51 feet (average two years in Caribbean), BB, CC some locations, SK, MH, PROV split or full, REFR. Bases: Guadeloupe, Martinique, Fort Lauderdale, St. Martin, Tortola. Best boats: Fountaine-Pajot 38 to 46 feet; Lagoon 41, 47 feet; Privilege 37, 48, 51 feet. Prices tend to be high (37-footer $3,400-5,500).

For well-to-do charterers looking for comfortable, spacious craft, the Catamaran Company is hard to beat. Its fast, stable, and well-appointed catamarans include some very large crewed yachts, such as Dennis Conner's Privilege 51. The shallow draft makes anchoring a snap, and families with small children like the deck space and absence of heel while under way. This company recently reopened its St. Martin base. All boats carry windsurfers and electric refrigeration. Larger boats have skippers, cooks, and even air-conditioning.

GPSC Charters, Ltd.

600 St. Andrews Rd., Philadelphia, PA 19118
800-732-6786 or 215-247-3903
www.gpsc.com

Founded 1976; 92 GPSC yachts and associated fleets, 31 to 65 feet (average six years or less), BB, CC, SK, FLO, MH, PROV, REFR larger yachts, TRAV. Bases: Croatia (30-Zadar, Trogir), France (11-St. Tropez), Greece (70-Athens, Rhodes), Italy (10-Sardinia), Portugal (6), Spain (15), Turkey (20). Best boats: Express 510, Sun Magic 44 feet, Baltic 40 feet. Pricing is below average (Greece: 44-footer $2,520-3,360).

Based in Greece, GPSC is one of the largest, most experienced charter operators in Europe. It specializes in Croatia, France, Greece, and Spain. GPSC is a very good choice for a flotilla charter in the eastern Mediterranean, with major bases at Athens, Rhodes, and Marmaris, Turkey.

The boats tend to be a bit older than ones at leading Caribbean charter bases. GPSC owns its Greek yachts, and it partners with other operators in western Europe.

The Moorings

19345 U.S. Hwy. 19 N., 4th Fl., Clearwater, FL 33764
800-535-7289 or 727-530-5424
www.moorings.com

Founded 1970; 770-plus yachts, 30 to 50 feet (average two years), BB, CC, SK, CB, DIO, MH, PROV split or full, REFR, TRAV. Bases: Australia (12), Bahamas (35), Baja (20), Florida (15), France & Corsica (60), Greece (25), Grenada (50), Martinique (50), New Zealand (20), St. Lucia (50), St. Martin (70), Spain (40), Tahiti (40), Tonga (20), Tortola (350). Best boats: Moorings 413, 362; 3800 cat, 4500 cat. Pricing: above average (Caribbean: 46-footer $2,950-5,500).

The Moorings rules the roost in the British Virgins and also serves exotic, less-crowded areas like Baja, Tahiti, and Tonga. Prices are fairly high, but its yachts are fitted with features such as power windlasses and extra ventilation. It now offers two-tiered pricing: Exclusive Line yachts are all less than two years old; Club Line vessels are two to four years old and cost about 20 percent less per week.

Novice charterers can choose from a number of smaller yachts in the fleet, and on the first day of a charter, they are provided with a complimentary skipper. The Moorings runs the Club Mariner program for people who want to combine a land-based resort holiday with a cruise aboard a skippered yacht. For nonsailors, powercats are popular.

Because the yachts see heavy use in the most active cruising grounds, you benefit by chartering early in the season, when the boats are in top condition. Keep in mind that Moorings has the youngest fleet, overall, of any major charter company. Normally, no boat is kept in service longer than four years.

Quest Marine Group (VIP Sail & Power Yacht Charters)

2401 W. Bay Dr., Ste. 410, Largo, FL 33770
800-524-2015 or 727-559-7142
www.vipyachts.com

Founded 1979; 38 yachts, 37 to 54 feet (average two years), BB, SK, CB, DIO, PROV deluxe, REFR, TRAV. Bases: eastern end of St. Thomas and Tortola. Best boats: new Jeanneau boats. Pricing: below average (44-footer $2,950-5,200).

VIP is the oldest and largest operation in the U.S. Virgin Islands cruising trade. Its charters can be much cheaper than the Moorings, yet the standard of boat maintenance and customer service is high. As with any charter in the Virgins, expect crowded anchorages in peak season. VIP provides 14-foot hard-bottomed inflatables, with 15-hp motors, on most charters.

Sun Yacht Charters

P.O. Box 4035, Portland, ME 04101
800-772-3500 or 207-253-5400
www.sunyachts.com

Founded 1978; 400 yachts, 35 to 63 feet (average two years), BB, CC, SK, CB, DIO, MH, PROV full or deluxe, REFR, TRAV. Bases: Antigua (15), Croatia (10), France & Corsica (20), Guadeloupe (25), Martinique (50), Puerto Rico (15), St. Martin (60), Seychelles (5), Spain (10), Tahiti (25), Tortola (100), Turkey (25), Union-Grenadines (10), Australia and Greece through affiliates. Best boats: Lagoon 38 cat, Jeanneau Sun Odyssey 40, Sun

Odyssey 43. Pricing: above average, but tiered (40-footer $2,170-4,200).

Sun Yacht Charters operates roomy, comfortable French boats. It charters all of the most popular cruising grounds, and the yachts come well-equipped, particularly in the Caribbean.

Its rates represent good value, with tiered pricing based on vessel age: Premier (under two years), Classic (three to five years), Value (five-plus years). Sun offers nice extras, such as a complimentary skipper to the first anchorage. It also offers superb crewed charters on 72- to 140-foot luxury yachts.

In 2000, Sun Yachts was acquired by the same ownership group as Sunsail. At press time, however, the two companies maintained separate operations.

Sunsail

980 Awald Rd., Suite 302, Annapolis, MD 21403
800-327-2276 or 410-280-2553
www.sunsail.com

Founded 1974; 800 yachts, 24 to 55 feet (average five years and less), BB, CC, SK, FLO, CB, DIO, MH, PROV, REFR on most, TRAV. Bases: Annapolis (15), Antigua (50), Australia (50), Croatia (20), England & Scotland (15), France (15), Greece (65), Guadeloupe (40), Maldives (12), Martinique (40), New Zealand (20), St. Martin (60), St. Vincent (50), Seychelles (10), Spain (15), Thailand (12), Tonga (10), Tortola (120), Turkey (50), and

others. Best boats: Oceanis 411, 461; Beneteau 50. Pricing: average (44-footer $2,100-3,800).

With 29 fleets, Sunsail is the biggest charterer in the world. It has long been a top choice for cruising the Mediterranean. In the Caribbean, it maintains a large fleet at six island bases, and it runs the best bareboat operation going in exotic Thailand. Sunsail's many smaller yachts are ideal for flotilla sailing. They also make good choices for couples who want to sail on their own, or for families on limited budgets.

Sunsail runs a remarkably professional program, and its peak-season rates are lower than those of such competitors as the Moorings. Great for families are Sunsail's ten **Watersports Beach Clubs**—nine summer facilities in Greece and Turkey, as well as a year-round Caribbean club in Antigua. Sunsail and Sun Yachts are now sister companies, but they maintain separate fleets.

Tortola Marine Management (TMM) Bareboat Vacations

P.O. Box 3042, Road Town, Tortola, British Virgin Islands
800-633-0155 or 284-494-2751
www.sailtmm.com

Founded 1979; 70 yachts (all sail), 36 to 51 feet (average five years and less), BB, SK, CB, DIO, MH, PROV, REFR all boats, TRAV. Bases: Belize, Grenadines, Tortola. Best boats: Lagoon 470 cat,

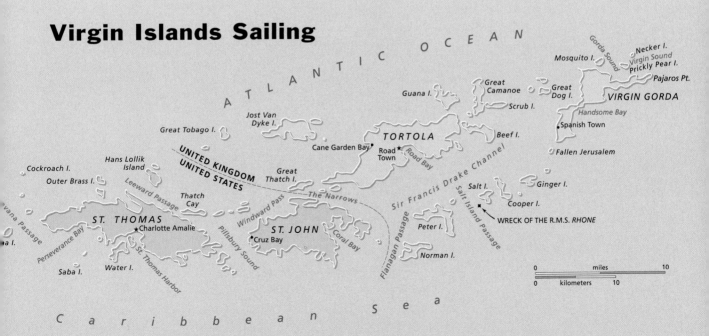

Virgin Islands Sailing

ATLANTIC OCEAN

Mosquito I.

Gorda Sound

Necker I.

Virgin Sound

Prickly Pear I.

Pajaros Pt.

Guana I.

Great Camanoe

Great Dog I.

VIRGIN GORDA

Scrub I.

Handsome Bay

Spanish Town

Jost Van Dyke I.

Great Tobago I.

TORTOLA

Beef I.

Fallen Jerusalem

Cane Garden Bay

Road Town

Road Bay

Sir Francis Drake Channel

Cockroach I.

Hans Lollik Island

UNITED KINGDOM

UNITED STATES

Great Thatch I.

Salt I.

Ginger I.

Outer Brass I.

Leeward Passage

The Narrows

Salt Island Passage

Cooper I.

Thatch Cay

Windward Pass

WRECK OF THE R.M.S. RHONE

Havana Passage

ST. THOMAS

★ Charlotte Amalie

Pillsbury Sound

ST. JOHN

★ Cruz Bay

Coral Bay

Flanagan Passage

Peter I.

Saba I.

Water I.

St. Thomas Harbor

Perseverance Bay

Norman I.

0 — miles — 10

0 — kilometers — 10

Caribbean Sea

Athena 38 Cat, Jeanneau Sun Odyssey 45.2. Pricing: average (42-footer $3,995/$2,375).

Rated best in the British Virgin Islands by *Cruising World* magazine, TMM is "large enough to serve, but small enough to care." Customers receive personalized treatment, and the yachts are carefully matched to meet the needs of your group.

The yachts come very well-equipped for the price. All have electronics, powered dinghies, and refrigeration. Kayaks, windsurfers, and scuba gear are available. Half of TMM's fleet are modern multihulls, and some of the bigger cats boast generators, air-conditioning, and dive compressors. ASA charter certification courses are also offered.

TMM serves the Grenadines and Belize as well. It maintains the best fleet in Belize—a unique destination with hundreds of unpopulated cays and almost unlimited miles of protected sailing inside the largest barrier reef in the Western Hemisphere.

WINDJAMMERS AND CREWED CHARTERS

Windjammers and Tall Ships

If you want to recapture the romance of the age of sail while letting a skilled crew do all the work (and cook gourmet meals), we recommend a windjammer or tall ship vacation. Windjammer and tall ship cruises are available worldwide, from the snug harbors of Maine to the tropical islands of the South Pacific.

CALIFORNIA

Nautical Heritage Society

1064-B Calle Negocio, San Clemente, CA 92673
800-432-2201 or 949-369-6773
www.californian.org

The Nautical Heritage Society offers winter and spring day cruises aboard the 145-foot tall ship *Californian,* an authentic replica of an 1848 vintage Revenue Marine Service cutter. This is the only regularly scheduled windjammer program on the West Coast. Programs range from a four-hour, $75-per-person sail to three- to nine-day offshore cruises for $140 per day, on a shared-cabin basis. In winter the ship is based in southern California, and in summer she sails from Monterey Bay and San Francisco.

CARIBBEAN

Windjammer Barefoot Cruises

P.O. Box 190120, Miami Beach, FL 33119
800-327-2601 or 305-672-6453
www.windjammer.com

If you are looking for a floating Club Med, this is it. Windjammer Barefoot Cruises (WBC) operates five upgraded 200- to 282-foot windjammers, all set up for serious partying. The ships sail mostly at night, allowing you time to frolic on the beach or party at more than 50 ports of call (including St. Martin, Antigua, Grenada, Tortola, St. Lucia, St. Vincent, Martinique, Dominica, St. Barts, Anguilla, Saba, Statia, St. Kitts and Nevis). Island destinations vary from trip to trip, but all cruises take you to a new port of call each day. WBC's 6- or 13-day cruises start at a reasonable $900 per person for a private cabin, including food and a "daily ration of grog."

WELL-HEELED: A 41-FOOT KETCH LEAVES THOMAS POINT
LIGHT ASTERN IN THE CHESAPEAKE BAY OF MARYLAND.

MAINE

Maine Windjammer Association

P.O. Box 1144, Blue Hill, ME 04614
800-807-9463 or 207-374-2993
www.sailmainecoast.com

Maine is the center of windjammer sailing in the United States. A fleet of classic 70- to 140-foot sailing vessels ply the waters here every summer, under the guidance of skilled skippers and professional crews. The typical schooner cruise lasts three or six days, averaging $350 for the shorter trip and $700 for the six-day voyage, and each vessel accommodates between 20 and 40 customers, usually in private cabins. The food is consistently excellent, and most cruises offer traditional lobster-bakes.

You will have more fun if you book your cruise to coincide with a summer windjammer event. In mid-June, Boothbay hosts Windjammer Days, featuring a sail parade and onshore festivities. During the last week of June, the Maine Windjammer Association conducts the Great Schooner race, an all-day run in Penobscot Bay. The second week of September sees the fleet converge at the headquarters of *Wooden Boat* magazine, on Eggemoggin Reach, for a waterfront celebration.

The association represents 13 sailing ships, including the *Angelique* (95 feet), *J.& E. Riggin* (89 feet), *Mary Day* (90 feet), *Nathaniel Bowditch* (82 feet), *Grace Bailey* (80 feet), *Timberwind* (70 feet), *Victory Chimes* (132 feet), *American Eagle* (92 feet), and *Heritage* (95 feet).

INTERNATIONAL TALL SHIPS AND OCEAN PASSAGES

Ocean Voyages

1709 Bridgeway, Sausalito, CA 94965
800-299-4444 or 415-332-4681
www.oceanvoyages.com

Ocean Voyages books individuals and groups aboard vessels sailing in the waters of the Caribbean, the Mediterranean, the Pacific Northwest, the Galápagos Islands, Mexico, Australia, the Indian Ocean, Chilean Patagonia, New Zealand and the South Pacific, Europe, and Pitcairn. These blue-water cruises are perfect for people who lack the skills to charter on their own or who prefer to sail in destinations not served by charter bases. Ocean Voyages includes classic tall ships and square-riggers among the vessels it represents.

Star Clippers

4101 Salzedo Ave., Coral Gables, FL 33146
800-442-0551 or 305-442-0550
www.starclippers.com

Star Clippers maintains a fleet of modern, white-hulled giants flying up to 54,000 square feet of canvas. The 439-foot, square-rigged *Royal Clipper*, launched in spring 2000, is the world's largest true sailing ship. For under $3,000 you can join her crew of 100 on a 21-day trans-Atlantic voyage from Cannes (France) to Barbados. Week-long cruises in the Caribbean start at about $1,500 per week. Another tall ship in the Star fleet, the 360-foot *Star Flyer*, was the first commercial sailing ship to make a trans-Atlantic voyage with passengers since the turn of the 19th century.

Star Clippers lets you relive the great epoch of sail on its short cruises in the Caribbean, Mediterranean, and Far East, and on the longer, transoceanic passages, including an Indian Ocean crossing from Thailand to Greece via the Suez Canal. Though true windjammers, the vessels offer comfortable cabins and first-class dining, plus free dinghy sailing, water-skiing, and windsurfing. They are even PADI-certified dive resorts, offering scuba diving for a modest extra fee.

CREWED CHARTERS

With bareboat operators, company size generally assures a certain level of quality and service. But some of the best crewed charter operations are small, perhaps just a husband and wife team. And finding a top-flight small operator isn't easy, because the good ones do not need to advertise; they get all the business they can handle from word of mouth. Here it is essential to get the advice of reputable charter brokers such as those listed below. Although a 34- to 40-foot yacht is ideal for a two-couple bareboat vacation, crewed charters in the 50- to 70-foot range are preferable. With a yacht of this size, three couples can each have a private cabin, there will be a full-time cook aboard, and the vessel can easily carry fishing tackle, dive gear, and windsurfers without compromising deck space.

Crewed Charter Agencies

Blue Water Yacht Charters

3725 212th Street S.E., Bothell, WA 98021
800-732-7245 or 425-481-9757
www.yachtworld.com/bluewateryachtcharters

Blue Water specializes in the Pacific Northwest, Alaska, Mexico, and the South Pacific, although yachts are available worldwide.

Jubilee Yacht Charters

P.O. Box 1358, 497 Yacht Harbor Dr., Osprey, FL 34229
800-922-4871 or 941-966-1563
www.jubileeyachtcharters.com

Superb yachts in France, Greece, and Turkey make Jubilee a top choice for sailing in the Mediterranean. It also offers New England and Caribbean charters, and it can book bareboat charters.

Lynn Jachney Charters

P.O. Box 302, Marblehead, MA 01945
800-223-2050 or 781-639-0787
www.lynnjachneycharters.com

Lynn Jachney specializes in premier crewed yachts, offering an excellent choice of vessels for sailing in the Caribbean, the Mediterranean, New England, and the Pacific Northwest.

Nicholson Yacht Charters

29 Sherman St., Cambridge, MA 02138
800-662-6066 or 617-661-0555
www.yachtvacations.com

Nicholson is the oldest and possibly the best source for deluxe crewed charters. All boats have a full-time crew and cook. Hundreds of yachts operate in the Caribbean, the Mediterranean, the South Pacific, and New England.

Paradise Connections

41 Water Isle, St. Thomas, USVI 00802
877-567-9350 or 340-774-1111
www.paradiseconnections.com

Paradise specializes in the Caribbean, with 150 yachts evenly distributed between the Windwards and Leewards.

CHOOSING A CHARTER COMPANY

Here are the most important factors to consider before you book any bareboat or crewed charter trip. Attention to these details will help you avoid the most common problems charterers encounter.

Choose a charterer with a proven track record. Look for a bonded company that has been in business for at least ten years. Although longevity is no guarantee of quality, you will avoid the typical problems that are associated with start-ups.

Ask about the age and condition of the yachts. Pick a company that can give you a boat under five years old, if at all possible. Bareboats take a lot of abuse, and a craft can become a headache after a few seasons of use. You generally get a better quality boat by chartering early in the season or soon after new boats have been delivered.

Learn the hidden costs in advance. Quoted prices typically omit provisioning, charter taxes, land accommodations, and extras such as windsurfers or dive gear. That said, don't be too cheap. Seasonal discounts notwithstanding, you generally get what you pay for when chartering.

Find out what qualifications are required. Almost all bareboat companies will ask you to provide a sailing résumé establishing that you have experience on a yacht of the size you plan to charter. When you arrive at your destination, you will be checked out on the water, and a skipper will be put on board if necessary.

Find out the best season to sail. Ask about wind, weather, and the water temperatures before you go. In much of the Caribbean, the best sailing is in the late spring when prices are lower and the anchorages are far less crowded.

Ask for references from past customers. Before you put down a deposit, talk to people who recently chartered the same type of yacht in the same area. You will learn things no brochure would reveal.

SAILING SCHOOLS

Annapolis Sailing School
P.O. Box 3334, Annapolis, MD 21403
800-638-9192 or 410-267-7205
www.annapolissailing.com

Founded in 1963, the Annapolis Sailing School conducts programs in Annapolis, Maryland, St. Petersburg, Florida, and St. Croix in the U.S. Virgin Islands. Annapolis offers a full range of classes, including one of the best bareboat charter certification programs. Courses range from two to eight days and cost $280-2,500. Highly recommended is the learn-to-sail cruising vacation, a great way for novices to explore the Caribbean with an experienced instructor on board. In Maryland the school offers powerboat handling schools, two- to five-day Kidship programs for ages 5 to 15, and Chesapeake Bay tours by sail or power with lodging at shoreside B&Bs. The Chesapeake tours cost $900 for two days or $1,900-3,200 for five days (depending on extras), all with on-board sailing instruction.

Chichester Sailing Centre
Chichester Marina, Birdham,
Chichester, West Sussex
PO20 7EL, England
01144-1243-512557. Fax 01144-1243-512570

Since 1954, the center has offered sailing instruction year-round in Chichester Harbor, the Solent, the English Channel, and off Brittany. Along with day classes, offshore training cruises are offered starting at $500 for five days, all-inclusive. This traditional, full-service sailing academy is located in the heart of England's yachting world. It is a member of the Royal Yachting Association (RYA). The center also offers skippered charters.

Club Nautique
1150 Ballena Blvd., Suite 161,
Alameda, CA 94501
800-343-7245 or 510-865-4700
www.clubnautique.net

With 45 yachts from 23 to 47 feet, Club Nautique (CN) operates one of the larger training fleets on the West Coast. It runs basic classes in windy San Francisco Bay, as well as intensive offshore cruising courses in the bay and nearby coastal waters (starting at $595). The CN Bareboat Certification course, one of the few such programs that carry much weight with big charter companies, is highly recommended. Bareboat courses begin at $895.

J World, the Performance Sailing School
P.O. Box 1509, Newport, RI 02840
800-343-2255 or 401-849-5492
www.paw.com/sail/jworld

J World offers comprehensive sailing instruction, including the most thorough race training available, in weekend and week-long programs. Instructors include world-class sailors with strong teaching skills. Seminars are offered year-round at San Diego, January through April in Key West, April through October in Annapolis, and May through August in Newport. J World conducts its well-known racing clinics in J-24s and similar boats (five days, $795). It also offers live-aboard cruising classes that teach students how to safely charter their own vessels. Cost will be roughly $1,375 for five days, or $825 for three days.

Offshore Sailing School
16731 McGregor Blvd., Ft. Meyers,
FL 33908
800-221-4326 or 941-454-1700
www.offshore-sailing.com

Training programs include Learn to Sail, Bareboat Cruising Preparation, Live-aboard Cruising, Performance Sailing, and Racing. We recommend the Caribbean Learn to Sail program, a great way to enjoy the bareboat experience without the worry. Offshore operates from eight bases: Captiva Island, St. Petersburg, Newport, New York Harbor, Stamford, Chicago, the Florida Keys, and Tortola in the British Virgin Islands. Prices start at $1,395 a week, including lodging. Yachts are well-maintained 27- to 43-footers.

Sailboats, Inc.
250 Marina Dr., Superior, WI 54880
800-826-7010 or 715-392-7131
www.sailboats-inc.com

Sailboats, Inc., operates the largest sailing school in the midwestern United States. It specializes in introductory courses that combine home study, four hours dockside instruction, and twenty hours on the water. This initial course, which can be taken as a three-day vacation curriculum, costs $795 and certifies a student to charter from the company's fleets in Wisconsin, Ontario, and the Chicago area. Sailboats also offers an advanced blue-water cruising course and a special preparation seminar for Caribbean chartering.

Womanship
137 Conduit St., Annapolis, MD 21401
800-342-9295 or 410-267-6661
www.womanship.com

Founded in 1984, Womanship is a unique sailing program run by women for women. Expert, USCG-certified female instructors teach general sailing plus cruising skills (navigation, sail trim, docking, maintenance) for bareboat certification. Courses range from 2 to 15 days and start at $272; teaching is personalized and noncompetitive. Womanship also runs land-based and live-aboard programs in the Virgin Islands, the Bahamas, the Chesapeake Bay, Florida, New England, California, the Great Lakes, and the Pacific Northwest. Overseas programs include Sail & See cruises in Greece, New Zealand, and Turkey.

SAILING RESOURCES

Bareboat Certification
If you have never bareboated, it is a good idea to take a bareboat certification course. Earning your certificate will not guarantee that you can charter on your own because most charter companies still put a skipper on board the first day unless you have a strong sailing résumé. Most better programs follow the American Sailing Association (ASA) certification standards,

but the best schools go beyond ASA minimums. A good program spans a couple of weekends and includes an offshore cruise. You get training in sail handling, anchoring, coastal navigation, radio etiquette, emergency procedures, and boat maintenance and repair. A basic bareboat course will train you to operate a boat up to 30 feet. After chartering a 30-footer two or three times, you may want to pursue your advanced certificate, which covers yachts up to 50 feet overall. Keep in mind that even with an advanced certificate, you will usually be asked to do a quick boat-handling drill on the water before you leave the charter base.

Sailing Resorts

Sunsail (*800-327-2276. www.sunsail.com*) operates ten land-based sailing resorts, nine in the eastern Mediterranean and one in Antigua. You can sail dinghies, small cats, and windsurfers, or enjoy short overnight cruises on skippered yachts. This is a good choice for families with small kids or those who love to sail but prefer shoreside lodging.

Britain's **Neilson** (*120 St. Georges Rd., Brighton, BN2 1EA, England. 01144-1273-626-283 or 284. www.neilson.co.uk*) operates fine sailing resorts in Greece, Spain, Turkey, and the Caribbean (Dominican Republic, Grenada). You can sail dinghies, catamarans, and windsurfers under the guidance of instructors certified by the Royal Yachting Association.

ONLINE

BVI Welcome Online
www.bviwelcome.com

Along with general travel info for the British Virgins, BVI Welcome lists charters, marinas, and anchorages, plus diving and windsurfing options.

pyacht.com
www.pyacht.com

The latest and greatest e-commerce site for yachties, pyacht.com is an online chandlery with a vast gear inventory for everything from dinghies to ocean racers.

Sail 4U
www.sail4u.be

This Benelux website offers charter listings for virtually every destination you can imagine, plus articles from the leading European sailing journals.

World Wide Sail
www.duhe.com

World Wide Sail lists hundreds of crewed and bareboat charters in all oceans.

YachtLink
www.yachtlink.com

This site is a large, searchable directory of charter agencies and crewed charters, mostly in Europe. It includes listings of used boats for sale worldwide.

BOOKS

Cruising Guide to the Virgin Islands by Simon and Nancy Scott (Cruising Guide Publications, 8th. ed., $17.95. P.O. Box 1017, Dunedin, FL 34697. 800-330-9542 or 813-733-5322) is essential for sailors in both the British and the U.S. Virgin Islands.

Cruising Guide to the Caribbean by William Stone and Anne Hayes (Sheridan House, 1991, $39.95. 145 Palisade St., Dobbs Ferry, NY 10522. 914-693-2410) is the most complete and authoritative guide to cruising in the Caribbean.

Cruising Guide to the Leeward Islands by Chris Doyle (Cruising Guide Publications, 3rd ed., $19.95. 800-330-9542) is a detailed resource with good listings of uncrowded anchorages.

Cruising Guide to Southern California's Offshore Islands by Brian Fagan—a veteran blue-water sailor—is the definitive guide to the region. $24.95.

Imray Piloting Guides provide excellent information on sailing in Europe, including the British Isles and Eastern Europe. About $60 to $70 from **Armchair** in Seattle (2110 Westlake Ave. N., Seattle, WA 98108. 800-875-0852 or 206-283-0858) or Bluewater Books & Charts (1481 S.E. 17th St. Causeway, Fort Lauderdale, FL 33316. 800-942-2583).

World Cruising Routes by Jimmy Cornell (International Marine, McGraw-Hill, $49.95. Blue Ridge Summit, PA 17294. 800-233-1128) details nearly 500 long-distance sailing passages. Cornell's *World Cruising Handbook* provides information on currency, customs, climate, medical facilities, visa requirements, and radio communication protocols.

VIDEO

Bareboat Charter Checklist. This short video covers boat inspection and daily maintenance, and it also offers tips on provisioning and choosing personal gear. $24.95 from Bennett Marine Video (8436 W. 3rd St., #740, Los Angeles, CA 90048. 800-733-8862).

WOMAN OVERBOARD!

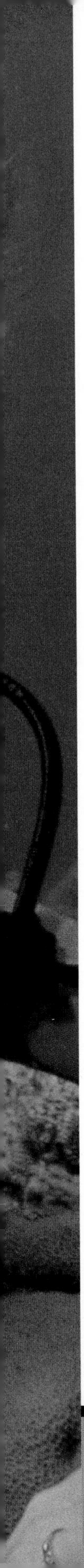

DIVING ALLOWS US TO EXPLORE A NEW WORLD, A WEIGHT-
LESS ENVIRONMENT UNLIKE ANYTHING ABOVE THE SURFACE.
The underwater realm teems with life—brilliantly colored fish,
exotic flora, and fascinating marine creatures such as dolphins,
sharks, and manta rays—providing an endless source of learning
and discovery. • With most of the planet covered by water, the
variety of possible diving destinations is infinite. It is in the tropics,
however, that most divers experience the ultimate in underwater
enjoyment. In the warm, clear waters of the tropics, fish school by
the thousands. Radiant corals are everywhere, and shipwrecks rest at
the bottom of the sea waiting to be explored. • On the following
pages you'll find a comprehensive guide to the top dive destinations
around the globe, along with advice on how to get the best deals on
dive adventures, how to travel to the world's remaining underwater
frontiers, and which outfitters offer services for children, nondivers,
and snorkelers. The ultimate goal is for everyone on your trip to
experience the awesome beauty and stunning diversity of the world
beneath the sea.

LEFT: A DIVER AND A POTATO COD FACE OFF ON AUSTRALIA'S GREAT BARRIER REEF.
BELOW: THE CORAL OF THE SOLOMON ISLANDS

Scuba Diving

Shark Diving

Catching Some Rays

Stay in School

Reef Madness

Adventure can be at your door every day. It is a spirit.
PHILLIPE JEANTOT (DIVER AND YACHT RACER)

Nine Delicious Ways to Dip into Diving

The conditions that make for great diving—warm, translucent water, good weather, and tropical locales—also make for a terrific getaway vacation. You'll find great bargains at the big Caribbean resorts, while exotic destinations such as Borneo and Micronesia promise true underwater adventure.

FIJI
South Pacific Paradise

Ask divers who have sampled most of the world's leading dive spots where they would go for a perfect dive vacation, and more often than not Fiji is the answer. Topside, Fiji is Polynesia at its best—unspoiled and uncrowded. The water is warm and clear, and there is every imaginable shape and variety of coral in all colors of the rainbow. The variety of dive sites is staggering—from the air, Fiji appears as a vast patchwork of coral covering hundreds of square miles.

Fiji is one destination where there is no clear choice between land-based and live-aboard diving options. Living aboard the dive boat allows you to explore the more remote dive sites and log the most dives per day. On the other hand, you will miss the experience of living on a tropical island, which is one of the best reasons to visit Fiji. The outer islands are quiet, idyllic retreats where civilization truly slips from your consciousness. And the Fijians are a wonderful people, fun loving and warmhearted.

Most of Fiji's premier dive spots are clustered among the northern group of islands, including **Vanua Levu, Matangi,** and **Taveuni.** The dive resort of choice—and the best for experienced divers—is the **Taveuni Island Resort** (*877-828-3864. www.divetaveuni.com*). Although the currents can be strong, Taveuni's diving is among the best in the world, and the lodge has been recently upgraded. The **Namale Plantation** (*800-447-3454 or 808-871-5986. www.maui. net/~fiji/namale.html*) is a bit more luxurious and a good all-around resort. If you're taking a family vacation, consider the **Jean Michel Cousteau Fiji Resort** (*San Francisco, CA. 800-246-3454 or 415-788-5794. www.fijiresort.com*), which offers plenty of topside activities, including a resident marine biologist and a staff of children's activity counselors.

Those with limited time may prefer to dive from the main island of Viti Levu. Despite strong currents, the Beqa Lagoon is easily the best dive area accessed from Viti Levu, boasting fascinating cuts, passages, and overhangs, and vividly colored soft coral walls. **Marlin Bay Resort** (*Newport Beach, CA. 800-542-3454 or 679-304042 in Fiji. www. marlinbay.com*) is the only hotel on the tiny, unspoiled island of Beqa. It offers daily dive trips to the lagoon as well as package holidays, including surfaris. Lagoon dive trips can also

be arranged with **Aqua Trek** (*Centra Hotel. 800-541-4334 or 011679-450022*). The cost is about $80 to $110 per day (two tanks).

Divers seeking a live-aboard option can choose between the two leading dive boats—the 85-foot M.V. *Princess II* and the 106-foot *Fiji Aggressor*. The *Fiji Aggressor* (*Seattle, WA. 800-247-3483. www.divetropical.com*) boasts the best onboard facilities and it ventures to the least crowded dive sites. The cost for a weeklong package is $2,300. The M.V. *Princess II* (*Boulder, CO. 800-576-7327. www. princessii.com*), based at Matangi Island, visits only the northern islands, including the Somosomo Strait. It offers combined land and live-aboard vacations, however, and it is less expensive than the *Fiji Aggressor*.

Trips start at approximately $2,040 for seven nights, including air flights within Fiji. Another vessel, the *Hana Nai'a* (*Niwot, CO. 800-854-3454. www.seafiji.com/ liveaboards.htm*), based in Lautoka, costs about $2,500 for seven nights and $3,600 for ten nights, including transfers to Lautoka. From Lautoka, it travels to Namena, Wakaya, Gau, and other prime areas of the northern group. You can book your holiday directly with the outfitter or through an agency such as **Tropical Adventures** (*800-247-3483*) or **Sea Fiji Travel** (*800-854-3454*).

INDONESIA
Diving Dreamland

For diversity of species—in the water, on land, and soaring overhead—you just can't beat the Indo-Pacific. Scientists estimate that for every 50 species of tropical fishes, ferns, orchids, or birds in the Caribbean, you will find 500 in the Indo-Pacific. Those impressive numbers translate into an exotic and fascinating marine life as well as a rich topside culture—the makings of world-class adventure.

Though land-based options are available, a live-aboard tour is the best way to explore Indonesia, a collection of about 15,000 islands. In addition to the convenience and appeal of virtually round-the-clock diving, the uncrowded islands and the undiscovered dive sites are all easily accessible. On an Indonesian live-aboard expedition, more often than not, the divers from your boat will be the only ones in the water with you. This is the kind of solitude you'll not be able to find in the Caymans or at Cozumel.

Many good dive vessels operate from the island of Bali. The *Sea Contacts I & II* offer dedicated dive trips around Bali and in nearby waters for about $225 per day. Also consider a dive voyage on the *Pelagian*, a beautiful boat delivering all the amenities for $2,750 per week. It sails June through October, the best dive months in the region. For more information or to book, contact **Tropical Adventures** (*800-247-3483. www.divetropical.com*) or **Deep Discoveries, Ltd.** (*Mulhurst Bay, AB, Canada. 800-667-5362 or 780-389-4408. www.deepdiscoveries.com*).

If you prefer to spend more time shoreside, there are some attractive land-based tours that will still let you sample the spectacular diving found in this part of the world. **Manado,** on the north side of Sulawesi, has several fine dedicated dive resorts, as well as a full range of hotels. At the **Kungkungan Bay Resort,** designed by and dedicated to divers, a seven-day package with 12 dives costs $1,575. The **Murex,** a family-run resort, offers a diving package priced at $100 per day. Either hotel can be booked through Tropical Adventures. For a more Western-style resort experience, the **Tafik Ria Hotel** offers a seven-night package, including dinners, for $800.

From the bustling waterfront city of Manado, you can also make an easy day trip to **Bunaken Island Marine Park.** An extensive fringing reef borders the park. Beyond, there's a steep drop-off where divers often catch a glimpse of large pelagics—whales, mantas, and whale sharks. Big schools of jacks and barracuda are an everyday occurrence. Inside the reef, it's a tropical aquarium—more species of coral and fishes than can be counted.

BAJA MEXICO
Latin Getaway

The water is neither as clear nor as warm as in the Caribbean or Indo-Pacific, but it doesn't really matter. Big sea creatures are what Baja diving is all about—sea lions, mantas, and schooling hammerheads, even whales.

The two major dive hubs in the southern Baja California Peninsula are **Cabo San Lucas** and **La Paz.** In Cabo, the oldest and by far the best dive shop is **Amigos Del Mar,** which coordinates the diving at many of the major resorts. In La Paz, a half day to the northeast, the diving is done from beach resorts, such as the **Hotel Las Arenas** and **Hotel Los Arcos.** Although the shoreside resorts are appealing, for serious divers, a live-aboard is the best way to go. An ocean-going dive vessel can access all the better known Sea of Cortez sites, such as the **Salvatierra** wreck, **El Bajo** seamounts (mantas and hammerheads), and **Los Islotes Island** (sea lions), which are quite a distance from the beach resorts. **Baja Expeditions** (*San Diego, CA. 800-843-6967*

or *858-581-3311. www.bajaex.com*) runs seven-day live-aboard trips on the 80-foot *Don Jose*. Although the *Don Jose* is an older vessel, it is air-conditioned and the crew is excellent. The cost runs from $1,300 to $1,700 per person.

For those with limited time, Baja Expeditions offers day trips on their quick *Rio Rita* and even faster *La Tina* dive boats. These relatively speedy craft cut the time spent on passages so that you can reach one of the more popular dive spots quickly and enjoy three dives in a single day. Cost is $115 per day including air tanks and two meals. We recommend you bring your own buoyancy compensator, regulator, and gauges, although rentals are available.

If you're willing to make a longer, eight- to ten-day offshore trip, you can experience what one world-renowned underwater photographer called the "best place I have ever dived." **Socorro** and **San Benedicto Islands**—part of the Revillagigedo chain—are located in the Pacific, about 250 miles south of the tip of Baja California. A trip out to these volcanic islands offers the chance to get up close and personal with giant mantas, schools of hammerheads, whale sharks, bottlenose dolphins, tiger sharks, schools of tuna, and more. The best time to visit the Revillagigedos is late fall, when the water is warmer—usually about 80° F—the season has ended, and the visibility averages 100 feet. Only a few live-aboards have permits to run dive trips to this protected area. Our first pick is the 112-foot **Solmar V** (*Pacific Palisades, CA. 800-344-3349 or 310-459-9861. www.*

solmar.com). Based in Cabo San Lucas, this luxurious live-aboard boasts 12 air-conditioned staterooms, each with a private bath. The crew is first-rate, with knowledgeable dive-masters from Amigos Del Mar. A nine-day trip runs $2,475, with about 22 divers on board. After June, the price drops to $1,715 for seven days.

Manta Magic

There's something about diving with gentle sea creatures that has an almost universal appeal. For a thrilling adventure that could easily be added on to a family vacation, try the **manta ray night dives** on the Big Island of Hawaii.

Surrounded by very deep water—approximately 18,000 feet—the Hawaiian Islands are a natural magnet for large sea creatures. Green and hawksbill turtles, spinner and other species of dolphins, and the occasional whale share these waters with more than 600 species of reef fishes. While Hawaii's bigger sea creatures tend to prefer deep waters, the **Kona Surf** hotel has discovered a clever way to attract some impressively big pelagics—notably Pacific manta rays—close in to shore for night feeding. Strong spotlights illuminate the water, attracting large swarms of plankton, and these in turn attract the mantas. Although the wingspan of a Pacific manta averages 5 to 8 feet across, some of the creatures can measure as much as 14 feet. Watching them swoop in from the darkness, gliding, even somersaulting through the sea, using their fins to funnel water and plankton into their open mouths, is a thrill that you won't soon forget.

In Kona's manta encounter programs, divers typically gather in a circle on the bottom and shine their dive lights into the center of the open water column to concentrate the plankton and to allow the mantas plenty of room to maneuver. All operators offering this night manta dive follow established guidelines. Protecting the animals is the primary focus of these rules, so touching the mantas is strictly prohibited. A number of dive operators in Kona offer manta dives, and it's advisable to make reservations, especially during peak season. Price averages $60-$100, depending on extras, operator, and season. With **Jack's Diving Locker** (*Kailua-Kona, HI. 800-345-4807 or 808-329-7585. www.divejdl.com*), the trip runs $85 for a two-tank/two-location adventure that includes a light supper. Jack's price includes tanks and weights; the rest of the gear can be rented for another $15-$20. Typically you'll do one late-afternoon dive at another Big Island site, then move to the Kona Surf for the evening's main attraction. This is an excellent way to get comfortable if you haven't made many night dives , or if it's been awhile since you were last in tanks.

Another outfitter, **Eco-Adventures,** located at the King Kamehameha Hotel in Kailua-Kona (*800-949-3483 or 808-329-7116. www.eco-adventure.com*), charges $97 for a two-tank manta dive. Snorkelers are $65, and the dive boat holds 20 people at full capacity. You can also book manta encounter dives through **Red Sail Sports** (*San Francisco, CA. 877-733-7245 or 808-885-2876. www.redsail.com*). While most of the Kona-based dive operators offer a manta ray night dive, not every dive shop leads a tour each night, so be sure to make advance reservations.

BAHAMAS
Diving with Dolphins

If you have a limited amount of vacation time and are looking for a truly unique underwater experience, we recommend you head straight for the Bahamas. There, in the waters off **Grand Bahama Island,** divers can experience the special thrill of open-ocean diving with dolphins.

The Bahamas' leading dive-with-dolphins program is offered by the **Underwater Explorers Society** (*Freeport. 800-992-3483 or 242-373-1244. www.unexso.com*). Since 1969, UNEXSO has offered a two-part program involving dolphins rescued from captive environments. In the trainer assistant program, both divers and nondivers interact with dolphins in a protected inlet in Sanctuary Bay. This cost is $179 and is limited to four participants a day; this ensures that the dolphins are not overwhelmed by human contact.

Much more exciting than the training assistant program, however, are the open-ocean dolphin and reef dives.

UNEXSO's dolphins are released into the ocean, where they rendezvous with the dive boats a mile offshore. Under the supervision of the dolphin handlers, a maximum of 12 divers feed the animals and swim alongside them for short distances. It is all fairly businesslike but it is still the experience of a lifetime for most divers. The dolphin dive is one part of a five-dive package costing $170. The program operates year-round.

If UNEXSO's dolphin dive is not the natural encounter you have in mind, it is also possible to dive with wild dolphins off Grand Bahama, although contact with the creatures is not a sure thing. One of the Bahamas' leading live-aboards, the 80-foot catamaran *Bottom Time II,* makes regular five-to ten-day trips to the shallow banks north of Grand Bahama—the favored playground of schools of wild spotted dolphins. On a good day, dolphins surround the boat by the time the anchor is secure. The wild mammals, familiar with the operation, circle around the dive ladders and often swim close to the divers during the entire session. The *Bottom Time II* is fast, stable, and very comfortable. It has 15 private cabins and all the amenities, even an onboard film lab. A typical seven-day dolphin adventure runs $1,295. Contact **Bottom Time Adventures**(*Ft. Lauderdale, FL. 800-234-8464 or 954-921-7798. www.bottomtime2.com*).

If a land-based trip is more to your liking, contact **Neal Watson's Undersea Adventures** (*Ft. Lauderdale, FL. 800-327-8150. www.nealwatson.com*). Watson offers a seven-night dive/hotel package that includes a one-day dolphin interaction for $1,085.

CAYMAN ISLANDS
Divers' Disneyland

The Caymans are the most popular dive destination in the Caribbean, and despite the number of people who flock there, few better aquatic playgrounds exist in the Northern Hemisphere. The water is warm, the wall-diving is world-class, and the visibility is consistently excellent—the best in the central Caribbean. While the Caymans have countless good dive sites, Grand Cayman can be crowded. Those in the know prefer to spend most of their diving time on **Cayman Brac** and **Little Cayman.** The coral is less chewed up, and there are more fish. Little Cayman's **Bloody Bay Wall** is spectacular, while favorites on Cayman Brac include **Sea Fan Wall** and **Butterfly Reef.**

No trip to the Caymans would be complete, however, without a chance to dive with stingrays in the shallows of **Grand Cayman's North Sound.** Here, at Stingray City and Sand Bar, divers can hand-feed the rays in crystal-clear 10-to 15-foot waters. This is a real crowd-pleaser, an opportunity to interact with surprisingly intelligent creatures that seem to enjoy their encounters with humans. **Treasure**

Island Divers (*800-872-7552. www.tidivers.com*) visits the sound three times a week. Diving costs $50, snorkeling is $30. And since you'll be on Grand Cayman, don't miss the famed **North Wall.** It starts fairly deep, at 70 feet, so you must monitor your dive times carefully.

The quality of the dive shops in the Caymans is high, a result of the intense competition. You won't go wrong with any of the top operators, including **Bob Soto's Diving, Ltd.,** (*800-262-7686. www.bobsotosdiving.com.ky*); and **Red Sail Sports** (*877-733-7245 or 345-949-8745. www.redsail.com*). Both are based on Grand Cayman.

It bears repeating: If you want to log the most dives each day, then book a live-aboard. **Brac Aquatic's** *Little Cayman Diver II* (*800-544-2722*) has been called the Caribbean's best boat, while the *Cayman Aggressor IV* (*800-348-2628*) is also excellent—less luxurious perhaps, but far more stable. Or you can book through **Dive Tours** (*Spring, TX. 800-433-0885 or 281-257-1771. www.divetours.org*), which operates out of Little Cayman. The company's seven-night trip aboard the 110-foot *Aggressor* runs $1,900. This spacious vessel boasts excellent chefs, nine staterooms with bath and shower, sundeck, and hot tub. Dive Tours also offers great deals on air tickets to the Caymans.

MICRONESIA
Lagoonatics

In Greater Micronesia, especially the islands of **Truk, Pohnpei,** and **Yap,** and the **Republic of Palau,** you will find unequaled wreck-diving, great visibility, large sea creatures, and dense schools of tropical fish.

Truk (or "Chuuk," as locals say), the site of one of World War II's great air and sea battles, is a wreck-diving site without peer. In all, there are more that 80 wrecks suitable for divers; you could spend a month here and not see it all. And Truk's underwater world is more than just rusting hulks. Over time the wrecks have become artificial reefs alive with corals and sea life. According to *Scuba Times Magazine,* "Truk Lagoon is the absolute ultimate....Dive it and be spoiled forever." Unfortunately, most wrecks are fairly deep—between 60 and 90 feet—so the lagoon is not the best destination for novices.

In order to spend the maximum amount of dive time exploring the most interesting wrecks, you should seriously consider a live-aboard. Your choices are the 170-foot *Thorfinn,* the 107-foot *Truk Aggressor II,* and the new *Odyssey.* All are comfortable, well-equipped vessels with knowledgeable crews. Though the *Thorfinn* stays in the lagoon,

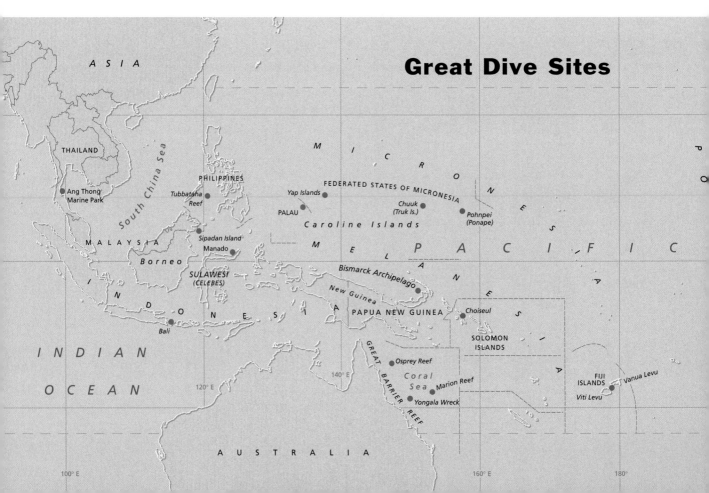

Great Dive Sites

the *Aggressor* visits the outer atolls and reef walls every week, providing a refreshing break from wreck-diving. The *Aggressor* also features double staterooms with private baths. An eight-day *Aggressor* live-aboard trip runs about $2,395, while the *Thorfinn*—which is 60 feet longer and very spacious but is older—runs about $2,300. To book a trip or for more information, contact **Tropical Adventures** (*800-247-3483. www.divetropical.com*).

After Truk, the Republic of Palau is greater Micronesia's leading attraction. Indeed, Palau has been ranked as one of the best all-around dive sites in the world. A large atoll with over 200 islands, Palau offers incredible diversity. The variety of dive spots in a small area is staggering, with 60 great drop-offs starting at surface levels and falling to 1,000 feet. The water is 82° F, with visibility typically 125 to 200 feet. Palau boasts a dozen blue holes, and a famed five-chambered cave system. The sea life is superb—clams that weigh 1,000 pounds, thick schools of reef fish, and large pelagics.

The best land-based dive operation in Palau is **Sam's Dive Tours**. Its divemasters know all the top sites, it employs fast, modern dive boats, and it offers high-end equipment, including nitrox tanks. If you prefer a live-aboard, **Peter Hughes Diving** (*Miami, FL. 800-932-6237 or 305-669-9391. www.peterhughes.com*) operates a superb vessel in Palau, the 138-foot *Sun Dancer II*. A gorgeous vessel launched in 1994, the *Sun Dancer* features air-conditioned staterooms, onboard photo lab, and user-friendly dive tenders. Trips run from $1,100 to $2,200 for seven days. Peter Hughes is the only operation with permits to dive all of the Palauan states, including Helen's Reef and the Southwest Islands. Trips are offered year-round with prices starting at $2,400 per person for seven days; ten-day packages run $3,100 to $3,300. From July 30 through October 22, similar trips are half the price.

Another fine live-aboard choice for Palau is the six-passenger, 60-foot *Ocean Hunter*. A one-week charter runs approximately $2,400 per person. This luxurious smaller boat can sit on the dive site so you don't have to swim long distances or be ferried, allowing you to rack up more dives each day.

If you have time left after Truk and Palau, we recommend a three-day visit to Yap. Yap's Mil Channel is perhaps the best place in the world to see giant mantas in the open ocean; close encounters are virtually guaranteed. While you can make your own arrangements with a number of Yap-based dive

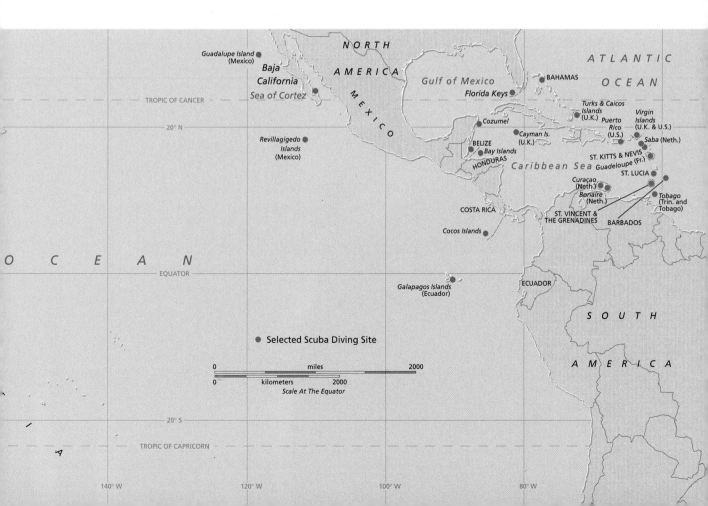

Shark Diving

The possibility of encountering a shark can fill a diver with both fascination and fear. For many seasoned divers, nothing can top a shark-diving adventure as the ultimate underwater thrill. Of course, not all sharks are the predators movies portray them to be. According to experts, the majority of sharks that you'd encounter while diving, including whale sharks and hammerheads, are generally not dangerous. But because of the many types of shark-diving expeditions you can choose from, you'll undoubtedly witness awesome behavior, from the teeth-baring aggressiveness of the great white shark to the dominance behavior of the female hammerhead, who performs a reverse flip with a full twist to warn off other females.

If a front row seat to such displays is what you're after, any number of outfitters will be happy to set you up. On the wild side are encounters with the deadly and fearsome great white shark. Great whites are distributed widely throughout the world's oceans, but the hot spot is in South Australia. There, from the safety of a metal cage, divers can experience the fury of a 15-foot great white from just an arm's length away.

If sharing personal space with huge sharks is what you seek but you don't want to be confined in a steel cage, consider a whale shark adventure. Unlike their smaller cousins, 25-foot whale sharks are not carnivores but filter-feeders, filtering plankton from the water using gill rakers. Consequently they are actually quite docile and tolerant of divers. With their distinctive spotted grey coloration, whale sharks are among the most beautiful creatures in the sea. In recent years, Western Australia and Baja California, have been reliable destinations for spotting whale sharks, although these mysterious giants can be elusive. Baja also offers diving with schools of hammerhead sharks—usually composed mostly of females—at a variety of sites.

Some favorite dive tour organizations that specialize in shark trips include:

Mad Dog Expeditions

132 E. 82nd St., New York, NY 10028
212-744-6763
www.mad-dog.net

Mad Dog, a firm specializing in highly exotic dive travel, leads a variety of shark dives, including a ten-day Great White Shark Expedition in the waters of South Africa. The program includes cage diving and surface activities with the South African Great White Shark Research Institute.

San Diego Shark Diving Expeditions

6747 Friar's Road, Suite 112
San Diego, CA 92108
888-737-4275 or 619-299-8560
www.sdsharkdiving.com

GRAY REEF SHARK OFF BIKINI ATOLL, MARSHALL ISLANDS

This company offers cage diving with steel-suited divemasters working outside the cage. The popular California trips (one, three, or four days) offer plenty of shark interaction and start at just $260. International dive expeditions, up to 13 days in length, are offered in South Africa (great whites), Cocos Island (hammerheads), the Galápagos, the Seychelles (whale sharks), Thailand, and Mexico. For novice divers, we recommend the whale shark expeditions in Baja's Sea of Cortez. Using spotter planes and an 80-foot live-aboard base, this trip is limited to just 14 divers. Advanced divers will enjoy Mexico's Islas Revillagegedo, home to schooling hammerheads and giant manta rays.

White Pointer Cage Diving & Sport Fishing

P.O. Box 2426, Port Lincoln, South Australia 5606. 011618-8682-2425. www.seachart.mtx.net

White Pointer offers close encounters with the feared great white shark. Divers observe the great whites from the safety of a sturdy dive cage. Skipper/owner Bruce Bennett is one of the most experienced operators running shark dives in the Southern Hemisphere. The chances of sighting great whites are better in this part of the world than any other. The four- to six-day charters cost $1,800-2,000 (AUS) per diver. Charters are normally limited to four divers so you get plenty of time in the cage and more elbow room topside.

operations (Manta Ray Bay Hotel & Yap Divers and Fish 'n Fins are among the best), it is easier and not much more costly to book a package vacation through a mainland dive agency such as Tropical Adventures or **Dive Tours** (*Spring, TX. 800-433-0885 or 281-257-1771. www.divetours.org*).

AUSTRALIA
The Great Barrier Reef and Coral Sea

Australia has much to recommend it as a premier dive destination: The Great Barrier Reef and the legendary Coral Sea, water that is a warm 75° to 85° F, visibility that ranges from good to spectacular, and enough outstanding dive sites to last a lifetime. Dive outfitting is extremely competitive in Australia, so you can generally find any type of trip you want at surprisingly low prices. Cairns (pronounced cans) in Northern Queensland is Australia's dive mecca, and here you will find superb vacation values.

A half-dozen excellent dive shops, such as **Down Under Dive** and **Mike Ball Dive Expeditions,** line the waterfront in Cairns, making comparison-shopping easy and productive. The most popular offerings are three- to five-day Barrier Reef live-aboard trips, typically priced at around $500 to $750—which is a good 20 percent less than similar trips advertised by American dive agencies. During three to four days offshore, you can sample a host of Barrier Reef sites, making a half-dozen dives a day—more if you add night dives. First-time divers can also enroll in a certification course in Cairns that concludes with a three-day offshore trip to the reef.

While the Barrier Reef is excellent by any measure, if you are looking for the maximum quantity and variety of sea creatures, you should head much farther offshore, out to the Coral Sea. The water is very warm, and during the best seasons visibility can exceed 200 feet. The seamounts of **Marion Reef** are magnets for aquatic life, attracting everything from schooling tropicals to whale sharks. Many experts believe that the wreck of the *Yongala* (sunk during a 1911 cyclone) is the single best dive in the world. It is virtually guaranteed that you will see vast numbers of fish and large pelagics, and visibility is regularly 200 feet or better between August and November. Visit the *Yongala* in June to observe schools of 25-foot-long mickey whales.

For those seeking an extended dive trip aboard a first-class vessel, try **Mike Ball Dive Expeditions** (*Richmond, BC, Canada. 800-952-4319 or 011617-4772-3022 in Australia. www.mikeball.com*). Mike Ball offers excellent multiday trips aboard luxurious twin-hulled dive craft, namely the 100-foot *Spoilsport,* the 90-foot *Supersport,* and the 70-foot *Watersport.* These large catamarans are fast, comfortable, stable, and have many special features ideal for diving. Departing from Townsville, the *Spoilsport* sails out to the Coral Sea on a seven-day voyage starting from around $1,420. The *Tara II*, another good live-aboard vessel with an expert crew, also offers dive trips to the Great Barrier Reef year-round. To book, contact **Tropical Adventures** (*800-247-3483. www.divetropical.com*).

Australian dive trips can be booked through agencies such as the ones mentioned above. However, you can save plenty if you bargain directly with the Aussie dive shops, such as **Down Under Dive, Pusa Dive,** and **Don Cawley Underwater Aquatics,** located on the Cairns waterfront or in Townsville.

GALÁPAGOS ISLANDS
South American Spectacle

This locale is a fantasy world for divers accustomed to nothing but small fish. Along with dense schools of tropical fish, there are numerous sea turtles, sea lions, and large pelagics. Many Galápagos dive sites harbor distinctive animal groups—such as schooling sharks, penguins, or even the marine iguanas, remarkable creatures found nowhere else on Earth. Nothing can prepare you for your first underwater encounter with an iguana. With their human-like limbs, they look like small green frogmen. Unafraid and largely uninterested in humans, they permit divers to approach as they bottom-feed. It's tough diving, however, as the iguanas stick to shallow waters with lots of surge.

Since the Galápagos are maintained as a wilderness preserve, there are no beach resorts. Therefore, all diving is done from live-aboard vessels. The M.V. *Mistral* is a top recommendation; it is a modern, comfortable, air-conditioned 74-foot, 12-passenger vessel. The *Mistral* has twice the cruising speed of other vessels, allowing much shorter crossings (most travel is at night). The *Mistral's* cruises (seven nights cost $2,200; ten nights, $3,150) reach the northern islands, **Wolf** and **Darwin,** where the schooling hammerheads gather.

The *Aggressor I* and *II* are also good choices. Both *Aggressors,* though slower than *Mistral,* have able crews, comfortable cabins with bath and shower, air-conditioning, sun deck, and hot tub. Either vessel costs $2,700 per week. Another option is the M.S. *Lammer Law,* a 93-foot sailing trimaran. An impressive sight under sail, this huge, dedicated dive yacht carries up to 18 passengers, at a rate of $2,530 for seven nights. The *Lammer Law's* wide, stable platform and vast deck space make it ideal for families with kids. Galápagos live-aboard dive trips can be booked through many agencies, including **Tropical Adventures** (*800-247-3483. www.divetropical.com*) and **Dive Tours** (*800-443-0885. www.divetours.org*).

Choosing a Dive Tour Operator

At the most popular dive spots, such as the Cayman Islands and Cozumel, you'll find as many as two dozen dive companies eagerly competing for your business. Choosing the best dive operation isn't always easy. But doing your homework—including reading the information below—can help you plan a rewarding getaway.

Land-based vs. Live-aboard

In many of the world's top dive spots, a live-aboard trip beats a land-based dive vacation hands down. On a live-aboard, you spend the maximum amount of time in the water. If you get up early, and dive shallow, it's quite possible to do six dives a day from a well-equipped dive boat. At a land resort, by contrast, you're lucky to get in three dives per day, since so much time is lost in transit. Even the best live-aboards get claustrophobic, however, so plan to take some shore leave after five to six days.

Dive Boat and Divemaster

Not all dive boats are created equal. A premium vessel should have an onboard compressor, and be able to carry at least 40 reserve tanks. Boats with large reserve air chambers are the best; they allow the speediest refills, and you don't have to lug so many tanks aboard. Select an easy-to-board vessel with a large, open gear-donning area. Stability and deck space are also important, and here, a big catamaran can't be beat. At sea, comfort counts; hot showers and private cabins are worth the extra cost. Divemasters come in all varieties, from superb to downright dangerous. If possible, choose a dive program that uses Western divemasters. They tend to be more safety-conscious and professional.

Variety in the Dive Sites

No matter how spectacular, any dive site becomes old hat quickly. Select a dive trip that visits a variety of locations, preferably at least two sites per day. Try to mix reef diving with wall diving, and add something of special interest, such as a lobster hole or shipwreck. Choose a locale where there's plenty to see above 45 feet. In general, shallow dives offer more clarity, color, and sea life. Your air supply will also last longer near the surface.

Recreational Options

Even in the best locations, you may grow tired of diving after three or four days. On a live-aboard, you'll want to return to shore for a respite. At a land-based resort, you may want to try another sport, or simply do nothing for a spell. Many tours offer a discount for days that you don't dive. Or, it may be possible to combine diving with sailing, fishing, or windsurfing, all for a single price.

Earning Your Dive Certification While on Vacation

Even if you've never dived before or your certification has lapsed, you can still enjoy a rewarding dive vacation. Most good dive centers around the world offer certification courses for first-time or out-of-practice divers. PADI or NAUI certifications are the most widely recognized, so select a PADI or NAUI training facility if possible. Before you choose a course, comparison shop with these points in mind. How much does the complete course cost, including the ocean dives? How many hours are spent in the pool versus the open water? Is the training pool deep enough to permit proper equalization? (It should be at least 8 feet deep.) What dive gear are you required to buy, and does the shop offer discounts on these items? How many years has the facility been in business, and how experienced are the instructors? Can you get a partial refund if you cannot complete the course? How many students are in each class? (The fewer the better, and never more than ten per instructor.) If the course involves boat dives, how many per day are you allowed? How much does it cost to add extra dive days once the course is complete?

The better dive shops will give reassuring answers to all these questions. When booking a foreign dive training program, however, try to avoid full payment in advance, and make sure that your spot is guaranteed. You don't need to purchase lots of costly gear before you go. Do obtain a top-quality mask that fits perfectly. But until you've decided how serious a diver you want to become, you probably should not invest in a custom wet suit, or expensive gauges and dive computers.

DIVE TRAVEL AGENCIES

The following agencies can book land-based or live-aboard dive trips worldwide, from air transport to lodging. Some, such as Tropical Adventures, specialize in live-aboards, while others, such as Island Dreams, focus on major land resorts. Don't assume that even the best agencies have firsthand knowledge of foreign dive operations, however, and remember that you may save as much as 10 to 20 percent on the cost by contacting dive shops directly.

Deep Discoveries, Ltd.
3A 1st Ave. N., Mulhurst Bay, AB T0C 2C0, Canada. 800-667-5362 or 780-389-4408
www.deepdiscoveries.com
DESTINATIONS: Costa Rica, Dominica, Fiji, Honduras, Indonesia (Bali, Manado), Malaysia, Maldives, Philippines, Seychelles, Tabago.

Specializes in more remote, less-traveled dive venues, most of which are land based. Agents develop custom itineraries and can create vacations that combine diving with rafting, kayaking, or biking.

Island Dreams Tours & Travel
8582 Katy Freeway, Suite 118
Houston, TX 77024. 800-346-6116 or 713-973-9300. www.islandream.com
DESTINATIONS: Australia, Belize, Bonaire, Cayman Islands, Cozumel, Fiji, Guanaja, Honduras, Indonesia, Malaysia, Roatan, Sipadan Island, Solomon Islands, Vanuatu.

Offers very competitive prices to Caribbean dive destinations and caters to divers looking for top dive destinations worldwide. All diving options are offered, from live-aboards to the best dive resorts. Agents are experienced divers.

Landfall Productions, Dive & Adventure Travel
855 Howe Ave., Suite 5
Sacramento, CA 95825.
800-525-3833 or 916-563-0164
www.landfallproductions.com
DESTINATIONS: Baja, Bay Islands, Belize, Bequia, Bonaire, BVI, Caymans,

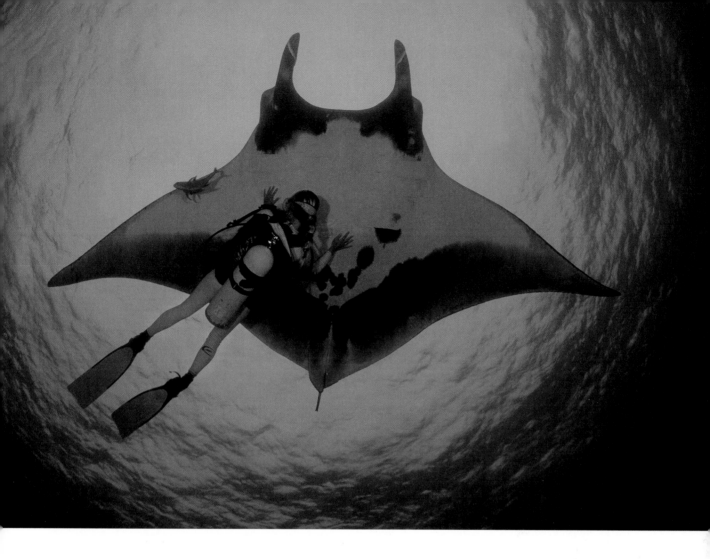

Cozumel, Costa Rica, Dominica, Fiji, Galápagos, Grenadines, Indonesia, Micronesia, Roatan, St. Kitts-Nevis, St. Lucia, St. Vincent.

Offers value-oriented, land-based and live-aboard trips. It is the largest and oldest dive tour operator for St. Vincent and the Grenadines, and runs a strong program in the Galápagos.

PADI Travel Network

30151 Tomas St.
Rancho Santa Margarita, CA 92688
800-729-7234 or 949-858-7234
www.PADI.com

DESTINATIONS: Australia, Bay Islands, Belize, Bonaire, Caymans, Cozumel, Curaçao, Fiji, Galápagos, Indonesia, Micronesia, Philippines, New Guinea, Red Sea, Thailand.

The most recognized dive qualification worldwide.PADI Travel Network books dive trips to roughly a hundred resorts worldwide. It offers quality resorts and very attractive prices, but its customer service could be improved.

Sportours

2335 Honolulu Ave., Montrose, CA 91020
800-774-0295 or 818-553-3333
www.sportours.com

DESTINATIONS: Africa (East and South), Australia, Caribbean, Central America, Indian Ocean, Mexico, Micronesia, Red Sea, South America, South Pacific, Southeast Asia.

Offers two decades of experience and a commitment to quality, customized tours. The staff visits and dives the venues it promotes, and it favors environmentally conscious dive operations. Customized trips and discount airfares available also.

Tropical Adventures

111 2nd Ave. N., Seattle, WA 98109
800-247-3483 or 206-441-3483
www.divetropical.com

DESTINATIONS: Africa, Australia, Baja, Belize, Bonaire, Caymans, Costa Rica, Cozumel, Fiji, Galápagos, Hawaii, Indonesia, Micronesia, Papua New Guinea, Red Sea, Seychelles, Solomon Islands.

The only agency offering regularly scheduled trips to East Africa. Agents have dived the regions in which they specialize.

GALLERY & FREE DIVING

Blue-water Hunting—Hold Your Breath!
Blue water hunting combines the challenge of free diving—diving without gear—with the thrill of big game fishing. Armed with only a camera or spear and a lung-full of air, divers pursue giant gamefish miles from shore, in deep waters often inhabited by man-eaters such as great whites.

Diving without gear rewards divers with rare aquatic experiences. Imagine a 200-pound tuna towing you across the surface or having a 500-pound marlin circling you in pursuit of a 50-pound yellowfin. In the waters off Baja Mexico or Australia, lucky blue-water divers ride whale sharks or giant manta rays.

TWO CREATURES WITH SELF-CONTAINED UNDERWATER BREATHING APPARATUS

Great Dive Sites Worldwide

Water Temp./ Visibility	Best Season	Recommended Dive Shops	Recommended Live-aboards	Accommodations	Package Per Week

AUSTRALIA (GREAT BARRIER REEF) *Lots of fish despite heavy dive traffic. Incredible diversity of corals and marine life. Worth a dive: Cod Hole, Osprey, Bougainville, and Flynn Reefs. The reef is far enough offshore that you should go for at least 3 days at a time. Avoid the 1-day programs; they're too rushed.*

| 73-85/50'-120' | Aug.-Dec. | Deep Sea Divers Den, Pro Dive (Cairns) | *Nimrod Explorer, Spoilsport, Supersport* | Many budget hotels on Cairns waterfront, live-aboard recommended | $1,400 (avg.) |

AUSTRALIA (SOUTH CORAL SEA) *Lihou Reef, Yongala wreck ranks among world's top 10 dive sites. Unreal visibility on the far offshore sites, with amazing fish numbers. Marion Reef has 220' pinnacles. Yongala wreck is a virtually guaranteed superb dive for clarity, sea life, and number of animals.*

| 75-80/70'-200' | Aug.-Dec. | Mike Ball Dive Expeditions, Don Cawley Underwater Aquatics | *Spoilsport, Undersea Explorer* | Exmouth Hotel | $1,000 (3 days) LB $2,970 (10 days deluxe) LA |

BAHAMAS *With 890 islands, the Bahamas offer incredible diversity—deep and shallow reefs, countless wrecks, blue holes, caves. Long Island is popular for wall and wreck diving. Enjoy dive sites from the James Bond film, and Shark Reef off Long Island. Winter can be too cold.*

| 68-85/70'-125' | All (summer best) | Neal Watson's Undersea Adventures, UNEXSO | *Bottom Time II* | Stella Maris, Divi Bahamas Resort | $1,295 LB $1,395-1,595 LA |

BAJA (SEA OF CORTEZ) *Best diving in north Pacific. Manta rays, dolphins, whales, sea lions. Great wreck dive: the Salvatierra. El Bajo seamount has schooling hammerheads. For safety, go with U.S.-based tour. Live-aboard is best, but East Cape hotels have good gear and decent divemasters.*

| 68-78/30'-70' | All (summer best) | None recommended | *Don Jose, Baja Expeditions* | Melia Cabo Real, Hotel Punta Pes Cadero | $1,295-1,695 LB $1,600 LA w/AIR |

BAJA (REVILLAGIGEDO ISLANDS) *Socorro and San Benedicto Islands, 250 miles SW of Baja, are renowned for giant mantas and big pelagics, plus whale and tiger sharks, hammerheads, sailfish, marlin, and tuna. A 9-day trip contains about 7 full days of diving. A trip for experienced divers.*

| 65-80/50'-150' | Nov.-May | Baja Expeditions | *Solmar V, Don Jose* | Solmar Hotel | $2,475 (9-10 days) LA |

BELIZE *Lighthouse Reef is world-class. Great site variety. Try Southwest Cut, Long Cay Wall, Blue Hole, Half Moon Cay Wall. Huge fish by Caribbean standards. Richest fish diving in Caribbean. Excellent coral and good numbers of large pelagics. Massive drop-offs. Remote islands are best.*

| 80/90'-125' | All (summer best) | Blue Hole Dive Center | *Belize Aggressor* | Turneffe Lodge, Ramada Inn, Lighthouse Reef Resort | $850-1,350 LB $1,895 LA |

BERMUDA *Excellent wreck diving, including the schooner Montana, the iron-hulled Constellation, and the Confederate blockade runner Marie Celestia. Mostly boat diving, but easy day-trip access. Bermuda's fringing reef has snagged its fair share of shipwrecks—as many as 350 identified.*

| 60-80/70'-100' | May-Nov. | Fantasea Diving, Scubalook, Blue Water Divers | None | Grotto Bay Beach Hotel, Princess Hotel, Sonesta Beach Hotel | $1,540-2,000 |

BONAIRE *NW end of island near Washington Park is best. Great numbers of fish, sharks, mantas, lovely corals. Nearby Klein, Curaçao, also has fine, unspoiled reefs. One of the better Caribbean areas for visibility, with good drop-offs, but stay away from the reefs near the major hotels.*

| 80/90'-125' | All | Peter Hughes Divers, Dive Bonaire (Divi), Capt. Don's | None | Capt. Don's Habitat, Sand Dollar Condos | $800-1,200 LB |

CALIFORNIA (CHANNEL ISLANDS) *Probably the best dive area on the West Coast, but weekends can be crowded. Anacapa, San Miguel, and San Nicholas have seals, otters, and lobsters. Kelp Forests. Winter water is cold, but very clear. Recent moratorium on abalone.*

| 52-64/30'-100' | All | Anacapa Dive Center, Sport Channel Divers, SB Aquatics | *Truth Aquatics* | Live-aboard only | $620 (4 days) |

CAYMAN ISLANDS (GRAND CAYMAN, LITTLE CAYMAN, CAYMAN BRAC) *Many rank Bloody Bay Wall on Little Cayman among the world's top 10 sites. Superior spots on Cayman Brac: Sea Fan Wall, Garden Eel Wall, Butterfly Reef. Many dive sites are crowded. Don't miss Stingray City.*

| 80+/80'-200' | All | Treasure Island Divers, Red Sail Sports, Bob Soto's Diving | *Little Cayman Diver, Cayman Aggressor* | Hyatt Regency (Grand), Tiara Beach Hotel (Brac), Pirate's Point (Little Cayman) | $2,795 (10 days w/AIR) LB $1,895 LA |

CURAÇAO *Desert island with good diving and pleasant weather in a European setting. Excellent shore diving on the fringing reef. Mushroom Forest has great star corals. Sandy's Plateau, with easy beach access, is a good beginner's site (corals are signposted). Marine reserve in south of park.*

| 75-80/60'-100' | All | Peter Hughes/Princess Lanhuis Daniel, Underwater Curaçao, Atlantis Diving | None | Princess Beach Hotel & Casino, Lion's Dive Hotel and Marina Guest House, Lanhuis Daniel | $850-1,100 (w/diving) LB |

COSTA RICA (Cocos Island) *Open water with strong currents. Countless big animals—turtles, mantas, whale sharks, huge pelagics. Deep shelf is suited for experienced deep-water divers only. Ultimate big-animal adventure for experienced deep-water divers. Don't expect much near surface.*

| 80/50'-100' | Nov.-Aug. | Scuba Safaris, Tropical Adventures | *Okeanos Aggressor, Undersea Hunter* | Cocos Island Resort | $2,795 LB (9 days) LB $2,995 (10 days) LA |

COZUMEL *80,000 divers a year have reduced the fish, but great wall diving remains at Santa Rosa and Palancar. Excellent coral mounts at Columbia Shallows. For a bargain, go with a package. Almost all drift diving—the current does the work. Caribbean Divers has fast boats to the reefs.*

| 75-82/50'-100' | All | Caribbean Divers Intl., Fantasia Dive, Chino's Scuba Shop | *Aggressor* | Casa Del Mar, La Ceiba | $580-717 |

Water Temp./ Visibility	Best Season	Recommended Dive Shops	Recommended Live-aboards	Accommodations	Package Per Week
DOMINICA *Soufrière Bay on leeward shore is a submerged volcanic crater with excellent wall diving—giant barrel and plentiful tube sponges, plus black coral. Champagne site has underwater hot springs. Off Castle Comfort Lodge is a reef with pipefish, banded morays, batfish. Fewer than 4,000 divers a year.*					
78-82/80'-100'	All	Dive Dominica, Nature Island Dive	None	Castle Comfort Dive Lodge, Castaways Beach Hotel, Anchorage Hotel	$950-1,150 LB
EGYPT *Ras Mohammed and nearby sites are busy, and the closest reefs are somewhat chewed up. However, Tiran Straits and the Dunraven (plus Thistle-gorm wrecks) are still super. Try the Brothers dive site near Hurghada for its sheer drop-off with long walls, pelagic animals, and 100-foot visibility.*					
68-85/80'-100'	All	Sinai Divers, Tropical Adventures	*Ghazala Voyager, Royal Emperor*	Sharm El Sheikh Hotel	$895 LB $1,295 (avg.) LA
FIJI *The northern islands (Taveuni, Matangi, Aamea) are truly world-class with superb coral, profuse marine life, and amazing visibility. Beqa Lagoon is tops on the main island. Fiji is still an unspoiled paradise. The people are wonderful. Consider a live-aboard to explore smaller islands and outer reefs.*					
73-76/100'-200'	All (rain Jan-Feb)	Dive Taveuni, Beqa Divers	*Nai'a, MV Princess II, Fiji Aggressor*	Namale Plantation, Raffles Gateway, Jean Michel Cousteau Fiji Resort	$2,000 LB $2,040-2,400 LA
FLORIDA KEYS *Many great wrecks, such as the Duane, the Bibb, and the Eagle. Wreck diving is superb throughout the Keys, and the corals are surprisingly good. Visibility and fish populations are not outstanding, however. Reefs worth exploring include Crocker, Alligator, Molasses, and Sombrero.*					
72-88/40'-100'	All	Dive Key West, Divers Den	N/A	Casa Marina, Quality Inn	$146-446 per day LB
GALÁPAGOS *A marine-mammal mecca. Darwin Island offers sharks, whale sharks, turtles, rays, huge schools of fish, numerous sea lions, iguanas, penguins. April and May are warmest. Extraordinary mass and variety of sea creatures. Where else can you swim with iguanas and penguins? Don't expect vivid coral.*					
68-78/60'-100'	Oct.-May	Dive Tours, Tropical Adventures	*Mistral, Galápagos Aggressor I & II, Lammer Law*	Live-aboard only	$2,695
HAWAII (KONA) *A hundred excellent dive sites with lava tubes, caves, abundant fish. All dive sites are close to shore. Puffers, eels and octopus are common. Dive mornings to avoid the trade winds. Kaiwi Point offers caverns and arches. Dive Makai is superb—very skilled and conscientious.*					
75-81/50'-100'	All	Dive Makai, Jack's Diving Locker, Red Sail	*Kona Aggressor II*	King Kamehameha, Kona Reef	$1,500 LB $1,895 LA
HAWAII (MAUI) *Fish life is somewhat depleted, but there are a multitude of interesting sites near shore, including Lanai underwater park. A fine choice for dive training. Maui is a multisport paradise. Dive one day and windsurf the next. Coral is abundant, and the package prices can't be beat.*					
74-80/50'-100'	All	Maui Dream Divers, Maui Dive Shop	None recommended	Plantation Inn (Lahaina)	$945 (for two people) LB
INDONESIA (BORNEO, SIPADAN) *"No other spot on the face of the planet has more marine life than this island," says the World Wildlife Fund of Borneo. Expect to see turtles, tropical fish, schooling barracuda, sharks, superb coral. Sipadan—2,800-foot seamount flared at the top—is a magnet for marine life.*					
80+/40'-50'	All (low visibility Aug.-Sept.)	Sipadan Mabul Divers, Dive Indonesia	Sea Contacts I & II, Pelagian	Sipadan Mabul Resort	$995 LB $2,750 LA
INDONESIA (MANADO, SULAWESI) *A popular dive destination, Manado on the island of Sulawesi has a protected marine park with a large fringing reef—lots of soft corals, then a steep drop-off. Bunaken Island boasts an excellent variety of tropical fish, sharks, rays, and turtles.*					
80s/150'	Oct.-April	Deep Discoveries, Tropical Adventures	*Sea Contacts I & II, Pindito*	Murex Manado Diving Resort, Manado Beach Hotel	$500-900 LB $1,575 LA,
KENYA *Watamu Bay and Kisite-Mpunguti Marine Parks offer quality diving with fish everywhere. Top Spots: Big 3 Caves (Watumu), Shimoni Reef (Kisite), Pemba Island. Dolphins, mantas, whale sharks and other big sea creatures abound. Clouds of reef fish on Pemba Island. Still undiscovered.*					
75-80/50'-100'	All	Turtle Bay Divers at Hemingway's	*MV Kisiwani*	Hemingway's (Malindi), Shimoni Reef Hotel, Manta Reef Lodge (Pemba Island)	$950 LB, $1,100-1,375 LA
MALAYSIA *Sea life is abundant—rays, turtles, humphead wrasse, dogtooth tuna and hammerhead. Try Tenggol Island, wreck diving off Labuan Island and Kota Kinabalu. Several live-aboards operate in this area, but none are handled by U.S. dive wholesalers.*					
80s/100'	Mar.-Oct.	Asian Overland Services, Dive Discoveries	None	Layang-Layang Resort	$850 LB
MALDIVES *A tropical paradise of 1,100 islands with first-rate diving. Wreck dives on Male near the airport; unforgettable reefs in outer atolls. Lion's Head in the Male Atoll has baby blue tangs, gray reef sharks. At Guraidhoo in Vaavu Atoll, try Bodu Ghaa (the Big Mushroom), a bommie with a soft coral fringe.*					
78-82/120'-150'	Dec.-April	Tropical Adventures, Deep Discoveries	*Manthiri, Mandivaru*	Live-aboards only	$2,750 (9 nights) LA
MARSHALL ISLANDS *The lagoon at Bikini Atoll has WWII wrecks from Japan, the U.S., and Germany. Try Mili Atoll for a close-up look at a giant clam farm and Robinson Crusoe living. An up-and-coming destination, the Marshalls have Micronesian diving with virtually no tourist infrastructure. Yet.*					
82-85/100'+	April-Nov.	Marshall Dive Adventures	None	Bikini Resort, Anrohasa, Robert Reimers	$630-1,350 LB
NORTH CAROLINA *Civil War wrecks along the Outer Banks (200-mile-long barrier islands). The U-85 (an intact German sub 14 miles off Nags Head) has exposed torpedo tubes and deck gun. Some dives are at—or beyond—the sport-diving limit, so use extreme caution regarding currents, cold, and depth.*					
mid-60's/ Variable	May-Oct.	Outer Banks Dive Center	None	Manteo Elizabethan Inn, Nags Head Inn	$77-97 (per day) LB

Water Temp./ Visibility	Best Season	Recommended Dive Shops	Recommended Live-aboards	Accommodations	Package Per Week
PALAU *Spectacular walls and limestone formations. Top spots: Blue Holes, Chandelier Cave. Lots of color, and many fish, sharks, and turtles. Yap extension offers rays. Incoming tide brings clear water and truly spectacular wall diving. Great diversity of dive sites.*					
80-83/90'-150'	Sept.-May	Fish 'n Fins, Peter Hughes Diving	*Thorfinn, Palau Aggressor, Sun Dancer II*	Palau Pacific, Marina Hotel, Sunrise Villa	$2,295 LB
PAPUA NEW GUINEA *A true diving frontier. Walindi and Banana Reefs and Rabaul wrecks are world-class. Prolific sea life: huge fish, manta rays, whale sharks, killer whales. Richly colored, large coral masses. PNG topside is a great cultural experience, but land resorts are unreliable.*					
75-82/70'-150'	All (rain Nov.-Jan.)	Walindi Plantation, Rum Runner	*MV Felorina, MV Sheretan*	Walindi Plantation, Peter Hughes	$1,800 LB $2,100 LA
PHILIPPINES (TUBBATAHA REEF) *Tubbataha, accessible only by live-aboard, is on many top 10 lists for its 500-foot vertical walls, schools of giant mantas, tropical fish by the thousands. Great abundance of life—large and small. If the coral is stunning, the volume of fish, especially at night, is phenomenal.*					
85/100'-200'	March-June	Aquaventure, Whitetip Divers	*Island Explorer, Nautika*	Coconut Plantation, Dive Discovery (agent)	$970 LB $1,260 LA
ROATAN & GUANAJA (BAY ISLANDS) *Noted for wall diving, plus spur and grove system. Top spots: Mary's Place, Valley of Kings (Coco Resort), and Prince Albert wreck. Great sea fans and sponges. Abundance of crevices, caves, and drop-offs within 30 feet of surface make this a great site for novices.*					
78-82/50'-90'	All	Inn of Last Resort, Posada Del Sol (Guanaja)	*Bay Islands, Aggressor III*	CoCo View, Anthony's Key, Capt. Ron's Reef Resort	$900 LB $1,495-1,895 LA
SABA *The best of the Dutch Antilles. Large fish for the Caribbean. Pristine reefs, with good pinnacles and drops. You always need a boat, reefs are deep and Saba has no beaches. Saba is one of the great undiscovered Caribbean dive areas. On a live-aboard, you can also visit the Lesser Antilles and BVI.*					
75-85/70'-125'	All	Saba Deep Dive Center	*Antilles Aggressor, Sea Dancer, Caribbean Explorer*	Juliana's Apartments, The Cottage Club	$800-1,225 LB $1,250 LA
SEYCHELLES *The granite geology offers arches, pinnacles and sheer walls, all covered with brilliant coral. 100 varieties of coral, 900 species of fish. Outer islands (Aldabra) are rich, virgin coral atolls. Visibility is superb. Don't miss Amirantes and Aldabra outer isles.*					
70-80/70'-200'	All	Coral Strand Hotel (Ultramarina)	*Indian Ocean Explorer*	Coral Strand Hotel, Des Roche Resort, La Digue, Frigate Island (super expensive— $1,200 per night).	$800 LB $1,750 LA
SOLOMON ISLANDS *Great wall and drift dives, neon coral, many undived WWII wrecks. Large numbers of mantas, sharks, large schooling fish. Outstanding invertebrate life makes for great night dives. Many virgin reefs and scores of wrecks to explore. Malaria is a real risk here. Not for beginners.*					
75-80/70'-150'	All	Dive Gizo, Solomon Sea Divers Mundo	*MV Bilikiki, MV Spirit of Solomons, Solomon Aggressor*	Live-aboard recommended Gizo Hotel	$2,295 (10 days) LA
ST. VINCENT & GRENADINES *Thirty-three islands and cays. Vertical walls, caves and big reefs, most virtually untouched by divers. St. Vincent has black-sand beaches, waterfalls, nightlife. St. Vincent and the Grenadines are not the best in the Caribbean, but the diving is still very good and dive sites are not crowded.*					
70-80/30'-80'	All	Dive St. Vincent	N/A	Grandview Beach Hotel, Umbrella Beach Hotel	$592-1,135 LB
SUDAN (RED SEA) *Big walls covered with soft corals, hammerheads, mantas, incredibly profuse reef fish. One of the top three places in the world in all categories—color, clarity, big animals, steep walls, numbers of fish. Live-aboards depart from Sharm El Sheik, Egypt. Truly an ultimate dive destination.*					
73-83/90'-150'	May-Oct.	None recommended	*Colona IV*	Sheraton Heliopolis	$1,695 (islands) LB $2,500 (Red Sea) LA
THAILAND *The Similan Islands and Angthong Marine Park are undiscovered gems. Crystal water, abundant coral, and wild granite and limestone formations. No crowds ever. Southern Thailand is cheap and diving is still relatively rare. Go with a local dive shop ($120/day) for the best dive value in the world.*					
70-82/70'-150'	Mar.-Oct.	Phuket Scuba Diving	*MV Fantasea 2000, Pelagian Club, Aqualand*	N/A	$1,650 LB $3,250 (11 days) LA
TOBAGO *Diving from traditional fishing craft and pirogues designed for local conditions. Spectacular natural rock formations off Charlotteville, huge mantas in Speyside, enormous brain coral and sea turtles near Little Tobago. Some heavy currents. Definitely off the beaten path.*					
78-82/80'-130'	Jan.-May	Tobago Dive Experience, Aqua Marine Dive Ltd., Man Friday Diving	Shore diving or 5-minute boat ride	Ocean Point Hotel, Manta Lodge	$750-1,000 LB
TRUK *Truk Lagoon offers spectacular wreck diving. Feb., March, Sept., and Oct. have best visibility, but June through Sept is the calmest period. 60+ divable wrecks. You'll want to get off Moen Island, where all the hotels are located. Try a 3-island tour with Pohnpei and Palau, or visit Yap for mantas.*					
80/80'-150'	All	Blue Lagoon	*Thorfinn, Truk Aggressor*	Blue Lagoon	$2,295 LB $1,795 LA
TURKS & CAICOS *General Caribbean reef life, good drop-offs, nice shallows, fine beaches, great place to combine beachcombing and sun worshipping with diving. Perfect place for couples or family to enjoy a vacation in paradise.*					
75-80/90'-125'	Mar.-Nov.	Peter Hughes Diving	*Sea Dancer, Turks & Caicos Aggressor, Wind Dancer*	Divi Resort (Erebus)	$1,795 LB $1,695 LA
YAP *Over 50 dive sites, but no crowds. In Mil Channel, Manta Ridge is a cleaning station, as well as an excellent feeding location, for the big oceanic flyers. Unspoiled Sunrise Reef boasts enormous hard coral formations of table, lettuce, and staghorn varieties. To spot a manta, plan on diving at least 4 days.*					
78-83/100'	Nov.-Mar.	Yap Divers in the Manta Ray Bay Hotel, Jeremy Stein's BlueDiving Club & Rainbow Divers	*MV Blue Explorer*	Manta Ray Bay Hotel	$965 (5 nights) LB $1,699 LA

Free divers hunt the open ocean, far from the security of reefs. A dive usually reaches 30 feet and lasts for 90 seconds, with just 20 to 30 seconds spent recovering between dives. The typical free diver wears a wet suit, weight belt, mask and snorkel, and powerful 3-foot-long free diver fins. To help play and land large gamefish, the diver trails a buoy-equipped line.

Obviously, the sport involves considerable risk. Marlin have been known to turn and gore their stalkers. Shallow-water blackout kills several divers every year. Line tangles are a constant threat. And each year motorboats take their toll on divers forced to surface under passing vessels. For a definitive look at the thrills, techniques, and dangers of the sport , read *BlueWater Hunting and Freediving* by veteran bluewater free diver Terry Maas (*Bluewater Freedivers. 888-511-1199. www.freedive. net*).

TRAVEL TIPS

What to Bring
If you're planning a trip to a remote destination, bring along this essential gear:

Mask and Snorkel—Keep them in plastic boxes for protection, and bring a spare mask if you're a hard fit.

Buoyancy Compensator/Backpack (BC)—Can be rented, but they are often old, ill fitting, and may leak.

Regulator—Bring your own regulator, equipped with octopus backup. Don't trust a rental unit.

Gauges (depth, air pressure)—Bring your own depth gauge or a dive computer. Some rental gauges are unreliable.

Dive Watch and Compass—Keep a cheap, plastic, waterproof watch as a backup timer. Tape your compass to protect the crystal in transit.

Lycra Skin Suit—In the tropics, a skin suit is all that most people need for a bit of warmth and protection from coral.

Dive Computer—Few remote locales offer good rentals, so bring your own.

Lights—Bring a high-quality lamp to help illuminate your gauges in murky water. Chemical light sticks are great marker lights on night dives.

Gloves—Bring both a neoprene set and a lighter cloth pair for the tropics.

TRAVEL SAFETY

Do not dive immediately before or after flying; wait 24 hours. If you plan on diving a remote area, obtain divers' accident insurance, which covers decompression sickness, ear problems, emergency evacuation, and other diving-related injuries. Insurance is available from PADI (*800-223-9998. www.padi.com*), Divers' Alert Network (*800-446-2671. www. diversalertnetwork.org*), and Divers' Security Insurance (*800-288-4810*).

ONLINE

Rodale's Scuba Diving Online
www.scubadiving.com

Operator listings, events, gear reviews, and a searchable dive travel database.

PADI
www.PADI.com

Information on certification courses, a directory of PADI-affiliated dive centers, and a calendar of scuba-related events.

Three Routes Worldwide SCUBA Diving Directory
www.3routes.com

Addresses and phone numbers for more than 4,000 dive charters, resorts, and liveaboards worldwide.

Ocean Planet
http://seawifs.gsfc.nasa.gov/ocean__planet.html

An online version of the Smithsonian's Ocean Planet exhibition, featuring movies, photos, and text.

Scuba Central
www.scubacentral.com

Travel advice, gear reviews, and scuba-related websites and e-mail lists.

MAGAZINES

Scuba Diving offers useful information, maps, and charts. Special issues detail equipment or international destinations. *Dive Travel* features articles and destination planners. *Ocean Realm* runs serious marine articles and spectacular photos.

BOOKS

Pisces' *Diving and Snorkeling Guides* detail dive venues worldwide. Available at **Lonely Planet** (*800-275-8555. www. lonelyplanet.com*).

Guidebooks from **Aqua Quest** (*800-933-8989. www.aquaquest.com*) feature dive site data plus topside coverage.

Best Publishing (*800-468-1055. www.diveweb.com/best*) offers titles on wreck diving to medical and safety issues.

TAKE A BOW

EA KAYAKING IS A GREAT WAY TO EXPLORE REMOTE COASTAL WATERS FROM THE ARCTIC TO THE TROPICS. More stable and considerably more comfortable than white-water kayaks, modern sea kayaks hold two people and plenty of gear. Novices can easily paddle the forgiving craft, and the pace of most guided trips is slow and easy. • The aquatic equivalent of backpacking, sea kayaking lets you travel light—and under your own power. You'll journey close to nature, observing the local wildlife and scenery from a floating observation platform that can navigate waterways inaccessible to other craft. Some favorite kayak cruising grounds are the South Pacific, where you can island hop and seek out corals and tropical fish; the inlets of the Pacific Northwest and the golden coast of Mexico's Baja California peninsula, where you can track migrating whales; and the rugged Maine coast, with its myriad coves, hidden harbors, and islands just off shore. • Vacation packages to these and other great sea-kayak destinations are described on pages 230-237, followed by a resource list of leading sea-kayak outfitters worldwide. And don't miss the Travel Tips on page 240; they'll help you choose just the right craft for your oceangoing adventures.

LEFT: A SEA KAYAK IN KAUAI, HAWAII, MIMICS DOLPHIN DESIGN.
BELOW: PORTAGE ACROSS TIDAL-ZONE SEAWEED, PENOBSCOT BAY, MAINE

Sea Kayaking

NW Passages

Sea Fiji

The Maine Thing

Paddle Whales

Believe me, my young friend, there is nothing—absolutely nothing—half so much worth doing as simply messing about in boats.
KENNETH GRAHAME

Sea Kayak Escapes: A Magnificent Seven

Sea kayaks are not for the Inuit alone. Touring by kayak, whether on your own or with a commercial outfitter, requires no superior training or strength. Like backpacking, sea kayaking takes you to realms beyond the reach of mechanized transport, to the wild places not yet spoiled by civilization. And for the adventurer on a budget, the price is right: Most organized sea-kayak trips cost less than $130 per day.

BAJA CALIFORNIA, MEXICO
Seagoing Serenity

If there is an ideal sea kayaking destination, Baja California may be it. The water is warm, the wildlife is varied and abundant, and countless inlets and beaches beckon the explorer. A host of quality outfitters lead kayak trips to Baja year-round, but most tours take place during Mexico's warm winters. Some tours focus on wildlife and whale-watching, while others emphasize the exploration of remote coves and out-of-the-way beaches.

Baja is the winter breeding ground for a number of large whale species, including grays. **Bahía Magdalena (Magdalena Bay),** far south on the west side of the peninsula, boasts the largest concentrations of gray whales on the Pacific coast. Each year, from late January through early March, **Baja Expeditions** (*San Diego, CA. 800-843-6967 or 858-581-3311. www.bajaex.com*) conducts seven-day kayak trips from La Paz to Magdalena Bay and back. Past customers have given these trips rave reviews, and many participants have returned a second time. Baja Expeditions also takes sea kayakers to **Isla Espíritu Santo,** a beautifully isolated island on the gulf coast near La Paz. With a major sea lion rookery, crystal blue waters, and numerous sea caves, this little island is a snorkeler's paradise. The Magdalena Bay trip costs $1,200; the seven-day Isla Espiritu Santo expedition runs $895.

Trudi Angell—a soft-spoken woman who knows every inch of the east coast from **Bahía Concepción (Conception Bay)** to La Paz—is a legend in Baja. Her tour company, **Paddling South** (*Calistoga, CA. 800-398-6200 or 707-942-4550. www.tourbaja.com*), runs multiday trips along the **Golfo de California** from October through May. Tours start in Loreto and work their way south along 40 miles of remote, unspoiled coastline. Some trips visit Isla Don Zante and Isla Carmen, both rich in marine life. Paddling just 5 miles each day leaves plenty of time for snorkeling on the reefs, day-hiking on the shore, and enjoying the meals—especially the local seafood—that are a highlight of Paddling South tours. Seven- to nine-day trips cost $895-995; ten- to fourteen-

day trips cost $1,295 (both include two nights at a hotel and transport in Loreto). Compared with Baja Expeditions, the program is more adventurous; no motorized support boat is used, and Paddling South avoids highly touristed destinations.

Tofino Expeditions (*Seattle, WA. 800-677-0877 or 206-517-5244. www.tofino.com*) runs more than 30 guided kayak trips to the Golfo de California every winter. With Loreto as a starting point, Tofino runs trips to **Isla Carmen,** the **Sierra de la Giganta coast,** and the **Gold Coast** north of Loreto. All Tofino tours visit remote hideaways rarely frequented by other groups. The tours are self-contained (no noisy outboard launches) and emphasize low-impact camping; the food, however, is surprisingly deluxe. The pace is an easy three to four hours of paddling per day, making Tofino's program a good choice for novice kayakers. Trips last eight days and range from $990 to $1,200.

North Star Adventures (*Flagstaff, AZ. 800-258-8434 or 520-773-9917. www.adventuretrip.com*) is another fine kayak tour operator with years of experience in Baja. Offering eight-day, small-group trips for $1,400 per person, North Star runs tours to remote, unspoiled areas north of La Paz. You'll explore the Sierra de la Giganta coastline and paddle to a variety of small islands with few inhabitants. Highlights include snorkeling with sea lions at **Los Islotes** rookery—an amazing experience. The guides are seasoned pros, and all trips are supported with a small *panga*, or motorized skiff, that is run by a local crew.

If you're looking for a shorter trip, **Aqua Adventures Kayak School** (*San Diego, CA. 800-269-7792 or 858-272-0800. www.aqua-adventures.com*) offers two reasonably priced five-day Baja kayaking tours. The Loreto trip, which explores from Puerto Escondido to the islands of Don Zante and Carmen, costs $675, while the **Bahía de los Angeles** trip, visiting islands in the bay, costs just $595 (the latter tour includes transport from San Diego). Aqua Adventures also runs outstanding weekend trips to scenic spots such as the rock gardens along northern Baja's Pacific coast. For those with limited time, these are great weekend getaways.

COSTA RICA
Paddling to the Ocean

Costa Rica is Central America's natural wonderland, a unique showcase of scenery and wildlife. Anything you can imagine—volcanoes, cloud forests, raging white water, idyllic beach resorts—can be found here. This ecological diversity—combined with a network of exciting rivers, lush jungle parks, and beautiful beaches on both the Caribbean and Pacific coasts—makes Costa Rica a sensational paddling destination. Because most of the country's rivers are relatively short and located near a coast, it is even possible to paddle from the highlands to the sea in a single trip.

One of the few Costa Rica-based companies offering multiday ocean kayak adventures is **Serendipity Adventures** (*Ann Arbor, MI. 800-635-2325 or 734-995-0111. www. serendipityadventures.com*), which runs wilderness voyages in the Golfo de Nicoya on the Pacific coast. Serendipity's three-day **Pacific Islands** program is suitable for paddlers with limited experience. Novices kayak along the coast and camp on small islands within a wilderness preserve. Paddlers confident in open ocean and surf will enjoy the six-day **Around the Horn** journey: It starts out in Paquera, where the first trip ends, and visits more rugged, exposed coastal zones. These trips are more akin to expeditionary voyages than the typical kayak cruise. You won't see other paddlers, and you'll enjoy exceptional natural beauty. The price for the guided three-day trip is $3,630 for four paddlers; the guided six-day cruise costs $8,100 for four.

Costa Rica Experts (*Chicago, IL. 800-827-9046 or 773-935-1009. www.crexpert.com*)—in conjunction with Ríos Tropicales, Costa Rica's leading river outfitter—offers a stimulating ten-day trip that combines coastal kayak trekking with river exploration. After arriving in San José, participants journey to the secluded **Playa Quesera** just outside the **Curu National Wildlife Refuge**. From this base camp, the group explores the coastline by kayak on day trips, with opportunities to swim, snorkel, fish, and practice surf kayaking.

The river adventure starts with participants' running the Class III **Río Reventazón,** which passes through verdant riparian scenery. Afterward, the group enjoys hot meals and traditional hospitality at a comfortable riverside lodge. The next two days are spent on the Class III-IV **Río Pacuare,** a jungle river renowned for its waterfalls and natural waterslides. Strong paddlers kayak the river in white-water boats, while others join Ríos Tropicales' rafters for the descent. Either way, participants relax after a hard day of river-running with hot meals, cold *cerveza,* and accommodations in rustic riverside bungalows. The cost for eight days and nine nights is $1,150, including equipment, guides, lodging, most meals, and transport in Costa Rica.

TWO-PERSON KAYAKS BREAK THE GLASSY SURFACE OF THE SEA AROUND ISLA BOTA IN BAJA CALIFORNIA.

BRITISH COLUMBIA
Odyssey with Orcas

The sheltered waters of the **Inside Passage** between Vancouver Island and mainland British Columbia provide a near-perfect venue for kayak touring. The summer weather is warm, calm, and dry, and hundreds of great campsites speckle the remote stretches of the British Columbia coast. While navigating the inlets and small islands between Vancouver and the northern coast, kayakers can enjoy watching eagles soar overhead. Porpoise sightings are commonplace too.

The biggest thrill, however, is interacting with the orcas that frequent the area. Attracted by the summer salmon runs, more than 200 of these whales visit the Inside Passage during the season, traveling in family groups called pods. Sea kayakers can accompany an orca pod for days, frequently venturing within a paddle length of the mammoth creatures. Experienced tour leaders are often able to identify particular whales that return to the same waters year after year.

Seattle's **Northern Lights Expeditions** (*Bellingham, WA. 800-754-7402 or 360-734-6334. www.seakayaking.com*) has offered orca-watching kayak trips since 1983. The guides know the best places to find orcas, and they have even gone so far as to outfit their kayaks with hydrophones, allowing you to eavesdrop on the whales as they communicate with one another underwater. Northern Lights' six-day trips require no special kayaking skills—only a love of nature and a hearty appetite. (At your campsites, which may include old Kwakiutal Indian villages, you'll be treated to fresh-caught salmon and halibut, among other regional specialties.) Trips run weekly from mid-June through mid-September and cost about $1,200, all-inclusive.

If you yearn to do more exploring after a week with the whales, consider Northern Lights' **Lost Islands Adventure.** Six times a year, the outfitter leads experienced kayakers to remote and wild stretches of the British Columbia coast. Most of the campsites are abandoned Indian villages, and the paddling is somewhat more strenuous than on the Inside Passage trips. Of the exact destination—which requires a fly-in by seaplane—a Northern Lights spokesperson would say only this: "It's an area that has rarely seen kayakers in the past, and we want to keep it that way for as long as possible. So its exact location will remain a mystery until you arrive." The six-day Lost Islands getaway costs $1,400.

Northern Lights also offers a sea kayak vacation based at a luxury lodge on a private island in Farewell Harbor. This is a great choice for families or for those seeking first-class amenities with their paddling holiday.

Pacific Rim Paddling Company (*Victoria, B.C., Canada. 250-384-6103. www.islandnet.com/~prp/*), operated by Heidi Krogstad and Dugald Nasmith from a base in Victoria, British Columbia, has offered wilderness kayak tours since 1984. Its guides are among the most knowledgeable in the business. Dedicated to the ethic of low-impact camping, Pacific Rim trips are limited to ten clients supported by two guides—often Krogstad and Nasmith themselves. As a bonus, the cuisine is outstanding—which helps explain why more than half of Pacific Rim Paddling Company's clients are personal friends or repeat customers.

During the summer months, Pacific Rim stages trips to six areas of the British Columbia coast, including all the major orca-watching spots. Tours include six-day, $690 trips to western Vancouver Island's **Barkley Sound,** to **Johnstone Strait,** and to the **Broughton Island archipelago** at the mouth of Kingcome Inlet. Pacific Rim also puts on 7- to 14-day excursions (starting at $1,100) in the **Queen Charlotte Islands,** near the Alaskan Panhandle.

In addition to its home-water programs, the company runs winter-season trips in Baja and Tonga. It also periodically offers special tours, such as a six-day bed-and-breakfast trip that explores Norway's **Solund Islands.**

Tofino Expeditions (*Seattle, WA. 800-677-0877 or 206-517-5244. www.tofino.com*) is another veteran outfitter that ushers sea kayakers into the pristine cruising grounds of the Pacific Northwest. In addition to whale-watching trips, Tofino's guides lead kayak cruises through British Columbia's Inside Passage (Queen Charlotte Strait) and the Queen Charlotte Islands. Benefiting from decades of experience, Tofino Expeditions crafts well-planned itineraries and staffs them with able guides.

If you want to explore remote, unspoiled territory, Tofino can take you to the **Gwaii Haanas National Park Reserve and Haida Heritage Site** (*Box 37, Queen Charlotte, B.C. 250-559-8818. www.harbour.com/parkscan/gwaii*), as well as to British Columbia's remote central coast, known as the Great Bear Rain Forest. There you will venture deep into wild habitats, still virtually untouched by humanity. All of Tofino's trips, which range in price from $1,000 to $1,450 for six to eight days, are genuine wilderness expeditions: The prospect of sighting another pod of paddlers during your journey is unlikely.

NEW ZEALAND
Tasmanian Daredevils

With more than 1,000 miles of coast girding a landmass the size of California, New Zealand offers a wealth of sea kayaking opportunities. Of these, **Abel Tasman National Park,** located on the South Island's north coast, is probably New Zealand's premier sea kayaking destination.

Sheltered from storms, Abel Tasman enjoys some of the best weather in the country. Passages are relatively short along a scalloped coastline of myriad small coves and bays blessed with golden-sand beaches. Solitude is guaranteed: Many of the park's remote beach camps are accessible only from the ocean. Ancient, subtropical forest grows right down to the shoreline, sheltering more wildlife than you'd be likely to see on the North Island. To top it all off, the coast faces away from the prevailing westerly winds and therefore experiences very little swell activity, making this a safe haven for less experienced kayakers.

Ocean River Sea Kayaking (*Motueka, New Zealand. 01164-3527-8266. http://webnz.com/ocean_river*), the original kayaking concession in Abel Tasman National Park, is the top choice for a guided sea kayak trip there. Ocean River's three-day **Enchanted Coast** trip showcases most of the park, covering the coastline from the town of Totaranui in the north to the town of Marahau in the south. The trip begins in Totaranui and travels south along the coastline to Tonga Island, visiting a fur seal rookery, the **Tonga Island Marine Reserve,** and the granite Tonga Arches along the way. The next day, kayakers explore tidal lagoons, reefs, and small coves. On the third day, the group passes the **"Mad Mile"**—a rugged, exposed section of coast with offshore reefs and two sheltered bays (watch out for rough seas when the winds are onshore or easterly). After each day's passage, participants set up camp on a remote beach, then hike in the coastal bush or just relax by the side of the ocean. The cost is $475 (NZ) per person, including food, guide, and all gear.

Another worthy itinerary (and Ocean River's most popular) is the three-day combination **Paddle-and-Walk Trip**—a bargain at $250 (NZ) per person (though you must provide your own food). This trip combines sea kayaking along a sheltered section of the coast with easy hiking along the famous **Abel Tasman Coastal Track.** In addition to multiday trips, Ocean River provides daily rentals for experienced kayakers.

Another good outfitter, **Abel Tasman Kayaks** (*Motueka, New Zealand. 0800-527-8022, toll-free in NZ, or 01164-3527-8022. www.kayaktours.co.nz*), offers a four-day, fully catered trip that is a comfortable way to see this beautiful region. Reversing Ocean River Adventure Company's route, this trip begins in Marahau. Paddlers travel north, kayaking to nearby islands, fine beaches, and lagoons (with optional detours up rivers), and visit the Tonga Island Marine Reserve. Guests spend two nights camping and one night in a lodge before returning to Marahau by boat. The price for gear, guide, and all catered meals is $630 (NZ). Abel Tasman Kayaks also offers guided day trips throughout the season for about $90 (NZ), as well as kayak rentals.

To explore another remote corner of New Zealand, consider a kayak cruise through the **Marlborough sounds,** which comprise Queen Charlotte Sound, Keneperu Sound, and Pelorus Sound. This region, a sheltered archipelago on the northern tip of New Zealand's South Island, boasts more than 540 square miles of hidden inlets, secret coves, and pristine beaches. Paddling in the sounds is easy; another small island or sheltered harbor is always only minutes away, so you never have to make long passages across open ocean.

With its calm waters and many good campsites, this little-known part of New Zealand is a great destination for a self-guided tour—easily one of the best sea kayaking areas in the Southern Hemisphere. And when you feel like trading your sleeping bag for a bed, you can cruise to a nearby island farm where homestay lodging is available at reasonable rates. Both kayak rentals and guided tours can be arranged through **Marlborough Sounds Adventure Company** (*Picton, New Zealand. 01164-3573-6078. http://marlboroughsounds.co.nz*). A guided trip will set you back about $80 (NZ) per day, including kayak rental and two meals. Custom itineraries and powerboat shuttles to nearby islands can be arranged on request.

If you plan to tour New Zealand's North Island, **New Zealand Adventures** (*John Day, OR. 541-932-4925. www.teraki.co.nz/seakayak*) offers an all-time favorite trip. It runs from Matauri Bay, on the northeastern tip of the island off the Bay of Islands, and takes kayakers on a 45-mile paddle north to Whangaroa Harbor, paralleling a remote and unspoiled stretch of the northeast coast. On this trip you spend two days on the **Motukawanui Islands,** about 2 miles offshore, then explore the volcanic rock gardens of the **Mahinepua Peninsula.** Expect excellent snorkeling and beachcombing—not to mention sumptuous beach picnics. In addition to its standard kayak tours, New Zealand Adventures offers a **Master's Kayak Tour** for those over 50. Basic tours cost $750 (NZ) for six days and $1,200 (NZ) for ten days; the master's tour runs $800 (NZ) for five days. Prices include all food and equipment.

FIJI
Wild Idyll South

If you're looking for a true Polynesian paradise, forget Hawaii or Tahiti and head straight for Fiji. Long recognized as a world-class dive venue, Fiji is also an excellent kayaking destination, with scores of idyllic islands, spectacular coral reefs, and warm, crystal-clear waters. Apart from the main island of Viti Levu, most of Fiji has escaped commercial tourist development. On the outer islands, life is quiet and simple. You can still walk down a perfect white-sand beach and not see another soul, or wade onto a reef at sunset and pluck a dinner lobster from the sea. And the Fijians are among the friendliest people on Earth.

Though most Westerners visit Fiji to dive, surf, or bask on the beach, the country's patchwork of closely placed islands makes it ideal for sea kayak cruising. Unless you bring your own craft, however, you must go with a commercial outfitter: There are no kayak rentals in Fiji. Of the several companies that run guided sea kayaking trips here, three are recommended: Southern Sea Ventures (based in Australia), Fiji by Kayak (based in Fiji), and Kayak Kadavu (based in Hawaii).

For novice paddlers who want a relatively slow-paced adventure, the tour offered by **Southern Sea Ventures** (*McMahon's Point, NSW, Australia. 800-387-1483 or 416-633-5666*) is the best choice. You spend ten days in the **Yasawa Group,** a chain of 16 small islands covering a 50-mile stretch of the Pacific. For eight days you paddle and sail double kayaks among the islands, camping on pristine beaches and visiting small island villages. The azure waters lapping the reefs defy description: With visibility approaching 200 feet, the sensation evokes paddling in a gigantic swimming pool. Additional highlights of the trip include Turtle Island (where the 1980 stinker *Blue Lagoon* was filmed) and the wild limestone caves of Sawa-i-lau Island. Trips cost approximately $1,400, with departures every month from May through October.

Kayak Kadavu (*Kahului, HI. 800-588-3454 or 808-871-5986. www.fiji-kayak-kadavu.com*) offers week-long trips around **Kadavu,** the fourth largest island in the Fijian chain. A beautiful, unspoiled island, Kadavu is often cooler than the more frequented islands to the north. Kayakers set out from the northern tip of Kadavu, then paddle their way along the isle's western coast, gliding past stretches of white-sand beaches sheltered by coral reefs. There is great snorkeling just 20 feet off the beach, with clear water and exotic, colorful fish and corals. The barrier reef shields boaters from heavy surf, making for smooth, safe kayaking. You'll have many opportunities to stop at palm-fringed villages, where the islanders demonstrate why Fijian hospitality is famous worldwide. A journey like the one described above costs $1,650 for seven nights; multiple trips are scheduled year-round.

Experienced dive-travel operator **Sea Fiji Travel** (*Niwot, CO. 800-854-3454 or 303-652-0751. www.seafiji.com*) offers sea kayaking adventures for those who want to experience Fiji on the water as well as beneath it. Custom sea kayaking trips originate in the Savusavu township on the island of Vanua Levu and travel to remote areas around the island. Participants camp within or near small villages. All equipment is provided, including single or double kayaks, as well as meals and resort accommodations on

the first and last nights of your stay. These trips are fun and keep a modest pace that is suitable for family groups. Week-long trips in **Natewa Bay** run from June through August; they can be extended by tacking on a dive trip, or they can be customized with mountain biking, rain forest treks, or family ecotours. The cost for a week of kayaking is approximately $950 per person.

MAINE
Transatlantic Tranquillity

The rugged coast of Maine is the right place to recharge your batteries. Conifers run down to the water's edge, and hundreds of tiny islands dot the coastline. The seaside villages and fishing ports are quiet, small-scale, reminders of New England's past. Even the most popular resort areas are relatively unspoiled. Snug harbors—perfect for coastal exploring—seem to wait beyond every bend in the shore.

Most sea kayaking in Maine takes place in **Acadia National Park,** located near Bar Harbor, and along the **Maine Island Trail,** . a waterway that extends 325 miles from Casco Bay to Machias. Here, reasonably fit paddlers can range easily from island to island, camping overnight in the park and visiting small harbor towns to replenish supplies. When oceangoing grunginess sets in, you can always beach your craft and seek out the creature comforts of a seaside inn.

Paddling is easy in the calm waters off the Maine coast, but good equipment and careful preparation are essential. With so many islands clustered around the jagged coastline here, navigating the shore requires a modicum of skill. If this is your first coastal cruise, stay within the Mount Desert Island section of Acadia National Park, never venturing too far offshore. Notify park rangers of your itinerary when you arrive, and keep daily paddling distances fairly short—four to six miles or less—to avoid fatigue and the bad decisions that can stem from it. Detailed land maps are available from visitor centers in the park, but you should also obtain navigational charts and tide tables before you go.

Maine has many good kayak outfitters, but three stand out from the crowd: Maine Island Kayak Company, Maine Sport Outfitters, and Coastal Kayaking.

The leader of the three is **Maine Island Company** (*Peaks Island, ME. 800-796-2373 or 207-766-2373. www.maineislandkayak.com*). Guide Tom Bergh's knowledge of the region is peerless, his equipment is the best available,

LUG IT OR LEAVE IT: THE PURGATORY OF PORTAGE, MAINE

and his trips venture farther than those of other outfitters, allowing you to reach remote, untouristed islands. Maine Island's most popular trip leaves from a point near the town of Stonington on Deer Isle and paddles 8 miles offshore to little-known **Isle au Haut**—a sizable, picturesque island with freshwater lakes, cobblestone beaches, and abundant wildlife. For the next three to five days, participants explore Isle au Haut and smaller islands in the archipelago, paddling through clear, relatively calm waters by day and camping on the islands by night.

Adventuresome and experienced kayakers will enjoy Maine Island's three- to five-day paddle to **Bois Bubert**. The archetypal Northeast island, sparsely populated Bois Bubert has a tortured landscape of granite headlands, dense forests, and low-hanging mists. Starting from the town of Milbridge on Narraguagus Bay, this is a rewarding but demanding trip that involves fairly lengthy daily passages. Wind and wave conditions can be tough, but the scenery is easy on the eyes—and fellow travelers are scant to nonexistent. Both the Bois Bubert trip and the Isle au Haut excursion cost between $450 and $875.

For the serious adventurer, Maine Island runs a **Downeast Maine** expedition that explores the wilder coastline of northern Maine. This is a realm of exposed headlands, brawny outer islands, strong tides, and fierce weather. The occasional white-shell beach contrasts with volcanic rocks and sea caves, Nature Conservancy preserves, outer-island lighthouses, and grassy barrens dotted with wild sheep. This stretch can be foggy, but it is free from virtually all tourist traffic. The cost for five to six days is about $850 to $950. Maine Island Kayak Company also offers customized trips of any length for $125 to $175 per day, depending on group size and itinerary. Kayaks are fully equipped, speedy fiberglass boats (mostly singles).

Maine Sport Outfitters (*Rockport, ME. 800-722-0826 or 207-236-8797. www.mainesport.com*) runs one- to four-day tours for paddlers of all skill levels using both single and double kayaks. Trips depart May through September from the Maine Sport Outfitters store in Rockport. This outfitter offers an abundance of cruising options: Camp overnight on a secluded campsite in **Muscongus Bay,** or paddle from island to island, camping at different sites each night (lodge accommodations are also available). Day trips in **Camden Harbor** start at $30 for two hours, while overnight trips range from $250 to $495.

With a base at Bar Harbor near Acadia National Park, **Coastal Kayaking Tours** (*Bar Harbor, ME. 800-526-8615 or 207-288-9605. www.acadiafun.com*) enjoys access to all the waters surrounding the park: south through **Merchants Row,** down to the Deer Isle area, **Frenchman Bay,** and

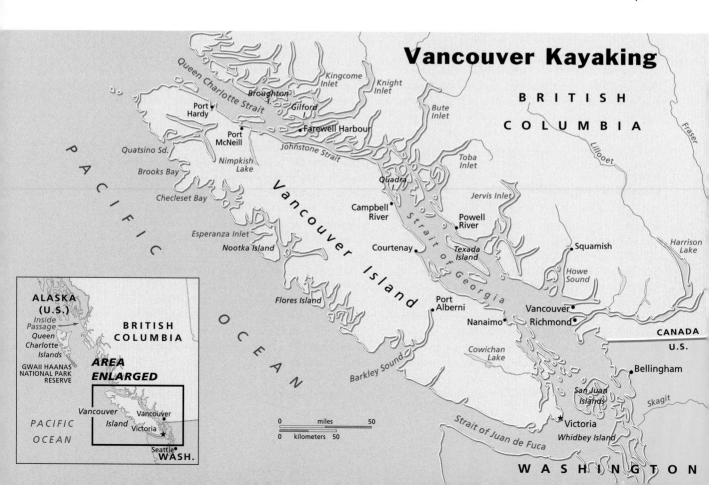

Blue Hill Bay. Offerings range from a 2.5-hour, $35 harbor or sunset cruise for $34, to three-day multi-island camping expeditions for $360.

BELIZE
Isthmus Be the Place!

Clear, warm waters sheltered by the world's second largest barrier reef make the tiny Central American nation of Belize an ideal playground for kayak touring. Paddlers find calm, inviting conditions as far as 35 miles offshore, providing unobscured views of underwater life. You can spend days paddling and snorkeling around Belize's patch reefs, home to countless varieties of corals and tropical fish. Inland, unlike many other tropical regions, Belize has preserved extensive tracts of virgin rain forest. Through these green jungles flow pristine rivers with challenging white water. This combination of inland and offshore paddling opportunities has distinguished Belize as an increasingly attractive destination for the adventurous kayaker.

Slickrock Adventures (*Moab, UT. 800-390-5715 or 435-259-3335. www.slickrock.com*) runs an active sea kayaking program from its resort at **Long Caye** (an atoll on **Glover Reef**), 35 miles off the central coastline of the mainland. Designated a national marine reserve in 1993, Glover Reef is one of the best places to view Belize's complex and varied underwater ecosystem. On Slickrock's six- or ten-day itineraries, participants set out from the outfitter's Water Sports Center on Long Caye for day trips to outlying islands. There you can relax on idyllic beaches, snorkel the patch reefs, or fish the flats right from your kayak. Choose a guided itinerary or set out independently. At night, paddlers return to the rustic but comfortable resort and bunk down in beach cabanas. The price for a six-day program is $1,150, while the ten-day program costs $1,695. This is a rewarding and relaxing introduction to tropical kayaking, and it is suited to paddlers of all levels—even first-timers.

Slickrock's nine-day, multisport trip combines kayaking with some of the many other adventures on tap in Belize. In just a week and a half, you can explore Mayan ruins, run jungle rivers, mountain bike in the rain forest, and sea kayak the atoll. The journey begins at the Chaa Creek Jungle Camp, then visits wildlife preserves and the Mayan ruins at **Xunantunich.** Next, participants make a 7-mile mountain bike ride through the jungle and citrus-orchard plantations.

Exchanging pedals for paddles, the group then voyages 12 miles by raft or kayak through the granite gorge of the **Macal River.** Pioneered by Slickrock, this is a high-energy run featuring 8 miles of Class III and Class IV white water (participants portage the Class V and Class VI runs), followed by an underground passage down a 5-mile section of the **Caves Branch River.** Navigating by headlamps, the group paddles through chambers filled with crystalline formations. The trip culminates with three days of sea kayaking from the resort on Long Caye. This insanely great adventure—one of the most entertaining multiactivity trips offered in the Western Hemisphere—costs roughly $1,950, all-inclusive.

Another company offering Belize kayaking tours is **Ceiba Adventures** (*Flagstaff, AZ. 800-217-1060 or 520-527-0171. www.ceibaadventures.com*). Both six- and ten-day holidays feature sea kayaking and a variety of other warm-water diversions on Glover Reef. This is more of a tropical vacation than a point-to-point trip; kayaking is the main focus, but plenty of time is spent snorkeling, fishing, beachcombing, and just getting away from it all. If you prize fun and relaxation above logging a lot of nautical miles, a Ceiba adventure is a good value at $1,150 for six days or $1,700 for ten days.

For those interested in a more structured, multisport vacation, Ceiba Adventures also offers a **Belize Adventure Week** similar to Slickrock's multisport program. Starting on the mainland, you'll explore a Mayan archaeological site, mountain bike through a rain forest, kayak some Class IV rapids on the Macal River, and navigate an underground river through a series of caves. The second half of the week is spent sea kayaking, snorkeling, windsurfing, and otherwise enjoying Glover Reef. The nine-day trip costs $2,000.

For a less expensive Belize vacation, consider booking a trip through **Reef-Link Kayaking** (*Ft. Dodge, IA. 515-576-1604 or 509-685-0713. www.seabelize.com*). Operated by Kirk Barrett—the author of *Belize by Kayak,* a guidebook available from the company—Reef-Link runs reasonably priced ($700) week-long kayaking trips out of **Ranguana Cay,** 20 miles offshore from Placentia Village. Small groups led by native guides paddle singles from cay to cay within the barrier reef. Paddling itineraries are flexible: They may feature snorkeling, fishing, or camping on idyllic islands. Be prepared to spend as much time underwater wearing a mask and fins as you will spend brandishing a double-bladed paddle in your kayak. A four-day mainland extension, which includes rain forest hikes and visits to the **Caracol** Mayan ruin and Belize's famed jaguar reserve, is available for an additional $300.

Reef-Link caters to independent kayakers, too. For $385, the company will launch you on a seven-day, self-guided tour. That price includes airport transfers, two nights' lodging in Placencia, round-trip boat transport to Ranguana Cay, use of a kayak for five days, and unlimited camping before or after the trip. Participants provide their own food and camping gear. Reef-Link also offers the best kayak-rental facility in Belize; its fully equipped boats include most touring gear.

How and Where to Float Your Boat

The world's premier sea kayaking companies appear below, along with some of their featured paddle trips.

Operating close to home or in far reaches of the globe, these outfitters can take you to sun-soaked tropical edens or to wild and unspoiled northern bays and inlets. Many popular sea kayak trips are sold out by summertime, so it's a good idea to nail down your float plans several months ahead of time.

CHOOSING A KAYAK OUTFITTER

When selecting a kayak outfitter, the **Trade Association of Paddle Sports** (*12455 N. Wauwatosa Rd., Mequon, WI 53097. 262-242-5228. www.gopaddle.org*) advises asking the following questions:

- How long has the company been in business? Many of the best outfitters have run trips for seven years or more.
- Does the outfitter maintain adequate liability insurance?
- Are the guides safety conscious? Do they wear life vests, for example?
- What will the wind and weather conditions be on the trip? Struggling against strong winds and currents is no fun—especially if this is your first kayaking trip.
- Is the company willing to provide references from past customers?
- What personal equipment are you expected to bring?
- Does the outfitter lead its own trips? Many American firms, for example, run trips through less skilled local outfitters in remote locales.
- Will the company furnish you with a complete itinerary before the trip?

Referrals for member outfitters in North America can be obtained by contacting the Trade Association of Paddle Sports. You may also request a free brochure, "Before You Go," which covers paddling technique, equipment selection, safety, and trip planning.

ALASKA

Alaska Discovery Wilderness Adventures
Juneau, AK. 800-586-1911 or 907-780-6226. www.akdiscovery.com

The exclusive on-site concession for guided sea kayak trips in Glacier Bay National Park. Five- and eight-day trips cost $1,700-1,995, including floatplane charter. Other kayak itineraries include Wrangell-St. Elias National Park (ten days, $2,200,

including bush plane charters), Glacial Giants and Hubbard Glacier (seven days, $1,895, including bush plane charters), and the Marine Mammal Discovery Trip featuring humpback whales (six days, $1,695).

North Star Adventures
Flagstaff, AZ. 800-258-8434 or 520-773-9917. www.adventuretrip.com

Low-impact wilderness kayak adventures in Prince William Sound and Kenai Fjords National Park (Aialik Bay). Logistics are well executed; guides are knowledgeable and safety-conscious. In Prince William Sound, the nine-day, $1,600 Knight Island trip visits remote, unspoiled regions. The week-long Aialik Bay trip offers whale-watching and spectacular scenery. Also: Winter kayak trips in Baja California.

Spirit Walker Expeditions
Gustavus, AK. 800-529-2537 or 907-697-2266. www.seakayakalaska.com

Fully outfitted kayak voyages through remote inlets and bays of southeast Alaska. Guides—all trained naturalists—lead two- to five-day whale-watching trips ($685-1,385) through Icy Strait off northern tip of Alexander Archipelago. Seven-day Myriad Islands expedition runs about $2,200, including wilderness floatplane drop-off and pickup. Spirit Walker also offers $120 day trips to Pleasant Island, where paddlers can see a variety of natural habitats.

CALIFORNIA

Aqua Adventures Kayak School
San Diego, CA. 800-269-7792 or 858-272-0800. www.aqua-adventures.com

Has run affordable weekend tours to northern Baja and elsewhere in Mexico since 1988. A wide variety of sites—the popular rock gardens among them—offer conditions suitable for all paddlers, including novices. Customized instruction is available. Sea and white-water kayak training at coastal locations costs $200 per weekend, including all equipment.

Monterey Bay Kayaks
Monterey, CA. 800-649-5357 or 831-633-2211. http://montereykayaks.com

Three-hour guided trips around Monterey Harbor for $50. Scenic, easy paddle with plenty of opportunities to view sea otters, sea lions, and harbor seals up close. Day rentals of standard or sit-on-top kayaks start at $25 per person. The three- or six-hour Elkhorn Slough tours, departing from Moss Landing, visit a unique ecosystem.

Southwind Kayak Center
Irvine, CA. 800-768-8494 or 949-261-0200. www.southwindkayaks.com

Features challenging trips to Santa Cruz Island and the Anacapa Islands (Channel Islands National Park) for intermediate to advanced paddlers. On the Anacapa Island trip, participants paddle 12 miles to one of the islands and camp overnight. Cost for the three-day Anacapa trip is $275. A two-day trip to nearby Santa Cruz Island is $240. Inland trips include a three-day exploration of scenic Lake Mead and a six-day canyonlands trip down Utah's spectacular Green River. Two-day, $220 intensive weekend sea kayak instruction off Newport Beach, San Onofre State Park, and Ventura.

CARIBBEAN & SOUTHEAST

Arawak Expeditions
Cruz Bay, St. John, USVI. 800-238-8687 or 340-693-8312. www.arawakexp.com

Offers $75 day trips and five- and seven-day guided tours in the U.S. and British Virgin Islands. Trips, which include visits to a number of islands and overnight camping, cost $945-1,145, all inclusive. A St. John Adventure Week features hiking, mountain biking, sea kayaking, and scuba diving from a camp with tent cottages.

Ecosummer Expeditions
Clearwater, BC. 800-465-8884 or 250-674-0102. www.ecosummer.com

Offers seven-day, $1,450 (US) and 14-day, $2,100 (US) kayak tours of the Exuma

A SAIL-FITTED KAYAK AND PINK FLAMINGOS SAIL ALONG THE YUCATAN COAST

Land and Sea Park in the Bahamas. Sails fitted to the kayaks speed paddlers along the 7- to 10-mile daily passages.

Gulf Coast Kayak

Matlacha, FL. 941-283-1125. www.gulfcoastkayak.com

Short trips in winter and spring in Matlacha Pass Aquatic Preserve, a back-bay mangrove estuary. Also unguided overnight camping trips to Cayo Costa State Park, a barrier island. For groups, three- to five-day Everglades tours are available. Guides are qualified naturalists. Standard and sit-on- top kayaks rent for $30-50 per day.

CENTRAL AMERICA & MEXICO

Baja Expeditions

San Diego, CA. 800-843-6967 or 858-581-3311. www.bajaex.com

Baja's oldest and largest adventure outfitter (bases in La Paz and San Diego) offers sea kayaking, scuba diving, and natural history cruises. Low client-to-guide ratio; support boat accompanies most tours.

Paddling South

Calistoga, CA. 800-398-6200 or 707-942-4550. www.tourbaja.com

Excellent 7- to 14-day ($800-$1,500) kayaking trips along Golfo de California from Loreto south, Oct.-May. Trips feature local culture, delicious food, leisurely paddling in remote areas. Horseback-riding option available, as well as all-women groups and private trips. Low-impact wilderness travel; no motorized support boats.

Slickrock Adventures

Moab, UT. 800-390-5715 or 435-259-3335. www.slickrock.com

From a private island base on Long Caye at Glover's Reef Atoll, leisurely sea treks suitable for all skill levels explore the Belize reef ecosystem. Trips run Dec.-Aug., starting at $1,250 for 8 days. Sea-land trips combine sea kayaking with other adventures, such as mountain biking, whitewater kayaking, caving, and treks to Mayan ruins. Nine-day trips cost $1,825-1,950.

EUROPE

Aventyrsresor Scandinavian Adventures

Stockholm, Sweden. 01146-8654-1155 or 01146-8654-1155. www.aventyrsresor.se

Tours through the 25,000 islets of the Stockholm Archipelago. Islands are wild and uninhabited but have no tides or dangerous currents. Sweden's access laws give paddlers a wide choice of routes and camping venues. Groups carry food and gear in their kayaks and camp out in tents. The three-day trips, suitable for novices of any age, cost about $350; four-day trips for more advanced paddlers run about $550.

Destinations Ireland and Great Britain

New York, NY. 800-832-1848, 800-169-0353 (toll-free in UK), or 212-265-0745. www.digbtravel.com

Week-long tours led by experienced Irish guides along Ireland's Connemara Coast, from Little Killary harbor in County Galway. The coastline boasts long, sheltered inlets and myriad small islands and bays. The $800 tour includes instruction and bed-and-breakfast accommodations. Also offers paddling trips in Great Britain.

HAWAII

Kayak Kauai Outbound

Hanalei, HI. 800-437-3507 or 808-826-9844. www.kayakkauai.com

Daily guided trips May-Sept. along the Na Pali Coast, notable for its sheer 1,000-foot cliffs, pristine beaches accessible only by sea, and spectacular waterfalls. Cost: $140 per person. One guided trip per day; unguided rentals start at $26 per day for a river kayak or at $35 per day for an ocean kayak.

Maui Sea Kayaking
Puunene, HI. 808-572-6299
www.maui.net/~kayaking

Maui's most experienced kayak outfitter runs mostly day trips on the island's lee side, using standard and sit-on-top kayaks. Cost: $65 per half-day, including lunch and all equipment. Overnighters include a romantic retreat for two and moonlight paddles.

MAINE & CANADIAN MARITIME PROVINCES

Coastal Adventures
Tangier, Nova Scotia. 877-404-2774 or 902-772-2774. www.coastaladventures.com

Tours visit the islands of the Nova Scotia archipelago, featuring great marine life, local seafood, and the chance to learn regional ecology from expert guides. Cape Breton tours paddle beneath 1,000-foot coastal headlands, where bald eagles soar overhead and pilot whales ply the warm (70°F) summer waters. Nova Scotia kayak-camping trips run three to seven days and cost $350-750; add about 10% for inn-to-inn tours. Newfoundland tour hits remote fishing outports, some with no road access and explores deep fjords.

Gros Morne Adventure Guides
Norris Point, Newfoundland. 800-685-4624 or 709-458-2722.
www.grosmorneadventures.com

Offers daily guided kayak tours, plus week-long Newfoundland sea kayaking tours in summer. The Notre Dame Bay expedition includes six days of island-hopping and exploring the rugged coast of Newfoundland; paddlers visit remote coastal islands and old fishing villages, with the option of hiking into coastal highlands, home to caribou herds. About $1,300 (CN).

Maine Island Kayak Co.
Peaks Island, ME. 800-796-2373 or 207-766-2373. www.maineislandkayak.com

Offers one- to ten-day kayak treks in expedition-equipped glass boats (mostly singles) in the Gulf of Maine and the Golfo de California. Leaders are Registered Maine Guides with extensive offshore experience. Instruction programs feature paddling skills, safety and rescue, seamanship, and surf and rock gardens. Customized trips available.

PACIFIC NORTHWEST

Ecosummer Expeditions
Clearwater, British Columbia. 800-465-8884 or 250-674-0102. www.ecosummer.com

Kayak adventures in the Johnstone Strait and the Queen Charlotte Islands (Gwaii Haanas), a rich natural habitat known for its intertidal zone. Orca-watching tours in Johnstone Strait run three to seven days and cost $425-925 (US). The Queen Charlotte trips (seven days at $1,060 or fourteen days at $1,775) feature World Heritage Native American sites, hot springs, and spectacular scenery. Sea kayaking tours also available in the Bahamas, Baja California, Ellesmere Island, Greenland, Patagonia (Chile), and Tonga.

Northern Lights Expeditions
Bellingham, WA. 800-754-7402 or 360-734-6334. www.seakayaking.com

Known for orca-watching trips, Northern Lights runs small-group tours all summer, using stable, two-person expedition kayaks. In addition to its $1,200 Inside Passage and $1,400 Lost Islands tours, the outfitter offers a unique seven-day fly-in kayak vacation at a deluxe lodge in northern British Columbia's Farewell Harbor (about $1,800; food, lodging, and kayaks included).

Tofino Expeditions
Seattle, WA. 800-677-0877 or 206-517-5244. www.tofino.com

Six- and eight-day tours to the north end of Vancouver Island and the central coast of British Columbia for $1,000-1,450. Also runs an eight-day trip to the Queen Charlotte Islands for about $1,300, including floatplane transport. Eight-day winter kayak trips to Baja California for about $1,100; destinations in the Golfo de California near Loreto include the Sierra de la Giganta coast (spectacular scenery), Gold Coast, and Isla Carmen. Nature lovers will like the January whale-watching trips to Magdalena Bay on Baja's Pacific coast.

SOUTH PACIFIC

Ocean River Sea Kayaking
Motueka, New Zealand. 01164-3527-8266. webnz.com/ocean_river

Guided sea kayak tours in remote, unspoiled Abel Tasman National Park on the South Island. This park offers remote, crystal-clear bays and harbors, wilderness solitude, and camping on uncrowded beaches. One- to three-day guided trips cost $65-270 (US); longer tours can be arranged. Free water-taxi service offered for returns on one-way trips. A three-day tour with overnights in lodges costs$420 (US). Kayak rentals will set you back about $20 (US) per day, with a 2-day minimum.

Southern Sea Ventures
McMahon's Point, NSW, Australia. 800-387-1483 or 416-633-5666. www.worldwidequest.com

Guided kayak expeditions in Queensland and Fiji, including a five-day trip to Hinchinbrook Island—one of the largest island national parks in Australia—and a seven-day, $1,060 trip to Hinchinbrook and associated islands. A ten-day trip to Fiji ($1,425) includes a mix of overnight stays in villages and on remote islands. All tours are self-contained—that is, paddlers carry their own food and gear.

TRAVEL TIPS

Kayaking Basics

Modern sea kayaks are made of polyethylene, Kevlar, or fiberglass. The latter two materials make for strong, long-lasting, and rigid watercraft, but they are susceptible to being damaged during transport or when landing on rocky shores. Polyethylene construction sacrifices stiffness and performance for impact resistance and economy.

Most touring kayaks have an enclosed cockpit, with a spray skirt to keep the water out. Open-cockpit designs are more comfortable, but for obvious reasons they are suitable for warm-water touring only. Solo kayaks range from 14 to 18 feet in length; doubles range from 18 to 23 feet long. Although a narrow kayak is faster, a wider boat is more stable and can hold more gear. Another kayaking truism: The shorter the craft, the easier it is to turn.

Novices should look for a relatively flat-bottomed design, which offers greater stability than a hull with a round bottom. Some "vee" in the design will make the kayak run straighter with less steering input.

Important Features

A rudder helps you paddle straight in crosswinds; it also prevents the boat from drifting when you need to keep your hands free. Hatches should be absolutely watertight, and big enough to hold all your gear. Good kayaks also feature watertight bulkheads, or vertical hull partitions; these add strength and prevent the craft from swamping if it capsizes.

Perhaps the most important cruising item is a well-formed, comfortable seat with decent back support. Don't buy any kayak with an uncomfortable seating position—it will feel worse with every mile you paddle.

Single vs. Double

Cruising singles are light and agile in the surf, whereas double kayaks offer greater speed, comfort, and stability. However, doubles are more difficult to turn than singles—and they can be more difficult to right when capsized. Like a tandem bicycle, a double is a good choice for a couple where one person is stronger—meaning the other might have trouble keeping up in his or her own kayak. Most doubles are fitted with rudders, and some have sailing rigs as well.

Collapsible Kayaks

For far-flung touring, try a collapsible kayak. Folding kayaks such as Feathercraft and Klepper can be broken down and stored in a case that is not much larger than an expedition backpack. Collapsible boats are costlier than rigid kayaks, however, and their design reduces their speed and ease of handling. A good compromise: a rigid kayak that breaks into sections for transport.

ONLINE

GASP Sea Kayaking Frequently Asked Questions (FAQ)
www.gasp-seakayak.org/faq/toc.html

This FAQ—the collected wisdom of the rec.boats.paddle newsgroup—is a great resource for everything from boat design to hypothermia prevention. Excellent advice on selecting the right boat and equipment.

InfoHub Canoeing and Kayaking Page
www.infohub.com/travel/adventure/recreation/kayaking.html

This site has an exhaustive list of kayak tour operators, plus a comprehensive set of links to other sites for information on equipment, paddling skills, safety, and kayaking associations. Worth a bookmark.

Internet Sea Kayaking Resources
http://www.ckf.org/other.html

California Kayak Friends created this list of Internet kayaking resources, including West Coast weather links.

Kayak and Paddling Store Directory
www.callamer.com/surf/kayak

Excellent directory of kayak and paddling shops, guides, and outfitters. Thorough list of North American paddling schools.

Sea Kayaker Magazine
www.seakayakermag.com

The online version of *Sea Kayaker* magazine offers boat and gear reviews, feature articles (including trip reports), club listings, and an index of articles.

PRINT

Complete Book of Sea Kayaking by Derek C. Hutchinson (Globe Pequot Press, 4th ed., 1994, $19.95). Graced with easy-to-follow text and illustrations, this is the best single book on sea kayaking. *Derek C. Hutchinson's Expedition Kayaking* (Globe Pequot Press, 4th edition, 1999, $19.95) offers more extensive coverage of open-sea paddling and advanced techniques than do most other books. (*888-249-7586. www.globe-pequot.com*)

The Essential Sea Kayaker by David Seidman (International Marine Publishers, 1997, $12.95) is a good overall introduction to the sport—highly recommended for novices. (*AdventurousTraveler.com. 800-282-3963. www.adventuroustraveler. com*)

Sea Kayaking—A Manual for Long Distance Touring by John Dowd (University of Washington Press, 5th ed., 1997, $18.95, 800-441-4115) is an excellent guide for planning a lengthy ocean passage.

Sea Kayaker. This bimonthly offers articles on kayaking destinations, equipment, navigation, and paddling skills. (*P.O. Box 17170, Seattle, WA 98107. 206-789-9536. www.seakayakermag.com*)

VIDEO

Performance Sea Kayaking: The Basics and Beyond ($29.95). This 58-minute video covers paddling skills, roll technique, surf entry, and self-rescue. In this case, pictures are worth a thousand words. (*AdventurousTraveler.com 800-282-3963. www.adventuroustraveler.com*)

PREPARING FOR SEA-KAYAK CAMPING TRIP AT STONINGTON, MAINE (PENOBSCOT BAY)

FORGET WHAT YOU'VE HEARD ABOUT OVERCROWDED SKI RESORTS. NORTH AMERICA BOASTS MORE than 600 of these snowy playgrounds, and some of the best remain relatively unheralded—and surprisingly uncongested.

• But how do you discover them? Ask even an experienced skier for the best places, and she or he is apt to list resorts within easy driving range. The same subjectivity creeps in when you ask skiing friends to evaluate one ski site relative to another; the response, though candid, is far from impartial—and nowhere near scientific. • That's where this chapter comes in: It profiles the top 20 North American ski centers, providing essential information on each one such as typical snow conditions, toll-free numbers, and type of runs maintained. Also spotlighted in the following pages are the continent's top ten all-around ski resorts, the ten best locations for beginning skiers, and a dozen hot spots for snowboarding. If you're headed outside North America, you'll also find a travel guide for skiing in Europe, as well as a comprehensive report on summer skiing and heli-skiing worldwide.

LEFT: SNOWBOARDER CLEARS A CLIFF AT SNOWMASS, COLORADO.
BELOW: RIDING TO THE RIM OF BRIDGER BOWL, MONTANA

Shred Factor 9

Heli-Skiing

Serious skiing is a gravity-fed reality check.
TREVOR PETERSON

Ski Resorts: The Top Ten

The best overall ski resorts in North America are described below. All ten of these resorts have something to offer skiers at any level; each resort excels in challenge, terrain variety, and snow quality. Whether you seek an adrenaline fix or just want to cruise on world-class runs with excellent snow conditions, these are the places to go.

MAMMOTH MOUNTAIN

Below an impressive two-mile ridgeline of big-drop cornices and narrow chutes, **Mammoth Mountain, California** (*800-626-6684. www.mammothmountain.com*) is a wide-open, above-tree-line playground for advanced skiers. Aptly named, Mammoth (and everything about it) is big—including a ski season that often lasts until June or July, a ski school with some 300 instructors, a lift system that spreads out the heavy crowds, and the largest fleet of Snowcats in the world. The latter maintain high-quality groomed snow all season long.

SQUAW VALLEY

The crown jewel of Tahoe ski areas, **Squaw Valley, California** (*800-545-4350. www.squaw.com*) spreads out over six peaks. For expert skiers, Squaw has it all: chutes, cornices, steeps, and bumps. The editors of *Skiing* magazine named Squaw the number one area for experts—particularly for its out-of-bounds runs, which have served as a training ground for such extreme skiers as Scott Schmidt. Permanent light fixtures have been installed for night skiing, while the KT-22 Express—a high-speed, quad chairlift—provides access to Squaw's longest big-bump runs.

ASPEN

With its many black-diamond runs and steep, narrow trails twisting down through the trees, **Aspen Mountain, Colorado** (*800-525-6200. www.skiaspen.com*) offers some of the most challenging conditions in the Rockies. The snow quality, terrain, and combination of powder and steep drops guarantee Aspen a spot high up on the list of North America's superlative ski areas. Comprising a little more than just 600 skiable acres, Aspen is relatively small. Its numerous expert runs, however, deliver as big a challenge as any you'll find at larger U.S. resorts.

VAIL

An excellent choice for families, the terrain at **Vail, Colorado** (*800-525-2257. www.snow.com*) is evenly distributed among beginner, intermediate, and advanced slopes. The legendary powder bowls on the mountain's back side constitute a destination for serious powder hounds. Vail also offers superb advanced-intermediate cruising runs and bump conditions.

SUN VALLEY

Sun Valley, Idaho (*208-622-2183. www.sunvalley.com*) has undergone some dramatic improvements. Several high-speed lifts have been added, new resort lodges have been constructed, and the snowmaking system has been upgraded. Despite the facelift, the resort still doesn't attract huge crowds—could it be the remote location?—but that just means there's more for anyone who manages to make it here. Experts spend their time skiing **Mount Baldy**— a towering slope with nearly 3,500 feet of steep, vertical terrain.

TAOS SKI VALLEY

Thanks to its southern latitude, **Taos, New Mexico** (*800-776-1111. www.skitaos.org*) offers a great combination of fair weather and light, dry powder to complement its steep terrain. The site's base elevation—more than 9,000 feet—puts the entire ski area above tree line. The majority of runs are designated "Expert," prompting top skiers to give Taos high marks for challenging terrain and open cruising.

SNOWBIRD

Boasting the most vertical feet in the state—and with nearly half its terrain designated "Advanced" or "Expert"—**Snowbird, Utah** (*800-453-3000 www.snowbird.com*) is a place where aggressive skiers can really rack up the mileage. The site's sheer variety—an array of steeps, bumps, tree skiing, and wide-open fields full of Utah's legendary light powder—also banishes boredom. Easy access from Salt Lake City and the extended skiing season round out the qualities that make Snowbird a top choice.

KILLINGTON

By sheer numbers alone, **Killington, Vermont** (*802-621-6867. www.killington.com*) rules in the East: It offers more lifts, more runs, more vertical feet, and more skiable terrain than any other ski area in the region. From the summit of Killington Peak, beginners can ski down runs as much as

10 miles in length. Killington is best known for its mogul slope, the steepest in New England; called the **Outer Limits,** it features bumps that are often taller than the skiers.

JACKSON HOLE

Set beneath the spectacular Grand Tetons, **Jackson Hole, Wyoming** (*800-443-6931. www.jacksonhole.com*) boasts stunning scenery and great snow. Yet skiers often pass it over for better-known ski areas in nearby Colorado and Utah. The result is a superior yet underutilized resort with small crowds and short lift lines. More than half the ski area is suitable for advanced skiers, making Jackson Hole one of the best places to push your skills to the limit.

WHISTLER & BLACKCOMB

With a combined skiing terrain of nearly 7,000 acres, **Whistler** and **Blackcomb, British Columbia** (*604-932-4222. www.whistler-blackcomb.com*) together form the largest ski resort in North America. Not surprisingly, there is plenty of skiing for all levels of ability. At the top of the mountains, experts will find steep chutes that debouch into broad powder bowls. And with a mile of vertical feet, advanced skiers can make continuous runs up to eight miles long.

Ten Best Resorts for Beginners

Let's face the facts: If you've been skiing for only a season or two, you don't need the longest runs, the deepest powder, or the biggest moguls. Instead, you are probably in the market for some gentle gradients, consistent, well-groomed trails, and plenty of room to practice your turns without being flattened by maniacal powderheads. The ten best places to practice and perfect your skiing skills in North America are listed below; for contact information on other resorts, see the chart on pages 248-49.

NORTHSTAR-AT-TAHOE

Although all major ski resorts in California have plenty of runs that are suitable for novices and intermediates, **Northstar** (*800-466-6784. www.skinorthstar.com*) is the clear destination of choice for not-ready-for-prime-slope skiers in the northern part of the state. The terrain is mostly intermediate, and the lower blue runs—with their reliable, superbly groomed snow—are as good as any in the West. For beginning skiers trepidatious about riding a chairlift, an airport-style conveyor belt called the **Magic Carpet** hauls you up the slopes with no midair dangling. Northstar has also expanded its snowmaking capacity and improved its back-side advanced runs. It's a solid choice for all classes of skiers.

INCLINED TO TAKE CHANCES: SHEER FUN AT CHAMONIX

BRECKENRIDGE

Despite its good reputation among strong skiers, **Breckenridge, Colorado** (*800-221-1091. www.breckenridge.com*) is not just for experts. The Peak Nine area, boasting a panoply of wide, well-groomed runs, is one of the best training areas in the state for novices and lower intermediates. Smooth, dry snow makes it easy to work on those parallel turns, while a high-speed quad chair means more time on the snow and less waiting. Many local hotels feature ski-in/ski-out access to the slopes.

BUTTERMILK

Part of the Aspen resort network, **Buttermilk, Colorado** (*800-525-6200. www.skiaspen.com*) took top honors in *SKI* magazine's ranking of ski schools nationwide. It also finished second (after Snowmass) as the country's best ski destination for families. With more than 200 instructors on hand—or should that be on foot?—classes are small, and even the best guides will teach beginners. All runs are easy to ski, and though the novices who make up half of Buttermilk's customers often clog the bottom of the hill, there's plenty of good skiing on the mountain's 43 trails.

COPPER MOUNTAIN

A favorite weekend resort, **Copper Mountain, Colorado** (*800-458-8386. www.ski-copper.com*) offers some of the most economical packages in the Rockies. Occasional skiers are the resort's bread and butter, and it caters to them with a fine network of long, wide novice trails. As you move east across the mountain, the trails get more difficult, meaning you need not choose between boring bunny hills and steep sections that will send you sprawling. Like nearby Vail, Copper Mountain has superb high-altitude snow conditions.

CRESTED BUTTE

For advanced novices seeking to practice their parallel turns, a superb network of long, smooth, "easy blue" runs is on tap at **Crested Butte, Colorado** (*800-544-8448. www.crestedbutteresort.com*). Long known as a great choice for intermediates—and, more recently, as the site of the U.S. Extreme Skiing Championships—Crested Butte now aims to attract first-timers with 150 acres of beginner terrain. As a further inducement, Crested Butte offers free skiing at certain times. Discount accommodations are also available.

SUNDAY RIVER

Rarely does **Sunday River, Maine** (*800-543-2754. www.sundayriver.com*)—one of the best training hills in the East—get overcrowded. It has smooth, well-groomed slopes, and a snowmaking capacity that covers more than 90 percent of the runs. Although most slopes here are

Skiing and Snowboarding

Map labels:

BRITISH COLUMBIA · Lake Louise · Whistler/Blackcomb · ALBERTA · CANADA · U.S. · Summit at Snoqualmie · WASHINGTON · MONTANA · Mont Tremblant · ME. · Sugarloaf · Sunday River · Mt. Hood · Bridger Bowl · Stowe · VT. · Killington · Stratton · Mt. Snow · Mt. Bachelor · OREGON · IDAHO · Sun Valley · Jackson Hole · WYOMING · New York · quaw alley · Northstar-at-Tahoe · Park City · Alta · Chicago · Sierra-at-Tahoe · Snowbird · Deer Valley · Steamboat Springs · Heavenly Valley · UTAH · Buttermilk · Vail · Breckenridge · ear Mt. · Mammoth Mt. · Snowmass · Copper Mt. · Aspen · CALIFORNIA · Crested Butte · COLORADO · Los Angeles · Taos Ski Valley · NEW MEXICO · ATLANTIC OCEAN · MEXICO · U.S. · CIFIC CEAN

miles 0–400
kilometers 0–400

Legend:
- Top ten all-around skiing resorts
- Top ten resorts for beginners and families
- Other skiing/snowboarding resorts

intermediate, skiers of all abilities will find enjoyable terrain and 2,340 feet of vertical drop.

DEER VALLEY

Distinguishing **Deer Valley, Utah** (*800-424-3337. www. deervalley.com*) are its smooth, well-groomed, wide-open slopes. These offer plenty of fun without pushing novices or intermediates past their limits. First-timers will enjoy **Wild West,** an area for beginners only: This is the place to improve your skills without thrashing yourself—or losing face. Deer Valley can also justifiably crow about its food and customer service, the best of any resort in the Rockies.

PARK CITY

The size and diversity of this facility means there's ideal skiing for everyone—even those working out of their wedge turns—at **Park City, Utah** (*800-222-7275. www. parkcity-mountain.com*). With 3,100 feet of vertical drop, Park City can seem like an experts' resort, but the open intermediate runs allow easy traversing if things get steep. Several new lifts have left more of the central runs free for entry-level skiers.

MOUNT SNOW

The broad and smooth lower slopes of **Mount Snow, Vermont** (*802-464-3333. www.mountsnow.com*) constitute one of the best areas in the East for skiers who want to progress beyond the rank of novice. Unlike some resorts that lavish their hardware budgets on lifts for advanced runs, Mount Snow features a wide variety of fast lifts on its gentler trails. The facility's fine cruising runs will keep the better skiers in your party happy as well. As a future site of the X-Games, Mount Snow has become one of the hottest snowboarding venues in the East.

STRATTON

The snow conditions can be a bit icy, but the gentle slopes and wide trails beckon novice skiers to **Stratton, Vermont** (*800-843-6867. www.stratton.com*). Let the hot dogs head to Killington while you take advantage of the space here—including a 45-acre section reserved for beginners—to practice your skills. The gondola and pleasant ski village are lagniappes that will appeal to all levels of skiers. Excellent nordic skiing is available nearby as well.

TWO STYLES CONVERGE IN SWITZERLAND'S JUNGFRAU.

Hot Spots = Cold Fun

Phone	Elevation	Runs	Beg./Int./ Adv. %	Lifts	Heli-ski/ Snowcat	Season/ Snowmaking %
HEAVENLY VALLEY P.O. Box 2180, State Line, CA 89449. www.skiheavenly.com. *Fantastic expert runs, but even novices can ski the top of the mountains.*						
M: 775-588-4584 R: 800-243-2836	3,500'	4,800 acres of skiable terrain. Groomed, open bowls with expert tree runs on Nev. side. Most beginner runs at top.	20/45/35	62-person tram, 3 HSQ, 9 triples, 7 doubles, 6 surface lifts	None	Nov.-May; 66%
MAMMOTH MOUNTAIN P.O. Box 24, Mammoth Lakes, CA 93546. www.mammoth-mtn.com. *Great runs, snow conditions & weather. Very long season.*						
M: 888-462-6668 R: 800-626-6684	3,100'	150 trails, mostly intermediate (up to 3 mi.), 3,500 acres SM. Major ski school with 300 instructors.	30/40/30	2 GON, 8 HSQ, 3 RQ, 7 triples, 7 doubles, 1 t-bar	None	Nov.-June; 12%
NORTHSTAR/TAHOE P.O. Box 129, Truckee, CA 96160. www.skinorthstar.com. *Good diversity & grooming. User-friendly for intermediates and families.*						
R: 800-466-6784	2,200'	63 trails (up to 3 mi.). North-facing bowls with good powder; back side with steep tree runs.	25/50/25	GON, 4 HSQ, 2 triples, 2 doubles, 2 surface	None	Nov. 21-Apr.; 50% of runs
SQUAW VALLEY Olympic Valley, CA 96146. www.squaw.com. *Among best U.S. resorts for skilled skiers. Great diversity, fast lifts; vistas and room galore.*						
R: 800-545-4350	2,850'	4,000 acres of open bowls. Most runs groomed; excellent advanced runs. Lighted night skiing	25/45/30	110-seat Tram, 1 Funitel, 4 HSQ, 8 triples, 8 doubles, 2 HS-6 paks, 4 surface. 49,000 skiers/hr. capacity.	None	Nov.-May; 350 acres
ASPEN MOUNTAIN P.O. Box 1248, Aspen, CO 81612. www.skiaspen.com. *Flashy crowd. Bell Mt. draws experts with its moguls, trees, and deep powder.*						
M: 970-925-1220 R: 800-525-6200	3,260'	675 acres of well-groomed, wide trails (up to 3 mi.) for intermediate to advanced. Adjacent Buttermilk Resort for novices.	0/35/65	Summit GON, 1 HSQ, 2 RQ, 4 doubles	Aspen Mountain Powder Tours, 800-525-6200	Nov.-Apr.; 33%
BEAVER CREEK P.O. Box 7, Vail, CO 81658. www.beavercreek.com. *Underrated; great intermediate skiing. Well-organized; cheaper than parent Vail.*						
M: 970-476-5601 R: 800-525-2257	3,340'	146 runs on 1,625 acres. Mostly intermediate, wide and groomed, but also challenging expert runs.	34/39/27	6 HSQ, 4 triples, 4 doubles, short lift lines. Very modern.	None	Nov.-Apr.; 38%
COPPER MOUNTAIN P.O. Box 3008, Copper Mtn., CO 80443. www.ski-copper.com. *No weaknesses. Mountain divided naturally for various skill levels.*						
M: 970-968-2882 R: 800-458-8386	2,601'	425 runs, 4 bowls on 1,453 acres, including 350 extreme. All types of terrain.	21/25/54	4 HSQ, 5 triples, 5 doubles, 5 surface, 1 kids' conveyor. Fast runs to bowls.	None	Nov.-Apr.; 15%
CRESTED BUTTE Box A, Mt. Crested Butte, CO 81225. www.crestedbutteresort.com. *An experts' playground, with plenty of steep chutes and open bowls.*						
M: 800-544-8448	3,062'	85 trails on 1,434 acres. Extensive expert terrain on the back side, with great open bowls and tree running.	15/44/41	3 HSQ, 2 triples, 3 doubles, 5 surface	None, but Snowcat	Nov.-Apr.; 21%
KEYSTONE/A-BASIN P.O. Box 38, Breckenridge, CO 80435. www.keystoneresort.com. *Great intermediate trail system. With SM, opens Halloween.*						
M: 800-248-0732	2,340'	116 runs on 1,861 acres. Open bowl, glade, and superbly groomed trails. North Peak moguls.	12/24/58	2 GON, 1 RQ, 5 HSQ lifts, 2 triples, 5 doubles, 7 surface	None	Oct.-June; 51%
SNOWMASS P.O. Box 1248, Aspen, CO 81612; www.skiaspen.com. *Huge complex, very popular intermediate runs & moguls. A real cruisers' mountain.*						
M: 970-925-1220 R: 800-766-9622	4,087'	82 runs on 3,010 acres. Fantastic array of wide-open intermediate runs (up to 4.16 mi.). Great expert runs.	10/52/38	7 HSQ, 2 triples, 6 doubles, 5 surface, short lift lines	None, but Snowcat	Nov-Apr; 130 acres
STEAMBOAT SPRINGS Steamboat Springs, CO 84087. www.steamboat-ski.com. *Short waits, great verticals. Major jet service. Above-average clientele.*						
M: 970-879-6111 R: 800-922-2722	3,660'	107 runs (up to 3 mi.) on 2,500 acres (1,500 groomed). Great advanced powder, glades & race trails. Open slopes.	15/54/31	GON, 2 HSQ, 1 RQ, 6 triples, 7 doubles, 3 surface. 29,300 skiers per hr. capacity.	Steamboat Powdercats, 800-288-0543	Nov.-Apr.; 15%
VAIL P.O. Box 7, Vail, CO 81658. www.snow.com. *No. 1 overall resort in SKI magazine writers' poll. China Bowl offers great backcountry powder.*						
M: 970-476-5601 R: 800-525-2257	3,300'	141 trails, 7,939 acres. 32/36/32, but many green runs up top. Best bowls in CO. Back side is challenging.	13/56/31	GON, 4 HSQ, 1 RQ, 6 triples, 6 doubles, 2 surface. Most hi-speed lifts in West.	None	Nov.-Apr.; 345 acres
SUN VALLEY P.O. Box 10, Sun Valley, ID 83353. www.sunvalley.com. *New lifts reduce wait time for superb, long runs. Good value among top ID. resorts.*						
M: 208-622-2183 R: 208-635-8261 or 800-786-8259	3,400'	78 trails on 2,054 acres. Groomed intermediate runs. Black-diamond bowls. Elkhorn resort nearby for novices.	36/42/22	7 Quads, 5 triples, 5 doubles, 2 surface. 10 minutes to top.	Yes for Heli-ski	Nov.-May; 30%

CODES: **M** (Main Phone), **R** (Reservation Phone); **GON** (Gondola), **HSQ** (High-Speed Detachable Quad), **RQ** (Regular Quad), **SM** (Snowmaking)

Phone	Elevation	Runs	Beg./Int./Adv. %	Lifts	Heli-ski/Snowcat	Season/Snowmaking %
SUGARLOAF *R.R. 1, Box 5000, Kingfield, ME 04947. www.sugarloaf.com. Big mountain with wide choice of black runs. Most complete SM in East.*						
M: 207-237-2000 R: 800-843-5623	2,837'	126 trails on 1,400 acres. Terrain from double diamond to 3-mi. cruising run. Mostly groomed. Many expert glades.	24/28/20 /18/10	2 HSQ, 2 RQ, 1 triple, 8 doubles, 1 surface	None	Nov.-Apr.; 92%
TAOS SKI VALLEY *P.O. Box 90, Taos Ski Valley, NM 87525. www.skitaos.org. Excellent terrain, but much of this mountain is quite difficult.*						
M: 505-776-2291 R: 800-776-1111	2,610'	72 lift-served runs on 1,094 acres. Great snow. Challenging expert runs. Lower trails crowded during earn-to-ski weeks.	24/25/51	4 RQ, 5 doubles, 1 triple, 2 surface	None	Nov.-Apr.; 39%
MT. BACHELOR *Box 1031, Bend, OR 97709. www.mtbachelor.com. Best resort in Pacific NW. Summit can be cold, but offers 360-degree views & great runs.*						
M: 800-829-2442 R: 541-382-2442	3,260'	70 runs on 3,683 skiable acres. Mostly groomed and intermediate. Spring is best.	15/60/25	7 HSQ, 3 reg. triples, 1 double, 2 surface	None	Nov.-July; No SM
ALTA *P.O. Box 8007, Alta, UT 84092. www.altaskiarea.com. Skiing the way God intended it: wild, open expert areas, great powder, and fine novice runs.*						
M: 801-742-3333 R: 801-942-0404	2,100'	40 trails, 2,200 acres, powder and groomed trails; mostly open and bowl skiing. Best for strong skiers.	25/40/35	2 triples, 6 doubles, 4 tows, trail to Snowbird	Wasatch Powderbird Guides (801) 742-2800	Nov.-Apr.; 27 acres
DEER VALLEY *Park City, UT 84060. www.deervalley.com. Better cruising runs, shorter lift lines than Park City. Pricey, but all amenities. Great food & service.*						
M: 435-649-1000 R: 800-424-3337	2,200'	87 trails on 1,750 acres. No long catwalks—just good, open downhills. Superb groomed powder; 6 bowls.	15/50/35	1 GON, 5 HSQ, 3 RQ, 8 triples, 2 doubles	None	Nov.-Apr.; 29%
PARK CITY *P.O. Box 39, Park City, UT 84060. www.parkcitymountain.com. Most variety in Utah. Nice long mogul runs. Fine bowl skiing.*						
M: 435-649-8111 R: 800-222-7275	3,100'	100 trails on 3,300 acres. 6 bowls, groomed runs, mogul and tree runs. Lighted night skiing.	18/44/38	4 HS-6 passenger, 1 HSQ, 1 RQ, 5 triples, 4 doubles	None	Nov.-Apr.; 15%
SNOWBIRD *Snowbird, UT 84092. www.snowbird.com. Huge skiable area, full range of terrain and conditions for all skill levels. Among top 10 in U.S.*						
M: 801-742-2222 R: 800-453-3000	3,240'	89 trails on 2,500 acres. Huge bowls. Groomed lower novice/intermediate runs from chairlifts.	25/35/40	125-person tram (inter/adv. terrain), 7 doubles, chute to Alta, 2 HSQ	Wasatch Powder Guides, 801-742-2800	Nov.-June; less than 5%
KILLINGTON *Killington Rd., Killington, VT 05751. www.killington.com. Longest run in U.S. (10-mi. Juggernaut). Longest season in East. Superb for all levels.*						
M: 802-422-3333 R: 802-621-6867	3,150'	7 mountains; 200 trails, 87 miles. Most intermediate, but ultra-steep runs for experts. Novice trails from summit.	50/18/32	2 GON, 6 HSQ, 5 RQ, 6 triples, 4 doubles, 7 surface, 6 slow quads.	None	Oct.-June; 72%
STOWE *5781 Mountain Rd., Stowe, VT 05672. www.gostowe.com. >50% of lifts exceed 1 mile. Big-mountain skiing & New England charm.*						
M: 802-253-3000 R: 800-247-8693	2,360'	48 trails on 480 acres. Great pro runs, plus long trails for novice/intermediate. Excellent grooming & SM.	16/59/25	HS GON, 1 HSQ, 1 triple, 6 doubles, 2 surface	None	Nov.-May; 73%
JACKSON HOLE *P.O. Box 290, Teton village, WY 83025. www.jacksonhole.com. Major verticals, wild chutes, good cruising routes.*						
M: 307-733-2292 R: 800-443-6931	4,139'	80 trails on 2,500 acres. Major steep and deep expert runs. Casper Bowl great for intermediate. Best snow on top.	10/40/50	1 GON, 1 HSQ, 63-seat tram, 2 RQ, 2 DQ, 1 triple, 4 doubles, 2 surface	High Mountain Heli-Ski, 307-733-3274	Dec.-Apr.; 5%
LAKE LOUISE *Box 5, Lake Louise, Calgary, AB, T0L 1E0. www.skilouise.com. Fabulous setting. Great for all levels. Sunshine Village, Mt. Norquay good too.*						
M: 403-256-8473 R: 800-258-7669	3,250'	105 named runs on 4,300 acres. Heaps of powder, long cruising runs. Novice runs off all lifts.	25/45/30	3 HSQ, 1 RQ, 2 triples, 2 doubles, 3 surface	See Heli-ski directory	Nov.-May; 40%
WHISTLER/BLACKCOMB *Whistler, B.C. www.whistler-blackcomb.com. No. 2 in SKI magazine. Great variety. Major new snowmaking at Blackcomb.*						
M: 604-932-3434 R: 604-932-4222	5,280'	> 200 marked trails, 12 Alpine bowls on > 7,000 acres. Superb grooming, heaps of snow. Off-piste, steep chutes for experts.	20/55/25	Ultra-modern lifts, 3 GON, 12 HSQ, 5 triples, 1 double, 12 surface (total)	Whistler Heli-skiing, 604-932-4105	Nov.-June; 530 acres
MONT TREMBLANT *3005 Chemin Principal, Quebec, J0T 1Z0. www.tremblant.ca. SKI readers rate it #1 in eastern North America. Longest run >3.5 mi.*						
M: 819-681-2000 R: 800-754-8736	2,131'	92 trails, 602 acres, trails newly widened. Good intermediate cruising runs. Lighted night skiing.	20/45/35	5 HSQ, 1 RQ, GON, 3 triples, 2 doubles	None	Nov.-May; 70%

Board to Death!

If you're looking for a new way to use your athletic abilities and want to try something that's exciting and fun, snowboarding may be your ticket to ride. No longer an underground sport banished to sledding hills and snow-covered golf courses, snowboarding has found acceptance at 98 percent of U.S. ski resorts. In fact, almost 500 resorts in the U.S. and Canada now rent boards and boots—and grant equal access to all downhill slopes. Snowboarders make up about one-third of visitors to Alpine resorts, and their numbers climb each year.

Although snowboarding has its fair share of hot dogs—a function of heavy crossover from skateboarding, a similar sport—today's snowboarders range in age from 6 to 65, and they come in all shapes and flavors. It's easy to see why so many people gravitate to the sport: Besides the sheer fun of speeding over snow, it's possible to become reasonably proficient after four or five trips to the slopes—an achievement made possible by breakthroughs in technology that have made the boards easier to control.

In contrast to skiing, crappy snow conditions are a snowboarder's dream. When the snow is heavy, wet, or deep—preferably all three—riders have more fun. Advanced boarders can handle even icy conditions.

According to expert ratings of conditions and accessibility for all levels, these are the best ski resorts for snowboarding:

SNOWBOARDING RESORTS

ALASKA

Eaglecrest Ski Area
907-790-2000
www.juneau.lib.ak.us/eaglecrest

Just 12 miles from downtown Juneau on Douglas Island you'll find the city's municipally owned ski area, a big mountain resort with small lift lines. Eaglecrest is known for its deep powder bowls and steep terrain, as well as its gentle beginner runs and exciting intermediate trails.

CALIFORNIA

Mammoth Mountain
800-626-6684
www.mammothmountain.com

Committed to snowboard-specific terrain, Mammoth Mountain Unbound Terrain Park's half-pipes draw riders of all ages and abilities with its mind-blowing jumps, hips, quarter-pipes, snake runs, and rollers.

Sierra-at-Tahoe, California
530-659-7453. www.sierratahoe.com

Voted one of the Top 50 Places to Ride by *Transworld Snowboarding* in 1999, Sierra-at-Tahoe boasts some legendary terrain parks. Challenges include the Gauntlet on the back side, an amazing half-pipe on Upper Main, and a big-time powder run through Avalanche Bowl. Overall, a little bit of something for both skiers and riders.

Bear Mountain Ski Resort
909-585-2519. www.bearmtn.com

Located northwest of Yosemite National Park, Bear Mountain has allowed snowboarding since 1988 on 100 percent of its runs. These include 31 snowboarding trails, two terrain parks, and four half-pipes. Music is played in the terrain park, and there are 25 snowboard shops within 10 miles. Snowboard clinics are offered twice a day, seven days a week. Quicksilver Terrain Park—a state-of-the-art facility that flows top to bottom in boarder-cross style—opened in 2000 with everything from berms, banks, jumps, and spines to quarter-pipes, kickers, and a 300-foot half-pipe.

COLORADO

Breckenridge Ski Resort
800-789-7669. www.breckenridge.com

In the mid-1980s, Breckenridge distinguished itself as the first major resort to allow snowboarding in the United States. Since then it has acquired a Super Dragon 2000 that is used to carve half-pipes with 15-foot-high walls. The resort now offers bowls, chutes, glades, powder pitches, bumps, and jumps, along with mellow cruising zones. Breckenridge has more than 2,000 acres of prime Alpine terrain stretching over four mountains. That spaciousness, combined with some great site engineering, translate into some of the best boarding in the Rockies.

Crested Butte Mountain Resort
800-544-8448 or 800-754-3733
www.crestedbutteresort.com

A family-friendly resort in a historically authentic mining town, Crested Butte is the last great Colorado ski town. It boasts 1,160 acres of skiable terrain, from gorgeous cruisers and easygoing slopes to an awesome snowboard park. Blanket all this with 25 feet of snow each winter, and you get an ideal venue for hardened shredheads and wobbly tyros alike. Crested Butte added a new half-pipe in the 2000 season.

OREGON

Mount Hood, Oregon
503-337-2230. www.mthood.com/snowboard

North America's only year-round ski area, 11,235-foot-high Mount Hood boasts the Ski Bowl—a snowboard park containing not only a boarder-cross but jumps, rail slides, and a humongous entrenched half-pipe. Race training takes place on Palmer and Zig Zag Glaciers, with free-riding on White River Glacier. Two express quad chairs and 2,500 feet of vertical make Mount Hood attractive for any winter activity. Free-riders spend most of their time in the park's Lower Palmer area, or in the public park on the Magic Mile.

VERMONT

Killington Resort
800-621-6867
www.ridekillington.com

Opening in mid-October and closing sometime in June, Killington posts the longest season in the East. According to *Snow Country* magazine, Killington is the favorite resort of East Coast riders. It has the most novice terrain in the East; intermediates will find an endless variety of new and challenging trails; and advanced skiers and riders can test their mettle on the largest advanced complex in the East.

STOP YOUR BIRCHING: BOARDER ROCKS THE WOODS AT TELLURIDE

For beginners, Killington's Learn to Ride program includes a three-hour clinic, rentals, and lift ticket for only $60.

Stowe Mountain Resort, Vermont
800-253-3000
www.stowe.com

Stowe has long been a leader in the growth and development of snowboarding in the U.S. *Snowboard Life* magazine has rated Stowe the Number 1 place to ride in the East, offering great terrain for snowboarders of all ages and ability levels. Check out the Jungle, an incredible terrain park. The Stowe Snowboard School, one of the nation's top snowboarding instructional centers, is dedicated to providing fun and fast improvement for riders. Stowe's new Pipe Dragon Groomer enables the resort to shape and groom the half- and quarter-pipes to world-class standards.

WASHINGTON

The Summit at Snoqualmie
206-236-7277
www.summit-at-snoqualmie.com

An hour's drive from Seattle, the Summit at Snoqualmie offers four mountains: Summit Central, Summit East, Summit West, and Alpental. Each has its own appeal, and all are open to snowboarders. The monster among them is Alpental, best suited to advanced and expert boarders and skiers with its 50 percent advanced terrain. In addition, the Summit at Snoqualmie has a new half-pipe and terrain park at Summit Central. At night, the Summit glows with lights for night skiing. Recent additions include two high-speed quad chairlifts and a rental shop featuring K2 snowboards.

CANADA

Lake Louise, Alberta
800-258-7669
www.skilouise.com

Located in Banff National Park in Alberta, Lake Louise Ski Resort offers jumps and bumps and big air. Juniper Jungle, the new terrain park for adventurous skiers and boarders, features a half-pipe, tabletops, big-air jumps, berms, banked turns, spines, quarter-pipes, hips, rail slides, and fun boxes. Completed in February 2000, the park is the largest in North America. Snowboarders can ride an impressive vertical drop of 1,950 feet from the bottom of Summit Platter to the base of the park on the front side of Whitehorn Mountain.

Whistler-Blackcomb Mountains, British Columbia
800-766-0449
www.whistler-blackcomb.com

Blackcomb offers all the challenge anyone could ask for. Riders can choose an intermediate or expert run through the park. On the expert side, expect monster tabletops and a couple of hips. On the intermediate side, you'll encounter loafs, tabletops, and spines of less intimidating size. Both parks have access to the World Cup pipe. A new beginner park/snowboard cross area—designed to help rookies practice before they hit the bigger stuff—can be found at the top of the Catskinner chairlift.

Whistler, British Columbia
To welcome the new millennium, Whistler unveiled a radical new Nintendo Terrain Park. Situated both left and right of the Green Acres run, it has doubled the ridable area on that part of the mountain. The expert line, on the left side of the park, features several huge pro-style jumps. On the right or intermediate side, riders encounter more of a free-ride experience. Whistler's half-pipe at the top of the Emerald chair provides access to the park.

European Ski Resorts: A Baker's Dozen

With so many fine ski areas in Europe, selecting a destination can be difficult—especially if you've never skied the Alps before. So we've done the heavy sledding for you, picking 13 resorts that offer world-class skiing, fine accommodations, and unrivaled après-ski attractions. All are four- or five-star sites, but some are best for experts, while others are suitable for all levels of skiers. In general, France offers the biggest resorts, with the steepest verticals and the most challenging off-*piste* (off-trail) skiing. Swiss ski areas tend to have equally impressive mountains, but more charm. In Austria you'll find good value, countless skiing options, and the relaxed feel of small villages. Italy has the lowest prices, the friendliest people, and the most consistent snow in the Alps.

AUSTRIA

ISCHGL

Ischgl, renowned for its consistently high-quality snow conditions, offers the après-ski opportunities of a larger resort with the rustic charm of an authentic Tirolean village. The **Silvretta ski area** nearby is large and modern by Austrian standards, but Ischgl and its surrounding hamlets constitute a skiing haven with its own distinctive identity. The town of Ischgl sits in a narrow valley at the base of some steep slopes that face north. From here, skiers ride one of three large gondolas to an upper plateau, where 40 lifts fan out to cover 120 miles of well-maintained ski terrain.

With nearly all its runs above 6,000 feet, Silvretta has the most reliable snow in the Tirol. As a result, its ski season often lasts a month longer than that of other resorts in the region. Beginners will find only a few long T-bar lifts, but these are conveniently located near the gondola stations and the on-mountain lodges.

Intermediates will particularly enjoy Ischgl. From the **Palinkopf Summit** at the west end of the slopes, intermediates can cruise on long, uninterrupted runs over treeless terrain. From the summit, skiers may also cross the Swiss border to visit the village of **Samnaun.** Thanks to its sunny southern exposure (not to mention its duty-free status), Samnaun is a popular lunch spot. A gondola returns skiers to the summit, but it often has long lines.

Expert skiers may wish to hire a guide to explore the off-*piste* skiing around Ischgl. Though relatively unheralded, this adventure offers real opportunities for untracked exploration.

The best accommodations in Ischgl are located near the center of the village and close to the gondola stations. The luxurious, modern Elisabeth Hotel is a top selection. The main gondola station is only a few steps from the back of the hotel, and the hotel bar is a popular après-ski hangout. Other, more traditional chalet-style accommodations include the Madlein, also just steps away from the gondola station, and the Goldener Adler, a 200-year-old chalet in the middle of the village. For these four-star hotels, expect to pay more than $250 per night in mid-season. Reservations should be made a year in advance.

Bed-and-breakfast lodges are more affordable; they start at around $60 per night.

A one-week ski pass for Silvretta (purchased locally) costs up to $250 in peak season. For more information about Ischgl, contact the local tourist office, **Tourismusberband** (*A-6561, Ischgl, Austria. 01143-5444-5266. Fax 01143-5444-5636*). Or book a package holiday with **Adventures on Skis** (*815 North Rd., Rte. 202, Westfield, MA 01085. 800-628-9655 or 413-568-2855. www.advonskis.com*).

KITZBUHEL

Easy access from Munich, a wide selection of intermediate runs, and the best night life among Austrian resorts are the claims to fame of **Kitzbuhel** resort. Although the snow can be thin on the relatively low-altitude (2,500- to 6,500-foot) slopes, the medieval town has a unique charm that draws skiers back time and again.

The focus of skiing at Kitzbuhel is the **Hahnenkamm**, the site of World Cup races each January. If you want to avoid the crowds, however, ski the **Ehrenbachhohe** in nearby Kirchberg, or try the 6,500-foot-high **Kitzbuheler Horn,** with its long but relatively easy intermediate trails.

World Cup races aside, Kitzbuhel is mostly an intermediate destination—at least when it comes to prepared trails. Off-*piste* fans can hire a guide (*about $110 per day; 6-8 people maximum*) to visit more challenging sections; the ski school gives group lessons in off-track skiing for about $55 per day. If you haven't booked a package tour, you can save quite a bit with the joint Kitzbuhel-Kirchberg lift pass (*3 days for about $100, 6 days for about $190*).

All kinds of accommodations can be found in Kitzbuhel, but a *Zimmer* (room) in a private home, farm, or apartment is usually warm, cozy, and spotless. This arrangement allows you to get by for less than $40 per person per day, including breakfast.

If you opt for a hotel, one of the best is the Goldener Greif. The traditional Hotel Landhaus Brauns in Kirchberg is conveniently situated close to the slopes. Budget (two-star) hotel packages begin at $290 per week; lifts cost an added $170 or so. Bargain-hunters should call **Tradesco Tours** (*310-649-5808. www.tradescotours. com*), which offers Kitzbuhel Ski Packages for less than $460 per week for bed-and-breakfast lodging and lifts. **Central Holidays** (*800-935-5000. www. centralholidays.com*) offers a week's skiing in Kitzbuhel starting at $800 per person, including lodging and round-trip airfare from New York, Newark, or Boston. **Holidaze Ski Tours** (*800-526-2827. www. holidaze.com*) also offers one-week, $1,000 ski tours to Kitzbuhel.

To get to Kitzbuhel/Kirchberg, fly to Munich and take the train from there. Contact the local tourist office, or **Fremdenverkehrsverband** (*Hinterstadt 18, A-6370 Kitzbuhel, Austria. 01143-5356-2155*), when you arrive.

ST. ANTON

In the Arlberg region of the Tirol lies **St. Anton,** one of the oldest—and busiest—Austrian ski resorts. You can ski dozens of runs from St. Anton proper, as well as hundreds of other runs in the nearby resorts of **St. Christoph, Stuben, Zurs,** and **Lech.** St. Anton offers Austria's largest ski school and perhaps the best skiing for intermediates in the Tirol. From St. Anton, take the cable car to the **Valluga** summit to enjoy a 9,000-foot, half-hour cruise to the valley below. The intermediate run from the **Gampberg** summit is outstanding, while experts will be challenged by the large mogul field accessed from the **Tanzboden** lift.

St. Anton is a charming but bustling community with a wide variety of accommodations. Bargain hunters prefer co-op apartments and small guesthouses; prices are lowest in the village of Stuben. If you want to go first class, try the Hotel Schwarzer Adler in St. Anton (*01143-5446- 22440. www.schwarzeradler.com*) or the Hotel Post in Lech (*01143-5446-22130*). A week-long package at one of these four-star hotels costs about $800-$1,000 per person, double occupancy (including meals and lifts). A six-day lift ticket good for the entire Arlberg area costs about $200.

To get to Arlberg, fly to Zurich, then take the express train to St. Anton or the *Arlberg Express* ski-bus to Lech. The tourist office can be contacted at A-6580 St. Anton am Arlberg, Austria (*01143-5446-22690. Fax 01143-5446-2532*). **Alphorn Tours** (*800-257-4647. www.alphorntours. com*) offers package tours to St. Anton and other Austrian resorts. Central Holidays (*800-935-5000. www.centralholidays. com*) offers a week's skiing and lodging in St. Anton starting at $1,000 per week, including lodging and round-trip airfare from New York or Boston.

ZELL AM SEE

A cornucopia of options—groomed trails, World Cup downhills, off-*piste* runs, and glaciers—qualify **Zell am See** as the ultimate Alpine ski adventure. The **Schmittenhohe** lifts give access to most of the best runs. Intermediate skiers will find an outstanding network of trails suited to their skills; experts can challenge themselves on the World Cup runs and a superb run down from the **Kapellenlift** summit. Nearby **Kaprun** is famous for its high-altitude glacier skiing. You can reach the Alpine center by cable car or by the Stanseil-bahn tunnel and ski down from there. The iron-thighed can take an aerial tram all the way to the top station at 10,000 feet.

Not only is this skiing great, it's cheap. A joint Zell-Kaprun seven-day pass, good for all 52 lifts at both resorts, runs about $165. Nor is there any shortage of places to stay. Most hotels and pensions are near the lifts, and you can even stay at a hotel right on the Kaprun glacier. If you have a rental car, another good choice is the tarn-side village of **Thumersbach** nearby.

In low- and mid-season, Zell am See offers a good all-in-one ski package, the **Schnee-Okay.** For about $350 per person, you get a regional six-day lift pass, seven nights' first-class lodging, and use of the regional ski shuttles. Less expensive plans, starting at $270, book you in pensions or B&Bs, but lifts are extra. Book local accommodations directly through the **Zell am See Kurverwaltung** (*Brucker Bundestrasse, A-5700 Zell am See, Austria. 01143-6542-47555. www.zellamsee.com*). Package tours can be obtained through **SnoSearch Ski Tours** (*800-628-8884. www.snosearchski-tours.com*). Starting at $650 per week (including lodging at a pension, transfers, and flight from New York, Newark, or Boston), the rates are attractive.

FRANCE

CHAMONIX

In the European Alps, France offers the biggest lift networks, the steepest verticals, and the most challenging off-*piste* and powder runs. Among the French resorts, in turn, the king of steep and deep is **Chamonix.** As soon as you visit, you'll understand why Chamonix was the first home of the Winter Olympics: The terrain rises abruptly on the outskirts of town into a wonderland of white verticals, topped by 15,800-foot-high **Mont Blanc.**

Though Chamonix boasts six separate ski resorts, the area is primarily geared for strong intermediate to advanced skiers. The showcase run is the 11-mile glacier descent from the **Aiguille du Midi,** skiable after February each year. You must possess strong skills, and a guide is required (*$220 for group of 4, plus $25 for one-way cable car*), but the passage down the **Vallée Blanche** and the **Mer de Glace** is one of the best skiing experiences on the planet. Another great expert run is the descent from the 10,600-foot-high station at **Les Grandes Monets.**

Nonexperts, too, can have fun at Chamonix, notably on the intermediate runs at **Planpraz** and the good blue trails at **Les Houches.** If you want to know what all the fuss is about, however, you should have black-trail skills.

Lift tickets at Chamonix are pricier than at the major Austrian resorts: $160 or so for a six-day pass in Chamonix resorts only, and $190 to ski all 12 resorts in the area. Lodging costs a bit more, too. Two-star hotels start at about $500 per person per week (including a six-day ski pass), while four-star hotels run about $850. The best hotels—the Mont-Blanc and the Auberge du Bois Prin, for example—run $200 and up per night, though prices are discounted in the low season. One-week ski packages at these four-star hotels cost $750-1,000 per person (including dinners and a six-day ski pass). Ski apartments start at about $300 per person per week, but they tend to be spartan. Both **Lindenmeyr Travel** (800-248-2807. *www.lindenmeyrtravel.com*) and SnoSearch Ski Tours (*see contact info above*) offer package tours for about $550 per week that include apartment rental and lift tickets. To rent a ski apartment online, try **Interhome** (*www.interhome.com*).

For information on Chamonix and all major French resorts, contact the **Chamonix Office du Tourisme** (*Place de l'Église, F-74400 Chamonix, France. 01133-4505-30024, late hours 01133-4505-30225. www.chamonix.com*).

LES TROIS VALLÉES

Although it's called **Les Trois Vallées,** the world's largest ski area encompasses four resorts: **Courchevel** (*01133-4790-80029. www.courchevel.com*); **Meribel** (*01133-4790-86001. www.meribel.net*); **Les Menuires** (*01133-4790-07300. www.lesmenuires.com*); and **Val Thorens** (*01133-7900-0808. www.valthorens.com*). Courchevel, the biggest and most cosmopolitan of the four, boasts facilities and runs on a par with those at Vail. The skiing here is mostly intermediate on superbly groomed slopes, though the **Col de Chanrossa** routes will challenge even the best skiers. Meribel also comprises mostly intermediate trails, but it offers easy access to the other ski areas in the region. Val Thorens and the newer resort of Les Menuires are the experts' destinations of choice; on tap at the former is some of the best summer skiing in France.

At Les Trois Vallées, diversity rules. More than 200 interconnected lifts and 375 miles of marked runs ensure that skiers will find exactly what they want, no matter what their skill level. For the average skier, Les Trois Vallées makes an excellent choice by virtue of its wide-open, relatively easy trails, all groomed to perfection (especially at Courchevel). Because the lifts are modern and efficient, lines are kept to a minimum.

Joint lift tickets valid for all area resorts run about $160 per week (prices are lower if you stick to a single resort). Most skiers stay in ski apartments, which outnumber hotel rooms four to one. Expect to pay about $550 per week for a small, two-person chalet. Comfortable rooms in luxury hotels cost $700-1,400 per week. Both apartments and hotel rooms are discounted heavily during special "White Weeks." Package tours with low-cost lifts and lodging are available from Lindenmeyr Travel (*contact info opposite*).

VAL D'ISÈRE

One of the legendary ski resorts of the European Alps, **Val d'Isère** is a magnet for downhillers eager to test their mettle. By purchasing a joint lift ticket to Val d'Isère and the nearby resort of Tignes, you can gain access to more than 100 lifts and 200 miles of groomed runs. Together these two ski areas form the **Espace Killy**—a tribute to Jean-Claude Killy, the local hero who swept the men's Alpine skiing events at the 1968 Winter Olympics in nearby Grenoble. Despite its reputation for advanced runs, Val d'Isère has a well-balanced combination of fun and challenging terrain for skiers of all abilities.

Novice skiers can enjoy the vast ski area without being relegated to the bottom of the mountain. A number of easy slopes at relatively higher elevations let moderately skilled skiers experience the good snow and great views that come with high-altitude skiing. And with almost half of Val d'Isère's terrain designated intermediate, skiers of modest ability can get the most out of the side-by-side resorts, making their way from one to the other via open boulevards.

For experts interested in pushing the skiing envelope until the glue melts from its seams, Val d'Isère offers classically steep Alpine chutes and cirques, bump skiing, powder skiing, and off-*piste* touring. Tignes and its immense **Grand Motte** glacier also provide possibly the best glacier skiing in the Alps.

Lodging is available throughout the valley. No matter where you are located, there is always a lift nearby, so many chalets offer ski-in and ski-out convenience. The local shuttle-bus system is excellent, too. If you are determined to go first class, the hotels Christiana and Les Latitudes offer four-star accommodations from about $170 per night. B&Bs in the area average $100-150 per night. A six-day ski pass for Val d'Isère and Tignes costs $200. **Central Holidays** (800-935-5000. www.centralholidays.com) offers a week's skiing starting at $1,150 per person, including B&B lodging, lift tickets, and round-trip airfare from New York, Newark, or Boston. For more information, contact the **Office du Tourisme** (73155 Val d'Isère, France. 01133-4790-60660. www.france-tourism.com).

ITALY

CERVINIA

With the Matterhorn looming above, you'll think you're in Switzerland, but **Cervinia**—offering both something more and something less than you'll get elsewhere in the Alps—is definitely Italy.

On the plus side, you'll see more sun and better weather than you would at nearby French or Swiss resorts. The snow has been much more reliable on the Italian side in recent years, and just about every outlay—from lift tickets to food and hotels—is less expensive.

The downside is that Cervinia's lifts lack the speed and capacity found in France or Switzerland (although a fine gondola now runs to **Plan Maison,** the main ski center), and many of the best expert runs do not open until late in the season. Still, this relatively new resort earns converts each season—even the French cross the border to ski Cervinia—and may offer the best overall skiing in the Alps for average skiers.

Most of Cervinia's slopes are broad, wide-open, and not too steep—ideal conditions for lower intermediates. Grooming is excellent. The lift system connects to **Val Tournache,** giving skiers a choice of 65 miles of marked trails served by six cable cars, a gondola, and 36 smaller lifts. The thrill of this hill is the descent from **Plateau Rosa** to Val Tournache. Where else can you cruise for 12 miles, enjoying a

5,000-foot vertical drop on a single run? Those seeking a stiffer challenge can ski the Zermatt side of the mountain, which offers steeper verticals and narrower runs.

A week's lift ticket at Cervinia also buys you a day's skiing at Courmayeur (*reviewed below*). If you're a patient shopper, you should be able to find some excellent bargains on packages. **Central Holidays** (800-935-5000. www.centralholidays.com) offers a week's skiing in the Italian Alps starting at $800 per person, including B&B lodging, lift tickets, and round-trip airfare from the East Coast.

If you book your own hotel, try to stay at the Hermitage—a five-star hotel just outside the village. Rates start at $250 per night, with two meals.

To get to Cervinia, it's best to fly to Milan and then drive a rental car (the local bus connections to Cervinia are unreliable). Access to the area from Geneva via the Mont Blanc tunnel is blocked until tunnel repairs are completed early in 2001.

CORTINA

Cortina d' Ampezzo is Italy's most fashionable luxury resort—a place where rich and glamorous members of Italian high society gather each winter to party and be seen. Skiing can be an afterthought amid the conspicuous consumption, yet Cortina possesses a relaxed atmosphere that belies its reputation for exclusivity. It is also surprisingly affordable, making it one of Europe's great ski values.

Cortina's major shortcoming is its remote location; reaching it requires a three-hour drive from Venice over steep and winding mountain roads. Still, its spectacular surroundings—the jagged pinnacles of the Italian Dolomites—set it apart as one of the most dramatically beautiful Alpine settings in the world. And let's not forget the skiing—an excellent mix of challenging terrain and mostly uncrowded slopes that are well worth the trip.

The ski area itself is quite large, spread over three mountains with more than 50 lifts. The town of Cortina sits in a valley at an elevation of less than 4,000 feet, but the bulk of the runs are located above 6,000 feet. Skiers must therefore take long lifts or gondolas to reach the lift network. The only ski runs within walking distance from the town center are some gentle cruising runs in the **Pocol** area, best suited for beginners. Intermediate and advanced skiers must choose among several poorly

linked outlying areas, making it difficult to move from one to the next. Shuttle buses are on hand, however, to ferry skiers to and from the slopes.

The closest intermediate slopes are in the **Socrapes** area, a few minutes from town, but more experienced skiers should not hesitate to explore the more distant runs. The **Passo Falzarego** area, offering some of Cortina's most sensational views, is 15 to 20 minutes away by bus. At the extreme opposite end of the ski area is the popular **Faloria Tondi** area, with moderate slopes set on a high plateau.

Expert skiers in Cortina usually seek out the steep, narrow chutes among the rocky crags that crown the mountaintops. Some of the best chutes are found along the ridges of the **Christallo** and **Tofana** summits, accessed by taking the gondola from **Col Druscie.** Expert skiers should hire a guide to take advantage of the excellent off-*piste* skiing. A Cortina lift pass gives skiers access to the 400-plus lifts in the greater **Dolomiti Superski** network.

After a day's skiing, visit the **Corso Italia**—a pedestrian-only thoroughfare lined with chic shops. Cortina's exceptional nightlife revolves around first-rate bars, restaurants, and all-night dance clubs. Accommodations to suit all budgets are available throughout the area, including a number of reasonably priced two- and three-star hotels near the town center. Weekly rates start as low as $550. A one-week ski pass is a reasonable $180. Less than $900 will buy you a package vacation with skiing, seven nights' lodging, and round-trip airfare from the eastern seaboard. Contact **Adventures on Skis** (800-628-9655 or 413-568-2855), **Central Holidays** (800-935-5000), or **SnoSearch Ski Tours** (800-628-8884).

COURMAYEUR

On the Italian side of Mont Blanc stands **Courmayeur,** Italy's premier ski resort. With lifts running as high as 11,000 feet, you can always find skiable snow. There is also a wide choice of runs, but most of them are suited for strong intermediates.

Courmayeur is split into two major sections: The bigger part stretches across the **Val Veny** from Mont Blanc. There, skiers take cable cars up to high bowls served by chairlifts. Beginners won't find much to their liking here, but the terrain is a confidence-builder for intermediates, who can rest on a number of plateaus separating the steeper sections. Snowmaking machinery is now available at the site, keeping the lower sections runnable even in dry years. The 8,500-foot-high **Cresta Youla** is probably the highest any intermediate will want to go; it allows a solid 3,600-foot vertical drop to **Zerotta**. Experts accompanied by a guide can take the cable car all the way up to **Crest Arp,** elevation 9,000 feet.

High-altitude fans will want to venture across the valley to ski the slopes of Mont Blanc itself. From the highest cable stop (11,000 feet), advanced skiers have a number of options: Ski back to Courmayeur (some of the best runs lace the trees), traverse the glacier face, or head to Chamonix.

Though lift tickets are only $185 for six days, you're still better off with a package that includes both lifts and accommodations. **Central Holidays** (*800-935-5000, www.centralholidays.com*) offers bargain packages starting at about $250 per person for lodging, six-day ski pass, and transfers, or $800 when you throw in round-trip airfare from New York City, Newark, or Boston.

The least expensive accommodations in Courmayeur are large apartment complexes such as the Residence les Jumeaux and the Residence Universo. The best rooms in town are at the Hotel Pavilion and the four-star Royal Hotel les Jumeaux, ideally situated near the lifts. Courmayeur is served by a private tourist agency, **VV Tours** (*Piazzale Monte Bianco 13, 11013, Courmayeur, Italy. 01139-01658-42060. www.courmayeurinitaly.com/regions/valsta*).

MADONNA DI CAMPIGLIO
Whereas Cervinia and Courmayeur are big—and getting bigger every season—**Madonna di Campiglio** has managed to retain its charm as a small Alpine ski village. Four local ski resorts encircle the town, and it's possible to circumnavigate the entire area via its 49 lifts and 90 miles of trails. The biggest ski area is **Groste,** famed for its three-mile gondola ride and correspondingly long cruising runs from an apex of 7,500 feet. You'll find tougher trails in nearby **Spinale,** among them rugged World Cup runs. Once you've exhausted the central ski basin, ride the linked lifts to the **Folgarida** and **Marilleva** resorts for another 20 lifts and more than 30 miles of prepared trails.

Though the Madonna area isn't noted for its off-*piste* pleasures or powder, you can get into pretty wild backcountry via a helicopter service run (one of the few in the Italian Alps) from **Campo Carlo Magna.**

No report on Madonna would be complete without some mention of the ambience. The village, hunkered by the shores of a scenic lake, is genuinely beautiful, its traditional architecture a refreshing change from the cookie-cutter concrete high-rises of overnight resorts. Topping it all off, the inhabitants of those houses are warm, helpful, and friendly.

A package vacation is probably the best way to ski Madonna di Campiglio and other Italian resorts. Central Holidays (*see contact info at left*) offers seven-day package tours to Madonna for about $1,100 per person, including lodging, two meals per day, transfers, and round-trip airfare from the East Coast. Lifts will set you back an additional $180. **SnoSearch Ski Tours** (*800-628-8884. www.snosearchskitours.com*) sells a package for $975 per person that provides lodging at the three-star Bella Vista Hotel.

SWITZERLAND

VERBIER
Many advanced skiers who've sampled resorts throughout Europe consider **Verbier** the best of the best. This reputation stems from its slopes (steep and challenging), its size (100 lifts connect four separate valleys), and its setting (among the most scenic high peaks of southwest Switzerland). Though Verbier can hardly be called a single-focus resort, it is best suited to skilled skiers; beginners and novices will find little but short bunny slopes to ski here. For experts seeking a real challenge, however—not to mention some unexcelled off-*piste* thrills—Verbier delivers.

The Verbier resort is the hub of a ski area that comprises the smaller resorts of **Thyon, Veysonna, Haute Nendaz,** and **Mayens.** Verbier proper offers the most modern lifts and longest trails. On Verbier's major expert runs—the **Tortin** descent from **Col des Gentines** is one—you'll find gradients of 30 degrees and up through narrow corridors, requiring quick, perfect turns. Those looking to push the off-*piste* envelope can sample deep powder and steep chutes on the upper reaches of the ski area. Easier skiing is found in Nendaz and Thyon, where the lifts are a bit slower but the slopes much less crowded, especially on weekends. Nendaz also offers cheaper accommodations than Verbier.

Verbier tends to be less expensive in the beginning of January and the end of March, when value weeks are scheduled. During this time you can pay $1,400 for seven nights' lodging in a four-star hotel with two meals a day, a six-day lift pass, and six half-days of instruction; the same package in a three-star hotel costs $1,000. At other times of the year, the most affordable lodging option is to rent a modern, ultraclean ski apartment through Verbier's computerized booking system. Many package tours house their guests in these apartments as well. Expect to pay from $300 to $600 per person per week for a studio apartment; lifts cost an additional $400 per week. Get in touch with SnoSearch Ski Tours (*see contact info at left*) for a ski package that includes either an apartment or a hotel stay.

Trains run directly from the Geneva airport to Verbier, which lies about an hour's drive from other major Swiss ski resorts and the charming cities of **Montreux** and **Lausanne**—both worth a visit when you've finished skiing. **Central Holidays** (*800-935-5000, www.centralholidays.com*) offers a week's skiing in Verbier starting at $1,150 per person, including round-trip airfare from major East Coast gateways. For further information, contact the local **Tourist Office** (*1936 Verbier 1, Verbier, Switzerland. 01141-267-6222 or 01141-2777-53888*).

ZERMATT
Zermatt places high on almost every skier's checklist:

Nestled at the foot of the Matterhorn? Check.

Classic, picturesque Alpine village? Check.

No cars allowed in town? Double-check!

The auto ban means taking a narrow-gauge railway or horse-drawn sleigh to arrive in Zermatt, where the conditions are varied enough to please skiers of all levels.

Beginners can practice on the gentle slopes of the **Klein Matterhorn** glacier and **Gornergrat**—true Alpine country, not mere bunny hills.

Intermediates will find an embarrassment of riches as well, from **Sunnegga** (sunny slopes and snowmaking) to the **Kumme area** (long, wide-open trails and short lift lines). There's nothing short about the cable-car ride to the top of the Klein Matterhorn at 12,500 feet, but the views from the summit are unreal, and you can descend the glacier—skiable year-round—from there. Alternatively, cross the ridge and ski down to Cervinia on the Italian side. To get back using the Italian lifts, however, you must first have purchased a special ticket in Zermatt.

And for advanced skiers? How about dozens of serious chutes and couloirs in the Sunnegga and Gornergrat areas, as well as on the Kumme side of the **Unterrothorn?** Mogul lovers will find plenty to ride home about, especially in the **Stockhorn** and **Rote Nasse** sections of the Gornergrat. The off-*piste* options, too, are virtually unlimited, with deep powder, cornice jumping, and even an overland run to **Saas-Fee.**

Hard-core adventure skiers may want to sample the **Haute Route**—a classic backcountry circuit that connects Saas-Fee, Zermatt, Courmayeur, and Chamonix. Guided Haute Route tours (guide salary, hut fees, and lift/transportation costs included) run $750-1,000 in Switzerland. Skiers must be strong in deep powder and on steep terrain, with the ability to climb 3,000 feet per day on skis. For information on UIAGM-certified guides in the Alps, contact the **UIAGM Secretary** (*Via Suot Chesas 6, Champfer, CH-7512, Switzerland. Fax 01141-8183-35680*).

Lodging in Zermatt is not cheap. The best hotels—the Mont Cervin and the Zermatterhoff—charge $250 or more per night in mid-season. Cheaper but still excellent are the Hotel Alpenhof and Hotel Monte Rosa (both under $200). With 10,000 apartment beds in Zermatt, you should be able to find one you can afford. Apartment prices begin at $170-235 per person per week, double occupancy; add $235 for a six-day lift ticket.

Zermatt's nightlife is active but not outrageous. Top après-ski pubs include the Old Zermatt and the Popular Pub. In the evening, try the jazz bar at the Hotel de Poste.

Package tours to Zermatt are offered by a number of operators, among them **ETT Tours** (*800-551-2085. www.etttours.com*); **Swiss Pak** (*800-688-7947. www.swisspak. com*), which offers round-trip air and hotel packages; and **Value Holidays** (*800-558-6850. valhol.com*). Call **Swissair** (*800-662-0021*) to request *The Alpine Experience,* the airline's free ski-package directory. For more information, consult the **Swiss Tourist Board** (*212-757-5944. www. myswitzerland.com*) or the **Zermatt Tourist Office** (*CH-3920, Zermatt, Switzerland. 01141-2796-70181. www.zermatt.ch*).

SKIERS SCALE A SPUR OF THE
AIGUILLE DU MIDI NEAR CHAMONIX.

Summer Skiing

Where do you go when the ski season ends at your favorite winter resort? Here are some great places to make tracks between June and September.

ARGENTINA

High in the Argentinian Andes lies South America's leading ski resort, **Las Lenas.** Located near the town of Mendoza, Las Lenas boasts a dozen lifts, 40 miles of trails, and 4,000 feet of vertical drop (starting from a height of 10,000 feet). The recipient of 250 inches of snow each year, Las Lenas offers excellent powder conditions and a reliable base from June through October. The quality of the skiing here has made Las Lenas the summer choice of the U.S., French, and Swiss Olympic teams. The bowls will remind you of Colorado's best.

Las Lenas is a 90-minute flight from Buenos Aires. Package tours and advance reservations can be made through **SnoSearch Ski Tours** (*13700 Alton Pkwy., Suite 158, Irvine, CA 92618. 800-628-8884 or 949-472-4682. www. snosearchskitours.com*). A seven-day vacation with six days' skiing costs about $1,900, including lifts, four-star hotel, and round-trip airfare from Miami.

AUSTRIA

Even if you miss Austria in the winter, plenty of skiing is possible in the summer. Choose from any of these five 9,000-foot destinations: **Hintertux,** at the end of the **Ziller Valley;** above **Innsbruck** in the **Stubai Valley;** above **Solden** in the **Oetz Valley;** at the end of the **Pitz Valley;** and under **Weissee Peak** in the **Kauner Valley.** For details, contact the **Austrian National Tourist Board** (*212-944-6880 or 310-477-2038. www.anto.com*). For info on summer snow conditions and current lift-ticket prices, contact the **Tirolian Tourist Board** (*Bozner Platz 6, A-6010 Innsbruck, Austria. 01143-512-5320*). The easiest way to ski Austria in the summer is to visit Kaprun. Lifts run year-round on glacier slopes beneath the 10,500-foot **Kitzsteinhorn.** For information, contact the **Fremdenverkehrsverband Kaprun** (*Postfach 26, A-5710, Kaprun, Austria. 01143-6547-8643*) or the Austrian Tourist Board. A good agency for Austrian ski holidays is **Adventures on Skis** (*815 North Rd., Westfield, MA 01085. 800-628-9655 or 413-568-2855. www.advonskis.com*).

360-DEGREE VIEW OF BRIGHTON, UTAH

CANADA

Canada's Whistler and Blackcomb Resorts, located side-by-side north of Vancouver, offer the most popular and extensive summertime skiing in North America.

Summer programs at Blackcomb cover virtually every type of skiing. Racing clinics, for example, are offered by **Salomon** (*800-265-7580. www.mprattsport.com*). Snowboard and free-style clinics are often held as well. Contact **Blackcomb Skiing Enterprises** (*Box 4545, Whistler, BC, V0N 1B4, Canada. 800-766-0449 or 604-932-3141. www.whistler-blackcomb. com*).

The longest running program at Whistler-Blackcomb is the **Dave Murray Summer Ski & Snowboard Camp** (*Box 661, Whistler, BC, V0N 1B0, Canada. 800-766-0449. www.skiandsnowboard. com*). This seven-day camp runs about $950 and is open to juniors only (ages 10-18).

CHILE

Chile has three principal ski resorts, all offering great snow and uncrowded slopes. The most popular are **Valle Nevado** and **Portillo.**

Valle Nevado offers dozens of well-marked runs, all above 10,000 feet, and miles of open terrain for experts. Valle Nevado was developed by the French operators of Les Trois Vallées. With 30,000 acres of skiable terrain able to accommodate 30,000 skiers at a time, it is one of the largest ski areas in the world. Skiers can have the vast ski area and its superb dry snow almost entirely to themselves. Visitors say the resort is like three Vails combined, offering the solitude of cross-country skiing with the convenience of lifts. Package tours run $2,500-3,100 per week with round-trip airfare from Los Angeles, or $1,500-3,100 with round-trip airfare from Miami. Heli-skiing is available as well. Contact **SnoSearch Ski Tours** (*800-628-8884. www.snosearchskitours. com*).

Portillo is Chile's oldest resort, and European experts favor its world-class downhill runs. It offers a low-key setting with some of the most challenging skiing in the Southern Hemisphere, including great heli-skiing. A week's skiing at Portillo starts at about $800 ($1,800 with round-trip airfare).

Termas de Chillan, another quaint resort, boasts South America's longest chairlift (1.5 miles long). From the top, you can ski 15,000 virgin acres with no one else in sight. Package prices begin at approximately $550 per week, including lodging, meals, and lifts. Contact **Adventures on Skis** (*800-628-9655. www.advonskis. com*).

FRANCE & SWITZERLAND

With a number of large glaciers in the French and Swiss Alps, you can ski year-round if you don't mind slightly unpredictable snow conditions. (A recent spate of hot, dry summers has caused many of the glaciers to recede, but plenty of snow remains up high.) For scenic splendor, head to Zermatt, Switzerland, and ski the **Klein Matterhorn Glacier,** served by a 12,000-foot-high cable car. In France, the **Tignes** resort operates an 11,000-foot lift year-round to the top of **La Grande Motte.** Package tours to these and other destinations can be arranged by **Adventures on Skis** (*815 North Rd., Westfield, MA 01085. 800-628-9655 or 413-568-2855. www.advonskis.com*).

For the ultimate summer ski experience in the Alps, hop a helicopter. **Air Zermatt** (*3920 Zermatt, Switzerland. 01141-2796-68686. www.rhone.ch/airzermatt*) offers Alpine heli-trips to some truly inspirational ski runs. Just the view from the drop points is worth the hefty price of admission: $450-650 per day.

NEW ZEALAND

Seasons are reversed south of the equator, so the "summer" skiing Down Under is always reliable. The major ski fields are above tree line, inviting skiers to enjoy wide-open runs with great vistas. The **Mount Hutt** resort is among the experts' choices for challenging skiing. However, high winds can close the resort a few days a month, explaining its Kiwi nickname: Mount Shut.

The **Cardrona** resort has the best intermediate skiing; nearly 1,300 vertical feet and wide-open bowls with dry, reliable snow make it a great place to improve your skills. Nearby **Treble Cone,** with 2,200 vertical feet and lots of moguls, is for rough-and-ready types. As with all New Zealand resorts, the skiing is above tree line.

A couple of hours away is **Queenstown,** the winter-sports hub of the South Island. Regular bus service takes skiers to the **Remarkables** and **Coronet Peak** ski areas. Snow conditions are likely to be better at the Remarkables, which offers some excellent and challenging black runs, although the slopes can get icy during the months of August and September.

Lift tickets at the majority of New Zealand skiing destinations cost around $40 per day. There are no on-site accommodations at the ski areas. However, lodging can be found in Queenstown, Wanaka, or nearby towns.

Deep powder, top-notch guides, and extraordinary views combine to distinguish New Zealand heli-skiing as world-class. **Harris Mountain Heli-Skiing** (*P.O. Box 634, Queenstown, New Zealand. 01164-3443-7930. www.new-zealand/hmh*) offers packages starting at about $300 per day, while an outlay of $2,500-3,200 will buy you a mind-boggling **Odyssey Week:** Seven days of guided heli-skiing, 75,000 vertical feet of runs, plus all meals and accommodations.

UNITED STATES

With several permanent glaciers, Oregon's 11,235-foot-high **Mount Hood** is North America's only year-round ski area. It once served as the summer training ground of the U.S. Olympic Ski Team. **Timberline Lodge** ski resort (*503-272-3311. www. timberlinelodge.com*) operates six chair lifts on Mount Hood, which beckons summer skiers with 1,500 vertical feet of skiing on 1,000 skiable acres. Fireplace rooms run $180 per night. Timberline Lodge also features a four-star restaurant. From the **Palmer Glacier** snowfield, Timberline hosts a number of camps for both skiers and snowboarders.

The **Timberline Summer Race Camp** (*503-231-5402, www.timberlinelodge.com*), Mount Hood's longest-running racing camp, also operates from the Palmer Glacier snowfield. TSRC participants ski on courses using the latest in breakaway gates configured for slalom, GS, Super G, NASTAR, and even dual racing courses. Experts show you how to bolt from the starting gates and how to select the best lines through each course. Videotape analysis of each skier's performance is also included in the program.

For nonracers striving to improve their skills, TSRC offers week-long programs on skiing bumps, jumps, and varied terrain and snow conditions. The cost for the one-week TSRC camp, including six nights' lodging and five days of lifts, is $980 per person. TSRC programs are offered between June and September.

Helicopter Skiing Worldwide

Here are some of the best heli-skiing services worldwide. Some of these operators also offer Snowcat service, fixed-wing air taxis, or snowmobile tows for snowboarders. In addition, many of the larger resorts profiled in this chapter operate their own Snowcat shuttles.

For a comprehensive list of helicopter skiing operators around the world, check out **Ski Central's** heli-ski directory (*www.skicentral.com/heliski.html*) or **HyperSki's** Heli-skiing and Snowcat Skiing List (*www.hyperski.com; click on the "Heli-Ski" button*). Ski Central maintains more than 50 links to heli-ski companies, while Hyperski offers brief but handy reviews of heli-ski and Snowcat operators in Canada, the United States, New Zealand, and the Himalaya.

CANADA

Canada is the heli-skiing center of North America. It offers the longest runs, deepest powder, and the most experienced flight services. Here you'll find most of the top heli-skiing operations in the business. If 15,000 vertical feet (**VF**) a day sounds attractive to you, contact one of the operators listed below. March usually offers the best overall conditions. *Unless otherwise noted, all prices are in U.S. dollars.*

ALBERTA

Assiniboine Heli Tours
1225 Railway Ave., Unit 1, Canmore, AB,
T1W 1R4, Canada
800-824-9721 or 403-678-5459
www.assiniboinehelitours.com

Seven-day package with all the vertical you can ski, $4,100; three-day package with 43,000 VF guaranteed, $1,900. Price per day for three runs: $375, plus $50 per extra 3,000 VF. One- to seven-day packages, including accommodations, meals, four runs, and lunch: $300 to $4,000.

BRITISH COLUMBIA

Canadian Mountain Holidays
P.O. Box 1660, Banff, AB, T0L 0C0
Canada
800-661-0252 or 403-762-7100
www.cmhski.com

Though its office is in Alberta, CMH is largely a British Columbia operation, with 11 lodge bases in B.C. Founded in 1965, CMH has many years of experience in the Canadian Rockies: Bugaboos, Gothics,

Bobbie Burns, Cariboos, Monashees, Revelstoke, Valemont, Kootenay, McBride, and Galena. Most routes are for experts only. Grades of 40 to 60 percent are not uncommon. One of the most radical runs, Steep and Deep, is 3,300 VF at an average grade of 78 percent. Seven days, with meals, lodging, and 100,000 VF: $2,700-$5,275 per person. An Intro Week is also offered for strong intermediates, with seven days' skiing on more moderate terrain. The average number of runs that you will ski per day is 8 to 10. Three-, four-, and seven-day packages are available in Kootenay.

Mike Wiegele Helicopter Skiing
P.O. Box 159, Blue River, B.C.
V0E 1J0, Canada
800-661-9170 or 250-673-8381
www.wiegele.com

Monashees and Cariboos (in BC). Deep, dry powder. Chutes, tree runs, and glacier routes for experts and strong intermediates. Among the most challenging heli-skiing in the world. Packages with meals and lodging: three days, 42,000 VF (30,000 guaranteed), $1,800-2,000; five days, 70,000 VF (50,000 guaranteed), $2,700-2,900; seven days, 100,000 VF (80,000 guaranteed), $3,500-4,300). A mix of 19 chalets and a large, comfortable lodge with European chefs make this a deluxe experience is quite deluxe.

Purcell Helicopter Skiing, Ltd.
P.O. Box 1530, Golden, B.C.
V0A 1H0, Canada
877-435-4754 or 250-344-5410
E-mail: purcell-heli-skiing@rockies.net

150 routes in the Purcell Range for experts and strong intermediates. A full day of heli-skiing, including lunch and three runs, costs $300. Packages with meals and lodging: three days with 29,500 VF, approximately $1,200-1,370; five days with 49,000 VF, approximately $2,000-2,300; seven days with 21,000 VF, approximately $4,500-$5,100. Additional runs $65 (CN) for every additional 1,000 meters. The number of runs skied per day ranges from three to six. December through May.

Robson Heli-Magic
P.O. Box 18, Valemount, B.C.
V0E 2Z0, Canada
250-566-4700
www.robsonhelimagic.com

A three-day package with 29,000 VF costs $1,500; a five-day package with 49,000 VF is $2,500; and a seven-day package with

68,000 VF is $3,500. Extra lifts are priced at about $14 per additional 1,000 feet. The price for a single day is $370, which includes four runs. On average, most clients ski six runs per day.

Selkirk Tangiers Heli-Skiing, Ltd.
P.O. Box 130, Revelstoke, B.C.
V0E 2S0, Canada
800-663-7080 or 250-837-5378
www.selkirk-tangiers.com

Selkirk and Monashee Ranges. 1,550 square miles of bowls, trees, and glaciers, all with deep, dry powder. Seven days with meals and lodging at the **Hillcrest Resort Hotel**, 30-plus runs: 100,000 VF, $3,600; five days, $2,700. Skiers can expect three to five runs per day.

Whistler Heli-Skiing
P.O. Box 368, Whistler, B.C.
V0N 1B0, Canada
888-435-4754 or 604-932-4105
www.heliskiwhistler.com

Coastal Mountain Range. Heli-skiing from the Whistler resort runs about $475 per day, which includes 8,000 to 10,000 VF. Most skiers work in three or four runs per day.

NEWFOUNDLAND

Blomidon Cat Skiing
P.O. Box 941, Corner Brook, NF
A2H 6J2, Canada
709-783-2712
www.catskiing.net

Backcountry skiing in the Long Range Mountains of Newfoundland. Snowcat skiing costs $140 per person per day, including shuttle transfer from hotels to Snowcat center, guides, snacks, and lunch. Maximum of nine skiers per group with an average of 10 runs and 14,000 VF per day. Group discounts and fat ski rentals available.

UNITED STATES

ALASKA

Alaska Backcountry Adventures
P.O. Box 362, Kenai, AK 9963
888-283-9354 or 907-835-5608
www.alaskabackcountry.com

Skiers can purchase various packages here. A guided heli-lift is $70, while a guided skiplane lift is $50. A full day's skiing costs $420, which includes six runs. Expect to ski about six to eight runs in the course of a good day, though skiers may take as many lifts a day as they like.

COLORADO

Telluride Helitrax

P.O. Box 685, Telluride, CO 8143
800-831-6230 or 970-728-4904
www.tellurideoutside.com

San Juan and Uncompahgre National Forest high-altitude (13,000') powder. The cost for skiing per day here is $650, which includes an average of 10,000-12,000 VF. Skiers can expect to ski about five to six runs per day. Each additional run costs $75.

IDAHO

Sun Valley Heli-Ski Tours

P.O. Box 978, Sun Valley, ID 83353
800-872-3108 or 208-622-3108
www.svheli-ski.com.

This company serves the Boulders, Smokies and Pioneer Ranges. Virgin corn powder. Only 4 skiers per guide. Expect to average 5 runs per day, totaling 10,000-12,000 VF; cost is $600 per day. Call for information on group discounts. Also heli-lift ski touring, ski mountaineering, and snowshoeing. Skiers can also helicopter to a yurt in the Pioneer Mountains, which sleeps six to eight people.

MONTANA

Montana Powder Guides

15792 Bridger Canyon Rd., Bozeman, MT 59715
406-587-3096

Generally 6 runs per day, priced at $625 for each hour of helicopter use. Excellent guides.

NEVADA

Ruby Mountain Heli-Ski

P.O. Box 281192, Lamoille, NV 89828
702-753-6867 or 7628
www.helicopterskiing.com

Open, high-altitude bowls and dry, light powder good for novice to expert heli-skiers. A three-day package with 39,000 VF costs $2,600. A one-day package with 13,000 VF is $875, including fat-ski rental. Snowcat backup for bad weather. Good skiers should have time to complete a minimum of eight runs in a single day.

UTAH

Wasatch Powderbird Guides

P.O. Box 920057, Snowbird, UT 84092
801) 742-2800
www.heliskiwasatch.com

Since 1973. Wasatch Range. Small groups with guide. Dry, light powder. A full day

with seven runs and 15,000 VF costs $560-630. Extra runs cost $50. Charter helicopters, serving up to 12 skiers, cost $3,300 and up.

WASHINGTON

North Cascade Heli-Skiing

P.O. Box 367, Winthrop, WA 98862
800-494-4354 or 509-996-3272
www.heli-ski.com

Eighty routes through Okanagan National Forest. Full-day, 5 runs with guide, 10,000 VF guaranteed is $575; extra runs $60. Three-day package (with lodging and meals), 30,000 VF is about $1,930-$2,055. One-day heli-lift nordic telemark program, 4,000 VF, costs $155 per person.

WYOMING

High Mountains Helicopter Skiing

P.O. Box 173, Teton Village, WY 83025
307-733-3274. www.heliskijackson.com.

Snake River and Palisades Ranges. Access powder bowls good for both experts and intermediates. Full-day, 6 runs, 12,000-15,000 VF is $530; extra runs $65. Ski package, with 5 nights lodging and 3 days of skiing, runs $1,805-$1,930, depending on season.

HELI-SKIING SEXTET, BRITISH COLUMBIA

INTERNATIONAL

AUSTRIA
Wucher Helicopter
A-6713 Ludesch, Austria. 01142-5550-3880.
www.wucher.at

ITALY
Monterosa Express
P.O. Box 78, Courmayeur, Italy. 01139-1658-43737 or 01139-1658-84828

NEW ZEALAND
Harris Mountain Heli-Skiing
Box 634, Queenstown, New Zealand
01164-3433-7930.
www.new-zealand/hmh
Heli-skiing packages start at about $300 per day.

SWITZERLAND
Air-Glaciers SA
P.O. Box 27, Civil Airport 1951, Sion, Switzerland
01141-2732-91415
www.airglaciers.ch

Air Zermatt
Postfach 3920 Zermatt, Switzerland
01141-2796-68686
www.rhone.ch/airzermatt

Ski Travel Agencies

The agencies listed below specialize in package ski vacations (hotel, airfare, and lift tickets). Most of these agencies book trips to destinations in North America and abroad, and many of them can arrange off-*piste*, heli-skiing, and wilderness skiing tours. It is wise to call two or three agencies to compare prices.

The following codes are used to describe specialty tour offerings and destinations served: heli-skiing (**HS**), ski mountaineering (**SM**), Argentina (**AR**), Austria (**AU**), Canada (**CAN**), Chile (**CH**), France (**FR**), Italy (**IT**), Japan (**JP**), Germany (**GR**), Morocco (**MO**), New Zealand (**NZ**), Norway (**NO**), Spain (**SP**), Switzerland (**SW**), United States (**US**).

Adventures on Skis (*815 North Rd., Westfield, MA 01085. 800-628-9655 or 413-568-2855. www.advonskis.com*)
HS, SM; AU, CAN, FR, IT, SW, GR, SA, western US. Excellent agency. Very good programs for Europe, especially Austria. Good values and customer service.

Alphorn Ski Tours, Inc. (*P.O. Box 5036, Incline Village, NV 89450. 800-257-4676 or 775-832-2577. www.alphorntours.com*).

HS, SM; AR, AU, CAN, CH, FR, IT, SW, SA, NZ. Austrian specialist; good choice of lodgings.

Central Holidays (*120 Sylvan Ave., Englewood Cliffs, NJ 07632. 800-935-5000 or 201-228-5244. www.centralholidays.com*). AU, FR, IT, SW. Many years in business. Solid choice for European ski packages, particularly in Italy.

Holidaze Ski Tours (*810 Belmar Plaza, Belmar, NJ 07719. 800-526-2827 or 732-280-1120. www.holidaze.com*). AR, CH, AUS, FR, NZ, SP, SW. Many years in business; reliable, with good rates. Wide range of resort options in Europe.

SnoSearch Ski Tours (*13700 Alton Parkway, Ste. 158, Irvine, CA 92618. 800-628-8884 or 949-472-4682. www.snosearchskitours.com*). HS; AR, AU, CH, FR, GR, IT, SA, SW. Agents know their stuff. Attractive pricing. Very good choice for South America.

Sportours (*2335 Honolulu Ave., Montrose, CA 91020. 800-660-2754 or 818-553-3333, www.sportours.com*). OP, HS; AUS, CH, FR, IT, NA, NZ, SA, SW, US. Well-established agency that covers the globe. Also books dive, golf, and tennis travel.

Value Holidays (*10224 N. Port Washington Rd., Mequon, WI 53092. 800-558-6850 or 262-241-6373. www.valhol.com*). AU, FR, NZ, SW. Represents all the marquee resorts in Austria, France, and Switzerland. Good rates.

TOURISM OFFICES

ARGENTINA
Argentina Govt. Tourist Office, 12 West 56th Street, New York, NY 10019. 212-603-0443. www.wam.com.ar/tourism

AUSTRIA
Austrian Nat'l Tourist Office, P.O. Box 1142, New York, NY 10108. 212-944-6880. www.anto.com; or P.O. Box 491938, Los Angeles, CA 90049. 310-477-2038. Austrian snow reports (24 hours): 212-944-6880, ext. 993 or 310-479-0940

CHILE
LAN-Chile Tourist Information Desk, 9700 South Dixie Hwy., Suite 640, Miami, FL 33156. 800-995-4888, 800-244-5366, or 305-671-5018.

FRANCE
French Govt. Tourist Office, 444 Madison Ave., 16th floor, New York, NY 10022.

212-838-7800. www.fgtousa.org; or 9454 Wilshire Blvd., No. 715, Beverly Hills, CA 90212,. 310-271-666. For brochures and info, call 410-286-8310.

GERMANY
German Nat'l Tourist Office, 747 Third Ave., New York, NY 10017. 212-661-7200. www.germany-tourism.de

ITALY
Italian Govt. Travel Offiice, 630 Fifth Ave., No. 1565, New York, NY 10111. 212-245-4822; or 12400 Wilshire Blvd., No. 550, Los Angeles, CA 90025. 310-820-1898. www.italiantourism.com

NEW ZEALAND
New Zealand Tourism Board, 501 Santa Monica Blvd., Suite 300, Santa Monica, CA 90401. 800-388-5494 or 310-395-7480. www.purenz.com

NORWAY
Norwegian Tourist Board, P.O. Box 4649, Grand Central Station, New York, NY 10163. 800-346-3436 or 212-885-9700. www.norway.org/travel, www.nortra.no

SWEDEN
Swedish Tourist Board, 655 Third Ave, New York, NY 10017, (800) 346-3436, (212) 885-9750, www.gosweden.org

SWITZERLAND
Swiss Nat'l Tourist Office, 608 Fifth Ave., New York, NY 10020. 212-757-5944. Fax 212-262-6166; or 501 Santa Monica Blvd., No. 607, Santa Monica, CA 90401. 310-640-8900. www.myswitzerland.com

MAGAZINES

Powder (P.O. Box 58144, Boulder, CO 80323-8144. 800-289-8983) is the magazine of choice for experts. Many outstanding photo essays of backcountry/extreme skiing and exotic locations worldwide. Seven issues per year.

SKI magazine (P.O. Box 52031, Boulder, CO 80321. 800-678-0817) covers the entire skiing scene: resorts, heli-skiing, and après-ski lifestyle. Authoritative training tips and expert gear reviews. Eight issues per year.

Skiing magazine (P.O. Box 51555, Boulder, CO 80322. 800-678-0817) is intended for more serious skiers. In addition to covering ski equipment, clothing, and fitness, it features articles on ski adventures worldwide. Seven issues per year.

GoSki
www.goski.com

Well-organized database of skiing/snowboarding equipment and resorts around the world. The quantity of resort reviews, though great, is somewhat inconsistent in quality.

MountainZone
www.mountainzone.com/ski/

Features ski and snowboard competition coverage, plus off-*piste* skiing and telemarking (with instructional tips and gear reviews). Also posts reports from overseas ski-mountaineering expeditions.

Ski Central
www.skicentral.com

This site allows you to search 5,000-plus ski-related pages—everything from heli-skiing operators to news groups. A great place to start your research.

Ski In
www.skiin.com

Extensive information on 3,000 ski resorts worldwide in English, French, and German. Contains recommendations from top-rated guidebook, *Where to Ski,* 1996 Edition.

Ski Map Server
www.skimaps.com

A collection of ski-area trail maps from around the world.

Ski Net
www.skinet.com

In this huge skiing database—created by the editors of *SKI* and *Skiing* magazines—you'll find snow reports, news from ski areas, travel and lodging information, World Cup coverage, instructional advice, an interactive resort finder, and a buyer's guide containing product advice and equipment tests.

SkiResorts.com
www.skiresorts.com

Hot ski-travel deals, plus personalized snow reports, trail descriptions, event listings, and nightlife info for more than 600 resorts worldwide.

Breakthrough on Skis by Lito Tejada-Flores (Vintage Books, 1994, $13). Renowned ski instructor Lito Tejada-Flores tells interme-diate skiers how they can advance to black diamond runs. The author advocates relaxed skiing—using form and gravity rather than brute force to carve perfect turns.

Ski Europe by Charles Leocha (World Leisure Corp., $19.95). Regularly updated, this is the best handbook for discount schussing on the Continent.

Skiing America by Charles Leocha (World Leisure Corp., $21.95). Vacation planning guide for downhill, cross country, and snowboarding at more than 100 North American ski resorts.

Skiing USA: The Insider's Guide by Clive Hobson (Fodor Sports, $18). This is a good summary of runs, lifts, lodging, and off-the-slope facilities at 30 top ski resorts in the U.S., but it does not contain any trail maps.

The Good Skiing & Snowboarding Guide 2000 by Peter Hardy and Felice Eyston, eds. (Overlook Press, 1999, 624 pages, $27). This global guidebook reviews and rates the top 600 ski resorts world-wide. Europe receives the most coverage. Complete profiles of each resort include news on recent upgrades, ski instruction, lodging, and après-ski opportunities, accompanied by full-color trail maps. A great resource.

The Times Ski Guide by David G. Ross, ed. (Skiers Holiday Guide Club, $19.95). Pro-duced by the staff of the *London Times* and *Sunday Times,* this is the only book that covers all the major resorts in both Europe and North America. The book includes large trail maps for most resorts and detailed summaries of resort facilities and hotels.

Real Action Pictures, Inc. (*707 15th Ave. S.W., Calgary, AB, T2R 0R8, Canada. 800-565-7777*) offers a complete catalog of videos featuring dramatic extreme skiing and snowboarding action filmed on location both in North America and in Europe.

Video Action Sports (*200 Suburban Rd., Suite E, San Luis Obispo, CA 93401. 800-727-6689 or 805-543-4812. www. videoactionsports.com*) offers a full line of skiing and snowboarding videos, including feature films from Warren Miller and Greg Stump. Highly recommended is *Breakthrough on Skis,* a two-tape version of the book of that name by Lito Tejada-Flores.

The Whiteout Series from **Extreme Explorations** (*611 East Kings Rd., North Vancouver, BC, Canada, V7N 1J4. 604-987-1625*) is an entertaining instructional video collection filmed on location in some of the world's most beautiful ski areas. The videos cover everything from the basics to extreme skiing and snowboarding.

APRÈS-SKI PATROL, CANAAN VALLEY, WEST VIRGINIA

SPORT PARACHUTING TAKES MANY FORMS: SKYDIVING, TANDEM JUMPING, BASE JUMPING, SKYSURFING, freestyle, and formation flying. For hundreds of thousands of people—from the nervous student taking her first tandem jump to former President George Bush, who jumped to celebrate his 75th birthday—skydiving is the quintessential risk sport. Adventurers who have tried every action sport under the sun claim that nothing beats the adrenaline rush of leaping into thin air 2 miles above the ground, then free-falling through it at more than 100 miles per hour. • For those who want to experience the sport without lengthy training, tandem jumping has put skydiving within reach. Linked to an expert jumpmaster, a rank novice can enjoy the thrill of free fall and the pleasure of canopy flying. • At the other end of the spectrum, the challenges of skysurfing, freestyle, and formation work offer new frontiers for expert parachutists. Given skydiving's extensive television exposure in recent years—from soft-drink commercials to the Extreme Games—more and more thrill seekers around the world can be expected to take to the air. For those who want to experience life to its fullest, skydiving is the ultimate E-ticket ride.

LEFT: DIVING FROM A DE HAVILLAND BEAVER INTO THE SKY OVER PALAU IN THE WESTERN PACIFIC. BELOW: SKYSURFING ABOVE FRANCE.

Bungee Jumping

BASE Jumping

Skysurfing

If riding in an airplane is flying, then riding in a boat is swimming.
If you want to experience the element, get out of the vehicle.
THE SKYDIVING ARCHIVE

Skydiving Primer

This is it, the real thing: Jumping out of an airplane with nothing but a few ounces of nylon between you and the void. For most of the human race, skydiving represents a danger line that cannot be crossed. Surprisingly, however, modern training methods, advanced equipment, and closely supervised instruction have transformed the sport of parachuting into something far safer than you might imagine.

Currently, in the United States, more than 300,000 jumpers make more than 3.25 million jumps each year, with about three dozen fatalities. Over the last five years, only one jump in 95,000 has resulted in death, and only 14 percent of fatalities are students. Statistically, you're safer skydiving than driving to work in many parts of the country. Jump schools are better than ever before, equipment is safer and easier to use, and new techniques such as tandem jumping and Accelerated Freefall (AFF) have made it possible for novice jumpers to enjoy the most exciting aspects of the sport. Today, on a tandem jump, even a first-timer can experience the thrill of free fall while in the secure grasp of two expert jumpmasters.

SELECTING A PARACHUTING SCHOOL

Sport parachuting is regulated by the **U.S. Parachuting Association** (*1440 Duke St., Alexandria, VA 22314. 703-836-349. www.uspa.org*). Most USPA Group Member training centers are reputable and maintain high professional standards. There are differences between schools, however, so you will want to choose a training program carefully. The most important factors to consider when selecting a jump school are safety record, quality of instruction, aircraft, equipment, and scheduling convenience.

Safety. Ask about the number of mishaps associated with the training program and how serious they were. High-quality drop zones will have logged thousands of training jumps without serious injury. Programs using static lines, which tether your parachute to the airplane and automatically open the chute when you jump, tend to have more minor injuries such as twisted ankles, for example.

Instructional Quality. Given the risks inherent in skydiving, it is obviously in your best interest to enroll in a well-established jump school that employs full-time, professional jumpmasters/instructors. The most qualified instructors will have logged a thousand jumps or more. Tandem and AFF classes should be taught only by jumpmasters specifically certified in these disciplines.

Aircraft. Two engines are better than one. Turbocharged or multiengined planes can take you higher in less time than small, normally aspirated Cessnas or similar aircraft. With larger aircraft, you typically jump from higher altitudes (12,500 feet versus 9,000 feet), allowing more free-fall time. And since big planes climb faster, it takes less time to reach your jumping elevation.

Equipment. Don't enroll in a school that uses old-style round canopies. In fact, the USPA now requires square parachutes and easy-to-manage piggyback chute packs for all its group member schools. Square parachutes fly better and land more easily. You'll also want to select a jump school that keeps its equipment (chutes, harnesses, and jumpsuits) in top condition. Ask if the school has an FAA-certified senior rigger on staff—your life depends on him or her.

Scheduling. Many smaller schools are part-time operations that are open only a few days a month. This can be inconvenient, and it will slow down your progress as a jumper. Major jump centers such as Skydive City in the east, or Perris Valley Skydiving in the west, operate six or seven days a week, and always have jumpmasters and aircraft ready to go.

YOUR FIRST JUMP

All training programs, whether traditional static line or AFF, begin with ground school. You will spend approximately five hours learning the principles of skydiving, basic safety techniques, rigging, and landing skills. In a scene reminiscent of those shown in films of World War II paratroopers, it was once common to practice a hard-impact landing and ground roll by jumping off a 10-foot concrete wall. But with the advent of square parachutes, those days are gone: You descend slowly enough to land easily on your feet.

After completing ground school, you have three choices for your first actual jump: tandem, AFF, or static line. Static line jumping is the simplest—you are physically attached to your aircraft by a tether that opens your chute as soon as you are clear of the plane. Because this allows for no free-fall time, however, most jump centers are phasing out static line jumping and concentrating instead on tandem and AFF jump training.

Bungee Jumping

The bungee jumping craze has cooled a bit from its height a few years ago, but this wild pastime is still very much alive worldwide. Although many of the better bungee centers now also offer exciting gravity rides such as canyon swings, cable "zipline" rides, and even "reverse bungee" catapults, a face-first bungee dive is still the biggest adrenaline rush. For a full rundown on bungee opportunities worldwide, check out www.bungeezone.com.

New Zealander and bungee entrepreneur A.J. Hackett *(www.ajhackett.com)* has developed commercial jump sites throughout the world. One of the tallest and most amazing is the Nevis High-Wire outside Queenstown in New Zealand's South Island. For about $170 (US), you can make a 440-foot jump over a steep-walled gorge.

Take It to New Heights

For the most visually spectacular bungee experience, head to Africa's Victoria Falls, one of the seven natural Wonders of the World. Victoria Falls Bridge spans the no-man's-land between Zambia and Zimbabwe. Daring jumpers launch off the bridge in heart-stopping 364-foot swan dives. The Victoria Falls jump is run by a group of expatriate New Zealanders, known appropriately as African Extreme. This group also engineered the world's biggest commercial jump—an astounding 708 feet from the Bloukrans River Bridge near Capetown, South Africa. The Bloukrans jump attracted over 10,000 jumpers in its first year alone, and may be the most outrageous adventure currently sold in the world.

TAKING THE PLUNGE OVER A TRIBUTARY OF LAKE TAUPO, NEW ZEALAND

An At-Your-Own-Risk Sport

There are no uniformly enforced standards for equipment testing, licensing, personnel training, or insurance in the bungee industry worldwide. Accidents can and do happen. While bungee experts differ as to the security of chest harnesses versus Kiwi-style ankle jumping, any good bungee operation should maintain fail-safe systems with built-in redundancy. This should include, at a minimum, the use of multiple locking carabiners, and careful monitoring of the number of uses and the condition of the bungee cord. The best jump centers employ multiple backups.

Before you jump, also be sure the company you select complies with all local laws. Outside the United States, legal regulation ranges from strict to none at all. The listing of jumping centers provided below is for informational purposes only; we do not recommend or endorse any jump center and offer no opinions as to their safety or reliability.

Major Bungee Jumping Centers

UNITED STATES
A. J. Hackett Bungy (Las Vegas, NV. 702-385-4321. www.ajhackett.com.) 171-foot tower jump. Cost: $79.

Adrenaline Dreams Adventures (Pittsburgh, PA. 412-367-4301. www.adrenalindreams.com) 250–foot Buffalo Creek Bridge jump. Cost: $525 for up to six jumpers, unlimited jumps.

Bungee Masters/Bungee.com (Fairview, OR. 503-520-0303. www.bungee.com) 200-foot bridge jump. Cost: $75 for one jump, $99 for tandem.

Bungee Squaw Valley (Tahoe City, CA. 530-583-4000) 80-foot tower jump. Cost: $50 for first jump, $20 for repeat jumps.

CANADA
Bungy Zone (Nanaimo, BC. 800-668-7771 or 604-753-5867. www.bungyzone.com) 140-foot bridge jump over Nanaimo River. Water dip option. Cost: $95 (CN).

Great Canadian Bungee (Nepean, ON 613-725-9192. http://infoweb.magi.com/~bungee/) 200-foot "Goliath" jump into water. Cost: $99 (CN).

AFRICA
African Extreme (Livingstone, Zambia. 01126-0332-4156; in South Africa, 01127-2172-4516. www.zamnet.zm/zamnet/extreme/bungi.htm) 364-foot Victoria Falls Bridge jump. Also Oribi Gorge and South African bridge sites. Cost: $95

Face Adrenaline (Capetown, South Africa. 01127-2171-25839. www.faceadrenalin.com) 708-foot Bloukrans River Bridge jump. Also 213-foot Gouritz River Bridge jump. Costs: $30 for Gouritz, $95 for Bloukrans.

UNITED KINGDOM
British Elastic Rope Association (Oxford, England. 01144-1865-311179) Promulgates safety standards and offers insurance for affiliated clubs. Call for affiliated bungee operations in the U.K.

McBungee & Bungee Inc. (Multiple locations. 01144-1895-833-067. www.bungeeinc.co.uk) Helicopter jumps and 197-foot crane. Cost: £40.

EUROPE
A.J. Hackett Bungy (Normandie, France. 011-33-231 663 166. www.ajhackett.com.au) 209-foot jump from the Vaiduc de la Soueuvre in the French countryside. Cost 365FF-480FF.

Adventure World (Interlaken, Switzerland. 01141-3382-67711. www.adventureworld.com) 330-foot or 590-foot jump from cable gondola. Cost: 100 SF.

Jochen Schweizer Bungee Jumping (Munich, Germany. 01149-8960-60890. www.jochen-schweizer.de) Sites in Italy, Munich, Austria, with options including crane, bridge, tower, and a 1,640-foot helicopter jump.Cost: 50-250 DM.

Sports Unlimited (Hepberg, Germany. 01149-8456-1222. www.SportsUnlimitedEvent.de) A.J. Hackett crane (425 feet) and helicopter (1,300 feet) bungee jumping. Cost: 50DM and up.

Vertige Aventures (Grenoble, France. 01133-4764-74280. www.bungeejump.com, www.vertigeaventures.com.) 338-foot Ponsonnas Bridge jump. Also 443-foot Le Sautet Bridge jump. Cost: 420FF, 700FF for tandem.

OCEANIA
A.J. Hackett Bungy (Queensland, Australia. 01161-7405-77001. www.ajhackett.com.au) 144-foot rain forest tower jump near Cairns. Cost: $99 (AU) or unlimited one-day jumps for $110 (AU).

A.J. Hackett Bungy (Queenstown, NZ. 01164-3442-7100. www.ajhackett.com) Three NZ jump options: 143-foot bridge jump ($90), 229-foot canyon jump ($154), 440-foot high-wire jump ($299).

Static Line Jumping

During conventional static line training, your parachute is opened by a tether attached to the aircraft. You will make a minimum of five solo jumps with the static line, leaving the aircraft at an altitude of about 3,500 feet. After half a dozen or so static line jumps, you will make your first free jump from about 4,000 feet, experiencing about ten seconds of free fall. You then jump from progressively higher altitudes, working up to about 9,000 feet and 45 seconds of free fall. It typically takes about 15 jumps before you complete your training and are certified to jump without supervision. The entire 15-jump static line training program costs about $1,650 at most jump schools.

Tandem Jumping

Tandem jumping is a reassuring way to make your first jump. This user-friendly mode of skydiving allows a person with absolutely no prior jumping experience to enjoy the thrill of free fall without worrying about making a mistake in the air. His or her instructor makes all the critical decisions, and deploys the canopy after the free-fall period. Following an introductory ground session, the tandem instructor and the student board the plane together. While airborne over the drop zone, the two will physically link their jumping harnesses, using high-strength carabiners to attach the back of the student's harness to the front of the instructor's rig. The jumpmaster/instructor carries an extra-large, two-person parachute designed expressly for tandem jumps. At the instructor's command, teacher and student jump from the aircraft and free-fall for 30 to 60 seconds before the instructor pulls the rip cord. Next, during the approximately four minutes the tandem team spends floating under the deployed canopy before touching down, the instructor demonstrates how to steer the parachute.

Tandem jumping is ideal for those who feel they'd never have the nerve to leap out of a plane on their own. While not all training centers offer tandem jumping yet, it is becoming increasingly popular. Some schools now even require a tandem jump as a prerequisite to a student's first free-fall jump. More than 20,000 tandem jumps were made in 1999, with a remarkable safety record.

If you're looking for the best way to sample skydiving for a minimal investment, tandem jumping is probably the route to take. An introductory session and one tandem jump will typically cost $150 to $200, including all equipment and basic instruction.

Accelerated Freefall

After you've tried a tandem jump, the next step for most skydiving students is an Accelerated Freefall (AFF) jump. This technique has eclipsed the conventional static line training

BASE JUMPING INTO A RAINBOW, ANGEL FALLS, VENEZUELA

method in North America's top jump schools. With AFF, a novice has a chance to enjoy free fall —the most exhilarating aspect of the skydiving experience—right away.

During initial AFF training, you will jump with two specially certified jumpmasters from about 9,000 feet. All three of you exit the plane at once, with your instructors holding on to your arms and/or harness during the free fall. When you have reached minimum altitude, the jumpmasters will tell you to pull your rip cord. If you have problems, the instructors will pull the cord for you. As a final safety measure, all students (whether AFF or otherwise) must be equipped with an Automatic Activation Device (AAD) that automatically deploys the canopy at minimum-safe altitude in the event the student is unable to do so.

After three to four jumps with two instructors, you will progress to one-on-one AFF jumps. Typically, after about 10 AFF jumps with one instructor (about 12 AFF jumps total), you will be approved to jump solo. At this point you can jump without any air-to-air supervision. You will still carry an AAD safety system, however.

Initial AFF jumps, including ground school, cost between $270 and $330. Additional jumps average $200 with two jumpmasters and $160 with one jumpmaster. Typically, it will cost between $1,500 and $2,000 to complete the dozen or so AFF jumps you must make before you are allowed to jump solo. The price varies based on how quickly the student progresses and the altitude of the jumps.

Obtaining a License

The next stage in your training is obtaining your **Class A parachute license.** To reach this level, most beginners require about 20 jumps, including the initial AFF jumps. The Class A license is your ticket to fly. It will permit you to pack your own parachute and make unsupervised jumps at USPA drop zones throughout the country. You will also be eligible for USPA liability insurance as a Class A licensee.

EQUIPMENT

After 10 to 20 jumps, if you decide to continue with the sport, you'll want to purchase your own equipment. As with any high-risk sport, choose top-quality gear. Here's what you can expect to pay to outfit yourself for the sport: primary parachute, $900 to $1,400; reserve parachute, $600 to $900; harness/container system, $1,100 to $1,350; Automatic Activation Device (AAD), $1,150; altimeter, $140 to $175; jumpsuit, $180 to $300; helmet, $50; goggles, $25. New, the entire outfit runs about $4,500 to $5,000. Used equipment is available, but have it thoroughly inspected and approved by an FAA-certified senior rigger at a jump site before you purchase it.

The use of an AAD such as Airtec's sophisticated CYPRES system is now mandatory at many of the more progressive parachuting centers. The AAD is a backup system that is installed on a parachute rig. These devices have been around for 30 or more years and have proven valuable in saving lives. They work by sensing the airspeed and altitude of a free-falling body. In the event the person passes through a preset altitude (usually 1,000 feet) or at a minimum safe altitude (no less than 750 feet as calculated by air pressure, rate of descent, and other factors) at a high rate of speed, the AAD activates the reserve parachute. Recent refinements have made this important safety device more reliable than ever, ensuring canopy deployment even if a jumper is unconscious or injured.

PRICE OF ADMISSION

Skydiving is not an inexpensive sport. Once you've completed your initial training and can jump without instructor assistance, however, the cost is comparable with other action sports such as rafting or scuba diving—about $100 to $200 per day, depending on the number of jumps. Once you're certified to make solo free-fall jumps, expect to pay about $15 to $20 for a typical 10,500- to 13,500-foot jump. At organized **jumpfests,** or "boogies," jump fees are often discounted. If you don't have your own gear, add the cost of rental equipment, which can range from $30 to $80 per day.

INSURANCE

Virtually all first-jump programs offer a 45-day student medical insurance policy available through the USPA. After the first jump, continuing students should become USPA members at an annual cost of $46. This membership provides $50,000 of insurance coverage for liability and property damage; medical coverage is available for an additional fee. To qualify you must be a USPA member at the time of the loss and students must jump under the supervision of a certified USPA jumpmaster at a USPA Group Member drop zone. Check your personal medical insurance to see if it covers minor injuries, such as sprained ankles, that are not covered by the USPA group policy. And before you jump, check to see whether skydiving is an excluded activity on your own medical or life insurance policies.

BASE JUMPING

Once the basics of jumping become old hat, some thrill seekers turn to BASE jumping, the most radical of the parachute sports. BASE is an acronym for Building, Antenna, Span, Earth, and the name accurately describes the central difference between this form of jumping and skydiving: Rather than jumping from aircraft, BASE enthusiasts leap from stationary objects such as bridges or buildings or from natural precipices.

BASE jumping is a particularly dangerous pastime because the parachute is deployed at very low altitudes, leaving little room for error. BASE jumpers have leaped from **Angel Falls** in Venezuela—at 3,212 feet, the world's tallest waterfall—and from the top of the 1,350-foot-high World Trade Center in New York City. But the biggest organized gathering of BASE jumpers—and thus far the only one that is legally sanctioned—takes place annually on the third weekend of October at the **New River Gorge Bridge** in Fayette County, West Virginia. There, for one day each year, hundreds of jumpers leap from the center of the 876-foot-high span. The so-called **Bridge Day Festival**—actually a local celebration of the anniversary of the completion of the bridge—now attracts thousands of curious onlookers and plenty of media attention.

Jumpers flock to Bridge Day for good reason: The New River Gorge Bridge offers a fairly high takeoff point, and, unlike a cliff, waterfall, or tall building, the yawning airspace beyond the arched span provides clear, unobstructed sailing for the descent. But the landing area is tight, and is surrounded by trees, rocks, and fast water, so accurate landing skills are important—and experience with water landings is a plus.

Obviously, this adventure is only for experts with lots of jumping experience. Sky divers leaping from airplanes typically deploy their parachutes at a minimum of 2,000 to 2,500 feet, leaving them ample time to deploy a reserve chute if the main canopy malfunctions. When making a BASE jump at a site like New River Gorge Bridge, there is typically not enough time to deploy a reserve parachute. The implication is clear: If your primary chute malfunctions, the chances of survival are slim.

Still, serious injuries (apart from a few broken ankles) are uncommon on Bridge Day, in large part because participants must be veteran parachutists schooled in the special skills needed to jump this location. For them, the jumpfest at New River Gorge Bridge is a great celebration of the sport. It offers the best opportunity to experience BASE jumping legally, with support and emergency services close at hand.

SKYSURFING

Skysurfing is a sport for the new millennium. This super-charged form of skydiving combines the speed of auto racing, the precision of gymnastics, and the exhilarating rush of bungee jumping. Like a sky diver, you jump out of an airplane, but with an additional piece of equipment: A board, much like a snowboard, is attached to your feet.

The skysurfer hooks his or her feet to the board, then typically hops out of the aircraft in a standing position. While plunging earthward at speeds of 120 mph or more, the skysurfer performs a crazed aerial ballet. Much of what skysurfers do is not completely new; freestyle sky divers can perform many of the same maneuvers using their bodies alone, including 360-degree spins, multiple somersaults, and dizzying pirouettes. However, the addition of a flyable footboard adds a new measure of speed and daring to the free-fall experience.

Although some sky divers think the board is just for show, it actually helps the skysurfer attain far greater lateral speed than the human body could achieve alone. Skysurfers literally fly across the sky, performing their aerial gymnastics. In addition, they cover greater distances at higher speeds than can free-fall jumpers. Another obvious difference is in landing, which is the biggest challenge when it comes to handling the board—the skysurfer must either cut it loose just before touching down or land on soft ground or water. While small parachutes are often used to recover sky boards, some new designs are so light they can float gently to earth after release.

When skysurfing began in the early 1980s, "air surfers" experimented with foam boogie boards during free fall. A breakthrough came in 1987, when French parachutists skydived in a standing position using conventional, rigid surf-boards with foot attachments. Since then, sky boards have gotten lighter and smaller each year. The current hot setup resembles a small snowboard with soft bindings and cutaways to release the board. Sky boards are now strong, high-tech platforms of honeycomb composites and carbon fiber.

The sport hit the big time in 1990, when pioneering French skysurfers, including future world champion Patrick de Gayardon, performed their amazing aerial tricks on Asian and European television. Over the decade, skysurfing grew rapidly: 1993 marked the first official **Skysurfing World Championships,** and in 1994, de Gayardon and other enthusiasts skysurfed during the opening ceremonies of the 1994 Winter Olympics in Lillehammer. Today there are both men's and women's world championships.

ESPN's **Extreme Games** (the "X Games") further popularized skysurfing, leading to new professional standards: Competitors are now judged on maneuvers performed in real time and filmed live by a "partner" cameraman.

As routines become increasingly complex, performing (or filming) the sport in competition demands extraordinary skill. Even today there are just a handful of skysurfers who can master the most difficult maneuvers. With a growing worldwide audience for the sport, however, new talents will undoubtedly emerge, and they will likely push the sport to even greater limits. Just remember that skysurfing is dangerous; accidents have claimed the lives of some of the most famous and skilled enthusiasts in recent years.

FORMATION FLYING

If you want to increase your skydiving skills—and thrills—but don't feel quite ready for BASE jumping or skysurfing, formation flying may be for you. This style of skydiving brings together two or more jumpers in the air, flying relative to one another to create different formations.

Freefall formation flying is performed in the same belly-to-earth position taught to students. As jumpers become more skilled in this style, they learn to alter their individual fall rates to match those of other sky divers. The jumpers exit the airplane as a group and maneuver themselves into position. Holding on to each other's wrists or to fabric "grips" that are sewn onto their jumpsuits, the group creates a pattern in the sky, such as a star. In competitive formation skydiving, the goal is to build as many formations as possible, one after the other, within a set time limit.

A variation on this theme is canopy formation skydiving, which differs from the free-fall form in two distinct ways: The sky divers in the formation are under open canopies from the start, and the formations are typically built vertically rather than horizontally.

The sky divers leave the aircraft one at a time in quick succession, and immediately open their parachutes. Once everyone is out, the jumpers build formations by flying relative to one another and connecting at points on the parachute itself, on other jumpers' suits, or on the parachute lines. In competition or just for fun, jumpers can try to build a succession of different formations, see how fast they can build single patterns, rotate jumpers within formations, or see how many people they can get into one large formation.

For information on all forms of parachuting, contact the **U.S. Parachuting Association** (*1440 Duke St., Alexandria, VA 22314. 703-836-3495. www.uspa.org*). For current information about skysurfing and BASE jumping, go to www.frc.ri.cmu.edu/~belboz/skydive/skysurf.html and www.afn.org/skydive/base/. You can also pick up a copy of Dan Poynter's classic book, *Parachuting: The Skydiver's Handbook* (800-727-2782). ESPN's website boasts skysurfing content, including air-to-air video clips from recent X Games and profiles of the competitors. Go to http://espn.go.com, then search for "skysurfing."

Skydiving Directory

There are hundreds of parachuting schools and drop zones where you can receive skydiving training from certified instructors. Not all parachuting schools offer AFF and tandem jumping yet, so be sure to ask about these options before you make a long drive to a jump site. Your local Yellow Pages contain jump school listings under "Parachute Schools," or sometimes under "Skydiving."

Below, we list some of the most active drop zones registered with the USPA as Group Members. (USPA Group Members have pledged to follow USPA Basic Safety Requirements and recommendations for student and advanced sky divers, and to offer first-jump courses taught by USPA-rated instructors.) You can obtain a complete directory of USPA Group Member drop zones across the country by contacting the **USPA** (*1440 Duke St., Alexandria, VA 22314. 703-836-3495. www.uspa.org*).

Note that these resources are provided for information purposes only, based on listings supplied by the USPA. For updates, check www.uspa.org/Group-Membership. This listing does not constitute an endorsement or recommendation of any facility included here and does not make any representations regarding these operators' safety practices or the quality of their professional activities.

CENTRAL NORTH

Aerodrome Sky Sports
5169 State Road 227 S., Richmond, IN 47374
888-234-5867 or 765-939-2939
www.aerodromeskysports.com

AerOhio Skydiving
11746 E. Easton Road, Rittman, OH 44270
800-726-DIVE or 330-925-3483
www.jumptoday.com

Parahawks Skydiving Center
Marine City Airport, Marine City, MI,
810-781-5867 or 810-765-3242 (drop zone)
www.parahawks.com

Skydive Chicago
3215 E. 1969th Road, Ottawa, IL 61350,
815-433-0000
www.skydivechicago.com

Skydive Hutchinson
760 Airport Rd. SW, Hutchinson, MN 55350.
877-587-5875 or 320-587-5875
www.skydivehutch.com

Sky Knights
East Troy Mun. Airport, W1341 Hwy. L
East Troy, WI 53120
800-382-4883 or 414-642-9494
www.skydiveskyknights.com

CENTRAL SOUTH

Ags Over Texas
Coulter Airfield, 6120 Hwy. 21 E.
Bryan, TX 77808
409-778-0245. www.agsovertexas.com

Alabama Skydiving
250 Airport Road, Pell City, AL 35128
800-332-JUMP or 205-884-6937
http://members.aol.com/alskydivng

Skydive Dallas
R.R.2 Box 15, Whitewright, TX 75491
903-364-5103 or 972-251-5093
www.skydivedallas.com

Skydive Houston
Skydive Houston Airport, Waller, TX 77484
800-586-7688
www.skydivehouston.com

Skydive Kansas
1613 E. Laing, Osage City, KS 66523
913-723-3483
www.skydivekansas.com

Skydive St. Louis
14026 Airport Road
Bowling Green, MO 63334
573-324-3334
www.skydivestl.com

Skydive Tulsa
19502 E. Rogers Post Road, Suite 4
Claremore, OK 74017
918-885-4721
www.skydivetulsa.com

NORTHEAST

Chambersburg Skydiving Center
3506 Airport Rd., Chambersburg, PA 17201
800-526-3497 or 717-264-1111
www.skydivingcenter.net

Connecticut Parachutists
Ellington Airport, Rt. 83
Ellington, CT 06029
860-871-0021
www.angelfire.com/ct/skydive

Frontier Skydivers
3316 Beebe Road, Newfane, NY 14108
716-751-6170
www.skydivefrontier

Pepperell Skydiving Center
P.O. Box 279, Pepperell, MA 01463
800-759-5867 or 978-433-9222
www.skyjump.com

Skydive the Ranch
56 Sandhill Road, Gardiner Airport
Gardiner, NY 12525
914-255-4033
www.skydivetheranch.com

United Parachute Club
New Hanover Airport, Rt. 663 at Swamp Pike
Gilbertsville, PA 19525. 610-323-9667
www.skydiveupc.org

Winnipesaukee Skydiving Center
Moultonboro Airport, NH
603-476-5867. www.skydivenh.com

ROCKIES

Colorado Parachute Club
Ft. Collins-Loveland Airport
Loveland, CO 80538. 970-669-9966

Front Range Skydivers
P.O. Box 229, 15145 Calhand Hwy.
Calhand, CO 80808. 719-347-2035.
www.frontrangeskydivers.com

Skydive Idaho
4317 Aviation Way, Caldwell Airport
Caldwell, ID 83605. 208-455-0000
www.skydiveidaho.com

Skydive Lost Prairie
3175 Lower Lost Prairie Road
Marion, MT 59925
888-833-5867 or 406-858-2493
www.skydivelostprairie.com

Skydive New Mexico
Coronado Airport, 10000 Pan American
Fwy., Albuquerque, NM 87113
505-797-2167. www.skydivenm.net

Skydive Salt Lake
4500 N. Airport Road, Erda, UT 84074 800-447-5867 or 801-255-5867
www.skydivesaltlake.com

SOUTHEAST ATLANTIC

Carolina Sky Sports
P.O. Box 703, Hwy. 56, Louisburg, NC 27549
919-496-2224
www.vast.net/css

Skydive Carolina!
1903 King Air Drive, Chester, SC 29706
800-759-3483 or 803-759-3483
www.skydivecarolina.com

Skydive City
4241 Skydive Lane, Zephyrhills, FL 33540
800-404-9399 or 813-783-9399
www.skydivecity.com

Skydive DeLand
1600 Flightline Blvd., Deland, FL 32724
904-738-3539. www.skydivedeland.com

SkyDive the Point
Airport Road, West Point, VA
804-230-0729 or 804-785-4007
www.skydivethepoint.com

Skydive Sebastian
400 W. Airport Drive, Sebastian, FL 32958
800-399-JUMP or 561-388-5672
www.skydiveseb.com

Tennessee Skydiving Center
P.O. Box 674, Tullahoma Airport
Tullahoma, TN 37388
800-483-DIVE or 931-455-4574
www.tennskydive.com

WEST

Kapowsin Air Sports
27611 144th Ave. E., Kapowsin, WA 98344
800-268-6778 or 360-893-3483
www.skydivenet.com/kapowsin

Perris Valley Skydiving
Perris Valley Airport, 2091 Goetz Rd.
Perris, CA 92570. 800-832-8818 or
909-657-1664. www.skydiveperris.com

Skydance Skydiving
24390 Aviation Ave., Yolo Co. Airport
Davis, CA 95616
800-752-3262 or 530-753-2651
www.1800skydive.com

Skydive Arizona
4900 N. Taylor Rd., Eloy Airport
Eloy, AZ 85231. 520-466-3753
www.skydiveaz.com

Skydive Hawaii
Dillingham Airfield No. 1,
68-760 Farrington Hwy.
Mokuleia, Oahu, HI 96791
808-637-9700. http://skydive-hawaii.com

Skydive Las Vegas
806 Buchanan Blvd. No. 115-200, Boulder
City Airport, Boulder City, NV 89005
702-293-1860. www.skydivelasvegas.com

OH, CHUTE!

Skydive Monterey Bay
3261 Imjin Road, Marina, CA 93933
888-229-5867 or 831-384-3483
www.skydivemontereybay.com

Skydive Oregon
Skydive Oregon Airport, 12150 S. Hwy. 211,
Molalla, OR 97038. 503-829-5867.
www.skydiveoregon.com

NATIONAL PARACHUTING ORGANIZATIONS

The **U.S. Parachuting Association** (703-836-3495. *www.uspa.org*) is the central clearinghouse for parachuting information nationwide. It has the most up-to-date information on USPA Group Member jump schools, as well as scheduled jumpfests and skydiving competitions. **The Canadian Sport Parachuting Association** (*4185 Dunning Rd., Navan, ON, K4B 1J1, Canada. 613-835-3731. www.cspa.ca*) oversees all aspects of skydiving in Canada, much as the USPA does in the United States. The 60 or so CSPA-affiliated drop zones are listed at www.cspa.ca/en/MemberGroup/afflcspa.html.

Other important international parachuting associations are listed below. In most cases, the official association website lists drop zones within that country. Other international listings can be found at www.fai.org/fai__members/addresses.asp.

AUSTRALIA

Australian Parachute Federation Inc.
P.O. Box 144, Deakin, West ACT 2600,
Australia. 01161-2628-16830 or
15358. www.apf.asn.au

AUSTRIA

Österreichischer Aero Club
Prinz Eugen Strasse 12-P,
A-1040 Wien, Austria
01143-1505-1028. www.oe.aeroclub.at

DENMARK

Dansk Faldskaerms Union (DFU)
Idraettens Hus, Brøndby Stadion 20,
DK-2605 Brøndby, Denmark
01145-4326-2626. www.dfu.dk

FRANCE

Fédération Française de Parachutisme
35 rue Saint-George, F-75009 Paris, France
01133-1445-37500. www.ffp.asso.fr

GERMANY

Deutscher Fallschirmsport Verbande.V
Geschäftsstelle, Comotorstraße 5,
66802 Überherrn, Germany
01164-6836-92306
www.fallschirmsportverband.de

IRELAND

Parachute Association of Ireland
A.F.A.S. House of Sport, Long Mile Road
Dublin 12, Ireland. 01135-3145-09845
http://indigo.ie/~pai

ITALY

Aero Club d'Italia
Via Roberto Ferruzzi 38, 00143 Rome, Italy
01139-6519-59701. www.aeci.it

JAPAN

Japan Skydiving Association
Fujioka Airport, Tochigi-Ken
01181-2826-23810 or 01181-3033-58190
www.jin.or.jp/ffj

NETHERLANDS

Royal Netherlands Aeronautical Association (KNVvL)
Jozef Israëlsplein 8, 2596 AS
Den Haag, Netherlands
01131-7031-43600
www.parachute-nl.org

NEW ZEALAND

New Zealand Parachute Federation
P.O. Box 1153, Rotorua, New Zealand
01164-7345-7520
E-mail: nzpf@xtra.co.nz

NORWAY

Norsk Aero Klub
F/NLF, Postboks 383 Sentrum
0102 Oslo, Norway
01147-2310-2900. www.nak.no/fallskjerm

PORTUGAL

Federaçao Portuguesa de Paraquedismo
Travessa das Morenas, 15-A,
7000 ÉVORA, Portugal
www.fppq.pt

SWEDEN

Svenska Fallskärmsförbundet (SFF)
Idrottens Hus, S-123 87, Farsta, Sweden
01146-8605-6516. www.sff.se

SWITZERLAND

Aero Club of Switzerland
Lidostrasse 5, CH-6006
Luzern, Switzerland
01141-4131-2121. www.aeroclub.ch

UNITED KINGDOM

British Parachute Association
Wharf Way, Glen Parva
Leicester, LE2 9TF, England
01144- 116-278-5271. www.bpa.org.uk

DROP ZONES WORLDWIDE

Most of the foreign parachuting associations listed above maintain a directory of affiliated drop zones on their official website. To access this information, point your browser to www.skydiveworld.com/english/dropzones.htm. Skydive World's online archive lists drop zones on every continent, including hundreds of jump centers in major European countries. USPA-affiliated drop zones in the United States and overseas can be found at www.uspa.org/GroupMembers.

ONLINE

U.S. Parachuting Association Home Page
www.uspa.org

Start here for general information, safety tips, membership services, and a list of USPA-affiliated jump centers. The USPA site also features a good calendar of boogies and major jump competitions. The *USPA Skydiver's Information Manual* can be downloaded as a PDF file.

Drop Zone
www.dropzone.com

Home of the Skydive Ring, with links to over 150 related websites, dropzone.com features important skydiving competitions, a calendar of boogies, articles on safety and training, photo galleries, forums for discussing the sport, and a database of sky divers and drop zones.

Fédération Aéronautique Internationale (FAI)
www.fai.org/parachuting/

FAI is the international governing organization for aerosports, including parachuting. You'll find a list of events and a list of national parachuting clubs.

Skydive Archive
www.afn.org/skydive

This is the best resource on the web for specific disciplines such as relative work, freestyle, BASE jumping, and paraskiing. The Skydive Archive also includes the Rec.Skydiving FAQ, the most complete parachuting primer available online — it even includes a glossary of jump terms and slang. Every new jumper should read this FAQ in its entirety.

Skydive World
www.skydiveworld.com

SkyDive World boasts the Web's most complete list of drop zones worldwide. Every continent is represented, with hundreds of listings in Europe alone. You'll find a comprehensive calendar of boogies and competitions while the companion E-zine, *SkyXtreme.com,* offers insightful articles, message boards, and timely coverage

of parachuting events around the globe.

Skydive WWW
www.skydivewww.com

This site boasts an excellent collection of links to skydiving events, articles, and a searchable index of drop zones. Don't leave your airplane without it.

World Freefall Convention
www.freefall.com

The annual Freefall Convention, a ten-day event held in Quincy, Illinois, attracts thousands of sky divers from around the world. This site includes all convention activities, plus message boards, a photo gallery, and a multinational directory of sky divers.

BOOKS

Parachuting: The Skydiver's Handbook by Dan Poynter is a classic that belongs in every sky diver's library. The 8th edition, a 2000 release, features a new section on skysurfing and updated equipment reviews. $19.95 from **Para Publishing** *(P.O. Box 8206, Santa Barbara, CA 93118. 800-727-2782 or 805-968-7277 www.parapublishing.com)*

Parachuting Manual for Accelerated FreeFall covers all phases of AFF jumping, with photo-illustrated instructions on exits, hand signals, dive sequences, flying the canopy, emergency procedures, and more. This small (36-page) booklet was written by Jan Meyer, an AFF Instructor with more than 2,000 jumps. $3.95 from **Para Publishing** *(P.O. Box 8206, Santa Barbara, CA 93118. 800-727-2782 or 805-968-7277. www.parapublishing.com)*

The Parachute Manual, Vol. I & II by Dan Poynter covers everything there is to know about parachutes: packing, rigging, alterations, design, repairs, materials, regulations, manufacture, specifications, loft layout, rigging tools, and much more. The manual is used by the armed forces, the Forest Service, and foreign governments. The first volume covers round, military-style chutes; the second covers square, sport canopies. Each volume is $49.95 from **Para Publishing** *(800-727-2782)*.

MAGAZINES

Parachuting Magazine, the journal of the USPA, is free with your USPA membership. Nonmembers can order issues and obtain a directory of USPA Group Member jump centers by contacting the USPA *(1440 Duke St., Alexandria, VA 22314. 703-836-3495. www.uspa.org)*. This quality publication is full of useful information.

Skydiving Magazine is a monthly that features aerial photography, technical articles, and event reports. $16 per year *(1725 N. Lexington Ave., DeLand, FL 32724. 904-736-4793, www.skydivingmagazine.com)*

VIDEOS

Over the EDGE by Tom Sanders *(Aerial Focus, 1993, $29.95. 8 Camino Verde, Santa Barbara, CA 93101. 805-962-9911. www.aerialfocus.com)* is one of the most remarkable adventure videos ever created. This production features nonstop action including BASE jumping from Angel Falls, night jumping, and 40-man formation jumps.

Drop Zone with Wesley Snipes and *Point Break* with Keanu Reaves are two engaging feature films that can be rented at a local video center. Both action-adventure films feature outstanding skydiving footage shot by the world's best air-to-air photographers.

Skydive University offers a series of instructional videos and workbooks for learning basic body flight, formation skydiving, and canopy control. Each video combines computer-animated simulations and in-air footage to demonstrate the techniques. Contact Skydive University *(400 W. Airport Drive, Sebastian, FL 32958. 800-891-5867 or 561-581-0100. www.skydiveu.com)*.

SEE? I *TOLD* YOU THE FIRST STEP WAS THE HARDEST!

THERE'S NO DOUBT THAT SNOWMOBILING PROMISES THE THRILL OF SPEED. IT IS ALSO ONE OF THE MOST pleasurable ways to experience the frozen backcountry in winter— at your own pace. The greater mobility and freedom afforded by a snowmobile allow the rider to push deeper into the wildlands than is possible on skis or on snowshoes. • An extensive network of sledding trails now crisscrosses the United States and Canada, opening hundreds of thousands of square miles of remote country for exploration. To help you get on the right trail—either for a speed run or a slow ramble—this chapter spotlights eight fabulous snowmobile vacations, both domestic and international. You'll also find useful reviews of leading tour operators, plus additional sledding destinations across North America's snowbelt. • Remember that responsible snowmobiling preserves the environment: Keep to the trail, except in authorized off-trail areas. Stay within speed limits and respect other riders. Never drink and drive, always travel with a buddy—and beware of thin ice.

LEFT: RIDER CRESTS A RIDGE IN ALASKA'S CHUGACH RANGE.
BELOW: OFF-TRAIL SLEDDING AT TOGWOTEE MOUNTAIN, WYOMING

Trans-Québec

Teton Off Trail

Sledding Iceland

As with expeditions into the wilds when we have endured storms and rapids, cold and sleet...it is ultimately the good things we remember, not the bad.
SIGURD OLSON

Snow Guts, Snow Glory

The notion of touring by snowmobile may seem odd to some, but it's the only way to go if you want to cover more than a few miles of winter wilderness a day. You can cruise slowly through untracked territory and meditate on the scenery, or you can crank it up and enjoy a burst of speed on packed trails. Whatever your style, the best part is that you don't need to be experienced to enjoy a snowmobile trip such as one of the eight listed below. All you need is a sense of adventure, a love of the outdoors—and some very warm clothes.

QUEBEC
Valcourt Snowmobile Festival

Since the early 1990s, the **Grand Prix de Valcourt** has become the largest and most successful festival of its kind. Every February, hundreds of sledders from around Canada and the northeastern states gather here to participate in trail rides and races, plus a host of other winter sports.

A side attraction is the **J. Armand Bombardier Museum** (*450-532-5300*). The world's only museum dedicated to the sport, its exhibits include the first motorized sled, built more than 50 years ago by Canadian Joseph-Armand Bombardier.

Apart from scheduled events, snowmobilers have many sledding opportunities west and east of Valcourt. The **Trans-Quebec Snowmobile Trail system** crisscrosses the province's rural regions with more than 5,600 miles (9,000 km) of marked, double-lane trails, which are groomed nightly. You can cover a lot of ground in a day—and there's always a country inn or lodge nearby when you feel like taking a break.

While February snow cover is usually good, conditions can be unpredictable. Quebec's extensive trail system, however, virtually guarantees that you will never be at a loss for riding options.

For general information, contact **Tourisme Québec** (*Montreal. 877-266-5687. www.tourisme.gouv.qc.ca/snowmobile*). Ask for the snowmobiling travel brochure; the online database also lists hundreds of vacation possibilities.

Many fine tour operators do business in the province. Recommended is **Randonneige Québec** (*Sainte-Agathe-Des-Monts. 800-326-0642 or 819-326-0642. www.randonneige.com*). This firm offers outstanding inn-to-inn snowmobiling tours in the scenic **Laurentian Hills,** about 55 miles (90km) northwest of Montreal.

Farther north, above Quebec City, **Château Mont Sainte-Anne ski resort** (*Beaupré. 888-824-2832 or 418-827-5211. www.quebecweb.com/hcmsa*) offers snowmobile tours among its winter holiday packages.

ALASKA
Wilderness Sledding Tours

Alaska is still a wild frontier. The 49th state boasts some of the highest mountains, the biggest snowfields, and the most abundant wildlife in America. As a snowmobiling destination, Alaska promises unmatched natural beauty.

You can rent snowmobiles by the day in Anchorage. On the other hand, if you've spent the money to travel this far, you should head inland, where you'll find far fewer tourists.

A good spot is the **Denali National Park** region, which lies about halfway between Anchorage and Fairbanks along the **George Parks Highway. Gray Jay Snowmobile Tours** (*Cantwell. 907-768-2600. www.grayjay.com*) runs an excellent sledding program just outside the park.

You start at the cozy Gray Jay B&B in Cantwell, then head along the **Nenana River** to Lingcod Lake Camp, where sledders bunk down in heated tent cabins. From this base you explore vast, untracked snowfields against the spectacular backdrop of **Mount Deborah** and **Mount Haye.** This is world-class snowmobiling: The conditions are ideal, the wildlife is abundant—and the solitude is guaranteed.

Gray Jay's owners, Scott and Vivian Mayo, treat their guests like family. They offer three-, four-, and five-day packages from Lingcod Lake, plus day trips from Cantwell. A good choice is the five-day package, which lets you see more of this unspoiled and majestic region. The price is about $1,230, including lodging, meals, sled, and guide.

Southeast of Anchorage, **Senior World Tours** (*888-355-1686 or 419-355-1686. www.seniorworldtours.com*) offers a nine-day snowmobile outing each March. Senior World times its tour to coincide with the famed **Iditarod** dogsled race.

After a cruise on **Resurrection Bay** to view glaciers and whales, the group visits the starting point of the Iditarod, then moves on to Tolsona Lake Resort, where the backcountry leg begins. You snowmobile to Crosswind Lake Lodge near **Wrangell-St. Elias National Park.** The park contains the largest concentration of peaks above 10,000 feet in North America. From here you travel through wild

country that is home to moose, caribou, and wolves to reach Lake Louise Lodge. After returning to Tolsana Lake, you cross **Scott Ice Field** and visit the tanker port at **Valdez.** Winding up five days of riding, you head back to Anchorage. The cost is about $2,400 per person, all-inclusive from Anchorage.

For those on a tighter budget, **Custom Tours Alaska** (*907-272-7225. www.alaskalife.net/tours*) offers a four-day tour that follows the Iditarod Trail to Valdez; the cost is $1,300 per person, all-inclusive from Anchorage.

WYOMING
Jackson Hole Holiday

Tucked against the imposing peaks of the Teton Range, this famed skiing hot spot is also a superior snowmobiling venue. Jackson Hole offers a good network of groomed trails. But if you really want to have fun, get off the trail. That's where you'll find open bowls, alpine meadows, and steep mountain passes for roaming. You can also explore the **Gros Ventre Valley,** cut across to **Green River Lakes Basin—** or, if you're feeling adventurous, climb over 10,000-foot-high **Union Pass** to the **Continental Divide.**

For confirmed trail-runners, the best routes take you through **Grand Teton National Park** and the high country in the Gros Ventre region.

A favorite cross-country run begins in Togwotee and runs overland to **West Yellowstone** and **Yellowstone**

National Park. You can't do this in a day, so you'll need to stay at least one night in Yellowstone—although once you find out how good the sledding is here, you'll probably want to extend your stay to two or more nights.

The best bet for a package snowmobile tour in the Jackson Hole area is the **Cowboy Village Resort at Togwotee** (*Moran. 800-543-2847 or 307-543-2847. www.cowboyvillage. com*), formerly Togwotee Mountain Lodge. Located 48 miles northeast of Jackson Hole and 8,500 feet up, the resort has 300 miles of groomed trails and 2.5 million acres of ridable territory. (Most riding is done off trail.) The average annual snowfall here exceeds 50 feet.

Cowboy Village offers everything a sledder could want, including sled rentals, hot tubs, a full restaurant, and a bar. Not only that, but you can park your snowmobile right outside your front door. The rental equipment is excellent; each season the resort buys premium Polaris and Arctic Cat sleds.

An all-inclusive package (minimum four nights) ranges from $250 per day in the lodge to $270 per day in a log-cabin suite, with two meals daily, three days of riding, a guide, and airport transfers. (The larger the group, the lower the rate.) For an additional $100, the staff will transport your sled to Yellowstone park for two days of guided touring and a night at the Stagecoach Hotel in West Yellowstone. Expect to see moose, bison, elk, and other wildlife.

Senior World Tours (*Fremont, OH. 888-355-1686 or 419-355-1686. www.seniorworldtours.com*) also offers a

SYNCHRONIZED LIFTOFF FROM A CORNICE RIDGE AT THOMPSON PASS NEAR VALDEZ, ALASKA.

package tour based out of the Cowboy Village Resort at Togwotee. Cost for the six-day tour through the Tetons and Yellowstone country is about $1,650 per person, including lodging, sled rental, all meals except three lunches, and ground transfers. One satisfied client raved about this tour: "A snowmobiler's dream with breathtaking scenery and miles and miles of trails that you must experience to believe."

Decker Sno-Venture Tours (*Eagle River, WI. 715-479-2764. www.sno-venture.com*) offers a six-night Jackson Hole holiday package that features five days of snowmobiling, including two days in Yellowstone National Park. The price is approximately $755 per person; add $450 for sled rental.

Each spring Jackson Hole hosts a snowmobile hill-climb event. For general information about the area, contact the **Jackson Hole Chamber of Commerce** (*307-733-3316*).

YELLOWSTONE
Snowmobiling Paradise

Yellowstone is the Alice's Restaurant of snowmobiling. Whatever you're looking for—whether it's speed runs or slow rambles, marked trails or wilderness—you'll find it here. There are more than 500 miles (800 km) of groomed trails and virtually limitless off-trail possibilities. Powder hounds can explore 10,000 square miles of wilderness in two national parks and seven national forests.

Gateway to **Yellowstone National Park,** the little town of **West Yellowstone** is a haven for sledders. You can take your snowmobile just about anywhere—even on the city streets.

The park itself is probably the most distinctive snowmobiling site in the world. Although sledders are restricted to marked trails, these provide excellent access to Yellowstone's 10,000 thermal sites and abundant wildlife. Elk and moose frequent the rivers in the park, while bison often graze close to the trails.

If you are seeking open country, the seven national forests that adjoin the park are ideal. You can easily cruise for 100 miles without running into other vehicular traffic. Popular trips include the **Continental Divide Trail** and the run to **Two Top Mountain.**

The Continental Divide Trail is a relatively new, groomed-trail system that crisscrosses the Wind River, the Gros Ventre, and the Absaroka Mountain ranges. The trail winds through scenic high country, offering great views all along the way. Though sledders familiar with the area should be able to navigate the trail independently, it is recommended that first-time visitors or less experienced riders hire a guide. The cost is about $175 per day.

A number of companies offer guided tours and sled rentals in the Yellowstone region. The leading operator is **Old Faithful Snowmobile Tours** (*Jackson. 800-253-7130 or 307-733-9767. www.snowmobilingtours.com*). This company

employs excellent guides and books its customers into the best lodges available, including the Stage Coach Inn or Elk Ridge Lodge in Yellowstone and the Triangle C Ranch on the Continental Divide.

For first-time visitors, we recommend Old Faithful's four-day **Yellowstone Snowmobile Safari.** The cost is $1,200 per person, including sled rental, meals, lodging, and ground transportation from Jackson. If you've been here before or are looking for a more challenging, high-alpine tour, do the three-day **Continental Divide Tour** for $1,050 per person.

More economical packages are offered by **Yellowstone Adventures** (*West Yellowstone. 800-231-5991 or 406-646-7735. www.wyellowstone.com/ya*) and **Yellowstone Tour & Travel** (*West Yellowstone. 800-221-1151 or 406-646-9310. www.yellowstone-travel.com*).

Founded in 1973, Yellowstone Adventures offers package tours and daily Ski-Doo rentals. The three-day package, including lodging (double occupancy), and rental sled, costs $350 per person; a full week is $880 per person. You choose your accommodations: Mammoth Hot Springs Hotel or the more recent Old Faithful Snow Lodge in Yellowstone park.

YT&T offers three- to seven-day packages that range from about $650 to $1,300 per person, including lodging, guide, and rental sled with fuel. A popular add-on is a day in the **Island Park** area, with backcountry riding in national forests and an evening in a cozy lodge.

COLORADO
High Alpine Adventure

Sun, warm temperatures, and an endless supply of perfect powder: These are the elements that draw skiers to the Colorado Rockies. They also make for superb snowmobiling. Colorado has the right stuff for every kind of sledding—from wide, groomed valley trails to the high ridges of **Rocky Mountain National Park.**

The state's snowmobiling center is **Grand Lake,** a resort town that receives an annual average snowfall of 140 inches. Along with a snowmobile racetrack, Grand Lake offers 300 miles (485 km) of trails; of these, 135 miles (220 km) are groomed. Access couldn't be easier: You ride down the town's main street to connect with some of the area's best trails. Most of the better lodges will arrange snowmobile rentals for you.

From Grand Lake it's just a few miles along groomed trails to reach Rocky Mountain National Park. There you're treated to spectacular views from trails that rise more than 12,000 feet to the top of the Continental Divide. **Trail Ridge Road,** for one, takes you right through the heart of the park. Another great route is **Stillwater Pass.** On a clear day from the top of the pass, you can see 50 miles or more.

Off-trail riding here is hard to resist. The snow base is deep, but the consistency of the powder allows even novices to sled the wildlands with confidence. Some of the prettiest runs are in nearby **Arapaho National Forest,** but you'll also find great conditions in the **Roosevelt, Routt,** and **White River National Forests.**

In January and February, Grand Lake draws sledders with a variety of events, including snowcross races and snowmobile drag races. There is also a popular snow-sculpture contest and dog-mushing championship in February.

If you need a bed and a sled, **Driftwood Lodge** (*970-627-3654*) assists with nearby rentals. **Grand Lake Motor Sports** (*800-627-8834 or 970-627-3806*) also offers rentals. For more information, contact the **Grand Lake Area Chamber of Commerce** (*800-531-1019 or 970-627-3402. www.grandlakechamber.com*).

Elsewhere in the state, you'll find excellent sledding—and modest prices—at **Grand Mesa.** Colorado's best kept snowmobiling secret, located about 55 miles west of Grand Junction, Grand Mesa receives more than 35 feet of snow each year (and plenty of the stuff sticks around here well into June). The area boasts 300 miles (485 km) of trails and 800 square miles (1,300 sq km) of open riding range.

A good base from which to explore the area is **Grand Mesa Lodge** (*Cedaredge. 800-551-6372 or 970-856-3250. www.coloradodirectory.com/grandmesalodge*). This small resort features heated housekeeping cabins on scenic **Island Lake.** Rooms cost about $65 per couple per night; guided snowmobile tours are $70 for two hours, $140 for four hours.

There's plenty of good snowmobiling right outside your cabin door. Experienced sledders can also opt to ride the scenic **Sunlight to Powderhorn Trail,** which winds for 90 miles (145 km) between the **Sunlight Mountain Resort** (*Glenwood Springs*) and the **Powderhorn Ski Resort** (*Cedaredge. 970-268-5700*). This is the closest area if downhill skiing is your thing. For those who prefer cross-country, check out the ski-trail system at Grand Mesa Lodge, 8 miles from Grand Mesa.

If you want to try snowmobiling while vacationing at a winter resort, **Breckenridge** (*800-789-7669 or 970-453-5000*) is a good choice. **Tiger Run Tours** (*800-318-1386 or 970-453-2231. www.tigerruntours.com*) offers guided half-day snowmobile trips for all levels that take you up to 11,000 feet, where you'll enjoy spectacular views of the Continental Divide and its 14,000-foot-high peaks. Tours leave from **Dry Gulch,** a restored 1800s gold camp. (Shuttles operate from Breckenridge, Keystone, or Copper Mountain ski resorts.)

SLEDDERS MAKE TRACKS FOR HOME ON LABRADOR'S FROZEN CHURCHILL RIVER.

UTAH
Powder Highways

Utah has long been a top snowmobiling destination. The scenery is spectacular and the snow is reliably abundant. Moreover, the high altitude creates light, dry powder conditions, which are ideal for fast, off-trail exploration.

But Utah is more than a powder playground. The state has a well-developed network of snowmobile trails, including the **Utah-Idaho trail network**—one of the first interstate trail systems in the country. Sledders can explore 300 miles (485 km) of groomed trails that are accessible from more than 18 trailheads.

The canyonlands of southern Utah offer 25 miles (40 km) of groomed trails that run from **Monticello** down to **Blanding** (about 80 miles south of Moab). An excellent system of trails also leads to various points in the **Manti-La Sal National Forest's Abajo** and **La Sal ranges.** These are accessible by La Sal Mountain Loop Road.

In northern Utah, **Bridgerland** is an ideal area for snowmobile explorations. It offers both dramatic alpine scenery and consistently good snow throughout the winter. Bridgerland's best sites are the Wasatch-Cache National Forest, Bonner Hollow, Cascade Springs, and Little Deer Creek.

The Wasatch Range promises solitude and inspiring ridgeline vistas, while in nearby **Midway,** just outside Park City, you'll find open fields with 3 to 6 feet of powder—particularly at elevations above 6,000 feet. For those who wish to combine a snowmobiling trip with skiing, **Park City** is one of the premier ski areas in the state.

Other areas open to snowmobilers are **Color Country, Dinosaurland, Mountainland,** and **Panoramaland. Great Salt Lake Country,** a local favorite, invites riders to explore South Willow Canyon in the Stansbury Mountain Range. The diverse routes range from wooded mountains to rocky plateaus to alpine meadows.

If you're thinking of an extended sledding vacation, consider the **Homestead Resort** (*Midway. 800-327-7220, 435-654-1102, or 435-654-5813 for snowmobile center. www.homesteadresort.com*). Located 25 minutes from Park City, the Homestead's many amenities include a spa, sleigh rides, and guided tours. (Snowmobile and clothing rentals are available for tour participants only.) Round-trip tours range from one hour to all day and can cover 50 miles. Rates are $40 per hour for a solo rider ($60 per hour for doubles) or $145 for a full-day solo ride, including lunch. The best time to go is mid-December through mid-March.

For more information, contact the **Park City Chamber of Commerce** (*800-453-1360 or 435-649-6100. http://parkcityinfo.com*).

VERMONT
Winter in New England

Bountiful snowfall, more than 4,500 miles of trails, and a multitude of backcountry inns make Vermont a prime choice for a New England sledding holiday. The state's fine network of snowmobile trails is operated and maintained by the **Vermont Association of Snow Travelers** (*802-229-0005. www.vtvast.org*).

You'll find some of the best sledding near Vermont's downhill ski centers, which receive on average 300 inches of snow each season.

Jay Peak boasts the most natural snowfall of any ski area in New England—and it offers the region's best snowmobiling, with trails that will challenge the most experienced sledder. Near Jay Peak is an excellent system of groomed trails that extends across the border into Quebec. For trail maps or lodging information, contact the **Jay Peak Area Association and Welcome Center** (*800-882-7460. www.jaypeakvermont.org*).

Pittsfield, just beyond the Killington ski area, is another snowmobile venue that promises ample snow as well as access to many VAST trails. You can go your own way or join a guided tour, either through **Vermont Snowmobile Tours** (*800-286-6360. www.vermontsnowmobiletours.com*) or through **Killington Snowmobile Tours** (*802-422-2121. www.snowmobilevermont.com*).

Top-rated VST operates rental centers at Killington, Pico, and Okemo. The cost for a three-hour tour starts at $115 per person. KST also has several locations—Killington, Okemo, Stowe, and Sugarbush—so you can sample a variety of terrain. Tours range from a gentle, one-hour introductory tour for $50 per person to a challenging, two-hour **Radical Ride** for $90 per person.

The benefit of going with a commercial tour is that you gain access to the VAST trail network without obtaining a special permit. If you want to explore on your own, you must register your sled and pay a membership fee to VAST. Fees vary from $40 to $75.

You'll have no trouble finding a place to stay in the Pittsfield area. Popular among sledders is the Clear River Inn and Tavern (*Rte. 100. 800-746-7916*), a comfortable, full-service motel and restaurant.

Among the villages in Vermont's northeastern region (known as the Northeast Kingdom) that offer good sledding possibilities, **East Burke** is quaint—and relatively untraveled. It offers a nice network of trails as well as friendly accommodations. Other recommended locales include **Orleans, Essex,** and **Caledonia.**

Every February, the town of **Island Pond** hosts **Winterfest**—a celebration of both the season and the sport of snowmobiling.

ICELAND
Far Northern Exposure

If you're looking for an exotic sledding destination, Iceland is hard to beat. Located just below the Arctic Circle, the 300-mile-long island was formed from the lava flows of more than 200 volcanoes—many of which are still active.

Iceland's remarkably diverse terrain is ideal for snowmobiling. You'll find flat rangeland, rolling hills, steep peaks, glaciers, geysers, and volcanic craters of every size. For most of the year, this varied landscape is covered with snow that is smooth and firm, allowing you to venture far afield without bogging down. If you love to ride off trail on well-packed snow, Iceland is the place. Many sledders rank it above the best areas in Canada, Wyoming, and Minnesota.

Iceland's far northern latitude makes for long days in the late spring—ideal for touring at a leisurely pace and enjoying the spectacular scenery. Be sure to bring your camera; just about any route you travel promises fabulous views.

Hundreds of natural hot springs dot the countryside. After you've been on the trail for a few hours, a hot dip out in the wilderness is heaven. You can also warm up at one of the many climbers' huts you'll find near lakes and other scenic spots in the country's interior.

For information about a snowmobile-trekking vacation package, contact **Iceland Travel Ltd.** (*Lagmull 4, P.O. Box 8650, 120 Reykjavik. 01135-4585-4300. www.icelandtravel.is*) or **Austurlands Travel** (*Stangarrhylur 3A, 129 Reykjavik. 01135-4567-8545*).

Both companies can arrange multiactivity tours throughout Iceland. These might include snowmobile glacier tours, horseback riding, nordic skiing, or jeep safaris. Either outfitter will customize your itinerary to suit your adventure style and interests.

Highly recommended is a trip with **Glacier Tours Ltd.** (*01135-4478-1000. www.eldhorn.is/glaciert*). One of Iceland's leading winter adventure outfitters, Glacier Tours operates the Jöklasel alpine chalet at magnificent **Vatnajökull,** Europe's largest glacier. You can overnight at the chalet and explore the glacier by snowmobile or snowcat, or you can take a cruise on the glacier's lagoon.

If you prefer to deal with a North American company, **Decker Sno-Venture Tours** (*Eagle River, WI. 715-479-2764. www.sno-venture.com*) runs an eight-day snowmobiling safari in Iceland each April. The tour cost of about $2,700 per person includes lodging, most meals, snowmobile rental, fuel, guides, and airfare from New York or Minneapolis.

Decker can arrange a customized tour for five or more sledders in March or April. For general information regarding travel to Iceland, contact **Icelandair** (*800-223-5500. www.icelandair.com*).

Snowmobile Tour Operators

If you are hankering for a sled getaway, the companies listed below offer complete vacation tours, both near and far. In most cases, the package will get you a guide, a rental sled, fuel, lodging, and most meals. For a less expensive travel alternative, check out a "bring your own sled" tour. Looking to ride but lack a sled? North America's snowbelt has plenty of dealers and lodges that rent equipment by the hour or by the day.

Daily rentals range from about $70 for a basic, air-cooled 440 to $200 for a big water-cooled rig with extended tracks.

The Canadian exchange rate often means great deals on vacation packages, particularly in the province of Quebec, where you can choose from more than 200 "moto-neige" holidays.

For information, contact Tourisme Québec (*Montreal. 877-266-5687. www.tourisme.gouv.qc.ca/snowmobile*).

NORTH AMERICA

Decker Sno-Venture Tours
P.O. Box 1447, Eagle River, WI
715-479-2764. www.sno-venture.com

Since 1980 Richard and Audrey Decker have operated Sno-Venture Tours. If you're looking for new sledding frontiers, they can get you to the world's best sites.

Sno-Venture designs its tours to suit its clients' skill levels and speed preferences; equipment and routes vary. The company's impressive itineraries include Alaska, Wisconsin's northwoods, Yellowstone park/Jackson Hole, South Dakota's Black Hills, Minnesota, Michigan, western Montana, Ontario, Finland, and Iceland.

Domestic tours range from $575 to $675 per person per week; add about $400 for sled rental. International trips range from $2,200 to $2,800, including airfare, accommodations, most meals, and sleds.

International Snowmobile Tours, Inc.
427 Sycamore St., Chesterfield, IN 46017
800-378-8687 or 765-378-5074
www.iquest.net/isti

Although ISTI's niche is high-mileage adventures for seasoned riders, they also offer a variety of guided tours. Founded in 1980, the company uses the best hotels and restaurants; great food is the rule.

Experienced sledders will enjoy the six-day Gaspé Peninsula trip. This diverse, fast-paced, 1,200-mile (1,935 km) trip costs $825 per person, excluding sled.

The $825 **Quebec North Country Tour** takes intermediate riders from St. Donat to a 19th-century castle/casino on the banks of the St. Lawrence River.

A perennial family favorite is the seven-day **Ontario Snow Train Tour**. You ride north on the train, then return by snowmobiles through scenic backcountry. Two guides accompany the group, allowing those who prefer a slower pace to take their time. The cost is $695 per person, sled not included.

Along with the Great Lakes/Canada ride, ISTI offers a Colorado/Wyoming combo trip and a Yellowstone adventure each year.

Though the majority of customers bring their own machines, sled rental is available in most locations.

Most ISTI guided trips consist of 10 to 20 skilled riders who want to cover a lot of ground in mutual company.

Old Faithful Snowmobile Tours
P.O. Box 7182, Jackson, WY 83002
800-253-7130 or 307-733-9767
www.snowmobilingtours.com

The largest snowmobile tour operator in the greater Yellowstone area, Old Faithful has been in business since 1985.

Yellowstone Snowmobile Safari, the outfitter's most popular tour, costs $1,200 for four days or $950 for three days. (Although day tours are offered as well, you should spend at least three days here to do justice to this remarkable area.)

For seasoned sledders, the three-day Continental Divide program is recommended. The tour takes you along the Continental Divide Trail—a relatively new groomed-trail system that crisscrosses the Wind River, Gros Ventre, and Absaroka ranges.

As a grand finale, snowmobilers ride up Lava Mountain to an elevation of 10,500 feet (3,200 meters) and top off the tour with powder running in the Togwotee

Pass area. The cost is $1,050 per person.

Old Faithful's prices are fairly high, but the guides are first rate and you stay in the best lodges, including the Stage Coach Inn, Elk Ridge Lodge, and Triangle C.

Randonneige Québec
25 rue Brissette, C.P. 65, Sainte-Agathe-Des-Monts, Québec, J8C 3A1, Canada
800-326-0642 or 819-326-0642
www.randonneige.com

Randonneige is one of North America's best snowmobile tour operators. Tours follow the Trans-Québec trail system; the Laurentian section boasts 2,170 miles (3,500 km) of groomed tracks. This company delivers a quality vacation in all respects—food, lodging, guiding, customer service—with a French flair.

Along with day trips and weekend specials, the most popular trip is a three-day holiday. Ideal for families, it costs $600 per person, based on double occupancy.

Serious sledders wishing to travel farther and faster will enjoy the five-day, inn-to-inn ride. The cost is $1,100 per person, double occupancy.

All multiday tours feature fine backcountry inns, with private baths and quality dining. The six-night, superluxury "tour gastronomique" includes four-star hotels and gourmet cuisine.

With a fleet of 50 Arctic Cats, Randonneige can serve large groups; custom tours are a specialty. Guides speak four languages.

Rocky Mountain Recreation Tours
9918 71st Ave., Edmonton, Alberta
T6E 0W7, Canada. 780-448-5860
www.cycleworks.com/tourcomp.html

Premium riding sites, reasonable prices, and a state-of-the-art, 52-sled transporter are the hallmarks of this fine company.

Rocky Mountain specializes in larger group tours (30 or more riders) in the Canadian Rockies and West Yellowstone, Montana. The season runs from December through March.

The Canadian destinations—Valemount, Revelstoke, Hunters Range, Golden in British Columbia, and Blairmore in Alberta—are all superb.

Valemount's three distinct mountain ranges feature well-marked trails, while Revelstoke, with an annual snowfall exceeding 52 feet, promises excellent powder snow. Hunters Range and Golden offer high-alpine wilderness routes as well as easy trail-running. Blairmore's specialty is sunny skies and scenic ridge-running atop Crowsnest Pass.

Canadian tours range from two to seven days. The average cost is $100 (US) per person per day, including sled transport. Sled rentals are an additional $100-150 per day. All trips are self-guided.

Senior World Tours

2205 N. River Rd., Fremont, OH 43420 888-355-1686 or 419-355-1686
www.seniorworldtours.com

SWT offers complete snowmobile vacation packages in Alaska and Wyoming. The company accommodates all age groups, but it specializes in trips for individuals over the age of 49.

SWT's most popular tour is based at the Cowboy Village Resort at Togwotee near Jackson Hole, Wyoming. High in the Tetons at an elevation of 8,500 feet (2,600 meters), you can enjoy challenging alpine runs above tree line, power through virgin powder, or cruise for miles on established trails. The itinerary includes a visit to Yellowstone National Park.

Trips range from six to eight days. The cost is $1,200 to $1,700 per person, including lodging, meals, and sled rental.

Also recommended is Senior World's Alaska program. Designed for experienced sledders, the ten-day March tour includes a Resurrection Bay glacier cruise and a lodge-to-lodge loop tour starting at Tolsona Lake Resort, near Wrangell-St. Elias National Park. Trips depart from Anchorage and cost about $2,400.

Yellowstone Tour & Travel

211 Yellowstone Ave., W. Yellowstone, MT 59758. 800-221-1151 or 406-646-9310
www.yellowstone-travel.com

YT&T runs three- to seven-day snowmobiling vacations from West Yellowstone. The three-day trip, which includes guided riding through Yellowstone National Park and nearby Targhee National Forest, is a good choice for the novice snowmobiler. The price—less than $700 per person, double occupancy—includes lodging, snowmobile rental, a daily tank of gas, and riding gear (suit, boots, gloves, goggles, mask, and helmet). For an additional $10 to $50 a day, you can rent a more powerful snowmobile.

The six- and seven-day programs offer the same provisions. You can use the extra days to explore the Grand Canyon of the Yellowstone and sample the powder in Gallatin and Targhee National Forests on more than 1,000 miles (1,600 km) of groomed trails.

EUROPE

SCANDINAVIA

Norvista Travel Services
228 E. 45th St., New York, NY 10017
800-677-6454 or 212-818-1198
www.norvista.com

Norvista offers package snowmobiling holidays throughout Scandinavia. One popular tour is the **Arctic Snowmobile Safari.** Starting in Finland, you sled for four days, overnighting in chalets or in comfortable lodges. The cost is about $2,000, including airfare from New York. Norvista will also arrange custom itineraries.

FINLAND

Lapin Eräsafarit Ky
PL 15, FIN-99831
Saariselkä, Finland
01135-8166-68345
http://personal.inet.fi/business/esafaris/english

Lapin offers snowmobile safaris into Finnish Lapland. Choose from lodge-to-lodge tours or more challenging treks with wilderness camping and overnights in remote villages. Along with great sledding, you get a unique look at Sami culture.

ICELAND

Glacier Tours Ltd.
P.O. Box 66, 780 Hornafjör-ur, Iceland
01135-4478-1000. www.eldhorn.is/glaciert

This major Icelandic adventure-tour operator has special access to Vatnajökull glacier. Overnight at the Jöklasel chalet and enjoy the views from the restaurant—at 2,760 feet (840 meters), the country's highest in Iceland.

From March through September, Glacier offers snowmobile and snowcat tours around the glacier as well as cruises on the glacier's lovely lagoon.

NORWAY

Svalbard Polar Travel
Box 540 9171 Longyearbyen, Norway
01147-7902-3400
http://www.svalbard-polar.no/index__eng.html

Since 1990, SPT has led off-trail snowmobile tours on polar Svalsbard archipelago. The six-day **Snowmobile Safari** leaves from Longyearbyen and crosses glaciers and fjord ice to Barentsburg, Kapp Linné, and Tempelfjord. The cost is about $2,200 per person, including lodging, meals, sled rental, riding gear, and instruction for those with no previous driving experience.

SWEDEN

Svanrek AB-Arctic Adventures
Svanstein 318, S-957 94 Overtornea, Tornedalen, Sweden
01146-9272-0086 or 01146-7062-37711
www.svanrek.se

Svanrek AB offers guided snowmobile tours in the border region between Sweden and Finland. The popular two- or three-day backcountry safari takes riders from Svanstein to Rovanieme, Finland, with overnights in hotels. The cost is about $420 per person, including lodging, meals, sled, and fuel.

More adventurous snowmobile tours take you north of the Arctic Circle to Russia. These extended trips, with overnight camping, cover a maximum of ten days and 1,250 miles (2,000 km) and cost $2,500.

Svanrek will create a custom sledding itinerary for groups. The cost is about $2,300 per person per week, all-inclusive. (Just for the record, this outfitter also offers great hunting and fishing programs in the summer.)

Snowmobile Destinations

Of the hundreds of fine snowmobiling destinations in North America, here are some favorite recreational sledding spots. They all feature extensive trail systems, sled rentals, and a variety of quality accommodations. Some offer short, guided tours.

CALIFORNIA

Lake Tahoe

LOCATION: Lake Tahoe and Reno, NV.

TRAILS AND CONDITIONS: Groomed and ungroomed logging roads and trails. Deep powder, often steep terrain. Many groomed trails, suitable for all riders, extend from Zephyr Cove.

TOP DESTINATIONS: Tahoe Vista, Toiyabe National Forest, and for experienced sledders, ski resort to ski resort.

ATTRACTIONS: 8,400-foot-high

lookouts, with great views of Lake Tahoe, Squaw Valley, and Alpine Meadows. Guided two-hour trips on groomed and powder trails. World-class downhill skiing, Nevada gambling, and excellent tourist facilities.

SNOWMOBILE RENTALS/GUIDES: Snowmobiling Unlimited, P.O. Box 1591, Tahoe City, CA 96145, 530-583-5858; Zephyr Cove Snowmobile Center, 760 Hwy. 50, Zephyr Cove, NV 89448, 775-588-3833; DJ's Snowmobile Adventures, Mammoth, CA, 760-935-4480. www.snowmobilemammoth. com. (Mammoth is two hours south).

CONTACT: Lake Tahoe Reservations. 800-824-6348. www.tahoefun.org

CANADA

Lanaudière, Québec

LOCATION: Access trails from St.-Donat, 75 miles north of Montreal.

TRAILS AND CONDITIONS: 100 miles of groomed trails with superb sign-posting. Linked to vast Trans-Quebec trail system. Mountain, lake, and forest terrain.

TOP DESTINATIONS: Lake Ouareau, Mont-Tremblant Park.

ATTRACTIONS: Some of the best snowmobiling in Canada. Outstanding network of small inns and warming huts, numerous wilderness preserves and parks to tour. Mont Tremblant Park trails are superb.

SNOWMOBILE RENTALS/GUIDES: Sport & Marine MV, 1108 Principale, St.Donat, PQ, J0T 2C0. 819-424-3433. Guided tours: Randonneige Quebec, 800-326-0642 or 819-326-0642 www.randonneige.com

CONTACT: Tourisme Québec. 877-266-5687. www.tourisme.gouv.qc.ca/snowmobile.

IDAHO

Yellowstone/Teton Country

LOCATION: Northeast Idaho near Island Park area.

TRAILS AND CONDITIONS: 500 miles of groomed trails through flatlands, forests, mountains. Deep powder in high country; average snowfall 19 feet per year.

TOP DESTINATIONS: Two Top Mountain, Centennial Range, Island Park trail system; cross to Yellowstone over the Continental Divide.

ATTRACTIONS: Stunning scenery (Big Springs, Mesa Falls), deep powder, long season. Excellent ski resorts nearby (Big Sky, Grand Targhee). Good restaurants and hotels.

SNOWMOBILE RENTALS/GUIDES: Island Park Polaris, 3394 N. Hwy. 20, Island Park, ID 83429, 208-558-7390; Robin's Roost, HC 66, Box 10, Island Park, ID 83429. 208-558-7440

CONTACT: Island Park Chamber of Commerce. 800-847-4843 or 208-558-7755

MAINE

Millinocket

LOCATION: North of Bangor at the foot of Mount Katahdin.

TRAILS AND CONDITIONS: 300 miles of groomed trails to nearby Baxter and Lilly Bay State Parks, or north into Canada. Mountain trails tend to be uncrowded, with good snow all winter.

TOP DESTINATIONS: Mount Kineo, Baxter State Park area, Double Top Mountain.

ATTRACTIONS: Twin Pine Camp caters to sledders. Popular Katahdin Family Winter Fest in late February.

SNOWMOBILE RENTALS/GUIDES: New England Outdoor Center, P.O. Box 669, Millinocket, ME 04462, 800-766-7238 or 207-723-5438.

CONTACT: Katahdin Area Chamber of Commerce. 207-723-4443. www.katahdinmaine.com; Baxter Park Authority. 207-723-5140.

MICHIGAN

Keweenaw Peninsula

LOCATION: Northwest corner of the Upper Peninsula.

TRAILS AND CONDITIONS: 21 feet of annual snowfall. More than 250 miles of groomed, marked trails. Mostly rolling hills and backwoods.

TOP DESTINATIONS: Brockway Mountain (Copper Harbor), Agate Beaches, Calumet, Firesteel River Gorge.

ATTRACTIONS: Many quality resorts and active nightlife in Houghton. Organized snowmobile rallies.

SNOWMOBILE RENTALS/GUIDES: Dan's Polaris, 657 Erickson Dr., Atlantic Mine, MI 49905, 800-858-4869 or 906-482-6227.

CONTACT: Keweenaw Tourism Council. 800-338-7982 or 906-482-5240. www.portup.com/snow

NEW HAMPSHIRE

North Country

LOCATION: Just south of the Canadian border, New Hampshire's North Country is accessible via Pittsburg.

TRAILS AND CONDITIONS: 500 miles of groomed trails, mostly logging roads, connect to other trail systems in Canada, Maine, and Vermont. Many frozen lakes and rivers are passable. Terrain is mountainous.

TOP DESTINATIONS: Stub Hill, Magalloway Mountain, Mount Pisgah.

ATTRACTIONS: Great wildlife, good fishing, ice-skating, skiing nearby, many small towns for rest stops.

SNOWMOBILE RENTALS/GUIDES: Alpine Adventures, 603-745-9911, www.alpinesnomobiling.com; Trail Ride Rental, 25 Woodcock Dr., Pittsburg, NH 03592, 603-538-1161.

CONTACT: NH Snowmobile Association. 603-224-8906. www.nhsa.com

WISCONSIN

Wisconsin Dells

LOCATION: The Wisconsin Dells is the center of a five-county recreation area in south-central Wisconsin.

TRAILS AND CONDITIONS: More than 800 miles of marked, mapped, and professionally groomed trails. Frozen lakes, meadows, and hills. Trails are mostly wooded.

TOP DESTINATIONS: Castle Rock Lake, Corridor 21 Trail, Devil's Lake.

ATTRACTIONS: Nearby state parks with 25 miles of nordic ski trails. Christmas Mountain Village winter carnival and sled-dog racing. Downhill skiing at Christmas Mountain and Cascade Mountain.

SNOWMOBILE RENTALS/GUIDES: Chula Vista Resort, 4031 River Rd., P.O. Box 30, Wisconsin Dells, WI 53965. 800-388-4782 or 608-254-8366.

CONTACT: Wisconsin Dells Visitor Bureau. 800-223-3557 or 608-254-8088.

RIDER SAFETY

Most regional snowmobiling organizations offer clinics to teach beginners basic snowmobile operation and trail safety.

For more information and a directory of regional sledding groups, contact the **American Council of Snowmobile Associations** (*271 Woodland Pass, Suite 216, East Lansing, MI 48823. 517-351-4362. www.snowmobileacsa.org*).

EQUIPMENT

Sleds come in solo and two-person models. The solos are smaller, lighter, and generally more maneuverable.

Premium sleds offer luxuries, such as upgraded suspension and heated grips; look for these features when you rent.

Virtually all machines use light, powerful two-stroke engines. The hottest sleds feature larger, water-cooled engines, which deliver more punch for deep powder; these are best left to experienced sledders.

If you're traveling in deep powder, sleds with extended tracks float you higher—important when you're riding two-up (or two riders per sled) off trail.

Most late-model sleds feature electric starters. This is a big plus, but it is prudent to have a backup manual starter—particularly when you're riding in remote regions.

When traveling far off trail, take Global Positioning Satellite (GPS) system units, and ride in pairs so you can make it home if you have a serious breakdown.

CLOTHING

Snowmobiling is cold business. Layering is the way to go to stay warm and fight the wind-chill factor.

Start with a skin-lining bottom layer of polypropylene or thermax. Top that with a good snowmobiling suit. Wear polypropylene socks and make sure that your boots are completely waterproof and well insulated. If your toes still get chilly, you can buy thermal inserts, such as Hot Feet. Electric socks, vests, and mittens are another option, but your sled must be equipped with the necessary wiring. You should have a pair of good, insulated gloves made of Gore-Tex or some other breathable, waterproof material. Silk inner gloves add comfort and warmth.

A helmet is a must—preferably a full-face model. Even a low-speed fall can cause serious injury to a bareheaded rider. Along with their safety function, helmets also keep your head warm, make it easier to see, and reduce wind noise.

An electric, voice-activated intercom will allow you to speak with your passenger or another rider over the din of the sled engine.

ONLINE

American Snowmobiler Online
www.amsnow.com

This site's North American "Getaway Guide" is an excellent resource for trip planning. The guide profiles more than 100 popular sledding destinations in the U.S. and Canada. You'll also find links to major snowmobile clubs, plus a searchable archive of articles on technical topics.

Sled City
www.sledcity.com

Sled City is an online snowmobiling community. Resources include news features, trail reports, product information, race results, and message boards.

Snowmobiling Network
www.snowmobiling.net

A real time-saver, this site offers handy, comprehensive directories for snowmobiling in the United States and Canada. The information—snowmobile rental venues, sled clubs and dealers, guided tours, lodging, and more—is organized by state and by province. Click on a map to find the directory for any North American destination.

Snowmobile Online
www.off-road.com/snowmobile

This site offers sled reviews, trail reports, and a complete set of links to U.S. and Canadian snowmobile clubs; click on "Info Center."

Snowtracks Trail Reports
www.snowtracks.com

Snowtracks provides current trail conditions for 14 U.S. states and 5 Canadian provinces. Other features include a good list of North American snowmobile clubs. Trail maps are available for purchase online.

PRINT

Snowmobiling: The Sledder's Complete Handbook by David and James Hallam (Fun On Snow Publications, $14.95). Written by a snowmobiler with more than 30 years of riding experience, this book emphasizes preparedness, whether riding on or off trail. Safety lessons include avalanche awareness and winter survival.

You'll also learn proper techniques for turning in deep snow, riding steeps, extricating stuck sleds, and troubleshooting mechanical problems.

Annual Vacation Guide Directory (Ehlert Publishing, Maple Grove, MN. 612-476-2200. www.ehlertpowersports.com). Published by *Snowgoer* magazine, this resource features North American snowmobile destinations, reviews of new equipment, and a calendar of major events.

SnowRider Magazine (Boucher Publications, Ellington, CT. 860-871-2548. www.snowridermag.com). Six issues annually feature profiles of top North American sledding sites, the best trails, rental centers, and guided tours.

VIDEOS

American Snowmobiler Magazine (800-507-283. www.amsnow.com) offers a good selection of videos that feature equipment previews, action, and instruction.

Riding Safely in Avalanche Country (Friends of the Sun Valley Avalanche Forecast Center, c/o Environmental Resource Center, Ketchum, ID. 208-726-4333. www.avalanche.org. $15.95). This video shows you how to test snow for stability and how to evaluate avalanche risk based on terrain and snowpack. It also demonstrates effective avalanche rescue skills.

LONE SLEDDER ETCHES A SNOWFIELD AT COWBOY VILLAGE RESORT IN MORAN, WYOMING.

WAVE RIDERS DANCE WITH PRIMAL FORCES OF NATURE. SURFING, THE SPORT OF HAWAIIAN kings, is more than just a pastime. Surfing is a lifestyle — for some, a metaphor for existence. To challenge the power of waves requires special skills, strength, knowledge, and courage known previously by few. But with the advent of soft boards for beginners and the resurgence of easy-riding longboards, participation in the sport is expanding. • Unfortunately, the increasing number of surfers has meant overcrowding at the more popular and accessible breaks. For many veteran surfers, the congestion has spoiled the fun. Consequently, discerning wave riders are now traveling the globe to explore new surfing frontiers. (With two-thirds of Earth's surface covered by water, there are plenty of pristine alternatives on the horizon.) For instance, you can still find perfect, virgin breaks in exotic locales such as Indonesia, Fiji, and South America. And that's only a start. This chapter profiles some of the world's top surf spots and the organizations that can take you there, whether you're an old pro or just getting your feet wet.

LEFT: SURFER TED QUAKENBUSH GETS BARRELED, SANTA BARBARA.
BELOW: WAITING FOR THE HUGE TUBULAR WAVES THAT MAKE UP THE
BANZAI PIPELINE AT EHUKAI BEACH PARK ON OAHU.

*I get on the water and surf waves I know no human being
has ever surfed before. And that's a trip.*
GREGG HENDERSON

Eight Ultimate Surfaris

Riding a perfect wave in a tropical paradise is one of life's great pleasures. The ultimate surfing experience, however, does not demand that you compete with locals for that ride. Although some of the world's best surf happens to limn populated shores, with a little chutzpah and an eye for good surf you can usually catch a wave of your own in any of these hot spots.

HAWAII
Birthplace of Surfing

It's no wonder that Hawaiians have been surfing for centuries. The archipelago's clear, warm waters offer surfers some of the most beautiful and challenging waves on Earth. Of all the islands, **Oahu** ranks highest for variety and consistency. On the north shore, **Pipeline, Sunset**, and **Waimea** are famed proving grounds for world-class surfers, who come — generally between October and May — to test their skill on waves towering to 25 feet. **Surf and Sea** (*Haleiwa. 808-637-9887. www.surfnsea.com*) provides board rentals and surfing lessons, and information on the area's best breaks.

On Oahu's gentler south shore, **Waikiki's** unique reefs allow swells to break in slow, easy peels that start half a mile out. Ideal for beginners, the most popular spots are **Canoes** at **Waikiki Beach Center** and **Queens** at **Kuhio Beach Park.** You can rent boards and sign up for lessons right on the beach. The main surf spot on the island's west side is **Makaha,** where, depending on conditions, you can find a world-class big wave or a mellow roller.

The best surfing on **Maui** is at **Honolua Bay, Ma'alaea,** and **Hookipa.** If you are a novice, **Nancy Emerson School of Surfing** (*Lahaina. 808-873-0264. www.maui.net/~ncesurf*) offers guided tours of the island's surf breaks, as well as private and group lessons, plus international package tours for experienced surfers. Greg Unabia's **Soul Lifter/Soul Drifter** (*Kihei. 808-879-9194. About $125 per day*) specializes in customized surfaris, primarily on Maui, although Greg will also arrange tours on Oahu and **Kauai.**

The latter's main attraction for serious surfers is **Hanalei Bay** and **Tunnels.** Beginners can sign up for a group lesson with a seven-time world champion at **Margo Oberg Surf School** (*Donovan's near Poipu Beach. 888-384-8810 or 808-742-7588. www.brenneckes.com*)

If you want to sample breaks around the islands, **Honolulu Sailing Company** (*Kaneohe. 800-829-0114 or 808-239-3900. www.honsail.com. $160 per person per day*) offers a variety of surfaris around the outer islands of **Lanai,** Maui, **Molokai,** and Oahu.

INDONESIA
Exotic Breaks

For epic surf coupled with adventure, there is no better destination than Indonesia, famous for its finely formed and consistent swells. A good place to begin any Indonesian surfing tour is **Bali**—except during the dry season (*June-Aug.*), when tourists crowd the beaches. This fabled island challenges wave riders with big, fast waves that often break over jagged reefs. Bali's best surf spot is **Uluwatu** on the island's south coast. A headland here channels the main force of the swells, creating a world-class — and dangerous — left. Just down the beach from Uluwatu at **Padang Padang,** a big, hollow left breaks near a cliff. If you lose your board here, you can kiss it good-bye. A relatively safe alternative, except for the powerful riptide, is **Kuta Beach,** where you'll discover a California-like sand break not normally seen in Indonesia.

Moving on to **Java,** head for **Grajagan** (*Weekly rates: $500 to $550 per person*), a surf camp at the island's western tip. When the trades are blowing offshore and the swell exceeds 6 feet, Grajagan delivers a virtually perfect wave. The best spot is **Moneytrees,** located right in front of the camp and distinguished by a flawless, not-too-dangerous left. Expect crowds from May through September; however, there are enough waves here for all to enjoy. For travel arrangements to Grajagan, Bali, or **Lombok,** contact **WaterWays Travel** (*Van Nuys, CA. 800-928-3757 or 818-376-0341. www.waterwaystravel.com*) or **Surf Travel Company** (*Cronulla, NSW, Australia. 01161-295-274-722. www.surftravel.com*).

For Bali's surf minus its crowds , pack your boards (and malaria pills) and head to **Nias,** an island off the west coast of **Sumatra.** There are plenty of uncharted breaks along the beach here, but the main spot is **Lagundi Bay,** which features a notable right at its western end. When the swell hits 5 to 15 feet, the outside reef becomes a pounding, gaping barrel that can deliver rides as long as 100 yards. Simple lodging, including a surf camp, is available nearby. (*For information on camping or custom boat charters, contact Surf Travel Company, above.*)

A great way to explore Indonesia's surf spots is by charter yacht, which allows you the option of diving or kayak-

ing if the surf's not up. A favorite locale for yacht surfaris is the **Mentawai Islands,** southwest of Padang off the Sumatran coast. **Great Breaks International** (*Margaret River, Australia. 011-61-897-579-191. www.greatbreaks.com.au or www.mentawai.com. 11-day charters: $1,550-2,100 per person, excluding airfare*) is the only local charter company with a year-round, radio-equipped base in Padang; it is also fully licensed and endorsed by the Sumatran government. Other companies offering charters include **WaterWays** (*Mentawai, 12-day charter: $1,800-2,200, excluding airfare; Lombok to Sumbawa, 8-day charter: $1,000*) and **Surf Travel Company** (*charters to Mentawai and Sumatra; call for length and prices*). The latter uniquely lets you create a custom charter for five.

SOUTH AFRICA
Jeffreys Bay and Beyond

The Point at **Jeffreys Bay,** or "J-Bay," is remote, dangerous, fast—and beautiful. Here, on South Africa's southeast coast, offshore winds brush the cold, deep-blue water into towering dark tubes plumed with white spray. Since the 1960s, this perfect right-point break has attracted die-hard surfers from around the world. J-Bay's golden beaches are not for the fainthearted: Getting there requires a grueling series of flights, and once you arrive, you won't find much

beyond the beach; moreover, the surf is not consistent. But if you have the right conditions—and the right stuff to stay with the racing wave—J-Bay promises the ultimate surfer's high. By the time you hit that inside section (rightfully nicknamed "Impossibles"), you will know what it means to fly.

Surf conditions are best during South Africa's winter, or May through December. Bring a full wet suit and booties, because J-Bay is notoriously cold and sharky.

There are many other superb breaks near J-Bay, including **Cape St. Francis,** which was immortalized in the movie *Endless Summer.* To explore these and the rest of South Africa's surf scene, several outfitters offer a variety of options. **WaterWays Travel** (*see p.296*) has a 10-day surfari from **Cape Town** to J-Bay and back. The cost is $1,250 per person, including meals, surf guide, and local transportation. If you have more time, **Surf Travel Company** (*see p.296. $550 per person, excluding airfare*) features one- to four-week guided tours, including a basic budget surfari, of the region's best surf spots. **Morris Overseas Tours** (*Melbourne Beach, FL. 407-725-4809. www.morrisoverseastours.com*) offers a one-week tour for $2,000 per person, including airfare, transportation, and accommodations.

If you decide to extend your holiday while in the country or want to visit other Indian Ocean surf spots such as

TRYING TO STAY AHEAD OF THE JAWS, MAUI.

Madagascar or Mauritius, contact South Africa's **True Blue Surf Travel** (*Noordhoek. 01127-2178-92910. http:// home.global.co.za/~trueblue*).

CALIFORNIA
Santa Cruz & North Coast

Part beach place and part college town, **Santa Cruz** sits near the top of Monterey Bay, protected from the brunt of the storms that slam California's northern coast each winter. Santa Cruz offers fairly consistent, quality surf at its year-round breaks. The water is always cold, though, so you'll need a full wetsuit.

The most popular surf spot in Santa Cruz is **Steamer Lane,** located just north of the harbor at **Lighthouse Point.** An audience often watches from the cliff top, and the lighthouse contains a surf museum. Another excellent site is **Pleasure Point** (shown on maps as **Soquel Point**) on the east side of town. A huge, right-point reef break, Pleasure Point boasts a remarkable variety of takeoff areas, from hollow, wedging Sewer Peak on the outside to long, mellow First Peak on the inside. Heavily surfed, Pleasure Point attracts all levels of surfers. Farther north is **Davenport Landing,** a popular summer spot with a fun hot-dog wave that can deliver rides as long as 100 yards. This is a good spot for beginners.

Along the coast—especially the more exposed northern reaches of Santa Cruz County—you can find secluded coves with reef and point surf. Also expect colder and bigger waves. At **Half Moon Bay,** check out the newest challenge for big-wave riders: **Mavericks.** A heavy wave comparable to Waimea and Todos Santos, its long, walled-up right is the main draw—for the few who can ride it, that is. Mavericks breaks far out to sea over rocky reefs that have already claimed lives, including that of Hawaiian champion Mark Foo. Be prepared: This wintertime break is colored by gray skies, cold winds, icy seas, and black, 20-foot waves.

Santa Cruz is accessible and easy to do on your own. For equipment rentals and reliable information, try **Freeline Surf Shop** (*41st Ave. 831-476-2950*). **Club ED** (*5 Isbel Dr. 800-287-7873 or 831-459-9283. www.club-ed.com. $70 per hour or $300 per day*) rents equipment and gives lessons on **Cowell's Beach,** a great spot for beginners. Club ED also arranges custom tours of breaks from Big Sur to San Francisco. For small-group lessons with a local expert, contact **Richard Schmidt School of Surfing** (*236 San Jose Ave. 831-423-0928. www.richardschmidt.com. 1-hour lesson: $60 per person*).

BAJA, MEXICO
Best of the West

Baja is the first frontier that California surfers explored in search of the perfect wave. Armed with little more than a map, a Spanish phrase book, and the obligatory four-wheel-drive truck, adventurous wave riders have been migrating south for decades. (The tough rig is de rigueur if you want to tackle this desolate landscape of dry riverbeds, rocky

plateaus, miles of agave, and long, dusty tracks that lead from the main highway to the coast.) The best thing about Baja is its secluded beaches where the waves are good, the seafood is excellent, and the people are few. Many surf spots have primitive campgrounds, but you won't find much in the way of services, so pack all essentials.

Baja boasts many great breaks, some just an hour or two south of the border. From **Ensenada,** a short boat ride gets you to the island of **Todos Santos**—home of the big wave break known as "Killers." Much farther south at **Punto San Eugenio,** you'll find **Isla Natividad,** famed for its many fine breaks, including a right-hand barrel at the end of the landing strip. The only outfit that can fly you there is **Baja AirVentures** (*Chula Vista, CA. 800-221-9283 or 619-421-2235. www.bajaairventures.com*).

On the central coast, **Punta Abreojos** promises a barreling right point with a hollow, dangerous wave to challenge thrill-seekers. To the south, **Scorpion Bay** rewards those who survive the endless, punishing drive to the sea with its long right point. You'll find a good left point at **Punta Canejo,** along with a great lobster camp.

Because the tip of Baja is much more developed, you may have to share a wave; the water is considerably warmer, however, so you can fish or dive when the swells are off. The major surf spots are **Zippers** and **Shipwrecks**—both right-point breaks—and **Monuments,** an open-ocean, left-favoring reef break. All three produce good, 3- to 6-foot waves.

A self-guided surf trip through Baja is not for everybody. You must be prepared for *bandidos, federales,* heat, flies, bad roads, and virtually no medical facilities. To enjoy more waves with fewer hassles, it makes sense to go with a guided tour. **Baja Surf Adventures** (*Vista, CA. 800-428-7873 or 760-744-5642. www.bajasurfadventures.com. 3- to 7-day tours: $300-900 per person*) runs four-wheel-drive camping surfaris to many of the best spots in Baja, including Punta Abreojos, **Seven Sisters,** Scorpion Bay, and **Cabo San Lucas.** For those with less time and more money, Baja AirVentures (BAV) runs fly-in trips from San Diego to remote surf spots in Baja as well as to **La Unica,** BAV's all-inclusive adventure resort on the Golfo de California. When you're not surfing, this is a great place to fish, kayak, and dive. BAV's vacation packages include a four-day, $845 **Quick Getaway** to a private, quarter-mile right-point break, as well as a seven-day, $1,495 **Grand Tour** to Isla Natividad, Abreojos, and Scorpion Bay. **Solo Sports Excursions** (*Irvine, CA. 949-453-1950. www.solosports.net. Tours from $1,400 per person per week*) offers surfaris around Baja, some featuring surf clinics with touring pros. The wind-and-wave tours combine board-sailing and wave surfing.

FRANCE
Biarritz & Atlantic Coast

Biarritz, on France's Atlantic coast near the Spanish border, uniquely combines world-class beach breaks with Continental ambience. Nowhere else will you find such a mix of quality surf, medieval castles, topless beaches, great nightclubs, superb food, and a truly international crowd. The citizens of Biarritz seem to have embraced California-style surfing culture. Their city is beginning to feel like a surf town, complete with heavy tourism, parking problems, and crime. But there is also plenty of nightlife, making Biarritz a favorite stop for surfers on the pro circuit.

Sandbar beach breaks form the surf at **Grande Plage,** the main strand in Biarritz. Conditions are best from late summer to early fall, when the water is fairly warm. Low to mid-tides produce good rights and lefts, but the high tide here is not surfable. Unfortunately, the primary surf zone is restricted during the summer, and the remaining open areas get very crowded on weekends and holidays.

When the lineup gets too heavy at Biarritz, veteran surfers simply use the town as a base from which to explore other excellent spots nearby. **Hossegor,** for one, located just north of Biarritz, offers a thick, meaty beach break. Often bigger and more hollow than Biarritz, Hossegor is known for its tubes. Farther north and west of Bordeaux is **Lacanau.** Like Biarritz, it is on the pro circuit and can be crowded, but it gets good northern breaks.

To the south, the **Côte des Basques** is a local favorite for its good, but undefined, beach break surrounded by

BEEFCAKE ON THE SAND, HAWAII.

dramatic cliffs and beautiful villas. **Mundaka,** about an hour's drive across the border in Spain, is famous for its large, hollow, and fast left—and for the radical tide fluctuations that can pull you out to sea. This one is for advanced surfers only, but it's worth the trip for anyone who wants to watch these daredevils from the shore and enjoy some beautiful scenery at the same time.

For information, contact the **French Government Tourist Office** (*310-271-6665. Help line 900-420-2003 or 900-990-0040: 50 cents per minute*). Remember that the French go on holiday for the month of August; to avoid the crowds, travel earlier or later. **Morris Overseas Tours** (*407-725-4869. www.morrisoverseastours.com. 8-day tour: about $1,500 per person, including airfare*) recommends September and October: The water is still warm, the surf is good, and there's less competition for waves. Morris offers a surf-holiday package that includes France's Biarritz region as well as a few of Spain's hot surf spots, among them **Bilboa** and **San Sebastian** (**Donostia**) just across the border. You can surf a different break each day and enjoy Spain, where the prices are lower and the locals party 'til dawn.

TAVARUA, FIJI
Board in Paradise

This small, 30-acre island in the Fijian archipelago was the site of the first tropical surf resort. **Tavarua Surf Camp** still offers visitors an idyllic and carefree surf vacation. Recently upgraded to provide more amenities for visitors, this well-managed and now-more-comfortable resort promises plenty of food and entertainment—not to mention outstanding surf off the beach. And with the number of camp guests limited to 24, you are guaranteed uncrowded waves.

Tavarua's main surf spot, and also its best wave, is **Restaurants**—so named because its beautiful tubes peel off conveniently in front of the camp's eatery. Many of the pros regard Tavarua's consistent left as the best in the world. When the swell exceeds 4 feet, this is about as perfect a wave as you'll find anywhere.

Twenty minutes by boat from Tavarua, **Cloudbreak's** waves are larger and also significantly more dangerous because of the underlying reef, particularly when the swell is big and the water is shallow. The surf at Cloudbreak is unique in that it can hold a swell and then grow while maintaining its perfect, open-barrel form. At most times, to minimize the risk of injury on the reef, you need a boat to get in and out of this surf.

Tavarua is normally booked months in advance. To reserve a place, you must register with a group organized by a tour operator; Tavarua does not accommodate individual reservations. For information, contact Dave Clark at **Tavarua Island Tours** (*Santa Barbara, CA. 805-686-4551.*

Cost per person is $180 per day, including meals, lodging, and activities, or $2,300 for the first week, including airfare). **Global Surf Travel** (*877-787-3872. www.globalsurftravel.com*) also arranges some group trips to Tavarua, but its rates may differ.

If you can't get into Tavarua, Fiji has many fine alternative surf spots. Nearby **Namotu Island** (also called **Picnic Island**) has excellent surf. You can stay at **Namotu Surf Camp,** or **Plantation Island Resort** provides daily boat service to Namotu. Reservations for either may be made through Global Surf Travel (*see above*). Keep in mind that Namotu gets more crowded than Tavarua and that the island still allows some individual reservations, so you probably won't experience as much camaraderie as you would on a group trip to Tavarua.

Big-wave riders also flock to **Frigate Passage,** home of the "Fiji Pipeline." When conditions are right, this powerful and fast-forming left-reef break, similar to Cloudbreak, is one of Fiji's best waves. Frigate Passage is just a short boat ride from **Marlin Bay Resort** on Beqa Island (*800-542-3454; in Fiji, 679-304-042. www.marlinbay.com*). Frigate Passage is also accessible from Beqa's **Lalati Resort.** Situated on a white-sand beach, Lalati is probably a better option for families. There is also a surf camp serving Frigate Passage. The rates are substantially cheaper than Tavarua's, but you'll be sleeping in a tent rather than a bungalow, and the amenities are not quite as nice. For information, contact **Australia's Surf Travel Company** (*01161-295-274-722. www.surf-travel.com.au. $65 per person per day*).

Although Fiji's outer islands produce the finest surf, perfectly satisfying swells beckon on the main island of **Veti Levu** as well. A decent moderate wave graces the **Hideaway Resort** on the **Coral Coast,** while **Pacific Harbor** near Suva has a fairly mellow spot that breaks at 2 to 3 feet. When conditions are right on popular **Natadola Beach,** the **Sigatoka River Mouth** gets big; strong tidal action and hazardous reefs, however, make Sigatoka a destination for experts only.

All of these breaks are accessible from Veti Levu's coastal resorts. Though perhaps less than ideal for hard-core surfers, these resorts are worth considering, especially if you are traveling to Fiji with a family. They are centrally located and reasonably priced when booked through a reliable agency, such as **Fiji Reservations & Travel** (*Kahului, HI. 888-447-3454 or 808-871-5986. www.fiji-islands.com*). If you are interested in kayaking or diving, this agency can also arrange excursions from major resorts.

AUSTRALIA
Gold Coast & Beyond

Blessed with 25,000 miles of coastline, Australia suffers no dearth of surf. The most popular stretch of beach for surfing is along the eastern shore, on **Queensland's Gold Coast.** There, within a fairly small area, you'll find legendary

spots that have produced some of surfing's biggest names.

The Gold Coast is characterized by white-sand beaches set off by dark, volcanic rock and vivid, blue-green water. The fine sand makes for fast waves, though wave conditions can change quickly due to beach erosion. **Burleigh Heads** boasts a world-class, right sand-barrel, but the quality of the wave varies from year to year with the shifting bottom sands. This break attracts lots of spectators; when the waves are good, a festive atmosphere prevails.

Another Gold Coast hot spot is **Kirra Point.** Boasting one of the most desirable breaks for regular foots, Kirra offers a tube-oriented wave with a sand-dredging, gaping barrel that gains momentum as it peels down the point. Depending on your skill—or luck—this tube can be a board-breaking cruncher or a sublime experience. Kirra Point is usually crowded, but you can beat the crowd if you arrive early.

Also worthy of a stop is **Duranbah.** Technically part of New South Wales, Duranbah is generally considered part of the Gold Coast. One of the most consistent surf spots in the world, it takes all swells with right and left peaks that range from 6 to 10 feet. It also features one of the world's best beach breaks. Here you'll find perfect shifting and hollow peaks that wind both ways along the beach. With more than one takeoff spot, Duranbah can handle a crowd.

In December, **Wave Sense & Surf Schools International** (*Queensland, Australia. 01161-754-749-076. www.surf-better.com. $250 per person, including meals, accommodations, and local transportation*) offers extended camping surfaris for experienced surfers to breaks from the Gold Coast to northern New South Wales, including Duranbah. Each tour makes its base camp at **Lennox Head;** from there, participants take day trips to the various breaks. Throughout the season, Wave Sense also offers regular surf clinics in the **Noosa Heads** area.

Down the coast is **Byron Bay,** whose tranquil beaches and mellow surfing community have made it a surfer's mecca of sorts. Byron Bay's many coves feature quality point, reef, and beach breaks. **AAA Plus Surf Tours** (*Point Lonsdale, Victoria, Australia. 01161-352-583-026. Tours from $70 per day per person*) offers custom, small-group tours of Byron Bay's breaks as well as coastal areas to the south.

Not to be ignored, Australia's more remote west coast rewards adventuresome visitors with world-class surf in largely unpopulated, pristine settings. The swells here, which gather all the way across the southern Indian Ocean, can be huge and powerful. Be prepared to drive significant distances between breaks on poor and punishing roads. Towns, too, are few and widely scattered, so independent travelers must be equipped for emergencies. Before embarking for the west coast, first-time visitors should consult local surf shops for travel tips and information; check the Internet for listings. **RealSurf** (*www.realsurf.com*) provides daily surf reports for most of Australia. For additional Australian surf links, try **Surfer Resources** (*www.sdsc.edu/surf*).

Let's Go Surfin' Now

Whether you choose to travel with a tour or on your own, the one predictable factor in any surfing holiday is the unpredictability of the waves. But there are a few things you can plan in advance. One of them is finding the right tour to suit your style and expertise, especially if you are bound for exotic or remote locales such as Indonesia, South Africa, or Fiji. For more accessible surf spots — Santa Cruz, Hawaii, or Biarritz, for example — all you really need are a few tips and a local surf report. Additional information on surf camps, resorts, and travel agencies is available online at www.boardingamerica.com/surf/sf__camp.htm.

Baja Surf Adventures
Vista, CA. 800-428-7873 or 760-744-5642
www.bajasurfadventures.com

Since 1992, Baja Surf has offered camping tours to Baja's prime spots for surfers of all levels. Trips run from three days to a month. The company also operates a fully equipped surf camp 200 miles south of the border, near San Quintín. Baja Surf's head instructor, Bill Eastman, has more than 30 years of surfing experience.

Global Surf Travel
Maui, HI. 808-244-1677 or 877-787-3872; (in Australia) 01161-755-200-962
www.globalsurftravel.com

Owned and operated by surfers, Global offers regular group charters to Tavarua and Fiji, plus surf-holiday packages in Europe, the Americas, and the Pacific and Indian Ocean regions. This outfitter features budget camps and luxury boat charters in Indonesia, island fly-ins in Mexico, and excursions to Peru's Pico Alto Surf Camp.

Morris Overseas Tours
Melbourne Beach, FL. 407-725-4809
www.morrisoverseastours.com

One of the oldest surf-tour operators, Morris offers a wide range of trip options, both guided and unguided, at attractive prices. The main destination is Costa Rica, but Morris also provides complete surf-tour packages to Barbados, Ecuador, France and Spain (combined), Mexico, Panama, Peru, the Philippines, Puerto Rico, and South Africa. A typical package includes airfare, vehicle rental, lodging, and maps. Morris is a top choice for Europe as well as South Africa.

Solo Sports Excursions
Irvine, CA. 949-453-1950
www.solosports.net

If you're not the resort type, Solo Sports runs tours for serious surfers who prefer to move from spot to spot. This outfit knows the breaks and hauls its clients—surf teams and television casts and crews among them—in a six-wheel-drive airport transporter to wherever the swells are hitting. Solo Sports also offers windsurfing trips and surf-and-sail tours in Baja. Some trips feature coaching by noted pro surfers. All-inclusive tent-camping tours start at about $1,400 per week per person.

Surf Express
Satellite Beach, FL. 321-779-2124
www.surfex.com

Since 1986, Surf Express has offered customized guided and unguided surf vacations. Owner Carole Holland, whose son surfed the world circuit, knows the best spots, particularly in Central America; most of her staff are also experienced surfers. Costa Rica is the main destination, but Surf Express also covers Barbados, Chile, Ecuador, El Salvador, the Galápagos, Panama, Peru, and Puerto Rico. Holland's outfit will arrange everything from air travel and rental-vehicle reservations to a complete holiday package, depending on your needs.

Surf Travel Company
Cronulla, NSW, Australia
011 61-0-295-274-722. www.surftravel.com

Established in 1984, STC is the official ticket agent for the Australian Surfing Professionals tour circuit. The company offers a broad selection of surf tours throughout the Pacific and Indian Oceans, including Indonesia, the Maldives, Fiji, the Philippines, and the Society Islands. STC covers Indonesia especially well, with both land camps and boat charters. In Fiji, you can choose from several resorts. STC's rates, like its staff, are generally hard to beat.

WaterWays Travel
Van Nuys, CA. 800-928-3757 or 818-376-0341. www.waterwaystravel.com

This travel agency offers to set up just about any surfing vacation, from budget to deluxe. Destinations include Fiji, Indonesia, the Maldives, Western Samoa, Tonga, and Tahiti. Options in Latin America include Peru, with a lodge near Lima, and Ecuador's Galápagos islands. WaterWays offers self-guided packages, including airfare, rental vehicle, meals, and lodging. The staff is professional and knowledgeable about even the most exotic surf spots.

SURFING SCHOOLS

Beginning surfers can save time, avoid bad habits, and preserve their gear by taking some basic lessons from a qualified instructor. A good surf school can also help intermediate wave-riders kick those nasty habits and learn proper techniques for handling different boards and wave conditions. Some of the best schools around are described below.

Club ED International Surf School and Camps
Santa Cruz, CA. 800-287-7873 or 831-459-9283. www.club-ed.com

Established in 1989 by surfer Ed Guzman, Club ED offers private and small-group lessons at $70 per person. Special programs include Baja Surf Camps, held during the Thanksgiving and New Year holidays, and a Costa Rica Surf Camp in November.

Nancy Emerson School of Surfing
Lahaina, HI. 808-873-0264
www.maui.net/~ncesurf

Operating since 1972, Hawaii's leading surf school offers clinics for all levels. Emerson also has a school in Queensland, Australia (*01161-755-907-764*). In addition, Emerson runs tours to Fiji, Indonesia, the Maldives, and Vanuata.

Paskowitz Family Surf Camp
San Clemente, CA. 949-361-9283
www.paskowitz.com

The Paskowitz family founded this renowned center at San Onofre in 1972. Most students register for multiday programs; a five-day surf camp costs $900 per person. Annual winter surfaris include a Cabo San Lucas getaway.

Richard Schmidt School of Surfing
Santa Cruz, CA. 831-423-0928
www.richardschmidt.com

Super surfer Richard Schmidt has directed this excellent program since 1978. Two-hour small-group lessons cost $70 per person. Week-long clinics are $800 per person, all-inclusive with camping.

San Diego Surfing Academy
San Diego, CA. 800-447-7873 or 858-565-6892. www.surfsdsa.com

The academy runs a modern, video-supported clinic with ideal beginner breaks at Cardiff-by-the-Sea in summer and at Pacific Beach and Baja in winter. Lessons start at $25 per hour. Cardiff Surf Camps are $750 per person for one week.

BOOKS

Surfer's Start-Up: A Beginner's Guide to Surfing; Longboard Start-Up: A Guide to Longboard Surfing (Tracks Publishing, $11.95) Simple but solid, Doug Werner's books are well-written and illustrated with helpful photos.

Learn to Surf (Lyons Press, $12.95) James McLaren presents the basics without jargon or surf lingo. A great guide for beginners.

Caught Inside: A Surfer's Year on the California Coast (North Point Press, $12) Daniel Duane's book is an inspired account of a year spent surfing in Santa Cruz.

MAGAZINES

SURFER (800-289-0936. www.surfer-mag.com) and *Surfing* (800-777-5489. www.surfingweb.com) are the best general magazines. *SURFER*'s monthly journal, "The Surf Report," covers the international surf scene, from wave breaks to travel tips, including the best local surf shops. For traditionalists, *Longboard* (800-284-1864) is the voice of the longboard revival.

ONLINE

SUR4
www.sur4.com

Listings include regional surf and marine reports, plus information about surf schools, tours, and resorts; also, an international directory of surf shops.

Surfer Resources
www.sdsc.edu/surf

This site provides an extensive list of surf links, including international websites.

Surfline
www.surfline.com

Check here for accurate surf reports and forecasts for the U.S. mainland, Hawaii, the Caribbean, Mexico, and Central America. Or call 800-928-3463 or 900-976-7873.

Surflink
www.surflink.com

Real-time surf reports; 72-hour forecasts; surf cams; break profiles; competitions.

Surfrider Foundation
www.surfrider.org

Learn more about Surfrider's mission and conservation activities.

Wave Action
www.waveaction.com

This site features content, including photos and destination reports, from the monthly magazine of the same name.

VIDEOS

Learn to Surf and Ocean Safety with Richard Schmidt (60 min., Richard Schmidt. $25, 831-423-0928) Produced by one of the nation's best instructors and shot in California and Hawaii, this video is an excellent tool for newcomers to the sport.

Endless Summer (Available in video stores) Bruce Brown's 1966 classic film remains the standard by which all other surf movies are measured. Highlights include shots of "ultimate" breaks from California to Capetown. With the recent revival of longboarding, the film's surfing scenes no longer seem so dated.

LAST RIDE OF THE DAY ON MAKENA BEACH, MAUI

LOOSELY DEFINED, A TREK IS A WALKING TOUR THROUGH WILD OR PRIMITIVE AREAS. In contrast to the trailside meals and tent accommodations common on a backpacking trip, however, trekkers typically eat and sleep in shelters along the way. This eliminates the need to carry full camping gear—and lightens the trekker's load to only a few pounds. • The classic Himalayan trek takes you from village to village, over high alpine trails: You lodge with the locals, eating with them in the evenings and really getting a taste of their way of life. A trek through the European Alps follows similar kinds of trails, though in Europe you're more likely to spend the evenings in isolated hillside huts or chalets than in villages. • It's easy to organize your own locally guided trek in many locations around the world. But if this isn't for you, there is a popular alternative: You can book a package trek offered by one of the commercial outfitters profiled in the following pages. Whatever your preference, a trekking holiday can be the experience of a lifetime—and this chapter will get you off on the right foot.

LEFT: A WALK ON THE WILD SIDE IN JASPER NATIONAL PARK, ALBERTA.
BELOW: DAY-HIKING IN MOUNT TAMALPAIS STATE PARK, CALIFORNIA.

Guided Treks

Footloose Frolics

Polar Exploring

*The art of Himalayan travel—and indeed of all adventure—
is the art of being bold enough to enjoy life now.*
W. H. MURRAY

Eight Ways to Get Trekking

On city streets or in country lanes, walking brings you closer to the people and places around you. This is especially true when you walk through a less developed country: In places where most people lack cars and therefore get about on foot as well, you can absorb more of the local culture than is possible with any other mode of travel. In short, when you walk into the world of others, you see it through their eyes.

PERU
In the Footsteps of the Incas

For 400 years, **Machu Picchu**—the Lost City of the Incas—eluded western archaeologists. Now, you can discover this imperial city the same way they did: by trekking over the high mountain passes of the Peruvian Andes and along the Camino Inca—**the Inca Trail.**

Following ancient Inca roads and tunnels, the trail rises through cloud forests, condor habitats, and orchid zones to the spectacular 13,700-foot-high Warmihuanusca Pass. After five days of hiking—with nights spent in camps run by local Quechua Indians—you finally arrive at the stone archway called Intipunku: the "gate of the sun." Spread below you—more exotic than any Hollywood set—lies the sacred city of Machu Picchu.

Porters and pack mules carry most of your gear, but the Machu Picchu trek remains a demanding one. And though you will doubtless be anxious to reach this famous site, make sure you spend a few days in the cities first in order to acclimatize your body to the altitude.

Many U.S. outfitters operate Inca Trail treks. **Wildland Adventures** (*3516 N.E. 155th St., Seattle, WA 98155. 800-345-4453 or 206-365-0686. www.wildland.com*) offers a moderately priced package—$2,500 (including air travel within Peru)—from March through November. On Wildland's 15-day itinerary, you trek to Machu Picchu in five days, visit the ancient capital of Cuzco and the modern-day capital of Lima, then travel to the Tambopata-Candamo Reserve Zone. Located in the Amazon Basin, Tambopata-Candamo is a lively jungle habitat, teeming with monkeys and macaws. Wildland also provides optional trips to Manú National Park, which is perhaps the finest nature preserve in the Western Hemisphere.

For a cultural adventure, try Wildland's **Virgen del Carmen Trek**—a week-long procession through the mountains with Quechua Indians; the trek culminates in an Andean village with the celebration of the Virgen del Carmen festival. This one-of-a-kind trekking experience costs approximately $1,900, including local air transportation. From time to time, Wildland also operates a ten-day **Inca Trail Preservation Trek** in summer. The cost is around $1,900, which again includes local air transportation.

Although Machu Picchu is a magnificent destination, the popularity of the site means you will encounter many other trekkers along the way. To avoid the crowds at peak season—July and August—consider the High Andes Circuit Trek run by **Worldwide Adventures** (*1170 Sheppard Ave. W., Unit 45, Toronto, ON M3K 2A3, Canada. 800-387-1483 or 416-633-5666. www.worldwidequest.com*). This 25-day itinerary begins with an exploration of Cuzco and the Sacred Valley of the Incas before following little-used passes up into the magnificent Cordillera Vilcabamba. After a brief visit to Machu Picchu, participants board a train for their next destination: the 20,800-foot-high Nevado Ausangate. Trekkers enjoy spectacular vistas of alpine lakes and glaciers as they make their way along the flanks of the Ausangate. The High Andes Circuit Trek runs all summer and costs about $2,600.

NEPAL
The Annapurna Circuit and Points East

Many veteran trekkers consider the 200-mile **Annapurna Circuit** the ultimate long-distance trek in Nepal. The route encircles the Annapurna Himal—a collection of massive, snow-covered summits rising to around 25,000 feet. While walking the circuit's high mountain passes, you'll see remote villages, rice paddies, and ancient monasteries, as well as glaciers, pine forests, tundra, and the world's deepest valley.

As you begin your Annapurna trek—probably in the Marsyandi River Valley—give yourself time to get used to the elevation. Midway through the trip you'll encounter the Thorong La—at 17,769 feet above sea level, one of the most formidable passes in trekking. Start up the pass in the middle of the night, and you should clear the crest by daybreak. Your reward will shimmer before you: a breathtaking view of the world's tallest mountains glowing in the pastel light of dawn.

The descent on the other side of the pass is a steep one—to the town of Muktinath and its Hindu and Buddhist shrines. From there, you trek through the Kali Gandaki Gorge—a rugged valley three times as deep as the

Grand Canyon—toward Pokhara. Along the way, you'll be treated to continuous views of 26,810-foot Dhaulagiri and other peaks in the Annapurnas. Take time to enjoy the view; Pokhara is the last stop on the circuit before you return to Nepal's capital, Kathmandu.

For your trek in the Annapurnas, you can easily hire your own guide in Kathmandu, who will arrange lodging in villages along your route and cook your meals. Total cost, including lodging, will be $30 to $80 per person per day, depending on the degree of creature comforts you desire. If you prefer more security and structure, a host of seasoned outfitters can take you around the Annapurna Circuit. **Journeys** (*107 Aprill Dr., Suite 3, Ann Arbor, MI 48103. 800-255-8735 or 734-665-4407. www.journeys-intl.com*) offers a 29-day trek—with 19 walking days—that avoids the busy camps and trail bottlenecks. The trek, which takes place in spring and fall, costs $2,600.

One of the most experienced outfitters in Nepal is **Worldwide Adventures** (*800-387-1483. www.worldwidequest. com*). During March and October, Worldwide does the circuit in 26 days at a cost of $2,000. **Mountain Travel-Sobek** (*6420 Fairmount Ave., El Cerrito, CA 94530. 800-227-2384 or 510-527-8100. www.mtsobek.com*) has also been running the circuit for years, and trekkers highly praise its program. Trips run in either spring or fall and last 29 days. Costs start at $2,800 to $3,100, depending on the season and the size of the group.

Trekking activity in Nepal has increased dramatically in the past two decades. In 1972, 2,000 Nepali trekking permits were issued. By 1995, that figure had soared to 65,000. Now, in the peak season of October and November, the busiest trails in the Annapurna area resemble Yellowstone National Park in summertime—with more than 40,000 trekkers passing through annually. Some villages in the lower Annapurna region see as many as 250 trekkers camped out each day.

If you're looking for the road less traveled, don't despair. With 80 percent of commercial trekking confined to 10 percent of the trails, many regions of Nepal remain relatively undiscovered. One such area is the Jaljale Himal, a corner of eastern Nepal that hosts very little activity. Here, you can follow a high-ridge trail that makes for easy walking—and nearly continuous views of four of the world's five highest peaks: Everest, Kanchenjunga, Lhotse, and Makalu.

Above the Clouds (*115 Spencer Hill Rd., Hinesburg, VT 05461. 800-233-4499. www.aboveclouds.com*) pioneered walking tours to the Jaljale region in 1987. The company has a strong commitment to low-impact trekking and the preservation of the traditional Nepali way of life. It offers a fine itinerary and employs top guides, making it a clear choice for a guided trek in the Jaljales.

A TREKKER CROSSES A BAMBOO BRIDGE IN NEPAL.

After a few days' sight-seeing in Kathmandu, you and your trekking group will fly to the town of Tumlingtar, where the trek begins with an easy walk through flat, cultivated fields and across a river. The route visits a bazaar in the pretty town of Chainpur and then a Sherpa village before pushing on to the ridge that is the trekkers' highway above the clouds. The ridge trail takes you through isolated hill villages and a dense rhododendron forest to the Jaljale itself—a spiny mountain range that runs north-south for more than 25 miles.

Coming down from the trail, trekkers follow the Mewa River to the rarely visited town of Topke Gola. Few outsiders ever make it to this ancient trading center in **Xizang (Tibet),** a place where the rhythms of life have remained constant for centuries. The walking part of the tour concludes at Basantpur. From there, the group drives to Biratnagar for the return flight to Kathmandu.

The total adventure lasts 30 days, 23 of which are spent hiking. Trips depart in the fall, and the cost ranges from $2,600 to $3,000, depending on group size.

Another less traveled alternative is the ancient kingdom of Mustang. Perched on the Nepali border with Tibet, this mystery-shrouded region of the Himalaya remained closed to foreigners until 1992. Remote, exotic, and unspoiled, Mustang is a place where Tibetan Buddhism and culture have survived largely undisturbed.

Trekking groups fly from Kathmandu to Pokhara and then on to Jomosom, where the trek begins. Following footworn paths along rivers, cliffs, and high mountain passes, the route combines steep climbs into high altitudes with level passages over farmland. Trekkers visit village marketplaces and ancient monasteries—all set against the magnificent backdrop of Nepal's alpine scenery.

The trip concludes in the 16th-century fortress town of Lo Manthang, whence a helicopter ferries you back to Kathmandu. The trip lasts 18 days and costs $3,850 to $4,350, depending on group size.

If you decide that you'd prefer a longer trekking trip in Nepal—after all, you've traveled halfway around the world to get here—try the Mustang *and* Dolpo package offered by Above the Clouds. This epic journey, which spans 38 days and costs $5,800 to $6,750, augments Mustang with a tour of Dolpo, the dramatically beautiful region that inspired Peter Matthiessen's classic work *The Snow Leopard.* For other recommended treks in the Mustang region, contact Britain's leading trekking company, **Himalayan Kingdoms, Ltd.** (*20 The Mall, Clifton, Bristol BS8 4DR, United Kingdom. 01144-117-923-7163. www.himalayankingdoms.com*).

BHUTAN
Into a Mountain Kingdom

The truly adventurous Himalayan trekker may want to consider another alternative: Bhutan. Located to the east of Nepal, the kingdom of Bhutan is the least visited of the

Himalayan countries. Thanks to strict government regulations, the country is an unspoiled wilderness rich in flora and fauna. On a trek in Bhutan you will find much the same scenery and terrain that you would in Nepal—rain forests, fertile valleys, and glaciers reaching 24,000 feet—but you'll encounter few, if any, other Westerners. You will also witness dramatically less human impact of any kind: The forests remain uncut, covering about two-thirds of the total land area, and wildflowers—including orchids and the rare blue poppy—abound in the country's lush meadows and tropical foothills.

Presently, Bhutan has relatively few trekking areas open to visitors, but a handful of companies do offer guide services on these limited route options. A logical first choice is the outfit that pioneered trekking in Bhutan, **Himalayan Kingdoms, Ltd.** (*20 The Mall, Clifton, Bristol BS8 4DR, England. 01144-117-923-7163. www.himalayankingdoms.com*). The company's specialty is tailor-made trips. In 1999, a quarter of its clients—which have included the British Broadcasting Corporation and the Royal Geographical Society—opted for a custom itinerary.

Himalayan Kingdoms offers excellent regularly scheduled Bhutan treks, too. It runs a dozen or more trips to the mountain kingdom annually, with eight different itineraries. The company's challenging, 25-day **Hidden Kingdom Trek,** for example, explores the remote area around Chomo Lhari on the Bhutan-Tibet border. At around $5,400, the price is high, but this journey—set amidst Bhutan's highest peaks—is a special one that warrants the expense.

Another good choice for Bhutan is **Above the Clouds** (*115 Spencer Hill Rd., Hinesburg, VT 05461. 800-233-4499. www.aboveclouds.com*). It offers five different treks in the country, including a 20-day program called **The Complete Bhutan: West to East** and the spectacular 29-day **Bhutan: Laya and Lunana trek,** a journey across 16,000-foot-high passes into the wildest corner of Bhutan. There is also a ten-day option, timed to coincide with a number of major cultural festivals in Bhutan. The itinerary starts at $1,900—good value in a country where government levies have rendered tourism relatively expensive.

THAILAND
Hill-tribe Odyssey

Do you dream of escaping the world of laws, taxes, and government regulations? In the northwest corner of Thailand—near the junction of the Burmese, Thai, and Laotian borders, home to the celebrated hill tribes of Thailand—you can.

A visit to the mountain retreats of the hill tribes is a unique cultural odyssey. In this remote region, some modern conveniences are gradually being introduced—several villages now have electricity, for example, and a motorbike or truck will occasionally be seen in the larger settlements. For the most part, however, the people here live as they have for hundreds of years, their ancient culture intact.

The center for hill-tribe trekking is the city of **Chiang Mai** in northern Thailand, a day's bus ride from **Krung Thep (Bangkok)** or an hour by plane. A busy commercial center, Chiang Mai is a haven for budget travelers: At one of its many guesthouses, you can book a clean room with a private bath for less than $15 per night.

To find a trekking agency, head for the **Old City,** a walled enclosure on the eastern side of Chiang Mai. There, along **Chaiyapoom Road,** you'll discover a dozen agencies offering guided hill-tribe treks. Competition among these agencies keeps their prices extremely low: Expect to pay roughly $100 per person for a five-day, four-night trek. Price isn't everything, though; the key to finding the best trek is to locate a guide who has established relationships with the local tribes.

After floating to the trailhead on a bamboo raft, you will hike about 15 miles each day. Lunch is usually in a village along the route, with a cooked dinner at the evening's destination. Because you will be staying in village huts, you need carry only a day pack containing your own personal gear. In the winter, though, it's a good idea to bring a sleeping bag: The thatched walls of the huts provide no insulation against the cold night air, and you'll probably find nothing but thin blankets to keep you warm.

Many decent trekking companies run hill-tribe tours. Among them are **Asia Transpacific Journeys** (*2995 Center Green Ct., Boulder, CO 80301. 800-642-2742, 303-443-6789, or 1633. www.southeastasia.com*) employ both local guides and Thai-speaking western tour leaders, who will take you to places not overrun by tourists. If you prefer to combine a trek with a longer, more wide-ranging tour of Thailand, Asia Transpacific can customize an itinerary that includes a visit to the capital, Bangkok, and southern Thailand. In fact, all visitors to the country should explore the lush beaches and mysterious islands in the south.

Asia Transpacific offers a memorable **Explorer's Thailand** tour that captures the best of the north and the south of the country in a single 15-day holiday. The tour combines visits to Bangkok and the **Khao Sok National Park** rain forest with a four-day hill-tribe journey—during which you'll travel by foot, by bamboo raft, and by elephant. And that's only half the adventure: Trekkers also visit legendary **Phangnga Bay** for three days of sea kayaking and camping on remote islands. Depending on group size, the trips costs about $2,500, excluding local air transportation. Book early—this trip has sold out in seasons past.

In addition to its Thailand tours, Asia Transpacific

offers a wide range of guided holidays throughout Southeast Asia, including nearby **Myanmar (Burma)**, Cambodia, Laos, and Vietnam.

An essential piece of equipment for any trip to Thailand is *Thailand: A Travel Survival Kit* from Lonely Planet Publications (*800-275-8563. www.lonelyplanet.com*). Perhaps more than any other single motivator, this resource is responsible for the current mania among adventure travelers for all things Thai.

NEW ZEALAND
Milford and Routeburn Tracks

"The finest walk in the world." That description is frequently applied to the **Milford Track** in New Zealand, where a four-day trek will take you through the Southern Alps and past the fjords—33 miles in all—of the country's South Island.

You can backpack this trek on your own, carrying all your gear and sleeping in basic park service huts along the way. Or you can go with a guided group, staying in guest lodges and eating catered food. If you opt for the latter, you need not carry anything more than a day pack containing a change of clothes, a camera, some toiletries, and—yes—an umbrella. Although this trip is not particularly strenuous, it can be outrageously pluvial.

The trek starts with a boat ride across **Lake Te Anau,**

the gateway to **Fiordland National Park.** From there, the trail follows the Clinton River through deep canyons, glaciated valleys, and rain forests of tree ferns and beeches. Atop McKinnon Pass, your scenery meter may go into overload mode at the vistas of the park's fjords and the snow-capped peaks of the **Southern Alps.**

The Milford Track is so popular that it is often fully booked months in advance (most of the available spaces go to New Zealand's tour companies). To hike the Milford Track, you have two options. Each requires at least six months' notice.

For about $800 (US), you can sign up for a guided six-day tour. You will need to carry only a day pack, and at night you will lodge in deluxe chalets that provide meals and sleeping quarters.

If this sounds a bit too expensive, sign up for the **Freedom Walk,** a self-guided four-day hike. You carry all your own gear—including food and camping equipment—and bed down in rudimentary huts. The Freedom Walk is essentially a backpacking trip, except that you sleep indoors and pay modest hut fees for the privilege. Packs and other equipment can be rented from a number of shops in **Queenstown**—the departure point for the bus to Lake Te Anau.

Milford Track outings can be booked in the United

States. Contact the **New Zealand Tourism Board** (*501 Santa Monica Blvd., Suite 300, Santa Monica, CA 90401. 800-388-5494 or 310-395-7480. www.purenz.com*) for a list of booking agencies. Request the Milford Track information packet, and specify whether you want a guided tour or a self-guided tour. For reservations and information on self-guided treks, you can also contact the Department of Conservation's **Great Walks Booking Desk** (*P.O. Box 29, Te Anau, New Zealand. 01164-3249-8514. www.doc.govt.nz*).

Another trek in this part of the South Island that merits the blisters is the **Routeburn Track,** set amid the spectacular scenery of **Mount Aspiring National Park** and **Fiordland National Park.** The 25-mile Routeburn begins with a steady ascent through a forest of beech trees and along a river gorge. The trail then climbs to the 4,190-foot-high **Harris Saddle.** Here, hikers enter an Alpine world full of wildflowers and even wilder views: Below lies the richly forested **Hollyford Valley;** beyond that, the glaciated **Darran Mountains** stretch to the sea. The last part of the journey is an easy meander through woods and past waterfalls and lakes to the trail's end.

The Routeburn is best hiked in the austral summer—December through February. Snow blocks the track in winter, and parts of it are susceptible to avalanches. Independent travelers can do the Routeburn on their own. The trailhead is easy to access by bus from Queenstown, and for just $35 per night you can stay in four well-maintained huts that are supervised by wardens throughout the summer months. As on the Milford Track, however, keep in mind that these huts are far from luxurious. Even though they are equipped with stoves, running water, and flush toilets, the structures were designed for those interested in "backpacking with a roof."

If you want more comfort—not to mention privacy—sign up for a guided commercial trek. Trekkers on the guided tour stay in comfortable lodges, replete with private rooms, hot-water showers, and catered meals. If you can spare the time, consider hiking the **Grand Traverse,** a combination of the Routeburn Track and the **Greenstone Track.** This 45-mile trek crosses the Southern Alps, treating walkers to alpine views, riverside trails, and lakeside accommodations. Plan on taking five to six days to complete it.

Routeburn Walk Ltd. (*P.O. Box 568, Queenstown, New Zealand. 01164-3442-8200. www.routeburn.co.nz*) is the only guide service on the Routeburn and Grand Traverse treks. You can also contact the **New Zealand Tourism Board** for a list of booking agencies for Routeburn Walks Ltd., as well as application forms for independent treks (which should be reserved well in advance).

Hikers interested in independent treks can also contact the **Great Walks Booking Desk** for information and trekking applications.

AUSTRIA
Tyrolian Hut to Hut

Trekking through the Alps offers spectacular scenery devoid of the logistical hassles and health risks associated with trekking in Asia. Trekking without a guide is also easy—again, certainly not the case in the Himalaya.

Although commercial programs in the Alps have tended to concentrate on Switzerland (Bernese Oberland) and France (Haute Route), Austria is a wonderful choice for an Alpine trek. The prices here are lower than those in Switzerland or France, the people are friendly, and—most important—the huts tend to be less crowded during the busy summer season.

The Austrian hut system is remarkable. There are more than 500 huts in the Tirol region alone, and they range from basic to deluxe. All provide blankets and mattresses, and most serve food. At $18 to $30 per night, the cost of overnighting in a hiking hut is eminently reasonable. And if you join the **Austrian Alpine Club**—Der Oesterreichische Alpenverein—(*Wilhelm-Greil-Strasse 15, A-6010 Innsbruck, Austria. 01143-51258-7828*) you can get a discount of 50 percent on any stay in a club-managed hut. If you understand German, check out the catalog of huts online at www.alpenverein. at/huette/index.htm.

Caveat trekkor: Hiking in the Alps requires good conditioning. Most trails are located above 6,000 feet, and you may have to climb 2,500 feet or more to reach your destination. Offsetting that is the multiplicity of hiking options in Austria. Many huts can be reached in a short day hike from ridges served by cable cars or ski lifts.

More adventurous trekkers will want to sample the **Weitwanderweg**—a 750-mile-long pathway that traverses Austria from one end to the other. Not all of the Weitwanderweg is appropriate for trekking, but the section south of Innsbruck passes through the **Stubaier** and **Zillertaler Alpen** and the mountains around **Grossvenediger,** all of which are premier trekking destinations.

Planning your own Austrian Alps trek is easy. A comprehensive directory of huts and alpine clubs can be obtained from the **Austrian National Tourist Office** (*P.O. Box 1142, New York, NY 10108. 212-944-6880. www.anto.com*). Request the *Tirol Mountains* booklet, a 70-page guide to hiking and trekking in the Tirol that covers mountaineering schools, recommended hikes, huts, and local history. In Austria itself, there are numerous Tirol Tourism Offices with English-speaking staffers who can supply hiking maps and detailed information on local inns, guesthouses, and the hut network.

If you prefer a commercially guided trek, **Wanderweg Holidays** (*519 Kings Croft, Cherry Hill, NJ 08034. 800-270-2577 or 856-321-1040. www.wanderwegholidays.com*) offers the

SCALING THE SOUTHERN ALPS FOR A VIEW OF LAKE WANAKA

most itineraries and the longest season of any American operator serving the Tirol. During a typical weeklong Wanderweg holiday, you'll hike a variety of high-country routes, spending each evening in a comfortable chalet. The company stages its trips from early spring through fall at affordable rates.

In Austria, both the Tirol Tourism Offices and Austrian Alpine Club can direct you to local guides, who lead Alpine walking tours. These treks last two days to two weeks and suit wallets from fat to thin.

NORWAY
Mountains and Fjords

Blessed by glaciated mountains and world-famous fjords, Norway offers enough trekking options to last a lifetime. The Norwegians have done everything they can to maximize enjoyment of this wonderful natural environment. The country boasts a well-maintained system of trails and comfortable trekking lodges. Norway's numerous national parks have traceries of well-posted hiking routes, as well as virtually unlimited opportunities for off-the-beaten-path orienteering.

The government subsidizes an outdoors club called **Den Norske Turistforening** (*www.turistforeningen.no*), which offers guided treks at reasonable prices in most regions of Norway. DNT's guides are friendly and knowledgeable, and nearly all of them speak some English. Participants on DNT treks usually stay in fully provisioned lodges; many of these are traditional grass-roofed log farmhouses that have been converted into hikers' huts.

To join a DNT trek, you must be a member of the **Norwegian Hiking Association,** which you can join for approximately $45. Not surprisingly, most of your fellow trekkers on a DNT outing will be native Norwegians—and they hike at a fast pace. Don't let this worry you, though; DNT treks are not road races. Americans—even those who are quite fit—should simply plan on adding an hour to DNT's estimated daily hiking times. For more information, contact the **Tourist Board of Norway** (*212-885-9700. www.goscandinavia.com*).

One DNT trek in south-central Norway explores the mountainous **Rondane National Park.** The park is known for the beauty of its rugged scenery, where large terraces of sand and gravel are interspersed with narrow canyons, rivers, and steep-walled mountains. Scrub vegetation, dwarf birch, and heather are the dominant plants, while lichen-covered rocks—and often snow—cover the landscape.

As the heather and berry bushes turn color in the fall, Rondane grows resplendent with yellows and reds. In the summer, vibrant wildflowers spring up amidst the subtler hues of the perennials. The Rondane trek, which takes eight days and departs in June and August, costs in the region of $510 per person.

For hard-core hikers, DNT offers a rigorous itinerary that explores the **Jotunheimen range**—the so-called "home of the giants." Located approximately 50 miles southwest of Rondane National Park, Jotunheimen National Park is an impressive expanse of mountains, glaciers, lakes, and waterfalls.

The trek begins in the southern edge of the mountain range and ends with a climactic ascent of 8,100-foot-high **Galdhøpiggen**—the highest mountain in Norway. Challenging changes in elevation mark the route, which passes through alpine lakes and valleys, steep gorges, moors, snowfields, and high mountain ridges—all of them affording excellent views of Jotunheimens' glaciers and peaks. Four different trips—ranging in length from five to eight days and in cost from $380 to $510 per person—depart from June through August.

If you'd like to include a major fjord in your trek, consider DNT's **Aurlandsdalen** trip. Hiking through Norway's "great divide"—the mountain range that splits the country lengthwise into eastern and western halves—trekkers are treated to views of towering cliffs, plunging waterfalls, windswept plateaus, and valleys carpeted in green. As you hike through a variety of ecosystems, you'll travel from marshland to mountaintops, meandering along high ridges, lakeside routes, and cliffside paths.

The trip culminates at the head of the majestic 127-mile-long Sognefjorden. From there the group makes its way to Oslo, Norway's capital, on the famous Flåm railway; along part of the route, in 50 minutes of thrilling switchbacks, the train climbs nearly 3,000 feet over a 12-mile stretch of track. This strenuous, seven-day trip—costing around $670 per person, with departures in July and August—can be booked through **Borton Overseas** (*5412 Lyndale Ave. S., Minneapolis, MN 55419. 800-843-0602 or 612-822-4640. www.bortonoverseas.com*).

For a gentler pace, hikers may want to consider the **Heart of Norway Trek,** a six-day hike through Jotunheimen National Park offered by **Destination Wilderness** (*P.O. Box 1965, Sisters, OR 97759. 800-423-8868 or 541-549-1336. www.wildernesstrips.com*). The route runs through valleys populated with hanging glaciers and sparkling alpine streams. The pace is moderate, elevation gains are modest, and—on an optional seventh day—participants can cap off the trek by rafting the **Sjoa River** or climbing the **Glittertind,** Norway's second highest mountain. The trip costs $1,240 ($1,390 for the seven-day version) and features overnights in Norwegian lodges—some operated by DNT, others privately owned.

CHILE
Patagonian Wilderness

Patagonia is the Alps, Yosemite National Park, and Alaska all rolled into one. In **Torres del Paine National Park,** razor-sharp pinnacles of granite climb more than a mile high into the clouds, and Alaskan-scale glaciers cut through forested valleys on their way to the Pacific Ocean, where they calve enormous blocks of ice into the frigid waters of the sea. Among such icy progeny is the **Glacier Moreno**—a sheer wall of white the size of a city that dominates the horizon for miles.

Patagonia is spectacular, and it is cold. Any first-time visitor should be prepared for a harsh climate characterized by bone-chilling winds and extremely changeable weather conditions. In this southern stretch of the Andes, you can experience rain, snow, sleet, and sunshine in the span of a hour. As long as you keep this reality in mind—and don't expect to come home with a suntan—you'll not be disappointed.

Although Patagonia can't be considered a mainstream trekking destination, there is a good selection of commercially led trips. One noteworthy Patagonian trek is offered by **Wilderness Travel** (*1102 9th St., Berkeley, CA 94710. 800-368-2794 or 510-558-2488. www.wildernesstravel.com*). The company's 20-day expedition is a masterly blend of great scenery and high adventure.

In addition to four days in Torres del Paine (with overnights in a backcountry lodge) and four days camping near the **Fitzroy Massif,** participants visit **Lapataia National Park** along the Beagle Canal. They also sail up **Last Hope Sound** to the face of **Cerro Balmaceda**—the southern tip of Patagonia's continental ice cap.

This program runs from November through February and costs approximately $4,000. Condor sightings are virtually guaranteed during your stay; other indigenous species you're likely to spot include pumas, guanacos (Chilean llamas), and Andean foxes.

Of the American outfitters who run treks in Chile, few offer as many options as **Wildland Adventures** (*800-345-4453. www.wildland.com*). The company's five Patagonia itineraries range from lodge-based nature trips to adventurous hikes through remote backcountry. For the rugged traveler, Wildland's 12-day, $2,050 Torres del Paine trek takes participants through the heart of the park, where they feast their eyes on unforgettable scenery. The route passes beneath the granite walls and peaks of the **Torres** and **Cuernos del Paine,** skirting lakes, glaciers, meadows, and waterfalls.

Wildland's Torres del Paine trip offers outstanding photo opportunities, including a boat cruise across dramatic, iceberg-studded **Lago de Grey.** Wildland can augment any of its Patagonian peregrinations with other activities such as river rafting, horseback riding, or sea kayaking.

The Ultimate in Trekking Companies

In this section you'll find a list of trekking companies that run well-organized trips to exotic locations all around the world. Some tend to specialize in particular destinations—Asia and the Himalaya, for example—while other companies, covering more of the globe, can take you virtually anywhere.

Before leaving on a trek—even an independent one—you should contact the trekking companies below and study their catalogs carefully. Not only does the literature give you some good basic itineraries, it indicates routes overly trafficked by tourists: If you find ten companies going to the same place at the same time of year, you may want to steer clear of that location. Consider all options; there's plenty to see in Nepal or the Andes without having to follow in anyone's footsteps.

Above the Clouds
115 Spencer Hill Rd., Hinesburg, VT 05461
800-233-4499. www.aboveclouds.com
DESTINATIONS: Alps (Mt. Blanc), Bhutan, England, France, India (Ladakh), Italy, Nepal (Everest, Kanchenjunga), Patagonia (Chile, Argentina).
PROGRAMS: Unique itineraries in less traveled regions. Very knowledgeable staff and guides. Runs its own trips. 23 days in Nepal: approx. $2,900.

Adventure Center
1311 63rd St., Suite 200, Emeryville, CA 94608. 800-227-8747 or 510-654-1879
www.adventurecenter.com
DESTINATIONS: Alps, Borneo, Greece, India, Morocco (Atlas Mountains), Nepal (Everest, Annapurna Himal, Langtang Valley), New Zealand, Peru (Inca Trail), Portugal, Spain, Tanzania (Kilimanjaro), Thailand, Turkey (Lycia), Vietnam.
PROGRAMS: Vast inventory of trips from a number of operators worldwide. 23 days in Nepal: from $1,500.

Himalayan Kingdoms, Ltd.
20 The Mall, Clifton, Bristol BS8 4DR, England. 01144-117-923-7163
www.himalayankingdoms.com
DESTINATIONS: The Himalaya—Arunachal Pradesh, Bhutan, Garhwal, Himachal Pradesh, the Hindu Kush, the Karakoram, Ladakh, Mustang, Nepal, Sikkim, Tibet, Zanskar. Also China (Tien Shan), Mongolia, Thailand, and Vietnam.
PROGRAMS: Britain's leading trekking company, Himalayan Kingdoms pioneered routes in Bhutan and Tibet. It offers custom itineraries for private groups. 24 days in Nepal: approx. $2,900.

Himalayan Travel
110 Prospect St., Stamford, CT 06901
800-225-2380 or 203-359-3711
www.gorp.com/himtravel
DESTINATIONS: Africa (Morocco, Kilimanjaro), Alps, Bhutan, France, Great Britain, Greece, India (Ladakh, Sikkim), Italy, Nepal (Annapurna, Everest, Kanchenjunga), Peru (Huayhuash Range, Machu Picchu), Spain (Pyrenees, Sierra Nevada), Tibet, Turkey (Mount Ararat).
PROGRAMS: Experienced agency with attractive prices. Affiliated with many good foreign outfitters. 23 days in Nepal: $1,965.

Journeys
107 Aprill Dr., Suite 3, Ann Arbor, MI 48103
800-255-8735 or 734-665-4407
www.journeys-intl.com
DESTINATIONS: Argentina, Bhutan, Chile, Costa Rica, India (Ladakh), Indonesia (Irian Jaya), Kenya, Madagascar, Mexico, Namibia, Nepal (Annapurna Himal), Panama, Peru, Tanzania (Kilimanjaro), Tibet, Vietnam.
PROGRAMS: Able guides, many of them trained naturalists. Excellent customer support. 29 days in Nepal: $2,600.

Mountain Travel-Sobek
6420 Fairmont Ave., El Cerrito, CA 94530
800-227-2384 or 510-527-8100
www.mtsobek.com
DESTINATIONS: Africa (Kenya, Tanzania), Alps (Mont Blanc circuit, North Face Route), Bhutan, Canadian Rockies, Chile (Patagonia), France (Provence), Italy, Nepal (Annapurna Himal, Everest, Mustang), Papua New Guinea, Peru (Cordillera Blanca, Inca Trail), Spain, Switzerland, Tibet, Venezuela (Lost World). 29 days in Nepal: $2,800.

REI Adventures
P.O. Box 1938, Sumner, WA 98390
800-622-2236 or 253-437-1100
www.rei.com/travel
DESTINATIONS: Alps (Mont Blanc), Chile, France (Provence), Nepal (Annapurna Himal, Dolpo, Everest), Peru (Machu Picchu), Turkestan. Many other wilderness or inn-to-inn hiking programs in North America and Europe (Germany, Greece, Italy, Switzerland).
PROGRAMS: Trips are well planned with good logistics; multiactivity itineraries in Alaska, Belize, California, Hawaii, Canada, Costa Rica. 19 days in Nepal: $3,000.

Wilderness Travel
1102 Ninth St., Berkeley, CA 94710
800-368-2794 or 510-558-2488
www.wildernesstravel.com
DESTINATIONS: Africa (Kilimanjaro, Serengeti, Zimbabwe), Alps (Mont Blanc, Chamonix Haute Route, Bernese Traverse), Argentina (Patagonia), Borneo, Ecuador, England, France, India (Rajasthan), Indonesia, Iran, Italy, Jordan, Nepal (Annapurna Himal, Dolpo, Everest), New Zealand, Peru (Cordillera Blanca, Machu Picchu, Urubamba Valley), Spain (Basque region), Syria, Tibet (Lhasa), Turkey.
PROGRAMS: Good customer service and a wide choice of less traveled destinations. Strong in South America. 27 days in Nepal: about $2,300.

Wildland Adventures
3516 N.E. 155th St., Seattle, WA 98155
800-345-4453 or 206-365-0686
www.wildland.com
DESTINATIONS: Bolivia, Botswana, Chile, Ecuador (Amazon, Andes), Peru (Colca Canyon, Lago Titicaca, Manu National Park, Tambopata-Candamo Reserve Zone), Tanzania, U.S. (Alaska), Zimbabwe.
PROGRAMS: Many less traveled destinations. Strong emphasis on ecology and native cultures. Excellent local guides.

Worldwide Adventures
1170 Sheppard Ave. W., Unit 45, Toronto, ON M3K 2A3, Canada. 800-387-1483 or 416-633-5666. www.worldwidequest.com

SOLITUDE ON A BEATEN PATH IN MOUNT TAMALPAIS STATE PARK, CALIFORNIA

DESTINATIONS: Argentina, Bhutan, China, India (Ladakh, Sikkim), Nepal (Annapurna Himal, Dolpo, Everest, Langtang Valley, Mustang), Pakistan (K2), Peru (Cordillera Vilcabamba, Machu Picchu), Tibet, Vietnam.

PROGRAMS: Seasoned operator with strong program in South America. Worldwide's parent company, World Expeditions, is extremely active in Nepal. 23 days in Nepal: $2,400.

HONORABLE MENTIONS

Adventure Women (*15033 Kelly Canyon Rd., Bozeman, MT 59715. 800-804-8686 or 406-587-3883. www.adventure-women.com*) specializes in trips for women over 30; many popular walking itineraries.

Asia Transpacific Journeys (*2995 Center Green Ct., Boulder, CO 80301. 800-642-2742 or 303-443-6789. www.southeastasia.com*) is the top outfitter for Southeast Asia, especially Thailand and Indonesia. Excellent multiactivity and multicountry holidays.

Sierra Club Outing Department (*85 2nd St., 2nd Floor, San Francisco, CA 94105. 415-977-5630. www.sierraclub.org/outings*) offers walking tours and classic treks; among its trips are the Alps, Belize, Costa Rica, England, Guatemala, Mexico, Norway (fjord region), and Peru.

OUTFITTED TREKS

On virtually all commercial treks, you will be accompanied by a guide familiar with the region in which you'll be hiking. A good guide will have hiked the route at least once, and he or she will have arranged lodging in the villages or outposts on the itinerary. It is crucial that your guide speak the local language(s) or have an assistant who does.

Typically you'll stay in a hotel on the first and last nights of the trip. Field accommodations include tea houses, mountain huts, or even movable shelters such as yurts or tents. You'll sleep on mats or thin mattresses, with bedding provided by the outfitter. If you are headed for a cold area, bring a quality sleeping bag and perhaps a traveler's pillow as well.

Food becomes a major focus when you're walking 10 to 20 miles a day. Your guide or village host will prepare meals for the whole group, with hot, hearty food for breakfast and dinner. Before leaving home, stuff the corners of your pack with nonperishable goodies you're unlikely to find on the trail, such as nuts, candy, and chocolate.

The latest trend in commercial treks is the multiactivity tour. In Thailand, for instance, treks now feature elephant rides and cruises on bamboo rafts or long-tail boats. In South America, some deluxe treks include river rafting. Tours in New Zealand combine trekking with mountain biking or rafting. These options are fun, but they can boost a trek's price by 20 percent or more.

Before setting off on a commercial tour, try to talk with a few past customers; they're apt to share key information that appears in no catalog. Ask about what to wear, how much pocket money you'll need, what the weather was like, how steep (or how crowded) the trails are, how spartan or cushy the food and lodging. Satisfy yourself that this is the trip for you.

Don't rule out a tour because you think it might be too rough, however. The best treks are those that go to remote areas whose inhabitants don't see many western-

Polar Exploring

Cold, remote, and forbidding, the Earth's poles have galvanized explorers past and present. From quests by early navigators for the Northwest Passage to recent assaults on the North and South Poles by dogsled, snowmobile, and skis, polar exploration has long been considered the ultimate human challenge. Few have been equal to it: In 1995, to cite only the most recent example, no less an adventurer than Reinhold Messner—considered by many to be the greatest mountaineer of all time—failed in his overland attempt to reach the North Pole.

Where does that leave lesser mortals? For starters, definitely in need of some outside assistance. With the help of experts in polar exploration, you can experience the excitement of standing atop the world—or the challenge of venturing deep into the heart of Antarctica.

Each year, aerial expeditions transport well-heeled clients to the geographic North Pole, while hardy adventurers reach the magnetic North Pole by snowmobile. Getting to the South Pole—whose notoriously fierce and unpredictable weather makes an aerial approach risky—is a much more daunting proposition. Nonetheless, Antarctica is definitely on the adventure map: Every meridional summer (December 21 to March 20), special expedition cruises navigate the waters of the world's highest, driest, coldest, and windiest continent, while experienced mountaineering teams tackle its icy summits.

Speaking of steep, such adventures have lofty price tags. Antarctic cruises start around $9,000 per person, while a major Antarctic overland or climbing expedition can easily cost double or triple that amount. For those intent on experiencing the otherworldly beauty of the polar regions, however, the price of adventure is seldom too great. The companies listed below all specialize in polar exploration.

Arctic and Antarctic Adventure Programs

Adventure Network International
Canon House, 27 London End,
Beaconsfield, Bucks. HP9 2HN, United
Kingdom 01144-1494-671808
www.adventure-network.com

This is the best company providing support for serious overland or climbing expeditions in Antarctica. The company can handle everything from polar expeditions to snowmobile refueling, and it maintains a fleet of expedition aircraft flown by top wilderness pilots.

Quark Expeditions
980 Post Road, Darien, CT 06820
800-356-5699 or 203-656-0499
www.quark-expeditions.com

Quark specializes in travel to remote areas that are not normally accessible to tourists. The company makes up to five vessels available for expeditions to Antarctica and three to the Arctic. Ranging in length from 235 to 495 feet, the ships hold 36 to 108 passengers in moderate comfort. To reach the North Pole, Quark even uses a helicopter-equipped nuclear-powered icebreaker that once belonged to the Soviet Navy. Unless you have the wherewithal to charter your own submarine—Soviet or otherwise—this is the only way to reach the North Pole by sea.

MUSHING ACROSS THE CANADIAN ARCTIC

High Arctic International Explorer Services, Ltd.
P.O. Box 200, Resolute Bay, Northwest
Territories Z0A 0V0, Canada. 867-252-3875.

If you need a base facility for an expedition to the North Pole, contact High Arctic. For years this operation has supported successful polar expeditions, including many of the aerial assaults on the pole. High Arctic no longer offers guided polar trips, but it can help you organize a polar undertaking of your own. The company can also provide accommodations and expedition support. Lodging costs $170 (CN) per person per night, including all meals.

Mad Dog Expeditions
132 East 82nd St., New York, NY 10028. 212-744-6763. www.mad-dog.net

Ready for a dip in 28°F water with 200 feet visibility? If so, Mad Dog is for you. The company organizes ice-diving expeditions in the Canadian High Arctic—a unique trip for those seeking the ultimate in extreme underwater adventure. Trips operate in May and June and cost about $5,500 for a week of unlimited diving (or as much as you can stand).

ers. Naturally, such treks can be arduous: You may have to walk more miles, climb steeper hills, and carry a heavier pack; the days may be hotter, the nights colder, the beds harder. But enduring such hardships may give you the chance to experience societies not yet changed by the modern world.

TREKKING ON YOUR OWN

World-Class Destinations
for Independent Trekkers

There are alternatives to traveling in large groups or on well-trodden paths. Rather than booking a packaged trek through a travel company based in your home country, you can go it alone. In many parts of the world, it's no problem to sign on with a local outfitter or hire your own guide—and, if needed, a porter. Not only is this option cheaper, it puts you in control: You determine group size, distance, and pace.

Listed below are some top spots for do-it-yourself hikes, each with recommended treks and suggestions for the best guidebooks to help plan your trip. Most of these resources are available **AdventurousTraveler.com** (800-282-3963. *www.adventuroustraveler.com*). If you can't decide whether to trek independently or travel with an organized group, contact some of the better trekking companies serving your region of choice. Often they have the most recent information on environmental and political conditions in the trekking areas, and their literature describes each region's popular routes and cultural highlights. You can also use online bulletin boards to solicit first-hand reports from travelers who have recently returned from overseas. Active message boards can be found at Away.com and at America Online's Travel Channel.

THE ALPS

Guide Needed for Glacier Routes Only

RECOMMENDED TREKS: Mont Blanc circuit, Haute Route, Bernese Oberland (Alpine Pass Route).

WHEN TO GO: May through September (August is very crowded).

GUIDEBOOKS: *Chamonix-Mont Blanc: A Walking Guide* by Martin Collins (Cicerone Press, $22.95); *Chamonix to Zermatt: The Walker's Haute Route* by Kev Reynolds (Cicerone Press, $16.95); *Tour of Mont Blanc* by Andrew Harper (Cicerone

Press, $19.95); *Walking the Valais* by Kev Reynolds (Cicerone Press, $24).

CONTACT: **Switzerland Tourism** (*608 5th Ave., New York, NY 10020. 212-757-5944. www.switzerlandtourism.com*); **Fédération Française de la Randonnée Pédestre** (*14 rue Riquet, 75019 Paris, France. 011331-4489-9393. www.ffrp.asso.fr*).

CANADA

No Guide Needed

RECOMMENDED TREKS: Hundreds of superb trails snake through Glacier, Yoho, Kootenay, Banff, and Waterton National Parks, near the border between British Columbia and Alberta. Consult a guidebook for suggested routes. The towns of Golden and Radium Hot Springs in B.C. are convenient staging points.

WHEN TO GO: Mid-May through mid-September.

GUIDEBOOKS: *The Canadian Rockies Trail Guide* by Brian Patton and Bart Robinson (Summerthought Publishers, $14.95); *103 Hikes in Southwestern British Columbia* by Mary and David Macaree (The Mountaineers, $14.95).

CONTACT: **Super Natural British Columbia** (*800-663-6000. www.travel.bc.ca*); **Travel Alberta** (*800-661-8888. www.explorealberta.com*); **Mountain Equipment Co-op** (*Vancouver, B.C. 800-663-2667. www.mec.ca*).

TOO COOL: Heli-hiking is the newest way to explore B.C.'s high country. Contact **Golden Alpine Holidays** (*Golden. 250-344-7273. www.goldenalpineholidays.com*) or **Canadian Mountain Holidays** (*800-661-0252. www.cmhhike.com*). Canadian mountain trips cost $1,060 for three nights and $2,000 for six. Multiday trips include deluxe chalet lodging, helicopter flights, and all meals. Hikers carry only a day pack.

GREECE

No Guide Needed

RECOMMENDED TREKS: Crete, Pindos Mountains, Óros Olympos (Olympus), the Peloponnesus. Inexpensive pension (family hotel) accommodations are available, but stay away from the major tourist areas.

WHEN TO GO: April through October.

GUIDEBOOKS: *Rough Guide to Greece* by Ellingham, Dubin, Jansz, and Fisher

(Rough Guides, $19.95); *Trekking in Greece* by Marc Dubin (Lonely Planet, $15.95).

CONTACT: **Greek National Tourist Organization** (*645 5th Ave., New York, NY 10022. 212-421-5777. www.gnto.gr*).

JAPAN

No Guide Needed

RECOMMENDED TREKS: Japan Alps (Akaishi Mountains), Mount Fuji, Kiryu-Ashio, Nikko.

WHEN TO GO: Late spring, when the flowers are in bloom, through mid-fall.

GUIDEBOOKS: *Exploring Kiryu, Ashio, and Nikko: Mountain Walks in the Land of Shodo Shonin* by Michael Plastow (Weatherhill Press, $19.95); *Hiking in Japan: An Adventurer's Guide to the Mountain Trails* by Paul Hunt (Kodansha, $17).

CONTACT: **Japan National Tourist Organization** (*515 S. Figueroa St., Suite 1470, Los Angeles, CA 90071. 213-623-1952. www.jnto.go.jp*). Trail maps available.

NEPAL

Local Guide Recommended

RECOMMENDED TREKS: Annapurna Sanctuary, Everest Valley approach, Gorkha area loop.

WHEN TO GO: Travel in Nepal is possible year-round, but it's best to cross the high passes in early fall or late spring. In December and January, trek only in the lower elevations—those below 10,000 feet. Summer is the rainy season.

GUIDEBOOKS: *The Trekking Peaks of Nepal* by Bill O'Connor (Cloudcap, $24.95); *Trekking in the Annapurna Region* by Bryn Thomas (Trailblazer, $18.95); *Trekking in the Everest Region* by Jamie McGuinness (Trailblazer, $15.95); *Trekking in the Nepal Himalaya* by Stan Armington (Lonely Planet, $17.95).

CONTACT: Numerous guide services are available in Kathmandu. A guide and a porter can be engaged for a total of less than $45 per day. Alternatively, contact **Tibet Travels and Tours** (*P.O. Box 7246, Tridevi Marg, Kathmandu, Nepal. 0119771-249140. www.tibettravels.com*) when you arrive in Kathmandu.

NEW ZEALAND

No Guide Needed

RECOMMENDED TREKS: Nelson Lakes National Park, Mount Aspiring

National Park, Mount Cook Traverse, Routeburn Track, Milford Track. Advance reservations are recommended for the Routeburn and Milford routes, which operate commercially.

WHEN TO GO: Late February to early March (fall in New Zealand) is probably the best time. The sunshine is more consistent, and most of the tourists have gone.

GUIDEBOOKS: *Classic Tramps in New Zealand* by Constance Roos (Cicerone Press, $28.95); *Tramping in New Zealand* by Jim DuFresne (Lonely Planet, $17.95).

CONTACT: New Zealand Tourism Board (*501 Santa Monica Blvd., Suite 300, Santa Monica, CA 90401. 800-388-5494 or 310-395-7480. www.purenz.com*); **Great Walks Booking Desk** (*Dept. of Conservation, P.O. Box 29, Te Anu, New Zealand. 011643-249-8514. www.doc.govt.nz*).

NORWAY

No Guide Needed

RECOMMENDED TREKS: Rondane National Park, Jotunheimen National Park, Hardangerfjorden, Sognefjorden, Lofoten Islands.

WHEN TO GO: May through September.

GUIDEBOOKS: *Climbing in the Magic Islands: A Climbing and Hiking Guide to the Lafoten Islands of Norway* by Ed Webster (Nord Norsk Klatreskole, $35.95); *Mountain Hiking in Norway* by Erling Welle-Strand (Nortrabooks, $23.95); *Walking in Norway* by Constance Roos (Cicerone Press, $21.95) features 20 walking routes in the major mountain areas.

CONTACT: Tourist Board of Norway (*P.O. Box 4649, Grand Central Station, New York, NY 10163. 212-885-9700. www.goscandinavia.com*). See also **Den Norske Turistforening** (*www. turistforeningen.no*).

TASMANIA

No Guide Needed

RECOMMENDED TREKS: Overland Track (Cradle Mountain-Lake St. Clair National Park, Cynthia Bay-Mount Ossa), South Coast Track. On popular tracks, ask about the availability of the local trampers' shuttle service, which can drop you off at a trailhead and pick you up at appointed time.

WHEN TO GO: November through March. Conditions can be soggy at any time of the year, but February often sees the most sunshine. When it's rainy in the highlands it can be balmy on the coast, so try to stay flexible.

GUIDEBOOKS: *100 Walks in Tasmania* by Tyrone Thomas (Hill of Content Press, $15.95); *Tasmania: Australia Guide* by John Chapman (Lonely Planet, $14.95).

CONTACT: Australian Tourist Commission (*Environment and Land Management Department. Attn.: The Department of Lands, Parks and Wildlife, 134 Macquarie St., GPO Box 44A, Hobart, 7000, Tasmania, Australia. www.atc.net.au*).

TURKEY

Local Guide Recommended

RECOMMENDED TREKS: Lycia Lakes District, Taurus Mountains/Alagdaglar (Mount Ararat). Renting a car is advised if you plan to visit multiple locations in Asiatic Turkey.

WHEN TO GO: Travel is possible year-round, but late spring into early summer offers temperate conditions and the chance to see wildflowers.

GUIDEBOOKS: *The Mountains of Turkey* by Karl Smith (Cicerone Press, $29.95); *Mount Ararat Region* map and booklet (West Col Productions, $19.95; order from www.omnimap.com).

CONTACT: Turkish Government Tourist Office (*821 United Nations Plaza, New York, NY 10017. 212-687-2194. www.tourismturkey.org*). Visas available for $45.

TREK FREE

When and Why to Light Out on Your Own

Most commercially run treks cost $75 to $175 per day. This covers a guide, land transportation, food, and lodging. If you're willing to carry your own sleeping bag and some minimal cooking gear, however, you can follow the same routes as many of the commercial treks for a fraction of the price.

In Nepal, for example, you can easily hire your own guide in Kathmandu. This person will arrange lodging in villages along your route and cook your meals, keeping the total cost of the trek to as little as $25 per person per day.

In New Zealand, where some companies charge $100 or more per day to hike the Routeburn Track or the Milford Track, you can cover the same itinerary on a self-guided tour—staying at Alpine huts en route—for less than $35 per night. You'll need to carry only a sleeping bag and food (cooking gear is available in the huts).

On a hike through Austria or Switzerland, a little homework and some advance planning can yield a self-guided hut-to-hut trek that costs less than $40 per day, including food.

Economy is obviously the big reason to organize your own trek, but you should also consider the extra freedom you will have. If the weather turns bad in the high country, you can stay in town for another day or two, or try your hand at something else altogether, such as rafting or sailing. If you find yourself at ease in a particular area, you can prolong your stay there for a few extra days. This isn't possible with most organized treks, which hew to a rigid schedule.

You can also customize a trek to suit your own special interests. If rock climbing or glacier exploring is your thing, you can hire a guide in the Alps who will take you up the mountain to do just that. Even hookers can get into the act: In Canada, New Zealand, and Patagonia—all of which boast good high-country angling—avid anglers can round out a trek with a few days' fishing.

Travel Tips

GEAR

On most commercial treks, porters or pack animals will carry all communal gear and most of your equipment (sleeping bags, etc.), so you can make do with a small backpack. For cameras or water bottles—but not both!—a fanny pack is handy. If your trip is not supported by porters, you will need a sturdy, comfortable backpack to carry your own gear. Although internal-frame packs are best for steep trails, they fit so snugly on your back that they can turn you into a fountain of sweat. For heavy loads, therefore, choose an external-frame pack. If you'll be making a number of airplane flights, select a travelers' pack with a zippered cover to enclose the waistbelt and shoulder straps. The more your pack looks and acts like a suitcase, the easier it will be to manage in an airport.

HEALTH

Consult your physician about the immunizations you will need. For places like Tibet, you should get a full battery of inoculations before you depart—typhoid, tetanus, meningitis, and gamma globulin. Both aspirin and the diuretic Diamox can help reduce the effects of altitude sickness. Make sure your medical insurance covers overseas travel.

Gastrointestinal disorders caused by impure water are a real problem on international treks. Boil your water, use purification tablets, or carry a good water filter. Hepatitis can be waterborne; if you detect symptoms of the disease—chiefly jaundice, fatigue, abdominal pain, loss of appetite, and diarrhea—suspend your trek and seek medical attention.

Even when you take Chloroquine tablets or other prophylaxes, malaria remains a problem in tropical areas. New strains of the disease are resistant to many of the most common medicines. For that reason, sleep under netting, burn mosquito coils (they work), and apply insect repellent when you are in infested areas. For more information on travel health, check out www.cdc.gov/travel. This website, posted by the Centers for Disease Control, provides global vaccination requirements and reports on outbreaks of disease worldwide. Its "Traveler Checklist" also offers tips on how to avoid unsafe food and water.

ONLINE

Away.com
www.away.com

A comprehensive adventure travel site with scores of commercial treks worldwide.

Lonely Planet Home Page
www.lonelyplanet.com

This site features recent reports from travelers around the world.

Trekinfo.com
www.bena.com/nepaltrek

Log on to this site to learn about visa fees, trekking permits, routes, and cultural etiquette. Don't miss the FAQs on Nepal and the links to Nepalese trekking companies.

VisitNepal.com
www.visitnepal.com

VisitNepal.com includes a directory of local agencies and trekking-permit offices, plus advice on the trekking seasons, health and fitness requirements, and how to reach remote areas in the Himalaya.

MAPS

A good map is the key to a great trek. Make sure your map shows elevations and important features such as river crossings. More than 90,000 maps covering virtually every corner of the planet are available from **Map Link** (*Santa Barbara, CA. 805-692-6777. www.maplink.com*).

BOOKS

Before you visit any trekking destination, pick up the appropriate *Travel Survival Kit* handbook published by **Lonely Planet Publications** (*Oakland, CA. 800-275-8563.www.lonelyplanet.com*). These invaluable little books deal with transportation, food, and lodging in faraway places. The following titles are also worth exploring:

Adventure Trekking: A Handbook for Independent Travelers by Robert Strauss (The Mountaineers, $14.95)

Chile and Argentina: Backpacking and Hiking by Tim Burford (Bradt, $17.95)

Climbing and Hiking in Ecuador by Rob Rachowiecki, et al (Bradt, $17.95)

Peru and Bolivia: Backpacking and Trekking by Hilary Bradt (Bradt, $17.95)

Trekking in East Africa by David Else (Lonely Planet, $17.95)

Trekking in the Everest Region by James McGuinness (Trailblazer, $15.95)

Trekking in the Indian Himalaya by Garry Weare (Lonely Planet, $17.95)

Trekking in the Karakoram and Hindukush by John Mock (Lonely Planet, $16.95)

Trekking in the Nepal Himalaya by Stan Armington (Lonely Planet, $17.95)

Trekking in the Patagonian Andes by Clem Lindenmayer (Lonely Planet, $17.95)

Walking Austria's Alps: Hut to Hut by Jonathan Hurdle (The Mountaineers, $14.95)

Walking the G.R. 5: Lake Geneva to Mont Blanc; Modane to Larche; Larche to Nice (Robertson McCarta Ltd., 3 vols., $23.95)

END OF THE PATH: A HIKER TAKES A LOAD OFF IN DEATH VALLEY, CALIFORNIA.

CHAPTER

22

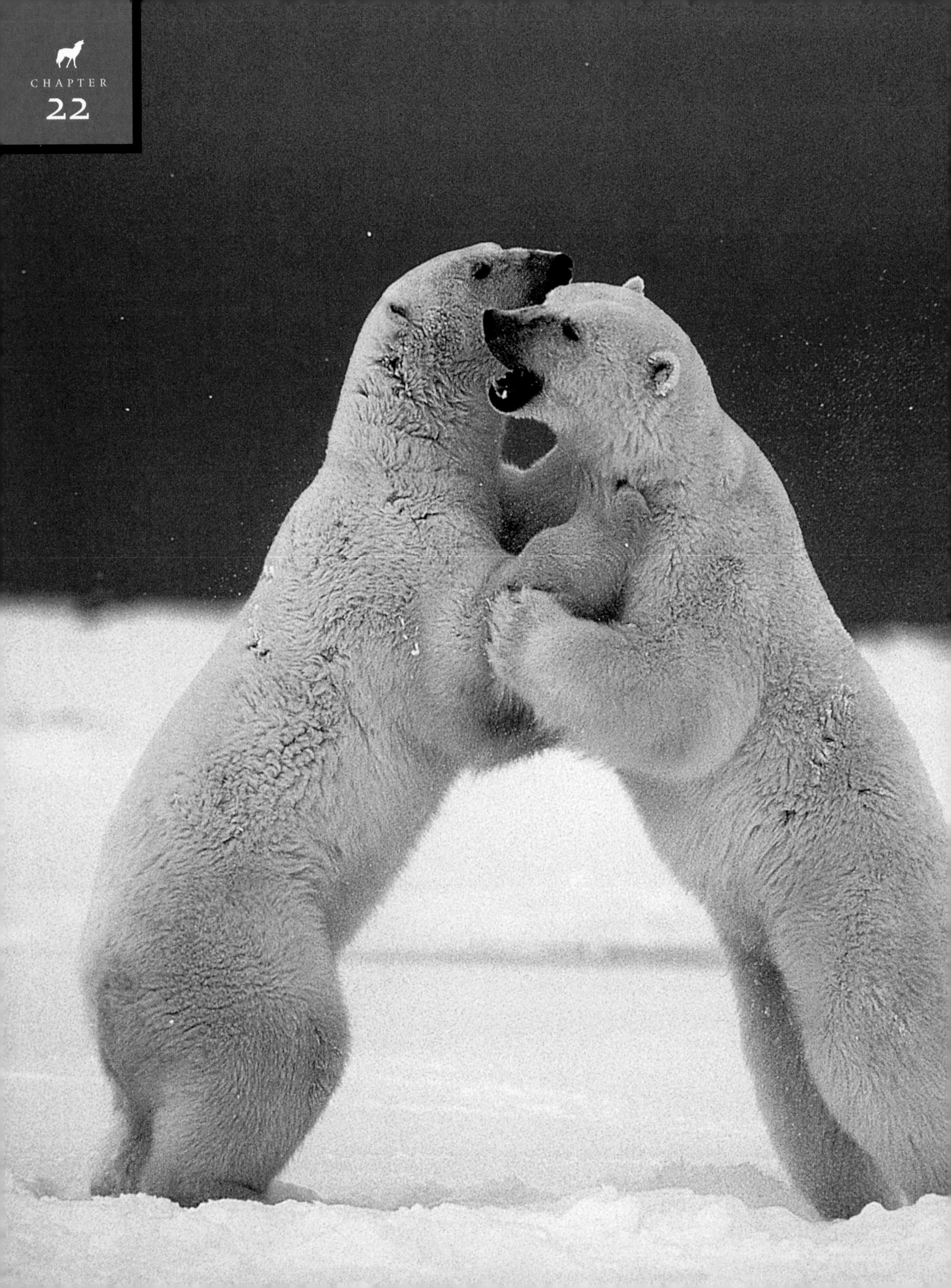

I T'S SAFE TO SAY THAT MOST PEOPLE LOVE LOOKING AT ANIMALS. PERHAPS IT IS SIMPLY OUT OF WONDER AT their diversity. Or maybe it's out of some deep sense of kinship. Whatever the allure, the fact is, watching animals in the wild— whether on land or on sea, in the far north or in the tropics—is an exhilarating experience. And you can do it virtually anywhere in the world. • Hundreds of nature outfitters offer at least as many varia- tions of wildlife tours, from polar bear odysseys in the Arctic to whale-watching cruises in Mexico to lemur-spotting expeditions in Madagascar. And if getting the animals on film is your primary focus, you'll find agents that cater to photographers. • This chapter offers recommendations for some of the world's best wildlife tours—both short outings as well as extended trips. You can choose your comfort zone: Trips range from rugged wilderness adventures to luxury vacations with all the amenities. You'll also find practical information on how to select the right tour, when to go, and what to take. • Note that this chapter does not include Africa. To learn about safari tours on that continent, see pages 180-195.

LEFT: YOUNG, MALE POLAR BEARS SPAR IN CANADA'S ARCTIC.
BELOW: SWIMMING WITH DOLPHINS IN THE FLORIDA KEYS

Wildlife Encounters

Dolphin Swims

Seals on Ice

Whale-Watching

Tropical Tours

Dogsledding

When you are close to nature you can listen to the voice of God.
HERMANN HESSE

Ultimate Wildlife Tours

A wildlife expedition need not be an expensive or laborious undertaking. But to see the greatest variety and number of creatures, you need to go where the wild things are—in their natural habitats, away from civilization. Granted, you may have to travel a bit farther and spend a bit more, but the rewards will be worth the extra effort. Read on for suggestions on where in the world you can encounter the most wildlife.

GALÁPAGOS ISLANDS
Ecuador's Garden of Eden

It's easy to lapse into superlatives when describing the Galápagos Islands. Many believe that the islands constitute the world's single richest sanctuary for land and aquatic wildlife. This place has it all: unusual flora, fantastic bird populations, sea lions, giant tortoises, and marine iguanas—creatures found nowhere else on the planet. For ardent naturalists, the Galápagos are a must-do adventure destination.

The entire chain of islands is maintained as a wilderness preserve, with only a few small settlements. To get there, you must first fly to Quito, Ecuador. A connecting flight then carries you 600 miles west to the landing strip on Isla Baltra, where most visitors transfer to a waiting yacht for the next three days to three weeks. Although some itineraries include a few days in hotels or camping, expect to spend most of your time sailing from island to island aboard ship, which lets you see more of the islands' environments and their distinctive natural features.

Outlying **Islas Española** and **Genovesa (Hood and Tower Islands),** for instance, are home to exotic marine iguanas and populations of blue- and red-footed boobies. **South Isla Plaza** hosts numerous land iguanas and colonies of friendly sea lions. **Isla Santa Cruz,** site of the **Charles Darwin Research Station,** is one of the largest islands and one of the few with acceptable hotel accommodations. A diving mecca, **Isla Santa María (Floreana Island)** offers extensive coral reefs, a wealth of tropical fish, and sandy beaches. **Isla San Salvador (James Island)** is noted for its diverse bird population, including the Galápagos hawk, as well as colonies of playful fur seals. Backpack trips are a feature on **Isla Isabela,** which is dominated by the still-active **Alcedo Volcano**—habitat of the giant tortoise.

A number of outfitters conduct nature-study tours of one to three weeks in the Galápagos Islands. Highly recommended is the 13-day **Ultimate Galápagos** trip offered by **Wilderness Travel** (*1102 Ninth St., Berkeley, CA 94710. 800-368-2794 or 510-558-2488. www.wildernesstravel.com*) from March through July. The tour visits a dozen islands and costs $3,550-4,000 per person, depending on group size.

Less expensive, but quite good, is the 13-day trip with **Wildland Adventures** (*3516 N.E. 155th St., Seattle, WA 98155. 800-345-4453 or 206-365-0686. www.wildland.com*). The itinerary features a 10-day, multi-island cruise and a hike to the **Sierra Negra Volcano.** The cost is $2,300 per person.

Both companies provide comfortable sailing yachts and expert naturalist guides from the Darwin Research Station.

INCA (International Nature and Cultural Adventures, *1311 63rd St., Emeryville, CA 94608. 510-420-1550. www.incafloats.com*) offers the widest variety of Galápagos tours, with more than 80 trips scheduled year-round. Typically, you travel with 8 to 14 fellow passengers, accompanied by a licensed naturalist, on a large sailing or motor yacht. The average price for 11- to 14-day itineraries is about $4,000 per person.

INCA also offers 11- or 14-day chartered dive trips for experienced divers. Other options include combination land and sea itineraries. The **Galápagos with Amazon Jungle** trip runs about $4,500 to $4,900 per person for 15 to 17 days; the 14-day **Galápagos with Ecuadorian Countryside** tour costs about $4,250.

Private charters may be arranged through **Tumbaco** (*7855 NW 12th St., Ste. 221, Miami, FL 33126. 800-247-2925 or 305-599-9008. www.quasarnauticatumbaco.com*)—the U.S. agent for **Quasar Nautica,** an Ecuadorean company that owns nine boats serving the Galápagos. Most trips are one week in length and cost $2,100 to $3,050 per person. Tumbaco's high-quality vessels feature comfortable cabins, skilled crews, and naturalist guides.

MADAGASCAR
Zoological Wonderland

Naturalist Alfred Russell Wallace called Madagascar "one of the most remarkable zoological districts in the world." The world's fourth largest island, located 250 miles off the East African coast, Madagascar is home to countless exotic plant and animal species—80 percent of which are indigenous.

The best time to travel here is from April to October, when the weather is relatively cool and dry. The climate varies around the island, though; it tends to be cooler in the

central highlands, drier in the southern desert, and more humid on the east coast.

Madagascar is practically synonymous with lemurs. Its mountains and jungles are home to the world's largest, and most diverse, population of these long-tailed, arboreal primates. Some species are found nowhere else on Earth. Resembling a cross between a raccoon and a teddy bear, they range from the tiny mouse lemur to the chimp-size giant indris.

This island nation has dedicated much of its interior as parkland or wildlife reserves, affording excellent opportunities to view lemurs, chameleons, and other unusual species.

Be sure to visit **Montagne D'Ambre National Park** on the island's northernmost tip. The rain forest here boasts fantastic orchid gardens, an impressive waterfall, dozens of bird and reptile species, and an assortment of lemurs.

Other highlights include several of the island's wildlife reserves: **Périnet** (**Aralamozaotra**) features one of Madagascar's most accessible rain forests, where you can see nine species of lemurs, numerous bird species, and large chameleons. **Berenty,** on the banks of the **Mandrare River,** is internationally acclaimed for its rare flora and fauna. Here you can find ring-tailed lemurs, rare sifakas, flying foxes, and exotic bird species.

Travel time to Madagascar is three hours by air from Nairobi, Kenya. Among the outfitters who can get you there is **Lemur Tours** (*501 Mendell St., Unit B, San Francisco, CA 94124. 800-735-3687 or 415-695-8880. www.lemurtours. com*). The Madagascar specialist, Lemur offers quite a few 7- to 13-day ecotours throughout the year. Prices vary widely according to itinerary.

If you're planning an East African safari, consider adding a side trip to Madagascar with the seven-day **Périnet-Berenty tour,** a good value at about $1,700 per person, all-inclusive, from **Antananarivo.** Lemur Tours also runs bird-watching, cultural, and other specialty tours.

Journeys (*107 Aprill Dr., Ste. 3, Ann Arbor, MI 48103. 800-255-8735 or 734-665-4407. www.journeys-intl.com*) offers excellent nature-study programs in Madagascar. Participants explore some of the island's most beautiful and remote regions. Tours, generally 10 to 11 days in duration, are scheduled year-round, but it is recommended that you plan your trip between April and November.

MARINE IGUANA GRAZES ON ALGAE IN THE GALÁPAGOS.

Suitable for all ages, Journey's trips feature easy day hikes, with overnights in lodges or in modest hotels. Tours range from about $2,000 to $2,325 per person (land cost), including park fees. Custom itineraries can be arranged.

BAHAMAS
Swimming with Dolphins

A number of programs invite you to cavort with captive dolphins in enclosed pens. But the Bahamas is one of the few places where you can free-float with the creatures in the open ocean. Since 1987, **Underwater Explorers Society (UNEXSO),** a Freeport-based dive center, has offered such a program for certified divers.

Several times a week, UNEXSO's trained dolphins are released into the sea. Dive boats carry participants to a rendez-vous point—a coral reef located a mile from shore. Supervised by handlers, divers (maximum of 10 per group) swim, in turn, with the dolphins for about 20 minutes.

The animals are friendly and responsive to hand signals, which divers are taught prior to embarking. It may be routine for the dolphins to act on signal command, but for humans, the experience of communicating with these intelligent, docile creatures is extraordinary. The program is offered year-round; the cost is about $170 per person.

For nondivers, UNEXSO offers a bargain-priced **Dolphin Close Encounter** program at **Sanctuary Bay,** where you can visit with the animals while standing waist-deep in a pool of salt water. The two-hour program runs four times daily; the cost is about $40 per person.

For more information about these programs, contact **UNEXSO** (*P.O. Box 22878, Ft. Lauderdale, FL 33335. 800-992-3483 or 954-351-9889 in Florida, 242-373-1244 in the Bahamas. www.unexso.com*).

You can also dive with wild dolphins off **Grand Bahama Island,** but encounters are less certain here. An 80-foot-long live-aboard catamaran called the *Bottom Time II* makes regular excursions to the shallow banks off **the Bimini Islands,** the favored playground of some very friendly spotted dolphins. On a good day, they will have surrounded the boat by the time the anchor is secure, and they proceed to circle the dive ladders and swim close to divers throughout the session.

The *Bottom Time II* is stable, fast, and comfortable. It features 15 private cabins plus all the amenities, including a film lab. A seven-day dolphin adventure typically costs about $1,300 per person. Contact **Bottom Time Adventures** (*P.O. Box 11919, Ft. Lauderdale, FL 33339. 800-234-8464 or 954-921-7798. www.bottomtime2.com*).

If you are interested in a more serious, extended excursion, the **Oceanic Society** (*Fort Mason Center, Building E, San Francisco, CA 94123. 800-326-7491 or 415-441-1106. www.oceanic-society.org*) runs several expeditions to study dolphins off Grand Bahama Island. These include seven-day cruises in May, July, and August.

These expeditions are conducted as part of an ongoing research effort focused primarily on the behavioral ecology of spotted dolphins. Noninvasive observation techniques are emphasized.

Participants need not be certified divers; all you require are a snorkel and fins. One former participant described the experience this way: "The water was the temperature of my skin, and I lost all sense of boundaries. A five-foot dolphin calf came to me and started corkscrew turns down to the ocean floor. I circled with him, down, then catapulted to the surface, exhausted and delighted."

Your home at sea for the week-long excursion is a comfortable, 68-foot motor yacht. The cost is $1,640 per person, with two guests per cabin.

YELLOWSTONE NATIONAL PARK
America's Wildlife Headquarters

North America's hallmark species—deer, moose, elk, bear, buffalo—all reside within Yellowstone's 2.2 million acres of geysers, mountains, and meadowlands. Their numbers alone are impressive: 30,000 elk, 2,100 bison, an estimated 200 grizzlies, and countless smaller species.

Summer crowds overwhelm the park's major tourist attractions, but you can easily escape the crowds if you're prepared to venture into Yellowstone's 3,500 square miles of backcountry.

Hiking the backcountry is the best way to observe Yellowstone's animals. With 1,210 miles of trails, foot travelers have plenty of options.

One essential day hike is a walk through **Hayden Valley,** Yellowstone's garden and home to the park's largest bison herd. Another scenic day hike is the **Mary Mountain Trail**.

Pebble Creek Trail, which begins a mile or so from the northeast entrance, is a good overnight excursion. You are likely to encounter large groups of elk, moose, and buffalo; black and grizzly bears may be observed here as well.

For a longer trip, take five days to walk the length of the **Thorofare Trail.** From the trailhead on **East Entrance Road,** it winds along the shore of **Yellowstone Lake,** providing good views of eagles and ospreys, and possibly bears.

Yellowstone is a high-altitude wilderness, with wintry storms often blowing up as late as June. The best months to hike the backcountry are August and September: Rivers and streams are lower, the insect count is down, and the weather is more hospitable. Snow flurries are possible at any time of year, so take warm clothes for layering and a good tent—no matter what the weather forecast.

For more details on wilderness hiking in Yellowstone, contact **Backcountry Information** (*Yellowstone National Park, WY 82190. 307-344-2160. www.nps.gov/yell*). Ask for the free information packet and trip planning guide.

In summer, you can easily view the park's wildlife on your own. During the winter, however, when many of the main roads are closed, it is recommended that you go with an outfitter.

An excellent winter tour is offered by **Joseph Van Os Photo Safaris** (*P.O. Box 655, Vashon Island, WA 98070. 206-463-5383. www.photosafaris.com*). Noted photographer Perry Conway leads small groups of amateur photographers to observe elk, deer, bison, bighorn sheep, and other wildlife.

This seven-day tour is offered in January or February and departs from Mammoth Hot Springs (the closest airport is Bozeman, Montana). The cost is about $2,400 per person.

ALASKA
Land of the Midnight Sun

The combination of plentiful wildlife and vast tracts of protected lands (**Denali National Park and Preserve** is larger than Massachusetts) makes Alaska the perfect destination for nature travelers.

Arctic National Wildlife Refuge, America's largest at 19.8 million acres, is one of the finest wildlife-viewing areas in North America. For one thing, there are no permanent human settlements here. Dozens of species—wolf, bear, caribou, and Dall sheep among them—thrive in this vast wilderness.

In the spring, you can witness one of nature's spectacular events: the annual migration of the 180,000-head Porcupine caribou herd. Each year at this time, the herd heads north across the refuge to its Arctic calving grounds.

Several small Alaskan outfitters can guide you to the herd on a custom basis. Or you can sign up for a **Dog Sled Expedition on the North Slope** with **Sourdough Outfitters** (*P.O. Box 26066, Bettles, AK 99726. 907-692-5252. www.sourdough.com*).

Participants fly in to a base camp in the refuge. From there, in groups of six, you travel by dogsled through the high valleys to look for caribou, as well as for wolves, wolverines, arctic fox, musk ox, and other mammals.

The week-long winter trip costs about $2,590 per person. In August, a reverse migration trip is offered for $2,000.

The late-season herds are smaller, but the animals themselves, with their mature antlers and lush winter coats, are more impressive.

If you want to see Alaskan wildlife under less rigorous conditions, **Mountain Travel-Sobek's** 11-day **Wild Alaska** trip might fit the bill.

In the words of one guest, this tour is "a terrific alternative for people who don't want to go on 1,200-person cruise ships, but don't want to camp out for two weeks." What you get is an easy, half-day rafting trip through the fjords of the scenic **Kenai River,** hiking and rafting in **Matanuska Valley,** and two full days at **Wrangell-St. Elias National Park and Preserve.** Plus, you overnight in lodges, cabins, or hotels. The cost, after you get yourself to Anchorage, is about $3,200 per person. For information, contact **Mountain Travel-Sobek** (*6420 Fairmont Ave., El Cerrito, CA 94530. 800-227-2384 or 510-527-8100. www.mtsobek.com*).

If you want to narrow your focus, bear-watching is big business in Alaska. The Alaskan brown bear is the world's largest carnivorous land mammal. And the best spot in the world to watch bears is along the banks of the **McNeil River** in **Katmai National Park and Preserve's Kamishak Bay.**

During the annual chum-salmon run (early July through mid-August), scores of Alaskan browns visit the riverbanks to fish and feed. It's not unusual to see as many as 30 bears within 100 yards. Visitors can watch the bears safely from a few yards away. This is possible because the animals are accustomed to being observed; they have not learned to associate humans with food; and the salmon streams are so productive that the bears would rather fish than beg for handouts (feeding the bears is strictly prohibited).

Access to the **McNeil River State Game Sanctuary** is closely controlled by the Alaska Department of Fish and Game. Only 10 visitors are allowed per day, by permit only; four-day permits are drawn from a lottery.

To enter, send $25 (this entry fee is nonrefundable) to the **Alaska Department of Fish and Game** (*333 Raspberry Rd., Anchorage, AK 99518. 907-267-2179. www.state.ak.us/adfg*). Applications must be received before March 1. Be aware that the state of Alaska receives an average of 2,000 applicants for 240 permits.

If you're lucky enough to get a permit, your base at McNeil will be **Chenik Camp.** For reservations and information about air shuttles, contact **Kachemak Bay Wilderness Lodge** (*China Poot Bay, P.O. Box 956, Homer, AK 99603. 907-235-8910. www.xyz.net/~wildrnes*).

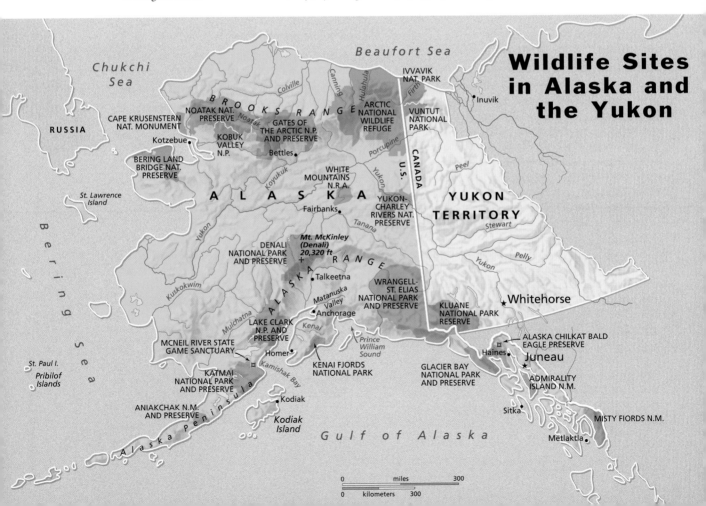

Wildlife Sites in Alaska and the Yukon

Another option for bear lovers is a **Brown Bears of Katmai National Park Photo Safari**, offered by **Joseph Van Os Photo Safaris** (*206-463-5383. www.photosafaris.com*). These popular six-day tours visit the **Brooks River** in Katmai, where visitors can observe the bears at close range.

Participants stay at the **Brooks Lodge**—which happens to stand just a few hundred yards from some of the bears' favorite salmon runs. The one drawback is that Brooks can get crowded during the peak season (*late June and July; late Aug.-early Sept.*). The trip costs about $2,100 per person.

Alaska Photo Tours (*P.O. Box 141, Talkeetna, AK 99676. 800-799-3051 or 907-733-3051. www.alaska.net/~photoak*) offers a similar bear-watching trip in **Kodiak** and coastal **Katmai.** Photographer Steve Gilroy guides groups through remote wilderness areas, where you can photograph brown bears without fighting the crowds.

Along with bears, Alaska is also the place to observe eagles in the wild. Each year during the November salmon run, more than 3,000 bald eagles gather in the **Alaska Chilkat Bald Eagle Preserve** in the Chilkat Valley. A birdwatcher's dream, the preserve is also home to thousands of swans, terns, cranes, geese, and songbirds.

Recommended outfitters for eagle tours in the Chilkat Valley are **Chilkat Guides, Ltd.** (*P.O. Box 170, Haines, AK 99827. 907-766-2491., www.raftalaska.com*) and Alaska Photo Tours (*see contact info above*).

From May through mid-September, **River Adventures** (*P.O. Box 556, Haines, AK 99827. 800-478-9827 or 907-766-2050. www.alaskarivertours.wytbear.com*) offers daily jet-boat outings into an otherwise inaccessible corner of the valley. The cost is a modest $70 for a three- to five-hour trip on the Chilkat River.

Another major eagle-nesting ground is **Prince William Sound.** You'll also see peregrine falcons, wild swans, puffins, and many other species of birds, as well as an array of mammals. Alaska Photo Tours (*see contact info above*) offers an outstanding and popular program that combines a cruise of the sound with a week in Denali National Park. This 12-day combination trip costs about $4,500 per person.

CANADA
Animals of the Arctic

One of Canada's most popular, and photogenic, denizens of the wild is the polar bear, a highly intelligent hunter that rules the high Arctic.

To see this creature in its natural habitat, head to **Churchill, Manitoba.** Each summer, as the pack ice retreats on **Hudson Bay,** polar bears gather by the hundreds along the bay's southern shore to hunt for seal and fish. The bears make their maternity dens just south of Churchill, where visitors can observe the mothers tending their cubs.

The best time for bear-watching is just before the winter freeze in October, when seals converge in the last few open waterways, attracting large numbers of bears.

Several outfitters offer polar bear expeditions. **Travel Wild Expeditions** (*P.O. Box 1637, Vashon Island, WA 98070. 800-368-0077 or 206-463-5362. www.travelwild.com*) offers an excellent seven-day trip for serious bear-watchers. Participants fly to Churchill, where they board giant, four-wheel-drive "tundra buggies" that enable safe—and warm—viewing of the animals at close range.

The best light for photographing the bears is in early morning and late afternoon. To accommodate shooters, Travel Wild runs a **Buggies and Bunkhouse** combination tour. The cost for the week-long trip is $2,395 per person; the nine-day bunkhouse trip is $3,295, all-inclusive, from Winnipeg, Manitoba. Trips run in October and November.

If the Travel Wild tour is beyond your means, **Adventure Canada** (*14 Front St. S., Mississauga, ON L5H 2C4. 800-363-7566 or 905-271-4000. www.adventurecanada.com*) offers outstanding four- and seven-day polar bear expeditions to the western shores of Hudson Bay near Churchill. Tundra buggies transport guests, who are accompanied by world-class guides and photo instructors Mike Beedel and Bonnie Chartier, both of whom have extensive Arctic experience.

Adventure Canada delivers an outstanding polar bear experience at reasonable cost. The four-day trip is about $1,200 per person ($1,850 for seven days), excluding airfare. Trips run in late October.

During autumn, the annual caribou migrations in Canada's **Yukon** and **Northwest Territories (NWT)** draw wildlife watchers from around the world. The sight of hundreds of thousands of animals traversing the landscape is truly awe-inspiring.

Wild and beautiful **Ivvavik National Park** in the northwest corner of the Yukon is the setting for a recommended caribou-watching adventure: **Ecosummer Expeditions** (*P.O. Box 1765, Clearwater, BC V0E 1N0. 800-465-8884 or 250-674-0102. www.ecosummer.com*) runs a 12-day **Caribou Trails** trek near the **British Mountains** in August, just as the autumn colors begin to change. The cost is about $2,275 per person, from **Inuvik**, NWT.

Ecosummer's July float trip on the **Firth River** offers an opportunity to view caribou from a raft. The tour takes you through river canyons and tundra valleys. Besides caribou, expect to see Dall sheep, musk ox, and moose along the river—and beluga whales and seals on the coast.

A shorter caribou encounter in the NWT can be had with **Raven Tours** (*P.O. Box 2435, Yellowknife, NWT. X1A 2P8. 867-873-4776. www.raventours.yk.com*). This agent offers half-day tours to view the 500,000-head Barrenground caribou herds. The tour departs from a comfortable lodge outside

Yellowknife, where you board an expedition skiplane to fly over the open wilderness. When caribou are spotted—typically clustered in groups of 100 to 200 animals—the plane lands so passengers can get a closer look. Day trips run from mid-December to mid-April and cost about $300 per person.

If you prefer a remote Arctic wildlife experience, **Adventure Canada** (*800-363-7566. www.adventurecanada.com*) runs a **Pond Inlet Floe Edge** expedition to the top of **Baffin Island.**

The highlight of this exciting program is a journey to the edge of the pack ice by snowmobile and sled with Inuit guides. Wildlife sightings are unpredictable, but the possibilities include bowhead and beluga whale, walrus, snow goose, snowy owls, arctic fox, peregrine falcon, gyrfalcon, and rough-legged hawk.

The cost for this nine-day trip from Pond Inlet is about $3,200 per person. On occasion, Adventure Canada also schedules exclusive women's trips to Baffin Island.

In July and August, **Arctic Odysseys** (*2000 McGilvra Blvd. E., Seattle, WA 98112. 800-574-3021 or 206-325-1977. www.arcticodysseys.com*) features a nine-day **Baffin Island Summer Wildlife and Cultural Odyssey** from Ottawa. This multidimensional trip offers an opportunity to observe wildlife in the far north. It also introduces participants to traditional Arctic culture in an Inuit summer encampment. Travel is by boat; the cost is $3,850 per person.

SEAL-SIGHTING
The Far North

When it comes to wildlife-watching, baby seals steal the show. If you want to visit the pups on their own turf, the way to go is the annual **Seal Watch,** operated by **Natural Habitat Adventures** (*2945 Center Green Court S., Ste. H, Boulder, CO 80301. 800-543-8917 or 303-449-3711. www.nathab.com*).

This five-day tour takes you to Canada's **Gulf of St. Lawrence** to observe a colony of newborn harp seals—among nature's most irresistible creatures. A helicopter delivers participants to the ice floes of the **Îles de la Madeleine (Magdalen Islands),** where you approach within a few feet of the wide-eyed "white coats."

The trip costs about $1,900 per person, including one helicopter flight to the ice; there is an additional charge of $350 to $450 for each additional heli-trip. Tours are scheduled during the month of March.

A similar trip to the Magdalen Islands is offered by **Adventure Canada** (*800-363-7566. www.adventurecanada. com*). This harp seal photo tour also runs for five days and costs about $1,900 per person.

In terms of quantity, you will see more seals in Alaska. For example, **St. Paul Island**—part of the **Pribilof**, or **Fur Seal, Islands** in the **Bering Sea**—is home to some 800,000 northern fur seals, as well as more than 200 species of birds.

Still relatively unknown and sparsely visited, these islands promise an amazing display of seals in undisturbed natural habitat. **World Express Tours** (*P.O. Box 2819, Kirkland, WA 98083, or 200 West 34th Avenue, Ste. 412, Anchorage, AK 99503. 800-544-2235 or 425-827-7557. www. worldexpresstour.com*) features three- to six-day trips to St. Paul Island in summer. Land costs are $900 to $1,400 per person, including overnight lodging in Anchorage.

If the habitat of harp and fur seals is restricted to far northern hinterlands, other seal species worth observing inhabit less remote locales.

On the west coast, North America's largest sea lion and sea elephant rookeries are easily accessible. California's **Channel Islands National Park,** located just a few hours from Los Angeles, is an excellent spot to view seals, sea lions, and elephant seals.

Among the Channel Islands, **Santa Cruz** receives the most visitors because of its easy beach landing, good hiking trails, and reliable dolphin and sea lion sightings.

A popular tour is a day trip to the **Anacapa Islands.** Here you can observe sea lions basking on the rocks and playing in the many coastal coves.

Serious seal-watchers will want to head farther offshore to **Santa Barbara Island,** a major gathering site for sea lions. Overnight camping is permitted on both Anacapa and Santa Barbara.

San Miguel Island to the north is the ultimate seal haven. Five different species of seals, sea lions, and elephant seals inhabit the rugged shoreline by the thousands. Though you can explore San Miguel on foot, the largest rookeries—including the seal-breeding grounds at Point Bennett—are off-limits to hikers. In fact, you'll see more if you stay aboard a boat, most likely one operated by **Island Packers** (*1867 Spinnaker Dr., Ventura, CA 93001. 805-642-1393 or 805-642-7688 for info. line. www.islandpackers.com*). Licensed as a concessionaire by Channel Islands National Park, Island Packers provides transport to all the islands. Trips to San Miguel run April through October; the cost is $90 per person, with overnight camping.

Condor Cruises (*The Sea Landing, Santa Barbara Marina, Santa Barbara, CA 93101. 888-779-4253 or 805-882-0088. www.condorcruises.com*) also offers modestly priced day trips to the Channel Islands year-round.

WHALE-WATCHING
Baja and the California Coast

By most counts, Mexico's ruggedly beautiful Baja California peninsula is among the best whale-watching sites in the world. Every winter, hundreds of gray whales migrate down the Pacific coast to winter in southern Baja's warm lagoons—watery nurseries for the female grays and their calves.

On the low-lying west coast—distinguished by long sandy beaches, pounding Pacific surf, and sheltering lagoons—**Laguna San Ignacio** is the hub of whale activity. Along the calmer east coast, which is lapped by the warm waters of the **Golfo de California** (the world's largest deep-water gulf), whales congregate around **Isla Espíritu Santo.**

Two main factors make this a prime area for watching whales: The animals gather in great numbers, and they remain in the same lagoon for an extended period of time.

Highly recommended for a superlative Baja whale-watching experience is the **Whales of Baja** trip with **Natural Habitat Adventures** (*800-543-8917. www.nathab.com*). This tour takes you to Laguna San Ignacio, where you can see scores of gray whales as well as bottlenose dolphins. The five-day excursion, which is offered in early spring, is limited to 20 people and costs about $2,400 per person. The point of departure for the trip is **Loreto, Mexico.**

A less expensive but still high quality alternative is an eight-day cruise on a large motor yacht with **Baja Expeditions** (*2625 Garnet, San Diego, CA 92109. 800-843-6967 or 858-581-3311. www.bajaex.com*). In motorized skiffs known as *pangas* that are launched from the yacht, guests observe blue, gray, and humpback whales in their winter harbors. Whale-watching cruises run from January through February and range in price from about $1,800 to $2,000 per person, depending on cabin class.

Baja Expeditions also offers satisfying, land-based whale-watching from a fairly deluxe, shoreside tent camp. Activities include snorkeling and naturalist-guided panga trips on **Bahía Magdalena (Magdalena Bay)** and Laguna San Ignacio. This holiday costs about $1,200 for the week.

Absent the time or the means for an extended vacation, you can observe the same gray whales during their northbound or southbound migrations through **Santa Barbara Channel.** In seasons past, mammoth blue whales—the largest mammals on earth—have also been spotted, generally during summer and fall. Day trips are offered by **Island Packers** (*805-642-1393. www.islandpackers.com*) out of Ven-

THE CORRECT WAY TO SHOOT A MAGNIFICENT FRIGATEBIRD

tura (*July-Sept. for blue whales, Jan.-March for gray whales*).

From February to April (for gray whales) and from July to September (for humpback and blue whales), **Condor Cruises** (*888-779-4253. www.condorcruises.com*) runs whale-watching excursions to the Channel Islands aboard the 88-foot-long *Condor*. Day trips cost $65 for adults, $35 for children; if you don't see any whale action, you receive a "whale check"—good for a free return trip. Early March is generally the best time to see migrating gray whales.

Pacific Northwest

To find wild orca whales, the best place to look is in the bays and inlets of Canada's Pacific northwest. You can spot them from any sizable boat, but if it's a closer encounter you're after, consider whale-watching by sea kayak.

An excellent agent for kayak-camping tours is David Arcese's **Northern Lights Expeditions** (*P.O. Box 4289, Bellingham, WA 98227. 800-754-7402 or 360-734-6334. www.seakayaking.com*). You explore the **Inside Passage,** which runs between **Vancouver Island** and the mainland of **British Columbia,** in close proximity to the whales. For the past several seasons, Northern Lights guides have been able to identify many individual orcas that return to these waters every year. The week-long tour costs about $1,200 per person.

Northern Lights also does a special seven-day trip at the end of the season. In lieu of camping, kayakers stay in **Farewell Harbour Lodge.** The cost of this tour, complete with hot tubs, is $1,795.

If you don't want to paddle, charter the *Spirit Bear,* Northern Lights' 40-foot yacht. It's a great way to see the whales and bears—without getting wet. Week-long charters (maximum four people) range from $6,000 to $7,000 per week.

Another fine yacht-based orca-watching trip is the **Queen Charlotte Islands Tour** with **Adventure Canada** (*800-363-7566. www.adventurecanada.com*). Each summer, a dozen passengers cruise to prime orca waters aboard the *Ocean Light II,* a 71-foot sailing yacht. The vessel follows pods of whales through inland waterways along British Columbia's coast. Hydrophones enable guests to hear the whales communicating underwater. This eight-day tour departs from **Vancouver;** the cost is about $2,000. Reserve early.

Alaska

Alaska's waters abound with assorted whale species. Many whale-watching options are available, from luxury nature cruises to coastal kayak expeditions.

One particularly good trip—highly recommended for nature photographers and natural history buffs—is offered by **Alaska Photo Tours** (*800-799-3051. www.alaska.net/~photoak*). Scheduled to coincide with peak humpback

activity, this seven-day **Southeast Explorer** tour visits prime humpback habitats where sightings are virtually guaranteed. The cost is about $2,500 per person.

The company also features an 11-day **Natural History Explorer** adventure that combines a **Prince William Sound** cruise—watch for humpback and orca whales—with a trek through **Denali** park. This trip costs $4,300.

Also recommended is a tour with **Dolphin Charters** (*1007 Leneve Pl., El Cerrito, CA 94530. 800-472-9942 or 510-527-9622. www.dolphincharters.com*). This seasoned operator has been running outstanding Alaskan nature cruises since 1976. Dolphin's able crew includes a professional photographer, an expert biologist, and an accomplished chef. While you're at sea, humpbacks and orcas are the focus; however, this 7- to 10-day cruise (*$2,700-3,600*) also includes day hikes and other terrestrial adventures.

If photography is your priority, **Joseph Van Os Photo Safaris** (*206-463-5383. www.photosafaris.com*) does a nine-day humpback tour in June and July. From Juneau, you travel on a 60-foot boat specially outfitted for photographers. The vessel's course is plotted to maximize photo opportunities; this includes navigating icy fjords and getting close to the animals. The price is about $3,000 per person.

Hawaii

If watching whales in frigid, arctic waters doesn't grab you, you do have other options: whale-watching in the tropics, for instance. Many marine mammals, including humpbacks, migrate to winter breeding grounds far to the south.

Each year, the Hawaiian islands are visited by families of humpback whales. A great way to see them is on a short cruise with **Captain Zodiac** (*P.O. Box 5612, Kailua-Kona, HI 96740. 800-422-7824; or 808-826-9371 on Kauai, 808-329-3199 on Hawaii. www.planet-hawaii.com/zodiac*). You have a choice of exploring Kauai's south coast or Hawaii's Kona Coast, with time out for snorkeling.

Expert guides pilot Zodiacs—small, motorized, inflatable boats—to within 100 yards of the whales, or close enough to feel the spray when they breach. The boats are equipped with hydrophones. The four-hour trips—offered twice daily, from December through April—cost $70.

If you are interested in a longer trip, **Hawaiian Adventure Tours** (*P.O. Box 1269, Kapa'au, HI 96755. 800-659-3544 or 808-889-0227. www.hawaiianadventuretours.com*) features an **Earth, Fire, and Sea Multi-Sport Adventure.** This versatile package combines sea kayaking, mountain biking, whale-watching, wilderness hiking, and volcano exploration.

Trips run year-round; the best time for whale-watching is January through March. The six-day trip costs about $1,050. A 10-day trip to Kauai, Maui, and Hawaii, with bed-and-breakfast accommodations, runs $1,800.

INDONESIA
Home of Vanishing Species

This vast archipelago is home to some of the most exotic creatures on earth. Many species are endemic, including the rare and threatened Javanese rhino. (The last 40 or 50 of these animals survive in the confines of **Ujung Kulon National Park** on the west end of **Java.**) Indonesia is also the last sanctuary of the orangutan and the Komodo dragon, a fabled link to the age of the dinosaurs.

These giant monitor lizards are found only on Komodo, a small volcanic island 200 miles east of **Bali.** They can grow 12 feet in length and have been known to attack humans, although birds and small mammals are their preferred fare.

If you're interested in a dragon trip, do the 13-day **East Indies Sea Trek** with the **Adventure Center** (*1311 63rd St., Ste. 200, Emeryville, CA 94608. 800-227-8747 or 510-654-1879. www.adventurecenter.com*).

Participants travel by schooner outfitted with eight two-berth cabins, visiting the islands of **Bali, Lombok, Sumbawa,** and **Komodo.** You stop for a day or two on each island to explore villages, trek inland, or snorkel in the warm, clear waters. Highlights include observing the dragons in their native habitat on Komodo and touring a sultan's palace in **Sumbawa Besar.** The price is $1,680 per person, excluding airfare. Food and on-board accommodations are better than backpacker fare, but don't expect haute cuisine or luxury cabins.

Borneo, the third largest island in the world, is a land of mystery. Famed for its dense rain forest, Borneo is now an exciting destination for adventure travelers.

The island's wildlife population is among the richest in the world, with an extraordinary number and diversity of animals. It is the last stronghold of the "old man of the forest"—the beguiling and endangered orangutan.

The **Wild Indonesia** tour run by **Asia Transpacific Journeys** (*2995 Center Green Ct., Boulder, CO 80301. 800-642-2742 or 303-443-6789. www.southeastasia.com*) is a magical, multifaceted adventure that focuses on **Bali, Irian Jaya, Komodo, Borneo,** and **Java.**

This is an active but comfortable trip that introduces you to the colorful cultures of Indonesia, as well as to many of the archipelago's resident creatures—among them orangutans, Komodo dragons, proboscis monkeys, long-tailed macaques, silver leaf monkeys, giant hornbills, banteng cattle, and more. Trips run from late spring through summer. Land cost for two weeks is about $3,000; for three weeks, about $4,000.

Asia Transpacific is one of the best tour operators for Southeast Asia. It can extend your itinerary to include stops in Malaysia, Thailand, Vietnam, or other destinations.

ORANGUTAN ON THE INDONESIAN ISLAND OF BORNEO

Nature to Go

Nature tour operators are nearly as diverse as the wildlife they promote. Some agents specialize in soft adventure vacations that deliver wilderness with creature comforts, while others offer active, rugged trips that promise more creatures than comfort. Most outfitters employ trained naturalists and use local guides on international tours. There's an itinerary out there for every traveler—if you know where to look. Listed below are some of North America's leading ecoagents—to get you started on your way.

The recent boom in ecoadventure travel has seen an explosion in the number of wildlife tour operators. Wherever in the world you want to go, however remote the locale, there's an agent waiting to take you to the animals. With so many options available, choosing the right outfitter and itinerary can be overwhelming. Here are some tips on getting back to nature—without getting ripped off.

First, research all the possible options available for your particular destination. The most popular wildlife-viewing areas, such as Alaska, Baja, and the Galápagos, are each served by a dozen or more major tour operators.

Prices vary widely depending on the amenities provided and the mode of transport. A whale-watching trip in Baja, for example, might cost $150 per day if you kayak but much more if you cruise.

Second, before you part with that deposit, find out who will actually be leading the tour and what sort of experience and expertise they have. In many cases, the company that advertises a trip is not the agent in the field. The last thing you want is to be stranded in the hinterland with an irresponsible or inexperienced guide.

Third, know what your focus is for the trip—it may, for example, be observing particular species or taking photographs. Look for an outfitter that caters to your special interest, such as a photo safari. The more specifically you can define your requirements, the better the chances of finding the right outfitter.

Finally, make sure you know the full price of the tour. To attract clients, many outfitters advertise a pared-down price that belies unavoidable additional expenses. Ask whether the company charges a small-group supplement (typically $300-400 extra), inland air charters ($200-300), ground transportation, and meals.

ABEC's Alaska Adventures

1550 Alpine Vista Ct., Fairbanks, AK 99712
907-457-8907. www.abecalaska.com

One of Alaska's oldest and most established wilderness guide services, the company specializes in rafting, kayaking, canoeing, and backpacking trips in the Brooks Range, a high-Arctic tundra ecosystem. Species for observation include caribou, grizzlies, wolves, musk ox, moose, Dall sheep, fox, wolverine, and lynx. The guides are experienced Alaskans who really know the backcountry. Trips are geared for fit and active outdoor travelers; nearly 60 percent are repeat customers or referrals. ABEC's trips range from 7 to 22 days and cost $1,300-$3,000.

Adventure Canada

14 Front St. S., Mississauga, ON
L5H 2C4 Canada
800-363-7566 or 905-271-4000
www.adventurecanada.com

Since 1987 Adventure Canada has been a leading choice for a Canadian wildlife experience. It runs more than 25 land trips a year throughout Canada, plus **tall ship cruises** in the Caribbean with a naturalist and a marine biologist. This company is a good pick for soft-adventure types; almost all trips feature comfortable lodges. For those who prefer to rough it, Adventure Canada offers a nine-day Baffin Island hiking and camping trip. Guides are expert naturalists or photographers—or both. Groups are small, typically 8 to 14 people.

Alaska Photo Tours

P.O. Box 141, Talkeetna, AK 99676
800-799-3051 or 907-733-3051
www.alaska.net/~photoak

This aptly named company is the top choice for an Alaskan photo safari. Destinations include Katmai National Park, Denali National Park and Preserve, Kodiak Island, Prince William Sound, the Pribilof Islands, Kenai Fjords National Park and Preserve, the Inside Passage, and Chilkat Eagle Preserve. Tours are scheduled for optimal viewing of wildflowers, autumn colors, and wildlife activity. Professional photographer Steve Gilroy guides the trips. Custom programs in Kodiak and coastal Katmai are designed to facilitate the photographing of brown bears away from crowds. Marine cruises use private vessels and Zodiac launches to get near the action. Top trips include the **Autumn Extravaganza,** combining Denali and Kenai Fjords parks, and the **Natural History Explorer** in July.

Arctic Treks

P.O. Box 73452, Fairbanks, AK 99707
907-455-6502
www.arctictreksadventures.com

This family operation is run by Jim Campbell and Carol Kasza. Since 1979, Arctic Treks has offered outstanding summer hiking and rafting programs in Alaska's Brooks Range. Strongly recommended is a float down the Hulahula River through the heart of the Arctic National Wildlife Refuge. Few trips offer a better combination of mountains, wilderness, and wildlife. Offered in June, this 10-day trip coincides with the summer migration of the Porcupine caribou herd; the cost is about $2,900. Arctic Treks also runs float trips down the Noatak, Canning, and Kongakut Rivers. Custom trips are a specialty: Hikers can choose from challenging alpine routes or day hikes from a high-Arctic base camp. These trips run in spring and fall, the best times to view caribou, bears, and wolves.

Earthwatch Institute

3 Clocktower Pl., Suite 100 Maynard, MA
01754. 800-776-0188 or 978-461-0081
www.earthwatch.org

Founded in the 1970s, Earthwatch is one of the largest private sponsors of field-research expeditions in the world. Its combination of high adventure and scientific research has attracted volunteers and won respect in the scientific community. Earthwatch currently sponsors more than 150 research projects worldwide. These range from saving endangered rhinos in Africa to monitoring wild dolphins off the coasts of New Zealand and Florida—projects that are cosponsored by the National Geographic Society. Far from reveling in a luxury vacation, participants work side-by-side with scientists for two weeks or more; the team usually stays in modest field stations or tent camps. Tax-deductible fees for the programs typically run $1,600 for a two-week session.

Ecosummer Expeditions
P.O. Box 1765, Clearwater, BC
V0E 1N0 Canada
800-465-8884 or 250-674-0102
www.ecosummer.com

Ecosummer Expeditions is one of Canada's most respected wilderness outfitters. It offers many fine nature tours, from yacht cruises to rugged overland treks, in the high Arctic, eastern Canadian Arctic, and Central and South America. Ecosummer has pioneered 95 percent of its itineraries, including the fjords of Ellesmere Island, the Mayan Mountains in Belize, and kayaking in the high Arctic. This solid company is highly recommended for any of its destinations. Groups are small, with one professional guide-naturalist for each five participants.

Lindblad Special Expeditions
720 Fifth Ave., New York, NY 10019
800-397-3348 or 212-765-7740
www.expeditions.com

Founded by Sven-Olof Lindblad in 1979, Lindblad Special Expeditions organizes ship-based nature voyages and land journeys all over the world. Led by skilled naturalists and historians, Lindblad tours visit remote, often unique, ecosystems, many of which can be reached only by sea. Comfortable expedition vessels—the *Sea Lion, Sea Bird, Caledonian Star,* and *Polaris*—feature fine cuisine and able crews. All boats are outfitted with Zodiac launches to transport passengers closer to the wildlife action. A sampling of Lindblad trips includes whale-watching in Mexico's Baja California, Alaska's Inside Passage, Costa Rica's national parks, Antarctica, and the Galápagos Islands.

Mountain Travel-Sobek
6420 Fairmont Ave., El Cerrito, CA 94530
800-227-2384 or 510-527-8100
www.mtsobek.com

The nation's oldest small-group adventure tour operator, Mountain Travel-Sobek runs adventure trips all over the world. Itineraries include jungle destinations, raft trips, African safaris, and mountain treks. The company's focus is on the quality of the traveler's wildlife experience—with participation, rather than passive observation, being the objective of every trip. All tour guides are experts in their field, be it anthropology, botany, zoology, or another profession.

Nature Expeditions International (NEI)
7860 Peters Rd., Plantation, FL 33324
800-869-0639 or 954-693-8852
www.naturexp.com

Nature Expeditions gears its international trips to travelers who want adventure by day and comfort at night. NEI emphasizes small groups and a quality experience. Staff tour leaders are qualified naturalists; most are fluent in the particular region's local language. Most tours cover a variety of ecosystems—for example, NEI's Australia trip visits the Blue Mountains, the Red Desert, Daintree Rain Forest, and Great Barrier Reef.

Joseph Van Os Photo Safaris
P.O. Box 655, Vashon Island, WA 98070
206-463-5383
www.photosafaris.com

If you're serious about photographing exotic wildlife, this is the operator to go with. Each year, the company sees more than 1,000 repeat customers. Van Os's leadership and its access to prime wildlife-viewing areas are key to its successful programs. Also, the company has pioneered many new destinations for photo safaris. Trips are designed expressly for nature photography: The guides are experienced photographers and naturalists, and the itineraries allow the maximum number of shooting days. Most groups are small, with no more than eight clients per guide.

Victor Emanuel Nature Tours (VENT)
P.O. Box 33008, Austin, TX 78764
800-328-8368 or 512-328-5221
www.ventbird.com

Established in 1975, VENT is the oldest and largest specialty agency for bird-watchers, with a loyal customer following. The company also offers a variety of general wildlife tours, from the Arctic to the Amazon. VENT trips tend to sport higher price tags than most—but the perks include excellent food and lodging and expert guides.

Wilderness Travel
1102 Ninth St., Berkeley, CA 94710
800-368-2794 or 510-558-2488
www.wildernesstravel.com

What sets this outfitter apart from the rest is its guides: Specialists all, most hold degrees in their respective fields and many are renowned experts. Founded in the 1970s, Wilderness Travel annually offers about 120 small-group trips around the globe. Nearly 65 percent of this agent's clients are repeat customers. Wilderness Travel also sponsors special wildlife seminars with celebrated naturalists, such as Jane Goodall and Cynthia Moss. The **2001 Antarctic Odyssey** will be led by highly-regarded natural-history writer Barry Lopez and mountaineering giant Reinhold Messner.

Wildland Adventures
3516 N.E. 155th St., Seattle, WA 98155
800-345-4453 or 206-365-0686
www.wildland.com

Wildland Adventures specializes in multicultural and natural-history expeditions for active and inquisitive travelers who seek close encounters with wildlife as well as native peoples. The company's unique focus is on immersion and authenticity of experience. Participants seek to gain a deeper appreciation for their particular destination—no matter where in the world it is—on a Wildland Adventure tour than is possible on most other trips. Trips are led by experienced, local naturalists, who can expertly interpret the regional culture and ecology. Wildland Adventure is recognized as a leader in ecotourism because of its continued support of conservation and community-development projects in its host countries.

Dogsledding

In his 1911 push to the South Pole by dog team, explorer Roald Amundsen secured a place for dogsledding in the annals of high adventure. Nearly a century later, dogsledding competitions—epitomized by the **Iditarod**—remain a supreme challenge of stamina and courage: For two weeks, Iditarod mushers and their dog teams race night and day, braving subzero temperatures and cruel winds, to cover 1,000 or more miles of frozen wilderness.

Today the availability of different commercial tours enables you to enjoy the adventure of dogsledding without risking life and limb. You can mush a team for the afternoon or sign up for a challenging, week-long wilderness expedition.

Many fine dogsled operations, both in the United States and abroad, can introduce you to this unique winter activity. Most operators in the continental U.S. offer day and weekend trips. In Alaska, a number of kennels specialize in extended backcountry tours.

The best resource for information about dogsledding is *Mushing Magazine (P.O. Box 149, Ester, AK 99725. 907-479-0454. www.mushing.com)*. Published every two months, the magazine features an international directory of dogsled outfitters and a calendar of mushing events.

For a comprehensive index of mushers, check the Web (*www.dogsledrides.com*).

NORTH AMERICAN OUTFITTERS

Absaroka Dogsled Treks
Mark Nardin, Box 134, Pray, MT 59065
406-222-4645
www.dogsledrides.com/mt.html
Treks depart from Chico Hot Springs Lodge, near Yellowstone National Park.

Boundary Country Trekking
7925 Gunflint Trail
Grand Marais, MN 55604
800-322-8327 or 218-388-9972
www.boundarycountry.com
Extended treks, with overnights in heated cabins or yurts.

Dog Sled Rides of Winter Park
P.O. Box 304, Fraser, CO 80442
970-726-8326
Popular outfit near ski resort offers excellent short rides with experienced mushers.

Earthsong Lodge Dog Sled Adventures
John Nuremburg, Denali National Park,
P.O. Box 89, Healy, AK 99743
907-683-2863
www.earthsonglodge.com
The only dogsled concession in Denali.

Grizzle-T Dog and Sled Works
HCR-66, Box 39
Steamboat Springs, CO 80487
970-870-1782
Two-hour tours.

Husky Express
P.O. Box 176, Gardnerville, NV 89410
775-782-3047
www.highsierra.com/sst
Backcountry tours are offered in the eastern Sierra Nevada.

Jackson Hole Iditarod Sled Dog Tours
P.O. Box 5517
Jackson, WY 83001
800-554-7388 or 307-733-7388
www.jhsleddog.com
A good choice for alpine tours near the Continental Divide.

Krabloonik Dogsled
4250 Divide Rd.
Snowmass Village, CO 81615
970-923-4342
www.krabloonik.com
This outfitter runs excellent alpine tours in the Rockies.

Mahoosuc Guide Service
1513 Bear River Rd., Newry, ME 04261
207-824-2073
www.mahoosuc.com
Trips in Maine, Quebec, the Northwest Territories, and Baffin Island, with Native American guides.

Pintler Sled Adventures
Bob and Nancy Davis, 9010 Hwy. 1
West Anaconda, MT 59711
Instruction and drive-your-own-team.

Sourdough Outfitters
P.O. Box 26066, Bettles, AK 99726
907-692-5252
www.sourdough.com
Extended trips in Brooks Range and Arrigetch Peak region.

Washakie Outfitting
P.O. Box 1054, Dubois, WY 83001
800-249-0662 or 307-455-2616
www.dogsledwashakie.com
Excellent day trips and overnight trips in scenic Jackson Hole backcountry.

Wilderness Inquiry
808 14th Ave. SE
Minneapolis, MN 55414
800-728-0719 or 612-379-3858
Trips for all ages and abilities, including the physically challenged, in Minnesota, Canada, and elsewhere.

Wintergreen Dogsled Lodge
1101 Ring Rock Rd., Ely, MN 55731
800-584-9425 or 218-365-6022
www.dogsledding.com
The lodge runs both lodge-to-lodge and wilderness trips.

INTERNATIONAL OUTFITTERS

Arctic Odysseys
2000 McGilvra Blvd. E., Seattle, WA 98112
800-574-3021 or 206-325-1977
www.arcticodysseys.com
Traditional dogsledding in Northwest Territories and on Baffin Island with Inuit guide.

Borton Overseas
5412 Lyndale Ave. S.,
Minneapolis, MN 55419
800-843-0602 or 612-822-4640
www.bortonoverseas.com
Dogsled and komatik trips in Greenland and Scandinavia.

Great Slave Sledging Co., Ltd.
P.O. Box 1978, Yellowknife, NWT
X1A 2P5 Canada
867-873-6070
Cabin-to-cabin and wilderness tours in the Northwest Territories.

Italian Dogsled School
Località Case Sparse, 10
25056 Ponte di Legno, Italy
01139-0364-92231 for phone and fax
www.adamelloski.com
Instruction, rides, and races year-round in the Italian Alps.

Travel Tips

WHAT TO TAKE

Most outfitters furnish a list of items that you should pack for your trip. A word of advice: If yours is an active itinerary that will keep you on the move, be sure to pack lightly. Those "indispensable" items quickly become excess baggage after a few days of schlepping them around the wilds. When in doubt, leave it out.

If you're northbound for Alaska or Canada, even in summer, you will need to take warm clothing. Gore-Tex or insulated pants and jacket, rain gear, and wool socks are recommended. Also take sturdy, waterproof boots, with separate inner liners and insoles.

For trips to desert environments such as the Galápagos or Baja California, pack a good sunscreen and a hat. Also carry salt- or electrolyte-replacement tablets.

Finally, carry with you any medications and toiletries you require. Items that are vulnerable to moisture should be stored in plastic containers.

WHEN TO GO

Timing is everything on a nature trip. It can also be tricky. If you dream of witnessing a great annual wildlife event such as a caribou migration or the hatching of sea turtles, you have to travel at just the right time—which, in some cases, leaves you a small window of opportunity. If you miss it, you'll be disappointed.

Weigh your priorities. Traveling off-season usually means lower rates and fewer people. It can also mean less favorable weather or wildlife-viewing conditions, so do your research.

If optimal animal activity and climate are tops on your list, you'll probably pay more—and encounter more tourists, depending on the location.

ONLINE

Away.com
www.away.com

This site features thousands of ecotours offered by hundreds of operators worldwide. Use the trip-finder database, or browse the "Green Channel" for eco-sensitive guide services.

Dogsled Rides
www.dogsledrides.com

Listed here are more than 100 dogsled tour operators, mushing schools, and kennels in more than 20 states.

National Geographic Society
www.nationalgeographic.com

National Geographic's impressive website features current expeditions and highlights from NGS projects.

BOOKS

The Lonely Planet guidebook series is recommended for many areas mentioned in this chapter. You'll find reliable information presented in an easy-to-read format, with helpful maps.

For identifying wildlife, the Audubon Society's *Field Guide to North American Birds* and *Field Guide to North American Wildflowers* are good bets. Also have a look at National Geographic's *Field Guide to the Birds of North America.*

Adventuring in Indonesia: Exploring the Natural Areas of the Pacific's Ring of Fire by Holly S. Smith (Sierra Club Adventure Travel Guide, 1997, $14.40). The most comprehensive ecoresource for Indonesia.

Costa Rica: Adventures in Nature by Ree Strange Sheck (John Muir Publications, 1998, $18.95). An excellent guide to reserves, parks, and nature tours.

The Log from the Sea of Cortez by John Steinbeck (Penguin, 1995 reprint, $13). Steinbeck fans and armchair travelers will enjoy the writer's thoughtful musings on his 1940 trip to Mexico's Baja peninsula.

Travels in Alaska by John Muir (Houghton Mifflin, 1995 reprint, $19). A classic travel journal by a founding father of the environmental movement.

Voyage of the Beagle by Charles Darwin (Anchor, 1989 reprint, $9.50). The book in which Darwin introduced his theory of evolution was based on his findings in the Galápagos Islands.

DOGSLEDDING IN ALASKA

A HIGH-ADRENALINE DANCE WITH WIND AND WAVE, WINDSURFING IS THE MOST INTENSE AND ATHLETIC form of sailing. Also known as boardsailing, this challenging and exhilarating solo sport combines elements of skiing, surfing, and sailing. In the hands—and beneath the feet—of an expert windsurfer, the latest boards can perform loops, jump waves, and move across the water at speeds of 40 miles per hour. • The ease of transporting a windsurfing rig by airplane makes it possible to enjoy the sport throughout the world. In this chapter, you'll find information on top windsurfing spots from Aruba to Australia to the Aegean—ultimate destinations that deliver consistent wind, usually in a comfortable, warm-water setting. • This chapter also shows you how to find travel bargains, how to assess the leading tour operators, and how to maximize your windsurfing time by picking the best situated beachfront resorts. So whether you're an experienced windsurfer or a relative newcomer to the sport, grab a board, hoist your sail, and come ride the wind.

DANCES WITH WAVES: WINDSURFING IN MAUI, HAWAII

The only matter of consequence...is what I will do with my allotted time. I can remain on shore, paralyzed with fear, or I can raise my sails and dip and soar in the breeze.
RICHARD BODE

Seven Windsurfing Wonders of the World

A windsurfing vacation may be the ultimate action holiday, but it need not cost the world. You can enjoy this sport at a budget price, typically $600 to $1,000 for a full week, including lodging, equipment, and rental car. Moreover, because trade-wind conditions make for the best sailing, most top resorts are located in the tropics—where the sun and the sand make the prospect of sailing about as good as it gets.

ARUBA
Two-Sided Treasure

Ah, Aruba! Located only 12 degrees north of the Equator, this Caribbean island offers warm, crystal-clear water that rarely drops below 75° F and consistent winds that are a windsurfer's dream: The average wind speed, year-round, is more than 20 knots, though it can get up to 10 knots higher in June, the island's windiest month.

With winds like these—beloved of speed sailors—Aruba should be a destination for experts only. Not so. Although the northeastern flank of the long, narrow island is turned toward the prevailing trade winds, its sheltered, lee side to the southwest provides excellent flat-water sailing—made even better by the presence of a nearby reef that blocks the ocean swell.

A number of tour operators book windsurfing vacations in Aruba. The top choice is **Vela Windsurf Resorts** (*4604 Scotts Valley Dr., Scotts Valley, CA 95066. 800-223-5443 or 831-461-0820. www.velawindsurf.com*), which operates the **Fisherman's Huts Windsurf Center**—probably the best facility on the island. Located at the northwest end of Aruba, the center offers a variety of lessons taught four times daily. The cost for a seven-night package with accommodations and equipment is $630 to $1,750 for a double, depending on the season.

Also recommended is **Sailboard Vacations** (*193 Rockland St., Hanover, MA 02339. 800-252-1070 or 781-829-8915. www.sailboardvacations.com*), which offers packages that include lodging and equipment rental. The company's **Aruba Windsurfing Academy** provides high-quality instruction for all ability levels, with special clinics held in April, August, and December. Weekly rates, not including airfare or car rental, run $700 to $900 from mid-June to mid-December and $900 to $1,100 from mid-December to mid-June. Sailboard's equipment is new, and its accommodations are located quite close to the prime sailing spots, so—although it's convenient to have one—you don't absolutely have to rent a car.

Divi Aruba (*Al G. Smith Blvd. No. 93, Divi Village, Aruba. 011-29-782-3300. www.diviaruba.com*) also rents equipment and provides lessons. For your convenience, all gear at Divi Aruba is rigged and ready for use, and the instruction is top-rate.

Aruba has much to offer in addition to wonderful wind-surfing conditions, so if you're recovering from sunburn, blisters, or just plain fatigue, take time out to enjoy some of the island's other attractions. During the day you can relax in temperatures that average a balmy 82° F, with low humidity. And at night—when Aruba really comes to life—you can try your luck at one of the island's popular casinos, where the roll of the dice can be less predictable than the blow of Aruba's trade winds.

OREGON
Gorging on the Columbia River

Tricky, challenging—and very windy. That's how best to describe the Pacific Northwest's premier windsurfing destination: the **Columbia River Gorge.**

To sail the gorge, you'd better be pretty good. At the peak of summer, when the thermal winds are really pumping up the Columbia, expect a solid 20 to 30 knots, with some days of more than 40. And unlike in Aruba, should you take a tumble in the gorge, you won't find any nice sandy spots to cushion your fall.

Summer water temperatures are around 65° to 70° F near the banks, and most windsurfers get by with short-sleeved conventional wet suits. Air temperatures at this time of year are typically in the high 80s to 90s.

Experts will find good sailing from Swell City to the Hatchery. Windsurfers of all levels should head to the stretch between Rowena and Doug's Beach. Novices should make their way to Bingen and the Hood River Marina, the most popular spots on the river.

Doug's Sports (*101 Oak Ave., Hood River, OR 97031. 541-386-5787. www.hoodriverwindsurfing.com*) has the most complete line of windsurfing equipment in the area. **Big Winds School** (*207 Front St., Hood River, OR 97031. 541-386-6086. www.bigwinds.com*) offers lesson-and-rental packages and sells complete rigs and accessories. **Sailworld** (*112 Oak Ave., Hood River, OR 97031. 541-386-9400. www.sailworld.com*) is a retail windsurf shop that also books lessons. For more

details on the gorge and its sailing options, contact **Columbia Gorge Windsurfing Association** (*541-386-9225. E-mail: cgwa@gorge.net*).

Several comfortable hotels in the area cater to windsurfers. The **Windrider Inn** (*200 W. 4th St., The Dalles, OR 97058. 541-296-2607. www.gorge.net/cwindrider*) offers low weekly rates: $250 per room, based on double occupancy. For $49 to $150 per night you can get a double room at the **Hood River Hotel** (*102 Oak Ave., Hood River, OR 97031. 800-386-1859. www.hoodriverhotel.com*) or at the **Days Inn** (*2500 W. 6th St., The Dalles, OR 97058. 800-991-0801 or 541-296-1191*). **Gorge Central Vacation Rentals** (*877-386-6109 or 541-386-6109. www.gorgeres.com*) can book accommodations as well.

Those on a tight budget can camp at one of the many private resorts and state parks along the Columbia. Advance reservations are a must for most good camping areas. Contact the **Oregon State Parks and Recreation Division, Reservations Northwest** (*P.O. Box 500, Portland, OR 97207. 800-452-5687. www.prd.state.or.us*).

MAUI
Windsurfing Heartland

Sooner or later, every windsurfer goes to the Hawaiian island of Maui—and once you get there you'll understand why. The island offers good instruction, top equipment, and—most important—the right conditions: warm water and trade winds that blow at 15 to 25 knots nonstop.

For these reasons, Maui is one of the best places to learn the sport. The island also offers what experienced windsurfers look for in addition to strong, steady winds: a good selection of sea conditions, from flat (at **Kanaha** and **Kihei**) to big swells (at **Ho'okipa**) to a mixture of the two (at **Spreckelsville**).

Unless you've got a buddy with a condo on the windward side of the island, you're wise to book a windsurfing package through one of Maui's well-established shops. A package with condo and sailboard and car rental will cost approximately $900 per person for a week, based on double occupancy. The price will include a top-quality board complete with full rig—sail, boom, mast base, and roof racks for your car.

Remember this when booking your trip: Most of the action is on the windward, northern side of the island, near the airport. So if you have a choice, don't stay on the leeward side—or you'll be spending a couple of hours a day commuting to and from your sailing spot.

On Maui, the rental equipment is so new and so good that there's little reason to bring your own gear, other than personal items such as gloves, booties, and harness. The preferred

WINDSURFERS ANGLE ACROSS THE SWELLS OFF
HO'OKIPA BEACH, MAUI.

rental board is a 9-foot to 9-foot-4-inch production slalom, although longer boards are available for beginners. The latest custom wave boards can be rented as well. Sail choice is up to the individual, but on a typical Maui day most sailors will rig a slalom or wave sail in the 4-foot-5-inch to 5-foot-1-inch range, with women opting for a size smaller.

All the top windsurfing shops on the island offer package tours—and all provide excellent equipment and service. **Hawaiian Island Surf & Sport** (*800-231-6958. www.hawaiianisland.com*) has seven-night packages starting at approximately $570 that include accommodations, board and rig, and rental car with unlimited free mileage. **Maui Windsurf Company** (*800-872-099 or 808-877-4816. www.maui-windsurf.com*) offers a seven-night package—which includes lodging, windsurfing equipment, rental car with rack, and optional lesson programs—for $600 to $1,000 per person, based on double occupancy (price depending on the season). Other recommended windsurfing shops on the island are **Second Wind Sail & Surf** (*800-936-7787. www.secondwindmaui.com*) and **Hi-Tech Surf Sports** (*808-877-2111. www.maui.net/~htmaui*). For bookings, contact **Vela Windsurf Resorts** (*800-223-5443. www.velawindsurf.com*).

When booking your trip, consider spending a little extra to stay at a North Shore guesthouse—preferably one with its own beach. This way you won't have to fight the crowds at Kanaha or Spreckelsville. **Maui Windsurfari** (*800-736-6284. www.windsurfari.com*) offers an assortment of accommodations, with prices ranging from $45 to $1,000 per night. **Excursions Extraordinaire** (*800-678-2252 or 541-484-0493. www.mauiwindsurfing.com*) features a fantastic oceanfront, four-bedroom North Shore villa with pre-rigged gear. Total price is around $1,200 per person, based on double occupancy, for seven days of meals, equipment, lodging, and instruction.

DOMINICAN REPUBLIC
In the Caribbean, Life is a Cabarete

Cabarete in the Dominican Republic is the eastern Caribbean's top windsurfing destination. Reliable 20-knot side-shore winds can be expected five days a week from November to April and from June through August. Air temperature is in the high 70s to 80s year-round, and the water temperature is a warm 75° F even in winter.

The north shore of the Dominican Republic offers ideal conditions for all levels of windsurfers. An offshore reef keeps the water flat close to the beach even in high winds, offering a smooth surface on which beginners can practice—and on which experts can achieve some impressive speeds. Five hundred yards offshore, where the swell and wind-waves hit the reef, there is prime-time wave sailing—considered by many to be the best outside Hawaii.

Major air carriers serve the Dominican Republic, so you can bring your equipment without great difficulty—provided your board is less than 8 feet 6 inches long (larger boards will be surcharged). For a 160-pound sailor, a

4-foot-7-inch slalom sail is a good choice for summer, a 5-foot-2-inch for winter. With good package vacations available, however, you may want to leave all that gear at home.

Vela Windsurf Resorts (800-223-5443. www.velawind-surf.com) offers Cabarete holidays at beachfront condos and resort hotels. Cost per person for a double ranges from about $400 to $850 per week, depending on the season. This includes lodging and complete board and rig rental. **Sailboard Vacations** (800-252-1070. www.sailboardvacations. com) also offers competitively priced package holidays at a variety of Cabarete resorts.

Of all the windsurfing concessions, Vela's is the best. Its boards are new, light, and fast, and the sails are kept pre-rigged. At Cabarete, you won't get the up-to-date sails, masts, or boards that you might see in Maui, but overall the rental rigs are quite good—and far superior to what you'll find in most Club Med-type Caribbean resorts.

The popularity of Cabarete is increasing—and so, eventually, will its prices. For now, however, it offers great wind and water, and relatively uncrowded sailing.

AUSTRALIA
Windsurfing in the Land of Auz

With around 8,000 miles of coastline encircling a landmass nearly the size of the United States, Australia is a wind-surfer's dream. The best action on the continent, though, is on the west coast. And thanks to thermal conditions in the Australian interior—which pull in strong, reliable sea breezes from the Indian Ocean—the coastline around **Perth** is particularly good.

The prime windsurfing season here runs from October to November, with continued good conditions through February. Winds are usually offshore in the morning with a cool onshore breeze in the afternoon, averaging 18 to 25 knots in the Perth area and even more in some spots nearby.

Perth's Swan River is an excellent choice for flat-water sailing. Being rather shallow, it's a good choice for novices but has enough wind to satisfy stronger sailors. Try putting in at Pelican Point on the north bank of the river near the University of Western Australia. **Pelican Point Windsurfing** (01161-8938-61830) operates a windsurfing school here and also offers trips out to the nearby Keeling Islands. Chop jumpers should head to reef-free Leighton Beach, just north of Fremantle. Summer brings onshore winds of 18 to 25 knots and more, with ideal swells for "bump and jump" sailing on small boards.

A couple of offshore islands shield Perth from the largest swells traveling across the Indian Ocean. For serious wave-sailing, therefore, you'll have to travel a little to the north or south. About one hour north of Perth you'll find the small fishing town of Lancelin. The winds are stronger here than

in Perth, and the reefs produce 6- to 10-foot waves throughout much of the year.

Lancelin doesn't offer many amenities, but there are shops where you can buy spares and rent a basic rig. Once you leave Lancelin, though, things get desolate in a hurry. Don't venture into the hinterlands without reliable transport and plenty of water and fuel.

Farther north, about five hours from Perth, you'll arrive in the town of **Geraldton,** a popular windsurfing center with reliable southwesterly sea breezes that range from 15 to 25 knots. Good sites exist all along the coast here. Geraldton's hot spots are the lighthouse at Point Moore—usually the windiest spot in the area—and St. Georges Beach, a good choice for all skill levels. Sunset Beach at the north end of Geraldton offers side-onshore winds with good bump and jump conditions near the shore, and head-high surf on the reefs when a swell is running.

Sail West (P.O. Box 1459, Geraldton, Western Australia 6530. 01161-8996-41722. www.wn.com.au/sailwest/sailwest.htm) offers one- to four-week windsurfing packages on Australia's west coast. A one-week package with lodging in Perth and Geraldton, rental car, and equipment costs $475 to $610 (AU) per person, double occupancy.

South of Perth, the territory gets fairly wild and rugged, especially between Cape Naturaliste and Cape Leeuwin. Head off in that direction only if you're feeling particularly adventurous—and you're looking for truly big-wave action. At **Margaret River,** for example, you can usually find mast-high swells and strong onshore winds. The river is ideal for surfing in the morning and wave riding in the afternoon, when the wind picks up. But don't even think about sailing here unless you're very good: The tremendous swells and rocky outcrops have claimed several lives. If you intend to sail in this area, make sure you spend some time observing the locals first.

GREECE
Aegean Adventure

Scattered in the Aegean Sea between Greece and Turkey, the **Kykládes (Cyclades)** islands have long been a popular tourist haven. The region's reliable winds also make them an excellent choice for windsurfers. And though hard-core European windsurfers still opt for the Canary Islands, the Cyclades offer a less expensive alternative—with more to do when the wind doesn't blow.

That's not to suggest that you should be overly concerned about a lack of wind, however. Greece enjoys a remarkably consistent summer wind pattern—known as the Neltemi—that rolls in from the northern Aegean at 10 to 35 knots for 20 days a month on average, from May through October. And in the off-season—spring and fall—the region often

A WINDSURFER GOES AIRBORNE OVER THE OCEAN AT MAUI.

experiences scirocco winds from the deserts of North Africa.

The sciroccos also blow in serious wave sailors keen to pit their skills against the swells kicked up by the hot African winds blasting across the Mediterranean. Summer air temperatures in the Cyclades are usually in the mid-80s but can reach more than 100° F. The water is warm in late summer; before July, though, it can be cool enough to require a short-sleeved fullsuit and a vest for warmer days.

Páros, a six-hour ferry ride from Athens and the third largest island in the Cyclades, has developed into a premier international windsurfing destination. The most popular launch sites on Páros include Golden Beach and New Golden Beach, both located on the island's east side. Golden Beach is set within a bay, so there's plenty of flat water for slalom sailing. Other popular windsurfing beaches on Páros include Kolimbithres, near the picturesque village of Náoussa, and Poúnda, a mile from the airport.

And when the winds don't blow? There's still plenty to do: You can dive, water-ski, mountain bike, sightsee, or at night—all in the name of cross-training, of course—stretch your legs at any number of dance clubs.

Board rentals, sailing lessons, and lodging packages are offered by both **Sun Wind Surf Center** (*Golden Beach. 01130-2844-2900. www.greektravel.com/greekislands/paros/ sunwind*) and **Páros Surf Club** (*New Golden Beach. 01130-2845-2822 or 01130-1959-8317. www.parosurf.gr*).

While Páros has been garnering attention, nearby **Náxos** has quietly become a favorite spot for windsurfers. Windsurfing conditions here are pretty much like those at Páros: windy and for the most part flat. What distinguishes Náxos is its conspicuous absence of tourists. Lacking an airport, the island is accessible only by ferry. Once there, you'll probably need a car.

But if you make it, there should be no problem finding a room, even in June and July. If you choose to windsurf near the town of Náxos, the best spot is Aghios Yeórghios at the end of the bay. Again, the water is very flat and the conditions are suitable for good slalom sailing. At about $25 a night for two people, accommodations on Náxos are nearly negligible, and camping is always a popular alternative. Austria's **TraWell Surfreisen** (*Vienna, Austria. 01143-1505-0457*) runs a big program in Greece, with sailing centers in Náxos and four other Greek locations.

Mikrí Vígla, about 12 miles from the town of Náxos, may be the best windsurfing spot in all the Greek islands. Winds can exceed 40 knots, and waves can reach 6 feet. Although you can camp at Mikrí Vígla, you may decide not to: There are a number of beautiful waterside resorts here that cost $85 in the high season and just $35 at all other times. You can rent boards through the local hotels for roughly $50 per day.

The nearby islands of **Ios** and **Santoríni** are well worth a visit. The windsurfing isn't spectacular on either, but both islands are scenic and just a few hours from Náxos by ferry.

If you're reluctant to plan your own Greek windsurfing trip, **Neilson** (*Brighton, BN2 1EG, England. 01144-1273-626-283 or 284. www.neilson.co.uk*) offers a turnkey solution. This well-established British company operates four seaside resorts in Greece where you can enjoy a full range of activities, including windsurfing. The most popular high-wind location is Vasilikí on the island of **Lefkás,** in the Ionian Sea off the west coast of Greece. Here, from June through September, a reliable thermal pumps 22- to 27-knot side-shore winds across a wide, beautiful bay. No matter what your equipment preference, you'll be happy at Vasilikí, because Neilson offers more than 120 boards and rigs from all the top manufacturers.

A 14-day vacation costs roughly $850, which includes lodging, certified windsurfing instruction, unlimited use of equipment, and round-trip airfare from London. If you want to combine catamaran or dinghy sailing with your windsurfing vacation, you can visit Neilson's sailing resorts at Nidhrí, which is also on Lefkás, or Portochélion and Finikouda on the Greek mainland. At any of these locations, you'll enjoy the fellowship of other windsurfers from throughout the world.

The greatest expense associated with a vacation in the Greek islands is getting there. Once you arrive you can easily minimize your costs by heading for the more remote islands, where you won't have to sacrifice on the quality of accommodations or food. Room rates throughout the country more than double during July and August. Even so, prices are still reasonable—and you always have the option of camping.

Another way to significantly lower your accommodation costs is to stay in one place for a weekly rate. It's hard to resist the temptation to island hop, however. And there will always be some form of lodging on offer: When you arrive at an island, your ferry will be greeted by a handful of locals offering rooms for rent in the family home. This is often a sensible option. A room for two without a bath costs about $20, including breakfast.

BAJA CALIFORNIA
Escapades & Escapes

More laid back than Maui—and certainly less crowded—Baja California is a wonderful windsurfing getaway. The water is warm, the sun is golden, and the setting is interesting enough that you don't feel like you're wasting precious vacation time when the wind doesn't blow—or when you decide to blow off that day's windsurfing.

Not blessed with trade winds, Baja depends on local

RED SAIL, BLUE SEA: LONE SAILOR OFF THE BAJA COAST

thermals and storm winds to generate its breezes. As a result, conditions can be inconsistent. The best season for wind is winter—from late November through mid-February. At other times of the year, the air may barely stir for days on end.

When the wind *is* active, it often starts in the morning, at around 10:30 or so, and blows moderately—at 10 to 15 knots—for a few hours. It can then die down for a while, only to come back much stronger—sometimes at speeds as high as 18 to 25 knots. Generally, though, you should plan to use a sail one size bigger than you might at Maui. A 4-foot-7-inch to 5-foot sail works on most days. Remember, too, that the proximity of landmasses affects winds, and that one spot along the coast may be better than another only a short distance away.

The top windsurfing resorts cluster along the southern end of the Baja peninsula near La Paz. A good flat-water spot is **Bahía de la Ventana.** Chop jumpers will prefer Punta Chivato, Palmas de Cortez, and Playa Hermosa. You don't need to stick to the resort beaches, of course; if you've got wheels, load up your rig and go exploring.

A word to the wise: Baja is not a great place for beginning shortboarders. Many of the beaches receive a large swell, or have pretty steep chop that makes it tough to stay under control. Also, the water gets deep right off the beach, so Baja is much less forgiving for novice water-starters than Aruba or even Maui. If you're just starting on a shortboard, stay at a flat-water location such as Bahía de la Ventana—or, better yet, perfect your water starts before you arrive.

With prices less than $850 per week, double occupancy, there's no real incentive to shun a package tour. **Vela Windsurf Resorts** (*800-223-5443. www.velawindsurf.com*) offers a full-week package for $820 to $910 per person at the Playa del Sol in Los Barriles. Most packages offer roughly similar services: a beachfront hotel with pool, bar, and restaurant, high-quality rigs and boards, and instruction programs. In choosing a resort, it's hard to go far wrong. Last time we were in Baja, Vela had the newest equipment and best sail inventory. Remember, however, that nearly all visitors to Baja are fairly good sailors; this is not a locale that caters to first-time water-starters.

The tough choice is how long to stay. For accomplished intermediates, a week is about right. If the winds are strong, experts may want to stay as long as they can. Prices for food and drink tend to be lower than they are in Maui, and the atmosphere is definitely less intense; *"mañana"* is the watchword. When booking your trip, check for special offers on airfare, which may not be included in the package price. **Alaska Airlines** (*800-426-0333. www.alaskaair.com*) often has the best rates.

Top Spots to Catch the Wind

The great thing about windsurfing is that, on a planet covered mostly by water, there are so many places to do it.

Here is a selection of some of the best. All offer strong winds, good water conditions, comfortable

accommodations, and—for those inevitable lulls when the wind dies down—enjoyable shoreside diversions.

CARIBBEAN

BONAIRE

Less well-known than Aruba, Bonaire is the "other" Dutch windsurfing haven in the Caribbean with outstanding sailing. Peak winds are in May and June, and average air and water temperatures are in the low 80s. Consistent trade winds—between 12 and 25 knots—blow into a large, reef-protected bay, offering smooth conditions that are good for all levels of windsurfers. Outside the reef there is wave sailing for experts. Complete equipment and lodging packages start at approximately $650 per person per week, which includes car rental. Contact **Roger's Windsurf Place** (*Lac Bay, Bonaire, N.A. 800-225-0102 or 01129-786-1918 in Aruba. www.rogerswindsurf.com*) or **Sailboard Vacations** (*800-252-1070. www.sailboardvacations.com*). You will need a rental car on the island to reach the sailing areas.

BARBADOS

After Cabarete in the Dominican Republic, Barbados delivers the best wave sailing in the Caribbean—at Silver Sands, a reef about 1,000 yards offshore. Nearby Oistins Bay offers sheltered sailing in side-shore trade winds, averaging 15 to 25 knots in late spring and early summer. The best winds arrive in January and February, with a strong resurgence in June. Spring months are still good but somewhat less consistent. Water temperatures run in the 70s year-round. Convenient lodging can be had at the Sea Breeze Beach Hotel on Oistins Bay, where the **Windsurfing Club** provides rentals, including beginner and intermediate Mistral equipment. Package trips start at $600 per person, including lodging and equipment. Contact **Sailboard Vacations** (*800-252-1070. www.sailboardvacations.com*).

LAGO DE ARENAL, COSTA RICA

Beneath a volcano lies Lago de Arenal (Lake Arenal), one of the finest inland sailing sites in the world—a real bump and jump heaven. December through April, solid thermal-boosted trade winds run down the lake at 15 to 30 knots. When it really blows, it can get up to 35 knots, and the big chop demands expert skills. The lake is long and narrow with most activity clustered at the downwind end, where water temperatures peak in the mid-70s. The Rock River Lodge/Tico Wind (*E-mail: ticowind@compuserve.com*) has nice rooms and good equipment, and the **Tilawa Marina & Windsurf Center**—the largest facility on the lake—offers competitive prices on lodging and gear rental. Package holidays with lodging and all gear run $600-700 per week per person. Call **Costa Rica Reservations** (*800-566-6716. www.calypsotours.com*).

ISLA DE MARGARITA, VENEZUELA

Margarita offers strong and exceptionally consistent side-shore breezes. Trade winds build through the day, giving advanced windsurfers great bump and jump conditions in the afternoons. The ideal season is mid-Feb. to May, when winds average 25 to 35 knots. Expect 18- to 25-knot winds December through April and inconsistent breezes late summer through fall. The beach resorts are very comfortable and the lifestyle is more laid back than other tourist islands of the Caribbean. The water is a warm 85° F and shallow—typically, waist deep for at least 200 yards from the beach. For package tours contact **Casa Viento Enterprises** (*3223 4th St., Boulder, CO, 80304. 800-660-9463 or 303-447-2630; 01158-1669-56858 in Venezuela. www.sni.net/windsurf*). Room and equipment cost $375-485 per person weekly.

TOBAGO

Tobago is still relatively undiscovered among Caribbean sailing venues. Blessed by the same trade winds that sweep Aruba, Barbados, and Margarita, the island enjoys great sailing conditions—and lower prices than in the more popular spots. Expect fairly consistent conditions from February to May, averaging 18 to 20 knots. Then, during the late spring months, the trades build, averaging 20 to 22 knots until the rainy season starts in June and July. You can rent board and sail for around $275 for seven days from **Windsurf Tobago** (*Pigeon Point, Tobago, W.I. 868-639-3846. www.windsurftobago.com*). Lodgings at the Bellevista Apartments (*E-mail: bellevis@tstt.net.tt*) begin as low as $70 per night.

MAINLAND

CAPE HATTERAS, NORTH CAROLINA

The jewel of the mid-Atlantic coast, Cape Hatteras offers ideal beginner conditions on the flat, forgiving waters of Pamlico Sound. Farther offshore, more advanced sailors will find solid breezes into the low 20s, ideal for chop hopping and wave jumping. Best times are spring and fall, when the winds are up and water temperatures are in the mid 70s. For rentals, call **Windsurfing Hatteras** (*252-995-5000. www.windsurfinghatteras.com*). Accommodations are plentiful, particularly rental houses for six to eight people, which start at $1,000 per week. Book through **Hatteras Realty** (*800-428-8372. www.hatterasrealty.com*).

CORPUS CHRISTI, TEXAS

Rated the best flat-water site on the mainland by *Windsurfing Magazine*, Laguna Madre offers ideal conditions for all windsurfers. The sandy-bottomed lagoon (which is part of the Padre Island National Seashore) is just 3 to 5 feet deep for more than 1,000 yards—perfect for novices learning water starts. With warm, smooth water and steady, unobstructed winds averaging around 16 knots, seasoned windsurfers experience fantastic speedsailing. Summer offers the most consistent winds, but there is good sailing year-round. Rent complete rigs for $40 to $60 per day from **WorldWinds Windsurfing** (*800-793-7471 or 361-949-7472. www.coolcats*).

com/worldwinds). Or log on to the website of the Corpus Christi Windsurfing Association (*http://members.xoom.com/CCWA*).

NITINAT LAKE, BRITISH COLUMBIA

One of the most beautiful windsurfing spots in the world, Nitinat Lake is an inlet surrounded by an old-growth forest along the west coast of Vancouver Island. Serene and secluded, this may be the best kept secret in mainland boardsailing. A favorite of Canadian Olympic boardsailors, Nitinat is best sailed from May to Labor Day, when the wind averages 8 to 13 knots. Water temperature is 60° to 70° F, depending on the time of year. Restricted camping is allowed on the lake. Like most of the outfitters in this area, **Pacific Boarder** (*1793 W. 4th Ave., Vancouver, BC V6J 1M2, Canada. 604-734-7245. www.pacificboarder.com*) sells—but does not rent—equipment.

EUROPE

CANARY ISLANDS

Home of 11-time world champion Bjorn Dunkerbeck, Spain's Canary Islands offer world-class conditions. Europe's elite windsurfers often stay for a month or more each summer, when it blows 15 to 25 knots, five days a week. Gran Canaria is a good starting place. Dunkerbeck's parents own the Side Shore resort, which has bungalows, a pool-bar, and most conveniences. Contact **Side Shore** (*P.O. Box 135, San Augustin, Gran Canaria, Spain. 01134-9287-62022. www.neilpryde.com/hotspots/testcentres/sidecanaria.html*). The nearby islands of Fuerteventura and Lanzarote are the top spots, however, with their stronger winds and long, sandy beaches. Fuerteventura has the best facilities, including car rentals, numerous lodging options, and a good board shop in Corralejo.

PORTO POLLO, SARDINIA

Porto Pollo and all of northern Sardinia offer the best windsurfing in the western Mediterranean. Wind speeds average 15 to 25 knots, while summer water temperatures range from 66° to 70° F. Sail smooth water inshore or jump chop farther out. **Windsurfing Outfitters F2 School** rents boards and equipment. Food and lodging are inexpensive by European standards, thanks to the relatively weak local economy. A hundred and fifty yards from the beach, **Hotel Le Dune** (*08023 Porto Pollo, Palau, Sardinia, Italy. 01139-0789-704013. www.sardinia.net/tirso/alberg/ledune.htm*) provides great views of the bay and islands.

TOUR OPERATORS

Windsurfers will find that package vacations are major bargains. Hawaiian holidays, in particular, offer remarkable value—a week's lodging plus board, rig, and rental car averages around $850 per person, double occupancy. With this kind of value, it's crazy not to opt for a commercial operator for most destinations. Many of the best windsurfing tour companies run their own operations, although some merely act as a travel agent for local resorts. Often you will find that local windsurf shops also offer economical lodging and equipment-rental packages.

Excursions Extraordinaire
P.O. Box 5766, Eugene, OR 97405
800-678-2252 or 541-484-0493
www.mauiwindsurfing.com

Since 1986, Excursions Extraordinaire has pioneered many exciting new destinations, such as Costa Rica and Venezuela. Now it concentrates on Maui, windsurfing's mecca. The company's North Shore center—between Spreckelsville and Kanaha Beach Park—offers beachfront accommodations and arguably the best private launch on the island. Guesthouse lodging, all meals, gear rental, and instruction costs $1,200 per person for seven days. The boards are even prerigged for you each

THE FLIP SIDE OF WINDSURFING: HEELS OVER HEAD AT THE HATCHERY, COLUMBIA RIVER GORGE NEAR HOOD RIVER, OREGON

morning. And here you won't need a rental car: A short walk from your room or cottage will put you right on the beach. This is hard to beat for convenience. No fuss and no hassles mean more time for sailing.

Hawaiian Island Surf & Sport

415-A Dairy Rd., Kahului, HI 96732
800-231-6958 or 808-871-4981
www.hawaiianisland.com

Hawaiian Island has friendly service, superb equipment, competitive prices, and the largest rental-sail inventory on Maui. Conveniently located close to Kanaha Beach, Hawaiian Island offers an attractive package vacation. The company has eliminated the older vans from its rental car fleet; you can even get an Eddie Bauer Limited Edition SUV during your stay. Outstanding gear, fair prices, fast turnaround: For all these reasons, Hawaiian Island still leads the pack in Maui.

Maui Windsurfari

425 Koloa St., Unit 107, Maui, HI 96732
800-736-6284 or 808-871-7766
www.windsurfari.com

Maui Windsurfari features new equipment each year, including the latest custom and production boards, and a great sail inventory. Vacation packages are customized for each traveler from a wide selection of condo accommodations, as well as North Shore beachfront cottages and rentals. Lodging starts at around $45 per night. Maui Windsurfari's vacation-planning staff is professional and helpful. Instruction, usually on Fanatic production boards, is offered by Alan Cadiz's school, Hawaiian Sailboarding Techniques, which is the best program on the island.

Neilson

120 St. Georges Rd., Brighton BN2 1EG, England. 01144-1273-626-283 or 284
www.neilson.co.uk

This British company offers resort-based holidays covering the full spectrum of wind sports—from boardsailing to blue-water yachting. All major Neilson sailing centers, profiled on Neilson's website, offer good winds and warm waters. High-wind junkies should head to Vasilikí on the Greek island of Lefkás, which boasts winds of 25 knots and more, five days a week in summer. Certified instruction is available free of charge when you book a vacation, and many Neilson resorts have kids' clubs. This is the best choice if you want to combine catamaran or dinghy sailing with your windsurfing vacation.

Sailboard Vacations

193 Rockland St., Hanover, MA 02339

800-252-1070 or 781-829-8915
www.sailboardvacations.com

Since 1986, Sailboard Vacations has welcomed nearly 20,000 windsurfers to its Barbados, Bonaire, Cabarete, and Margarita resorts. Its primary focus, however, is Aruba. The company's lodgings on the island are situated right on the beach, prices are reasonable, and the Aruba Windsurfing Academy provides top-flight instruction. In Aruba, children 18 and under sail for free with a family lodging package. The travel staff is very knowledgeable and helpful. Sailboard's sailing centers feature new factory equipment: Fanatic (Aruba), Mistral (Barbados, Margarita), and BIC (Cabarete, Bonaire).

Solo Sports

1 Technology Dr., Suite E305, Irvine, CA 92618. 949-453-1950. www.solosports.net

Solo Sports runs a unique operation in Baja for adventurous windsurfers who want to travel off the beaten track and enjoy beach-camping. Employing a 16-passenger van, Solo Sports explores outstanding, remote sailing sites on Baja's Pacific coast south of El Rosario. Here you'll find some of the best wave sailing in North America. On the same tour you can combine boardsailing with surfing at famed breaks like Scorpion Bay and Abrejos. Regular clinics are hosted by noted professionals and boardsailing champions.

TraWell Surfreisen

Apfelgasse 6, A-1040 Vienna, Austria
011431-505-0457. www.trawell.at

If you want to sail in either Europe or Africa, TraWell Surfreisen is one of your best choices. Destinations include the Canaries, Cape Verde, Egypt, Greece, Rhodes, South Africa, Spain, and Turkey. In the Caribbean, TraWell also operates in Aruba, Barbados, Cabarete (Dominican Republic), and Margarita (Venezuela). The accommodations tend to be good. With well over 500 rigs each, TraWell's sailing centers in Egypt and Rhodes are some of the largest in the world. Boards and sails (mostly F2s and Mistrals) are a cut below what you get in Maui, but still very good. Because TraWell Surfreisen's website is in German, the best way to contact the company may be by fax (01143-1505-1224). If you prefer to call, the staff in Vienna also speaks good English.

Vela Windsurf Resorts

4604 Scotts Valley Dr., Scotts Valley, CA 95066. 800-223-5443 or 831-461-0820
www.velawindsurf.com

Founded in 1987, Vela is one of the biggest tour operators in Aruba, Baja, Cabarete (the Dominican Republic), Maui, and especially Venezuela—where it operates resorts and sailing centers serving Margarita, Islas Los Roques, and Isla Coche. Vela's Baja package is probably the best for intermediate to advanced sailors. In Maui, Vela works with the Maui Windsurf Company. Vela features prerigged equipment and a wide range of quality lodges in most of its destinations. Vela is a first-class operation.

Windsport Travel

115 Danforth Ave., Ste. 302, Toronto, ON M4K 1N2, Canada. 800-640-9530 or 416-461-3276. www.windsport-travel.com

WindSport is a travel bureau allied with Canada's leading boardsailing magazine. Its website features destination profiles of two dozen sailing venues. It can arrange air travel or complete boardsailing vacation packages for Aruba, Barbados, Bonaire, Cabarete, Margarita, and Maui. Given the favorable exchange rates with Canada, American travelers may find some bargains.

TRAVEL TIPS

Booking a package windsurfing tour is only part of planning the perfect windsurfari. You also need to know what to bring and how to transport your high-tech equipment. Here are some tips for globetrotting sailors.

What to Bring

On a package tour, it's not necessary to bring much of anything except a light wet suit and gloves and booties. Besides, the equipment you will rent—especially in Hawaii—is likely to be better and newer than what you have at home. If you do bring a board, make it an 8-foot to 8-foot-10-inch wave board—nothing bigger. Your package will cover the rental of a larger slalom/fun board. If you are going to a location where winds can be variable, you might bring along your sails. A 4-and-a-half-foot and a 5-foot-2-inch are the most versatile for trade-wind conditions. You probably won't bother to sail with anything bigger, and if you really need something smaller, it's always easy enough to rent one. Most windsurf rental shops offer a two-sail or one-sail package, which permits you to exchange sizes as needed. Don't bother to bring a mast, even a two-piece. But do pack a large board bag; it will come in handy when you're driving around looking for the best wind.

Gear Transport

Boards under 8 feet 6 inches can usually be shipped as part of your regular baggage allowance at no extra charge—or for a nominal fee at most. Larger boards may be subject to a significant surcharge. Some airlines have a surfboard-only policy, so remove the foot straps from your board to avoid surcharges. Use a padded board bag and make sure you cushion the board's nose, tail, and rails with foam tubing. Bubble wrap particularly fragile boards from nose to tail. And if you do plan to take a mast—which is *not* recommended—make sure it's a two-piece. Many airlines refuse to ship a full-length mast, no matter what you offer to pay.

Insurance

Because accidents happen, you should buy travel health insurance. While you're at it, get extra insurance for your equipment. The standard insurance offered by most air carriers will not cover the cost of the board alone, much less your whole inventory of sails and gear.

WINDSURFING GROUPS

American Windsurfing Industries Association
1099 Snowden Rd., White Salmon, WA 98672. 800-963-7873 or 509-493-9463 www.awia.org

Visit the AWIA website for a step-by-step guide to learning the sport. The site also contains a list of sailing schools, a calendar of clinics hosted by board and sail manufacturers, and information on major AWIA events such as the annual Windfest.

U.S. Windsurfing Association
P.O. Box 978, Hood River, OR 97031 800-872-1994 or 541-386-8708 www.uswindsurfing.org

This group promotes the sport nationwide and sponsors major competitions. Association members enjoy a variety of benefits, including travel discounts on airfare and hotels.

SAILING SCHOOLS

Bonaire, Netherlands Antilles
Bonaire offers exceptional training conditions: trade winds, shallow water, and a sandy bottom. The expansive, near-shore

Kite Surfing

Just when you thought you had seen everything, along comes kite surfing—the most amazing solo ocean sport in years. Part sailing, part surfing, and part waterskiing, kite surfing has taken the Hawaiian Islands by storm. With just a modified surfboard and a fabric parafoil attached to a harness, kite surfers can travel across the surface of the water at speeds approaching 40 miles per hour.

The idea of propelling watercraft with kites is nothing new; yachters have toyed with the concept for centuries. However, a breakthrough came when a group of water-sport enthusiasts—perhaps temporarily short of a towboat or two—came up with the idea of using semi-rigid delta kites to pull water-skiers through the water. They tried it, and not only did it work—it was fast. With Cory Roeseler's KiteSki system, for example, a water-skier could zip along at around 30 miles per hour—and all without the roar and smoke of a diesel engine.

The kites proved difficult to launch, however, and were ill suited for use in ocean surf. Although some kite surfers have stuck with hard-wing kites, most have switched to a different "engine": a soft, fabric parafoil.

IF CHARLIE BROWN COULD SEE ME NOW: KITE SURFING IN MAUI

Attached to a harness with multiple control lines, the parafoil kite rides 70 to 100 feet in the air, normally in front of the kite surfer at an angle of about 45 degrees. The parafoil thus provides lift and thrust, both of which the surfer adjusts by flying the kite higher or lower. To steer the sailboard through the water, the surfer carves turns just like those of a regular surfboarder.

At first, kite surfers stayed in sheltered waters, where it was easier to master the sport. Things have changed since then: Experts can now perform amazing feats, thanks to the combined forward and vertical pull of the kite: Traveling as fast as a jet ski, kite surfers can jump off an ocean swell, elevate 50 feet or more in the air, and traverse 100 feet laterally before setting down on the water again.

Some practitioners—such as world champion Flash Austin—regularly challenge the epic surf of Hawaii. Ripping out through the shorebreak under full power, they pirouette in midair before coming back down on the face of a wave, which they then surf back to shore.

As with many other adventurous undertakings, there is an element of danger to this sport. Wipeouts happen. Modern kites are equipped with inflatable bladders, however, which the kite surfer can rapidly launch from the water's surface after a fall.

Kite-surfing equipment is built to endure high winds and strong waves. But modern parafoils can also operate in less extreme conditions. In fact, in the light to moderate winds typical of mainland and inland sailing sites, kite surfers outperform surfers equipped with conventional windsurfing rigs.

Whereas a windsurfer needs a solid 18 knots or more of wind to sail efficiently, kite surfers can perform effectively in as little as 10 knots. For this and other reasons, expect to see the sport grow in popularity—and for kite surfing to become increasingly visible in any place where water and wind combine.

To learn more about the sport of kite surfing, and the latest developments in equipment and gear, contact **Kitesurfing Hawaii** (350 Kulike Rd. Haiku, HI 96779. 808-573-6630. www.kitesurfing.com). The company's website also contains a dazzling gallery of kite-surfing action photos. For kite-surfing instruction, contact **Action Sports Maui** (206a Leinani Dr., Wailuku, HI 96793. 808-871-5857 or 808-283-7913. www.actionsportsmaui.com), where top pros teach classes ranging from one-hour safety sessions to five-day complete courses. Both Kitesurfing Hawaii and Action Sports Maui sell full kite-surfing rigs that include harness, controls, parafoil, and board.

flats may be the best spot in the Caribbean to learn to water-start. At **Roger's Windsurf Place** sailboard center (*800-225-0102. www.rogerswindsurf.com*) you learn in small classes with new, quality equipment. Roger's Windsurf Place operates year-round, with patient, professional instructors.

Corpus Christi, Texas

Blessed with a large, warm-water lagoon that stays shallow for more than 1,000 yards from the beach, Corpus Christi is a wonderful learning site. The winds are unobstructed and the water is smooth, allowing beginners to concentrate on fundamentals. Summer offers warm, steady winds—strong enough for water-starting without being overpowering. Contact **WorldWinds Windsurfing** (*800-793-7471. www.coolcats.com/worldwinds*).

Maui, Hawaii

Maui's top school is Alan Cadiz's **Hawaiian Sailboarding Techniques** (*800-968-5423 or 808-871-5423. www.hstwindsurfing.com*). A great windsurfer, and a patient, capable instructor, Cadiz may be Maui's best one-on-one teacher. His school employs two-way radios, video, and other progressive techniques that speed the learning process.

ONLINE

Windsurfer.com
www.windsurfer.com

This crowd-pleasing site features the fine AWIA learn-to-sail primer, travel and board reviews, tons of links, and a searchable online product catalog for boards, sails, and accessories. The weather page posts current data for multiple sailing areas in North America.

Windsurfingmag.com
www.windsurfingmag.com

Bookmark this quality site operated by the leading windsurfing magazine. It has up-to-date gear reviews, late-breaking news, and well-researched destination reports with local contact information you can't find anywhere else. The instruction section—for novices, intermediates, and experts—is a must-read.

Maui Windsurfing Report
www.maui.net/~mauiwind/MWR/mwr.html

A prized resource for any windsurfer interested in Maui. Along with weather, you'll find profiles of sailing sites, daily sailing reports, interviews, and a message board.

MAGAZINES

American Windsurfer (*Bayview Business Park No. 10, Gilford, NH 03246. 800-292-2772 or 603-293-2721. www.americanwindsurfer.com*). A great read for the armchair windsurfer, this bimonthly journal features solid writing and large, full-page photo layouts. Check out the website for back issues and some amazing photographs.

Windsport (*2255B Queen St. E., No. 3266, Toronto, ON, M4E 1G3, Canada. 800-223-6197. www.windsport.com*). A comprehensive Canadian windsurfing journal. *Windsport's* website features great video clips and two dozen firsthand destination reports that include photographs.

Windsurfing (*P.O. Box 420235, Palm Coast, FL 32142. 800-879-0480. www.windsurfingmag.com*). This magazine features equipment reviews and plenty of trip-planning information. Look for the annual travel issue, which profiles dozens of destinations.

VIDEO

Rip: A Windsurfing Video (*Naish Hawaii, $25.00. 808-262-6068. www.naish.com*) features legendary windsurfer Robby Naish, who takes viewers on a personal tour of his favorite windsurfing spots in the Hawaiian Islands. Slalom and wave-sailing action are filmed from the beach, from the water, and from the air—all accompanied by an excellent modern rock soundtrack.

WIND REPORTS

Wind Hot Line (*900-976-9463. www.windhotline.com*)
The Wind Hot Line operates weather stations in the mid-Atlantic area, the northeastern United States, and Canada. Founded in 1986, the Hot Line uses its own sensors, which are monitored by local forecasters. It offers wind reports and forecasts both by voice and over the Internet. The voice service costs $40 per year. Nonmembers can also get wind reports at a rate of $1.50 per minute.

Micro Forecasts (*900-860-0600. www.windsight.com*)
MicroForecasts offers accurate, real-time wind reports for the Columbia River Gorge, Puget Sound, the Oregon Coast, and San Francisco Bay. Voice service is available by calling 800-695-9703. The company's reports come from Windsight, which maintains a chain of sensors on the West Coast that are monitored by local meteorologists. Current wind reports are $1.95 per minute.

COMING TO GROUND: A WINDSURFER CALLS IT A DAY IN HAWAII.

THE SEARCH FOR NEW ADVENTURES IS NEVER ENDING. AT THE REQUEST OF READERS OF THE FIRST EDITION of this book, we have collected in this chapter a host of ultimate adventures that defy easy categorizing. Some of these are "soft adventures"—outdoor activities combined with a heavy dose of luxury. Others, such as bobsledding and air combat, can only be described as a tad insane. • There wasn't room to list every outré pursuit out there—wetboarding, extreme golf, and ultimate frisbee, for example, will all have to wait for the next edition—you'll still find some exciting new adventures, both mild and wild. In the luxury column, we've included barge and canal cruising. For those with a bent for exploration and discovery, we've added both dinosaur hunting and treasure hunting. And if your idea of adventure travel is to voyage into the past, you'll find guidance on how to board such vintage trains as the *Orient Express*. • Finally, we've added a section on fitness vacations—a trend that combines outdoor exertions with the restorative treatments of a health resort. And for those constantly on the prowl for something completely different, you'll also find a section on camel trekking in Australia, Africa, and India.

LEFT: YOU, TOO, CAN SHOOT THE OLYMPIC BOBSLED RUN AT LAKE PLACID. BELOW: PLACIDITY AT A SPA ON THE ST. LAWRENCE RIVER

Miscellaneous Madness

Spa vs. Spa

Digging Dinosaurs

One Hump or Two?

E. M. Frimbo Lives!

Air Combat

Student Vacations

Barging Right In

It's all right letting yourself go, as long as you can get yourself back.
MICK JAGGER

Women's Adventure Programs

Adventure is for everyone, regardless of age, sex, or physical abilities. As adventure recreation evolves from macho thrill seeking to a more universal pastime, outfitters are delivering tours expressly designed for women travelers. In this section we have profiled the best adventure-travel companies that cater to such groups. These organizations feature customized programs that are a better match for women than a "one-size-fits-all" approach.

Women-only trips offer a break from the responsibilities of work and family, along with an opportunity to learn wilderness skills in a supportive atmosphere. Although many of the clients on these trips are married professionals with grown-up kids, specialized programs also exist for singles, both straight and gay. The typical women's trip is a cooperative learning experience that allows participants to relax in a noncompetitive environment.

ADVENTURE ASSOCIATES

Specializing in small-group, ecosensitive trips in the Pacific Northwest and worldwide, **Adventure Associates** (*P.O. Box 16304, Seattle, WA 98116. 888-532-8352 or 206-932-8352. www.adventureassociates.net*) is run by a female owner-director with a wealth of travel experience worldwide. AA excels at customer service; 70 percent of its clients are repeat customers or referrals from past clients. Though AA offers co-ed trips as well, all-women adventures are now its major focus. Popular programs include kayaking in the San Juan Islands; hiking and camping in the North Cascades; lodge-based hiking in the Olympic Mountains and Grand Tetons; hiking and sea kayaking in Hawaii; Nordic skiing in Yellowstone; horse-assisted hiking in California's High Sierra; and backpacking on the Olympic coast. International offerings include wildlife-cultural safaris in Africa; multisport adventures in Costa Rica and New Zealand; trekking in Nepal and the Copper Canyon of Mexico; sailing in Greece and Turkey; wildlife cruising in the Galápagos; and sea kayaking in Baja. Many AA trips require peak fitness, but very few demand prior experience. For women in the market for their first major adventure vacation, this is a good choice. Highly recommended.

ADVENTURE WOMEN

Women over 30 (the average client is 50) turn to **Adventure Women** (*15033 Kelly Canyon Rd., Bozeman, MT 59715. 800-804-8686 or 406-587-3883. www.adventurewomen.com*) for its lineup of adventure-travel vacations worldwide. Since 1982, Adventure Women (formerly Rainbow Adventures) has staged active vacations built around sports ranging from camel trekking to jet boating. U.S. trips typically last seven to ten days, while trips to international destinations can run anywhere from ten days to three weeks. Prices range from $1,600 for a Baja kayaking adventure to $5,300 (airfare included) for a camel-trekking expedition to Timbuktu, Mali. First-timers should check out the multiactivity tour of Utah, where participants travel by foot, raft, jeep, and jet boat through three national parks. Adventure Women also offers a classic English-style safari through East Africa's big game parks and **Masai Mara Reserve.** The company's **Kenya Camel Safari** is its most popular overseas trip.

MARIAH WILDERNESS EXPEDITIONS

Since 1982, **Mariah Wilderness Expeditions** (*P.O. Box 70248, Pt. Richmond, CA 94807. 800-462-7424 or 510-233-2303. www.mariahwe.com*) has served more than 75,000 clients. The company specializes in unique trips for women; among these are one- to thirteen-day white-water rafting trips in California and elsewhere in the West, as well as active and soft adventure travel in Baja, Belize, Costa Rica, the Galápagos Islands, and Peru. **New Millennium and Beyond** trips include excursions to Australia, Bolivia, Chile, Peru, and Hawaii.

Mariah's women's trips cater to both straight and gay clienteles. The company's California rafting trips and Baja kayaking program are highly recommended. In addition to its extensive program for women only, Mariah throws open the following trips to all comers: white-water rafting on seven rivers in California and Oregon; full-service customized travel planning in Costa Rica.

OUTDOOR VACATIONS FOR WOMEN OVER 40

Another good choice for first-time adventurers is **Outdoor Vacations for Women Over 40** (*P.O. Box 200, Groton, MA 01450. 978-448-3331*). With guides providing all the instruction you'll need along the way, no previous outdoor experience is required to take part in these vacations.

Outdoor Vacations has offered its trips—for women and led by women—since 1982. Most of its guides are full-timers, and they boast a wealth of local knowledge. Groups are kept relatively small (12 to 14 women per tour, on average), creating a supportive atmosphere rich in camaraderie. The tours

generally avoid commercial destinations, and the accommodations tend to be rustic. Most participants sign on individually; the average age of customers is 58. One-week trips average $1,900, excluding airfare. Outdoor Vacations runs five to ten programs per year, with an emphasis on cross-country skiing, hiking, canoeing, and cycling. Canada is a popular venue for skiing and hiking.

WOMEN IN THE WILDERNESS

Although it is a destination-oriented company, **Women in the Wilderness** (*566 Ottowa Ave., St. Paul, MN 55107. 651-227-2284*) also teaches wilderness skills (firebuilding, tracking, living outdoors with minimal gear) and outdoor sports (paddling, dogsledding, sailing, hiking) in a nonstressful way. Women in the Wilderness (WIW) maximizes interaction with indigenous cultures by using local guides, eating local foods, and taking part in cultural activities. The clientele ranges in age from 16 to 92, but the majority are professional women 35 to 60 years old. Many WIW guides are professional women whose love of the outdoors has motivated them to lead trips. WIW runs about 30 trips each year, ranging from four to twenty-five days, at about $100 per day. The company's specialty is canoeing; its paddling trips in wildlife-rich northern Min-

nesota teach canoe skills for all levels, novice to expert. There's even a low-intensity program for cancer survivors. Although most WIW trips are in Minnesota and nearby Canada, WIW also offers trips to Peru, the Canadian Arctic, and the American Southwest.

WOMEN'S TRAVEL CLUB

Offering 20 or more itineraries to destinations worldwide, the **Women's Travel Club** (*21401 Northeast 38th Avenue, Aventura, FL 33180. 888-480-4448 or 305-936-9669. www. womenstravelclub.com*) leads tours ranging from the mild to the wild—that is, from spa vacations in the lap of luxury to rugged treks along the Inca Trail. The club publishes a newsletter for its members and posts bargain specials on its website.

Resources

For a bibliography of books on travel for women, go to www.womenstravelclub.com/suggested.html. Also recommended are *Women Travel* (edited by Natania Jansz and Miranda Davies), a compilation of letters written by women travelers from more than 60 countries, and *Travelers' Tales: Gutsy Women* by Marybeth Bond, a practical guide to leaving the beaten path behind.

MUD SLINGERS KICK BACK AT A SPA IN NOTRE-DAME-DU-PORTAGE, QUEBEC.

Fitness Vacations

Combine the boomer obsession with surface appearances and the mania for adventure travel and you get the fitness vacation—a holiday designed to relieve stress, tone the body, and rejuvenate the spirit. The typical escape offers a daily health regimen in a beautiful setting. Active vacationers can sign up for a wilderness fitness tour, while those seeking a more leisurely getaway can find a specialty resort designed to rejuvenate both body and spirit.

Global Fitness Adventures (*P.O. Box 330, Old Snowmass, CO 81654. 800-488-8747 or 970-927-9593. www.globalfitnessadventure.com*) organizes week-long retreats that combine adventure activities such as hiking, rafting, diving, skiing, and horseback riding with daily workouts, massage, yoga, and fitness or diet counseling. Special programs include meditation, Indian sweat lodges, and motivational seminars. You can create a custom trip or visit locations such as Aspen, Sedona, Lake Como (Italy), and Bali. The goal is to enjoy the outdoors while gaining control over stress and diet.

Backcountry health spas provide a full regime of body improvement in a setting of great natural beauty. Favorites include the **Mohonk Mountain House** in New York; **Canyon Ranch** in Arizona and Massachusetts; **Skylonda** in California; and **the Peaks** in Colorado.

RESOURCES

Fodor's Healthy Escapes by Bernard Bart (Random House, 1994) is a good guide to North American fitness vacations.

The Spa Finder (*free from Spa-Finders Travel, 91 5th Ave., New York, NY 10003. 800-255-7727 or 212-924-6800*) catalogs 200 spas worldwide. Its database has client comments.

For online recommendations: www.resort2fitness.com.

Island Fitness Travel (*Kennesaw, GA 30144. 877-290-1467 or 678-290-1424. www.discount-all-inclusive.com*) offers resort-based fitness vacations in the Caribbean. Special programs for triathletes and runners, plus tennis, scuba, and golf.

MountainFit (*P.O. Box 6188, Bozeman, MT 59771. 800-926-5700 or 406-585-3506. www.mountainfit.com*) features resort-based active vacations with daily hiking and occasional cycling, rafting, and rock climbing combined with fitness counseling and massage. Montana, Canadian Rockies, Arizona, Utah, Hawaii, Scotland, France.

Mountain Trek Fitness Retreat and Health Spa (*P.O. Box 1352, Ainsworth Hot Springs, B.C. V0G 1A0, Canada. 800-661-5161. www.hiking.com*) is a highly recommended deluxe Alpine lodge in the Kootenays that offers hiking and snowshoeing combined with massage, yoga, and healthful gourmet cuisine.

Scandinavian Special Interest Network (*38 Valley View Trail, Sparta, NJ 07871. 201-729-8961*) runs group tours that meld outdoor activities with visits to natural spas in Scandinavia and the Baltic.

Dinosaur Hunting

With the appearance of dinosaur movies and dinosaur theme parks, was the dinosaur adventure vacation far behind? Not very: The increased media focus on paleontology has spurred venturesome types to set off in quest of dinosaur bones and ancient fossils. They are motivated in part by the 1995 discovery in Patagonia of the remains of the largest carnivore ever to walk the Earth. That year, an Argentinian auto mechanic and amateur fossil hunter named Ruben Carolini came across the buried bones of a beast even bigger—and older, by about 30 million years—than *Tyrannosaurus Rex.* To honor the animal's size and finder, it was dubbed *Gigantosaurus Carolini.* The discovery led experts to predict that the dig site will yield many new dinosaur skeletons. If you get lucky, the next one could be named for you.

DINOSAUR ADVENTURES

When Arthur Conan Doyle wrote *The Lost World* in 1912, he set his fantastical tale of a dinosaur-filled valley in Venezuela. Ironically, some key dinosaur finds are now occurring in South America, in the remote deserts of Argentine Patagonia. The United States has also become something of a paleontological mecca, with dig sites disgorging the bones of ancient creatures in Wyoming, South Dakota, Montana, and Colorado.

Whether you want to dig dinosaurs close to home or journey to a distant fossil field, the options are multitudinous. An excellent resource for adventures in archaeology, paleontology, and other forms of scientific travel is *Transitions Abroad* (*P.O. Box 1300, Amherst, MA 01004. 800-293-0373 or 413-256-3414. www.transitionsabroad.com*), a directory of volunteer and learning vacations.

The following organizations offer dinosaur and paleontology trips and workshops:

Dinosaur Discovery Expeditions, sponsored by the Dinamation International Society (*550 Jurassic Ct., Fruita, CO 81521. 800-344-3466 or 970-858-7282. www.digdino.org*), are package dinosaur vacations led by paleontologist guides in Colorado, Argentina, China, Mexico, and Mongolia. On a summer dig in Colorado (*$975 for adults, $650 for children ages 6 to 11*), for example, dino-sleuths venture to the Mygatt-Moore Quarry near Grand Junction, where they master every aspect of paleontology, from unearthing bones and fossils to making plaster casts and cataloging discoveries.

Earthwatch (*680 Mt. Auburn St., Box 4033, Watertown, MA 02272. 800-776-0188 or 617-926-8200. www.earthwatch. org*) conducts a raft of paleontology projects each year. In recent years, sites have included Mexico, Argentina, South Dakota, and Utah. Volunteers work alongside expert scientists at some of the most famous dinosaur-hunting grounds on Earth.

The **Paleontology Field School** run by the **Museum of the Rockies** (*600 W. Kagy Blvd., Bozeman, MT 59717. 406-994-2251. www.montana.edu/wwwmor/*) offers one-day, two-day, and week-long dinosaur field-study programs for adults and teenagers. Based at rustic Camp Makela near Glacier National Park in Montana, participants work with Montana State University paleontologists at major digs. The field school's weeklong program, offered in June and July, costs about $1,200.

The University of California's **University Research Expeditions Program** (*1 Shields Avenue, Davis, CA 95616. 530-752-0692. http://urep.ucdavis.edu*) stages paleontology expeditions each summer at a variety of sites around the world.

Camel Safaris

There's no denying the high adventure quotient of a camel safari through the Australian outback. Introduced to Australia from Afghanistan in the 19th century as conveyances for mining gear in the arid interior, camels adapted so well to life in the outback that they are now permanent fixtures of the landscape. In recent years, they have even become popular tourist attractions.

Australian camel outfitters offer both one-day rides and multiday treks into the country's Red Centre. Being a camel jockey is unlike anything you've ever done. Larger and far more cantankerous than horses, camels demand some skill to control—and a good deal of courage and coaxing to reach full speed. Even when propped atop a custom saddle devised by an Aussie camel master, staying aboard a camel at full gallop is a challenge to say the least.

For a fascinating account of an odyssey with camels, read *Tracks: A Woman's Solo Trek Across 1,700 Miles of Australian Outback* by Robyn Davidson. The book's humor and insight set new standards in adventure storytelling when it appeared in 1980, and it remains valid today for its insights into the psyche and behavior of camels. Anyone contemplating a camel trek should consider this "must" reading.

In Africa, you can arrange camel adventures in Egypt, Morocco, Zimbabwe, and South Africa. The classic site for a dromedary jaunt is in Giza, just outside Cairo, where you can ride a camel in the shadows of the Great Pyramids (about $10 for two to three hours). **SafariCentre International** (*3201 N. Sepulveda Blvd., Manhattan Beach, CA 90266. 800-223-6046 or 310-546-4411. www.safaricentre.com*) offers a wide variety of African camel trips, including trans-Saharan camel expeditions along ancient routes once used by desert caravans.

In India, **Himalayan Travel, Inc.** (*110 Prospect St., Stamford, CT 06901. 800-225-2380 or 203-359-3711. www.gorp.com/himtravel.htm*) offers **Rajasthan Camel Safaris** through the **Great Indian Thar Desert.** This trek—a journey back in time—leads riders through a starkly beautiful desert landscape to meet nomadic tribes who rarely see outsiders.

For camel safaris in Australia, contact:

Outer Edge Expeditions (*45500 Pontiac Trail, Walled Lake, MI 48390. 800-322-5235 or 248-624-5140. www.outeredge.com*)

World Expeditions (*441 Kent St., Sydney NSW 2000, Australia. 01161-2-9264-3366. www.worldexpeditions.com.au*)

Treasure Hunting

There comes a time in every rightly constructed boy's life when he has a raging desire to go somewhere and dig for hidden treasure.
—Mark Twain

Long before adventure travel became an industry, people sought thrills—and found them—in the search for gold and other buried treasure. The quest for simultaneous excitement and enrichment lives on in the form of modern-day gold-prospecting expeditions.

The most successful treasure hunters are professionals who invest many years—and millions of dollars—in their search for gold and precious artifacts. In the Caribbean, for example, famed treasure hunter Mel Fisher used marine archaeology and salvage teams to locate such fabled Spanish galleons as the *Neustra Señora de la Atocha* and her sister ship, the *Santa Margarita.*

What does it take to recover sunken treasure? Planning, perseverance, money, and (above all) luck. Fisher spent 15 years and hundreds of thousands of dollars to find the *Santa Margarita*, but the payoff was a $20 million bonanza in gold, silver, and 17th-century artifacts. Five years later, Fisher topped that by pinpointing the *Atocha*, whose cargo of emeralds and gold and silver coins represents the richest treas-

ure discovered since King Tut's tomb was opened in 1922.

Despite the successes of "celebrity" salvage experts such as Fisher, hundreds of millions of dollars in sunken treasure still lies buried beneath the waves. In 1995, for instance, the Japanese submarine *I-52* was found lying on the seafloor in 17,000 feet of water 1,200 miles off the Cape Verde Islands. The sub holds more than two tons of gold bullion that never reached its intended destination in Germany, where it was to finance an Axis plot.

Such revelations suggest that a good deal of underwater treasure awaits discovery to this day. True, most hunts for priceless pirate troves are high-tech ventures funded by deep-pocketed investors, but amateurs can still dive into the action. Many institutions conduct programs in aquatic archaeology at sites ranging from the Florida Keys to Alexandria, Egypt. **Earthwatch** (*680 Mt. Auburn St., P.O. Box 4033, Watertown, MA 02272. 800-776-0188*) organizes archaeology expeditions each year to sites around the world (most of these are academic programs rather than salvage operations).

Not all treasures are man-made, of course, and **Rocky Mountain Treasure Expeditions** (*P.O. Box 234, Loveland, CO 80539. 970-669-0361*) runs expeditions to recover those that come right out of the ground. On prospecting adventures in Montana and the Southwest, participants head for the hills in quest of gemstones, gold, silver, and rare fossils (large crystals have topped the list of recent finds). Customized trips combine rock hunting with gold panning. For more information about the occult world of treasure hunting, consult the following resources:

Resources

Nuggets of treasure-hunting data can best be mined online. The **Treasure Hunters Bulletin Board** (*www.melfisher. com/bbfram.html*) contains some fascinating reports of recent discoveries worldwide. Other websites worth a visit are **International Treasure Hunters Exchange** (*www.treasure.com*), **Mel Fisher's Treasure Site** (*www.melfisher.com*), and **TreasureNet** (*www.treasurenet.com*).

You can also learn about sunken treasure from the following books:

The Treasure Diver's Guide by John S. Potter is the book that inspired Mel Fisher. Though out of print, it's worth searching for on the Advanced Book Exchange (*http://abe.com/*).

A Shipwreck Guide to the Bahamas, Turks and Caicos, 1500 to 1990 by Tony Jaggers is available from the author (*P.O. Box 1386, Ft. Pierce, FL 34954. 407-595-0379*).

Ship of Gold in the Deep Blue Sea by Gary Kinder.

The Spanish Treasure Fleets can be ordered from Timothy Walton (*1390 Chain Bridge Rd., Suite 250, McLean, VA 22101*).

Vintage Rail Tours

[N]o good train ever goes far enough, just as no bad train ever reaches its destination soon enough.

—Paul Theroux

People become train buffs for a panoply of reasons. Some are drawn to the drama of a big, noisy steam locomotive chuffing down the tracks, while others long to experience the romance—and comfort—of luxury travel from a distant era. In some parts of the world, such as Siberia, railroading remains the primary mode of transportation.

Recognizing the special allure of train travel, soft adventure travel companies have made available a wide range of exciting rail-borne excursions, both in the United States and overseas. Whether you are a budget backpacker on the Eurail circuit or a seasoned traveler seeking the opulent elegance of the *Orient Express*, opportunities for classic railroading holidays abound.

HOW TO HOP ABOARD

Here are some of the most enjoyable iron-horse adventures worldwide. Each trip combines spectacular scenery with vintage or historically significant railcars or locomotives. The trans-Canadian run on VIA Rail appears first because many railroading experts consider it to be North America's premier train ride.

All year long, **VIA Rail Canada** (*Montreal, Quebec. 800-561-9181. www.viarail.ca*) runs three passenger trains a week from Vancouver to Toronto along a sensational route through the Rocky Mountains that is without parallel in North America. For those who want to understand why previous generations looked on train travel as romantic rather than rigorous, VIA Rail is a trip back in time. The 1950s-vintage passenger cars are spotless and authentic.

One of the most scenic routes in North America is operated by the **Alaska Railroad Corporation** (*Anchorage, AK. 800-544-0552 or 907-265-2494*), whose trains run from Anchorage or Seward to Fairbanks, passing Denali National Park and Preserve, Denali (Mount McKinley), and the Talkeetna River along the way. Trains depart daily from mid-May through mid-September. The fare is $125 each way; group rates are available. Rolling stock consists of diesel locomotives and modern coaches.

A historical and fully refurbished narrow-gauge line, the **Durango & Silverton Railroad** (*Durango, CO. 888-872-4607 or 970-247-2733. www.durangotrain.com*) is the pride of Durango. In the early summer, the train makes a serpentine crawl along the lip of a nearly vertical gorge containing a torrent of raging Class V white water. In winter, the itinerary

Miscellaneous Madness

is reduced to an out-and-back trip that takes passengers only as far as Cascade Canyons, but the trip is spectacular nonetheless—a photographer's dream—and can be completed in the space of a few hours. Equipment includes classic steam locomotives, vintage coaches, a snack-bar car, and a vintage caboose.

The reborn **Orient Express** (*800-524-2420 or 01144-2780-55100. www.orient-expresstrains.com*) sets the standard for style and bygone elegance. Although an airplane flight will get you from Paris to Istanbul more quickly and cheaply than the four-day, $5,000 voyage aboard the *Orient Express,* you'll miss the stopovers in Budapest, Transylvania, and Bucharest along the way. Equipment: Late 19th-century-style luxury coaches and sleepers; vintage or modern locomotives, depending on the section of the run.

To recapture the luxury made famous by the golden age of rail travel, board a steam-powered run from Capetown, South Africa, to spectacular Victoria Falls and beyond. The trip is organized by **Rovos Rail** (*African Safari Consultants, 800-529-2376 or 818-225-0391. www.classicsafaris.com*). For budget travelers, the **Zimbabwe State Railway** also operates a vintage narrow-gauge steam train through elephant country to the falls. Equipment includes 1920s-era steam locomotives and vintage luxury coaches.

The **Sierra Madre Express** (*Rail Travel Center, Brattleboro, VT. 800-458-5394 or 802-254-7788. www.railtravelcenter.com*) is a privately chartered train that tours Mexico's scenic Copper Canyon, hauling renovated lounge cars and Pullman sleepers from the *Super Chief, Empire Builder,* and other historic trains. The trip includes all meals and a variety of off-train expeditions. Equipment: Diesel locomotive, Pullman sleeping and dining cars.

Many other tourist railroads offer memorable day trips. A favorite is New Zealand's **Taieri Gorge Limited** (*Dunedin, New Zealand. 01164-3477-4449. www.taieri.co.nz*), a 48-mile-long rail venture through a spectacular South Island gorge (the ride earned New Zealand's Transportation Tourism Award in 1998.) For information on hundreds of other novelty trains—from Switzerland's **Appenzeller bahnen** to Australia's **Zig Zag Railway** in New South Wales—visit **Tourist Railways Worldwide** (*www.railserve.com/tourist*) or **Tourist Railways North America** (*www.trainweb.com/touristrailways*).

PLANNING YOUR TRIP

If you have already narrowed down your destination, contact a major rail line such as **Amtrak** (*800-872-7245*), **Eurail Pass** or **BritRail** (*both 800-551-1977*), **Scandinavian Rail-Pass** (*800-345-1900*), or **European Rail Authorities** (*800-542-6212*). Those heading to Europe should consult Kathryn Turpin's *Eurail Guide Annual: Traveling Europe and the World by*

Train. A good online supplement to Turpin's book, offering up-to-date route maps and train schedules, is *How to Travel Europe by Train* at www.eurorail.com/planindx.htm. A wealth of rail-travel information is also available from the **Society of International Railway Travelers** (*1810 Sils Ave., No. 306B, Louisville, KY 40205. 800-478-4881 or 502-454-0277. www.trainweb.com/irtsociety*). The society's monthly newsletter (*$59 per year*) is tops in its field; in addition, society members are eligible for discounts on rail bookings in the United States and abroad.

For package rail tours, try one of the following specialty-travel agencies. Among them, they should be able to get you anywhere on the planet that two rails reach.

Trains Unlimited Tours

P.O. Box 1997, Portola, CA 96122. 800-359-4870 or 530-836-1745 in the United States, 800-752-1836 in Canada. www.trainsunltdtours.com

Since 1985, Trains Unlimited has offered railfan and tourist-railroad tours in Argentina, Bolivia, Canada, Chile, Ecuador, Guatemala, Mexico, Peru, and the United States (Alaska, California, Colorado, and New Hampshire). The tour director, who retired after 27 years as a conductor with the Western Pacific and Union Pacific Railroads, has made more than 100 trips to Latin America. Trains Unlimited boasts an in-depth knowledge of the rail industry that informs all its tours. The company has chartered more than 540 trains on 105 rail lines in 26 countries, and it maintains an excellent working relationship with railroads worldwide.

Rail Travel Center

139 Main St., Brattleboro, VT 05301. 800-458-5394 or 802-254-7788. www.railtravelcenter.com

Rail Travel Center (RTC) operates fully escorted and independent tours, primarily by rail, in North America, Europe, Australia, New Zealand, and Asia. Familiar with the best rail tours on most continents, the company packages a broad range of itineraries to suit most budgets. Recommended trips include **Mexico's Copper Canyon,** the **Grand Teton-Yellowstone** tour, and the **Grand Rail Circle** tour in the Canadian Rockies. Unlike other travel agencies, RTC understands the special interests of railfans and can organize special charters on legendary trains all over the globe.

Europe Train Tours

198 E. Boston Post Rd., Mamaroneck, NY 10543. 800-551-2085 or 914-698-9426.

This well-established agency represents many of the most prestigious novelty trains worldwide. Ask about such classic rides as the U.K.'s *Royal Scotsman,* Spain's *Al-Andalus Express,* or southern Africa's *Pride of Africa* (Rovos Rail).

Air Combat

Pilots are getting the adrenaline-pumping rush of *Top Gun*-style dogfights at airfields across North America. Aspiring Navy fliers, perhaps? Nothing of the sort; these fly-boys and girls are amateurs who have paid for the privilege. After learning basic flight skills and air-combat strategies in ground school, they strap themselves into powerful, highly maneuverable military training aircraft and take to the skies for a dogfight: There, when a pilot scores a "hit" with his or her laser "guns," the victim emits a telltale plume of white smoke. On-board video cameras record every move.

The rapid growth of the air-combat industry underscores the extreme excitement delivered by these ultimate airborne adventures. Most first-timers are amazed by the G-forces the aircraft produce—and by the emotional intensity of the aerial joust. Although no prior flight training is required in order to participate, the program is decidedly not for the faint of heart.

The leading air-combat programs appear below. Most employ military-trained pilots and fly SIAI-Marchetti SF.260s—sleek Italian fighter-trainers with side-by-side seating for pilot and client. Traditionalists may prefer programs that utilize planes with classic inline military seating, such as the T-34 trainer. Either way, you're in for the ride of your life.

Air Combat USA

P.O. Box 2726, Fullerton, CA 92837
800-522-7590 or 714-522-7590
www.aircombat.com

Air Combat has flown more than 20,000 guest-pilots since 1989, using its patented dogfighting program in which laser "guns" and target receptors mounted on Marchetti 260s activate a smoke trail (and an alarm siren in the victim's headset) in response to a "hit." The program, starting at $800 per half-day session, serves a dozen cities nationwide. Virtually all Air Combat instructors are former fighter pilots.

Incredible Adventures

6604 Midnight Pass Rd., Sarasota, FL 34231
800-644-7382 or 941-346-2488
www.incredible-adventures.com
Some of the most mind-blowing experiences in this book are on tap at the aptly named Incredible Adventures. This unique but pricey program (its adventures cost $5,000 and up) offers high-altitude aerobatic flights with top Russian pilots in MiG-29s, MiG-25s, Su-27s, and other exotic jet aircraft. An even more outrageous option is the **Edge of Space** flight, in which you ride a MiG-25 at Mach 2.8 to an altitude of nearly 17 miles. At the apex of its parabola, the plane noses over and you experience the weightlessness of zero gravity. Incredible Adventures also offers acrobatic flights over Capetown, South Africa, in classic British jet fighters.

Texas Air Aces

8319 Thora Lane, Hangar A5, Spring, TX 77379
800-544-2237 or 281-379-2237
www.airaces.com
Texas Air Aces fly the T-34—a fully aerobatic military trainer aircraft. Participants fly from the front seat beneath a bubble canopy. The site, located about 40 minutes from downtown Houston, also offers formation flights. Demonstration programs start at $450, while a half-day session of air combat will set you back $695.

Student and Youth Vacations

Most of the adventures listed in this book are designed primarily, if not exclusively, for adults. There is no good reason, however, that teenagers cannot enjoy diving a lagoon, climbing a mountain, or paddling a river. In most cases, teens have more than enough physical strength and energy to thrive in the outdoors—and their enthusiasm for adventure runs high. With this in mind, a host of organizations now offer adventure programs tailored to younger minds and bodies. These programs allow teens to train and socialize with their peers. The result: fast, fun progress—and a sense of accomplishment that carries into later years.

The teen-oriented adventure companies profiled below are not your father's summer camp. They give teenagers the opportunity to spend a week to nine months sailing the Caribbean, hiking the Alps, or exploring the backcountry of Hawaii. Such experiences can be transformative, giving teens a love of the outdoors that lasts a lifetime.

ACTION QUEST

Most programs at **Action Quest** (*P.O. Box 5517, Sarasota, FL 34277. 800-317-6789 or 941-924-6789. www.actionquest.com*) are designed for 13- to 19-year-olds. They feature sailing, scuba diving, windsurfing, waterskiing, and lifeguarding in a two- or three-week yacht-based learning vacation that costs $2,800 to $4,200.

In 1997, Action Quest added a college-level, semester-long program that offers academic credit. Semester students sail yachts through the Caribbean, enjoying outdoor activities while being trained in oceanography, navigation, marine biology, leadership, and communications.

In 1999, Action Quest launched a nine-month-long high-school program that gives teens a year of schooling while they live on board a large schooner in the Caribbean.

Scuba and sailing certification are available on all programs. Participants maintain equipment and keep the yacht shipshape; they also serve a stint in each job on board, including that of skipper. The goal of the program is to increase self-esteem, motivation, independence, problem-solving abilities, and responsibility. Action Quest operates in the British Virgin Islands, the Leeward Islands, the Mediterranean, the Galápagos, Fiji, Tahiti, and Australia. This strong, well-established program is highly recommended.

ADVENTURE PURSUITS-TEEN WILDERNESS

A diverse, positive, outdoor-adventure experience for ages 13 to 18 is furnished by **Adventure Pursuits-Teen Wilderness** (*4101 Suncrest Dr., Fort Collins, CO 80525. 800-651-8336 or 970-226-4543. www.apadventures.com*). Teens from around the world join small groups that undertake a multitude of activities in scenic wilderness areas of Colorado, Utah, and the Pacific Northwest. Each adventure is designed to deliver age-appropriate challenges and successes, maximizing the fun for a specific age group. In order to offer something for every active teen, courses vary in length and locale. Past participants have praised the leadership, group spirit, and activity planning of this program, which is a great confidence-builder for teens.

AMERICA'S ADVENTURE/VENTURE EUROPE

Since 1976, **America's Adventure/Venture Europe** (*2245 Stonecrop Way, Golden, CO 80401. 800-222-3595 or 303-526-0806. www.aave.com*) has offered 18- to 40-day hands-on camping adventures for teenagers. The destinations are diverse, ranging from the Swiss Alps to the beaches of Hawaii. Each program features popular outdoor activities that build individual abilities as well as teamwork skills. AAVE's programs are popular with teen participants, who hail from all over the world.

The program, accredited by the American Camping Association, is run by enthusiastic, capable adult leaders who limit group size to a maximum of 15. Destinations include the United States (Alaska, Colorado, Hawaii, Utah, and Washington), France, Italy, Scandinavia, Spain, and Switzer-

land. A typical program lasts four weeks and costs about $3,500; longer or shorter programs are available as well.

Especially noteworthy is the 21-day **Ultimate Hawaii** trip, which combines sailing, mountain biking, sea kayaking, ocean sports, and backpacking. On the opposite side of the globe, AAVE offers **Academic Adventure** programs that feature a month's immersion in the French or Spanish language at a cost of $4,400. There may be no better way for teens to learn a foreign tongue than while enjoying outdoor adventures.

OUTWARD BOUND

Founded in 1941, **Outward Bound** (*100 Mystery Point Rd., Garrison, NY 10524. 800-243-8520 or 914-424-4000. www. outwardbound.org*) now encompasses more than 30 schools and training centers worldwide, 27 of them in North America. The core of the Outward Bound experience is still a one-to four-week wilderness adventure in which students learn self-sufficiency in the outdoors, but that theme now has many variations: Programs focus on ocean skills, rock climbing, river rafting, winter camping, canoeing, mountaineering, sea kayaking, sailing, desert backpacking, cross-country skiing, and dogsledding. Three-month semester courses are also available, as are specialty programs for families and young adults.

Outward Bound enjoys an excellent reputation for safety and professionalism. All instructors have Red Cross training and are certified in CPR, and the typical staff-to-student ratio is one to three. For more information, see pages 155-156.

TRAILMARK OUTDOOR ADVENTURES

Multiactivity summer adventure trips for youths ages 12 to 17 have been offered by **Trailmark Outdoor Adventures** (*16 Schuyler Rd., Nyack, NY 10960. 800-229-0262 or 914-358-0262*) since 1985. Destinations include New England, the Pacific Northwest, southwest Colorado, and the northern Rockies.

A typical Trailmark program is an active, challenging co-ed tour during which 18 students (grouped by age and led by three adults) spend 15 to 35 days traveling in passenger vans from one wilderness destination to another, undertaking a new adventure almost every day. These may include white-water rafting, backpacking, rock climbing, mountain biking, and horseback riding. Overnights are spent in public or private wilderness campsites.

The 28-day New England trip features rock climbing, ropes courses, canoeing, white-water rafting, road biking, mountain biking, windsurfing, Rollerblading, and a service project. Trips range in price from approximately $1,500 to $3,100.

Barge and Adventure Cruising

On a luxury cruise along the inland waterways of Europe, the pace is leisurely, the cuisine is superb, and the "back-yard" view of the countryside is unique. There are all types of cruises, from barges to powered yachts and from budget programs with shared accommodations to luxury craft fit for a king and queen. Those with extra-deep pockets can even arrange a vacation that combines barging with ballooning—or with overnight stays in spectacular castles.

Too sedentary to qualify as adventure travel, you say? Think again. Seasoned blue-water sailors who have sought out the experience as a break from the bareboat-charter routine say an inland cruise can be outstanding. For them, it constituted both a relaxing holiday and a true cultural adventure, one that brought new landscapes—and new discoveries—every day of the journey. Many veterans of barge cruises add that they have never eaten so well in their lives.

Many brokers offer European barge cruising, so it pays to shop around. Don't be shy about requesting any special items, such as side trips to historic castles or other sites. To book barge and canal cruises in Europe (including the British Isles and Ireland), contact any of these companies:

Le Boat (*10 S. Franklin Tpk., Suite 204B, Ramsey, NJ 07446. 800-992-0291 or 201-236-2333. www.leboat.com*)

European Waterways (*140 E. 56th St., New York, NY 10022. 800-217-4447 or 212-688-9489. www.europeanwaterways.com*)

French Country Waterways, Ltd. (*P.O. Box 2195, Duxbury, MA 02331. 800-222-1236 or 781-934-2454*)

Remote Odysseys Worldwide (*P.O. Box 579, Coeur d'Alene, ID 83816. 800-451-6034 or 208-765-0841. www.rowinc.com*) runs luxury barge tours and adventure cruises in the Turkish Mediterranean on 50- to 80-foot-long motor-sailors.

Outside Europe, **Ocean Voyages** (*1709 Bridgeway, Sausalito, CA 94965. 800-299-4444 or 415-332-4681. www.oceanvoyages.com*) offers unique adventure cruises under sail or power. Representing yachts, tall ships, and myriad inland and blue-water cruising craft, Ocean Voyages claims that it can book passage on anything that floats. For more information on chartered yacht vacations, see pages 196-211.

Authoritative and unbiased information on cruises of all kinds is floated monthly by *The Shipboard Cruiser* newsletter. To read sample features or subscribe online ($46 per year), visit www.shipboardcruiser.com. *The Shipboard Cruiser* offers ship reviews as well as late-breaking news on cruise itineraries and ship inspections. Reviews of cruise packages by passengers who have taken them are posted online by the **Cruise Review Library** (*www.travel-library.com/cruise*).

Bobsledding

For a true adrenaline rush, nothing beats a high-speed run in an Olympic-class bobsled. Lake Placid, site of the Winter Olympics in 1932 and 1980, offers bobsled rides for the public in both summer and winter. In 1999, Lake Placid unveiled a 20-million-dollar luge-and-bobsled track designed for the 2000 Goodwill Games. You can ride nearly the full length of the Olympic racing run, reaching speeds of up to 80 miles per hour. (To lessen the terror, start lower down the track.) On the longer runs, expert drivers pilot the sleds. On the shorter, slower runs, participants use a self-guided sled. Call **Lake Placid Information** (*800-462-6236*) and select the Mount Van Hovenberg Luge and Bobsled Run (*ext. 251*), or call the bobsled facility (*518-543-4436*).

Out west, Salt Lake City boasts a high-tech bobsled run created for the 2002 Winter Olympics. For $125, you can shoot the full run in a four-person Olympic-style bobsled, sandwiched between a professional driver and brakeman who handle such essential chores as steering and stopping. The four-person sleds reach speeds of 70 to 80 miles per hour during their runs, with G-forces that rival those of a fighter jet. Alternatively, you can run the course solo in a rocket sled—the poor man's luge—that costs less then $30 per glide but still reaches speeds up to 40 miles per hour. Call the **Utah Winter Sports Park** (*435-658-4220*) for reservations for either the four-man or solo sled.

In Canada, head to Calgary Olympic Park, site of the 1988 Winter Olympics, for a ride on the Bob Bullet. This unique, 60-mile-per-hour bobsled operates much like a roller coaster—all you do is hang on and enjoy the ride. It costs about $30 for the first run, a bit less for repeat rides. Minimum age is 16. If you're certifiably crazy, you can ride a one-person luge down the last third of the bobsled run—500 feet of insanity with five curves. With your body just inches from the ice, it will seem like you're going 100 miles per hour; in reality, the luge never exceeds 35 miles per hour during its 30-second run. For more information, call **Calgary Olympic Park** (*403-247-5480 or 8811*).

World-class European bobsled runs are open to amateur adventurers in Lillehammer, Norway (year-round), La Plagne, France (summer and winter), and Innsbruck (Ischgl), Austria (winter). At both Lillehammer and Innsbruck you can blast down full Olympic runs in competition-grade sleds piloted by expert drivers at speeds up to 85 miles per hour. Run maps, track specifications, and contact information for these and other bobsled tracks worldwide can be accessed at www.bobsleigh.com/tracks.html.

For more on competitive bobsledding, contact the **U.S. Bobsled Federation** (*P.O. Box 828, Lake Placid, NY 12946. 800-262-7533 or 518-523-1842. www.usabobsled.org*).

TRAVEL TIPS

More Mad Miscellany

To provide unique vacation opportunities not available through conventional travel services, specialized companies have sprung up that cater to extremely focused clienteles. Some of the leading specialty travel agencies and consultants are listed below. Although a few of these offer their services free of charge, others levy a consulting fee that must be paid by the client.

Battlefield Tours: Valor Tours (*415-332-7850*)

Garden Tours: Coopersmith's England (*415-669-1914*)

Golf Tours: Francine Atkins' Scotland/Ireland (*800-742-0355*); Golfpac (*407-260-2288*); ITC Golf Tours (*800-257-4981*)

Gourmet Tours: Cuisine International (*214-373-1161*)

Same-Sex Travel: International Gay & Lesbian Travel Association (*800-448-8550*)

Singles Travel: Connecting Solo Travel Network (*604-737-7751*)

Tennis Tours: Championship Tennis Tours (*800-468-3664*)

ONLINE

Among the best websites for specialty travel is **Outdoor Adventure Online** (AOL keyword: "Outdoor Adventure"). Other prominent websites devoted to travel are:

Adventure Travel
www.specialtytravel.com

Budget Travel
www.lonelyplanet.com

City Database
www.excite.com/travel/

European Train Schedules
www.eurorail.com/skedintr.htm

Round-the-World Travel Guide
www.travel-library.com/rtw

Special Needs Travel
www.access-able.com

Tourist Trains, North America
www.trainweb.com/touristrailways;
www.railterminal.com/map.shtml

Tourist Trains, Worldwide
www.railserve.com/tourist

Train Travel
www.trainweb.com/travel

Women's Travel
www.womenstravelclub.com

World Travel
http://travel.yahoo.com

PRINT

A great resource for archaeology, paleontology, and other science-related travel adventures is the directory of volunteer and learning vacations put out by **Transitions Abroad** (*413-256-3414. www.transitionsabroad.com*). This directory lists hundreds of programs offered by nonprofit and academic institutions worldwide. Many of the programs offer academic credit, and their overall price is often much less than you would pay through a conventional commercial tour.

The *Specialty Travel Index* (*800-442-4922. http://specialtytravel.com/*), published twice a year, is a comprehensive directory of adventure companies. Available both in print and online, it contains hundreds of recreational opportunities.

The Adventurous Traveler Bookstore (*800-282-3963. www.adventuroustraveler.com*) is a treasure trove of travel books, maps, and videos. Footloose types can browse thousands of titles and order online; overnight shipping is available.

SHIPBOARD VACATIONS

Cruise Critic
www.cruisecritic.com and on America Online

Research Ship Departures
Oceanic Information Center at http://diu.cms.udel.edu/ships/world-wide__ships.html

The Shipboard Cruiser
www.shipboardcruiser.com

Small Ship and Freighter Cruises
www.smallshipcruises.com

TELEVISION

With the explosion of new cable channels, you can now view adventure-oriented programming almost 24 hours a day. A favorite program, *Great Sports Vacations*, provides in-depth analysis of exciting vacation opportunities around the globe. Unlike the typical adventure travelog, *Great Sports Vacations* offers specific, detailed information that helps you plan an itinerary. *Great Sports Vacations* is broadcast in the United States over the **Prime Network**. Other shows to look for are *National Geographic Explorer*, the *Lonely Planet* on the **Travel Channel,** and various adventure programming on the **Outdoor Life Network** (OLN). *Preview Vacations*, broadcast on the **Travel Channel**, offers special deals on cruise and hotel packages.

PALOMETA FISH COME NOSE TO TOES WITH TOURIST, ST. JOHN, U.S. VIRGIN ISLANDS.

EXPERIENCED TRAVELERS DON'T SWEAT EVERY DETAIL OF A TRIP. NOR DO THEY ATTEMPT TO PLAN EACH stop on the itinerary beforehand. Seasoned globetrotters *do* pay great attention, however, to the things that really matter: travel documents, money, communications, and insurance. You should do the same. By taking care of these essentials before you leave, you can get off the plane, train, or boat feeling confident that you can handle anything else that comes your way. • This chapter tells you how to obtain your passport and visas, how to convert money abroad, how to select traveler's and health insurance, and what to do in case of emergencies. Two final sections consider discount travel and travel for those with special needs. • Although the chapter focuses on travel in exotic places, most of the information applies to any foreign trip. Things happen when you travel— whether striking off on your own up the Zambezi or booking a place on a package tour to Cancun. That's part of the thrill. So plan what you can, be prepared to deal with changes as they arise— and enjoy the adventure.

LEFT: JAPANESE RAIL ADVENTURE AT 160 MILES PER HOUR
BELOW: RIDERS TRACK THE ROUTE OF THE *COAST STARLIGHT*.

Let the tourist be cushioned against misadventure, but your true traveler will not feel that he has had his money's worth unless he brings back a few scars.
LAWRENCE DURRELL

Passports and Visas

If you plan to travel outside North America, you will need a passport. Keep this valuable document on you at all times when abroad; carrying it in a small passport purse secured around your neck or leg and hidden beneath your clothing is a good idea. As a backup proof of citizenship, bring along a xerox of the identification pages of your passport, an expired passport, or a certified copy of your birth certificate. Carry this item separate from your other papers or give it to a traveling companion for safekeeping.

First-time Passport Applications

All American citizens, including children, are required to obtain passports in their own names for identification while traveling abroad and for reentry into the United States. Unless specifically authorized by a passport-issuing office, no person may have more than one valid, or potentially valid, U.S. passport of the same type at any time.

If you are applying for your first U.S. passport—or if your passport was issued more than 12 years ago—you must apply for it in person. You may do so at one of the more than 2,500 courthouses and 900 post offices that accept passport applications. Or you may apply at one of the 13 regional passport agencies listed on page 99. Call the largest regional post office in your area or look in the Blue Pages of your phone book.

Processing time is normally about two weeks. However, you should apply for your passport at least four to six weeks before any international travel. You will need to provide the following documents:

1. **Proof of United States citizenship** or nationality. Acceptable documents include a certified copy of a birth certificate for all applicants born in the United States; a Certificate of Naturalization or Citizenship; a previous U.S. passport.

2. **Proof of identity** (a photo ID with a signature), such as a previous U.S. passport; a Certificate of Naturalization or Citizenship; a valid driver's license; or a valid government, military, or corporate identification card.

3. **Two identical passport photographs** taken within the last six months. The photographs must be 2 inches by 2 inches. In addition, the photographs must be front views—showing the full face—and taken against a plain white background.

4. **Completed passport application** form that contains all the requested information—except your signature. You must sign the form in the presence of an authorized executing official.

5. **Social security number**: Although not required for issuance of a passport, the Internal Revenue Service requires all passport applicants to provide it. Passport Services routinely passes this information on to the IRS. Any applicant who fails to provide the information is subject to a $500 penalty enforced by the IRS.

Passport Renewals

Applicants who have had a previous U.S. passport issued within the past 12 years—and who were 16 or older when the passport was issued—may be eligible to apply for a new passport by mail. They may do so provided that their name has not changed and that they can submit their most recent passport. They may also apply in person. Documents required for renewals include:

1. **Most recent U.S. passport**

2. **Two passport photos**

3. **A completed passport application** form that contains all the requested information and is signed and dated. Ask your travel agent, post office, or courthouse for an application form. Or you can order a form by calling the passport agency nearest you.

Mail the completed application and attachments to:

National Passport Center
P.O. Box 371971
Pittsburgh, PA 15250-7971

Passport Fees

Passport fees for initial passports are $60 if you are 16 years of age and over, $40 if you are 15 years and under. Passport renewal fees are $40 for all ages. Make your check or money order payable to Passport Services. Note: Fees are subject to change.

What If You Need a Passport in a Hurry?

If you are leaving on an emergency trip within five working days, apply in person at the nearest passport agency and present your tickets or travel itinerary from an airline, as well as the other required items. However, don't just show up at the agency: Make sure you call ahead and set up an appointment. (At many of the country's passport offices, in fact, appointments are now mandatory for all visits.)

For passport renewals, you can send your application by overnight express mail, along with a check and a request for the passport's return by mail. Whether you apply in person or renew by mail, you will have to pay a $35 expediting fee, in addition to all other applicable fees. Be sure to include your dates of departure and travel plans on your passport application: Applications are processed according to the departure date indicated on the application form. If you give no date, the passport agency will assume that you have no immediate travel plans.

Passport forms can be obtained by calling the passport agencies or the **National Passport Information Center.** You can also download forms from the Internet at http://travel.state.gov.

Passport Agencies

Passport agencies tend to have extremely long lines during the busiest months, typically from January through July. To avoid lengthy waits, you may want to apply at the nearest courthouse or post office that accepts passport applications, where you'll generally find shorter lines. (You can get a list of these locations by visiting the following website: http://travel.state.gov/passport__services.html.)

If you prefer to apply at one of the passport agencies, contact one of the following:

BOSTON Passport Agency
Thomas P. O'Neill Federal Building
10 Causeway St., Suite 247
Boston, MA 02222
617-565-6990

CHICAGO Passport Agency
Kluczynski Federal Building
230 S. Dearborn St., Suite 380
Chicago, IL 60604
312-341-6020 for appointment (mandatory)

HONOLULU Passport Agency
First Hawaiian Tower
1132 Bishop St., Suite 500
Honolulu, HI 96813
808-522-8283

HOUSTON Passport Agency
Mickey Leland Federal Building
1919 Smith St., Suite 1100
Houston, TX 77002
713-751-0294 for appointment (mandatory)

LOS ANGELES Passport Agency
Federal Building
11000 Wilshire Blvd., Suite 13100
Los Angeles, CA 90024
310-575-5700 for appointment (mandatory)

MIAMI Passport Agency
Claude Pepper Federal Office Building
51 SW First Ave., 3rd Floor
Miami, FL 33120
305-859-2705

NATIONAL Passport Information Center
31 Rochester Ave.
Portsmouth, NH 03801
603-334-0500

NEW ORLEANS Passport Agency
Postal Services Building
701 Loyola Ave., Suite T-12005
New Orleans, LA 70113
504-412-2600

NEW YORK Passport Agency
Rockefeller Center
630 Fifth Ave., Suite 270
New York, NY 10111
212-206-3500 for appointment (mandatory)

PHILADELPHIA Passport Agency
U.S. Custom House
200 Chestnut St., Room 103
Philadelphia, PA 19106
215-597-7480

SAN FRANCISCO Passport Agency
Tishman Speyer Building
525 Market St., Suite 200
San Francisco, CA 94105
415-538-2700 for appointment (mandatory)

SEATTLE Passport Agency
Henry Jackson Federal Building
915 Second Ave., Suite 992
Seattle, WA 98174
206-220-7788

STAMFORD Passport Agency
One Landmark Square
Broad and Atlantic Sts.
Stamford, CT 06901
203-356-1444 for appointment (mandatory)

WASHINGTON Passport Agency
1111 19th St. NW, Room 300
Washington, D.C. 20522
202-647-0518

SPECIAL ISSUANCE Agency
1111 19th St. NW, Room 300
Washington, D.C. 20522
Applications for diplomatic, official, and no-fee passports

All offices, except the special issuance, maintain a 24-hour automated information line. The service provides general passport information, passport agency locations, hours of operation, and information regarding emergency passport services during nonworking hours. Some agencies require appointments, which you must schedule by calling a separate number.

VISA REQUIREMENTS FOR OVERSEAS TRAVEL

How to Determine If You Need a Visa

In some countries, you never need a visa. In others, you always need one. And in still others, it depends on how long you are planning to stay.

For example, American passport holders do not need a visa to visit Canada or most countries in Latin America and Western Europe. However, there are still dozens of countries throughout the world where you must obtain a visa for any visit. These places include Australia, China, Egypt, India, Kenya, Morocco, and Tanzania, as well as Russia and most former communist bloc nations. Then there are certain countries—such as Nepal, New Zealand, and Thailand—where you may visit for a certain amount of time without having to secure a visa.

Because the visa policies of foreign governments change regularly, be sure to check the requirements before you depart. Often, the national tourism board of the country you plan to visit can give you an answer. However, to be sure about current visa requirements, inquire directly with the relevant foreign embassy or consulate. As a rule of thumb, if you are planning to travel anywhere outside Canada, Latin America, or Western Europe, double-check with the embassy or the consulate to ensure that you do not need a visa.

An official summary of visa requirements for Americans traveling overseas is available for 50 cents from the **U.S. Consumer Information Center** (*Dept. 361C, Pueblo, CO 81009. 719-948-3334. Ask for the "Foreign Entry Requirements"*). Or, try the U.S. Department of State website (*http://travel.state.gov/foreignentryreqs. html*), which also provides the addresses of foreign embassies and consulates where visas may be obtained.

The Embassy Page (*www. embassyweb.com*) carries contact information for all foreign embassies and consulates in the United States, too. In addition, this website offers a searchable database of 50,000 addresses, phone numbers, and e-mail addresses of diplomatic posts worldwide, plus links to other important international travel websites.

Getting Required Visas

You will need visas for many countries in Asia, for most African and Middle Eastern countries, and for most remaining communist nations. Visa requirements vary widely from country to country, so be sure you know what you need before you submit your application. It is strongly advised that you contact the embassy or consulate of the country you plan to visit to obtain its current visa policies.

Allow three to five working days to obtain a visa if you apply in person at the foreign embassy or consulate. Be aware that many foreign countries require visa applications to be submitted during particular business hours or days of the week. Allow up to three weeks if you submit your visa application by mail.

For around $20-40 per visa, you can make life easier by having a commercial visa agency obtain your visas for you. These services are reliable, but if you need expedited processing you may have to pay as much as $100 extra. Remember, though: even if you pay for expedited service, you will not receive your visa until the foreign embassy or consulate staff processes the visa application—so always give yourself a few extra days.

Normally you are required to send the agency your completed visa applications, valid passport, and payment in advance. Always use registered or certified mail when transmitting your passport and supporting documents. With that understood, here is a list of agencies that will obtain your visas.

Commercial Visa Services

Express Visa Service, Inc.

2233 Wisconsin Ave., Suite 215
Washington, DC 20007
202-337-2442. www.expressvisa.com
The top-rated company, Express Visa Service, also has offices in Chicago, Houston, Los Angeles, Miami, New York City, and San Francisco.

Intercontinental Visa Service

L.A. World Trade Center, 350 S. Figueroa St., Suite 185, Los Angeles, CA 90071
213-625-7175. www.ivisaservice.com

Visas International

6525 Sunset Blvd., Los Angeles, CA 90028. 800-638-1517 or 323-462-3636

Communications and Finances

Affording travel is a matter of priorities. Many people who 'can't afford a trip' could sell their car and travel for two years.
—Rick Steves

MONEY MATTERS

Traveler's Checks

American Express traveler's checks are still the most widely accepted checks throughout the world. Visa, Thomas Cook, and Barclay's are not-so-close seconds. Wherever you get your traveler's checks, however, make sure they are in U.S. dollars, which will serve you better than any other currency, except in Britain.

When getting your traveler's checks, select mostly $50 and $100. Many foreign banks and hotels charge per-check. Always be prepared to show your passport when changing money or cashing checks.

If you find that you need more money than anticipated—and you have an American Express card—there's another option while abroad: Once every seven days, you can write a personal check to obtain up to $1,000 in American Express Traveler's checks. This is the simplest and best way to get more money when you're away from home. American Express offices will also cash cardholders' home-bank personal checks for up to $200 in local currency.

Many major airports now feature Express ATMs that issue American Express or Visa traveler's checks and charge them to your credit cards. This is fast and handy. The transaction fees you pay when obtaining traveler's checks by ATM are generally comparable with normal bank charges, unless your financial institution issues the checks without charge.

Keep records of when and where you spend your traveler's checks; also, keep a list of your checks' serial numbers separate from the checks themselves. Try to use the checks in numerical order, which will simplify your record keeping. Finally, write down the phone number to call in case your checks are lost or stolen.

To obtain American Express checks, call 800-673-3782 in the United States; elsewhere, consult the nearest American Express office.

Credit Cards

Don't travel anywhere abroad without a major credit card (Mastercard, Visa, or American Express)—preferably a gold or silver model. These cards are recognized worldwide, and you'll find them extremely useful wherever there are phones and banks. You can get a cash advance with a Mastercard or Visa at most commercial banks in the world, and these cards can also access ATMs in many countries.

Credit cards offer other important advantages to the traveler. Many premium cards now provide free travel accident insurance up to one million dollars. Most gold cards also cover car rental insurance deductibles up to a specified amount—although in some foreign countries you may have to pay an insurance surcharge.

Read your cardholder's terms and conditions carefully to determine the extent of rental insurance coverage. If there is any question about coverage, ask your issuing bank for a coverage declaration in writing. To avoid fraudulent billings, keep your receipts and write the local exchange rate on the receipt to avoid any confusion.

Every world traveler should have an American Express card—not just to charge purchases but also to take advantage of the company's worldwide travel services. With an American Express card, you can cash personal checks, book flights, and get emergency money and assistance if your valuables are lost or stolen. The ability to cash a personal check overseas can be a real lifesaver. And for this, American Express is the only game in town—whether you're in London or Kathmandu.

Currency Exchange

Before you depart, try to change about $150 into the currency of the country you'll be visiting. This will get you through air-ports and train stations more quickly and with fewer hassles.

If the currency you need is not readily available stateside, then change $20 to $50 as soon as you get off the plane. Despite what you hear, airport exchange rates are usually not all that bad. In fact, in some places—Austria is one—the airport rates are identical to what you will receive at a bank in town.

You can find lists of exchange rates in the financial section of major newspapers. Internet users can access worldwide rates at www.oanda.com or consult America Online (keyword: "currency converter").

When you're abroad, shop around before exchanging large sums. Most money changers in modern countries post their exchange rates, so it's easy for you to compare one bank with another. But make sure that you know the service charge as well as the rate of exchange. Also, you'll benefit by exchanging at least $100 at a time, especially if there is a service charge per check. When you receive the foreign currency, count it carefully before you leave the premises.

If you are exchanging U.S. dollars or deutsche marks in Russia or Eastern Europe, be aware that most money changers will not accept torn, crumpled, or ink-stained bills—even if they look fine by home-country standards. And although it's not a good idea to carry large amounts of cash overseas, sometimes there is an advantage to having greenbacks—or deutsche marks—in hand. In Eastern Europe, for example, the exchange rates for German and American currency are often significantly better than those for equivalent amounts in traveler's checks.

Bank Debit Cards and Overseas ATMs

Automatic teller machines are springing up all over Europe and Asia. From these handy machines you can withdraw foreign currency and pay for it automatically with your credit card. Some machines even let you make withdrawals with the ATM card issued by your bank in the United States.

There are advantages to using ATMs for currency transactions. First, the exchange rates tend to be quite good: In many cases, ATMs deliver a more favorable rate than you can get at banks, and they often charge a lower fee per transaction. Second, direct debits from your bank card avoid the carrying charges and access fees you may incur with a credit card.

COMMUNICATIONS

Phoning Home

When phoning home from abroad, you'll have one of two very different experiences. Either it will be easy, with a modern, direct-dial phone network and English-speaking operators, or it will be very difficult. There seems to be no middle ground.

Phones are hard to find in many countries, and they're often out of order. In addition, the operators may be unskilled and the connections poor. What's worse, you may have to wait in long lines in crowded post offices, and carry with you what feels like a ton of coins.

You can make calls from your hotel, of course. But if you're staying in a hotel in a developing country, always try to get the establishment's fee schedule in writing before making your calls.

Make sure to bring an AT&T, Sprint, or MCI-Worldcom calling card when you travel. It will be useful in Europe and in major cities throughout Asia. Visa and Mastercard are also good for placing calls from airports and hotels. Phoning to the States from Europe is relatively cheap, if you dial direct. Also, most Western European phone networks do not impose a flat fee for the first few minutes of overseas calls. So you can place a quick call home for very little money.

AT&T's USADIRECT service will connect you with an American operator or a prompt when calling home from more than 150 countries. Call 800-225-5288 for a pocket-size card listing all countries linked to USADIRECT and their respective access codes. You will be billed at the host country's USADIRECT rate, which is lower, in most cases, than going through the domestic operator. You will almost always save money by using USADIRECT when calling home from a hotel.

Be aware, though, that AT&T imposes a $2.50 fee for every USADIRECT call and a $5.00 fee for every collect call. It can also be costly to use USADIRECT or Sprint Express to dial from one foreign phone to another. For example, if you use USADI-RECT to call from France to Germany, you will be billed for multiple segments. Invariably, you will save money by using a local-money phone card for calling from one European nation to another or for calls within that country.

Calling within a Foreign Country

In most parts of Europe, as well as Australia and New Zealand, you will save money by using a regional telephone calling card. You can purchase these cards in various places, such as post offices, banks, and small stores.

In many European countries you can also use a Mastercard or Visa to make calls from many newer pay phones. The price varies widely, so keep your calls short. When using a hotel phone, be sure to know the charges *before* you dial. Deluxe hotels impose stiff fees to make long-distance calls, particularly if you are not a guest in the hotel.

Mail & Messages

American embassies will not hold mail or telephone messages for U.S. citizens abroad—except in the case of true emergencies, such as a death in the family. If you have an American Express card, however, American Express offices worldwide will receive and hold your mail, fax, and telegram messages. For mail, the sender should mark the envelope "Client Letter Service." Call American Express Customer Service (*800-528-4800*) for a worldwide list of participating offices.

AT&T also offers its "True Messages" service (*800-878-3123*), which allows those at home to record and send messages to any telephone worldwide. If no one is home, AT&T's computer or attendant will automatically redial every 30 minutes for 10 hours until the call goes through. The caller must have an AT&T calling card, the True Message option for his or her home telephone service, or a major credit card.

In most places in the world, you can receive mail addressed to you care of "Poste Restante" (general delivery). Although the name of the city, province, and country will probably be enough, try to supply the sender with the street address of the city's main post office as well. Your name should be printed in block letters and underlined. Note, too, that in Eastern Europe it is customary to place the surname first, followed by the first name—"Jones, Robert," for example. When receiving Poste Restante mailings, be sure to check under both your first and last name, especially in Asia.

Fax machines are not yet universal. In many Third World countries you will still have to rely on telexes and telegrams. Remember, though, most telegrams are not instantaneous, but require postal delivery at some point. Thus, allow three to six days

for a telegraphic message to reach a party in the United States.

Moreover, you'll find that it's often cheaper to telephone than to send a telegram or telex. In the countries of the former Soviet Union, many post offices offer e-mail service—which is cheaper than voice calls and faster and more reliable than sending telegrams.

E-mail

Sending e-mail over the Internet is the cheapest way to communicate with travelers overseas. Users with access to the Internet can send a text message of unlimited length for the price of a local phone call. This is far more economical than sending a fax, which typically costs around $3-5 per page to transmit internationally.

Your friends back home won't have trouble sending you e-mail if they have an account with any online service or Internet provider. The difficulty may lie on the other end: How do you receive your e-mail?

If you are a CompuServe member, you can log on to CompuServe while overseas via one of the service's many local access numbers. CompuServe, a subsidiary of America Online, currently maintains the largest network of local nodes, and its coverage in Europe and Asia is very broad.

If you don't bring your own computer with you, to retrieve your e-mail you will have to find a computer-equipped hotel or business center that will let you log on as a guest or that has its own e-mail address to which messages can be sent. Be aware that there may be a significant surcharge for such communications services. Alternatively, many post offices in Europe now offer e-mail reception services for both citizens and tourists.

Apart from finding a local access number to call, there are more mundane problems facing e-mail users on the road. Many overseas travelers soon learn to their dismay that their laptops and Personal Digital Assistants won't work for the simple reason that they can't plug them in. Because of plug incompatibility, they simply can't plug their computer into the wall socket or their modem cord into the phone outlet.

To solve the problem, you'll need specific adaptors for each country you visit. Thankfully, the travel accessories mail-order shop **Magellan's** (*800-962-4943 or 805-568-5400. www.magellans.com*) sells handy adaptor kits for both power and phone connections for all countries. For product specifications, contact the manufacturer of the adaptors, **TeleAdapt** (*408-965-1400. www.teleadapt.com*). The company offers over 40 different adaptors, including an alligator clip connection for the most primitive phone systems.

What is the future of electronic communications for travelers? Someday a network of satellites will offer global coverage for cellular phones and digital pagers. Technologies already exist to transmit voices over the Internet at the same low rate as text messaging. In order to take advantage of Internet voice transmission, however, both the sending and the receiving units must have dedicated Internet accounts and specially configured hardware and software. Very few such installations exist at present.

Security for World Travelers

The scientific theory I like best is that the rings of Saturn are composed entirely of lost airline luggage.

—Mark Russell

Coping with Emergencies

As mentioned above, American embassies and consulates worldwide will take emergency messages and relay them—as long as they have a reliable address. In cases of extreme need, the State Department Overseas Citizens' Services can send money to U.S. citizens abroad. This service can also assist Americans in accidents, disasters, or legal trouble, and inform families of injuries or deaths.

Contact **Overseas Citizens' Services** (*U.S. Dept. of State, Bureau of Consular Affairs, No. 4811, 2201 C St. NW, Washington, DC 20520. 202-647-5225 for hot line*). Also, before you leave for abroad, check on the current U.S. State Department Travel Advisories (*http://travel.state.gov/travel_warnings.html*).

American Express offices will send and receive important fax and mail messages, as well as help cardholders with lost passports, tickets, or credit cards. **Worldwide Assistance Services, Inc.** (*1133 15th St. NW, Suite 400, Washington, DC 20005. 800-821-2828 or 703-204-1897. www.worldwideassistance.com*) can also provide help. If you obtain coverage with the company before your departure, Travel Assistance will transmit messages, help replace lost passports and visas, provide legal assistance, and arrange emergency

evacuation or repatriation. The cost of coverage ranges from $23 for one week to $305 for three months.

Customs

You must declare all items you purchased overseas when returning to the United States. American citizens may bring $400 worth of articles into the country without paying duty (although this amount is higher for those returning from American Samoa and certain other locations).

If you mail back a parcel with a value exceeding $100 (gift) or $200 (nongift), the postal service will collect duty and a handling charge. However, if you are mailing back to the United States items that you bought there, you can avoid paying any duty by writing "American Goods Returned" on the box.

There is no limit on the total amount of money that you can bring in or take out of the United States. But if you transport more than $10,000 in currency on any occasion—either into or out of the country—you must file a report (Customs Form 4790).

To learn more about customs regulations, request the *"Know Before You Go"* brochure from the **U.S. Customs Service, National Dist. Center** (*317-290-3149, ext. 102*). This publication is also available online at www.customs.ustreas.gov.

Staying Healthy

Medical Insurance

Don't leave home without an adequate medical insurance policy—one that covers what you plan to do and where you plan to do it. This may sound obvious. However, many health policies exclude injuries sustained while scuba diving or parachuting, and they may cover only a few days of emergency care in a foreign health facility. And do not rely on Medicare: This government program does not cover foreign medical care at all.

Read your health policy carefully. If there are troublesome loopholes, go to a good agent and take out additional insurance. If you're planning an adventure trip to a remote location, be sure your medical insurance includes emergency medical evacuation. (A helicopter rescue in Borneo could cost thousands of dollars.)

If you're not satisfied with what your own insurer can provide, contact one or more of the following underwriters:

Travelex

11717 Burt St., No. 202

Omaha, NE 68154
800-228-9792
www.travelex-insurance.com

Travelex's Cruise & Tours program—as well as its Travel Assure Policy for independent travelers—offers comprehensive accident insurance for tourists that covers most medical and evacuation costs, baggage loss, and trip cancellation.

Wallach & Co.

107 West Federal St., P.O. Box 480
Middleburg, VA 22117
800-237-6615 or 540-687-3166
www.wallach.com

Under its Health Care Abroad program, Wallach & Co. offers comprehensive foreign medical care, emergency evacuation coverage, accidental death, and trip cancellation protection.

Worldwide Assistance Services, Inc.

1133 15th St. NW, Suite 400
Washington, DC 20005
800-821-2828 or 202-331-1609
www.worldwideassistance.com

Through its Travel Assistance Policy, this underwriter covers foreign medical expenses and emergency medical evacuation, and offers a 24-hour travelers' aid service to help with legal problems and lost passports and visas. You can also purchase coverage for trip cancellation, baggage loss, and death and dismemberment.

Immunizations

Consult with a medical professional before traveling to tropical or Third World destinations. If immunizations are required, your local physician or health clinic can administer the vaccinations you will need for your planned itinerary.

If you have not received boosters for tetanus/diphtheria and polio in the last ten years, it's a good idea to get them before you leave. For travel to rural areas or tropical regions, you will probably need vaccines for Hepatitis type A and typhoid.

If you travel in sub-Saharan Africa or in the Amazon Basin, add a yellow fever vaccine to the list. Malaria is a major health hazard in these areas, as well as in other rural parts of Latin America and in Southeast Asia. Before your departure, you must take antimalarial medication. This medication will not guarantee that you won't contract malaria, though, and you should also use insect repellents and mosquito bed nets once you get there.

Be sure to have all your immunizations

entered on an official vaccination certificate, which should also indicate when any further boosters are due.

General Health

To locate a good physician while you're abroad, contact the **International Association for Medical Assistance to Travelers** (*417 Center St., Lewiston, NY 14092. 716-754-4883*), which publishes a free global directory of Western-trained, English-speaking doctors. American Express cardholders can get physician referrals and immunization information from the **Global Assist Hotline** (*800-554-2639*).

A good health resource is *International Travel Health Guide* by Stuart Rose (Travel Medicine, 1995, $17.95. 800-872-8633 or 413-584-0381. www.travmed.com).

Jet Lag

When it comes to jet lag, the experts seem to agree that an ounce of prevention is worth a pound of cure. Avoid overeating before and after the flight—and the consumption of alcohol during the flight. Drink plenty of other fluids, however, and make sure to take extra doses of Vitamin B and Vitamin C.

Eyeshades and a U-shape neck support will help you sleep on the plane. As soon as you arrive at your destination—or as soon as is practical—go to bed and sleep until the local morning.

RISK MANAGEMENT

Traveler's Insurance

It's easy to obtain good, low-cost insurance for the most common accidents and mishaps that occur while vacationing. Your first step, though, is to find out how much coverage you—perhaps unknowingly— already have.

Your homeowner's insurance, for example, may already protect you against the theft of tickets and other valuables while you're away from home. Check your policy. And if you have a premium Visa or Mastercard, you probably have substantial accidental death and dismemberment coverage, as well as some protection for lost baggage and trip cancellation. American Express also provides its cardholders with some trip accident and baggage protection.

Adventuresome travelers should secure special coverage for trip cancellation and emergency evacuation. Many exotic trips require a significant, nonrefundable down payment. Trip cancellation insurance will

cover this loss if you have to back out at the last minute. Emergency evacuation insurance will cover the costs of being hauled out of the wilderness due to injury or environmental threat.

Separate trip accident insurance can be purchased from a number of carriers. In addition to those medical insurers listed above, comprehensive travel insurance packages are offered by the following companies:

Access America
P.O. Box 90315
Richmond, VA 23286
800-284-8300. www.accessamerica.com

Carefree Travel Insurance
The Berkeley Group
100 Garden City Plaza, P.O. Box 9366
Garden City, NY 11530
800-645-2424

Council on International Educational Exchange
205 East 42nd St.
New York, NY 10017
212-822-2600. www.ciee.org

Travel Guard International
1145 Clark St.
Stevens Point, WI 54481
800-782-5151 or 715-345-0505

Travel Insurance Pak
Travelers Insured International
52 South Oakland Ave.
East Hartford, CT 06128-0568
800-243-3174

Special Insurance Deals

The American Automobile Association's **Trip Assist Worldwide Protection Plan** is available to AAA members in many states for a special discounted rate. This program offers trip cancellation/interruption coverage, emergency medical coverage, and lost baggage protection—along with a 24-hour hotline to provide assistance with medical, legal, or other travel-related problems. Contact your local AAA office.

For teachers, enrolled students, and anyone under 26, affordable insurance is available from the **Council on International Education Exchange** (*212-822-2600. www.ciee.org*). When you purchase the council's $20 identification card, you are automatically enrolled in a comprehensive insurance plan covering accident, sickness, death and dismemberment, overseas medical and legal assistance services, and emergency medical evacuation.

This is a great deal, one of the better travel bargains available. The ID card also entitles the holder to many valuable discounts worldwide, including reduced-fare

air, train, and bus travel. In Egypt, for example, card-holders get as much as 50 percent off domestic airfares.

Driving Insurance

Major agencies such as Hertz or Avis provide both liability and property damage insurance when you rent a vehicle overseas. However, the size of deductibles varies dramatically from country to country, and there are many exclusions—such as cracked windshields in Australia—that can end up costing you plenty. Typically, you are responsible for the first $3,000 of losses, but policies change regularly and you must read the fine print.

Some rental agencies hold the renter liable for the entire amount of collision damages, up to the price of the vehicle. Unfortunately, paying with a premium credit card (such as Visa Gold) does not automatically cover the collision damage waiver (CDW) overseas, as it does in America. You should check with the financial institution that issues your credit card.

The American Express Gold Card, however, does automatically provide CDW coverage for vehicle rentals in many countries. The gold card delivers primary insurance—not merely the "excess" insurance that only kicks in if your own auto insurance will not pay. It is the cardholder's responsibility, though, to pay any costs to the overseas rental car company. You must then apply to American Express for reimbursement for the loss. Bear in mind that this reimbursement process involves a considerable amount of paperwork—and time—and you may want to purchase insurance instead.

If you plan to buy a vehicle overseas— or drive for an extended period of time in a number of foreign countries—you should obtain specialized insurance. Your regular insurer company may not be able to cover you for foreign travel, however. If so, two British firms can provide vehicle coverage for your overseas adventure. **Campbell, Irvine Ltd.** (*48 Earls Court Rd., Kensington, London W8 6EJ, U.K.*) will insure vehicles traveling anywhere in the world. **Hanover Park Insurance Brokers** (*Greystoke House, 86 Westow St., London SE19 3AQ, U.K.*) offers coverage throughout Europe and the Mediterranean.

You will have trouble insuring a vehicle overseas—or even renting one when you get there—unless you possess an International Driving Permit. You can get one easily from any AAA office nationwide before you depart. The fee is about $10 and you'll need two passport-size photographs. The permit is good for one year from the date of issuance.

If you contemplate riding any two-wheel motorbike while overseas—even a moped—make sure that you have a motorcycle endorsement in your International Driving Permit. It's true that in many tropical vacation areas, vendors will rent you a small motorcycle without requiring a permit. But if you drive without one, you can be in all kinds of trouble if you get into an accident: Your passport may be confiscated or you may be forced to pay excessive fines or damages.

Discount Travel Strategies

Airline travel is hours of boredom interrupted by moments of stark terror.
—Al Boliska

Have your plans for an ultimate adventure been grounded by the high price of flying? Take heart. With a little planning—and a little ingenuity—you can easily cut your air travel costs by as much as 30 percent. You'll find below a host of bargain-hunting tips that can help you reduce your major travel expenses and make that dream vacation affordable.

AIRFARE WHOLE-SALERS AND TICKET CONSOLIDATORS

Discount airfare consolidators—more commonly known as "bucket shops"—now thrive in every major U.S. city. The vast majority of their tickets are surplus seats that have been acquired wholesale from major carriers. Good bucket shops offer big savings, especially if you shop around and use good judgment. But don't expect them to do the many extra things that a good travel agency would normally do for you.

Though there may be some restrictions on your tickets, most bucket shops deliver what they promise—outstanding bargains. Be sure to ask which airline will be used, how long the quoted price is guaranteed, and who will provide any refund—the agency or the airline. Pick up the tickets yourself to avoid delays.

Airfare wholesalers and ticket consolidators purchase blocks of seats that are sold at 10 to 30 percent below the very lowest fares obtainable from regular travel agents or the airlines. If you have to fly on short notice, consolidator prices are hard to beat. With 48 hours notice, you can purchase tickets at 25 percent less than the airline's lowest seven-day advance purchase rate.

So what's the catch? Prices quoted in ads often omit required taxes. Many consolidators require cash payment or impose a 3 to 7 percent surcharge if you purchase your tickets with a credit card. And you sometimes can't get your money back if you miss the flight.

To find a discount shop in your area, check the newspaper classified advertisements and the Yellow Pages. The following companies are some of the leading ticket consolidators:

Cheap Tickets, Inc.
Los Angeles, CA
800-377-1000 or 818-765-3395
www.cheaptickets.com

This well-established agency has offices nationwide and a secure website for ticket orders 24 hours a day.

Council Travel Services
Los Angeles, CA
310-208-3551. www.counciltravel.com

With dozens of offices nationwide, Council offers some of the lowest advertised prices, with particularly attractive discounts for students and teachers. Council can issue Eurail passes on the spot.

Cut-Throat Travel Outlet
San Francisco, CA
415-989-8747

Specializing in around-the-world trips, this agency was highly rated by *USA Today*. It boasts experienced, intelligent personnel and good service. Ticket prices are not rock bottom, but are generally competitive.

New Frontiers USA
New York, NY
800-366-6387

Low fares to Europe, with particularly great fares to France.

There are many other reputable ticket wholesalers around the country. Check out he Sunday travel section of the major newspapers for some of the current deals. Online users looking for late-breaking travel bargains should consult America Online's Travel Forum (keyword: "travel forum"), which features a regularly updated Bargain Box with details on dis-counted airfares, both domestic and international.

Charter Flights

Available from most full-service travel agencies, charter flights offer the lowest confirmed reservation fares to popular destinations. There are drawbacks, however. You usually have to fix your departure and return dates well in advance, and you may have to pay a substantial fee to cancel or change your flights. In addition, you'll probably spend more time in line at the airport and—because charters aren't as organized as major airlines—run a greater risk of lost baggage.

Despite these shortcomings, millions of passengers fly on cheap charters every year, and the reliability records of charters compare favorably with many large carriers. Remember, too, that it is often possible to book only one leg of a two-way charter—sometimes for substantially less than half of the normal charter fee.

Here are some leading charter operators:

Council Charter
New York, NY. 212-822-2800

This popular charter company provides flights from the United States to Europe. Book well in advance.

Jet Vacations, Inc.
New York, NY. 800-538-0999

An Air France subsidiary, Jet Vacations, Inc., runs 747-charters from the East Coast to France, for approximately $250 and up each way.

Travac International
New York, NY. 800-872-8800 or 212-563-3304

Travac International concentrates on flights to Western Europe (prices to Switzerland are usually the lowest), the Middle East, and Africa.

Student Discounts

The following agencies specialize in cheap airfares as well as rail passes for students and persons 26 or under. Even when they cannot beat other consolidators' prices, these agencies can generally deliver student tickets with fewer restrictions, and their routings can be modified with only minimal fees.

STA Student Travel Network
STA Los Angeles (national headquarters)
Los Angeles, CA
800-777-0112 or 323-937-1150
www.sta-travel.com

STA is the student travel industry leader, offering a wide range of services. With more than 100 offices worldwide, STA can issue student ID cards on the spot and can book discounted flights to just about anywhere. STA discounts are available to enrolled students under 35 and to all persons under 26.

Council Travel Services

Los Angeles and offices nationwide
310-208-3551. www.counciltravel.com

Council Travel Services is a large agency, with numerous offices located throughout North America. It offers very good rates for student and teachers. Council's helpful website provides comprehensive travel resources.

Standby and Last Minute Travel

All of the following companies offer substantial discounts on airfares, cruises, and lodging to travelers who are able to travel on short notice. Most publish newsletters or maintain websites that list current bargains. Some charge an annual fee.

If you enjoy package vacations or cruise travel, there are many good bargains to be found. For example, a British website—www.lastminute.com—offers deep discounts on hotels, airfares, resort packages, entertainment, and even passage on the famed Orient Express. Other last minute travel bargains are offered by these travel clubs:

Last Minute Travel Club, Inc.

Woburn, MA. 800-527-8646

Mostly Boston departures. Specializes in air-and-hotel packages to the Caribbean and Mexico, as well as air connections to Western Europe. No fee.

Moment's Notice, Inc.

New York, NY. 718-234-6295
www.moments-notice.com

A well-established agency with mostly East Coast departures. Offers air-and-hotel packages and airfares to destinations worldwide (but not within the continental United States). Annual fee: $25 (which includes traveling companions).

Worldwide Discount Travel Club

Miami Beach, FL. 305-534-2082

Departures from Atlanta, Boston, Chicago, Los Angeles, Miami, and New York. Cruises and inclusive tours to all major destinations. Annual fee: $40 ($50 for a family).

Courier Services

If you're willing to give up your baggage allowance and travel with only a carry-on, you can fly to most foreign business centers for less than half the normal fare—and sometimes even for free. How? By traveling as a courier.

Using your baggage allowance for their overnight cargo, courier companies can subsidize your fare and still turn a profit. The main drawback—other than being forced to pack light—is that you may be asked to fly on short notice. However, you can give the courier company a general idea of your availability, and the company will usually try to accommodate you.

To get current updates on courier opportunities, prices, and flight schedules, you can join the **Air Courier Association** (*800-822-0888 or 800-693-8333*) or the **International Association of Air Travel Couriers** (*561-582-8320. www.courier. org*). The payment of a modest initiation fee and annual dues gives you access to a 24-hour courier hotline with current route-by-route information. These organizations know who is flying where at the lowest fares. The courier hotlines save you the hassle of calling courier company employees just to ascertain flight availability.

You may also consult *Air Courier Bargains* by travel agent Kelly Monaghan (Intrepid Trader, 1995, $14.95), a detailed guide to courier travel. Available from www.intrepidtraveler.com.

For immediate opportunities, check the travel classifieds in major U.S. cities, including New York, Los Angeles, Miami, Chicago, and San Francisco; look for a reference to "Courier." Or, you can contact the major courier services directly, at the addresses below.

Jupiter Air

Inglewood, CA. 310-670-5123
DESTINATIONS: Bangkok, Seoul, Tokyo. Requires two to four weeks advance notice.

NOW Voyager

New York, NY. 212-431-1616
DESTINATIONS: Amsterdam, Buenos Aires, Brussels, Caracas, Caribbean, Copenhagen, Frankfurt, Hong Kong, London, Oslo, Paris, Rio de Janeiro, Seoul.
The principal booking agency for courier companies flying from New York.

UTL Travel

San Francisco, CA. 650-583-5074
www.ufreight.com
DESTINATIONS: Manila, Singapore. Requires 4 to 30 days notice.

APEX Fares

If you don't know what an APEX fare is by now, you've probably paid too much for flight tickets. APEX—advance-purchase excursion—designates a discount ticket offered by a major international carrier for travelers who can book well in advance and return within a particular time limit.

With APEX, you can save as much as 30 percent over standard fares, though you will be charged a penalty if you have to change or cancel your ticket. Still, if you know exactly when you're going to travel, APEX is a good deal. To make a reservation, call your travel agent or call the major airlines directly through their toll-free numbers.

Air Shipping Tips

Let's see. You're headed off to New Zealand, and you want to bring your climbing gear, your mountain bike, and your surfboard with you. Can it be done? Yes.

Heavy articles that you can part with well ahead of time—such as your climbing gear—can be shipped by sea to your destination. (Allow five to ten weeks for delivery.) The Postal Service's sea mail is inexpensive for items weighing 40 pounds or less. Commercial shipping services are cheaper for heavier, bulkier items. You'll find their names and contact information in the Yellow Pages.

What about the mountain bike and the surfboard? With most airlines, you'll be able to check both in as luggage—as long as the total weight is less than 80 pounds. You'll have to partly disassemble the bike, however, and place it in a cardboard box or in one of the heavy plastic bags supplied by the airline. You can check the surfboard in as regular luggage—provided it is less than 8 feet long and is contained in a padded bag. The airline may charge a modest surcharge for the surfboard, perhaps around $25-40.

When transporting valuable sporting gear or camera equipment abroad, make sure to carry receipts, insurance inventories, or other written proof that the goods were originally bought in the United States. Otherwise, customs agents may impose duty on the items when you return to the country.

How about bigger problems—say, transporting several tons of climbing equipment to Tibet? Solving logistical questions like this is the calling of Britain's **Expedition Advisory Centre** (*1 Kensington Gore, London SW7 2AR, U.K. 01144-171-591-3030. www.rgs.org*).

Founded by the Royal Geographical Society more than a century ago, the Expedition Advisory Centre is staffed by experienced researchers and explorers. The company will consult with expedition leaders and recommend specialty services worldwide.

Physically Challenged and Special Needs

Whatever you can do, or dream you can, begin it. Boldness has genius, power, and magic in it.

—Johann von Goethe

Adventure travel is not just for the young, the fit, and the hardy. Persons with disabilities and special needs share the same love of adventure and outdoor activities as other members of society. In recent years, the travel industry has been improving the range of services available to clients with physical or cognitive limitations.

Special needs programs allow those with disabilities to enjoy a variety of outdoor activities, including rafting, canoeing, hiking, and horseback riding. Here are some of the leading tour operators offering customized programs:

Able Trek Tours
P.O. Box 384, Reedsburg, WI 53959. 800-205-6713 or 608-524-3021.

All trips are chaperoned vacations for people who require assistance traveling. Most travelers have mild to moderate developmental disabilities, but Able Trek Tours also welcomes the elderly and the mentally ill, as well as accompanying friends and family members.

This operation has been in business since 1992 and offers around 45 domestic and foreign vacations annually. Most trips are "mainstream," such as bus tours to national parks. However, Able Trek does offer outdoor activities, including dogsledding, cross-country skiing, hiking, and horseback riding.

Environmental Traveling Companions
Fort Mason Center, Bldg. C, San Francisco, CA 94123. 415-474-7662.

Environmental Traveling provides "shared adventures"—outdoor trips for people with special needs and for disadvantaged youth. Activities include rafting, sea kayaking, and cross-country skiing.

Most trips are in California, but the company occasionally runs trips to other locales in the western United States. Thanks to grants and subsidies, Environmental Traveling Companions is able to offer a sliding fee scale for special needs participants with limited funds.

Search Beyond Adventures
400 South Cedar Lake Rd., Minneapolis, MN 55405. 800-800-9979 or 612-374-4845

This culturally sensitive organization has specialized in trips for adults with physical and mental disabilities since 1979. Currently, it offers approximately 150 domestic and international tours every year, each ranging from 2 to 12 days.

In addition to its Minneapolis headquarters, Search Beyond maintains offices in Waltham, Mass., and Orlando, Fla. Tours are open to the general public. Customized trips can be arranged, and several wheelchair accessible trips are available. The staff is skilled and caring. While most of its trips are to urban centers, Search Beyond Adventures also offers canoe expeditions and camping trips.

Wilderness Inquiry, Inc.
1313 Fifth St. SE, Box 84, Minneapolis, MN 55414. 800-728-0719 or 612-379-3858
www.wildernessinquiry.org

Wilderness Inquiry is a nonprofit organization that emphasizes low-impact adventures for individuals with special needs. Both domestic and overseas trips feature a variety of activities, including camping, kayaking, canoeing, dogsledding, horse packing, rafting, hiking, and skiing. Among its destinations are Minnesota's Boundary Waters (in summer and winter), the Big Salmon River and Misty Fjords in Alaska, Utah's Canyonlands, the San Juan Islands, and Florida's Everglades.

Wilderness Inquiry does not simply run a few special tours for travelers with special needs, but instead incorporates them into all their programs. The staff is experienced and supportive, and all are trained in advanced first aid, CPR, and lifeguarding. Prices are about $100 per day.

ONLINE

For all those planning a trip, there is a vast amount of valuable, up-to-date travel information available online. Here are some important websites:

Centers for Disease Control (Travelers' Health)
http://www.cdc.gov/travel/travel
This site provides worldwide immunization requirements, regional health reports, and preventive medicine advice.

CityNet
www.excite.com/travel
CityNet covers over 5,000 cities around the world. Best for urban destinations, this website provides information on lodging, entertainment, business, government, and community services.

Consolidator Airline Travel Online
www.airlineconsolidator.com
This e-commerce site run by the leading fare consolidators sells tickets for 50 airlines, including British Airways, Continental, KLM-Northwest, and US Airways.

Fodor's Destination Guides
http://dest-excite.previewtravel.com
Detailed coverage of 200 destinations worldwide, mostly large cities. The primary focus of the site is hotels and restaurants.

Lonely Planet Travel Center
www.lonelyplanet.com
Containing highlights from Lonely Planet's award-winning guidebook series, this is a great resource for independent travelers venturing to exotic or Third World destinations.

Moon Travel Handbooks
www.moon.com
Moon's site offers informative articles from its popular travel guides, including Moon's Costa Rica Handbook.

The Embassy Page
www.embassyweb.com
Here you'll find a comprehensive, searchable list of embassies and consulates worldwide.

U.S. Department of State Travel Advisories
http://travel.state.gov/travel__warnings.html
This is the official U.S. Dept. of State website, which also provides information on passport and visa requirements.

MAGAZINES

Condé Nast Traveler (212-697-3132). Though aimed primarily at wealthy travelers, this handsome magazine offers practical advice for anyone venturing overseas. The magazine's ombudsman can help with travel disputes. Dial 800-967-4324 for the magazine's automated reader service line, or visit CNT's website at w.cntraveler.com.

Adventure magazine (*800-647-5463*), from the National Geographic Society, is a well-researched and beautifully illustrated adventure magazine featuring exotic and un-touristed destinations worldwide.

Lonely Planet Newsletter (*800-275-8555 or 510-893-8555*). This quarterly features articles written by the Lonely Planet staff and firsthand tips from travelers in the field. Free from Lonely Planet Publications, Oakland, CA.

BOOKS

The Traveler's Handbook, edited by Melissa Shales (now unfortunately out of print), covers personal security, airline travel, money matters, and countless other topics of interest to travelers. The appendices include listings of visa requirements, mailing regulations, contact information for embassies and consulates worldwide, and hundreds of travel publications. Try to get a copy of this book—every serious traveler should have one.

World Business Travel Guide by Uniglobe Travel International (Olympic Marketing Corporation, 1987, $2.99). Despite its title, this book is not just for briefcase toters. It includes customs and visa requirements, basic foreign language guides, and maps for 140 major cities worldwide. Available at major bookstores.

Journey of One's Own by Thalia Zepatos (Eighth Mountain Press, 1996, $16.95) is filled with practical information about overseas travel. The book has a special emphasis on traveling for women.

TRAVELER'S SURVIVAL KIT

Here are 15 easy-to-pack items that every traveler should carry—no matter what the destination or how long the trip:

Flashlight—preferably a mini-maglight or other sturdy, waterproof model. If you'll be camping, make sure to bring a small head-lamp as well.

Small folding umbrella—if your destination is anywhere but the Sahara, take this item with you on the plane.

Compact auto-focus zoom camera —it's unobtrusive and will give you great candid shots of locals, even if you just point and shoot without raising the camera to your eye. Make sure to bring spare batteries.

Plastic bottle of iodine—purifies water and—because you can see just where you've applied it—is one of the best antiseptics.

U.S. $10 bills—take them with you wherever you go. American dollars will get you to the airport and out of trouble—just about everywhere.

Medium-size clear, Tupperware box— use this for your medicines, pills, and other easy-to-lose items that should be kept dry. Another plus: Busy customs agents will appreciate this see-through item, too.

Travel clock/calculator—you will use the calculator constantly. Sharp makes a great combination alarm clock/calculator/ currency converter.

BIC pens and writing paper—if you visit the Third World, it'll break your heart to see so many kids without writing tools. Take these along as gifts.

AloeGator sunblock—this is one of the few nonirritating, waterproof sunscreens that really stand up to a full day on the water.

Casio—buy a $15 water-resistant watch as a backup, and set it to U.S. time. When it's time to leave, give it away to a local kid.

Wide adhesive tape—you will use this to repair your body and your gear. It can also secure valuables out of sight.

Sewing kit—make sure you have some good scissors, safety pins, and heavy thread, plus spare buttons.

Braided, stretchy clothesline—to dry those wet towels. Built-in loops let you hang small items without clothespins.

Toilet paper—don't count on anyone else (at your hotel or aboard your airplane) having it.

Leatherman tool—will fix broken luggage, slice a salami, scale a fish, and in Western Europe you can trade it for twice what you paid for it back in the States.

TRIP PLANNING

For current information on a variety of outdoor activities, consult **Patagonia's Guideline** (*800-523-9597*), a free phone-in service offering tips on where to go and what outfitters to use. Featured activities include: alpine and nordic skiing, backpacking, canoeing, fly-fishing, mountaineering, rafting, rock climbing, sailing, and white-water and sea kayaking.

If you're an American Express cardholder, ask for the free *American Express Traveler's Companion* (*American Express Customer Service. 800-528-4800*). This invaluable pocket guide covers all the essentials: passports, communications, health, emergency aid, and—of course— traveler's check refunds.

ALL CARRY-ON ITEMS MUST BE SECURELY STOWED.

◎ This icon indicates that an outfitter has agreed to provide either a discount of $30 or 5 percent of the trip price (at the outfitter's discretion) to any customer who presents a valid sales receipt for this edition of the *Ultimate Adventure Sourcebook*.

A.J. Hackett Bungy
P.O. Box 488, Bungy Center
Shotover Street, Queenstown
New Zealand
01164-3442-7100
www.ajhackett.com
ACTIVITIES: Bungee jumping,
mountain biking
DESTINATIONS: Australia, Bali,
France, Las Vegas, New Zealand

AAT King's Australian Tours
2300 East Katella Ave., Suite 450
Anaheim, CA 92806
800-353-4525 or 714-456-0501
www.aatkings.com
ACTIVITIES: 4WD, Outback
safaris, land tours
DESTINATIONS: Australia:
Kakadu, Northern Territory, Queensland, Red Centre (Alice Springs/Ayers
Rock), Tasmania, Victoria, and Western Australia

ABEC's Alaska Adventures
1550 Alpine Vista Court
Fairbanks, AK 99712
907-457-8907
www.abecalaska.com
ACTIVITIES: Backpacking, canoeing, kayaking, nature, rafting
DESTINATIONS: Alaska, Brooks
Range

Abercrombie & Kent
1520 Kensington Road
Oak Brook, IL 60521
800-323-7308 or 630-954-2944
www.abercrombiekent.com
ACTIVITIES: Cruising, hiking,
nature, safari, trekking
DESTINATIONS: Africa, the Americas, Asia, Europe, South Pacific

◎ **Above the Clouds Trekking**
115 Spencer Hill Road
Hinesburg, VT 05461
800-233-4499 or 508-799-4499
www.aboveclouds.com
ACTIVITIES: Cultural tours,
hiking, trekking
DESTINATIONS: Alps, Bhutan,
England, France, India, Italy, Nepal,
Patagonia (Argentina & Chile)

Above the West Ballooning
P.O. Box 2290
Yountville, CA 94599
800-627-2759 or 707-944-8638
www.nvaloft.com
ACTIVITIES: Ballooning
DESTINATIONS: Napa Valley, Cal-
ifornia

◎ **Action Quest**
P.O. Box 5517, Sarasota, FL 34277
800-317-6789 or 941-924-6789
www.actionquest.com
ACTIVITIES: Sailing, scuba diving,
windsurfing, youth programs
DESTINATIONS: Australia, BVI,
Fiji, Galápagos, Leeward Islands,
Mediterranean, Tahiti

Action Sports Maui
206a Leinani Drive
Wailuku, Maui, HI 96793
808-871-5857 or 808-283-7913
www.actionsportsmaui.com
ACTIVITIES: Kite surfing,
windsurfing
DESTINATIONS: Maui, Hawaii

Adirondack River Outfitters
P.O. Box 649, Old Forge, NY 13420
800-525-7238 or 315-369-3536
www.aroadventures.com
ACTIVITIES: Rafting
DESTINATIONS: New York: Black,
Hudson, Moose, & Sacandaga Rivers

**Adirondack Rock & River
Guide Service**
P.O. Box 219, Keene, NY 12942
518-576-2041
www.rockandriver.com
ACTIVITIES: Skiing, nordic
ski touring
DESTINATIONS: Adirondacks,
New York

Adrift Adventures
P.O. Box 192, Jensen, UT 84035
800-824-0150 or 435-789-3600
www.adrift.com
ACTIVITIES: Fishing, rafting
DESTINATIONS: Green, Gunnis-
son, & Yampa Rivers (CO, UT)

Adventure Associates
P.O. Box 16304, Seattle, WA 98116
888-532-8352 or 206-932-8352
www.adventureassociates.net
ACTIVITIES: Cruising, hiking,
nature, sea kayaking, women's
DESTINATIONS: Cascades, Costa
Rica, Galápagos, Greece, Mexico,
New Zealand, San Juan Islands,
Tetons, Turkey

Adventure Balloons
Winchfield Park, London Road,
Hartley Wintney, Hampshire, RG27
8HY, England, U.K.
01144-1818-400-108
www.adventureballoons.co.uk
ACTIVITIES: Ballooning
DESTINATIONS: England, Ireland, Normandy (France)

Adventure Canada
14 Front Street South, Mississauga,
ON, L5H 2C4, Canada
800-363-7566 or 905-271-4000
www.adventurecanada.com
ACTIVITIES: Hiking, cruising,
nature, trekking, windjammers
DESTINATIONS: Baffin Island,
Canada, Caribbean, Yukon

◎ **Adventure Center**
1311 63rd Street, Suite 200
Emeryville, CA 94608
800-227-8747 or 510-654-1879
www.adventure-center.com
ACTIVITIES: 4WD, nature,
trekking, safari
DESTINATIONS: Africa, the Alps,
Asia, Borneo, Central and South
America, Greece, India, Morocco,
Nepal, New Zealand, Peru, Portugal,
Spain, Tanzania, Thailand, Turkey,
Vietnam

**Adventure Network
International**
15A The Broadway, Penn Road,
Beaconsfield, Bucks, HP9 2PD,
U.K.
01144-1494-671-808
www.adventurenetwork.com
ACTIVITIES: Climbing, nature,
mountaineering, trekking
DESTINATIONS: Antarctica,
Patagonia

**Adventure New Zealand
Motorbike Tours**
P.O. Box 674, 82 Achilles Ave.,
Nelson 7001, New Zealand
01164-2196-9071 or 0-800-848-
6337; www.nzmctours.com
ACTIVITIES: Motorcycle touring
DESTINATIONS: North Island &
South Island, New Zealand

Adventure Pursuits
4101 Suncrest Drive
Fort Collins, CO 80525
800-651-8336 or 970-226-4543
www.apadventures.com
ACTIVITIES: Camping, hiking,
river sports, youth programs
DESTINATIONS: Colorado, Utah,
Pacific Northwest

Adventure Women
15033 Kelly Canyon Road
Bozeman, MT 59715
800-804-8686 or 406-587-3883
www.adventurewomen.com
ACTIVITIES: Womens' only: hiking, camel safari, nature, sea kayaking, trekking
DESTINATIONS: Australia, Africa,
Baja, Canyonlands, Colorado, Utah
and worldwide

◎ **Adventures on Skis**
815 North Road, Rt. 202
Westfield, MA 01085
800-628-9655 or 413-568-2855
www.advonskis.com
ACTIVITIES: Heli-skiing, skiing,
snowboarding
DESTINATIONS: Austria, Canada,
France, Italy, Germany, Switzerland,
South America

African Extreme
P.O. Box 60353
Livingstone, Zambia, Zambia
01126-332-4156
www.zamnet.zm/zamnet/extreme/
bungi.htm
ACTIVITIES: Bungee jumping,
rafting, safari
DESTINATIONS: Victoria Falls,
Zambia, Zimbabwe

Air Combat USA
P.O. Box 2726, Fullerton, CA 92837
800-522-7590 or 714-522-7590
www.aircombat.com
ACTIVITIES: Air Combat, flying
DESTINATIONS: California,
United States

◎ **Alaska Discovery
Wilderness Tours, Inc.**
5310 Glacier Highway
Juneau, AK 99801
800-586-1911 or 907-780-6226
www.akdiscovery.com
ACTIVITIES: Nature, sea kayaking,
rafting
DESTINATIONS: Alaska: Gates of
Arctic N.P., Glacier Bay N.P., Icy Bay,
Hubbard Glacier; Tatshenshini,
Alsek, Noatak, & Kongacut Rivers

Alaska Photo Safaris
P.O. Box 141, Talkeetna, AK 99676
800-799-3051 or 907-733-3051
www.alaska.net/~photoak
ACTIVITIES: Hiking, nature,
photo tours
DESTINATIONS: Alaska: Chilkat
Eagle Preserve, Denali N.P., Inside
Passage, Katmai N.P., Kenai Fjords
N.P, Kodiak Island, Pribilof Islands,
Prince William Sound

◎ **Alaska-Denali Guiding**
P.O. Box 566, 3rd. Street
Talkeetna, AK 99676
907-733-2649
www.denaliexpeditions.com
ACTIVITIES: Climbing, moun-
taineering, ski mountaineering
DESTINATIONS: Alaska: Denali
(Mt. McKinley)

◎ **All-Outdoors Rafting**
1250 Pine Street, Suite 103
Walnut Creek, CA 94596
800-247-2387 or 925-932-8993
www.aorafting.com
ACTIVITIES: Rafting
DESTINATIONS: 12 California
rivers, including American, Stanislaus, & Tuolumne

Alphorn Ski Tours, Inc.
P.O. Box 5036
Incline Village, NV 89450
800-257-4676 or 775-832-2577
www.alphorntours.com
ACTIVITIES: Heli-skiing, skiing,
ski mountaineering
DESTINATIONS: Argentina,
Austria, Canada, Chile, France, Italy,
New Zealand, Switzerland

Alpine Club of Canada
P.O. Box 2040
Canmore, AB, T0L 0M0, Canada
403-678-3200
www.alpineclubofcanada.ca
ACTIVITIES: Climbing, ice
climbing, mountaineering
DESTINATIONS: Canada, Rockies

◎ **Alpine Guides
(Mount Cook)**
P.O. Box 20
Mount Cook, New Zealand
01164-3435-1834
www.alpineguides.co.nz
ACTIVITIES: Climbing, ice climb-
ing, mountaineering, skiing
DESTINATIONS: Alaska, New
Zealand (Southern Alps)

◎ **Alpine Skills International**
P.O. Box 8, Norden, CA 95724
800-916-7325 or 530-426-9108
www.alpineskills.com
ACTIVITIES: Climbing, ice climbing,
mountaineering, skiing, snowboarding
DESTINATIONS: California,
European Alps, Mexican volcanoes,
Sierra Nevada

**America's Adventure/
Venture Europe**
2245 Stonecrop Way
Golden, CO 80401
800-222-3595 or 303-526-0806
www.aave.com
ACTIVITIES: Backpacking, hiking,
language immersion, sailing, sea
kayaking
DESTINATIONS: France, Italy,
Scandinavia, Spain, Switzerland,
United States (Alaska, Colorado,
Hawaii, Utah, Washington); not all
countries every year

◎ **American Alpine
Institute (AAI)**
1515 12th Street
Bellingham, WA 98225
360-671-1505 or 360-734-8890
www.aai.cc
ACTIVITIES: Climbing, ice climbing, mountaineering, trekking
DESTINATIONS: Bolivia, Canada,
Chile, Ecuador, European Alps, Mexico, Nepal, Peru, United States

**American River Touring
Association (ARTA) River Trips**
24000 Casa Loma Road
Groveland, CA 95321
800-323-2782 or 209-962-7873
www.arta.org
ACTIVITIES: Rafting
DESTINATIONS: Classic rivers in
California, Colorado, Idaho, Oregon,
Utah

**American Wilderness
Experience (AWE)**
P.O. Box 1486
Boulder, CO 80306
800-444-0099 or 303-444-2622
www.awetrips.com
ACTIVITIES: Canoeing, dogsled-
ding, horse riding, rafting, ranch
vacations, sea kayaking, snowmobil-
ing
DESTINATIONS: Canada, Costa
Rica, Mexico, and the United States
(Colorado, Montana, Hawaii,
Wyoming)

Anacortes Yacht Charters
P.O. Box 69, Anacortes Marina
2415 T Ave., Anacortes, WA 98221
800-233-3004 or 360-293-4555
www.ayc.com
ACTIVITIES: Charter sailing, cruising
DESTINATIONS: Pacific Northwest (British Columbia, San Juan
Islands, Washington)

**Anchor D Guiding
& Outfitting**
Box 656, Black Diamond, AB
ToL oHo, Canada
403-933-2867
www.anchord.com
ACTIVITIES: Horsepacking,
horse riding
DESTINATIONS: Kananaskis,
Alberta Rockies, Continental Divide

Annapolis Sailing School
P.O. Box 3334
Annapolis, MD 21403
800-638-9192 or 410-267-7205
www.annapolissailing.com
ACTIVITIES: Sailing, charter
sailing, sail training
DESTINATIONS: Annapolis
(MD), St. Petersburg (FL), and
St. Croix (USVI)

Aoraki Balloon Safaris
P.O. Box 75
Methven 8353, New Zealand
01164-3302-8172 or 0800-256-837
www.nzballooning.com
ACTIVITIES: Ballooning
DESTINATIONS: Canterbury
Plain, South Island, New Zealand

Arctic Odysseys
2000 McGilvra Boulevard East
Seattle, WA 98112
206-325-1977
www.arcticodysseys.com
ACTIVITIES: Arctic, dogsledding,
nature
DESTINATIONS: Alaska, Baffin
Island, Canada, Greenland, NWT,
Yukon

Arctic Treks
P.O. Box 73452
Fairbanks, AK 99707
907-455-6502
www.arctictreksadventures.com
ACTIVITIES: Hiking, nature,
rafting, trekking
DESTINATIONS: Alaska: Brooks
Range, Gates of the Arctic N.P., Arctic
N.W.R.; Hula Hula, Noatak, & Kon-
gakut Rivers

Arizona Raft Adventures, Inc.
4050 E. Huntington
Flagstaff, AZ 86004
800-786-7238 or 520-526-8200
www.azraft.com
ACTIVITIES: Rafting
DESTINATIONS: Grand Canyon,
Colorado River

Arizona River Runners
P.O. Box 47788
Phoenix, AZ 85068
800-477-7238 or 602-867-4866
www.raftarizona.com
ACTIVITIES: Motor rafting
DESTINATIONS: Grand Canyon
of the Colorado

Arizona Soaring
Estrella Sailport, P.O. Box 858
Maricopa, AZ 85239
520-568-2318 or 480-821-2903
www.azsoaring.com
ACTIVITIES: Gliding, soaring
DESTINATION: Arizona

◎ **Asia Transpacific Journeys**
2995 Center Green Court
Boulder, CO 80301
800-642-2742, 303-443-1633, or
303-443-6789
www.southeastasia.com
ACTIVITIES: Cultural, hiking,
kayaking, trekking
DESTINATIONS: Burma, Indonesia, Malaysia, Thailand, Vietnam

◎ **Asian Pacific Adventures**
9010 Reseda Blvd., Suite 227
Northridge, CA 91324
800-825-1680 or 818-886-5190
www.asianpacificadventures.com
ACTIVITIES: Cycling, mountain
biking
DESTINATIONS: China, India,
Mongolia, Russia, Thailand, Vietnam

Atalante
C.P. 701, 36037, Quai Arloing,
69256 Lyon Cedex 09, France
01133-4725-32480
www.atalante.fr
ACTIVITIES: 4WD, hiking,
canyoning, kayaking, mountaineer-

ing, rafting, ski mountaineering,
trekking
DESTINATIONS: Africa, Asia,
Europe, France, Mediterranean,
South America, Turkey

**Australian Motorcycle
Adventures (AMA)**
424 Samford Road, Enoggera,
Brisbane, Queensland 4051
Australia
01161-7385-53542
www.austmcycleadventures.com
ACTIVITIES: Motorcycle touring
DESTINATIONS: Cape York,
Queensland, Australia

Backcountry Bicycle Tours
1408 Gold Avenue, No. 6
Bozeman, MT 59715
800-575-1540 or 406-586-3556
www.backcountrytours.com
ACTIVITIES: Cycling, mountain
biking
DESTINATIONS: San Juan Islands, Glacier N.P./Canadian Rockies, Yellowstone, Bryce Canyon N.P.,
Zion N.P., Montana Rockies

◎ **Backroads**
801 Cedar Street
Berkeley, CA 94710
800-462-2848 or 510-527-1555
www.backroads.com
ACTIVITIES: Cycling, mountain
biking, walking
DESTINATIONS: Alaska, California, Colorado, Montana, New England, Rockies, Utah, Canada, and 26
other countries worldwide

◎ **Baja Expeditions**
2625 Garnet Avenue
San Diego, CA 92109
800-843-6967 or 858-581-3311
www.bajaex.com
ACTIVITIES: Scuba diving, sea
kayaking, whale-watching
DESTINATIONS: Baja, Mexico,
Sea of Cortez

Baja Off Road Tours
25108 Marguerite Parkway, Suite B-126
Mission Viejo, CA 92692
949-830-6569
www.bajaoffroadtours.com
ACTIVITIES: Off-road motorcycle
touring
DESTINATIONS: Baja, Mexico

Balloon Sunrise
41 Dover Street, Richmond,
Victoria 3121, Australia
01161-3942-77596
www.balloonsunrise.comau/~hotair/
ACTIVITIES: Ballooning
DESTINATIONS: Australia, Nepal

Ballooning Tyrol
Speckbacherstr. 33a, A-6380 St.
Johann in Tirol, Austria
01143-05352-65666
www.alpennet.com/ballooning-
tyrol
ACTIVITIES: Ballooning
DESTINATIONS: Tirolean Alps,
Austria, Kitzbuhel

Baobab Safari Company
210 Post Street, Suite 911
San Francisco, CA 94108
800-835-3692 or 415-391-5788
www.baobabsafaris.com
ACTIVITIES: Nature, safari
DESTINATIONS: East and Southern Africa

Barker-Ewing River Trips
P.O. Box 450
Jackson, WY 83001
800-448-4202 or 307-733-1000
www.barker-ewing.com
ACTIVITIES: Rafting
DESTINATIONS: Wyoming,
Snake River near Jackson, and
Main Salmon (ID)

**Beach's Motorcycle
Adventures, Ltd.**
2763 West River Parkway
Grand Island, NY 14072
716-773-4960
www.beachs-mca.com
ACTIVITIES: Motorcycle touring
DESTINATIONS: European Alps,
New Zealand, Norway

**Bermuda High
Soaring School**
P.O. Box 1510
Lancaster, SC 29721
803-475-7627
www.bermudahighsoaring.com
ACTIVITIES: Gliding, soaring
DESTINATIONS: South Carolina

Beyond Limits Adventures
P.O. Box 215
Riverbank, CA 95367
800-234-7238 or 209-869-6060
www.rivertrip.com
ACTIVITIES: Rafting
DESTINATIONS: American,
Kaweah, and six other California
Rivers

Bicycle Adventures
P.O. Box 11219
Olympia, WA 98508
800-443-6060 or 360-786-0989
www.bicycleadventures.com
ACTIVITIES: Cycling, mountain
biking
DESTINATIONS: California,
Hawaii, Pacific Northwest (U.S.
and Canada), Utah

**Big Five Tours & Expeditions,
Ltd.**
1551 S.E. Palm Court
Stuart, FL 34994
800-244-3483 or 561-287-7995
www.bigfive.com
ACTIVITIES: Nature, photo tours,
safari
DESTINATIONS: Egypt, Ethiopia,
Kenya, South Africa, Tanzania

Bike Riders Tours
P.O. Box 130254
Boston, MA 02113
800-473-7040 or 617-723-2354
www.bikeriderstours.com
ACTIVITIES: Cycling
DESTINATIONS: France, Ireland,
Italy, Maine, Martha's Vineyard/Nan-
tucket, Nova Scotia, Portugal, Prince
Edward Island, Spain

Bike Vermont
P.O. Box 207
Woodstock, VT 05091
800-257-2226 or 802-457-3553
www.bikevt.com
ACTIVITIES: Cycling
DESTINATIONS: Vermont,
New England

Bio-Bio Expeditions
Box 2028
Truckee, CA 96160
800-246-7238 or 530-582-6865
www.bbxrafting.com
ACTIVITIES: Kayaking, rafting
DESTINATIONS: California,
Chile, Nepal, Peru, Russia (Siberia),
Zambezi (Zambia)

◎ **Bombard Society**
333 Pershing Way, West Palm
Beach, FL 33401
800-862-8537 or 561-837-6610
www.bombardsociety.com
ACTIVITIES: Ballooning, gourmet
tours
DESTINATIONS: Austria, Czech
Republic, France, Italy,
Switzerland,Turkey

Borton Overseas
5412 Lyndale Ave., Minneapolis,
MN 55419
800-843-0602 or 612-822-4640
www.bortonoverseas.com
ACTIVITIES: Hiking, nature,
nordic skiing, safari
DESTINATIONS: Norway, Africa,
Scandinavia, Europe

**Bosenberg Motorcycle
Excursions**
Mainzer Strasse 54, 55545 Bad
Kreuznach, Germany
01149-6716-7312
www.bosenberg.com
ACTIVITIES: Motorcycle touring
DESTINATIONS: Germany, Swiss,
Austrian, French and Italian Alps,
Bavaria, Alsace

◎ **Boulder Outdoor Center**
2510 N. 47th Street, Boulder, CO
80301
800-364-9376 or 303-444-8420
www.boc123.com
ACTIVITIES: Canoeing, kayaking,
rafting
DESTINATIONS: Colorado
(multiple rivers)

**Boulder Outdoor
Survival School**
P.O. Box 1590
Boulder, CO 80306
800-335-7404, 303-444-9779, or
303-442-7425. www.boss-inc.com
ACTIVITIES: Outdoor skills,
Survival Training
DESTINATIONS: South Utah,
Canada, Mexico (Copper Canyon,
Sonora)

Bungy Zone
P.O. Box 399, Station A, Nanaimo,
BC, V9R 5L3, Canada
800-668-7771 or 604-753-5867
www.bungyzone.com
ACTIVITIES: Bungee jumping,
flying fox
DESTINATIONS: British
Columbia, Canada

Butterfield & Robinson
70 Bond Street, Toronto, ON, M5B
1X3, Canada
800-678-1147 or 416-864-1354
www.butterfieldandrobinson.com
ACTIVITIES: Bicycling
DESTINATIONS: Canada, France,
Asia, Africa, Central America, Europe,
the Pacific

◎ **Canadian
Mountain Holidays**
P.O. Box 1660
Banff, AB, T0L 0C0, Canada
800-661-0252 or 403-762-7100
www.cmhski.com
ACTIVITIES: Heli-skiing, skiing,
snowboarding
DESTINATIONS: Canadian Rock-
ies: Bugaboos, Gothics, Bobbie
Burns, Cariboos, Monashees, Revel-
stoke, Valemont, Kootenay, McBride,
Galena

Canadian River Expeditions
P.O. Box 1023, Whistler, B.C.
B0N 1B0, Canada
800-898-7238 or 604-938-6651
www.canriver.com
ACTIVITIES: Rafting
DESTINATIONS: Major rivers in
Alaska, British Columbia, Yukon

Canyonlands Field Institute
P.O. Box 68, Moab, UT 84532
800-860-5262 or 435-259-7750
www.canyonlandsfieldinst.org
ACTIVITIES: Ecology, nature,
outdoor skills
DESTINATIONS: Moab, Utah
and Colorado Plateau

**Caribbean Yacht
Charters (CYC)**
2401 W. Bay Dr., Ste 410
Largo, FL 33770
800-225-2520 or 727-559-7142
www.cycyachtcharters.com
ACTIVITIES: Charter sailing, cruising
DESTINATIONS: Virgin Islands,
Caribbean (BVI and USVI)

Central Holidays
120 Sylvan Ave.
Englewood Cliffs, NJ 07632
800-935-5000 or 201-228-5244
www.centralholidays.com
ACTIVITIES: Skiing, snowboarding
DESTINATIONS: Austria, France,
Italy, Switzerland

Class VI River Runners
Ames Heights Road, P.O. Box 78
Lansing, WV 25862
800-252-7784 or 304-574-0704
www.raftwv.com
ACTIVITIES: Rafting
DESTINATIONS: New, Gauley
(WV); Rio Grande (TX)

**Colgate's Offshore
Sailing School**
16731-110 McGregor Blvd., Ft.
Meyers, FL 33908
800-221-4326 or 941-454-1700
www.offshore-sailing.com
ACTIVITIES: Sailing, sail training
DESTINATIONS: Florida, Newport
(RI), New York Harbor, Stamford
(CT), Chicago (IL), Tortola (BVI)

**Colorado Mountain
School (CMS)**
P.O. Box 1846
Estes Park, CO 80517
970-586-5758. www.cmschool.com
ACTIVITIES: Climbing, ice climb-
ing, mountaineering, trekking
DESTINATIONS: Alaska, Col-
orado, Bolivia, Ecuador, Mexico

**Colorado River &
Trail Expeditions**
P.O. Box 57575
Salt Lake City, UT 84157
800-253-7328 or 801-261-1789

www.crateinc.com
ACTIVITIES: Rafting
DESTINATIONS: Alaska, Arizona,
Colorado, Utah Rivers

◎ **Cross Country Interna-
tional Equestrian & Walking
Tours**
P.O. Box 1170, Millbrook, NY 12545
800-828-8768 or 914-677-6000
www.equestrianvacations.com
ACTIVITIES: Horse riding,
walking, Western vacations
DESTINATIONS: USA, England,
Ireland, Scotland, Costa Rica, France,
Greece, Italy, Portugal, Spain

David Anderson Safaris
30 W. Mission, Suite 7
Santa Barbara, CA 93101
800-927-4647 or 805-563-7943
www.davidanderson.com
ACTIVITIES: Nature, safari, walking
DESTINATIONS: Botswana,
Kenya, South Africa, Zambia,
Zimbabwe

Decker's Sno-Venture Tours
P.O. Box 1447
Eagle River, WI 54521
715-479-2764
www.sno-venture.com
ACTIVITIES: Snowmobiling
DESTINATIONS: Alaska, Wiscon-
sin Northwoods, Yellowstone
Park/Jackson Hole, Minnesota,
Michigan, Montana, South Dakota,
Ontario, Finland, Iceland

Deep Discoveries, Ltd.
3A 1st Ave. N., Mulhurst Bay, AB
T0C 2C0, Canada
800-667-5362 or 780-389-4408
www.deepdiscoveries.com
ACTIVITIES: Scuba diving
DESTINATIONS: Fiji, Costa Rica,
Dominica, Honduras, Indonesia,
Malaysia (incl. Borneo), Maldives,
Philippines, Seychelles, Tabago

**Dinosaur Discovery
Expeditions**
550 Jurassic Ct., Fruita, CO 81521
800-344-3466 or 970-858-7282
www.digdino.com
ACTIVITIES: Dinosaur-hunting,
geology, paleontology
DESTINATIONS: Colorado,
Argentina, China, Mexico, and
Mongolia

**Dixon's Airplay
Paragliding & Flight Park**
P.O. Box 2626, Flagstaff, AZ 86003
520-526-4579. www.paraglide.com
ACTIVITIES: Paragliding
DESTINATIONS: Arizona,
Washington

**Don Donnelly Horseback
Vacations & Stables**
6010 S. Kings Ranch Road
Gold Canyon, AZ 85219
800-346-4403 or 480-982-7822
www.dondonnelly.com
ACTIVITIES: Horse riding, trail
ride, Western vacations
DESTINATIONS: Arizona: Monument Valley, Superstition Wilderness,
White Mountains, Mogollon Rim

Downstream River Runners
13414 Chain Lake Road
Monroe, WA 98272
800-234-4644 or 360-805-9899
riverpeople.com

ACTIVITIES: Rafting
DESTINATIONS: Eight rivers in
Oregon and Washington

**EagleRider
Motorcycle Rentals**
20917 Western Ave.
Torrance, CA 90501
800-501-8687 or 310-320-3456
www.hogrent.com
ACTIVITIES: Motorcycle touring
DESTINATIONS: Rentals from
Chicago, Las Vegas, Los Angeles,
Orlando, San Francisco

◎ **Earth River
Expeditions, Inc.**
180 Towpath Road
Accord, NY 12404
800-643-2784 or 914-626-2665
www.earthriver.com
ACTIVITIES: Rafting
DESTINATIONS: British Colum-
bia, Quebec, Yukon, Chile, Ecuador,
Peru, China, Tibet, Tanzania

**Earthsong Lodge
Sled-dog Adventures**
Denali National Park
P.O. Box 89, Healy, AK 99755
907-683-2644
www.earthsonglodge.com
ACTIVITIES: Dogsledding,
winter camping
DESTINATIONS: Alaska, Denali
National Park

Earthwatch
680 Mt. Auburn Street, Box 4030
Watertown, MA 02272
800-776-0188 or 617-926-8200
www.earthwatch.org
ACTIVITIES: Anthropology,
archaeology, marine mammals,
nature, research, safari
DESTINATIONS: Argentina,
Florida, Hawaii, Mexico, South
Dakota, New Zealand, Utah, and
many others worldwide

◎ **Eastern Mountain
Sports Climbing School**
Main Street, P.O. Box 514
North Conway, NH 03860
800-310-4504 or 603-356-5433
www.emsclimb.com
ACTIVITIES: Climbing, ice climb-
ing, mountaineering, winter skills
DESTINATIONS: New Hampshire,
New York (New Paltz), Connecticut
(West Hartford), Colorado (Boulder)

◎ **Ecosummer Expeditions**
5640 Hollybridge Way, Unit 130
Richmond, BC, V7C 4N3, Canada
800-465-8884 or 604-214-7484
www.ecosummer.com
ACTIVITIES: Hiking, nature, sea
kayaking, trekking
DESTINATIONS: Alaska, Pacific
Northwest, Queen Charlottes, Yukon,
Bahamas, Baja, Ellesmere Island,
Greenland, Patagonia (Chile), Nepal,
South America

Edelweiss Bike Travel
P.O. Box 2, A-6414 Mieming, Austria
800-582-2263 or 760-249-5825
01143-5264-5690
www.edelweissbike.com
ACTIVITIES: Motorcycle touring
DESTINATIONS: Africa, Austria,
France, Germany, Ireland, Italy, Mex-
ico, New Zealand, Spain, Switzerland,
United States

Epic Trails
7875 170th Place N.E.
Redmond, WA 98052
425-861-9969
www.serioussports.com/epictrails
ACTIVITIES: Cattle drive, horse riding, ranch vacations
DESTINATIONS: Saskatchewan, Canada into Northern Montana

◎ Equitour
P.O. Box 807, Dubois, WY 82513
800-545-0019 or 307-455-3363
www.ridingtours.com
ACTIVITIES: Horse riding, ranch vacations, trail rides
DESTINATIONS: Western U.S. States, Canada, Argentina, Australia, Austria, Chile, Costa Rica, England, India, Ireland, Italy, Greece, Portugal, Spain and worldwide

◎ Euro-Bike & Walking Tours
212 Sycamore Road, P.O. Box 990
Dekalb, IL 60115
800-321-6060 or 815-758-8851
www.eurobike.com
ACTIVITIES: Bicycling
DESTINATIONS: Belgium, France, Italy, Germany, Netherlands and all Europe

European Waterways
140 East 56th Street
New York, NY 10022
800-217-4447 or 212-688-9489
www.europeanwaterways.com
ACTIVITIES: Barge trips, yachting
DESTINATIONS: Belgium, England, France, Scotland

Europeds
761 Lighthouse Ave.
Monterey, CA 93940
800-321-9552 or 831-646-4920
www.europeds.com
ACTIVITIES: Bicycling, mountain biking
DESTINATIONS: France, Italy, Switzerland

Excursions Extraordinaire
P.O. Box 5766, Eugene, OR 97405
800-678-2252 or 541-484-0493
www.mauiwindsurfing.com
ACTIVITIES: Sailing, windsurfing
DESTINATIONS: Hawaii, Maui

Exum Mountain Guides
Grand Teton National Park
Box 56, Moose, WY 83012
307-733-2297
www.exumguides.com
ACTIVITIES: Climbing, ice climbing, mountaineering
DESTINATIONS: Grand Teton, Rockies, Tetons, Wyoming

Far Flung Adventures
P.O. Box 377, Terlingua, TX 79852
800-359-4138 or 915-371-2489
www.farflung.com
ACTIVITIES: Canoeing, cultural tours, kayaking, rafting
DESTINATIONS: Arizona, Colorado, New Mexico waterways, and many rivers in Mexico

◎ Fish Eagle Safaris
11191 Westheimer No. 349
Houston, TX 77042
800-513-5222 or 713-467-5222
www.fisheaglesafaris.com
ACTIVITIES: Hiking, nature, Safari
DESTINATIONS: Southern Africa (Botswana, Namibia, South Africa)

◎ Fishing International
P.O. Box 2132
Santa Rosa, CA 95405
800-950-4242 or 707-539-3366
www.fishinginternational.com
ACTIVITIES: Fishing
DESTINATIONS: Worldwide

Four Corners River Sports Paddling School
360 S. Camino del Rio
Durango, CO 81301
800-426-7637 or 970-259-3893
www.riversports.com
ACTIVITIES: Canoeing, kayaking, rafting
DESTINATIONS: Animas River, Whitewater Park, Durango, Colorado

Freedom Tours
P.O. Box 848
Longmont, CO 80502
800-643-2109 or 303-682-9482
www.indra.com/freedom/
ACTIVITIES: Motorcycle touring
DESTINATIONS: Arizona, Colorado, New Mexico, Utah, Southwest Nat. Parks

Frontiers
P.O. Box 959, Wexford, PA 15090
800-245-1950 or 724-935-1577
www.frontierstrvl.com
ACTIVITIES: Fishing, hunting, shooting sports
DESTINATIONS: Worldwide

Glacier Tours
P.O. Box 66
780 Hornafjö rur, Iceland
01135-4478-1000 or
01135-4892-9243
www.eldhorn.is/glaciert
ACTIVITIES: Hiking, Cruising, Snowmobiling
DESTINATIONS: Iceland

◎ Glacier Wilderness Guides & Montana Raft Co.
P.O. Box 330
West Glacier, MT 59936
800-521-7238 or 406-387-5555
www.glacierguides.com
ACTIVITIES: Fishing, hiking, rafting
DESTINATIONS: Montana, Flathead River

Global Surf Travel
P.O. Box 2639
Wailuku, Maui, HI 96793
877-787-3872 or 808-244-1677
in Australia: 01161-7552-00962
www.globalsurftravel.com
ACTIVITIES: Surfing
DESTINATIONS: Costa Rica, Fiji, Peru, and throughout the Pacific and Indian Oceans, Europe and the Americas

GPSC Charters, Ltd.
600 St. Andrews Road
Philadelphia, PA 19118
800-732-6786 or 215-247-3903
www.gpsc.com
ACTIVITIES: Charter sailing, cruising
DESTINATIONS: Greece, Croatia, France, Italy, Portugal, Spain, Turkey

Grand Canyon Expeditions Company
P.O. Box O, Kanab, UT 84741
800-544-2691 or 435-644-2691
www.gcex.com
ACTIVITIES: Dories, rafting
DESTINATIONS: Grand Canyon

Colorado River

Gray Jay Snowmobile Tours
P.O. Box 83
Cantwell, AK 99729
907-768-2600
www.grayjay.com
ACTIVITIES: Snowmobiling, winter camping
DESTINATIONS: Alaska, Denali area

Great Canadian Motor Corp.
P.o. Box 239
Revelstoke, BC, V0E 2S0, Canada
800-667-8865 or 250-837-6500
www.gcmc.com
ACTIVITIES: Motorcycle touring, snowmobiling
DESTINATIONS: Vancouver, Calgary, Alberta, BC, Canadian Rockies

Gunflint Northwoods Outfitters
143 S. Gunflint Lake
Gunflint Lodge
Grand Marais, MN 55604
800-362-5251 or 218-388-2296
www.gunflintoutfitters.com
ACTIVITIES: Camping, canoeing, fishing
DESTINATIONS: Boundary Waters Canoe Area, Minnesota

Hargrave Cattle & Guest Ranch
Thompson River Valley
300 Thompson River Road
Marion, MT 59925
406-858-2284
www.hargraveranch.com
ACTIVITIES: Cattle Drive, Horse Riding, Ranch Vacations
DESTINATIONS: Northern Montana, near Glacier Nat. Park

Harris Mountain Heli-Skiing
Box 634, Queenstown
New Zealand
01164-3433-7930
www.new-zealand/hmh
ACTIVITIES: Heli-skiing, skiing, snowboarding
DESTINATIONS: New Zealand, Southern Alps

Hawaiian Island Surf & Sport
415-A Dairy Road
Kahului, Maui, HI 96732
800-231-6958 or 808-871-4981
www.hawaiianisland.com
ACTIVITIES: Sailing, windsurfing
DESTINATIONS: Hawaii, Maui

Hidden Trails
5936 Inverness Street
Vancouver, BC, V5W 3P7, Canada
888-987-2457 or 604-323-1141
www.hiddentrails.com
ACTIVITIES: Horse riding, trail rides, ranch vacations
DESTINATIONS: Western U.S. States, Canada, Argentina, Australia, Austria, Chile, Costa Rica, England, India, Ireland, Italy, Greece, Portugal, Spain and worldwide

High Adventure
4231 Sepulveda Avenue
San Bernardino, CA 92404
909-883-8488
www.flytandem.com
ACTIVITIES: Hang gliding, paragliding
DESTINATIONS: California

High Angle Adventures, Inc.

178 Hardenburgh Road
Ulster Park, NY 12487
800-777-2546 or 914-658-9811
www.highangle.com
ACTIVITIES: Climbing, ice climbing
DESTINATIONS: Shawangunks, New York

High Island Ranch & Cattle Co.
346 Amoretti, Suite 10
Thermopolis, WY 82443
307-867-2374
www.gorp.com/highisland
ACTIVITIES: Cattle drive, horse riding, ranch vacations
DESTINATIONS: Wyoming

Himalayan Kingdoms, Ltd.
20 The Mall, Clifton
Bristol BS8 4DR, England, U.K.
01144-1179-237-163
www.himalayankingdoms.com
ACTIVITIES: Climbing, cultural tours, mountaineering, trekking
DESTINATIONS: All the Himalaya—Arunachal Pradesh, Bhutan, Sikkim, Tibet, Nepal, Mustang, Garhwal, Himachal Pradesh, Ladakh, Zanskar, Karakoram, Hindu Kush, China (Tien Shan), Outer Mongolia, Thailand and Vietnam

◎ Himalayan Travel, Inc.
110 Prospect Street
Stamford, CT 06901
800-225-2380 or 203-359-3711
www.gorp.com/himtravel.htm
ACTIVITIES: Cultural tours, hiking, safari, trekking
DESTINATIONS: Nepal and Himalayas; also Russia, Peru, Galápagos, India, Tibet, Bhutan, Pakistan, Thailand, Africa, Europe, Greece, China, Mongolia, Burma, Vietnam, Cambodia, Malaysia, Indonesia, Borneo, Galápagos, Amazon

◎ Holiday Expeditions
544 E. 3900 S.
Salt Lake City, UT 84107
800-624-6323 or 801-266-2087
www.bikeraft.com
ACTIVITIES: Bicycling, mountain biking, ranch stays, rafting
DESTINATIONS: Canyonlands, Colorado, Idaho, Utah

Holidaze Ski Tours
810 Belmar Plaza
Belmar, NJ 07719
800-526-2827 or 732-280-1120
www.holidaze.com
ACTIVITIES: Skiing, snowboarding
DESTINATIONS: Argentina, Austria, Chile, France, New Zealand, Spain, Switzerland

◎ Hughes River Expeditions
P.O. Box 217, Cambridge, ID 83610
800-262-1882 or 208-257-3477
www.hughesriver.com
ACTIVITIES: Fishing, rafting
DESTINATIONS: Idaho: Salmon, Snake (Hell's Canyon), Owyhee, Bruneau Rivers

Hurricane Creek Llama Treks
63366 Pine Tree Road
Enterprise, OR 97828
800-528-9609 or 541-432-4455
www.hcltrek.com
ACTIVITIES: Hiking, llama trekking
DESTINATIONS: Eagle Cap Wilderness Area, Hell's Canyon Nat. Rec. Area, Oregon

Hurunui Horsetreks
Taihoa Downs, Hawarden RD,
North Canterbury, New Zealand
01164-3314-4204
www.horseback.co.nz
ACTIVITIES: Farm stay, horse
riding, horse trekking, wagon train
DESTINATIONS: South Island,
Canterbury Plain Foothills, New
Zealand

Hyak River Adventures
203-3823 Henning Drive
Burnaby, BC, V5C 6N5, Canada
800-663-7238 or 604-734-8622
or 206-382-1311
www.hyak.com
ACTIVITIES: Nature, rafting
DESTINATIONS: Major rivers in
Alaska, British Columbia, Idaho,
Yukon

**Incredible Adventures -
MIGs Etc.**
6604 Midnight Pass Road
Sarasota, FL 34231
800-644-7382 or 941-346-2488
www.incredible-adventures.com
ACTIVITIES: Air combat, jet flying,
space rides
DESTINATIONS: Florida, Russia,
South Africa

**International Mountain
Climbing School (IMCS)**
2733 Main Street
North Conway, NH 03860
603-356-7064. www.ime-usa.com
ACTIVITIES: Climbing, ice climb-
ing, mountaineering, winter skills
DESTINATIONS: New Hampshire,
Guided Climbs many locations

**International Mountain
Guides (IMG)**
P.O. Box 246, Ashford, WA 98304
425-222-4958 or 360-569-2604
www.mountainguide.com
ACTIVITIES: Climbing, moun-
taineering, trekking
DESTINATIONS: Alaska, Andes,
Europe Alps, Antarctica, Bolivia,
Ecuador, Himalayas, Mexico, Peru,
Tanzania

**International School
of Mountaineering**
Hafod Tan-y-Graig, Nant Gwynant
Caernarfon, North Wales, LL55
4NW, U.K.
01144-1766-890-441
http://dspace.dial.pipex.com/ism
ACTIVITIES: Climbing, moun-
taineering, ski mountaineering
DESTINATIONS: Andes, Europe
Alps, Himalayas, HIndu Kush,
Karakoram, Khyrgystan, Nepal,
Switzerland, Tien Shan

**International Snowmobile
Tours, Inc. (ISTI)**
427 Sycamore Street
Chesterfield, IN 46017
800-378-8687 or 765-378-5074
www.iquest.net/isti
ACTIVITIES: Snowmobiling
DESTINATIONS: Canada, Col-
orado, Ontario, Gaspé Peninsula,
Quebec, Wyoming, Yellowstone

**Ishestar Icelandic
Riding Tours**
Baejarhraun No. 2, 220
Hafnarfjordur, Iceland
01135-4565-3044

www.ishestar.is
ACTIVITIES: Farm stay, horse
riding, horse trekking
DESTINATIONS: Iceland, Volcanic
zones and glaciers

◎ **Island Dreams
Tours & Travel**
8582 Katy Freeway, Suite 118,
Houston, TX 77024
800-346-6116 or 713-973-9300
www.islandream.com
ACTIVITIES: Scuba diving
DESTINATIONS: Australia, Belize,
Bonaire, Cayman Islands, Cozumel,
Fiji, Guanaja, Honduras, Indonesia,
Malaysia, Roatan, Sipadan Island,
Solomon Islands, Vanuatu

Island Fitness Travel
2932 Carrie Farm Road, NW
Kennesaw, GA 30144
877-290-1467 or 678-290-1424
www.discount-all-inclusive.com
ACTIVITIES: Biking, running,
swimming (triathlon); golf, tennis
DESTINATIONS: Caribbean
Island Resorts

Jackson Hole Llamas
P.O. Box 12500
Jackson, WY 83002
800-830-7316 or 307-739-9582
www.jhllamas.com
ACTIVITIES: Hiking,
llama trekking
DESTINATIONS: Montana,
Wyoming near Yellowstone Park

**Jackson Hole Mountain
Guides & Climbing School**
P.O. Box 7477, 165 N. Glenwood
Jackson Hole, WY 83001
800-239-7642 or 307-733-4979
www.jhmg.com
ACTIVITIES: Climbing, moun-
taineering, ski mountaineering
DESTINATIONS: Rockies, Tetons,
Wyoming

Jagged Globe
The Foundry Studios
45 Mowbray Street, Sheffield S3
8EN England, U.K.
01144-1142-763-322. www.jagged-
globe.co.uk
ACTIVITIES: Climbing, mountaineering, trekking
DESTINATIONS: India, Nepal,
Pakistan and ranges worldwide

Journeys International
107 Aprill Drive, Suite 3
Ann Arbor, MI 48103
800-255-8735 or 734-665-4407
www.journeys-intl.com
ACTIVITIES: Cultural tours, hik-
ing, nature, safari, trekking
DESTINATIONS: Belize, Nepal,
Tibet, Ladakh, Kenya, Peru, Ecuador,
Costa Rica, Madagascar, Patagonia,
Bhutan, Namibia, Tanzania, Vietnam,
Indonesia, Mexico, Guatemala,
Panama, Chile, Argentina, Irian Jaya

Kaibab Mountain Bike Tours
391 So. Main Street, Moab, UT
84532
800-451-1133 or 435-259-7423
www.kaibabtours.com
ACTIVITIES: Bicycling, mountain
biking
DESTINATIONS: Canyonlands,
Utah, Rockies

**Kaufmann's Streamborn
Fly Shop**
8861 S.W. Commercial Street
Tigard, OR 97223
800-442-4359 or 503-639-6400
www.kman.com
ACTIVITIES: Fishing, hunting
DESTINATIONS: Worldwide

Kayak & Canoe Institute
U. of Minn. (Duluth)
121 SPHC, 10 University Dr.
Duluth, MN 55812
218-726-6533
www.d.umn.edu/umdoutdoors/cou
rses/kci
ACTIVITIES: Canoeing, kayaking,
rafting
DESTINATIONS: Apostle Islands,
Boundary Waters, annual trips in
Rockies

KE Adventure Travel
1131 Grand Ave., Glenwood
Springs, CO 81601, U.K.
800-497-9675 or 970-384-0001
www.keadventure.com
ACTIVITIES: Mountaineering,
trekking
DESTINATIONS: Himalayas,
India, Nepal, Pakistan

◎ **Ker & Downey**
2825 Wilcrest Dr., Suite 600
Houston, TX 77042
800-423-4236 or 713-917-0048
www.kerdowney.com
ACTIVITIES: Hiking, nature, safari
DESTINATIONS: Botswana, East
and Southern Africa

Kitty Hawk Kites
P.O. Box 1839
Nags Head, NC 27959
800-334-4777 or 252-441-4124
www.kittyhawk.com
ACTIVITIES: Hang Gliding,
Paragliding
DESTINATIONS: North Carolina

Krabloonik Dogsled Rides
4250 Divide Road
Snowmass Village, CO 81615
970-923-4342 (kennel) or
970-923-3953 (restaurant)
www.krabloonik.com
ACTIVITIES: Dogsledding
DESTINATIONS: Rockies near
Aspen, Colorado

**Landfall Productions, Dive &
Adventure Travel**
855 Howe Avenue, Suite 5
Sacramento, CA 95825
800-525-3833 or 916-363-0164
www.landfallproductions.com
ACTIVITIES: Scuba diving
DESTINATIONS: Baja, Bay
Islands, Belize, Bequia, Bonaire,
BVI, Caymans, Cozumel, Costa Rica,
Dominica, Fiji, Galápagos,
Grenadines, Indonesia, Micronesia,
Roatan, St. Vincent, St. Lucia,
St. Kitts-Nevis

◎ **Lindblad
Special Expeditions**
720 Fifth Ave.
New York, NY 10019
800-397-3348 or 212-765-7740
www.expeditions.com
ACTIVITIES: Cruising, nature,
whale-watching
DESTINATIONS: Antarctica,
Alaska Inside Passage, Baja, Mexico,

Costa Rica, Galápagos Islands and
more

**Lookout Mountain
Flight Park**
7201 Scenic Hwy. 189
Rising Fawn, GA 30738
800-688-5637 or 706-398-3541
www.hangglide.com
ACTIVITIES: Hang gliding
DESTINATIONS: Georgia

◎ **Lotus Tours**
1644 N. Sedgwick Street
Chicago, IL 60614
312-951-0031
www.lotustours.com
ACTIVITIES: Motorcycle touring
DESTINATIONS: Africa, Australia,
Austria, Bhutan, Canada, Chile,
Egypt, France (and Corsica), Italy
(and Sicily), India, Israel, Italy, Jordan, Mexico, Morocco, Peru, Switzerland, Thailand, Tibet, U.K., U.S.A.,
Vietnam

Mad Dog Expeditions
132 East 82nd Street
New York, NY 10028
212-744-6763 or 212-744-6568
www.mad-dog.net
ACTIVITIES: Ice-diving, scuba diving, shark diving
DESTINATIONS: Canadian Arctic,
South Africa, South Pacific

Madawaska Kanu Centre
39 First Ave.
Ottawa, ON, K1S 2G1, Canada
613-594-5268
www.owl-mkc.ca
ACTIVITIES: Canoeing, kayaking
DESTINATIONS: Ontario,
Canada; Madawaska, Petawawa,
and Ottawa Rivers

Maine Island Kayak Co.
70 Luther Street
Peaks Island, ME 04108
800-796-2373 or 207-766-2373
www.maineislandkayak.com
ACTIVITIES: Sea kayaking
DESTINATIONS: Casco Bay,
Penobscot Bay, Maine, Nova Scotia,
Tusket Islands

◎ **Maine Windjammer Assoc.**
P.O. Box 1144, Blue Hill, ME 04614
800-807-9463 or 207-374-2993
www.sailmainecoast.com
ACTIVITIES: Cruising, sailing,
windjammer
DESTINATIONS: Maine Coast,
Caribbean in off-season

**Mariah Wilderness
Expeditions**
P.O. Box 70248
Pt. Richmond, CA 94807
800-462-7424 or 510-233-2303
www.mariahwe.com
ACTIVITIES: Rafting, nature,
trekking, womens' trips
DESTINATIONS: Baja, Belize, California, Costa Rica, Ecuador/Galápa-
gos, Hawaii, Oregon, Peru and others

Maui Windsurfari
425 Koloa Street
Unit 107, Kahului, Maui, HI 96732
800-736-6284 or 808-871-7766
www.windsurfari.com
ACTIVITIES: Sailing, windsurfing
DESTINATIONS: Maui, Hawaii

**Mike Wiegele
Helicopter Skiing**
P.O. Box 159
Blue River, BC, V0E 1J0, Canada
800-661-9170 or 250-673-8381
www.wiegele.com
ACTIVITIES: Heli-skiing, skiing,
snowboarding
DESTINATIONS: Canada, BC:
Monashees and Cariboos

Mission Soaring Center
1116 Wrigley Way
Milpitas, CA 95035
408-262-1055
www.hang-gliding.com
ACTIVITIES: Hang gliding,
paragliding
DESTINATIONS: California

Morningside Flight Park
357 Morningside Lane
Charlestown, NH 03603
603-542-4416
www.cyberportal.net/morningside
ACTIVITIES: Hang gliding,
paragliding
DESTINATIONS: New Hampshire,
New England

Morris Overseas Tours
400 Ave. B
Melbourne Beach, FL 32951
407-725-4809
www.morrisoverseastours.com
ACTIVITIES: Surfing
DESTINATIONS: Barbados, Costa
Rica, Ecuador, France/Spain, Mexico,
Panama, Peru, Philippines, Puerto
Rico, and South Africa

Mountain Guides Alliance
P.O. Box 266
North Conway, NH 03860
603-356-5310
www.mountainguidesalliance.com
ACTIVITIES: Climbing, ice
climbing, winter skills
DESTINATIONS: North Conway,
New Hampshire

Mountain Madness
4218 S.W. Alaska, Suite 206
Seattle, WA 98116
800-328-5925 or 206-937-8389
www.mountainmadness.com
ACTIVITIES: Climbing, moun-
taineering, trekking
DESTINATIONS: Bolivia, Ecuador,
Europe Alps, Kilimanjaro (Tanzania),
Nepal

◎ **Mountain Travel-Sobek**
6420 Fairmont Ave.
El Cerrito, CA 94530
800-227-2384 or 800-282-8747 or
510-527-8100
www.mtsobek.com
ACTIVITIES: Hiking, moun-
taineering, nature, rafting, trekking
DESTINATIONS: Africa (Kenya,
Tanzania), Bhutan, Canadian Rockies, China, Europe Alps, France, Italy,
Nepal, Pakistan, Papua New Guinea,
Peru, Patagonia, Spain, Switzerland,
Tibet, Turkey, Venezuela, Washington, United States

**Mountain Trek Fitness
Retreat & Health Spa**
Box 1352, Ainsworth Hot Springs,
BC, V0G 1A0, Canada
800-661-5161 or 250-229-5636
www.hiking.com
ACTIVITIES: Hiking, snow-

shoeing, yoga, massage
DESTINATIONS: Kootenay
Range, BC, Canada

Mountain Trip
P.O. Box 11809
Anchorage, AK 99509
907-345-6499
www.mountaintrip.com
ACTIVITIES: Climbing, moun-
taineering, ski mountaineering
DESTINATIONS: Alaska, Denali
Nat. Park, Mt. McKinley

Mountain Wings
150 Canal Street
Ellenville, NY 12428
914-647-3377
www.flightschool.net
ACTIVITIES: Hang gliding,
paragliding
DESTINATIONS: New York

MountainFit
P.O. Box 6188, Bozeman, MT 59771
800-926-5700 or 406-585-3506
www.mountainfit.com
ACTIVITIES: Fitness, massage, hik-
ing; limited biking, rafting, climbing
DESTINATIONS: Arizona, Hawaii,
Montana, Utah, Canadian Rockies,
France, Scotland

Nahanni River Adventures, Ltd.
Box 4869
Whitehorse, YT, Y1A 4N6, Canada
800-297-6927 or 867-668-3180
www.nahanni.com
ACTIVITIES: Canoeing, hiking,
nature, rafting, sea kayaking
DESTINATIONS: Alaska, Yukon
Arctic and sub-Arctic Rivers: Alsek,
Nahanni, Coppermine, Burnside,
Horton, and more

**Nancy Emerson
School of Surfing**
P.O. Box 463
Lahaina, Maui, HI 96767
808-874-1183
www.maui.net/~ncesurf
ACTIVITIES: Surfing
DESTINATIONS: Hawaii, plus
tours to Australia, Fiji, Indonesia,
Maldives, and Vanuata

Nantahala Outdoor Center
13077 U.S. Hwy. 19 West
Bryson City, NC 28713
888-662-1662 or 828-488-2176
www.noc.com
ACTIVITIES: Canoeing, kayaking,
rafting, sea kayaking
DESTINATIONS: Over 20 lakes
and rivers in NC, TN, SC, and GA,
plus Grand Canyon, Rio Grand,
Costa Rica, Honduras, Mexico and
other locations worldwide

**National Outdoor
Leadership School (NOLS)**
288 Main Street
Lander, WY 82520
307-332-5300
www.nols.edu
ACTIVITIES: Climbing, kayaking,
mountaineering, outdoor skills, ski
mountaineering
DESTINATIONS: Alaska, Arizona,
Baja, Cascades, Washington,
Wyoming, Australia, Canada, Chile,
Mexico

Natural Habitat Adventures
2945 Center Green Court South
Suite H, Boulder CO 80301
800-543-8917 or 303-449-3711
www.nathab.com
ACTIVITIES: Marine mammals,
nature, safari
DESTINATIONS: Magdalen
Islands, British Columbia, Costa
Rica, Botswana, Mexico

Neilson
120 St. Georges Road
Brighton, BN2 1EA, England, U.K.
01144-1273-626-283 or 284
www.neilson.co.uk
ACTIVITIES: Sailing, skiing,
windsurfing, yachting
DESTINATIONS: Britain,
Caribbean, Greece, Mediterranean,
Turkey

New England Outdoor Center
P.O. Box 669
Millinocket, ME 04462
800-766-7238 or 207-723-5438
www.neoc.com
ACTIVITIES: Kayaking, rafting
DESTINATIONS: Maine

Nichols Expeditions
497 N. Main Street
Moab, UT 84532
800-648-8488 or 435-259-3999
www.nicholsexpeditions.com
ACTIVITIES: Bicycling, mountain
biking, hiking, rafting, sea kayaking
DESTINATIONS: Alaska, Arizona,
Canyonlands, Colorado, Utah, Chile,
Costa Rica, Galápagos, Peru, Italy, Spain

North Cascade Safaris
P.O. Box 250
Winthrop, WA 98862
509-996-2350
E-mail: clod@methow.com
ACTIVITIES: Horsepacking,
horse riding
DESTINATIONS: Cascades,
Okanagan National Forest (Paysaten
and Lake Chelan Sawtooth Wilder-
nesses)

North Star Adventures
P.O. Box 1724
Flagstaff, AZ 86002
800-258-8434 or 520-773-9917
www.adventuretrip.com
ACTIVITIES: Sea kayaking
DESTINATIONS: Alaska,
Kenai Fjords, Prince William Sound,
Baja, Mexico

**North-Eastern
Motorcycle Tours**
P.O. Box 574
Saxtons River, VT 05154
802-869-3999
www.motorcycletours.com
ACTIVITIES: Motorcycle touring
DESTINATIONS: New England,
Adirondacks, Nova Scotia, New
Brunswick, Gaspé Peninsula
(Canada)

◎ **Northern Lights
Expeditions**
P.O. Box 4289
Bellingham, WA 98227
800-754-7402 or 360-734-6334
www.seakayaking.com
ACTIVITIES: Sea kayaking,
whale-watching
DESTINATIONS: British Columbia,
Inside Passage, Pacific Northwest

Northwest Outdoor Center
2100 Westlake Ave. N.
Seattle, WA 98109
800-683-0637 or 206-281-9694
www.nwoc.com
ACTIVITIES: Canoeing, kayaking,
sea kayaking
DESTINATIONS: Rogue
River (OR), Skykomish,
Wenatchee Rivers (WA)

**Nova, The Adventure
Company**
Chickaloon, AK 99674
800-746-5753 or 907-745-5753
www.novalaska.com
ACTIVITIES: Hiking, rafting,
trekking
DESTINATIONS: Alaska,
Chickaloon, Copper, Lionshead,
Matanuska, Six-Mile Creek,
Talkeetna, Tana Rivers

Ocean River Adventure Co.
Main Road, Marahau Beach
R.D. 2, Motueka, New Zealand
01164-3527-8266
www.seakayaking.co.nz
ACTIVITIES: Camping, sea kayaking
DESTINATIONS: New Zealand,
South Island, Abel Tasman Nat. Park

◎ **Ocean Voyages Inc.**
1709 Bridgeway
Sausalito, CA 94965
800-299-4444 or 415-332-4681
www.oceanvoyages.com
ACTIVITIES: Cruising, sailing,
windjammer
DESTINATIONS: Caribbean, the
Mediterranean, the Pacific North-
west, the Galápagos Islands, Mexico,
Australia, the Indian Ocean, Chilean
Patagonia, New Zealand and the
South Pacific, Europe

**Old Faithful
Snowmobile Tours**
P.O. Box 7182, Jackson, WY 83002
800-253-7130 or 307-733-9767
www.snowmobilingtours.com
ACTIVITIES: Snowmobiling
DESTINATIONS: Jackson and Yel-
lowstone areas, Wyoming

Orange Torpedo Trips
P.O. Box 1111
Grants Pass, OR 97528
800-635-2925 or 541-479-5061
www.orangetorpedo.com
ACTIVITIES: Kayaking, rafting
DESTINATIONS: Lower Klamath,
North Umpqua, Rogue (OR); Salmon
(Main & Lower) (ID)

Orion Expeditions, Inc.
5111 Latona Ave. N.E.
Seattle, WA 98105
800-553-7466 or 206-547-6715
www.orionexp.com
ACTIVITIES: Rafting
DESTINATIONS: Eight rivers in
Oregon and Washington

Otter Bar Lodge
P.O. Box 210
Forks of Salmon, CA 96031
530-462-4772
www.otterbar.com
ACTIVITIES: Kayaking, rafting,
River Training
DESTINATIONS: California,
Salmon River, Klamath River

Outback Ranch Outfitters
P.O. Box 384
Joseph, OR 97846
541-886-2029
www.catsback.com/outbackranch
ACTIVITIES: Fishing, horsepacking, horse riding, rafting
DESTINATIONS: Wallowa Mountains, Wenaha-Tucannon Wilderness (WA border), Hell's Canyon (ID border), Snake River in Hell's Canyon

◎ **Outdoor Adventure River Specialists (O.A.R.S)**
P.O. Box 67
Angels Camp, CA 95222
800-446-7238 or 800-346-6277 or 209-736-4677
www.oars.com
ACTIVITIES: Rafting, fishing
DESTINATIONS: California, Idaho, Oregon, Wyoming, and Utah

Outer Edge Expeditions
4830 Mason Road
Howell, MI 48843
800-322-5235 or 517-552-5300
www.outer-edge.com
ACTIVITIES: Dogsledding, nature, safari, rafting, trekking
DESTINATIONS: Borneo, Canada, Indonesia, Irian Jaya, Kenya, New Zealand, Patagonia, Peru, Turkey, Zambia

Outward Bound
100 Mystery Point Road
Garrison, NY 10524
800-243-8520 or 914-424-4000
www.outwardbound.org
ACTIVITIES: Youth camping, climbing, outdoor skills, rafting, sailing, skiing, trekking
DESTINATIONS: 30 training centers worldwide, 27 in North America

Ouzel Adventures
P.O. Box 827, Bend, OR 97709
800-788-7238 or 541-385-5947
www.oregonrafting.com
ACTIVITIES: Rafting
DESTINATIONS: Oregon Rivers: Deschutes, McKenzie, North Umpqua, Owyhee, Rogue; and Lower Salmon (ID)

Overseas Adventure Travel (OAT)
347 Congress Street
Boston, MA 02210
800-221-0814 or 617-346-6799
www.oattravel.com
ACTIVITIES: Cultural tours, nature, safari, walking
DESTINATIONS: Africa, the Americas, Asia, Europe

Paddling South
P.O. Box 827, Calistoga, CA 94515
800-398-6200 or 707-942-4550
www.tourbaja.com
ACTIVITIES: Sea kayaking, horse riding
DESTINATIONS: Baja, Mexico, Sea of Cortez

PADI Travel Network
30151 Tomas Street
Rancho Santa Margarita, CA 92688
800-729-7234 or 949-858-7243
www.padi.com
ACTIVITIES: Scuba diving, snorkeling
DESTINATIONS: Australia, Bay Islands, Belize, Bonaire, Caymans, Cozumel, Curaçao, Fiji, Galápagos, Indonesia, Micronesia, Philippines, New Guinea, Red Sea, Thailand

Pancho Villa Moto-Tours
4510 Hwy. 281 North #3
Spring Branch, TX 78070
800-233-0564 or 830-438-7744
www.panchovilla.com
ACTIVITIES: Motorcycle touring
DESTINATIONS: Mexico (Baja, Copper Canyon, Yucatan), South America (Chile, Argentina)

Paragon Guides
P.O. Box 130, Vail, CO 81658
877-926-5299 or 970-926-5299
www.paragonguides.com
ACTIVITIES: Hiking, mountain biking, skiing, nordic skiing, snow-shoeing
DESTINATIONS: Tenth Mountain Trail, Colorado Rockies

Paskowitz Family Surf Camp
P.O. Box 522
San Clemente, CA 92674
949-361-9283
http://members.aol.com/surfcamp
ACTIVITIES: Surfing
DESTINATIONS: Southern California, Baja (Cabo San Lucas), Mexico

Peregrine Outfitters
64 Ptarmigan Lane
Durango, CO 81301
800-598-7600 or 970-385-7600
www.peregrineriver.com
ACTIVITIES: Rafting
DESTINATIONS: Six rivers in Southwestern Colorado

Peter Hughes Diving
5723 NW 158th Street
Miami Lakes, FL 33014
800-932-6237 or 305-669-9391
www.peterhughes.com
ACTIVITIES: Scuba diving, whale-watching
DESTINATIONS: Dom. Republic, Belize, Curacao, Galápagos, Palau, Papua N. Guinea, South Pacific, Venezuela, Turks and Caicos

Pioneer Mountain Outfitters
3267 East, 3225 North
Twin Falls, ID 83301
208-774-3737 (summer) or 208-734-3679 (winter)
www.pioneermountain.com
ACTIVITIES: Fishing, horsepacking, horse riding
DESTINATIONS: Idaho, White Clouds Mountain, Sawtooths

Powder River Wagon Trains & Cattle Drives
P.O. Box 676, Broadus, MT 59317
800-492-8835, 800-982-0710, or 406-436-2404
www.powderrivercattledrive.com
ACTIVITIES: Cattle drive, horse riding, wagon train
DESTINATIONS: Montana

◎ **Quark Expeditions**
980 Post Road, Darien, CT 06820
800-356-5699 or 203-656-0499
www.quark-expeditions.com
ACTIVITIES: Polar cruises, nature
DESTINATIONS: Antarctica, Arctic, North Pole

Queensland Yacht Charters (QYC)
P.O. Box 293, Airlie Beach
Whitsunday, Queensland 4802
Australia
01161-7494-67400
www.yachtcharters.comau
ACTIVITIES: Charter sailing, cruising
DESTINATIONS: Australia, Queensland, Whitsunday Islands

Rail Travel Center
139 Main Street
Brattleboro, VT 05301
800-458-5394 or 802-254-7788
www.railtravelcenter.com
ACTIVITIES: Rail travel, train tours
DESTINATIONS: Canadian Rockies, Copper Canyon (Mexico), and elsewhere in Asia, Europe, Australia, New Zealand and the Americas

Rainier Mountaineering, Inc.
535 Dock Street
Tacoma, WA 98402
253-627-6242 or 360-569-2227
www.rmiguides.com
ACTIVITIES: Glacier travel, mountaineering, winter skills
DESTINATIONS: Alaska, Mt. Rainier, Washington

Randonneige Québec
25 rue Brissette, C.P. 65
Sainte-Agathe-Des-Monts
Québec, J8C 3A1, Canada
800-326-0642 or 819-326-0642
www.randonneige.com
ACTIVITIES: Snowmobiling
DESTINATIONS: Quebec, Canada

Rapp Guide Service
3635 County Road
Durango, CO 81301
877-600-2656, 970-375-1250, or 970-247-8923
www.rappguides.com
ACTIVITIES: Horsepacking, horse riding
DESTINATIONS: San Juan Nat. Forest, Continental Divide, Southwest Colorado

◎ **REI Adventures**
P.O. Box 1938, Sumner, WA 98390
800-622-2236 or 253-437-1100
www.rei.com/travel
ACTIVITIES: Hiking, kayaking, nature, trekking
DESTINATIONS: North America, France, Italy, Germany, Greece, Switzerland, Nepal, Chile (Patagonia), Peru, Turkestan

◎ **Rim Tours**
1233 So. Highway 191
Moab, UT 84532
800-626-7335 or 435-259-5223
www.rimtours.com
ACTIVITIES: Bicycling, mountain biking
DESTINATIONS: Canyonlands, Colorado Rockies, Moab area, San Juan Mountains, Utah

Rios Tropicales
P.O. BOX 526770
Miami, FL 33152
01150-6233-6455 in Costa Rica
www.riostropicales.com
ACTIVITIES: Kayaking, rafting
DESTINATIONS: Costa Rica: Pacuare, Reventazón, General Rivers

Riversport School of Paddling
P.O. Box 95, 355 River Road
Confluence, PA 15424
800-216-6991 or 814-395-5744
www.shol.com/kayak
ACTIVITIES: Canoeing, kayaking, rafting
DESTINATIONS: Maryland, Pennsylvania, West Virginia

Rocky Mountain Motorcycle Holidays
103-4338 Main Street, Suite 124
Whistler, BC, V0N 1B4, Canada
604-938-0126
www.rockymtnmoto.com
ACTIVITIES: Motorcycle touring
DESTINATIONS: Canada (Alberta, British Columbia)

Rocky Mountain Outdoor Center
10281 U.S. Highway 50
Howard, CO 81233
800-255-5784 or 719-942-3214
www.rmoc.com
ACTIVITIES: Rafting
DESTINATIONS: Eastern Slope of Rockies, Colorado

Rocky Mountain River Tours, Inc.
P.O. Box 8596
Boise, ID 83707
208-345-2400
www.rafttrips.com
ACTIVITIES: Rafting, fishing
DESTINATIONS: Idaho, Salmon Middle Fork

Rocky Mountain Worldwide Cycle Tours
Box 268, Garibaldi Highlands
Squamish, BC, V1L 4H6, Canada
800-661-2453 or 604-898-8488
www.rockymountaincycle.com
ACTIVITIES: Bicycling, mountain biking
DESTINATIONS: Canadian Rockies (Alberta, BC), Hawaii and six countries in Europe

Rod & Reel Adventures
566 Thomson Lane
Copperopolis, CA 95228
800-356-6982 or 209-785-0444
www.rodreeladventures.com
ACTIVITIES: Fishing, fly-fishing
DESTINATIONS: Worldwide

Rogers Bonaire Windsurf Place
Amboina No. 18, Kralendijk
Bonaire, N.A.
800-225-0102 or 01129-786-1918
www.rogerswindsurf.com
ACTIVITIES: Sailing, windsurfing
DESTINATIONS: Bonaire, Netherlands Antilles

◎ **R.O.W. (River Odysseys West—Remote Odysseys Worldwide)**
P.O. Box 579
Coeur d'Alene, ID 83816
800-451-6034 or 208-765-0841
www.rowinc.com
ACTIVITIES: Cruising, hiking, rafting, sailing
DESTINATIONS: Alaska, Idaho, Ecuador, Greece, Mediterranean, Turkey, with rafting on ten rivers in ID and MT

Saco Bound
P.O. Box 119
Center Conway, NH 03813
800-677-7238 or 603-447-2177
www.sacobound.com
ACTIVITIES: Canoeing, kayaking, rafting
DESTINATIONS: New Hampshire, New England

SafariCentre International
3201 North Sepulveda Blvd.
Manhattan Beach, CA 90266
800-223-6046 or 310-546-4411
www.safaricentre.com
ACTIVITIES: 4WD, cultural tours, nature, safari, trekking
DESTINATIONS: Africa, Asia, Central and South America, Europe and worldwide

Saga D'Aventures
46 bis rue de la Ré publique, 92170 Vanves, France
01133-1410-81490
www.webexpert.fr/raft
ACTIVITIES: Canoeing, canyoning, kayaking, rafting, river-boarding
DESTINATIONS: Europe, France, Italy, Morocco

◎ **Sailboard Vacations**
193 Rockland Street
Hanover, MA 02339
800-252-1070 or 781-829-8915
www.sailboardvacations.com
ACTIVITIES: Sailing, windsurfing
DESTINATIONS: Aruba, Barbados, Bonaire, Cabarete (Dom. Repub.), Margarita (Venezuela)

Salmon River Outfitters
P.O. Box 519, Donnelly, ID 83615
800-346-6204 or 208-325-3400
www.salmonriveroutfitters.com
ACTIVITIES: Kayaking, rafting
DESTINATIONS: Idaho, Main Salmon River

San Diego Shark Diving Expeditions
6747 Friar's Road, Suite 112,
San Diego, CA 92108
888-737-4275 or 619-299-8560
www.sdsharkdiving.com
ACTIVITIES: Scuba Diving, Shark Diving
DESTINATIONS: California, Costa Rica, Galápagos, Mexico, Thailand

Sawtooth Mountain Guides
P.O. Box 18, Stanley, ID 83278
208-774-3324
www.sawtoothguides.com
ACTIVITIES: Climbing, mountaineering, skiing, snowboarding
DESTINATIONS: City of the Rocks, Idaho, Sawtooth Mountains

Search Beyond Adventures
400 South Cedar Lake Road,
Minneapolis, MN 55405
800-800-9979 or 612-374-4845
www.searchbeyond.com
ACTIVITIES: Trips for disabled and special-needs clients
DESTINATIONS: Acadia Park (ME), Boundary Waters, Yellowstone, and many urban venues

Seminole Flying & Soaring
P.O. Box 120458, Claremont, FL 34712
352-394-5450. www.soarfl.com
ACTIVITIES: Gliding, Soaring
DESTINATIONS: Florida

Seneca Rocks Climbing School
P.O. Box 53, Seneca Rocks, WV 26884
800-548-0108 or 304-567-2600
www.seneca-rocks.com
ACTIVITIES: Climbing
DESTINATIONS: Seneca Rocks, West Virginia

Seneca Rocks Mountain Guides
P.O. Box 223, Seneca Rocks, WV 26884
800-451-5108 or 304-567-2115
www.senecarocks.com
ACTIVITIES: Climbing, Indoor Climbing Gym
DESTINATIONS: Seneca Rocks, West Virginia

Senior World Tours
2205 North River Road
Fremont, OH 43420
888-355-1686 or 419-355-1686
www.seniorworldtours.com
ACTIVITIES: Snowmobiling
DESTINATIONS: Alaska, Wyoming (Jackson, Yellowstone and Wind River Range), Ontario, Canada

Sierra Club Outings
85 Second Street, 2nd floor
San Francisco, CA 94105
415-977-5522 or 415-977-5630
www.sierraclub.org/outings
ACTIVITIES: Camping, hiking, trekking
DESTINATIONS: Alaska, California, Colorado, Idaho, Montana, Wyoming, Washington and worldwide

◎ **Sierra Mac River Trips**
P.O. Box 366, Sonora, CA 95370
800-457-2580 or 209-532-1327
www.sierramac.com
ACTIVITIES: Rafting
DESTINATIONS: California: North Fork American and Tuolumne Rivers

Sierra South Mountain Sports
P.O. Box Y, 11300 Kernville Road
Kernville, CA 93238
800-457-2082 or
800-376-7303 (store) or
760-376-3745
www.sierrasouth.com
ACTIVITIES: Canoeing, kayaking, rafting
DESTINATIONS: Kern River, Lake Isabella, California

Sky's The Limit Climbing School & Guide Service
HCR 33, Box 1, Calico Basin—
Red Rock, NV 89124
800-733-7597 or 702-363-4533
www.skysthelimit.com
ACTIVITIES: Climbing
DESTINATIONS: Red Rock, Nevada

◎ **Slickrock Adventures**
P.O. Box 1400
Moab, UT 84532
800-390-5715 or 435-259-3335
www.slickrock.com
ACTIVITIES: Caving, mountain biking, sea kayaking, trekking
DESTINATIONS: Belize, Central America, Canyonlands Area, Utah

SnoSearch Ski Tours
13700 Alton Parkway, Suite 158
Irvine, CA 92618
800-628-8884 or 949-472-4682
www.snosearchskitours.com
ACTIVITIES: Heli-skiing, skiing, snowboarding
DESTINATIONS: Argentina, Austria, Chile, France, Germany, Italy, Switzerland

Soar Minden
P.O. Box 1764
Minden, NV 89423
800-345-7627 or 775-782-7627
www.soarminden.com
ACTIVITIES: Gliding, soaring
DESTINATIONS: Nevada, Lake Tahoe area

Solo Sports Excursions
One Technology, Suite E305
Irvine, CA 92618
949-453-1950
www.solosports.net
ACTIVITIES: Kite surfing, sailing, surfing, windsurfing
DESTINATIONS: Baja, Mexico; Southern California

South Fishing
7101 SW 99th Ave.
Miami, FL 33173
800-882-4665 or 305-279-3252
www.southfishing.com
ACTIVITIES: Fishing
DESTINATIONS: Australia, Bahamas, Belize, Bermuda, Brazil, Costa Rica, Guatemala, Hawaii, Honduras, Mexico, Panama, South Pacific, Venezuela, Virgin Islands

Southwind Kayak Center
17885 Sky Park Circle
#A, Irvine, CA 92614
800-768-8494 or 949-261-0200
www.southwindkayaks.com
ACTIVITIES: Sea kayaking, kayaking
DESTINATIONS: California Coast and Islands, Green River (UT), Lake Mead

Sportours
2335 Honolulu Ave.
Montrose, CA 91020
800-660-2754 or 818-553-3333
www.sportours.com
ACTIVITIES: Golf, scuba diving, skiing, tennis
DESTINATIONS: Europe (Alps Countries), Africa (East and South), Central America, South America, Australia, Caribbean, Indian Ocean, Mexico, Micronesia, Red Sea, South Pacific, Southeast Asia

◎ **St. Elias Alpine Guides**
P.O. Box 111241
Anchorage, AK 99511
888-933-5427 or 907-277-6867
www.steliasguides.com
ACTIVITIES: Climbing, glacier travel, ice climbing, mountaineering
DESTINATIONS: Alaska, Colorado, Wrangell-St. Elias Nat. Park

Star Clippers
4101 Salzedo Avenue
Coral Gables, FL 33146
800-442-0551 or 305-442-0550

www.star clippers.com
ACTIVITIES: Sailing, cruising, scuba diving, windjammer
DESTINATIONS: Caribbean, Mediterranean, Far East including France, Greece, Thailand

Stonehearth Open Learning Opportunity
RR 1, Box 163, Conway, NH 03818
888-765-6633 or 603-447-6711
www.stonehearth.com
ACTIVITIES: Outdoor skills, wilderness medicine
DESTINATIONS: Colorado, New Hampshire, New Mexico, North Carolina and Wyoming, and Canada

Summits Adventure Travel
P.O. Box W
Ashford, WA 98304
360-569-2992
www.summitsadventure.com
ACTIVITIES: Climbing, mountaineering, trekking
DESTINATIONS: Andes, Argentina (Aconcagua), Canada, Ecuador, Europe Alps, Kilimanjaro, Peru

Sun Yacht Charters
P.O. Box 4035
Portland, ME 04101
800-772-3500 or 207-253-5400
www.sunyachts.com
Activities: Charter sailing, cruising
DESTINATIONS: Tortola, Antigua, Grenadines, Guadeloupe, Martinique, St. Martin, Puerto Rico, Croatia, French Med & Corsica, Seychelles, Spain, Tahiti, Turkey

◎ **Sundance River Center**
14894 Galice Road
Merlin, OR 97532
888-777-7557 or 541-479-8508
www.sundanceriver.com
ACTIVITIES: Kayaking, rafting
DESTINATIONS: Rogue River, Oregon, Idaho, Grand Canyon

Sunsail
980 Awald Road
Annapolis, MD 21403
800-327-2276 or 410-280-2553
www.sunsail.com
ACTIVITIES: Charter sailing, cruising
DESTINATIONS: Antigua, Guadeloupe, Martinique, Tortola, St. Martin, St. Vincent, Annapolis, Australia, Croatia, England, France, Greece, New Zealand, Thailand, Tonga, Turkey and others

Surf Express
Sea Park Plaza, 568 Highway A1A
Satellite Beach, FL 32937
321-779-2124
www.surfex.com
ACTIVITIES: Surfing
DESTINATIONS: Costa Rica, Barbados, Chile, Ecuador, El Salvador, the Galápagos, Panama, Peru, Puerto Rico

Surf Travel Company
P.O. Box 446, Cronulla Plaza, Cronulla, NSW 2230, Australia
01161-2952-74722
www.surftravel.com
ACTIVITIES: Surfing
DESTINATIONS: Pacific and Indian Oceans, Indonesia, the Maldives, Fiji, Philippines, Society Islands

**Sylvan Rocks
Climbing School**
P.O. Box 600
Hill City, SD 57745
605-574-2425
www.sylvanrocks.com
ACTIVITIES: Climbing
DESTINATIONS: Custer State
Park, Devils Tower, South Dakota

◎ **Telemark Inn & Llama
Treks**
RFD 2, Box 800
Bethel, ME 04217
207-836-2703
www.telemarkinn.com
ACTIVITIES: Hiking, llama
trekking
DESTINATIONS: Maine, Caribou
Speckled Wilderness Area

**Teton Wagon Train
& Horse Adventure**
Double H Bar, P.O. Box 10307
Jackson Hole, WY 83002
888-734-6101 or 307-734-6101
www.tetonwagontrain.com
ACTIVITIES: Horse riding,
wagon Train
DESTINATIONS: Jackson Hole,
Teton Nat. Park, Wyoming

Texas Air Aces
8319 Thora Lane, Hangar #A5
Spring, TX 77379
800-544-2237 or 281-379-2237
www.airaces.com
ACTIVITIES: Air combat, flying
DESTINATIONS: Texas

The Barge Cruise Company
2 Orchard Close
Felton, Bristol, BS40 9YS, U.K.
800-688-0245 or 01144-1275-474-
034. www.bargecompany.com
ACTIVITIES: Barge cruising
DESTINATIONS: England, France,
Holland, Ireland, and Scotland

The Catamaran Company
4005 N. Federal Highway, Suite
200
Ft. Lauderdale, FL 33308
800-262-0308 or 954-566-9806
www.catamaranco.com
ACTIVITIES: Charter sailing, cruising
DESTINATIONS: Ft. Lauderdale,
Guadeloupe, Martinique, St. Martin,
Tortola (BVI)

◎ **The Moorings**
19345 U.S. Highway 19 N.
4th Fl., Clearwater, FL 33764
800-535-7289 or 727-530-5424
www.moorings.com
ACTIVITIES: Charter sailing,
cruising
DESTINATIONS: Tortola,
Bahamas, Grenada, Martinique,
St. Lucia, St. Martin, Australia, Baja,
Florida, France & Corsica, Greece,
New Zealand, Spain, Tahiti, Tonga

The Rivermen
P.O. Box 220
Lansing, WV 25862
800-545-7238 or 304-574-0515
www.raftwv.com
ACTIVITIES: Rafting
DESTINATIONS: New, Gauley
Rivers (WV)

Timberline
7975 E. Harvard
Unit J, Denver, CO 80231
800-417-2453 or 303-368-4418
www.timbertours.com/tours
ACTIVITIES: Bicycling, hiking,
mountain biking, walking
DESTINATIONS: Colorado, Montana, Western U.S and Canada;
hiking in 34 different Nat. Parks

TMM Bareboat Vacations
P.O. Box 3042
Road Town, Tortola, BVI
800-633-0155 or 203-854-5131
www.sailtmm.com
ACTIVITIES: Charter Sailing,
Cruising
DESTINATIONS: Tortola BVI,
Belize, Grenadines

◎ **Tofino Expeditions**
P.O. Box 15280, Seattle, WA 98115
800-677-0877 or 206-517-5244
www.tofino.com
ACTIVITIES: Sea kayaking, whale-
watching
DESTINATIONS: Canada, Queen
Charlotte Strait, Vancouver Island,
Baja, Mexico, Sea of Cortez

Tom Brown's Tracker School
P.O. Box 173, Asbury, NJ 08802
908-479-4681
www.trackerschool.com
ACTIVITIES: Outdoor skills,
survival, tracking
DESTINATIONS: Pine Barrens,
New Jersey

◎ **Torrey Pines Gliderport**
2800 Torrey Pines Scenic Dr.,
La Jolla, CA 92037
858-452-9858. www.flytorrey.com
ACTIVITIES: Hang gliding,
paragliding
DESTINATIONS: San Diego,
California, Baja, Mexico

**Trailmark Outdoor
Adventures**
16 Schuyler Road
Nyack, NY 10960
800-229-0262 or 914-358-0262
www.trailmark.com
ACTIVITIES: Youth backpacking,
canoeing, mountain biking, horse
riding, rafting, rock climbing
DESTINATIONS: New England,
Pacific Northwest, Southwest
Colorado, the Northern Rockies

Trains Unlimited Tours
P.O. Box 1997, Portola, CA 96122
800-359-4870, 800-752-1836 (in
Canada), or 530-836-1745
www.trainsunltdtours.com
ACTIVITIES: Rail travel, train tours
DESTINATIONS: Argentina,
Bolivia, Canada, Chile, Ecuador,
Guatemala, Mexico, Peru and United
States (AK, CA, CO, NH)

TraWell SurfReisen
Apfelgasse 6
A-1040 Vienna, Austria
01143-1505-0457
www.trawell.at
ACTIVITIES: Diving, sailing,
windsurfing
DESTINATIONS: Canaries, Cape
Verden, Cuba, Egypt, Greece, Rhodes,
Spain, South Africa, Turkey, Cabarete,
Margarita, Aruba, Barbados

◎ **Tropical Adventures**
111 Second Avenue North
Seattle, WA 98109
800-247-3483 or 206-441-3483
www.divetropical.com
ACTIVITIES: Scuba diving
DESTINATIONS: Africa, Australia,
Baja, Belize, Bonaire, Caymans,
Costa Rica, Cozumel, Fiji, Galápagos,
Hawaii, Indonesia, Micronesia, Papua
New Guinea, Red Sea, Seychelles,
Solomon Islands

Turf Soaring School
8700 West Carefree Highway
Peoria, AZ 85382
602-439-3621
www.turfsoaring.com
ACTIVITIES: Gliding, soaring
DESTINATIONS: Arizona

UNEXSO
P.O. Box 22878
Ft. Lauderdale, FL 33335
800-992-3483 or 242-373-1244
www.unexso.com
ACTIVITIES: Scuba diving, marine
mammals
DESTINATIONS: Bahamas

Unicorn Balloon Company
15001 N. 74th Street, Suite F
Scottsdale, AZ 85260
800-468-2478 or 480-991-3666
www.unicornballoon.com
ACTIVITIES: Ballooning
DESTINATIONS: Arizona, Aspen,
Colorado

**United States
Parachuting Assoc. (USPA)**
1440 Duke Street
Alexandria, VA 22314
703-836-3495
www.uspa.org
ACTIVITIES: Parachuting, skydiving, skysurfing
DESTINATIONS: United States

Upp & Ner Balloons
P.O. Box 34032, S-100 26
Stockholm, Sweden
01146-8695-0100 www.uppner.se
ACTIVITIES: Ballooning
DESTINATIONS: Stockholm,
Uppsala, Gö teborg, Malmö , Kö penhamn, Sao Paulo (Brazil)

◎ **USA RAFT &
Appalachian Wildwaters**
P.O. Box 277
Rowlesburg, WV 26425
800-872-7238, 800-624-8060, or
304-454-2475. www.usaraft.com
ACTIVITIES: Kayaking, rafting
DESTINATIONS: New, Gauley,
Nolichucky Rivers and many other
runs in MD, NC, TN, WV

**Van Os Nature Tours/
Photo Safaris**
P.O. Box 655
Vashon Island, WA 98070
206-463-5383
www.photosafaris.com
ACTIVITIES: Hiking, nature,
photo tours, safari
DESTINATIONS: Africa, Alaska,
Antarctica, Australia, Borneo, Brazil
(Pantanal), Canada, Costa Rica, Mexico, Midway Island, Patagonia, Yellowstone N.P.

VBT Bicycling Vacations
P.O. Box 711
614 Monkton Road
Bristol, VT 05443
800-245-3868 or 802-453-4811
www.vbt.com
ACTIVITIES: Biking,
bicycle touring
DESTINATIONS: USA and
Canada, plus Austria, England,
France, Ireland, Italy, New Zealand,
The Netherlands, and Nova Scotia

Vela Windsurf Resorts
4604 Scotts Valley Dr.
Scotts Valley, CA 95066
800-223-5443 or 831-461-0820
www.velawindsurf.com
ACTIVITIES: Sailing, windsurfing
DESTINATIONS: Aruba, Cabarete,
Baja, Coche, Dom. Republic,
Margarita, Maui (Hawaii)

**Vertical Adventures Climbing
School & Guiding Service**
P.O. Box 7548
Newport Beach, CA 92658
800-514-8785 or 949-854-6250
www.vertical-adventures.com
ACTIVITIES: Climbing, rock-craft
DESTINATIONS: California, Idyllwild, San Jacinto Mountains, Joshua
Tree

Victor Emanuel Nature Tours
P.O. Box 33008
Austin, TX 78764
800-328-8368 or 512-328-5221
www.ventbird.com
ACTIVITIES: Birding, nature,
trekking, safari
DESTINATIONS: Africa, the Americas, Asia, and worldwide

**Wagons West -
Yellowstone Outfitters**
P.O. Box 1156, Afton, WY 83110
800-447-4711 or 307-886-9693
www.awe.com (broker)
ACTIVITIES: Horse riding, wagon
train, Western holiday
DESTINATIONS: Bridger-Teton
National Forest (Jackson, Wyoming)

Waitomo Adventures, Ltd.
P.O. Box 29, Waitomo Caves,
New Zealand
01164-7878-7788 or 0800-924-
8666 (NZ toll-free)
www.waitomo.co.nz
ACTIVITIES: Caving, rafting,
Spelunking
DESTINATIONS: Waitomo Caves,
New Zealand North Island

Wallaby Ranch, Inc.
1805 Dean Still Road
Davenport, FL 33837
863-424-0070
www.wallaby.com
ACTIVITIES: Hang gliding
DESTINATIONS: Florida

Wasatch Powderbird Guides
P.O. Box 920057
Snowbird, UT 84092
801-742-2800
www.heliskiwasatch.com
ACTIVITIES: Heli-skiing, skiing,
snowboarding
DESTINATIONS: Wasatch Range,
Utah

Washakie Outfitting
P.O. Box 1054
Dubois, WY 83001
800-249-0662 or 307-455-2616 or
307-733-3602
www.dogsledwashakie.com
ACTIVITIES: Dogsledding, fly
fishing, horsepacking, hunting
DESTINATIONS: Wyoming, Wind
River Range, Shoshone National
Forest, Togwottee Pass, Continental
Divide, Absorokas Range

WaterWays Travel
15145 Califa Street, No. 1
Van Nuys, CA 91411
800-928-3757 or 818-376-0341
www.waterwaystravel.com
ACTIVITIES: Surfing
DESTINATIONS: Fiji, Galápagos,
Indonesia, Maldives, Peru, Western
Samoa, Tonga, and Tahiti.

Western Hang Gliders
P.O. Box 828
Marina, CA 93933
831-384-2622
www.westernhanggliders.com
ACTIVITIES: Hang gliding,
paragliding
DESTINATIONS: California

Western River Expeditions
7258 Racquet Club Dr.
Salt Lake City, UT 84121
800-453-7450 or 801-942-6669
www.westernriver.com
ACTIVITIES: Motor rafting
DESTINATIONS: Colorado
(Grand, Cataract, & Westwater
Canyons) (AZ, UT, CO); Salmon
(Main and Middle Fork) (ID); Green
(UT)

◎ **Western Spirit Cycling**
478 Mill Creek Drive
Moab, UT 84532
800-845-2453 or 435-259-8732
www.westernspirit.com
ACTIVITIES: Cycling,
mountain biking
DESTINATIONS: Arizona (Grand
Canyon), Colorado, Idaho, South
Dakota (Black Hills), Utah (Canyon-
lands, Bryce, Zion, & Capitol Reef
N.P.s)

Whitewater Voyages
5225 San Pablo Dam Road
El Sobrante, CA 94803
800-488-7238 or 510-222-5994
www.whitewatervoyages.com
ACTIVITIES: Kayaking, rafting,
river camp
DESTINATIONS: More than
a dozen California rivers, north
and south

Wild Rose Outfitting
P.O. Box 113
Peers, AB, T0J 1W0, Canada
780-693-2296
www.wildroseoutfitting.com
ACTIVITIES: Fishing, horsepack-
ing, horse riding
DESTINATIONS: Willmore
Wilderness Park, northern edge of
Jasper N.P., Alberta, Canada

Wild Waters
1123 Route 28 at The Glen
Warrensburg, NY 12885
888-945-3420 or 800-867-2335
www.wild-waters.com
ACTIVITIES: Canoeing, kayaking
DESTINATIONS: Hudson River,
New York

Wilderness Alaska
P.O. Box 113063, Anchorage, AK
99511
907-345-3967
www.wildernessalaska.com
ACTIVITIES: Hiking, kayaking,
rafting, trekking
DESTINATIONS: Alaska, Arctic
N. W. R., Brooks Range Rivers
(Hulahula, Kongakut, Koyukuk,
Alatna, Killik, Noatak, & Kobuk)

Wilderness Inquiry
1313 Fifth Street SE, Box 84
Minneapolis, MN 55414
800-728-0719 or 612-379-3858
www.wildernessinquiry.org
ACTIVITIES: Camping, canoeing,
hiking, horsepacking, rafting, skiing
for both regular and special-needs
clients
DESTINATIONS: Alaska, Boundary Waters Canoe Area Wilderness
(MN), Canyonlands (UT), Everglades
(FL), San Juan Islands (WA)

**Wilderness Medical
Associates**
189 Dudley Road
Bryant Pond, ME 04219
888-945-3633 or 207-665-2707
www.wildmed.com
ACTIVITIES: Outdoor skills,
wilderness medicine
DESTINATIONS: Sites throughout
North America

**Wilderness Medicine
Institute, Inc.**
P.O. Box 9, Pitkin, CO 81241
970-641-3572
http://wmi.nols.edu
ACTIVITIES: Outdoor skills,
wilderness medicine
DESTINATIONS: Western U.S.
States, Australia, Costa Rica, Kenya
and South Africa

Wilderness Outfitters
3800 Rattlesnake Drive
Missoula, MT 59802
406-549-2820
www.recworld.com/wildout
ACTIVITIES: Fishing,
horsepacking, horse riding
DESTINATIONS: Bob Marshall
Wilderness Area, Montana

◎ **Wilderness Travel**
1102 Ninth St., Berkeley, CA 94710
800-368-2794 or 510-558-2488
www.wildernesstravel.com
ACTIVITIES: Hiking, nature,
Safari, trekking
DESTINATIONS: Africa, England,
Europe Alps, France, Italy, Turkey,
Ecuador, Patagonia, Peru, Borneo,
French Polynesia, Nepal, New
Zealand, India, Jordan, Syria, Tibet

◎ **Wildland Adventures**
3516 N.E. 155th Street
Seattle, WA 98155
800-345-4453 or 206-365-0686
www.wildland.com
ACTIVITIES: Hiking, nature,

trekking
DESTINATIONS: Alaska, Mexico,
Bolivia, Chile (Patagonia), Ecuador
(Galápagos, Amazon, Andes),
Peru, India, Nepal, Tibet, Botswana,
Madagascar, Tanzania, Zambia,
Zimbabwe and more

**Windjammer
Barefoot Cruises**
P.O. Box 120
Miami Beach, FL 33119
800-327-2601 or 305-672-6453
www.windjammer.com
ACTIVITIES: Cruising, sailing,
windjammer
DESTINATIONS: Caribbean
(50 ports of call)

WindSport Travel
115 Danforth Ave., Suite 302
Toronto, ON, M4K 1N2, Canada
416-461-3276 or 800-640-9530
in Canada
www.windsport-travel.com
ACTIVITIES: Windsurfing
DESTINATIONS: Aruba, Barbados,
Bonaire, Cabarete, Margarita
(Venezuela), Maui (Hawaii), Tobago

Windsports Soaring Center
16145 Victory Boulevard
Van Nuys, CA 91406
800-426-4454 or 818-988-0111
www.windsports.com
ACTIVITIES: Hang gliding,
paragliding
DESTINATIONS: California

Wintergreen Lodge
1101 Ring Rock Road
Ely, MN 55731
800-584-9425 or 218-365-6022
www.dogsledding.com
ACTIVITIES: Dogsledding,
ski touring, skiing
DESTINATIONS: Boundary
Waters Canoe Area Wilderness, MN

Women in the Wilderness
566 Ottowa Avenue
St. Paul, MN 55107
651-227-2284
niemi008@tc.umn.edu
ACTIVITIES: Canoeing, cancer
recovery, dogsledding, nature,
women's trips
DESTINATIONS: Canada
(south and Arctic), Minnesota,
Southwest USA, Peru

Women's Travel Club
21401 NE 38th Avenue
Aventura, FL 33180
888-480-4448 or 305-936-9669
www.womenstravelclub.com
ACTIVITIES: Cruising, hiking,
spa vacations
DESTINATIONS: Caribbean,
North America, South America

World Balloon Corp.
4800 Eubank Boulevard NE
Albuquerque, NM 87111
800-351-9588 or 505-293-6800
www.worldballoon.com
ACTIVITIES: Ballooning
DESTINATIONS: Albuquerque,
New Mexico

World Expeditions
3rd Floor, 441 Kent Street
Sydney, NSW 2000, Australia
01161-2926-43366
www.worldexpeditions.comau
ACTIVITIES: Camel trekking,
4WD, safari, trekking
DESTINATIONS: Africa, Asia,
Australia, Central and South America,
Europe, New Zealand

Worldwide Adventures
1170 Sheppard Avenue West
Toronto, ON, M3K 2G9, Canada
800-387-1483 or 416-221-3000
www.worldwidequest.com
ACTIVITIES: Hiking, kayaking,
nature, trekking
DESTINATIONS: Australia, Andes,
Argentina (Patagonia), Asia, Bhutan,
China, India, Nepal, Pakistan,
Sikkim, Tibet, Vietnam

Yamnuska, Inc.
P.O. Box 200
50-103 Bow Valley Trail
Canmore, AB, T1W 1N8, Canada
403-678-4164
www.yamnuska.com
ACTIVITIES: Climbing, glacier
travel, ice climbing, mountaineering,
winter skills
DESTINATIONS: Alberta, British
Columbia, Canada, Peru, Yukon

Yellowstone Llamas
P.O. Box 5042
Bozeman, MT 59717
406-586-6872
www.yellowstone-llamas.com
ACTIVITIES: Hiking, llama
trekking
DESTINATIONS: Montana near
Yellowstone Park

Yellowstone Tour & Travel
211 Yellowstone Avenue
West Yellowstone, MT 59758
800-221-1151 or 406-646-9310
www.yellowstone-travel.com
ACTIVITIES: Snowmobiling, skiing
DESTINATIONS: Montana,
Wyoming, Yellowstone area

**Yosemite Cross-Country
Ski School**
Yosemite Concession Services,
Yosemite National Park, CA 95389
209-372-8444 (winter only)
www.yosemitepark.com
ACTIVITIES: Nordic skiing,
ski mountaineering
DESTINATIONS: Yosemite N.P.,
Sierra Nevada, California

**Yosemite Mountaineering
School & Guide Service**
Yosemite National Park, CA 95389
209-372-8435 or 209-372-8344
www.yosemitemountaineering.com
ACTIVITIES: Climbing, moun-
taineering, ski mountaineering
DESTINATIONS: Yosemite,
Sierra Nevada, Sierra High Route

**ZOAR Outdoor
Paddling School**
P.O. Box 245
Charlemont, MA 01339
800-532-7483 or 413-339-4010
www.zoaroutdoor.com
ACTIVITIES: Canoeing, kayaking
DESTINATIONS: Massachusetts

N

O

P

Q

R

S

PHOTOGRAPHY

Cover (t-b) Doug Perrine/Innerspace Visions; Steve Bly; Brian Bailey/Adventure Photo & Film; Erik Aeder/Adventure Photo & Film; Bill Hatcher; **spine** Brian Bailey/Tony Stone Images; **back cover (t-b)** James Randklev/Tony Stone Images; Tom Bol; Bill Hatcher 2-3 Didier Givois; 4 le Kennan Harvey/Tony Stone Images; 4 rt (t-b) Andy Belcher/Adventure Photo & Film; Bill Curtsinger; Skip Brown; Gordon Wiltsie/Adventure Photo & Film; Andy Belcher/Adventure Photo & Film; 6 Brian Bailey/Tony Stone Images

Chapter 1: 8-9, 13, 21, 25 top Roger Mear/Tony Stone Images; 9 Sean Arbabi/Tony Stone Images; 11 Maria Stenzel; 12 Chris Noble/Tony Stone Images; 15 Chris Noble/Tony Stone Images; 17 top Bill Hatcher; **bottom** Kennan Harvey/Tony Stone Images; 19 Kennan Harvey/Tony Stone Images; 20 Bill Hatcher; 22 Andy Belcher/Adventure Photo & Film; 25 bottom Bill Hatcher

Chapter 2: 26, 31, 33 top, 35 top James Randklev/Tony Stone Images; 27 Issac Hernandez/Mercury Press; 29 Patrick Ward; 30 Manoj Shah/Tony Stone Images; 33 bottom Nancy Black/Mercury Press; 35 bottom Issac Hernandez/Mercury Press

Chapter 3: 36, 41, 51, 53 top Steve Bly; 37 Ray Gehman; 40 Skip Brown; 42 Robert M. Reynolds/Otter Bar Lodge; 44 Rich Reid; 45 Robert M. Reynolds/Otter Bar Lodge; 47 Robin Siegel; 49 Otter Bar Lodge; 50 Skip Brown; 53 bottom Todd Buchanan

Chapter 4: 54,59, 61 top, 63, 67 top, 69 top Bill Hatcher; 55 Chuck Haney; 57 Chuck Haney; 58 Travel International; 61 bottom Markham Johnson; 62 Mark Cosslett/Adventure Photo & Film; 65 David Epperson/Adventure Photo & Film; 67 bottom Bill Hatcher; 69 bottom Ace Kvale

Chapter 5: 70, 73 top, 75, 77, 79, 81 top Casa de Campo; 71 Stephen Pumphrey; 73 Dan Westergren; 74 Steve Bly/Tony Stone Images; 77 bottom Patrick Ward; 78 Donald R. Perry; 81 bottom Frank Jensen

Chapter 6: 82, 87, 93, 95 top Tom Bol; 83 Maria Stenzel; 85 Tom Bol; 89 Darrell Jones; 91 Ken Redding; 92 Maria Stenzel; 95 bottom Michael Melford

Chapter 7: 96, 101 Skip Brown; 97 Otis Imboden; 99 Thomas Ulrich/Adventure Photo & Film; 100 Skip Brown; 103 Otis Imboden; 105 Skip Brown; 107 both Skip Brown

Chapter 8: 108, 113, 115 top, 117, 121, 123 top James C. Richardson; 109 William A. Allard; 111 Gail Mooney; 112 Skip Brown; 115 bottom Sarah Leen; 116 David A. Harvey; 119 William A. Allard; 120 Richard Nowitz; 123 Sarah Leen

Chapter 9: 124, 127 top, 129, 133, 139 top Helge Pedersen; 125 Marty Evans/Adventure Photo & Film; 127 bottom Issac Hernandez/Mercury Press; 131 Pressenbild/Adventure Photo & Film; 132 Kevin Horan; 135 Helge Pedersen; 137 both Helge Pedersen; 139 Nicholas DeVore

Chapter 10: 140, 145, 147, 151 top Gordon Wiltsie/Adventure Photo & Film; 141 Maria Stenzel; 143 Didier Givois/Adventure Photo & Film; 144-5 Gary Brettnacher/Adventure Photo & Film; 146 Skip Brown; 149 Maria Stenzel; 151 bottom Scott Spiker

Chapter 11: 152, 157, 159, 161 top Maria Stenzel; 153 Bobby Model; 155 Tracker School; 156 B.O.S.S.; 161 bottom Bobby Model

Chapter 12: 162, 167, 171, 173, 175, 177, 179 top Yvette Cardozo/Tony Stone Images; 163 Brian Bailey/Tony Stone Images; 165 Chris Johns; 166 Dugald Bremner/Tony Stone Images; 169 Coco van Oppens/Mercury Press; 174 Chris Johns; 179 Dugald Bremner

Chapter 13: 180, 185, 189, 193, 195 top Steve Gilroy; 181 Theo Allofs; 183 Dan Westergren; 184 Theo Allofs; 187 Theo Allofs; 188 Theo Allofs; 191 Jannie Naude/CCA; 195 Jannie Naude

Chapter 14: 196, 197, 199 top, 201, 203, 205, 207, 209, 211 top Skip Brown; 199 bottom David Curran/Adventure Photo & Film; 202 Boken; 208 David A. Harvey; 211 Jodi Cobb

Chapter 15: 212, 217, 219, 221, 223, 227 top Doug Perrine/Innerspace Visions; 213 Wolcott Henry; 215 Wolcott Henry; 216 William R. Curtsinger; 220 William R. Curtsinger; 225 Dave Fleetham/Innerspace Visions; 227 Wolcott Henry

Chapter 16: 228, 233, 237, 239 top, 241 top Michael Powers/Adventure Photo & Film; 229 Skip Brown; 231 Rich Reid; 232 Greg Huglin/Adventure Photo & Film; 235 Skip Brown; 239 John Plummer/F Stock; 241 bottom Skip Brown

Chapter 17: 242, 247, 249, 251 top, 253, 259, 263 top Brian Bailey/Adventure Photo & Film; 243 Gordon Wilstie/Adventure Photo & Film; 245 Jan McBride/Adventure Photo & Film; 246 Thomas Ulrich/Adventure Photo & Film; 251 bottom Paul Chesley; 252 Jeff Curtis/Burton Snowboards; 254 Scott Spiker/Adventure Photo & Film; 257 Francois Causse/Tony Stone Images; 258 Joe McBride/Adventure Photo & Film; 261 Gary Brettnacher/Adventure Photo & Film; 263 Skip Brown

Chapter 18: 264, 271, 275 top Tom Sanders/Adventure Photo & Film; 265 Andy Belcher/Adventure Photo & Film; 267 Andy Belcher/Adventure Photo & Film; 268-9 Ken Fisher/Tony Stone Images; 270 Andy Belcher/Adventure Photo & Film; 273 Ken Fisher/Tony Stone Images; 275 bottom Joe McBride/Adventure Photo & Film

Chapter 19: 276, 281, 285, 287 top Steve Gilroy; 277 Richard Olsenius; 279 Steve Gilroy; 280 Richard Olsenius; 283 Sarah Leen; 287 bottom Richard Olsenius

Chapter 20: 288, 293, 297 top Rich Reid; 289 Macduff Everton; 291 Greg Huglin/Adventure Photo & Film; 292-3 Macduff Everton; 295 Rich Gilley; 297 bottom Skip Brown

Chapter 21: 298, 303, 305, 309 top, 311, 313 top Philip & Karen Smith; 299 David Epperson/Adventure Photo & Film; 300 Skip Brown; 304 Ace Kvale; 307 Skip Brown; 309 bottom David Epperson/Adventure Photo & Film; 310 Gordon Wiltsie/Adventure Photo & Film; 313 bottom Peter Essick

Chapter 22: 314, 319,321,323, 327, 329 top Norbert Resing; 315 Joel Sartore; 317 David Doubilet; 318 Joel Sartore; 322 Nature Expedition International; 325 Mattias Klum; 329 bottom Bruce Dale

Chapter 23: 330, 335, 337 top, 343 top Erik Aeder/Adventure Photo & Film; 331 Gary Brettnacher/Adventure Photo & Film; 333 Paul Chesley; 334 Robert Kendrick; 337 bottom Gary Brettnacher/Adventure Photo & Film; 339 Skip Brown; 341 Eric Sanford/Adventure Photo & Film; 342 & 343 bottom Skip Brown

Chapter 24: 344, 351, 355, 357 top Courtesy of ORDA; 345 Tomas Tomaszewski; 347 Tomasz Tomaszewski; 349 Ira Block; 350 Brian Skerry; 353 Jodi Cobb; 354 Courtesy Air Combat USA; 357 bottom David Doubilet

TEXT COPYRIGHT © 2000 PAUL MCMENAMIN AND BOKEN COMMUNICATIONS

COPYRIGHT © 2000 NATIONAL GEOGRAPHIC SOCIETY

All rights reserved. Reproduction of the whole or any part of the contents without written permission of the publisher is prohibited.

Composition for this book by the National Geographic Society Book Division. Printed and bound by R. R. Donnelley & Sons, Willard, Ohio. Color separations by Digital Color Image, Pennsauken, New Jersey. Covers printed by Miken, Inc., Cheektowaga, New York.

Visit the Society's website at www.nationalgeographic.com

Library of Congress Cataloging-in-Publication Data

McMenamin, Paul.
    Ultimate adventure: National Geographic ultimate adventure sourcebook / Paul McMenamin.
        p.   cm.
    Includes bibliographical references (p.)
    ISBN 0-7922-7591-8
    1. Outdoor recreation—Directories. 2. Travel--Directories.
    I. Title.

GV191.35 .M35 2000
796'.025--dc21

00-037979
CIP

CREDITS

Published by
NATIONAL GEOGRAPHIC SOCIETY

John M. Fahey, Jr.
President and Chief Executive Officer

Gilbert M. Grosvenor
Chairman of the Board

Nina D. Hoffman
Senior Vice President

William R. Gray
Vice President and Director, Book Division

Elizabeth L. Newhouse
Director of Travel Publishing

Allan Fallow
Editor

Marty Ittner
Art Director

Marilyn Mofford Gibbons
Illustrations Editor

Barbara A. Noe
Associate Editor

Carolinda E. Averitt,
Janet Cave, Roberta Conlan,
Robin Currie, Alison Kahn
Text Editors

Barbara Quarmby,
Lise Sajewski
Copy Editors

Josie Dean, Roxie France-Nuriddin, Karen Hayes,
Rebecca Mills, Jane Sunderland,
Mark Waner
Editorial Researchers

Carl Mehler
Director of Maps

Joseph F. Ochlak, chief;
Keith R. Moore, Nicholas
Rosenbach
Map Research

Gregory Ugiansky, chief;
Matt Chwastyk, Jerome N.
Cookson, Mapping Specialists,
XNR Productions
Map Production

Sharon Kocsis Berry
Illustrations Assistant

Lewis R. Bassford
Production Project Manager

Angela George
Editorial Assistant

Connie D. Binder
Indexer

Craig Battles
Susan Potter
Stephanie Sneddon
Research Assistants

Brian Fagan
Bibi Garcia Jordan
Susan Potter
Pamela Sneddon
Stephanie Sneddon
Contributors